SUICIDE SQUAD

BAD BLOOD

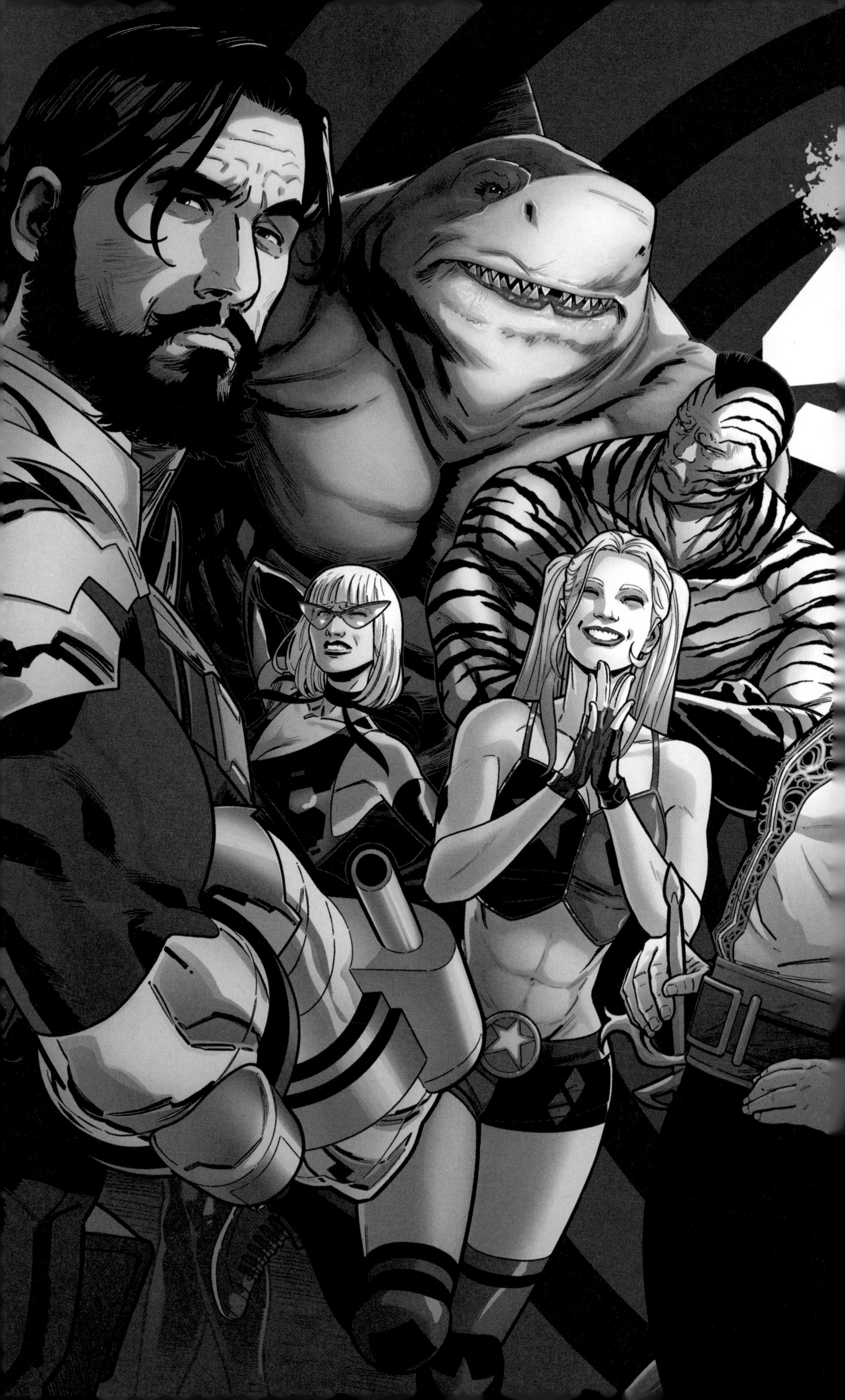

SUICIDE SQUAD
BAD BLOOD

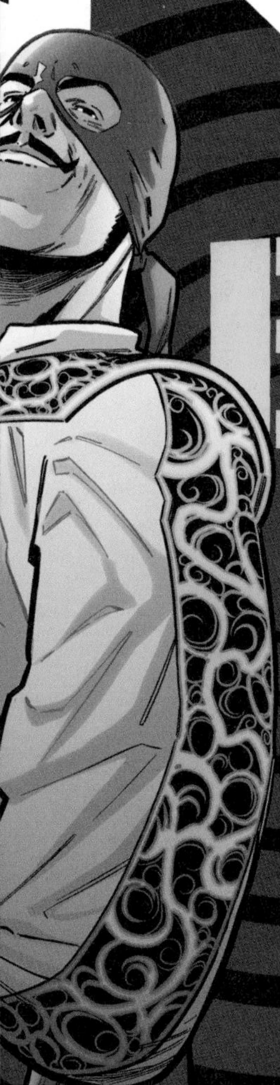

TOM TAYLOR
writer

BRUNO REDONDO
DANIEL SAMPERE
artists

JUAN ALBARRAN
inker

ADRIANO LUCAS
colorist

WES ABBOTT
letterer

BRUNO REDONDO
collection cover artist

Superman created by Jerry Siegel and Joe Shuster.
By special arrangement with the Jerry Siegel family.

ANDREA SHEA
Editor - Original Series & Collected Edition

STEVE COOK
Design Director - Books

MEGEN BELLERSEN
Publication Design

ERIN VANOVER
Publication Production

MARIE JAVINS
Editor-in-Chief, DC Comics

DANIEL CHERRY III
Senior VP - General Manager

JIM LEE
Publisher & Chief Creative Officer

DON FALLETTI
VP - Manufacturing Operations & Workflow Management

LAWRENCE GANEM
VP - Talent Services

ALISON GILL
Senior VP - Manufacturing & Operations

JEFFREY KAUFMAN
VP - Editorial Strategy & Programming

NICK J. NAPOLITANO
VP - Manufacturing Administration & Design

NANCY SPEARS
VP - Revenue

SUICIDE SQUAD: BAD BLOOD

DC Comics, 2900 West Alameda Ave., Burbank, CA 91505
Printed by Transcontinental Printing Interweb Montreal, A division of
Transcontinental Printing inc., Boucherville, QC, Canada. 2/25/22. First Printing.
ISBN: 978-1-77951-512-4

Library of Congress Cataloging-in-Publication Data is available.

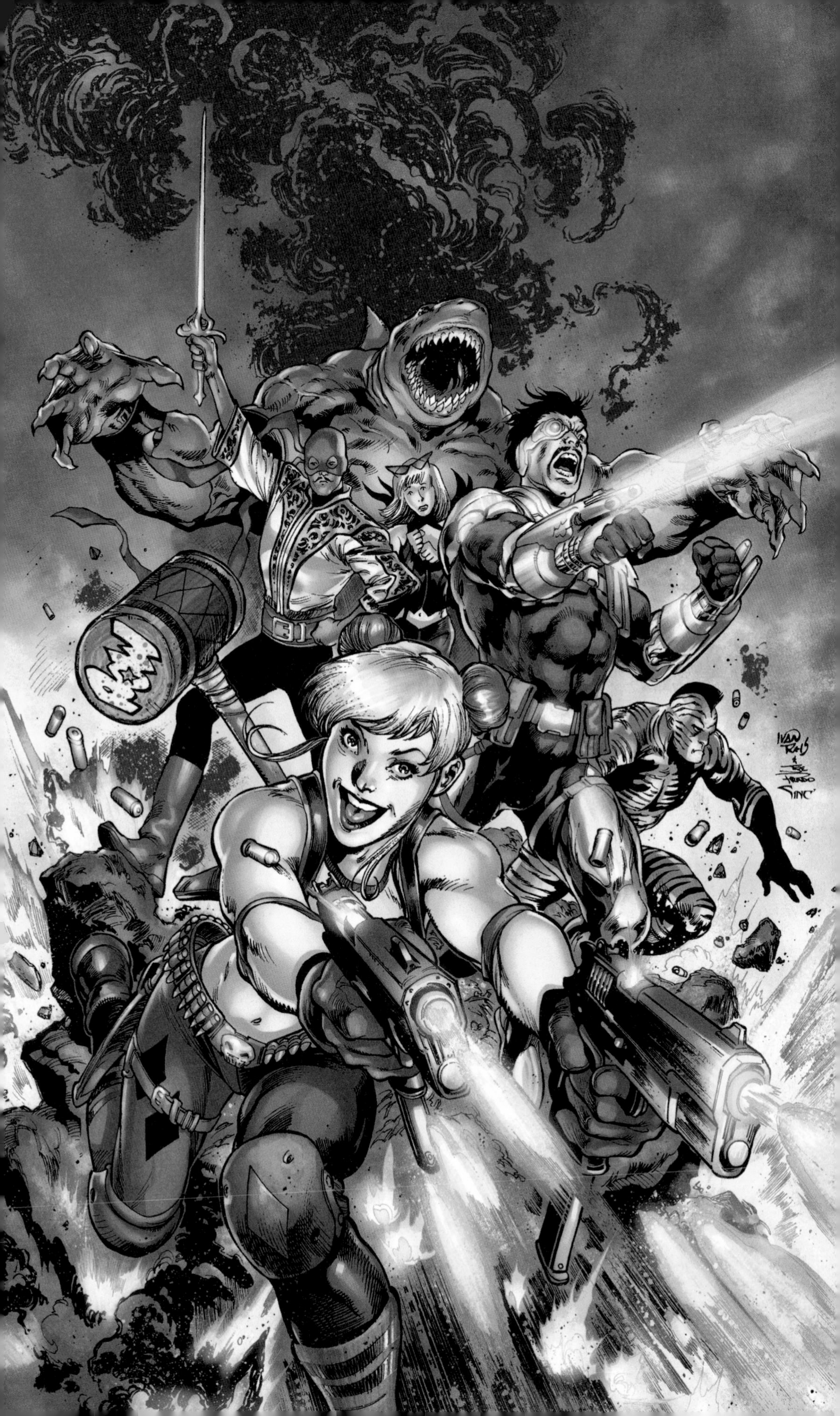

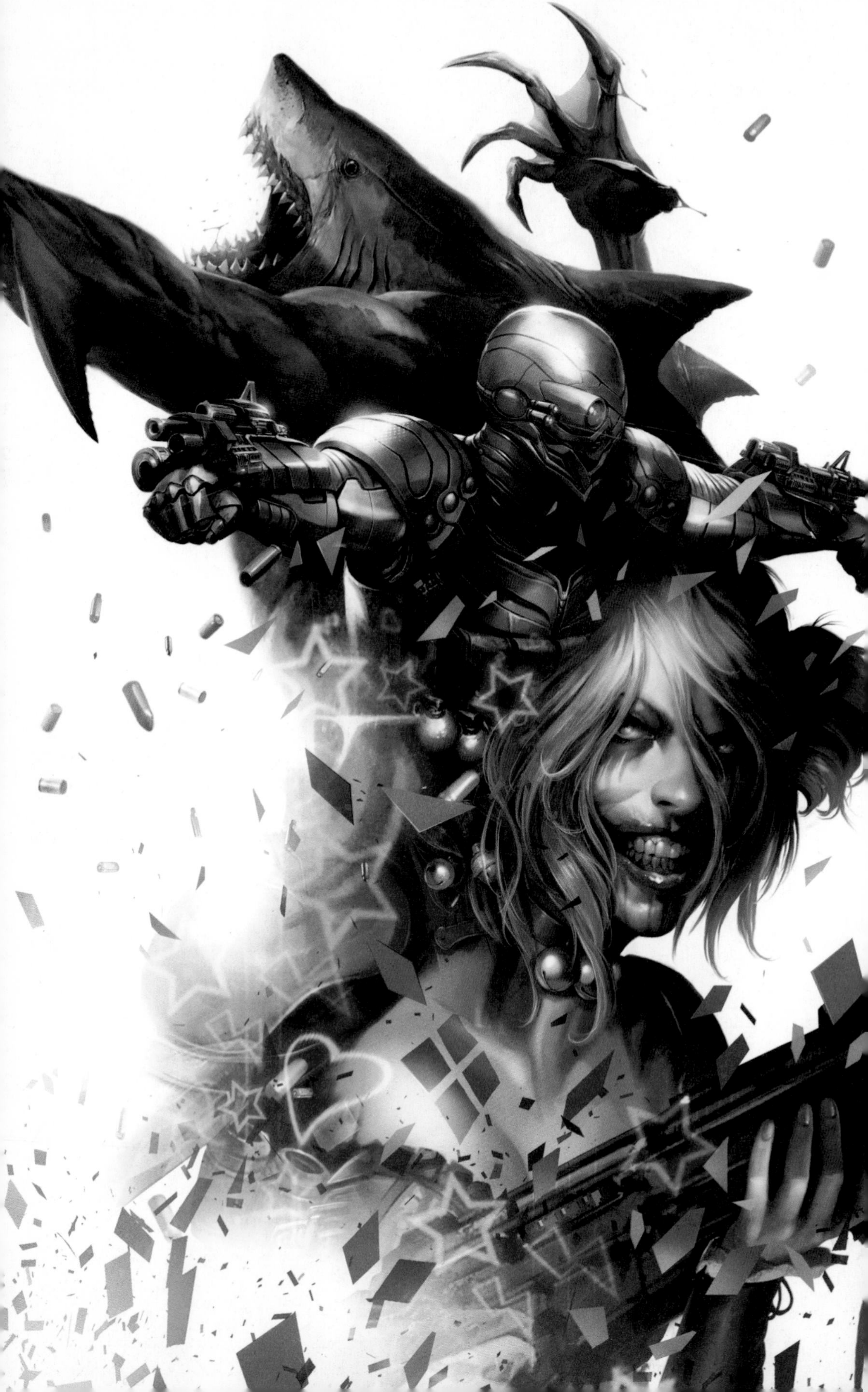

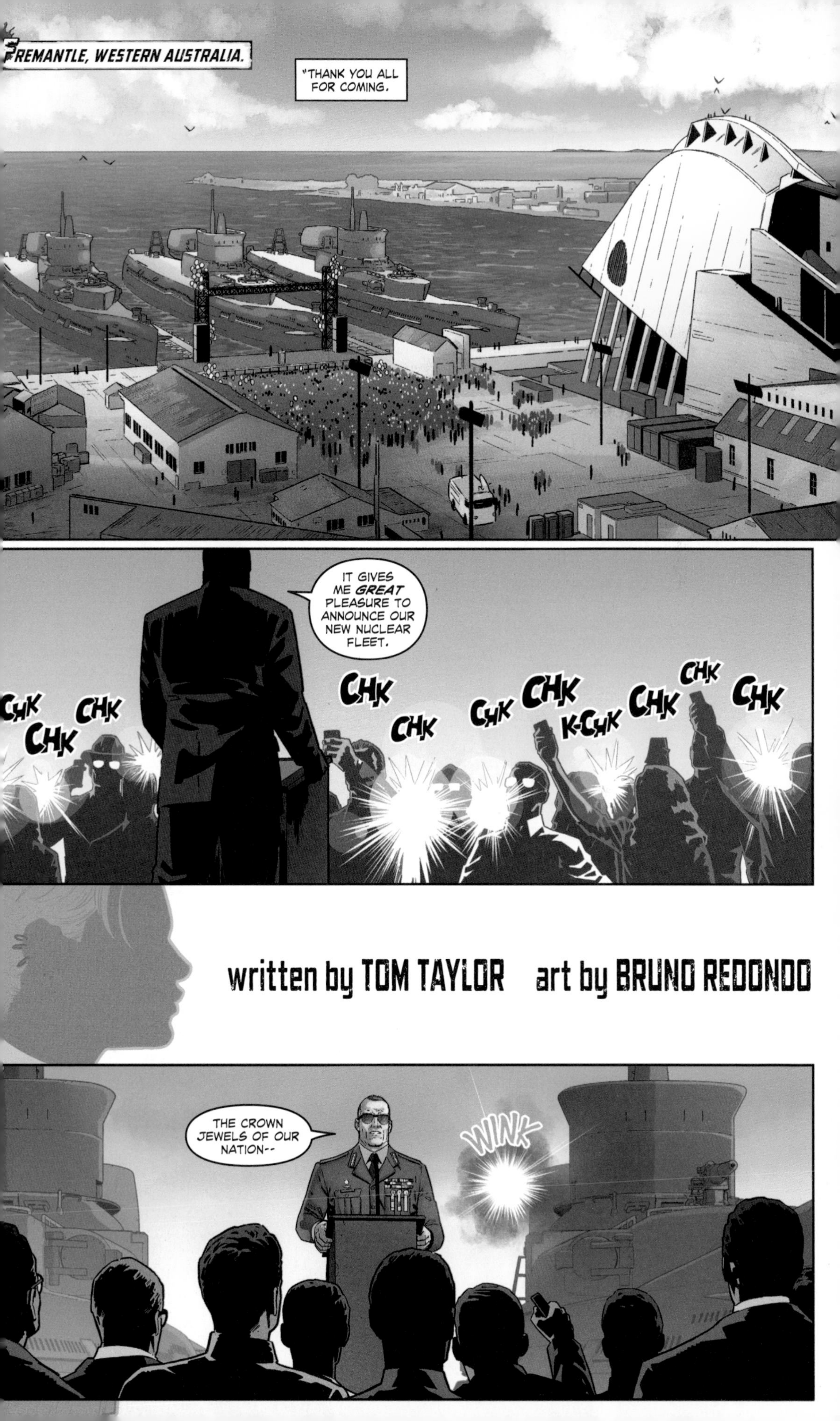
FREMANTLE, WESTERN AUSTRALIA.
"THANK YOU ALL FOR COMING.
IT GIVES ME GREAT PLEASURE TO ANNOUNCE OUR NEW NUCLEAR FLEET.
CHK CHK CHK
CHK CHK CHK CHK K-CHK CHK CHK CHK
written by TOM TAYLOR art by BRUNO REDONDO
THE CROWN JEWELS OF OUR NATION--
WINK

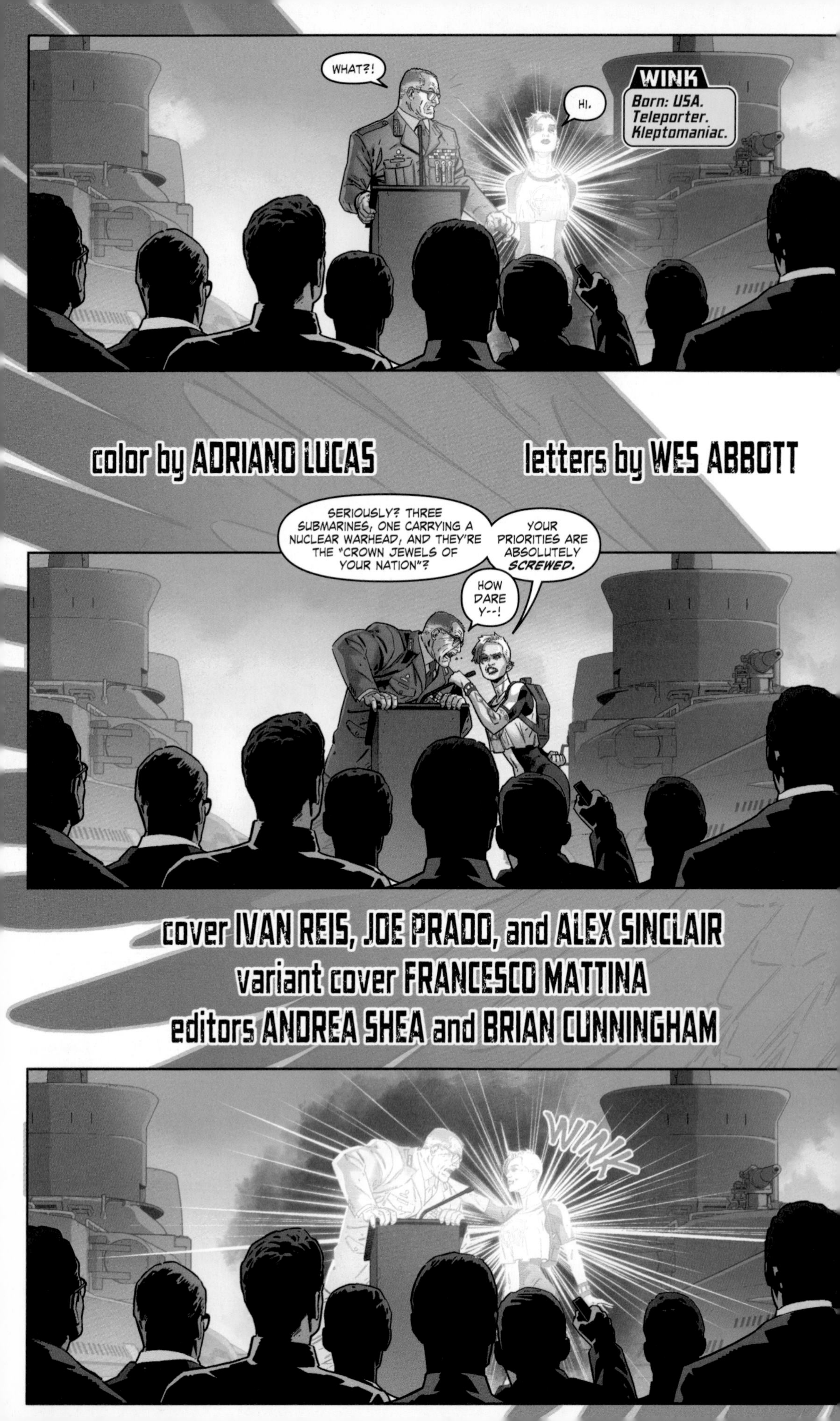
WHAT?!
WINK
Born: USA.
Teleporter.
Kleptomaniac.
HI.
color by ADRIANO LUCAS
letters by WES ABBOTT
SERIOUSLY? THREE SUBMARINES, ONE CARRYING A NUCLEAR WARHEAD, AND THEY'RE THE "CROWN JEWELS OF YOUR NATION"?
YOUR PRIORITIES ARE ABSOLUTELY SCREWED.
HOW DARE Y--!
cover IVAN REIS, JOE PRADO, and ALEX SINCLAIR
variant cover FRANCESCO MATTINA
editors ANDREA SHEA and BRIAN CUNNINGHAM
WINK

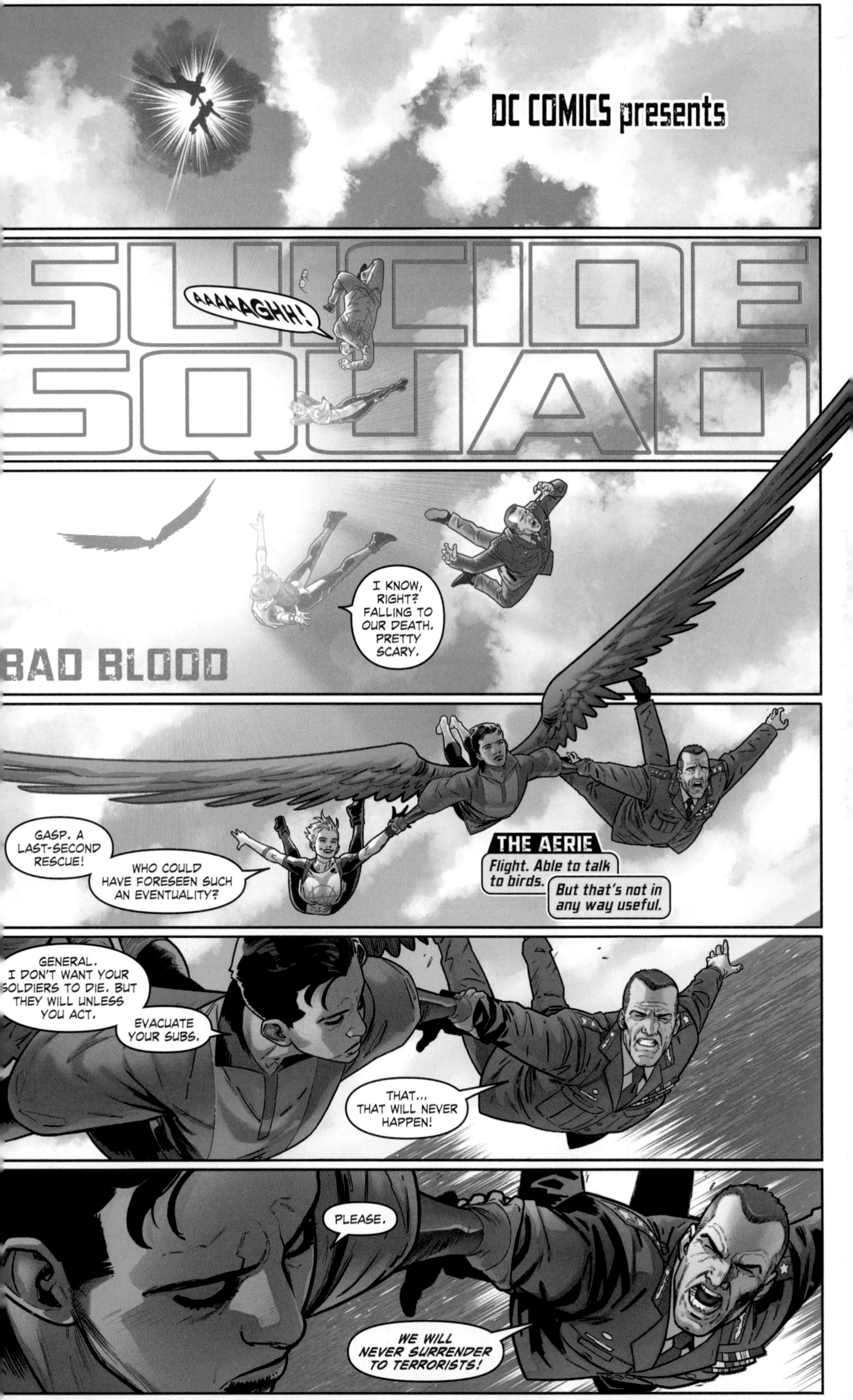
DC COMICS presents
SUICIDE SQUAD
AAAAAGHH!
BAD BLOOD
I KNOW, RIGHT? FALLING TO OUR DEATH. PRETTY SCARY.
GASP. A LAST-SECOND RESCUE!
WHO COULD HAVE FORESEEN SUCH AN EVENTUALITY?
THE AERIE
Flight. Able to talk to birds.
But that's not in any way useful.
GENERAL. I DON'T WANT YOUR SOLDIERS TO DIE. BUT THEY WILL UNLESS YOU ACT.
EVACUATE YOUR SUBS.
THAT... THAT WILL NEVER HAPPEN!
PLEASE.
WE WILL NEVER SURRENDER TO TERRORISTS!

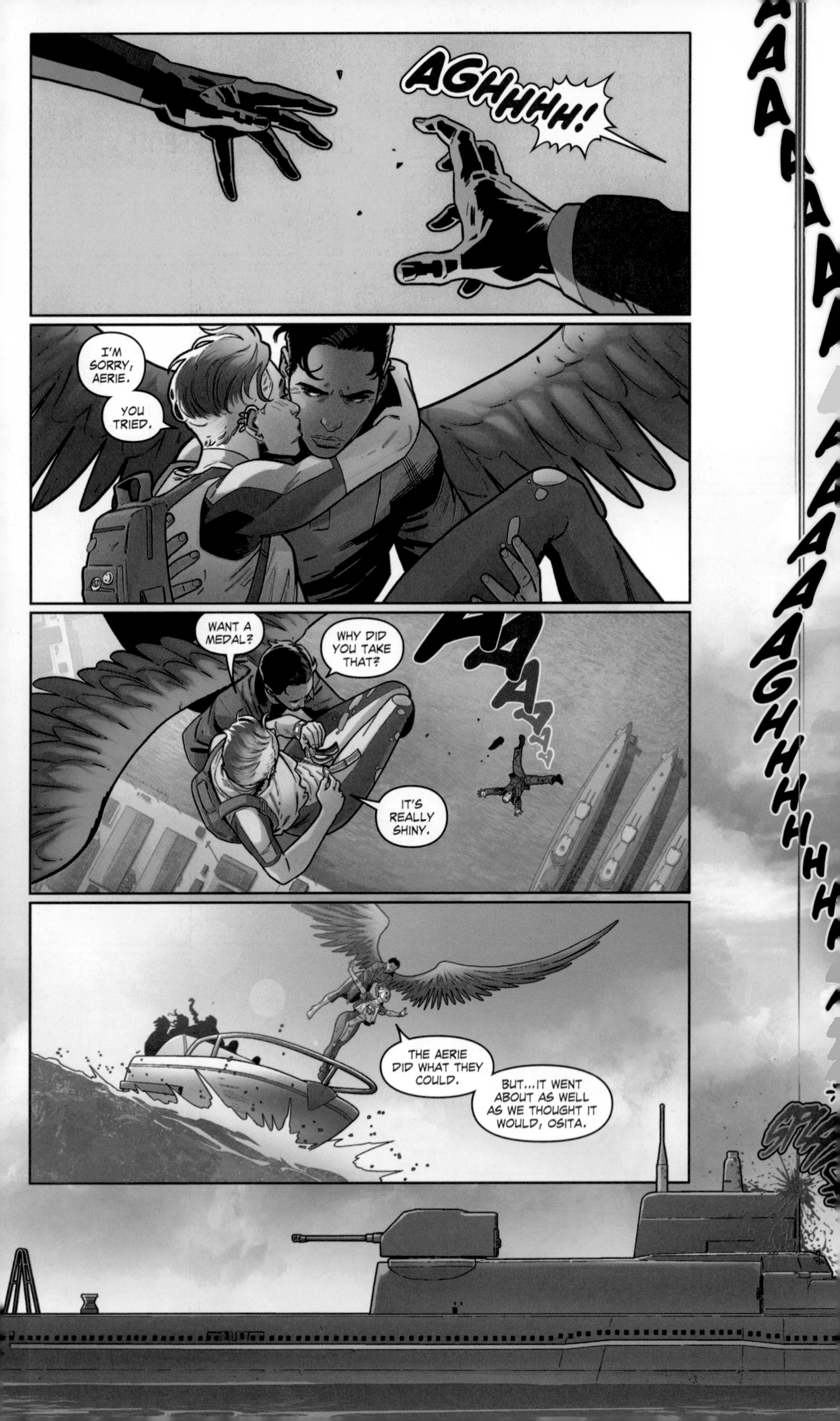

AGHHHH!
I'M SORRY, AERIE.
YOU TRIED.
WANT A MEDAL?
WHY DID YOU TAKE THAT?
IT'S REALLY SHINY.
THE AERIE DID WHAT THEY COULD.
BUT...IT WENT ABOUT AS WELL AS WE THOUGHT IT WOULD, OSITA.

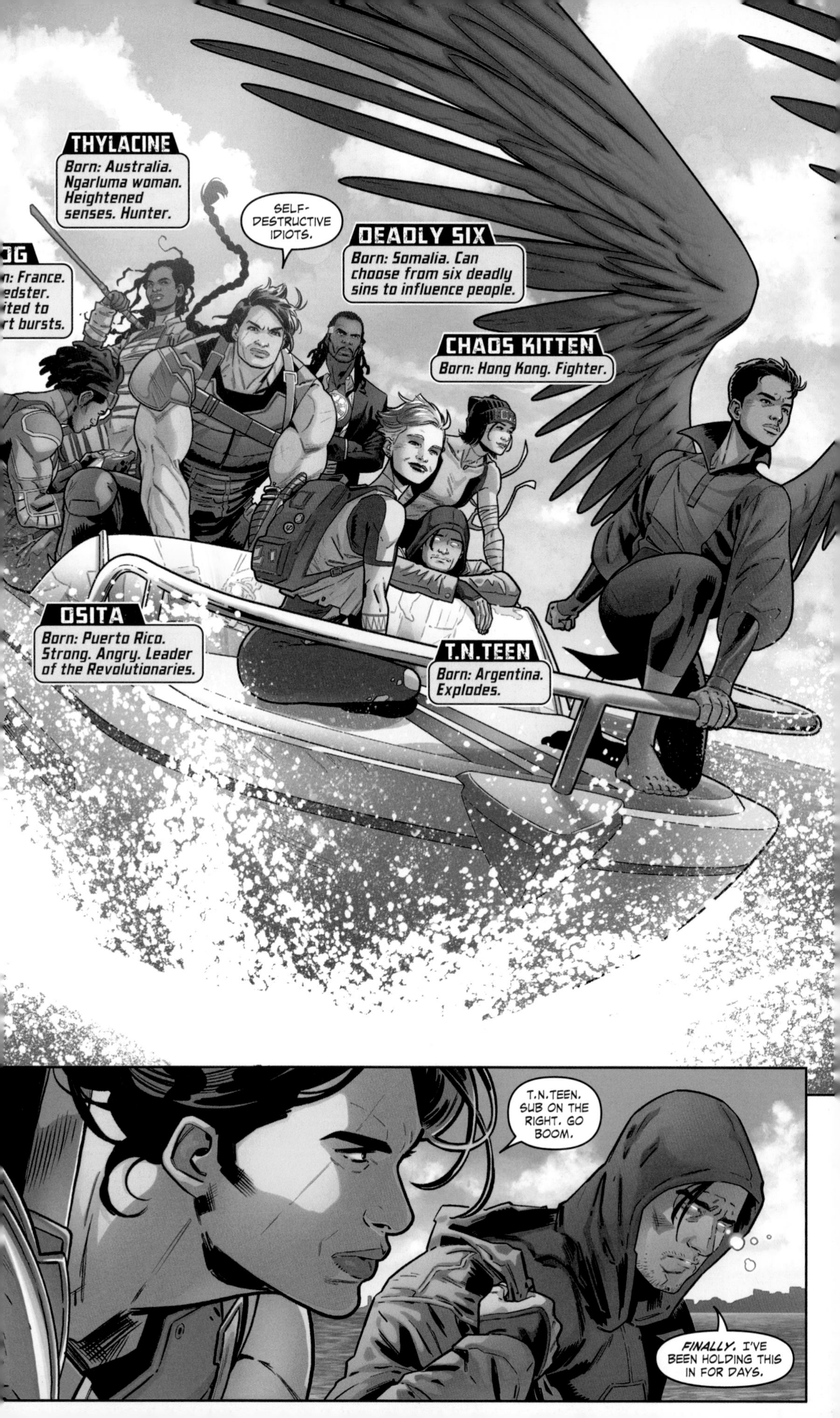
THYLACINE
Born: Australia. Ngarluma woman. Heightened senses. Hunter.
SELF-DESTRUCTIVE IDIOTS.
DEADLY SIX
Born: Somalia. Can choose from six deadly sins to influence people.
CHAOS KITTEN
Born: Hong Kong. Fighter.
OSITA
Born: Puerto Rico. Strong. Angry. Leader of the Revolutionaries.
T.N.TEEN
Born: Argentina. Explodes.
T.N.TEEN. SUB ON THE RIGHT. GO BOOM.
FINALLY. I'VE BEEN HOLDING THIS IN FOR DAYS.

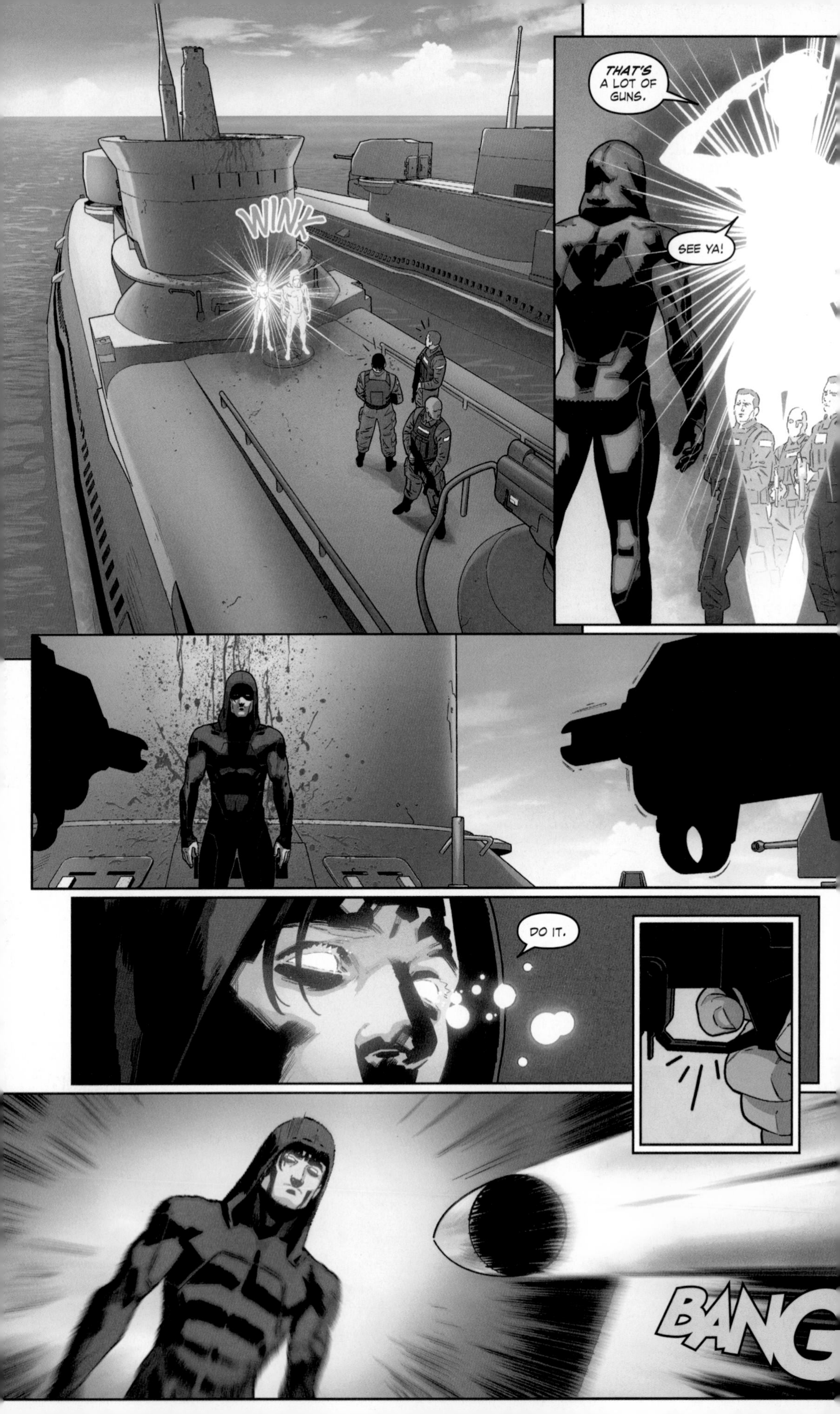
WINK
THAT'S A LOT OF GUNS.
SEE YA!
DO IT.
BANG

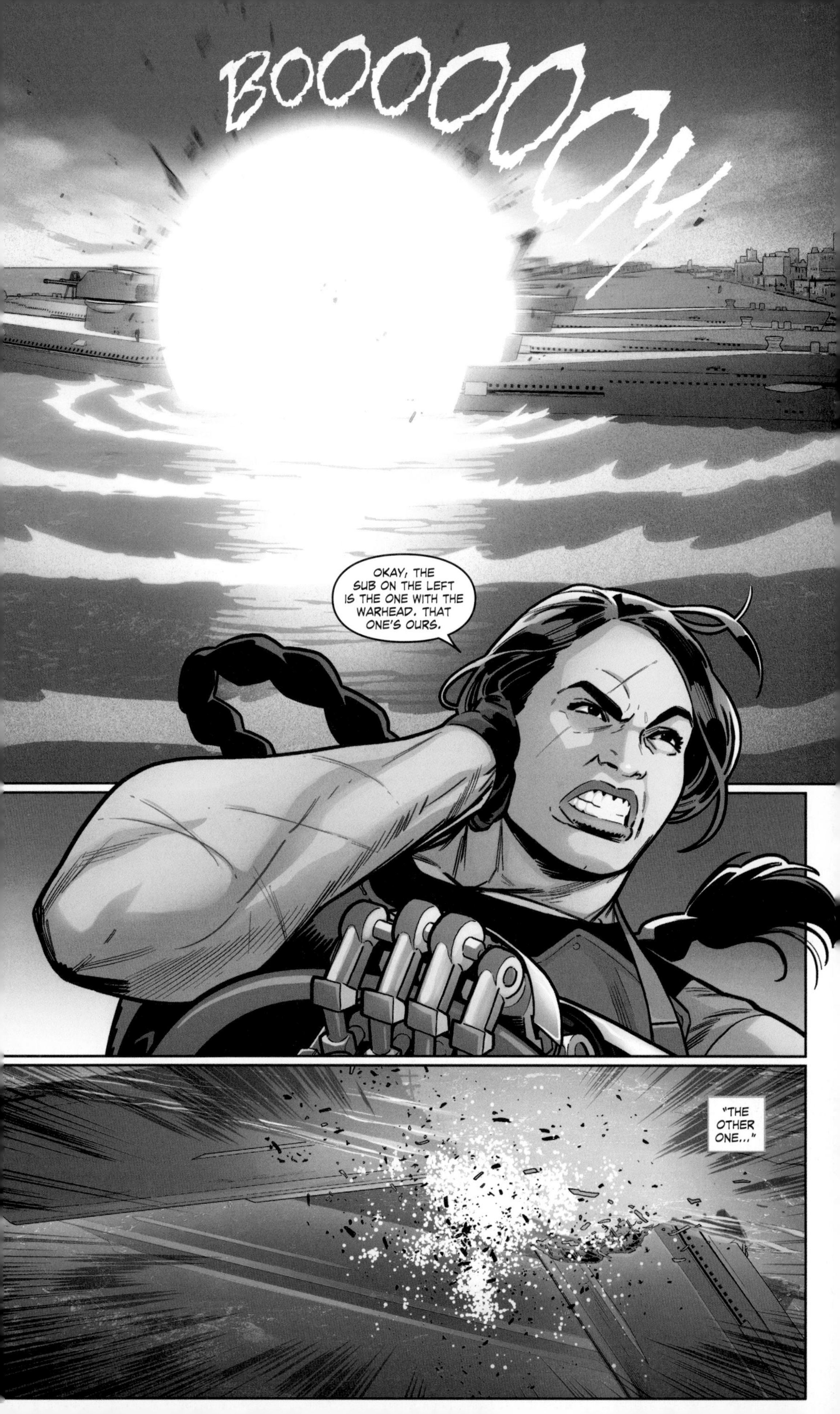
BOOOOOOOM
OKAY, THE SUB ON THE LEFT IS THE ONE WITH THE WARHEAD. THAT ONE'S OURS.
"THE OTHER ONE..."

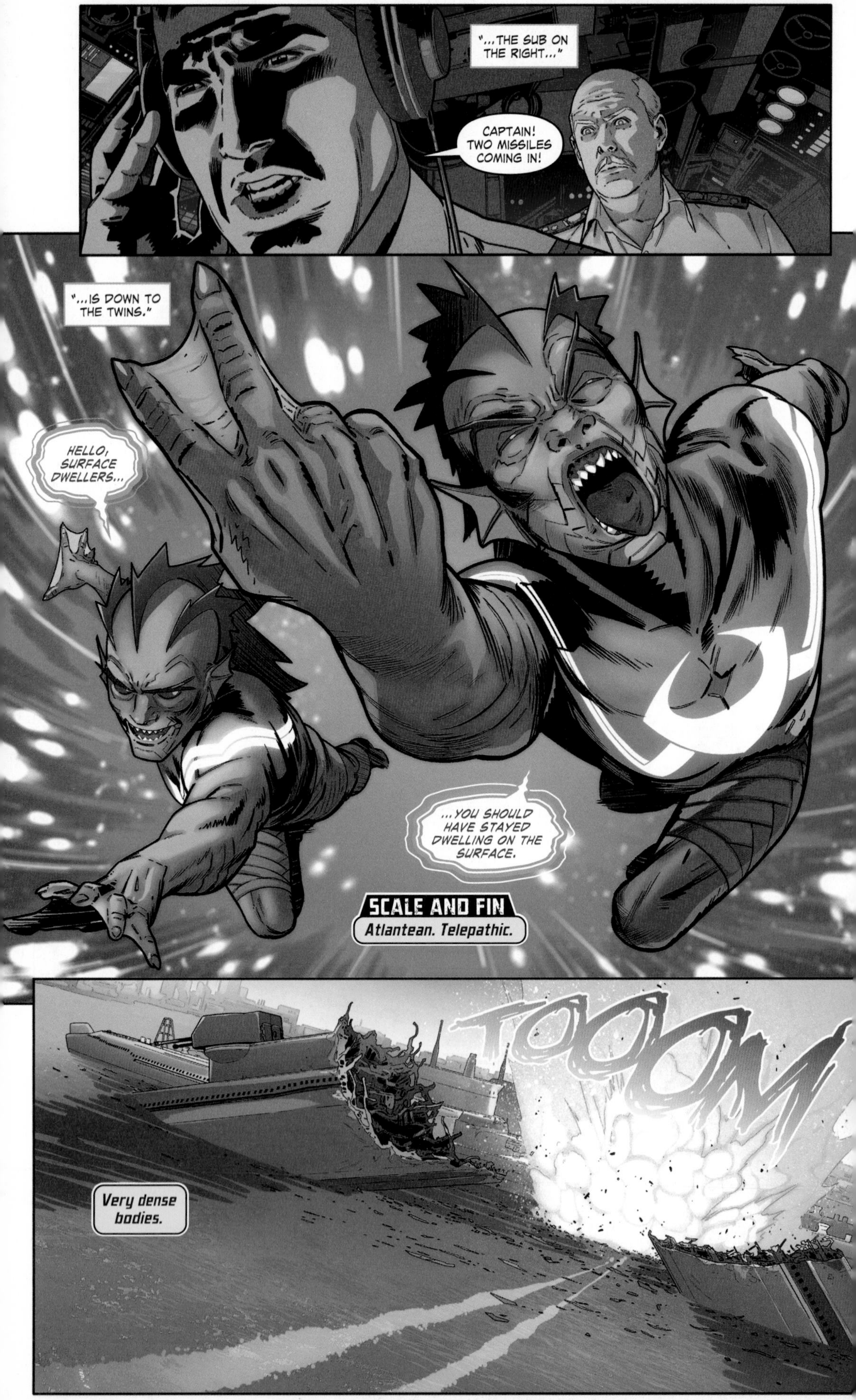

"...THE SUB ON THE RIGHT..."
CAPTAIN! TWO MISSILES COMING IN!
"...IS DOWN TO THE TWINS."
HELLO, SURFACE DWELLERS...
...YOU SHOULD HAVE STAYED DWELLING ON THE SURFACE.
SCALE AND FIN
Atlantean. Telepathic.
TOOOM
Very dense bodies.

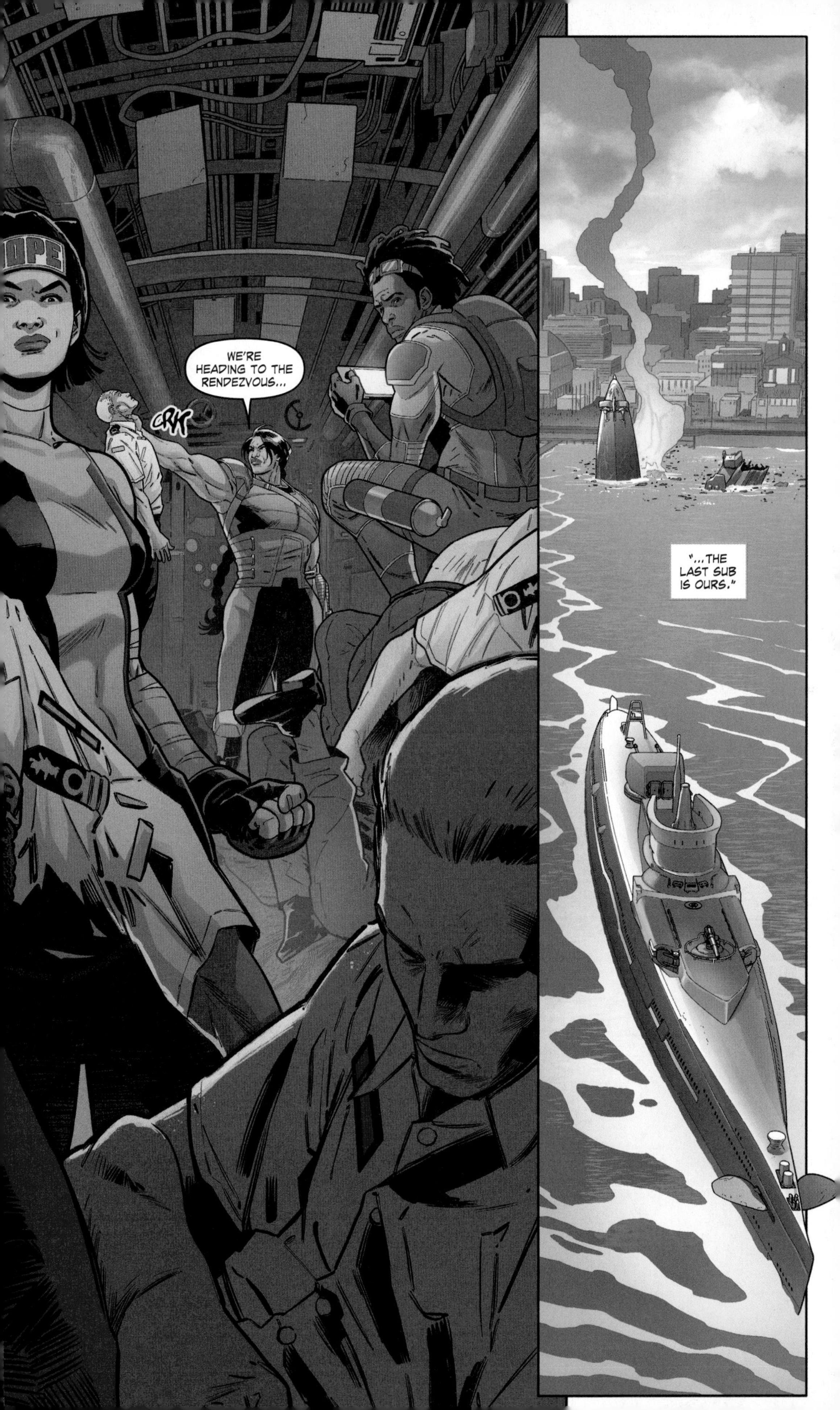
DOPE
WE'RE HEADING TO THE RENDEZVOUS...
CRK
"...THE LAST SUB IS OURS."

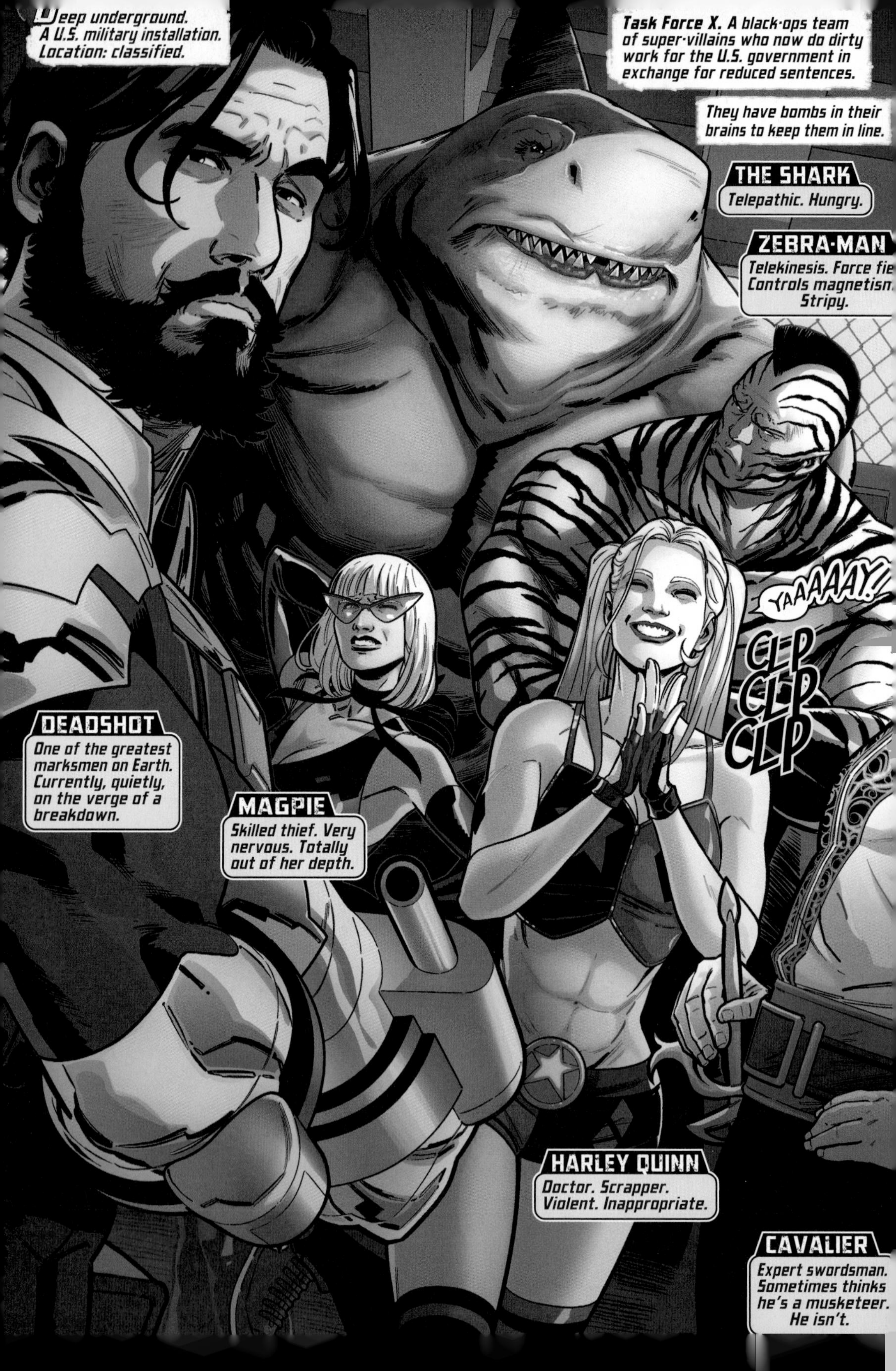
Deep underground.
A U.S. military installation.
Location: classified.
Task Force X. A black-ops team of super-villains who now do dirty work for the U.S. government in exchange for reduced sentences.
They have bombs in their brains to keep them in line.
THE SHARK
Telepathic. Hungry.
ZEBRA-MAN
Telekinesis. Force fie
Controls magnetism
Stripy.
YAAAAAY!
CLP CLP CLP
DEADSHOT
One of the greatest marksmen on Earth. Currently, quietly, on the verge of a breakdown.
MAGPIE
Skilled thief. Very nervous. Totally out of her depth.
HARLEY QUINN
Doctor. Scrapper. Violent. Inappropriate.
CAVALIER
Expert swordsman. Sometimes thinks he's a musketeer. He isn't.

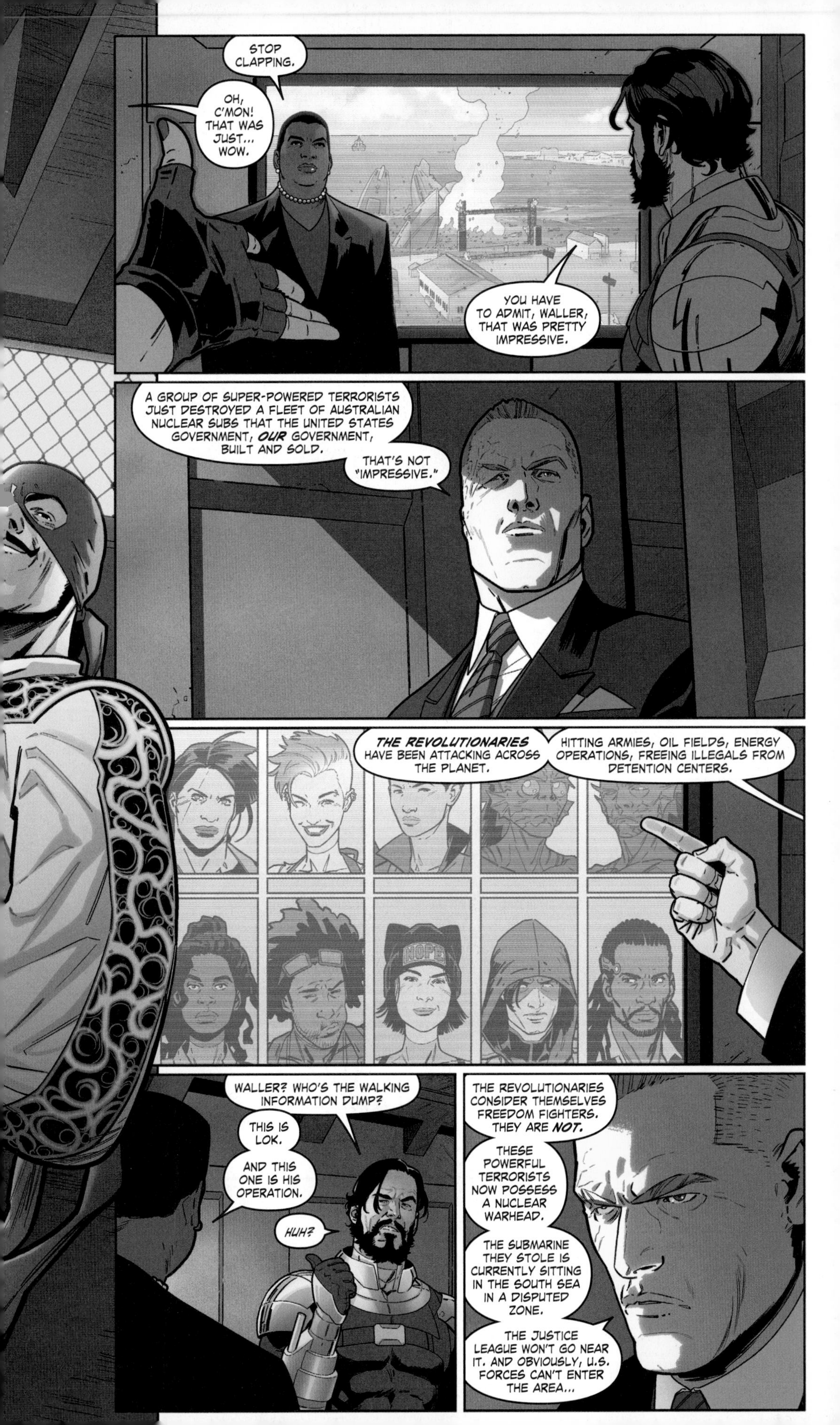
STOP CLAPPING.
OH, C'MON! THAT WAS JUST... WOW.
YOU HAVE TO ADMIT, WALLER, THAT WAS PRETTY IMPRESSIVE.
A GROUP OF SUPER-POWERED TERRORISTS JUST DESTROYED A FLEET OF AUSTRALIAN NUCLEAR SUBS THAT THE UNITED STATES GOVERNMENT, ***OUR*** GOVERNMENT, BUILT AND SOLD.
THAT'S NOT "IMPRESSIVE."
THE REVOLUTIONARIES HAVE BEEN ATTACKING ACROSS THE PLANET.
HITTING ARMIES, OIL FIELDS, ENERGY OPERATIONS, FREEING ILLEGALS FROM DETENTION CENTERS.
WALLER? WHO'S THE WALKING INFORMATION DUMP?
THIS IS LOK.
AND THIS ONE IS HIS OPERATION.
HUH?
THE REVOLUTIONARIES CONSIDER THEMSELVES FREEDOM FIGHTERS. THEY ARE ***NOT.***
THESE POWERFUL TERRORISTS NOW POSSESS A NUCLEAR WARHEAD.
THE SUBMARINE THEY STOLE IS CURRENTLY SITTING IN THE SOUTH SEA IN A DISPUTED ZONE.
THE JUSTICE LEAGUE WON'T GO NEAR IT. AND OBVIOUSLY, U.S. FORCES CAN'T ENTER THE AREA...

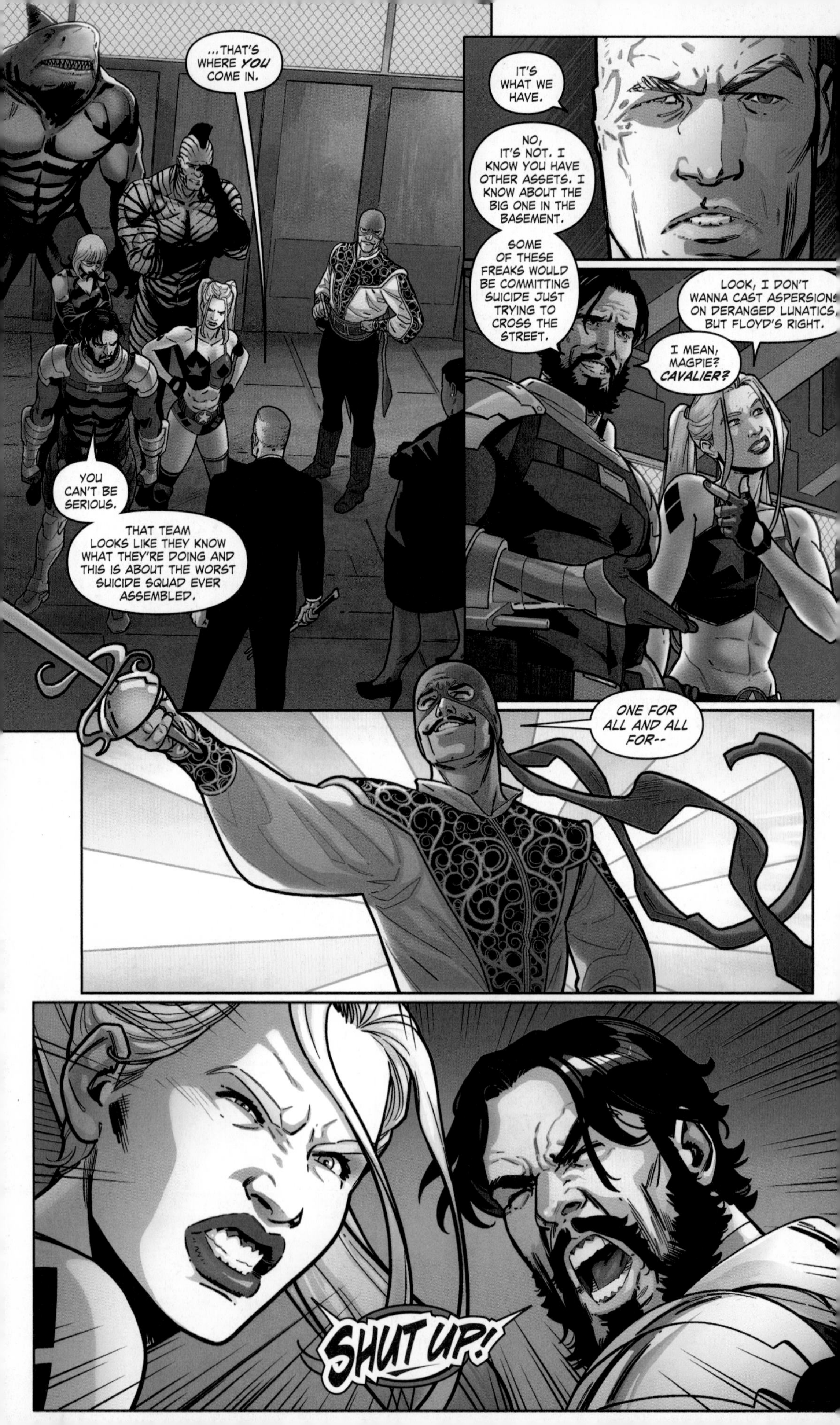
...THAT'S WHERE *YOU* COME IN.
YOU CAN'T BE SERIOUS.
THAT TEAM LOOKS LIKE THEY KNOW WHAT THEY'RE DOING AND THIS IS ABOUT THE WORST SUICIDE SQUAD EVER ASSEMBLED.
IT'S WHAT WE HAVE.
NO, IT'S NOT. I KNOW YOU HAVE OTHER ASSETS. I KNOW ABOUT THE BIG ONE IN THE BASEMENT.
SOME OF THESE FREAKS WOULD BE COMMITTING SUICIDE JUST TRYING TO CROSS THE STREET.
LOOK, I DON'T WANNA CAST ASPERSIONS ON DERANGED LUNATICS, BUT FLOYD'S RIGHT.
I MEAN, MAGPIE? *CAVALIER?*
ONE FOR ALL AND ALL FOR--
SHUT UP!

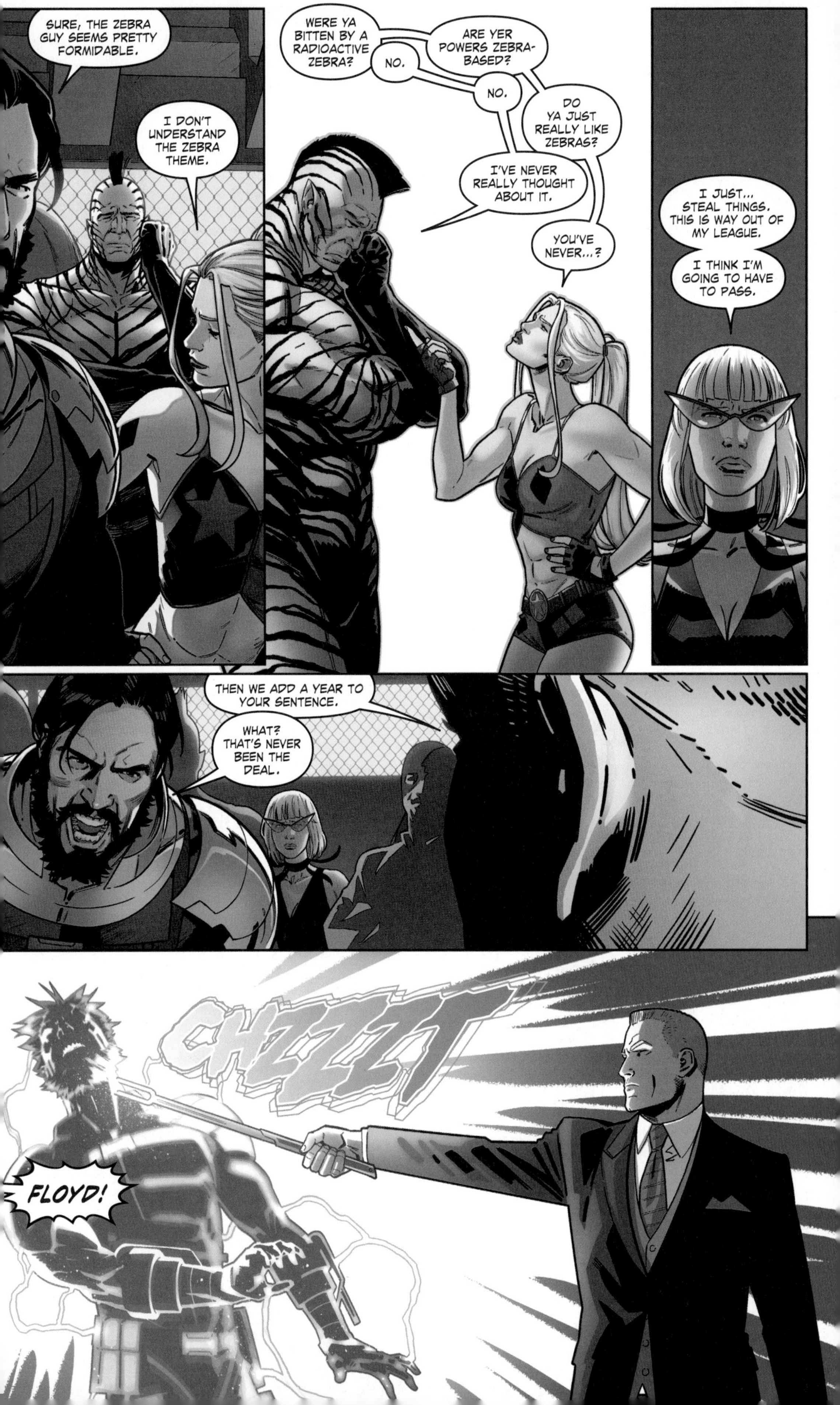
SURE, THE ZEBRA GUY SEEMS PRETTY FORMIDABLE.
I DON'T UNDERSTAND THE ZEBRA THEME.
WERE YA BITTEN BY A RADIOACTIVE ZEBRA?
NO.
ARE YER POWERS ZEBRA-BASED?
NO.
DO YA JUST REALLY LIKE ZEBRAS?
I'VE NEVER REALLY THOUGHT ABOUT IT.
YOU'VE NEVER...?
I JUST... STEAL THINGS. THIS IS WAY OUT OF MY LEAGUE.
I THINK I'M GOING TO HAVE TO PASS.
THEN WE ADD A YEAR TO YOUR SENTENCE.
WHAT? THAT'S NEVER BEEN THE DEAL.
CHZZZT
FLOYD!

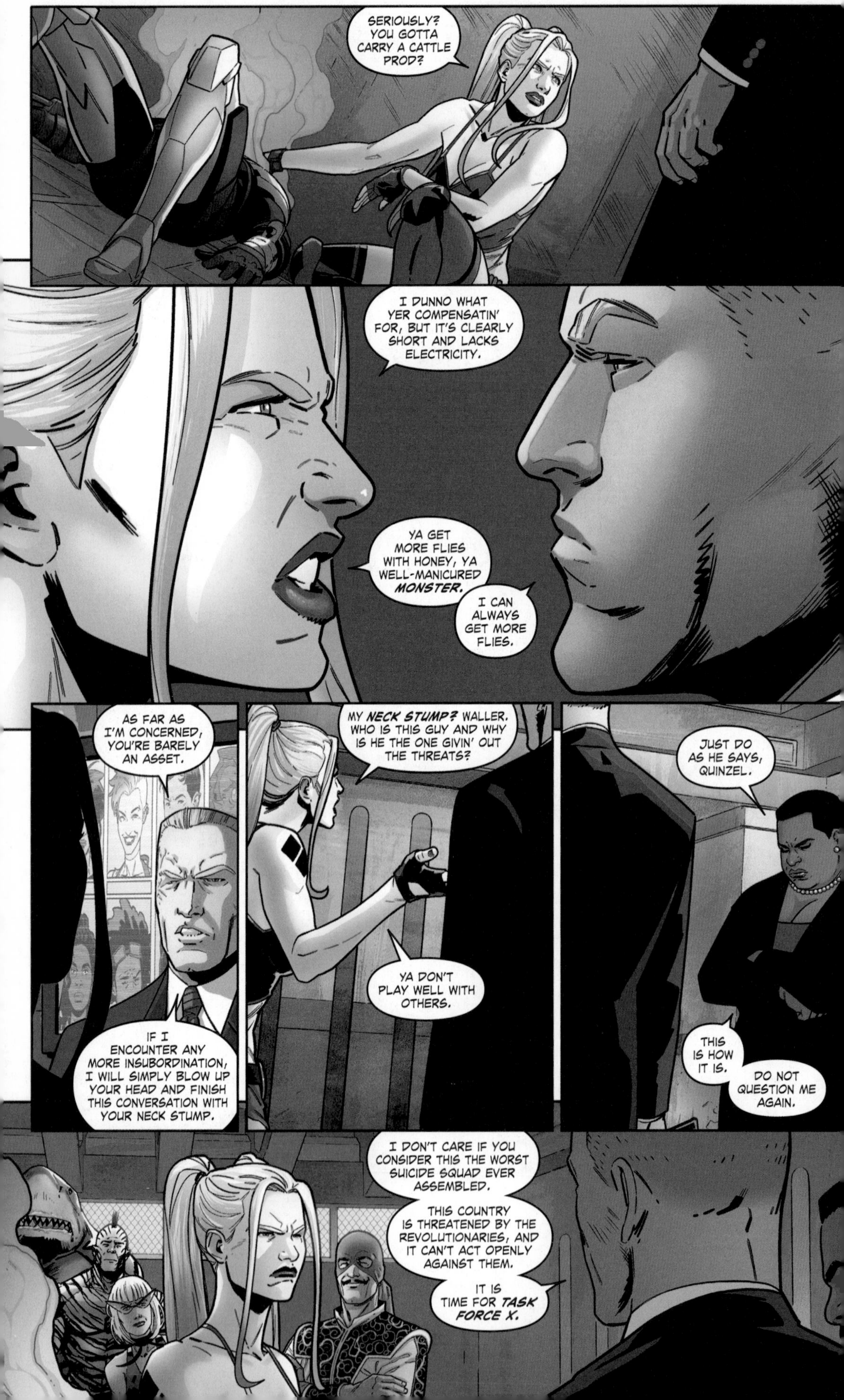
SERIOUSLY? YOU GOTTA CARRY A CATTLE PROD?
I DUNNO WHAT YER COMPENSATIN' FOR, BUT IT'S CLEARLY SHORT AND LACKS ELECTRICITY.
YA GET MORE FLIES WITH HONEY, YA WELL-MANICURED MONSTER.
I CAN ALWAYS GET MORE FLIES.
AS FAR AS I'M CONCERNED, YOU'RE BARELY AN ASSET.
IF I ENCOUNTER ANY MORE INSUBORDINATION, I WILL SIMPLY BLOW UP YOUR HEAD AND FINISH THIS CONVERSATION WITH YOUR NECK STUMP.
MY NECK STUMP? WALLER. WHO IS THIS GUY AND WHY IS HE THE ONE GIVIN' OUT THE THREATS?
YA DON'T PLAY WELL WITH OTHERS.
JUST DO AS HE SAYS, QUINZEL.
THIS IS HOW IT IS.
DO NOT QUESTION ME AGAIN.
I DON'T CARE IF YOU CONSIDER THIS THE WORST SUICIDE SQUAD EVER ASSEMBLED.
THIS COUNTRY IS THREATENED BY THE REVOLUTIONARIES, AND IT CAN'T ACT OPENLY AGAINST THEM.
IT IS TIME FOR TASK FORCE X.

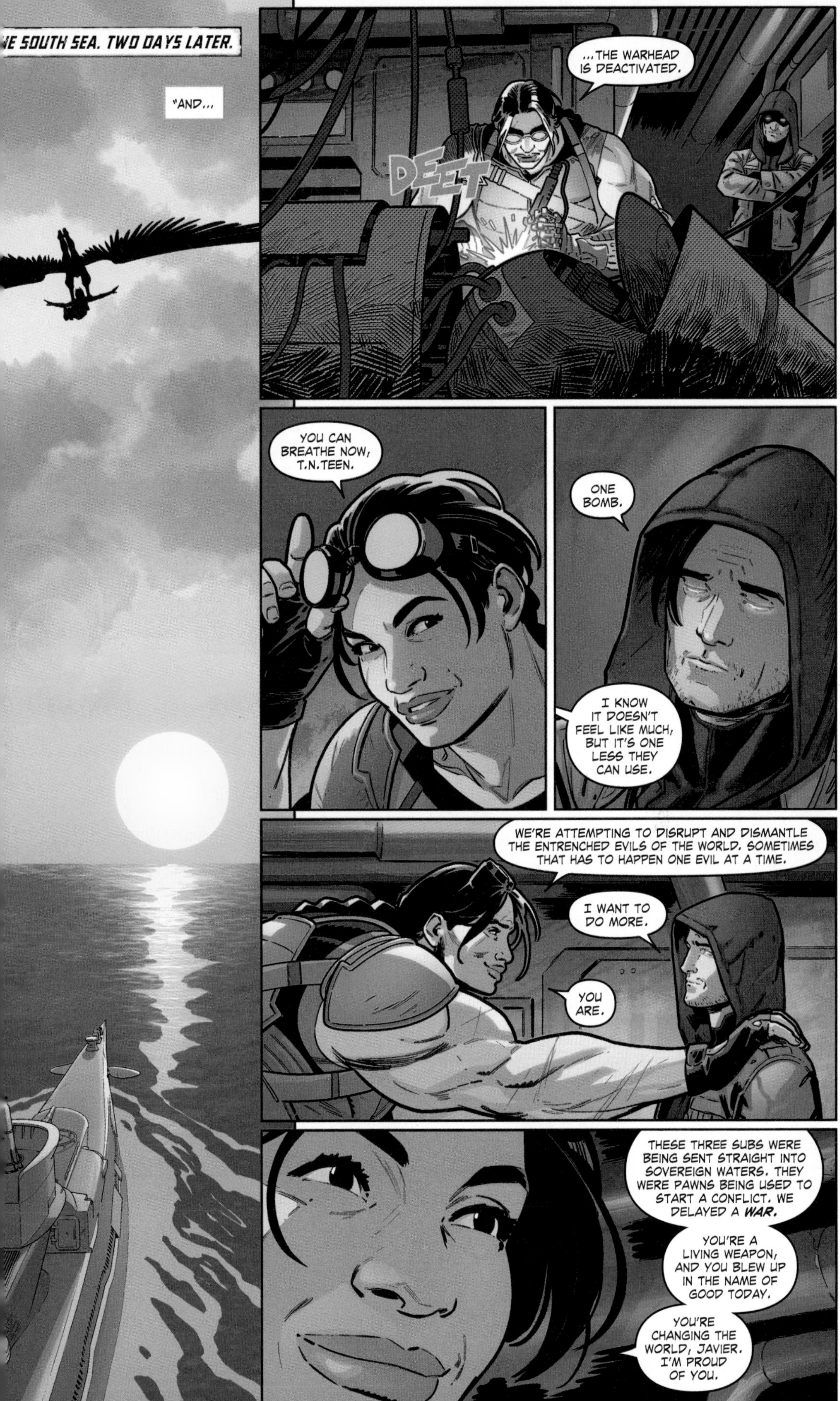

HE SOUTH SEA. TWO DAYS LATER.
"AND...
...THE WARHEAD IS DEACTIVATED.
DEET
YOU CAN BREATHE NOW, T.N.TEEN.
ONE BOMB.
I KNOW IT DOESN'T FEEL LIKE MUCH, BUT IT'S ONE LESS THEY CAN USE.
WE'RE ATTEMPTING TO DISRUPT AND DISMANTLE THE ENTRENCHED EVILS OF THE WORLD. SOMETIMES THAT HAS TO HAPPEN ONE EVIL AT A TIME.
I WANT TO DO MORE.
YOU ARE.
THESE THREE SUBS WERE BEING SENT STRAIGHT INTO SOVEREIGN WATERS. THEY WERE PAWNS BEING USED TO START A CONFLICT. WE DELAYED A WAR.
YOU'RE A LIVING WEAPON, AND YOU BLEW UP IN THE NAME OF GOOD TODAY.
YOU'RE CHANGING THE WORLD, JAVIER. I'M PROUD OF YOU.

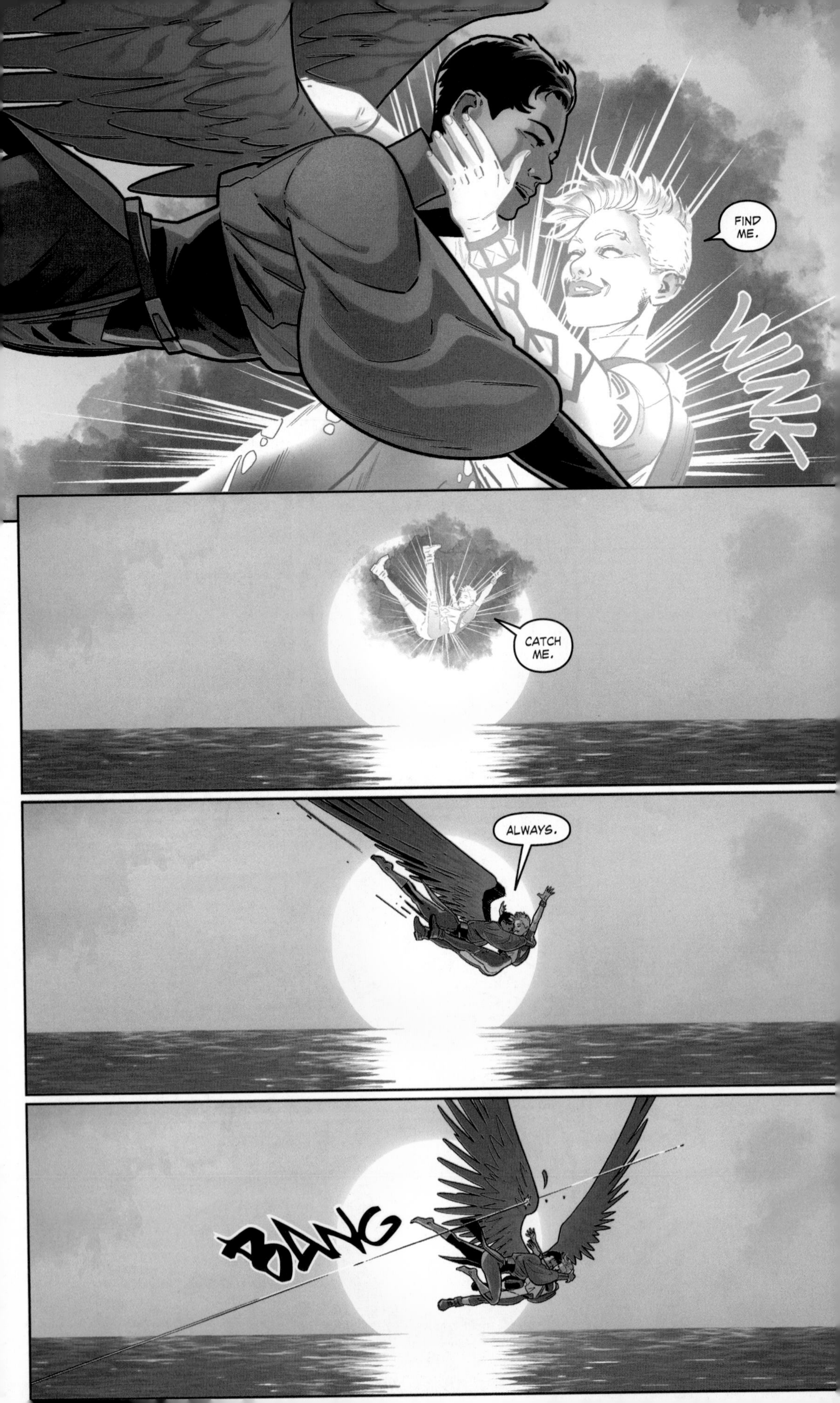
FIND ME.
WINK
CATCH ME.
ALWAYS.
BANG

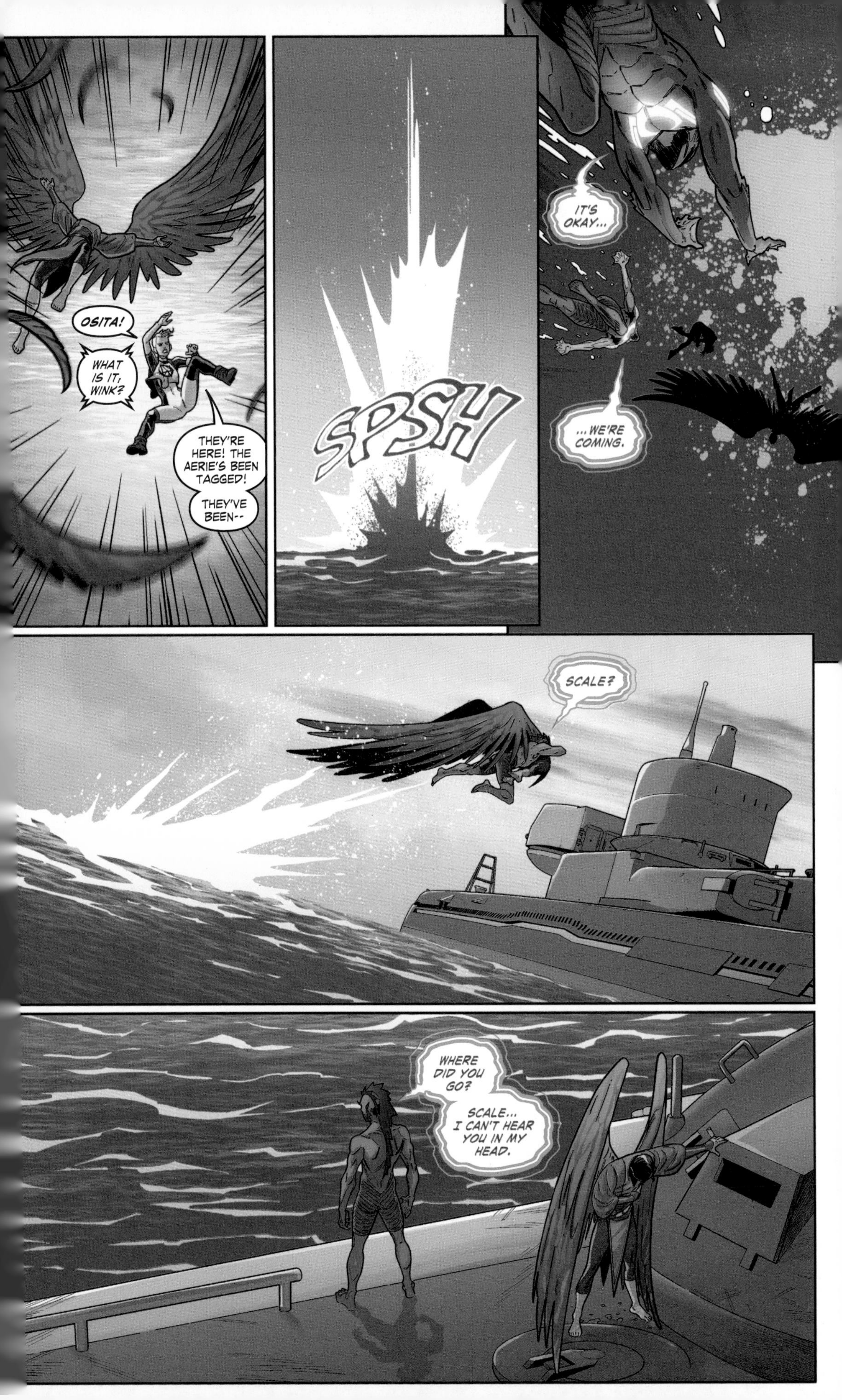
OSITA!
WHAT IS IT, WINK?
THEY'RE HERE! THE AERIE'S BEEN TAGGED!
THEY'VE BEEN--
SPSH
IT'S OKAY...
...WE'RE COMING.
SCALE?
WHERE DID YOU GO?
SCALE... I CAN'T HEAR YOU IN MY HEAD.

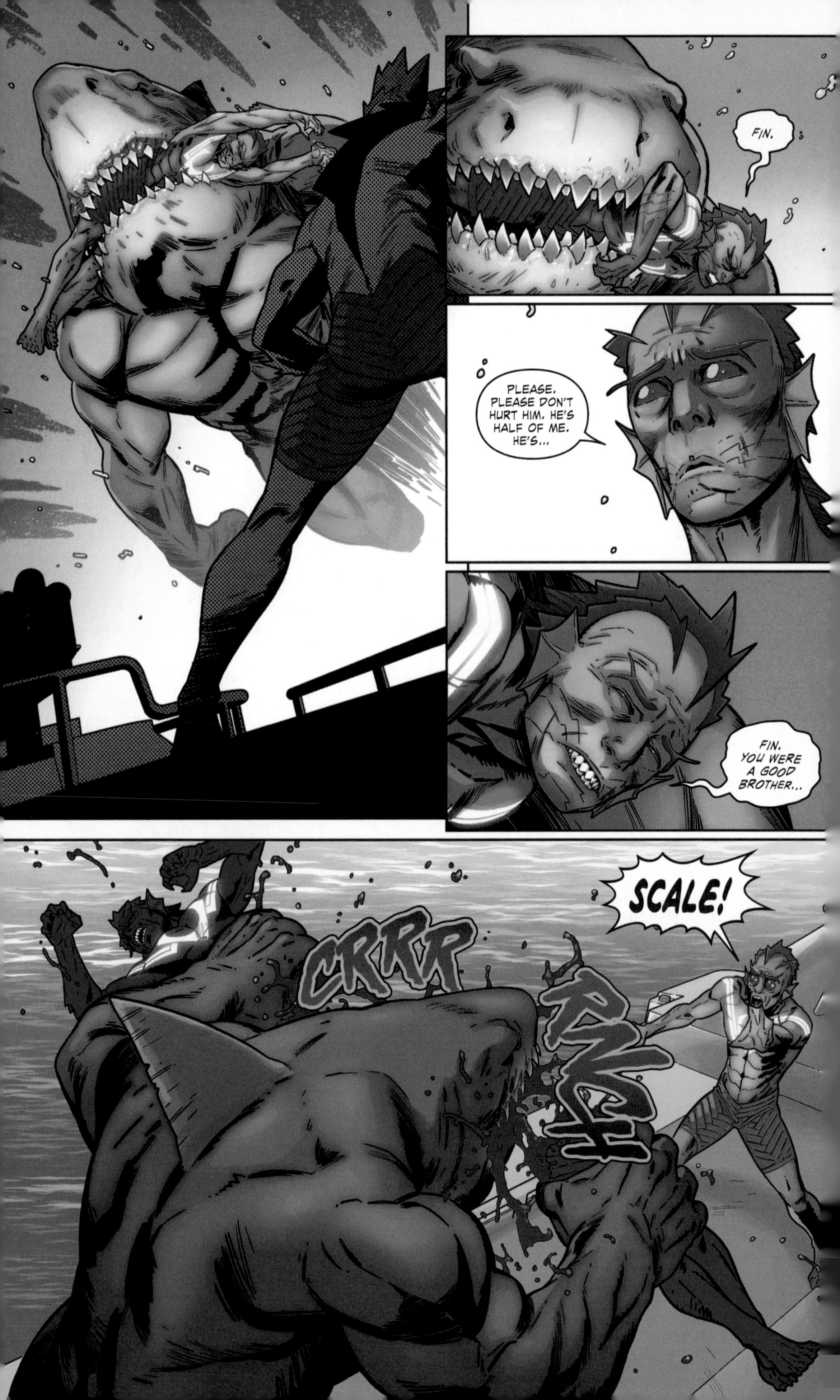
FIN.
PLEASE. PLEASE DON'T HURT HIM. HE'S HALF OF ME. HE'S...
FIN. YOU WERE A GOOD BROTHER...
SCALE!
CRRR
RNCH

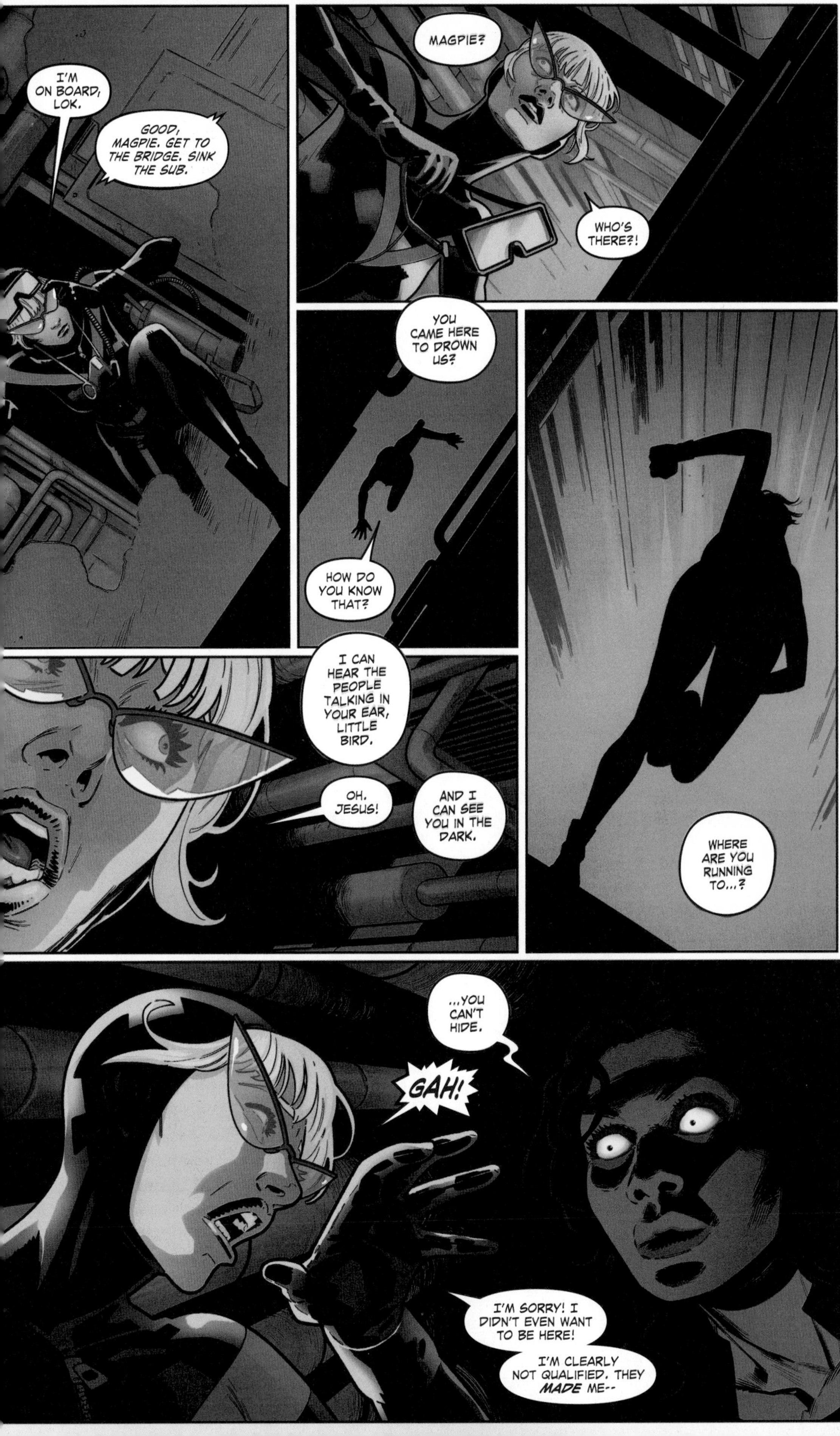
I'M ON BOARD, LOK.
GOOD, MAGPIE. GET TO THE BRIDGE. SINK THE SUB.
MAGPIE?
WHO'S THERE?!
YOU CAME HERE TO DROWN US?
HOW DO YOU KNOW THAT?
WHERE ARE YOU RUNNING TO...?
I CAN HEAR THE PEOPLE TALKING IN YOUR EAR, LITTLE BIRD.
OH. JESUS!
AND I CAN SEE YOU IN THE DARK.
...YOU CAN'T HIDE.
GAH!
I'M SORRY! I DIDN'T EVEN WANT TO BE HERE!
I'M CLEARLY NOT QUALIFIED. THEY *MADE* ME--

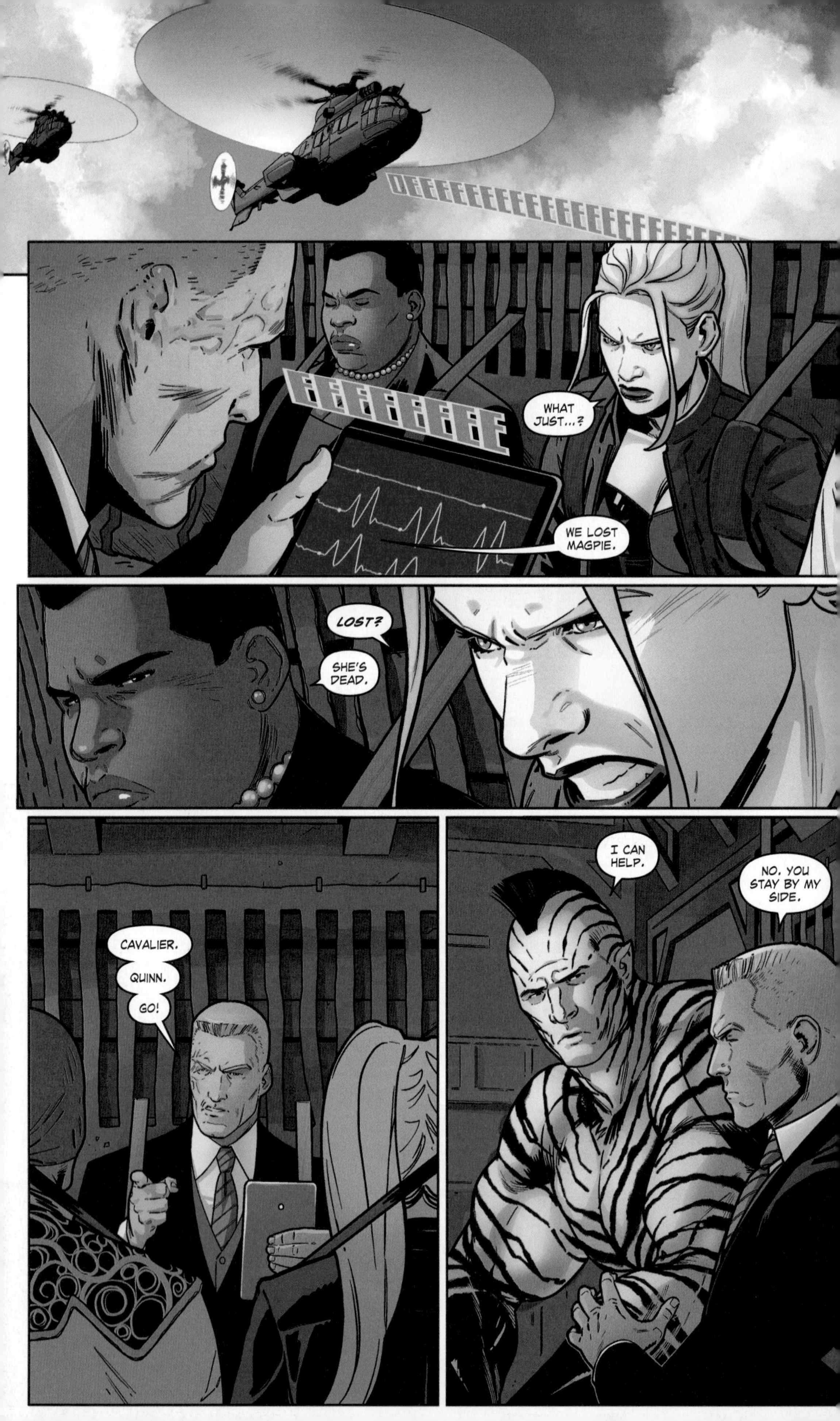
DEEEEEEEEEEEEEEEEEEEEEEEE
EEEEEEEE
WHAT JUST...?
WE LOST MAGPIE.
LOST?
SHE'S DEAD.
CAVALIER.
QUINN.
GO!
I CAN HELP.
NO. YOU STAY BY MY SIDE.

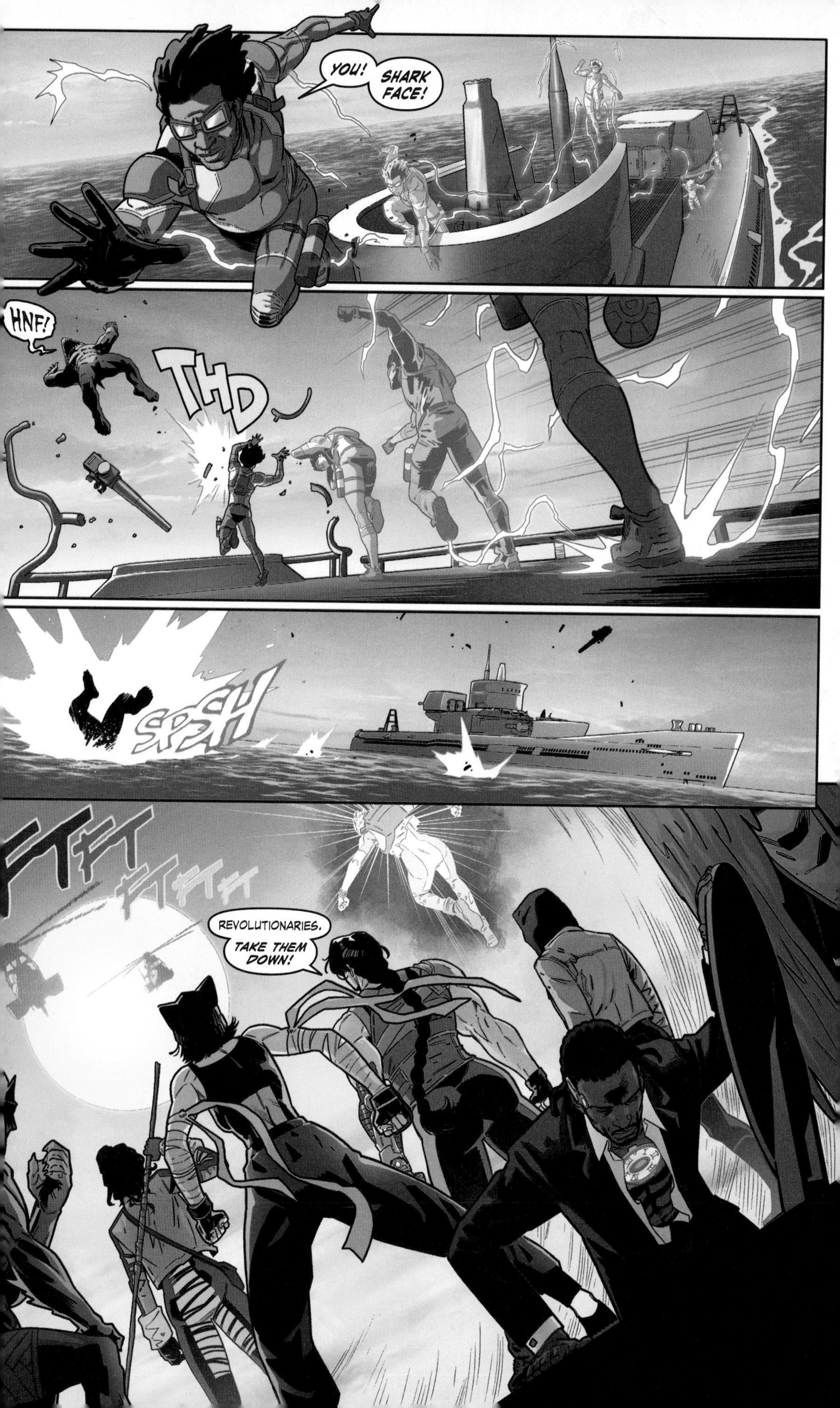
YOU!
SHARK FACE!
HNF!
THD
SPLSH
FFT FFT FFT FT
REVOLUTIONARIES.
TAKE THEM DOWN!

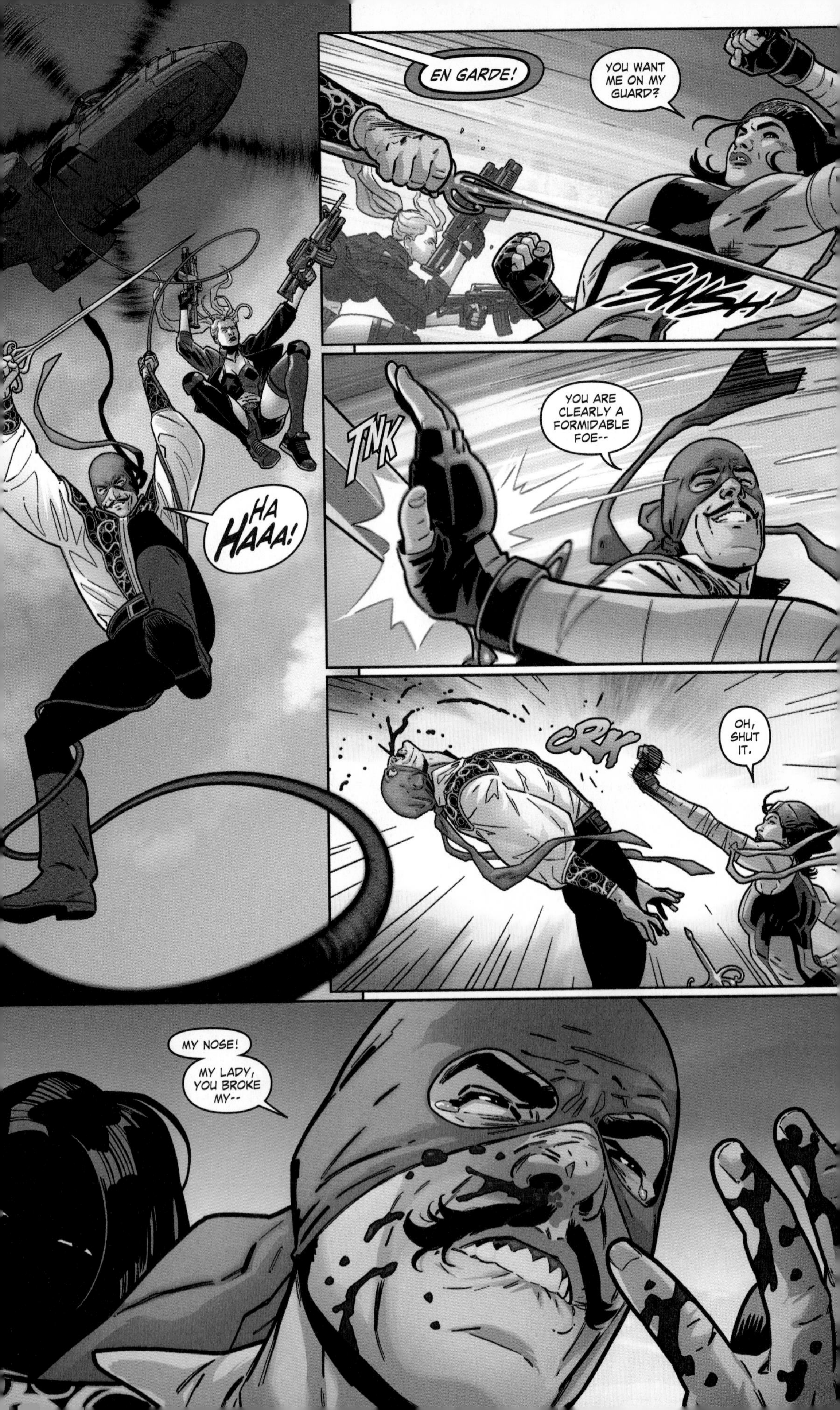
HA HAAA!
EN GARDE!
YOU WANT ME ON MY GUARD?
SNSH
TINK
YOU ARE CLEARLY A FORMIDABLE FOE--
CRK
OH, SHUT IT.
MY NOSE!
MY LADY, YOU BROKE MY--

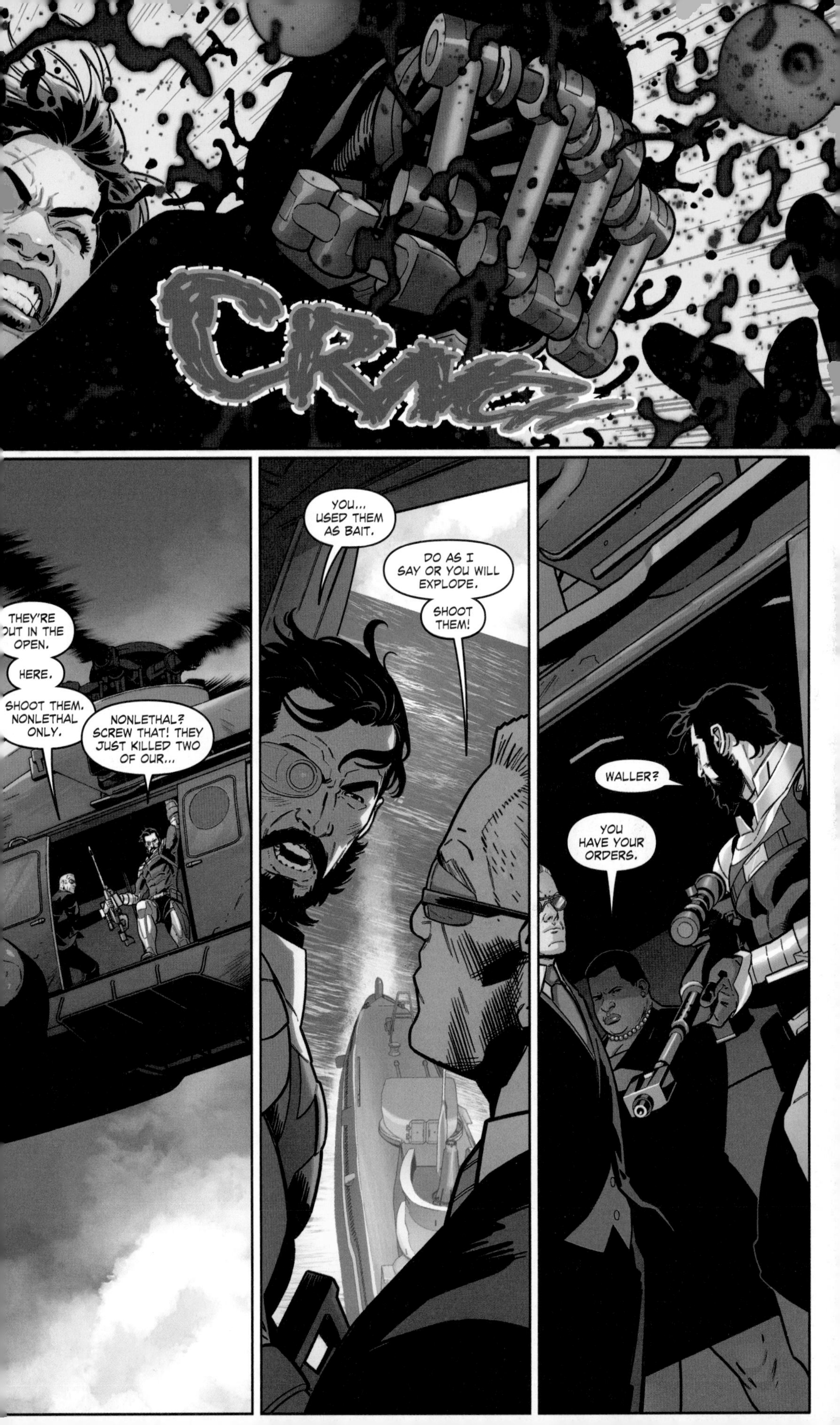
CRACK
THEY'RE OUT IN THE OPEN.
HERE.
SHOOT THEM. NONLETHAL ONLY.
NONLETHAL? SCREW THAT! THEY JUST KILLED TWO OF OUR...
YOU... USED THEM AS BAIT.
DO AS I SAY OR YOU WILL EXPLODE.
SHOOT THEM!
WALLER?
YOU HAVE YOUR ORDERS.

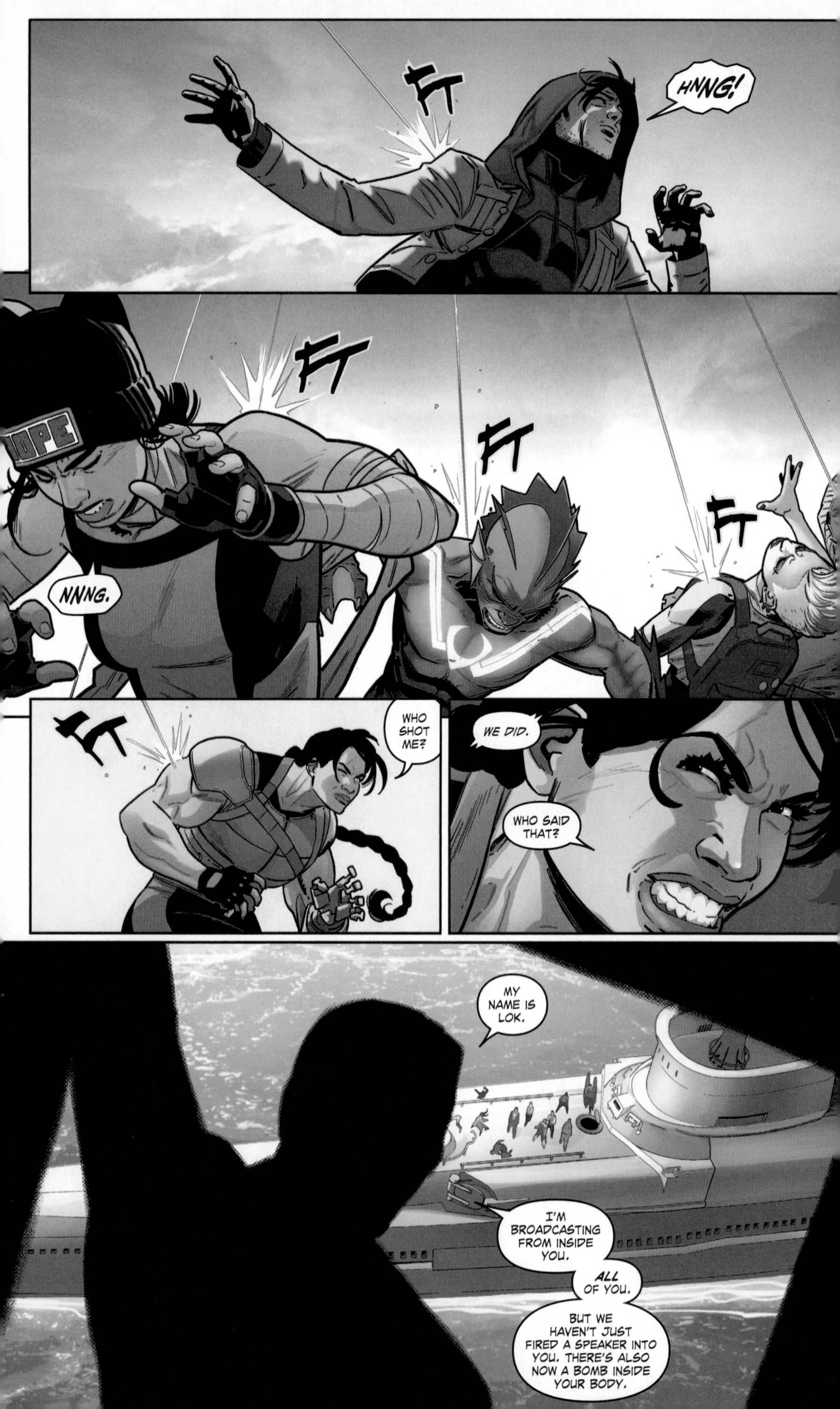
FT
HNNG!
FT
FT
FT
HOPE
NNNG.
FT
WHO SHOT ME?
WE DID.
WHO SAID THAT?
MY NAME IS LOK.
I'M BROADCASTING FROM INSIDE YOU.
ALL OF YOU.
BUT WE HAVEN'T JUST FIRED A SPEAKER INTO YOU. THERE'S ALSO NOW A BOMB INSIDE YOUR BODY.

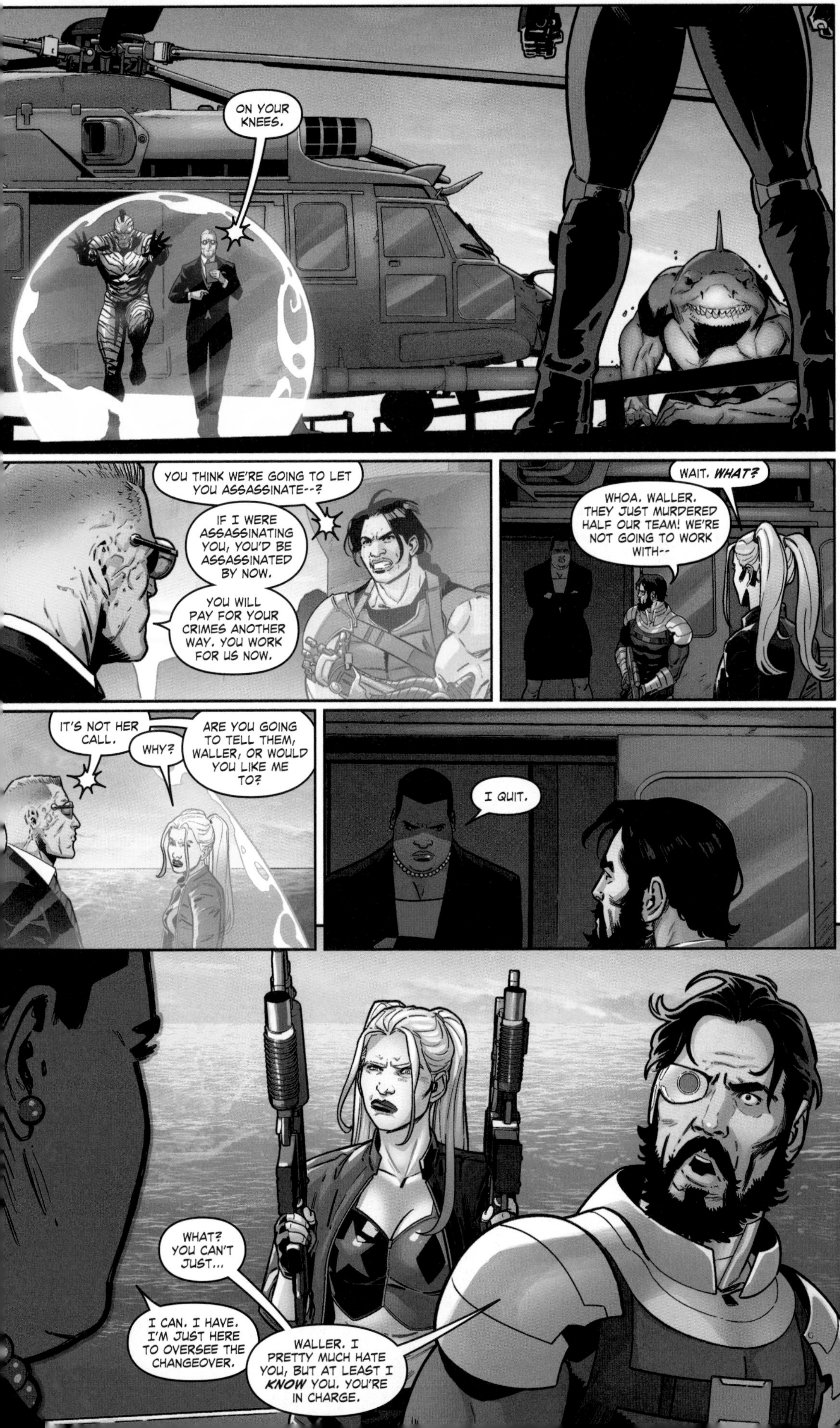
ON YOUR KNEES.
YOU THINK WE'RE GOING TO LET YOU ASSASSINATE--?
IF I WERE ASSASSINATING YOU, YOU'D BE ASSASSINATED BY NOW.
YOU WILL PAY FOR YOUR CRIMES ANOTHER WAY. YOU WORK FOR US NOW.
WAIT. *WHAT?*
WHOA. WALLER. THEY JUST MURDERED HALF OUR TEAM! WE'RE NOT GOING TO WORK WITH--
IT'S NOT HER CALL.
WHY?
ARE YOU GOING TO TELL THEM, WALLER, OR WOULD YOU LIKE ME TO?
I QUIT.
WHAT? YOU CAN'T JUST...
I CAN. I HAVE. I'M JUST HERE TO OVERSEE THE CHANGEOVER.
WALLER. I PRETTY MUCH HATE YOU, BUT AT LEAST I ***KNOW*** YOU. YOU'RE IN CHARGE.

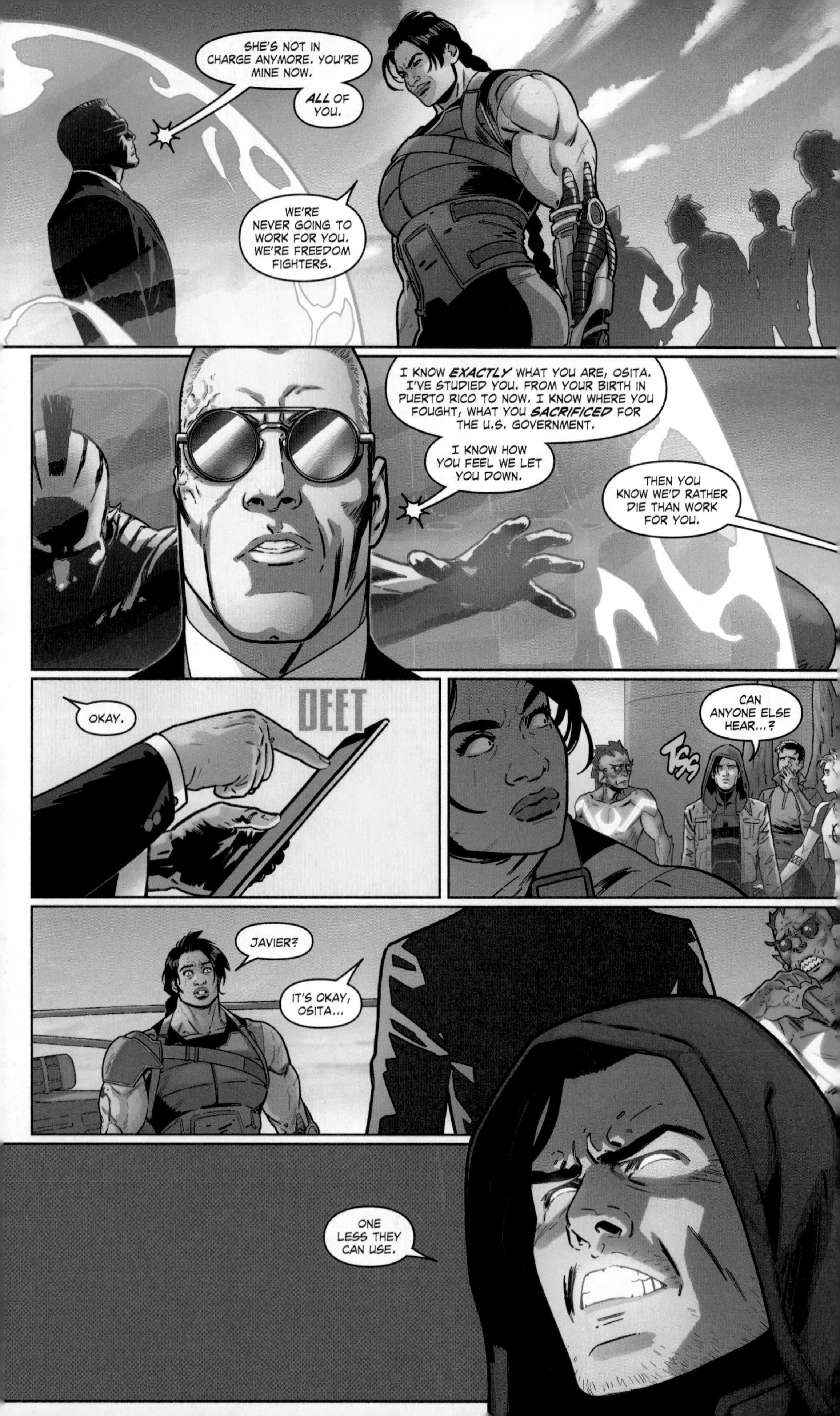

SHE'S NOT IN CHARGE ANYMORE. YOU'RE MINE NOW.
ALL OF YOU.
WE'RE NEVER GOING TO WORK FOR YOU. WE'RE FREEDOM FIGHTERS.
I KNOW EXACTLY WHAT YOU ARE, OSITA. I'VE STUDIED YOU. FROM YOUR BIRTH IN PUERTO RICO TO NOW. I KNOW WHERE YOU FOUGHT, WHAT YOU SACRIFICED FOR THE U.S. GOVERNMENT.
I KNOW HOW YOU FEEL WE LET YOU DOWN.
THEN YOU KNOW WE'D RATHER DIE THAN WORK FOR YOU.
OKAY.
DEET
CAN ANYONE ELSE HEAR...?
TSS
JAVIER?
IT'S OKAY, OSITA...
ONE LESS THEY CAN USE.

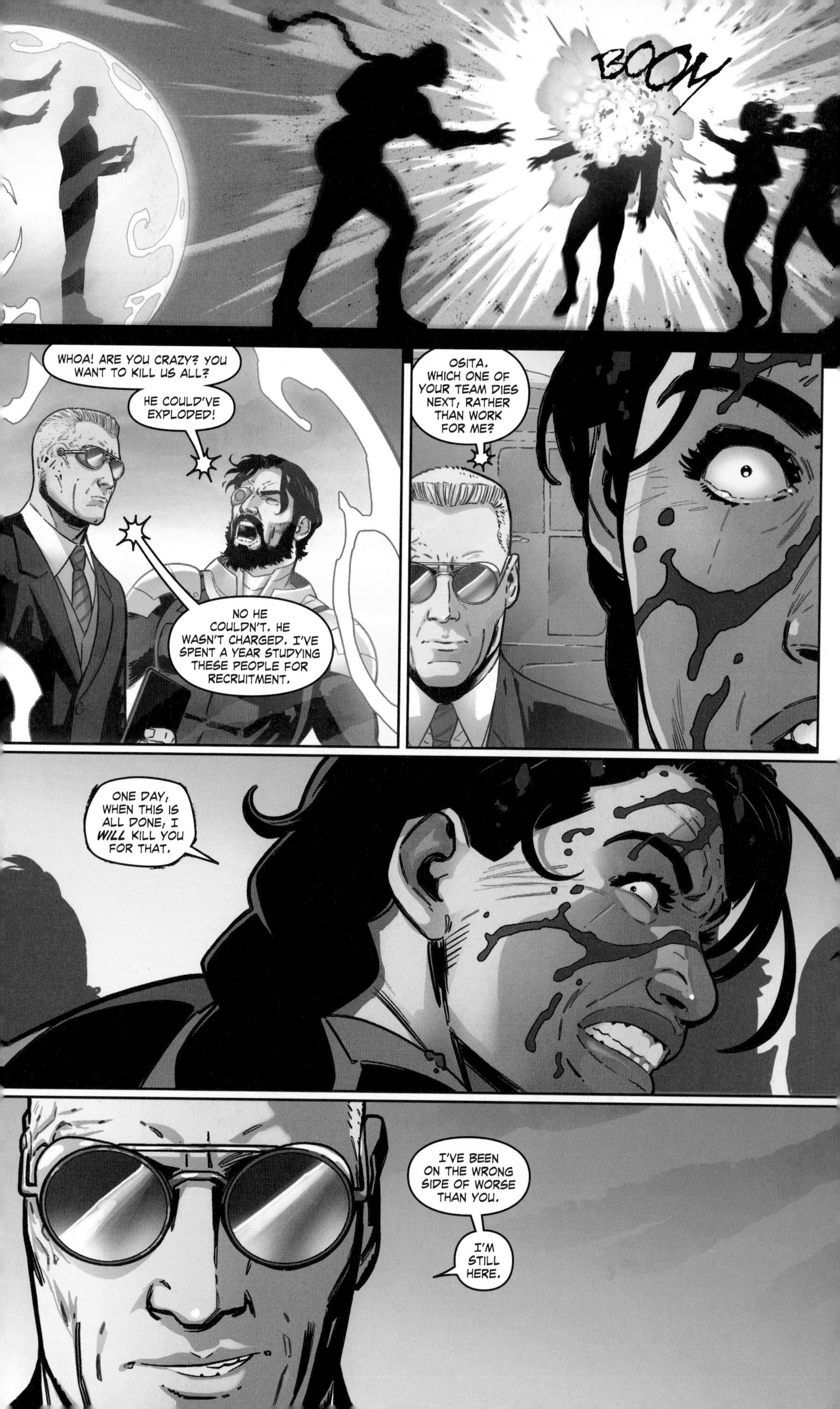
BOOM
WHOA! ARE YOU CRAZY? YOU WANT TO KILL US ALL?
HE COULD'VE EXPLODED!
NO HE COULDN'T. HE WASN'T CHARGED. I'VE SPENT A YEAR STUDYING THESE PEOPLE FOR RECRUITMENT.
OSITA. WHICH ONE OF YOUR TEAM DIES NEXT, RATHER THAN WORK FOR ME?
ONE DAY, WHEN THIS IS ALL DONE, I *WILL* KILL YOU FOR THAT.
I'VE BEEN ON THE WRONG SIDE OF WORSE THAN YOU.
I'M STILL HERE.

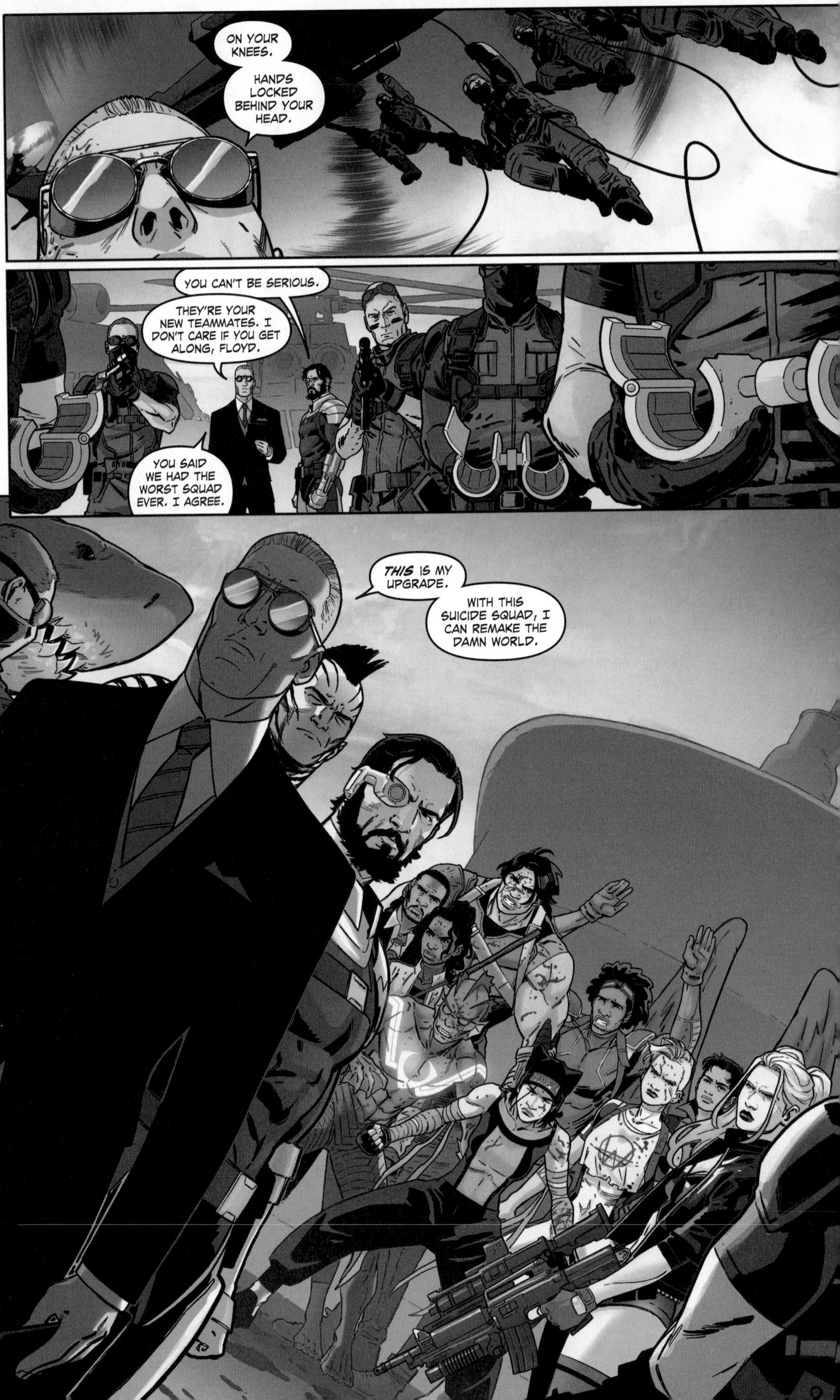
ON YOUR KNEES.
HANDS LOCKED BEHIND YOUR HEAD.
YOU CAN'T BE SERIOUS.
THEY'RE YOUR NEW TEAMMATES. I DON'T CARE IF YOU GET ALONG, FLOYD.
YOU SAID WE HAD THE WORST SQUAD EVER. I AGREE.
THIS IS MY UPGRADE.
WITH THIS SUICIDE SQUAD, I CAN REMAKE THE DAMN WORLD.

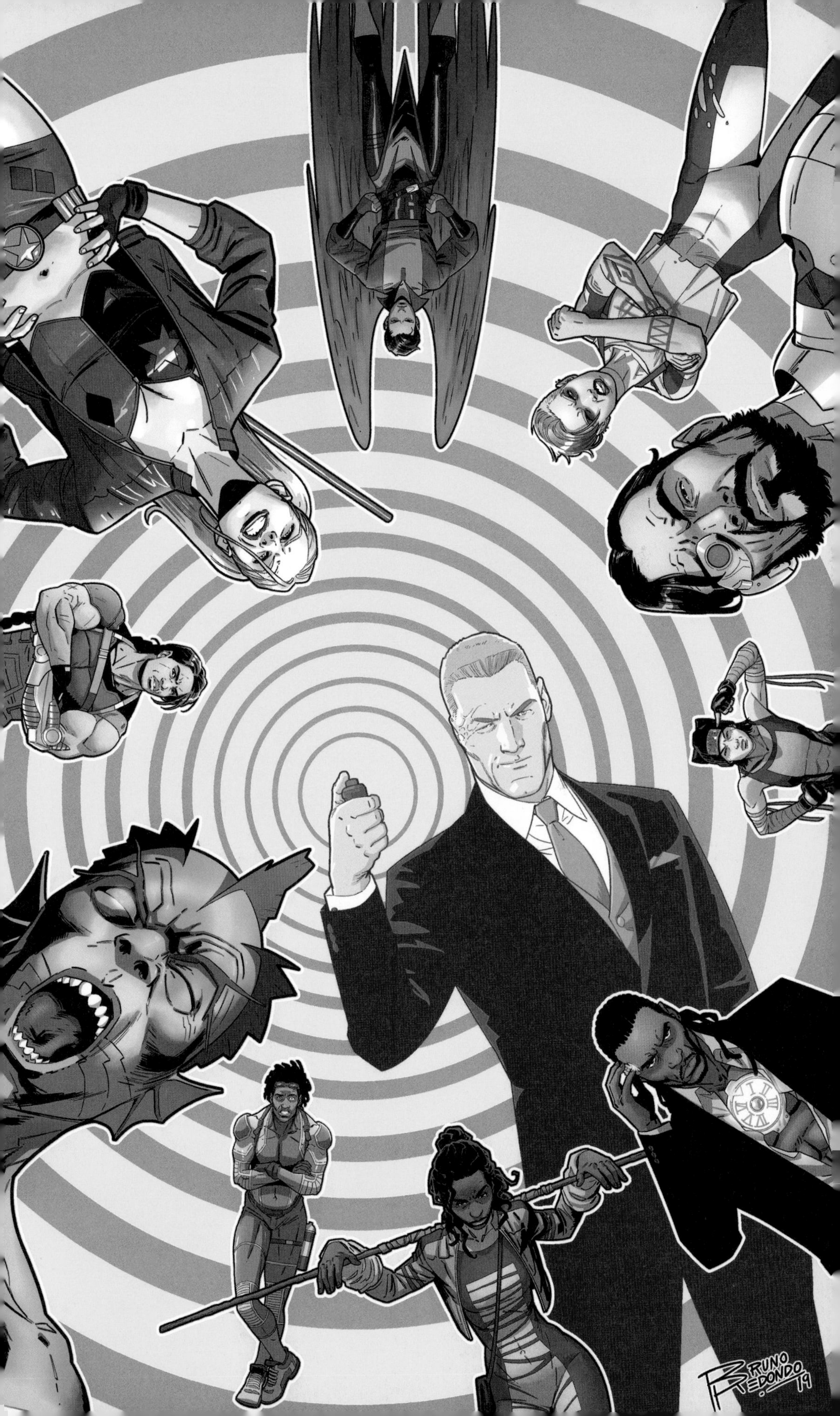
BRUNO REDONDO '19

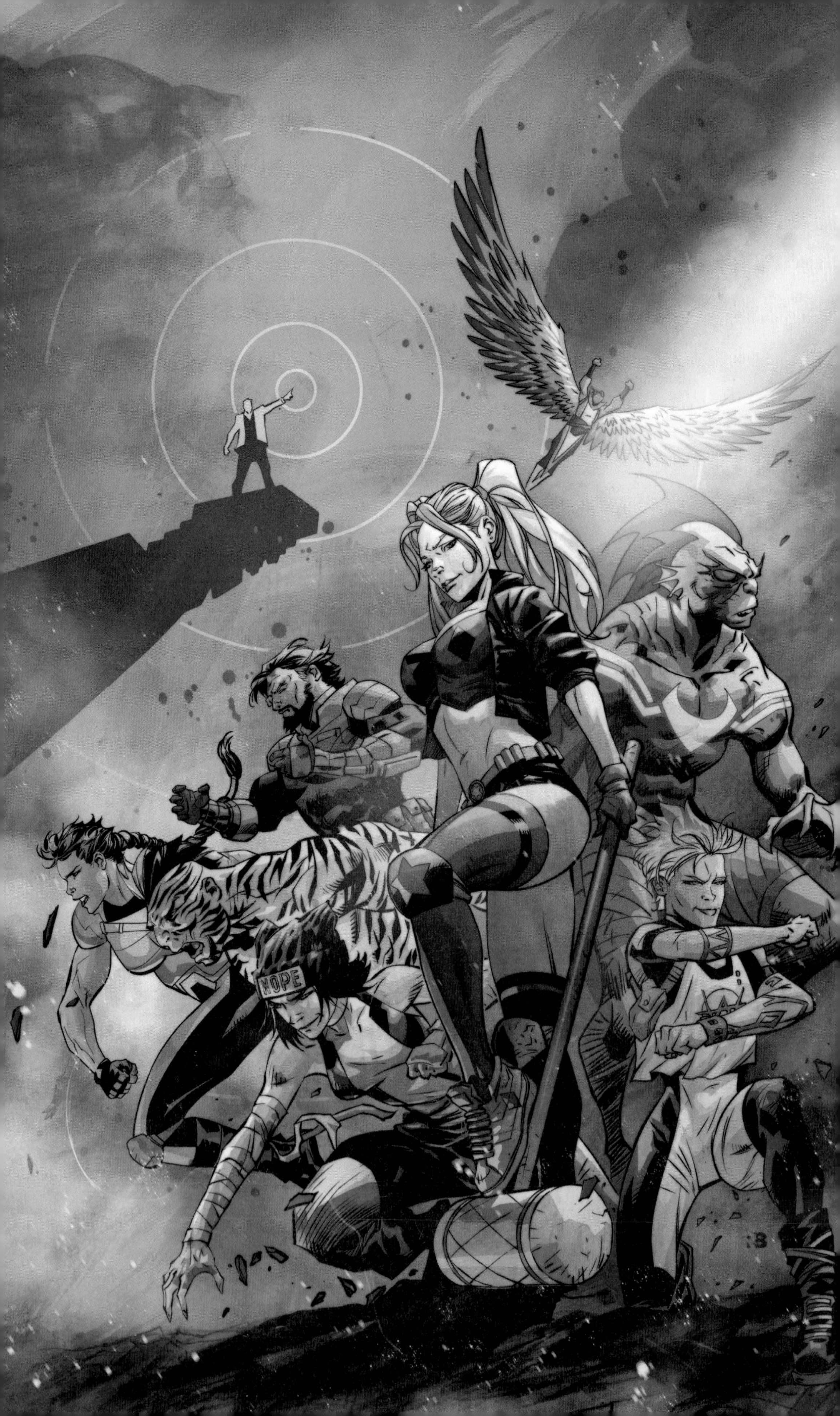
NOPE

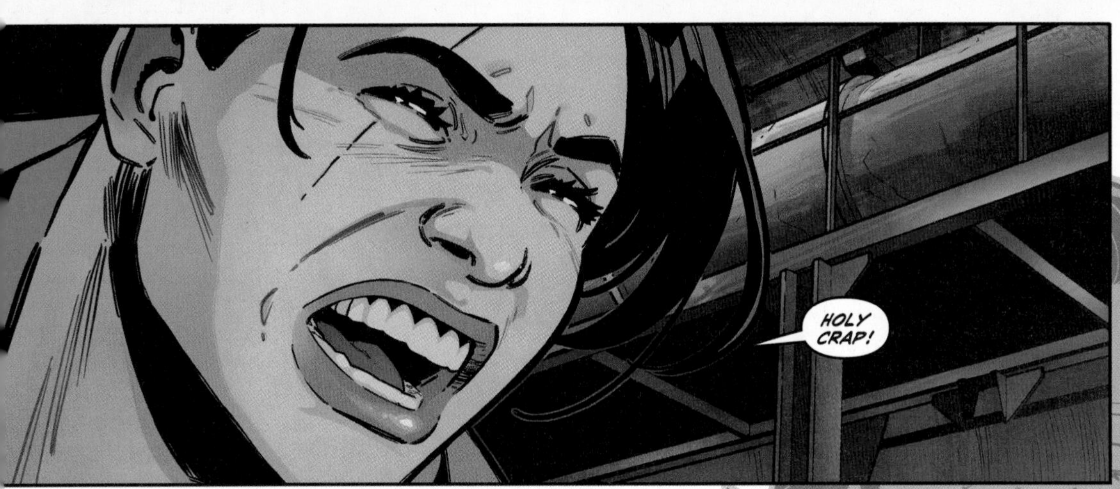
HOLY CRAP!

written by TOM TAYLOR

art and cover by BRUNO REDONDO

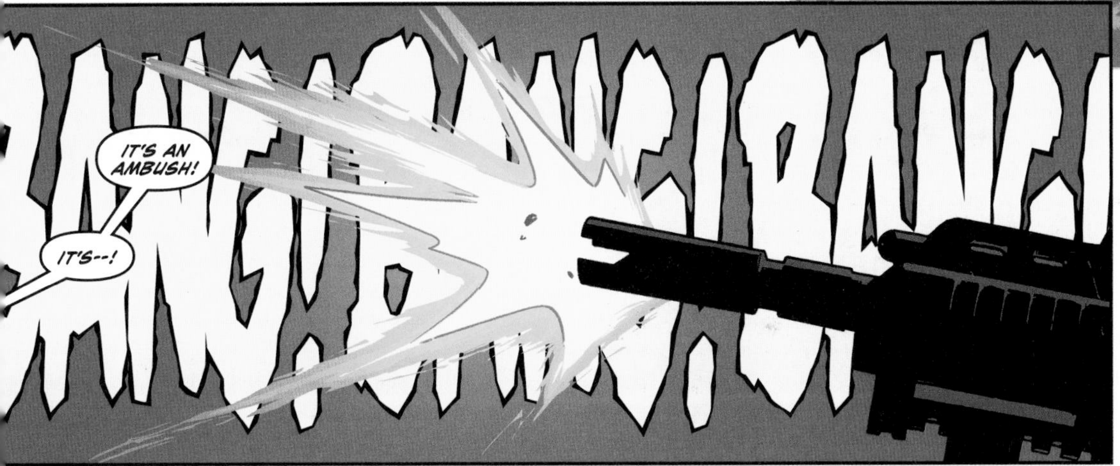
IT'S AN AMBUSH!
IT'S--!

color by ADRIANO LUCAS letters by WES ABBOTT

variant cover by RYAN BENJAMIN

editor ANDREA SHEA group editor ALEX R. CARR

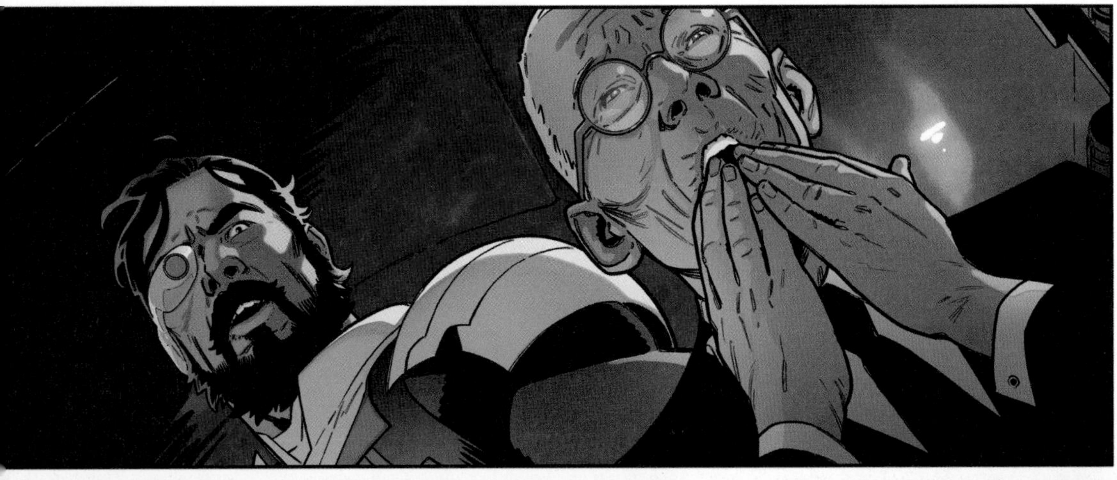

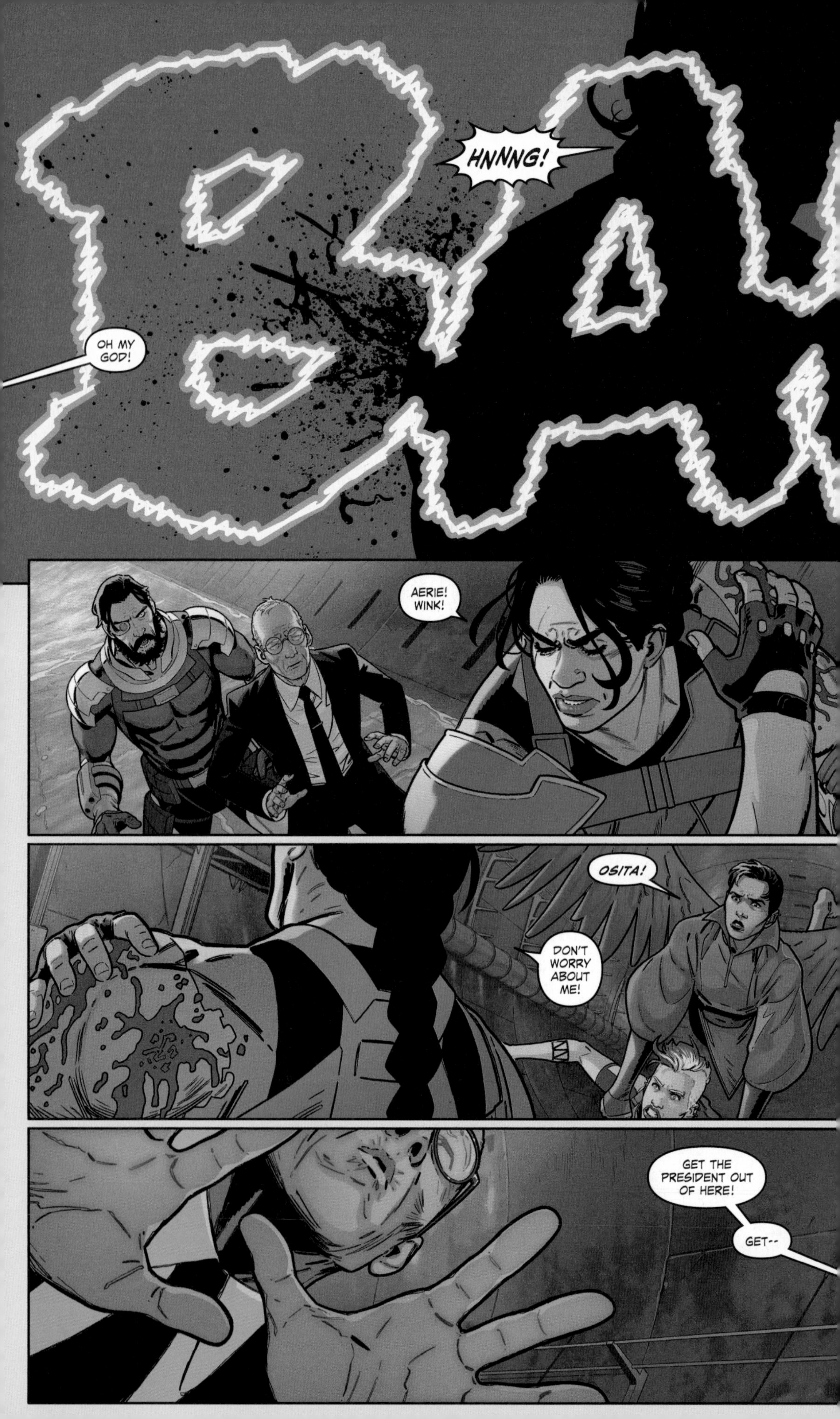
HNNNG!
OH MY GOD!
AERIE! WINK!
OSITA!
DON'T WORRY ABOUT ME!
GET THE PRESIDENT OUT OF HERE!
GET--

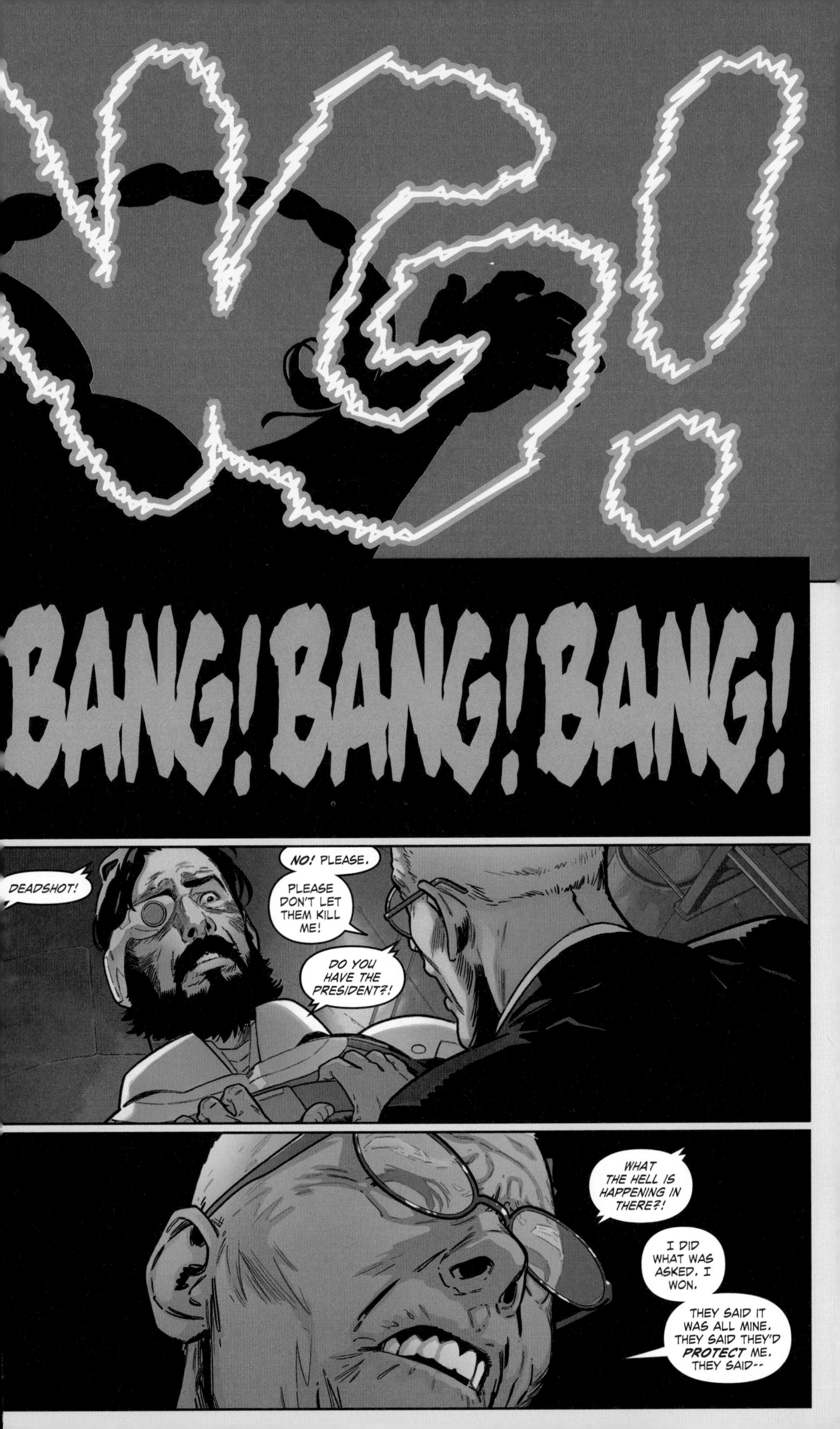
BANG! BANG! BANG!
DEADSHOT!
NO! PLEASE.
PLEASE DON'T LET THEM KILL ME!
DO YOU HAVE THE PRESIDENT?!
WHAT THE HELL IS HAPPENING IN THERE?!
I DID WHAT WAS ASKED. I WON.
THEY SAID IT WAS ALL MINE. THEY SAID THEY'D PROTECT ME. THEY SAID--

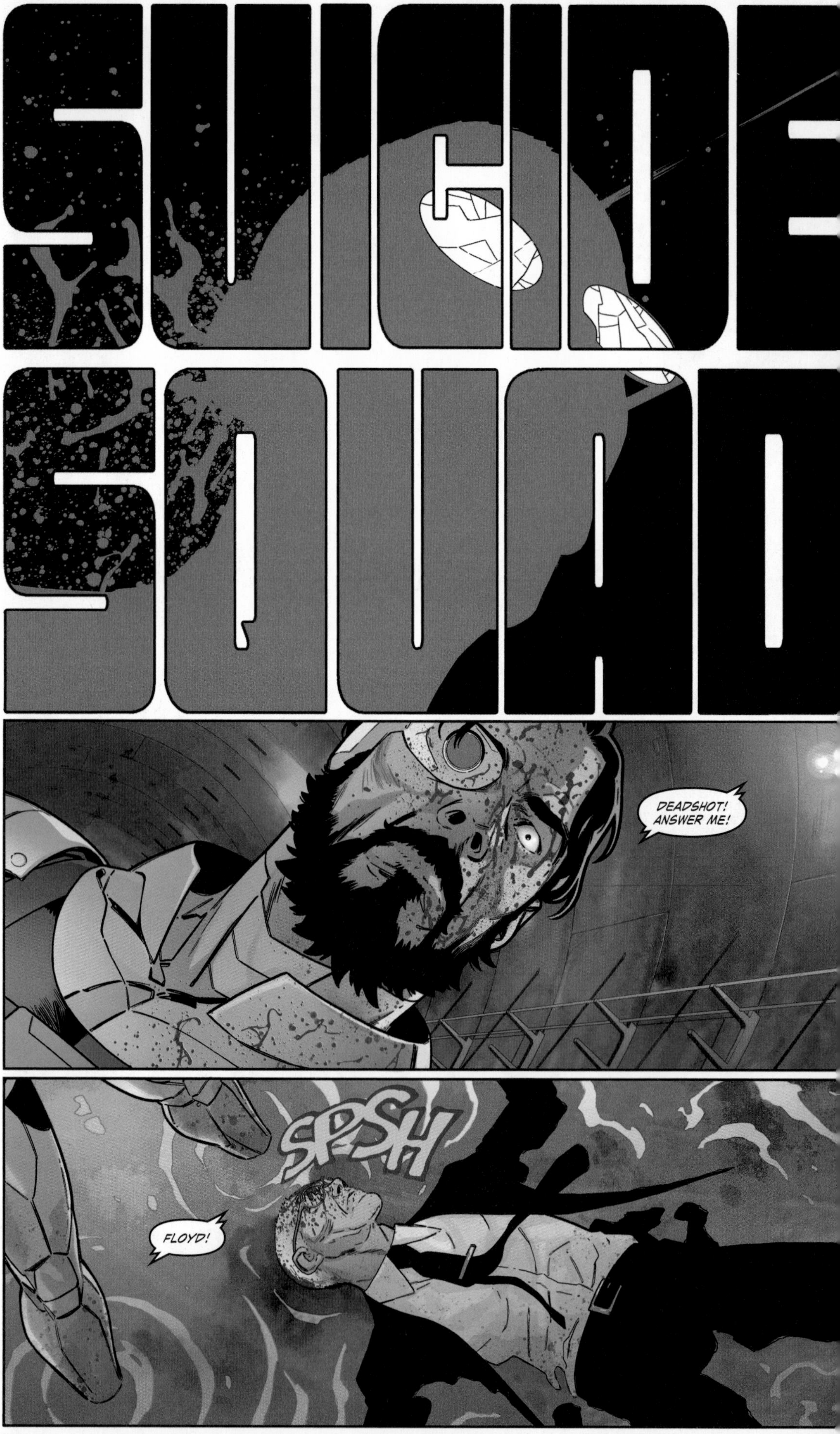
SUICIDE SQUAD
DEADSHOT! ANSWER ME!
SPSH
FLOYD!

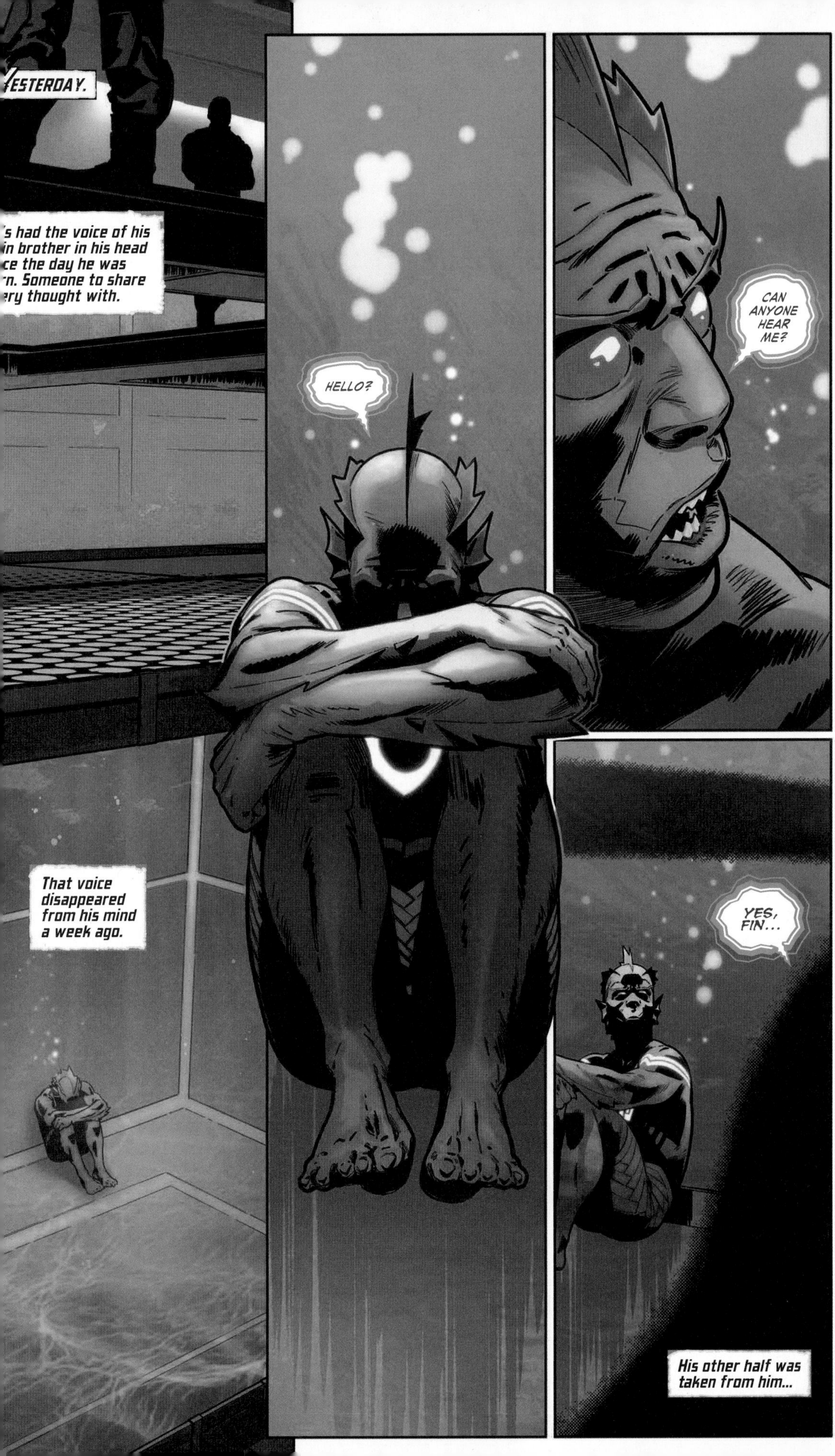
YESTERDAY.
'S HAD THE VOICE OF HIS
IN BROTHER IN HIS HEAD
CE THE DAY HE WAS
N. SOMEONE TO SHARE
RY THOUGHT WITH.
HELLO?
CAN ANYONE HEAR ME?
That voice disappeared from his mind a week ago.
YES, FIN...
His other half was taken from him...

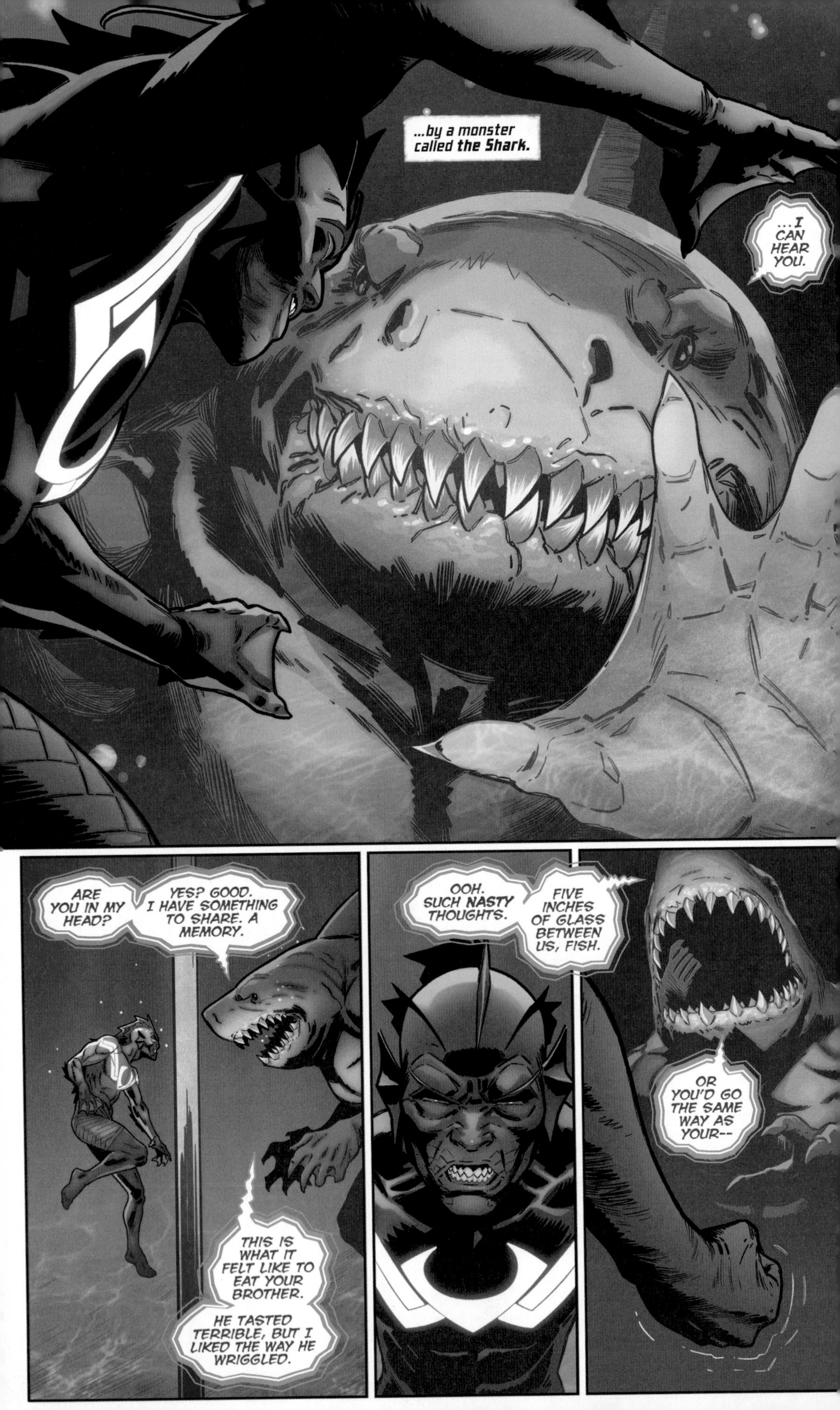
...by a monster called the Shark.
...I CAN HEAR YOU.
ARE YOU IN MY HEAD?
YES? GOOD. I HAVE SOMETHING TO SHARE. A MEMORY.
THIS IS WHAT IT FELT LIKE TO EAT YOUR BROTHER.
HE TASTED TERRIBLE, BUT I LIKED THE WAY HE WRIGGLED.
OOH. SUCH NASTY THOUGHTS.
FIVE INCHES OF GLASS BETWEEN US, FISH.
OR YOU'D GO THE SAME WAY AS YOUR--

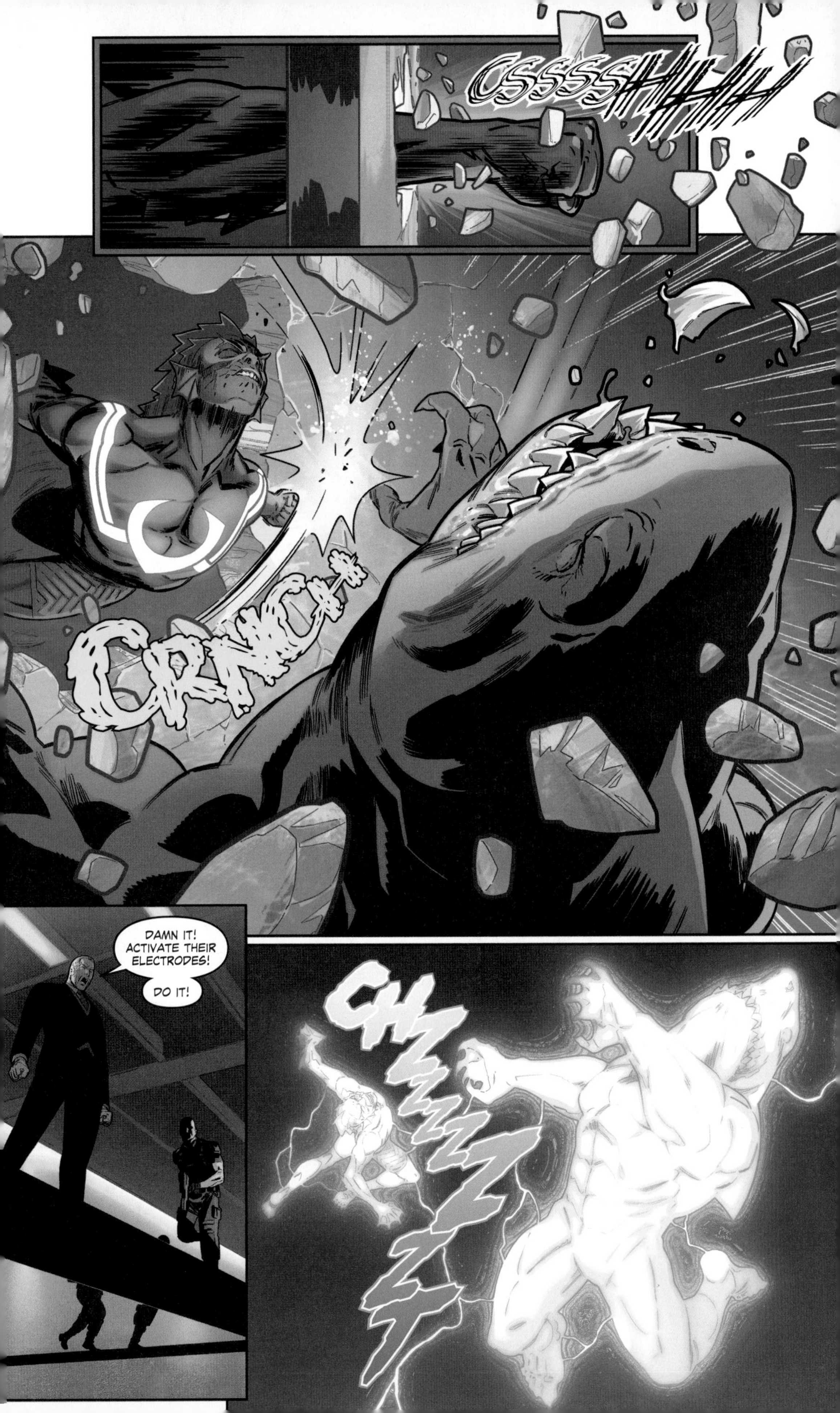
CSSSSHHHHH
CRNCH
DAMN IT! ACTIVATE THEIR ELECTRODES!
DO IT!
CHZZZZZZZT

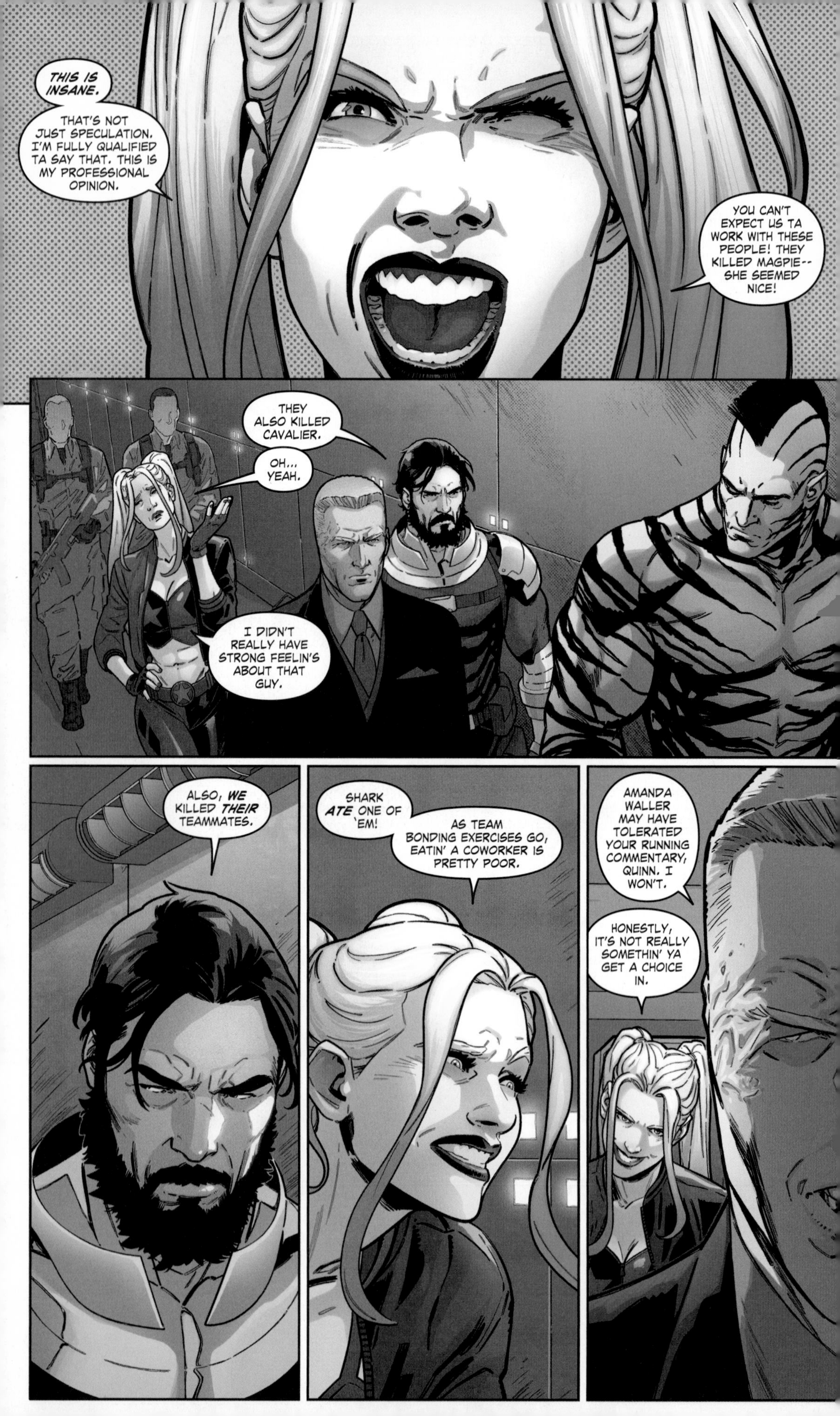
THIS IS INSANE.
THAT'S NOT JUST SPECULATION. I'M FULLY QUALIFIED TA SAY THAT. THIS IS MY PROFESSIONAL OPINION.
YOU CAN'T EXPECT US TA WORK WITH THESE PEOPLE! THEY KILLED MAGPIE-- SHE SEEMED NICE!
THEY ALSO KILLED CAVALIER.
OH... YEAH.
I DIDN'T REALLY HAVE STRONG FEELIN'S ABOUT THAT GUY.
ALSO, WE KILLED THEIR TEAMMATES.
SHARK ATE ONE OF 'EM!
AS TEAM BONDING EXERCISES GO, EATIN' A COWORKER IS PRETTY POOR.
AMANDA WALLER MAY HAVE TOLERATED YOUR RUNNING COMMENTARY, QUINN. I WON'T.
HONESTLY, IT'S NOT REALLY SOMETHIN' YA GET A CHOICE IN.

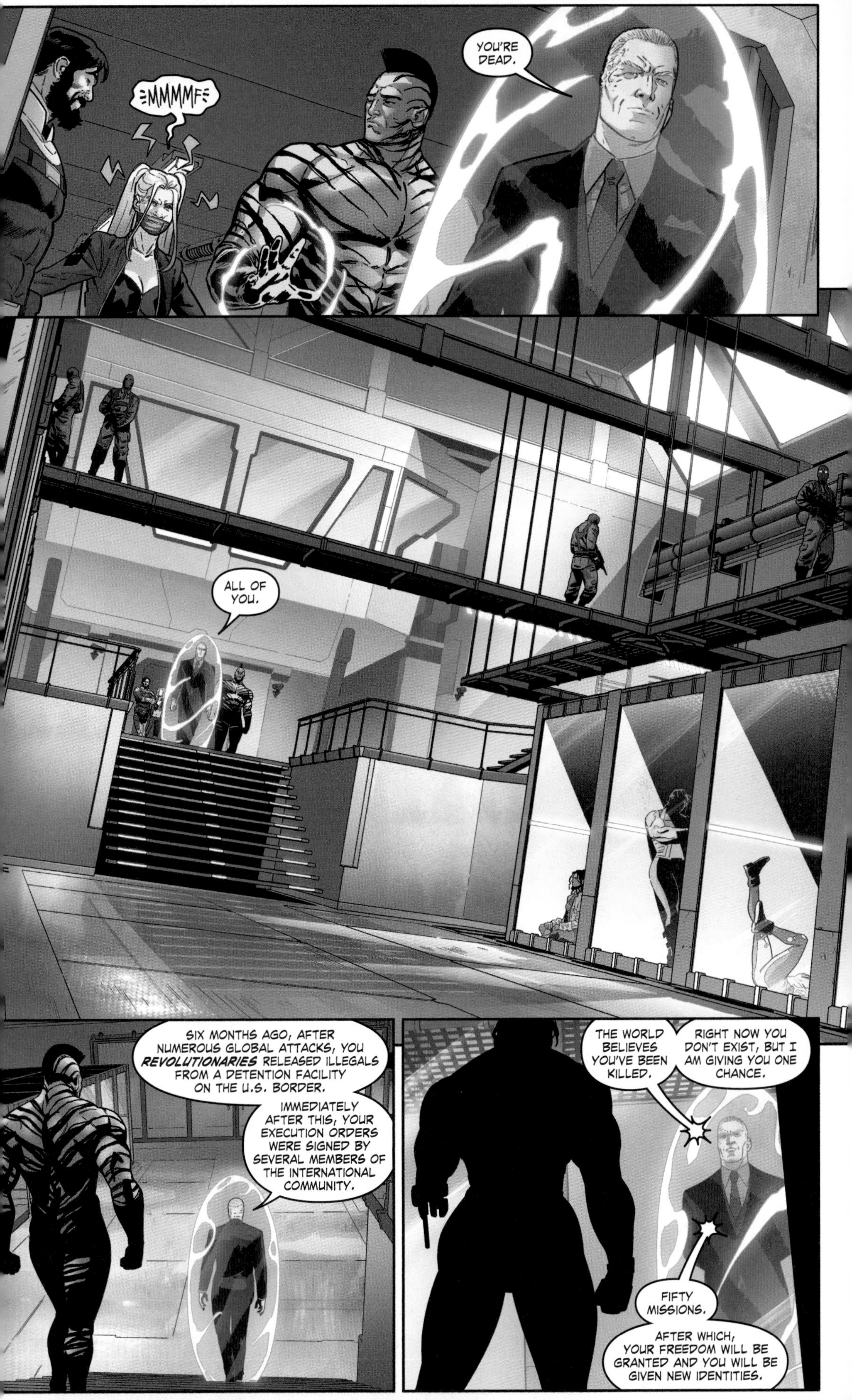
MMMMF
YOU'RE DEAD.
ALL OF YOU.
SIX MONTHS AGO, AFTER NUMEROUS GLOBAL ATTACKS, YOU REVOLUTIONARIES RELEASED ILLEGALS FROM A DETENTION FACILITY ON THE U.S. BORDER.
IMMEDIATELY AFTER THIS, YOUR EXECUTION ORDERS WERE SIGNED BY SEVERAL MEMBERS OF THE INTERNATIONAL COMMUNITY.
THE WORLD BELIEVES YOU'VE BEEN KILLED.
RIGHT NOW YOU DON'T EXIST, BUT I AM GIVING YOU ONE CHANCE.
FIFTY MISSIONS.
AFTER WHICH, YOUR FREEDOM WILL BE GRANTED AND YOU WILL BE GIVEN NEW IDENTITIES.

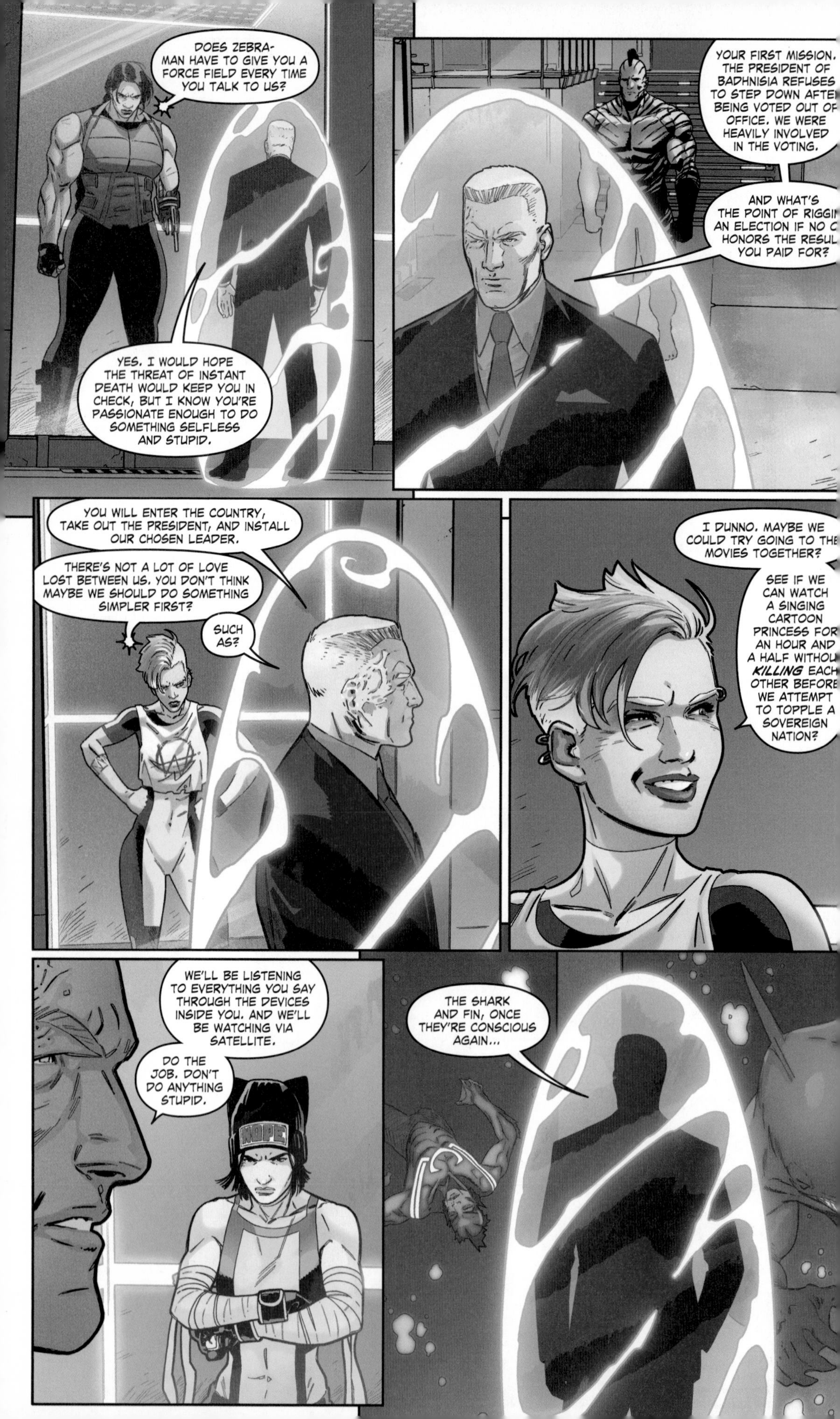
DOES ZEBRA-MAN HAVE TO GIVE YOU A FORCE FIELD EVERY TIME YOU TALK TO US?
YES. I WOULD HOPE THE THREAT OF INSTANT DEATH WOULD KEEP YOU IN CHECK, BUT I KNOW YOU'RE PASSIONATE ENOUGH TO DO SOMETHING SELFLESS AND STUPID.
YOUR FIRST MISSION. THE PRESIDENT OF BADHNISIA REFUSES TO STEP DOWN AFTE BEING VOTED OUT OF OFFICE. WE WERE HEAVILY INVOLVED IN THE VOTING.
AND WHAT'S THE POINT OF RIGGI AN ELECTION IF NO C HONORS THE RESUL YOU PAID FOR?
YOU WILL ENTER THE COUNTRY, TAKE OUT THE PRESIDENT, AND INSTALL OUR CHOSEN LEADER.
THERE'S NOT A LOT OF LOVE LOST BETWEEN US. YOU DON'T THINK MAYBE WE SHOULD DO SOMETHING SIMPLER FIRST?
SUCH AS?
I DUNNO. MAYBE WE COULD TRY GOING TO THE MOVIES TOGETHER?
SEE IF WE CAN WATCH A SINGING CARTOON PRINCESS FOR AN HOUR AND A HALF WITHOU KILLING EACH OTHER BEFORE WE ATTEMPT TO TOPPLE A SOVEREIGN NATION?
WE'LL BE LISTENING TO EVERYTHING YOU SAY THROUGH THE DEVICES INSIDE YOU. AND WE'LL BE WATCHING VIA SATELLITE.
DO THE JOB. DON'T DO ANYTHING STUPID.
NOPE
THE SHARK AND FIN, ONCE THEY'RE CONSCIOUS AGAIN...

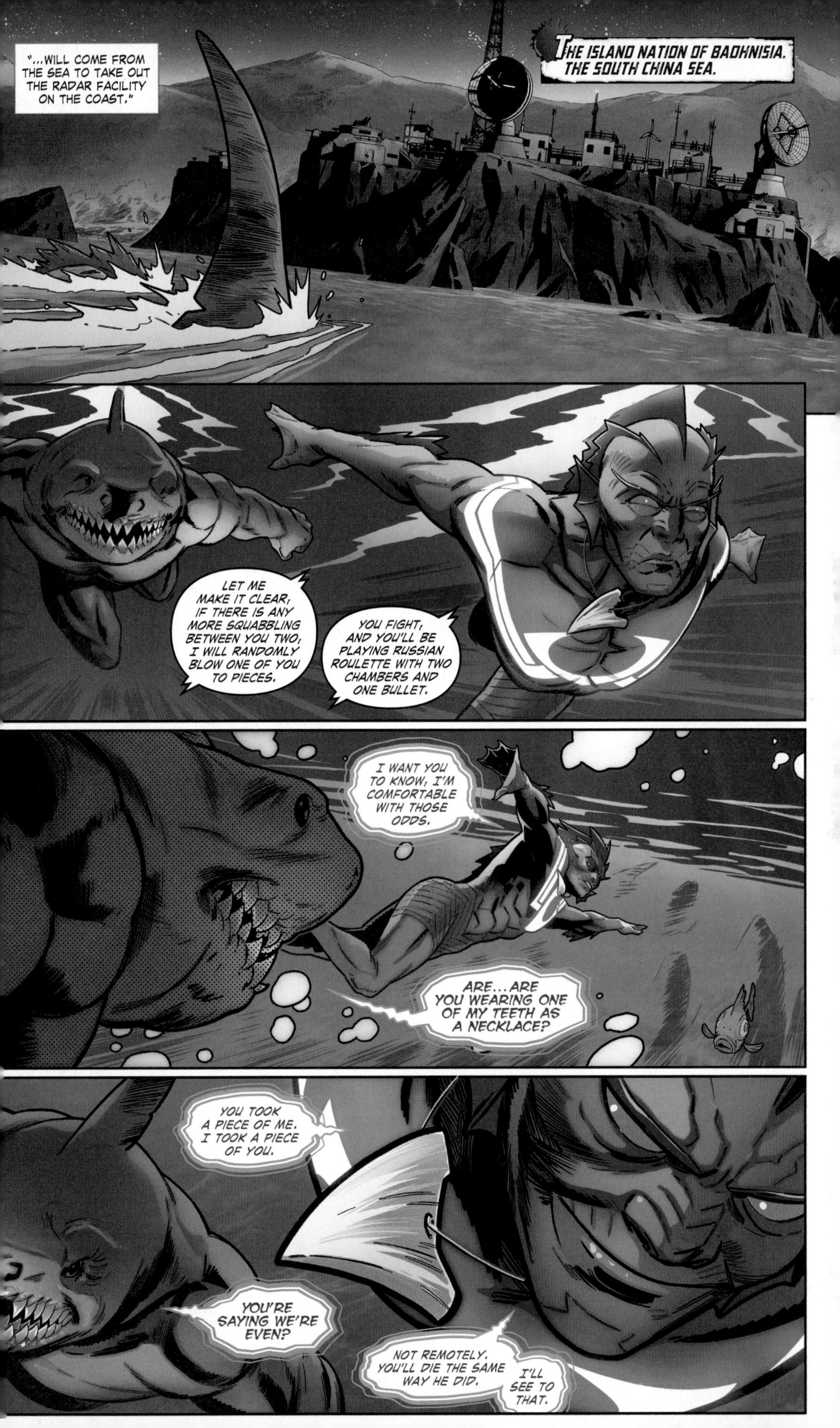
"...WILL COME FROM THE SEA TO TAKE OUT THE RADAR FACILITY ON THE COAST."
THE ISLAND NATION OF BADHNISIA. THE SOUTH CHINA SEA.
LET ME MAKE IT CLEAR, IF THERE IS ANY MORE SQUABBLING BETWEEN YOU TWO, I WILL RANDOMLY BLOW ONE OF YOU TO PIECES.
YOU FIGHT, AND YOU'LL BE PLAYING RUSSIAN ROULETTE WITH TWO CHAMBERS AND ONE BULLET.
I WANT YOU TO KNOW, I'M COMFORTABLE WITH THOSE ODDS.
ARE...ARE YOU WEARING ONE OF MY TEETH AS A NECKLACE?
YOU TOOK A PIECE OF ME. I TOOK A PIECE OF YOU.
YOU'RE SAYING WE'RE EVEN?
NOT REMOTELY. YOU'LL DIE THE SAME WAY HE DID.
I'LL SEE TO THAT.

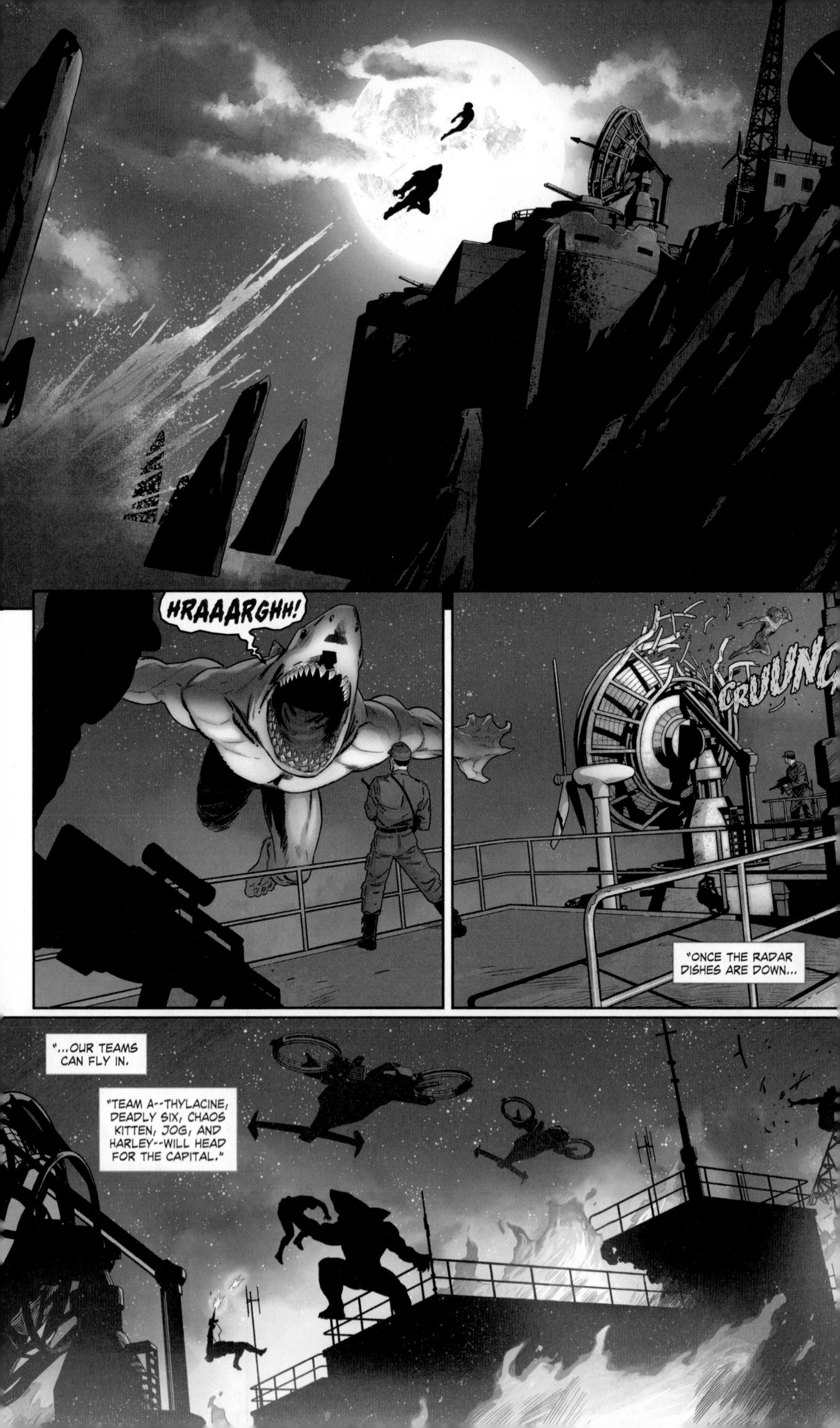
HRAAARGHH!
GRUUNG
"ONCE THE RADAR DISHES ARE DOWN...
"...OUR TEAMS CAN FLY IN.
"TEAM A--THYLACINE, DEADLY SIX, CHAOS KITTEN, JOG, AND HARLEY--WILL HEAD FOR THE CAPITAL."

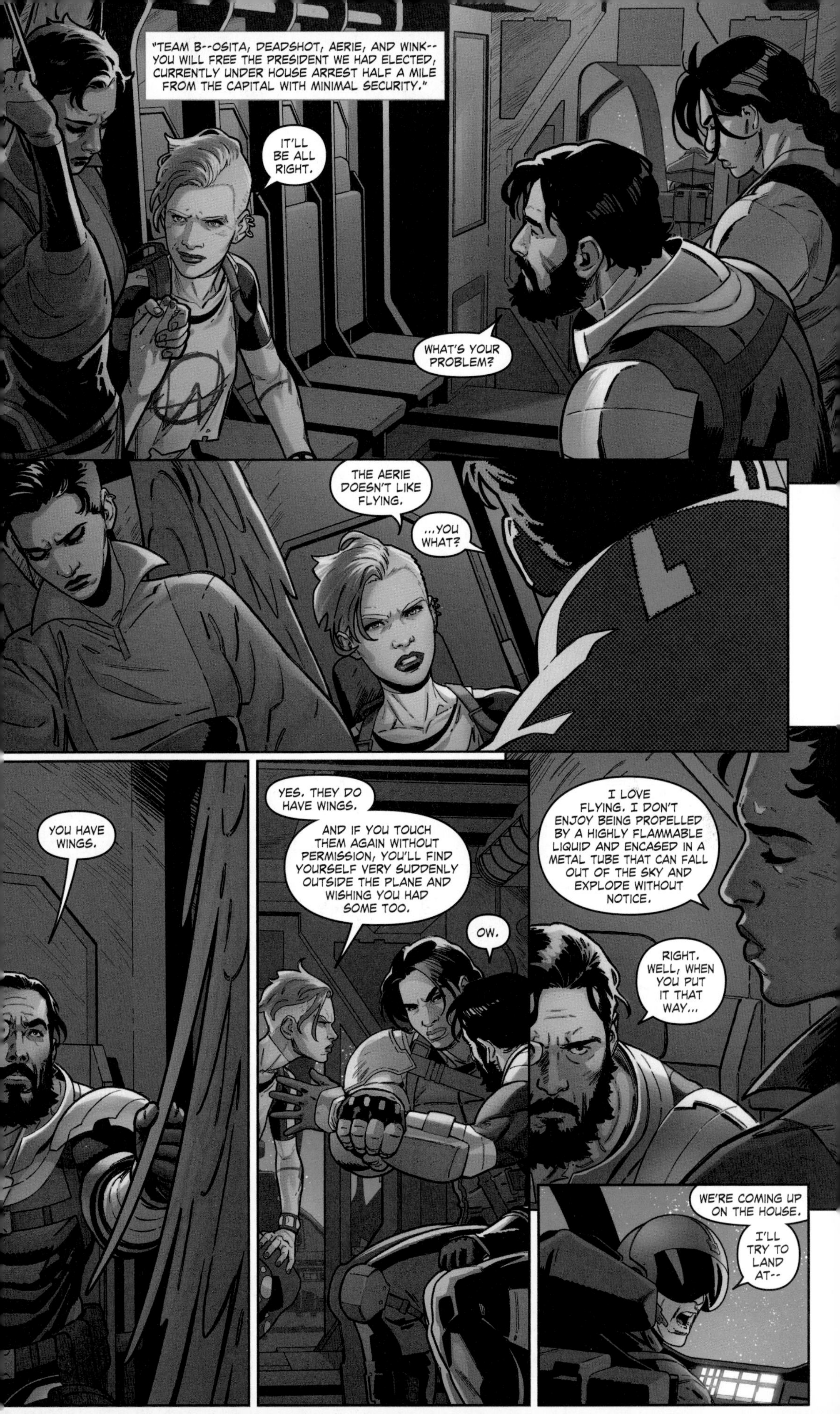
"TEAM B--OSITA, DEADSHOT, AERIE, AND WINK--YOU WILL FREE THE PRESIDENT WE HAD ELECTED, CURRENTLY UNDER HOUSE ARREST HALF A MILE FROM THE CAPITAL WITH MINIMAL SECURITY."
IT'LL BE ALL RIGHT.
WHAT'S YOUR PROBLEM?
THE AERIE DOESN'T LIKE FLYING.
...YOU WHAT?
YOU HAVE WINGS.
YES. THEY DO HAVE WINGS.
AND IF YOU TOUCH THEM AGAIN WITHOUT PERMISSION, YOU'LL FIND YOURSELF VERY SUDDENLY OUTSIDE THE PLANE AND WISHING YOU HAD SOME TOO.
OW.
I LOVE FLYING. I DON'T ENJOY BEING PROPELLED BY A HIGHLY FLAMMABLE LIQUID AND ENCASED IN A METAL TUBE THAT CAN FALL OUT OF THE SKY AND EXPLODE WITHOUT NOTICE.
RIGHT. WELL, WHEN YOU PUT IT THAT WAY...
WE'RE COMING UP ON THE HOUSE.
I'LL TRY TO LAND AT--

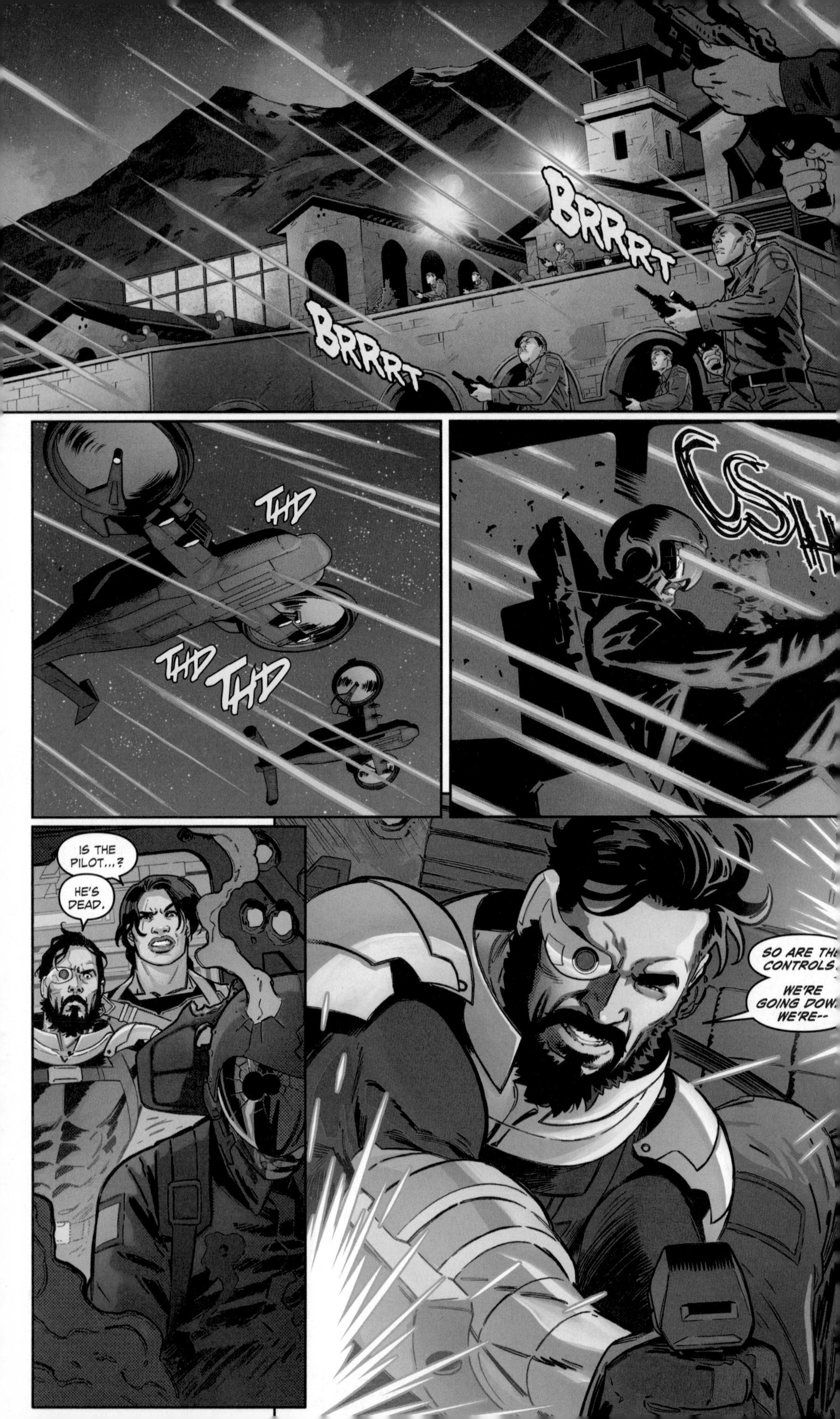
BRRRRT
BRRRRT
THD
THD THD
CSH
IS THE PILOT...?
HE'S DEAD.
SO ARE THE CONTROLS.
WE'RE GOING DOWN. WE'RE--

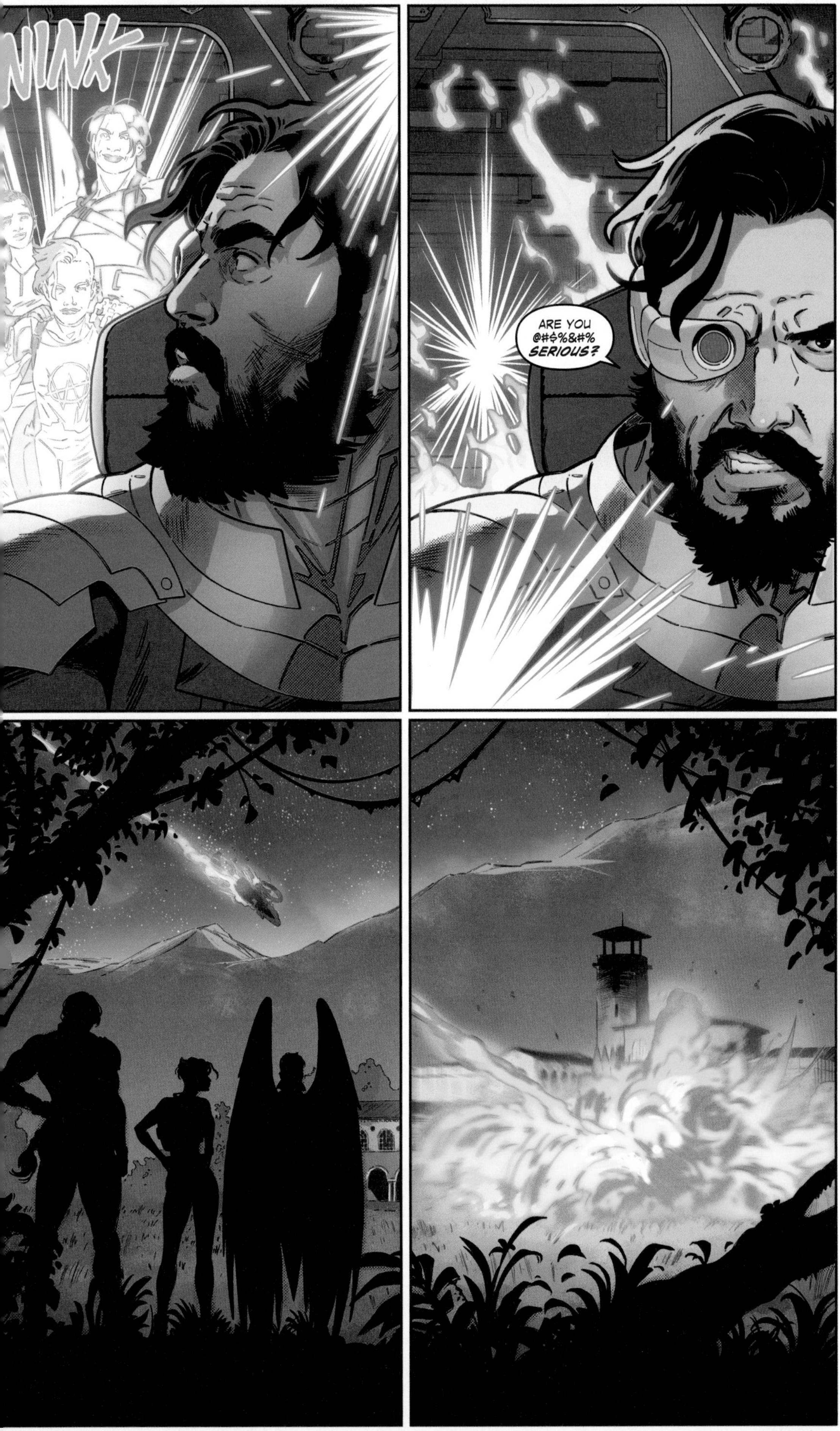
NINK
ARE YOU @#$%&#% SERIOUS?

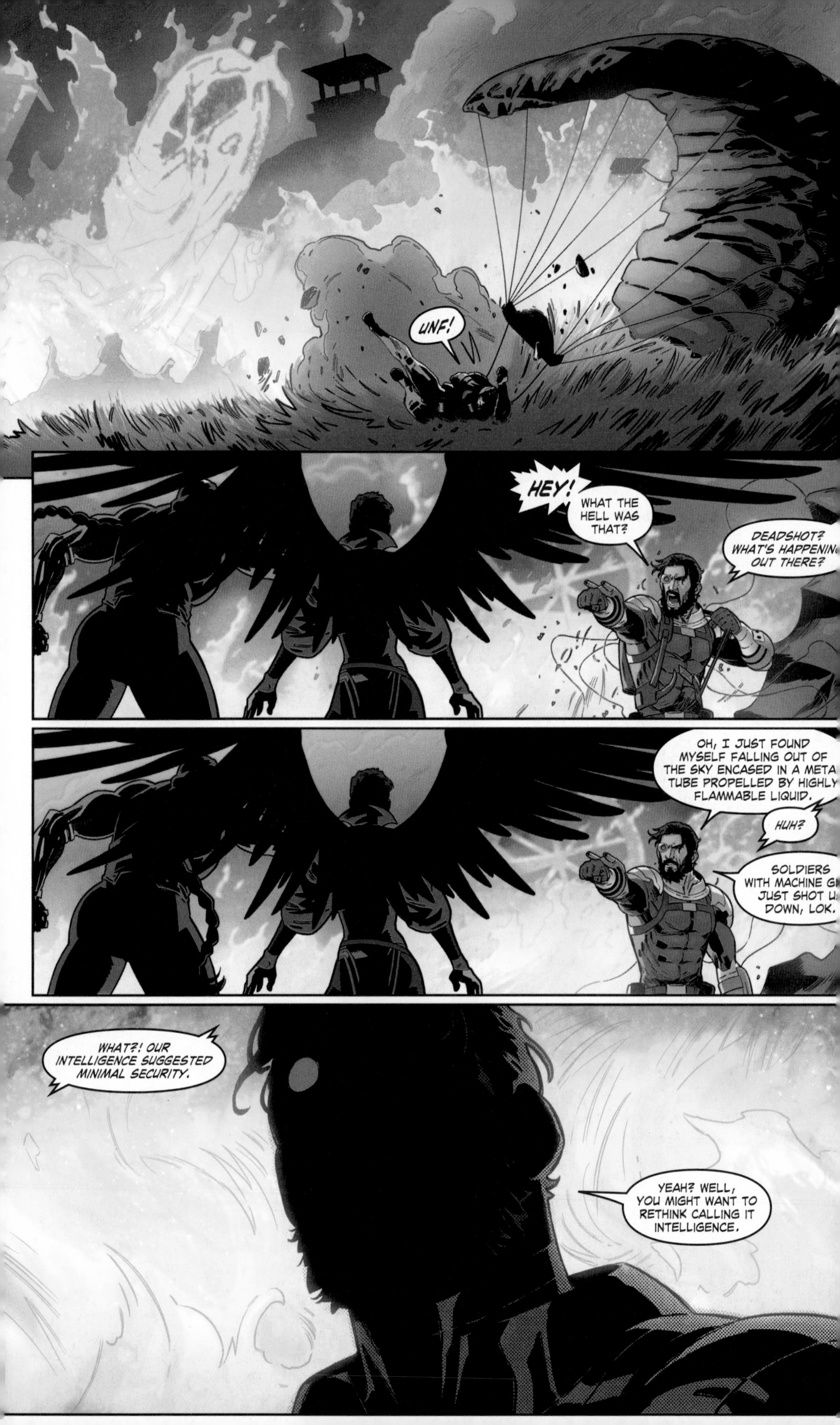
UNF!
HEY!
WHAT THE HELL WAS THAT?
DEADSHOT? WHAT'S HAPPENIN OUT THERE?
OH, I JUST FOUND MYSELF FALLING OUT OF THE SKY ENCASED IN A META TUBE PROPELLED BY HIGHLY FLAMMABLE LIQUID.
HUH?
SOLDIERS WITH MACHINE G JUST SHOT U DOWN, LOK.
WHAT?! OUR INTELLIGENCE SUGGESTED MINIMAL SECURITY.
YEAH? WELL, YOU MIGHT WANT TO RETHINK CALLING IT INTELLIGENCE.

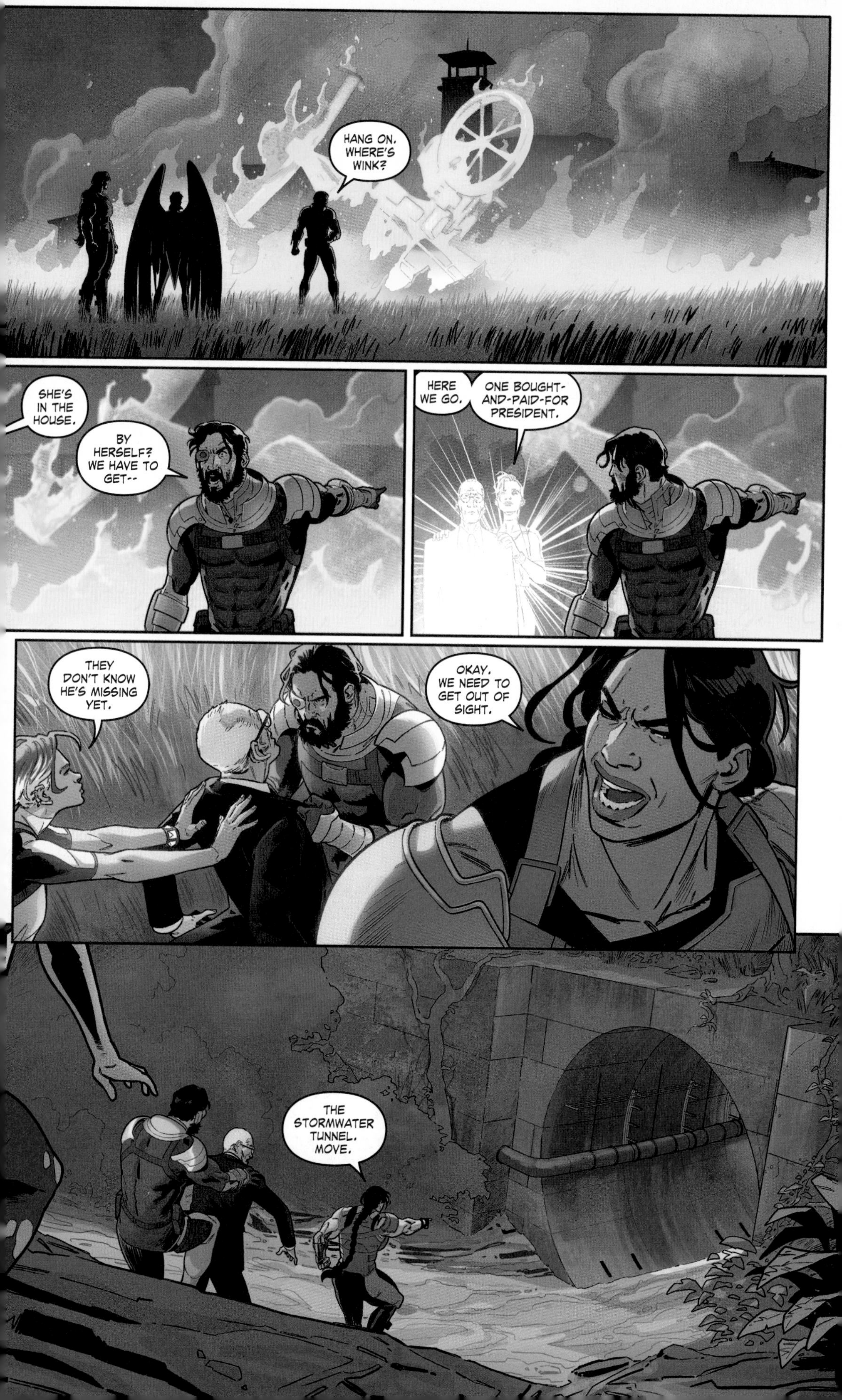
HANG ON. WHERE'S WINK?
SHE'S IN THE HOUSE.
BY HERSELF? WE HAVE TO GET--
HERE WE GO.
ONE BOUGHT-AND-PAID-FOR PRESIDENT.
THEY DON'T KNOW HE'S MISSING YET.
OKAY. WE NEED TO GET OUT OF SIGHT.
THE STORMWATER TUNNEL. MOVE.

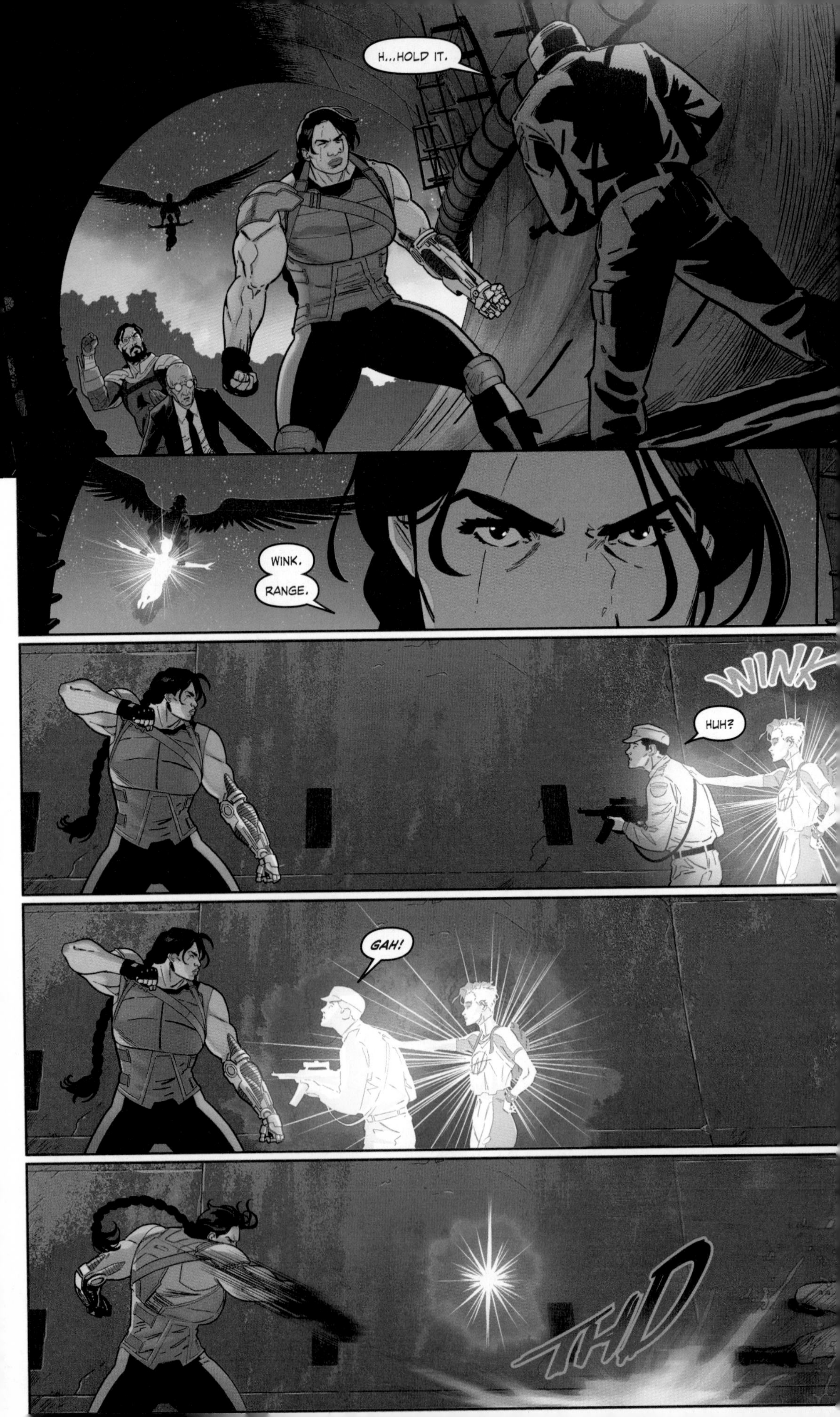
H...HOLD IT.
WINK. RANGE.
WINK
HUH?
GAH!
THD

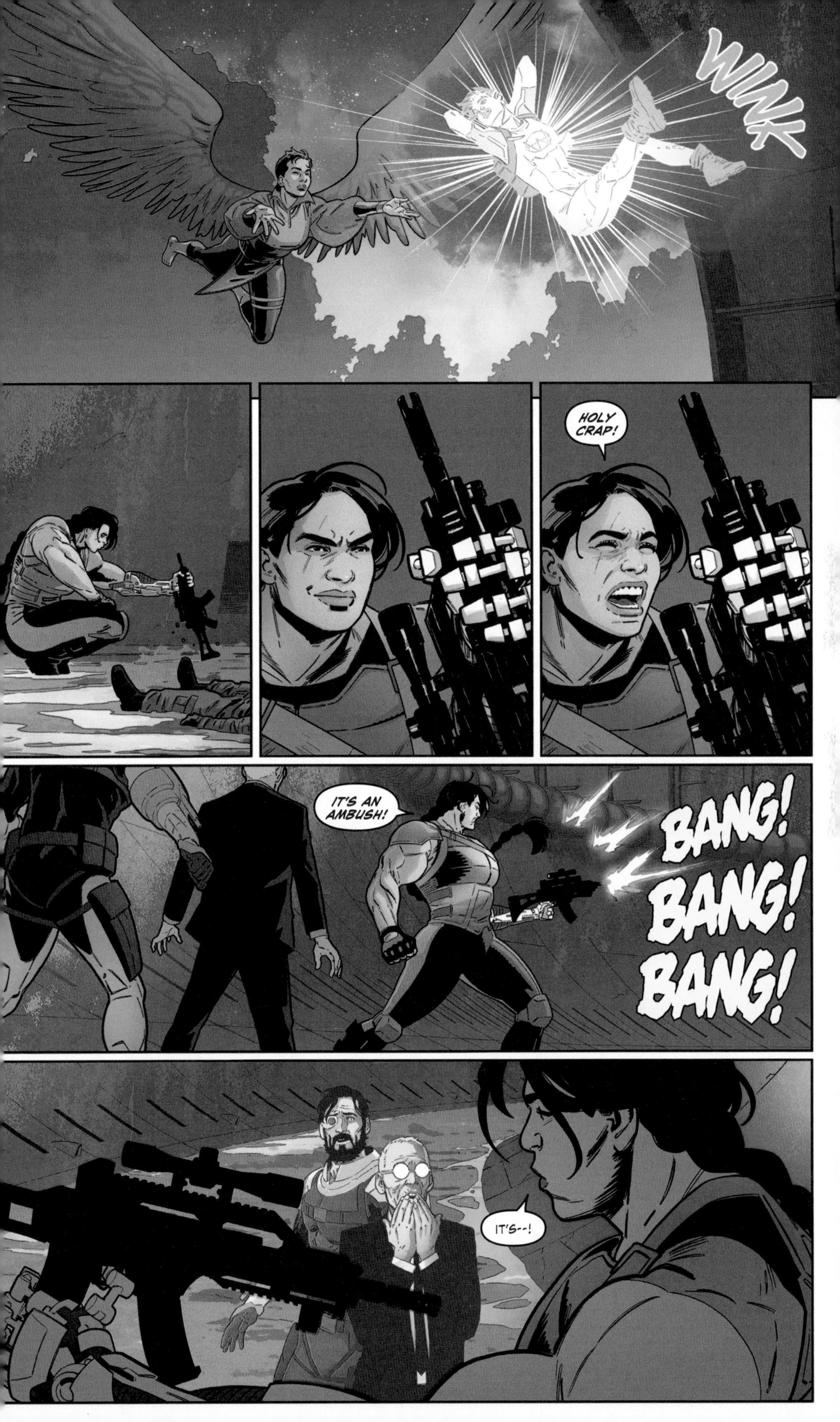
WINK
HOLY CRAP!
IT'S AN AMBUSH!
BANG! BANG! BANG!
IT'S--!

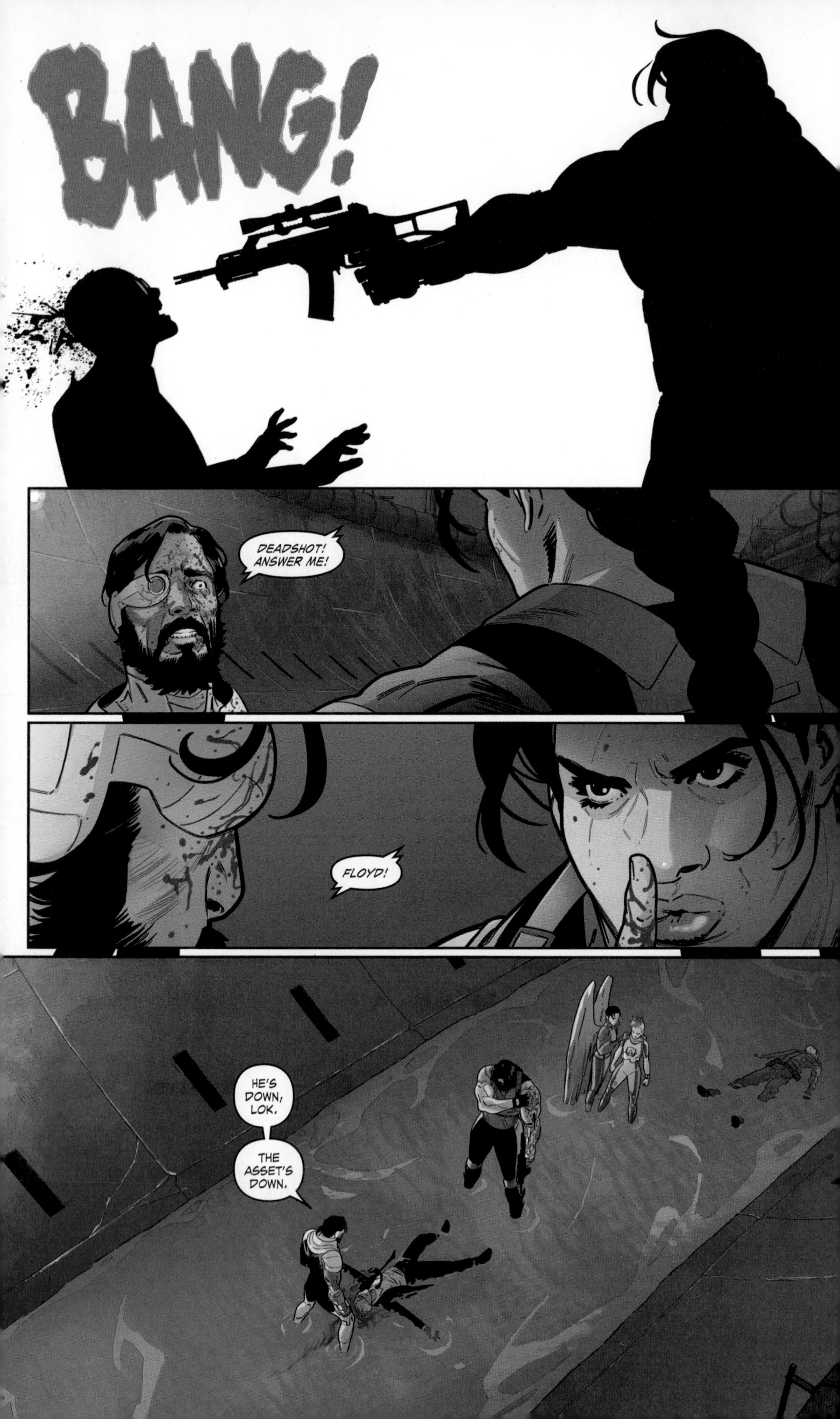
BANG!
DEADSHOT! ANSWER ME!
FLOYD!
HE'S DOWN, LOK.
THE ASSET'S DOWN.

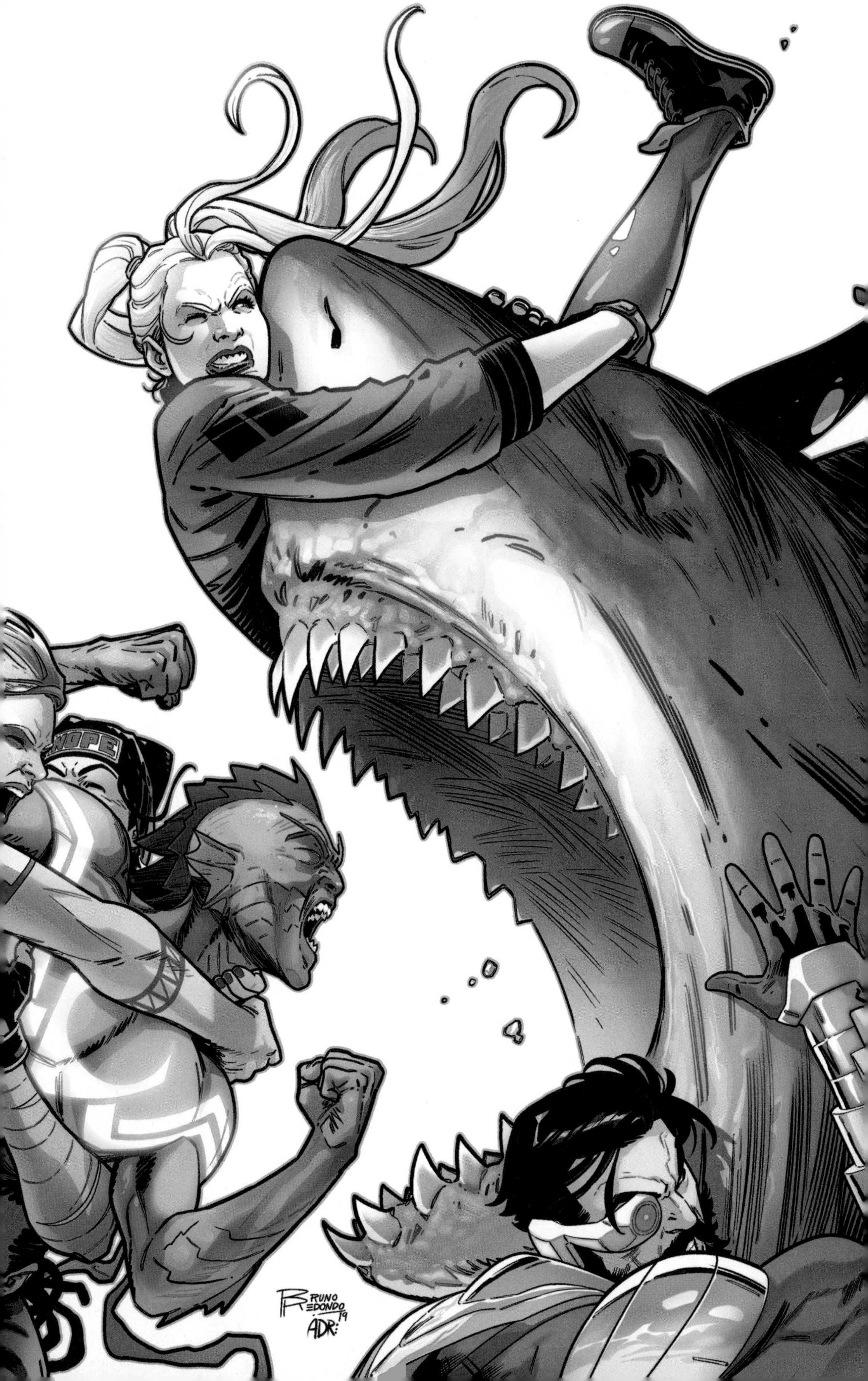
NOPE

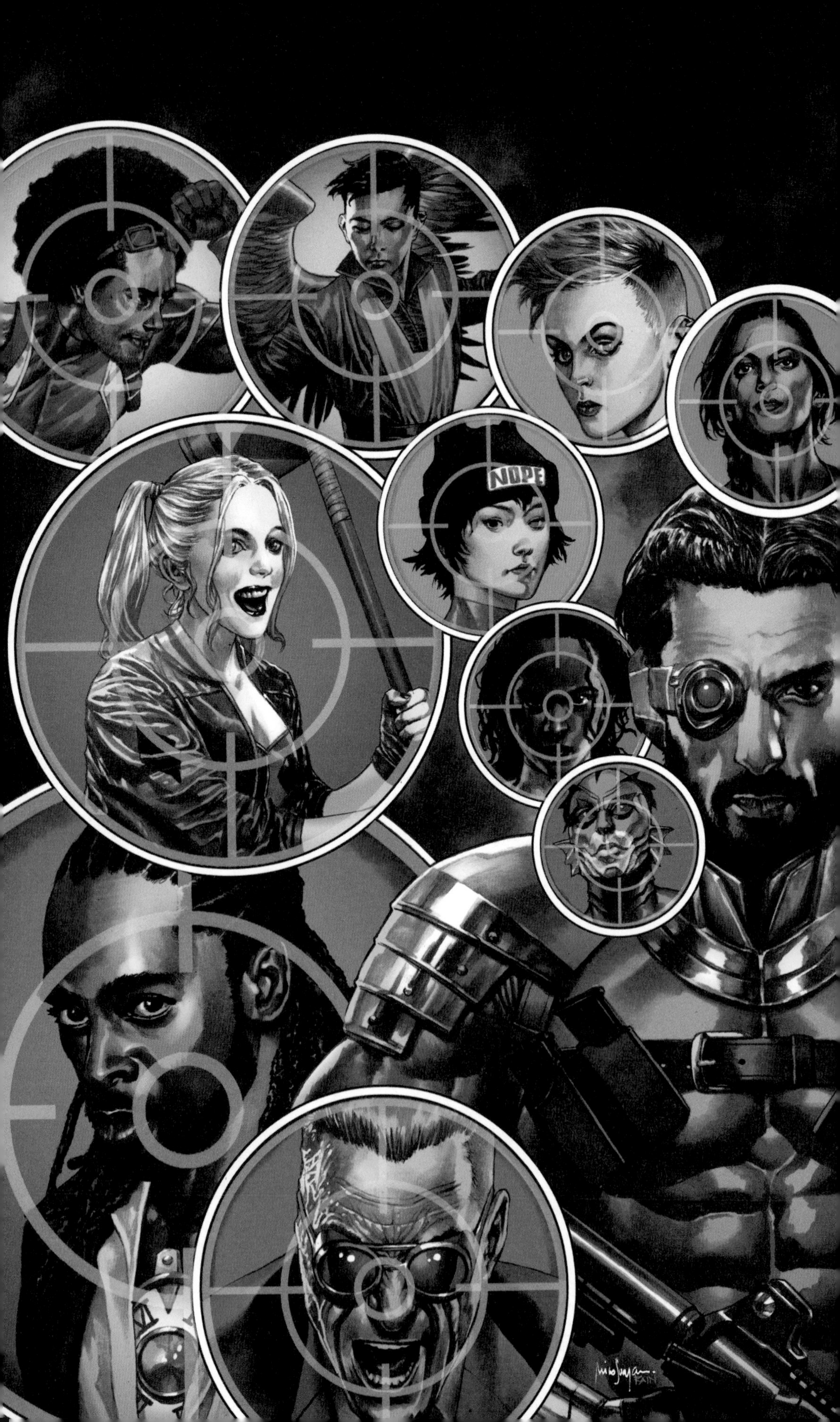
NOPE

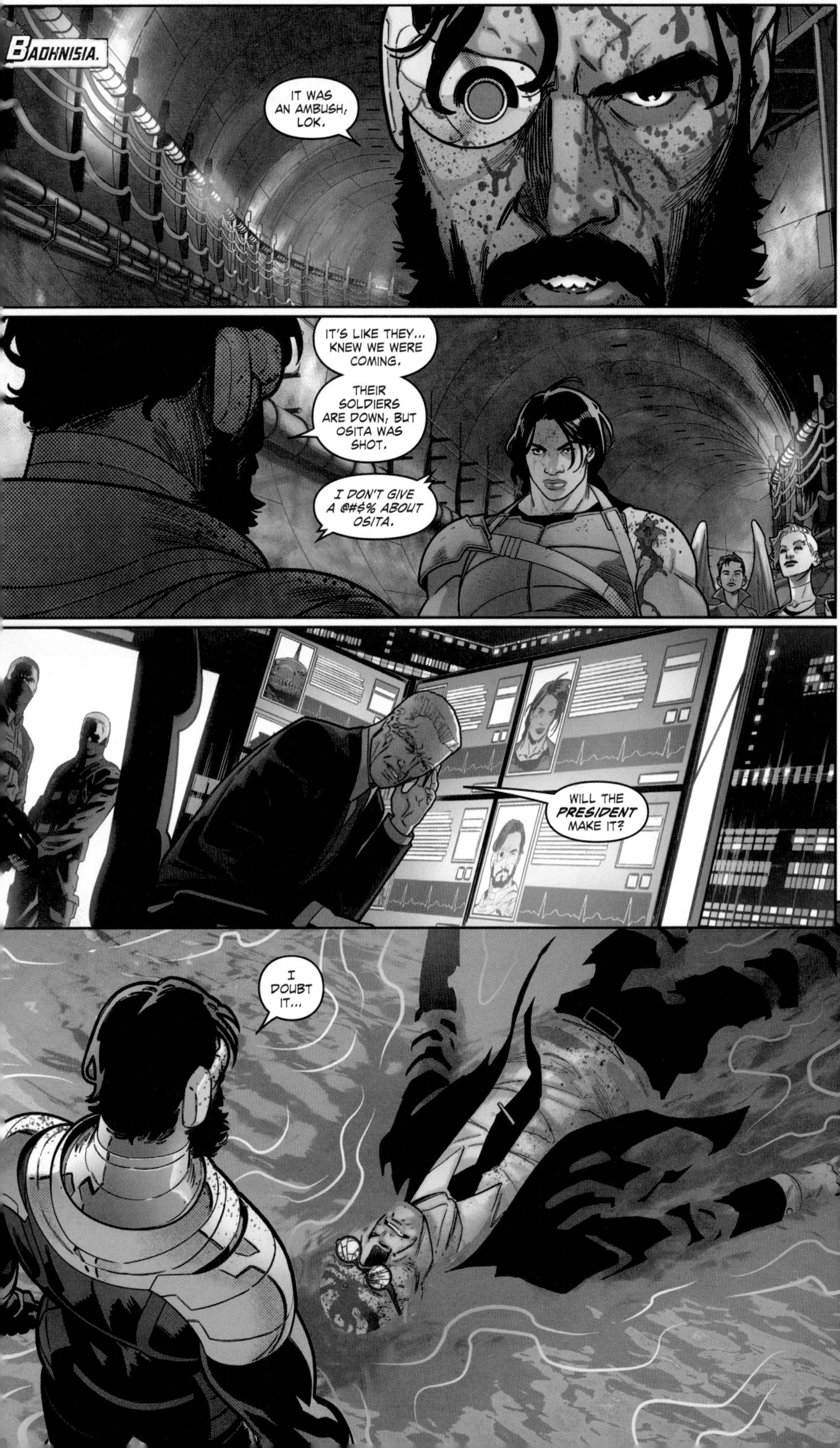
BAOHNISIA.
IT WAS AN AMBUSH, LOK.
IT'S LIKE THEY... KNEW WE WERE COMING.
THEIR SOLDIERS ARE DOWN, BUT OSITA WAS SHOT.
I DON'T GIVE A @#$% ABOUT OSITA.
WILL THE ***PRESIDENT*** MAKE IT?
I DOUBT IT...

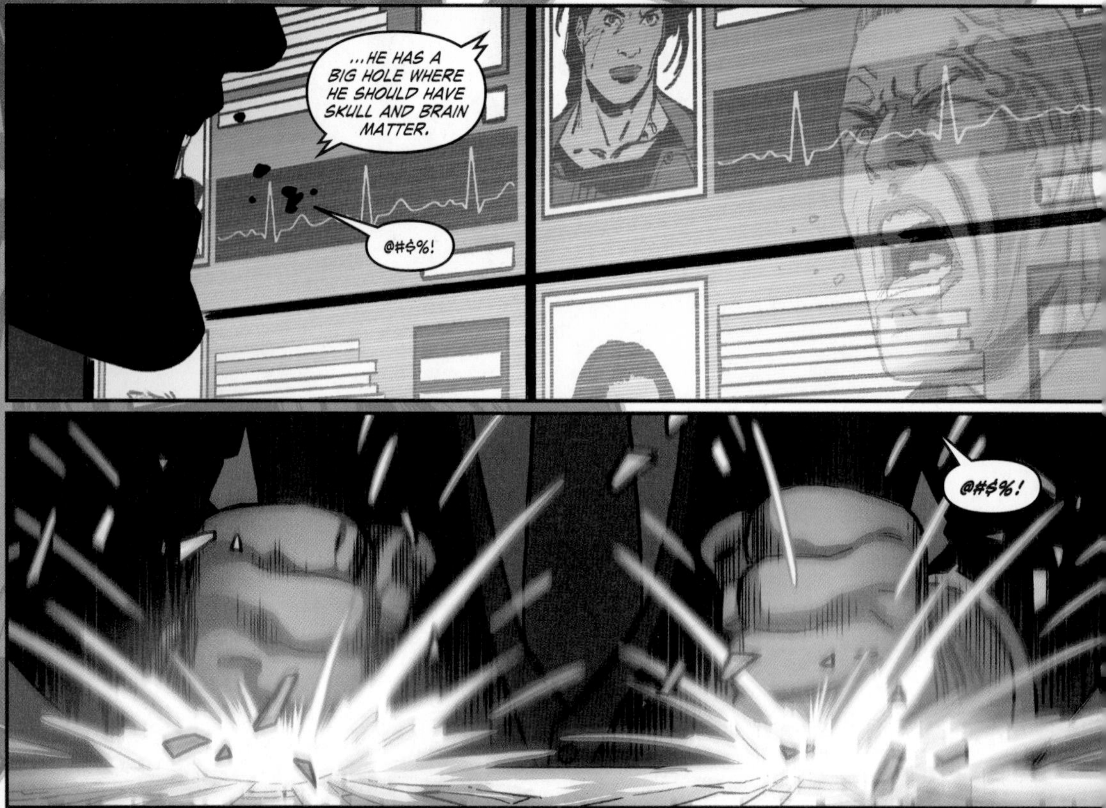
...HE HAS A BIG HOLE WHERE HE SHOULD HAVE SKULL AND BRAIN MATTER.
@#$%!
@#$%!

written by TOM TAYLOR

art by BRUNO REDONDO

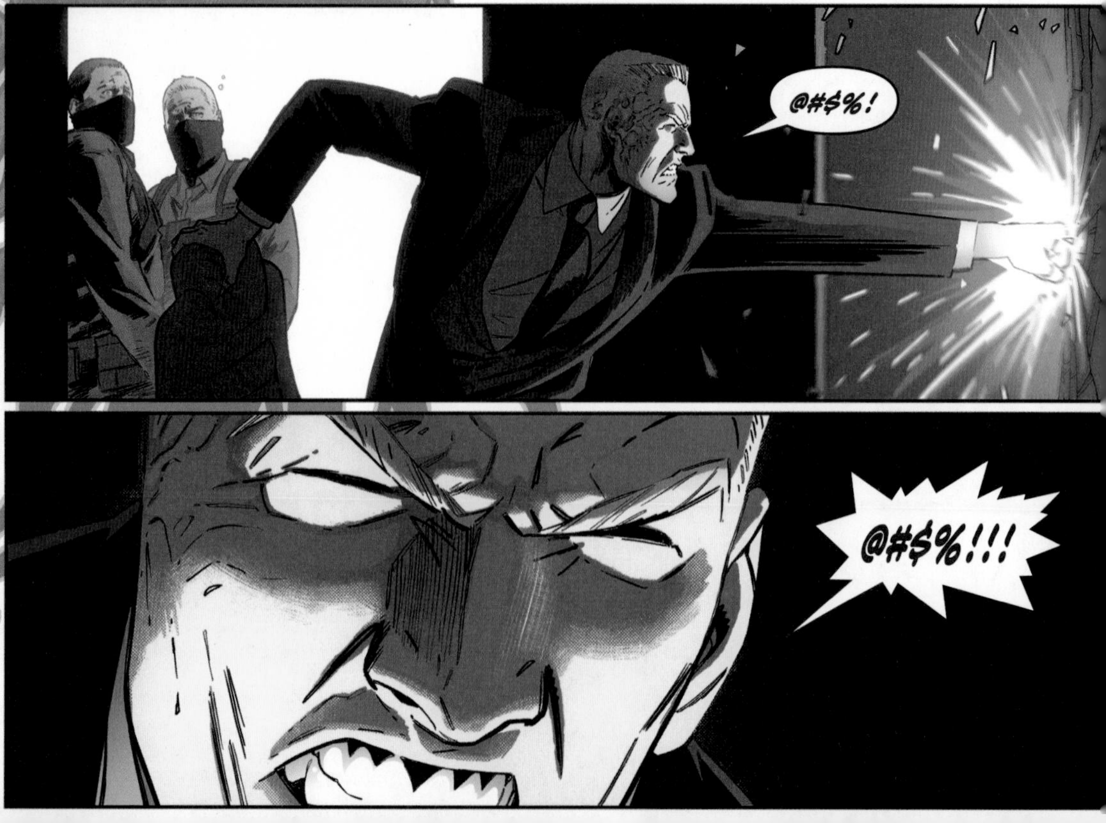
@#$%!
@#$%!!!

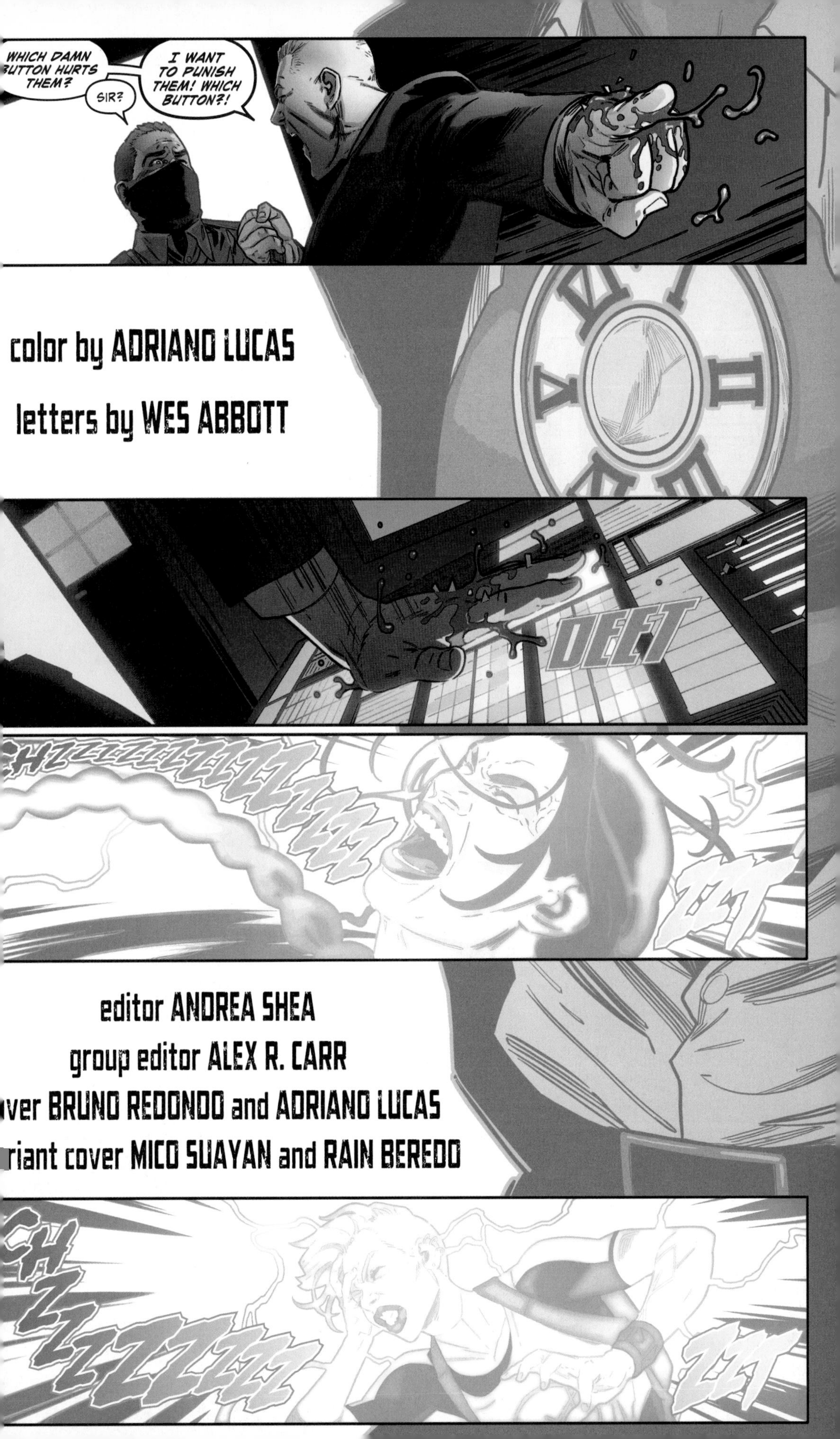
WHICH DAMN BUTTON HURTS THEM?
SIR?
I WANT TO PUNISH THEM! WHICH BUTTON?!
DEET
CHZZZZZZZZZZZZZZZZZZZ
ZZT
CHZZZZZZZZZZ
ZZT

color by ADRIANO LUCAS

letters by WES ABBOTT

editor ANDREA SHEA

group editor ALEX R. CARR

ver BRUNO REDONDO and ADRIANO LUCAS

riant cover MICO SUAYAN and RAIN BEREDO

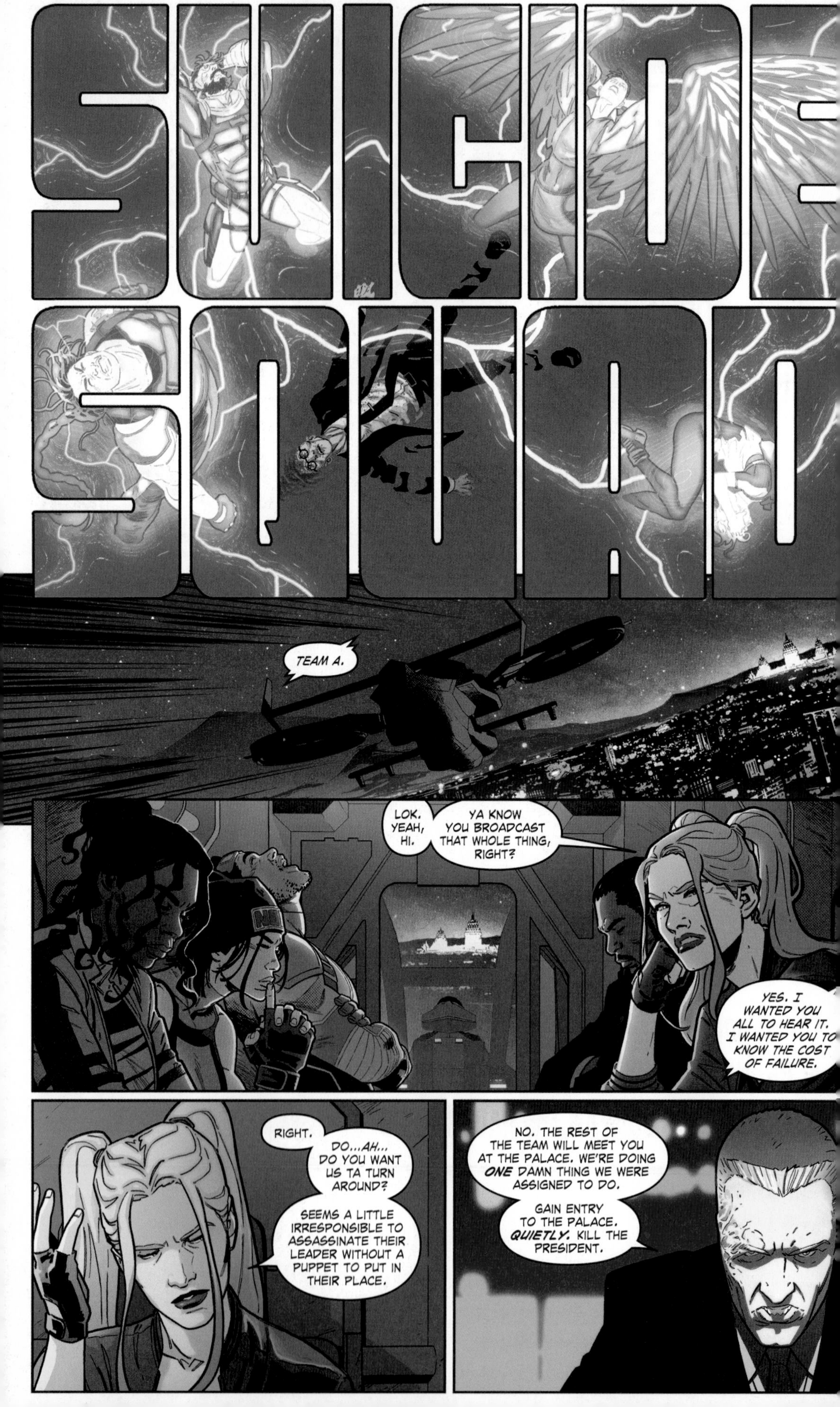
SUICIDE SQUAD
TEAM A.
LOK. YEAH, HI.
YA KNOW YOU BROADCAST THAT WHOLE THING, RIGHT?
YES. I WANTED YOU ALL TO HEAR IT. I WANTED YOU TO KNOW THE COST OF FAILURE.
RIGHT.
DO...AH... DO YOU WANT US TA TURN AROUND?
SEEMS A LITTLE IRRESPONSIBLE TO ASSASSINATE THEIR LEADER WITHOUT A PUPPET TO PUT IN THEIR PLACE.
NO. THE REST OF THE TEAM WILL MEET YOU AT THE PALACE. WE'RE DOING ONE DAMN THING WE WERE ASSIGNED TO DO.
GAIN ENTRY TO THE PALACE. QUIETLY. KILL THE PRESIDENT.

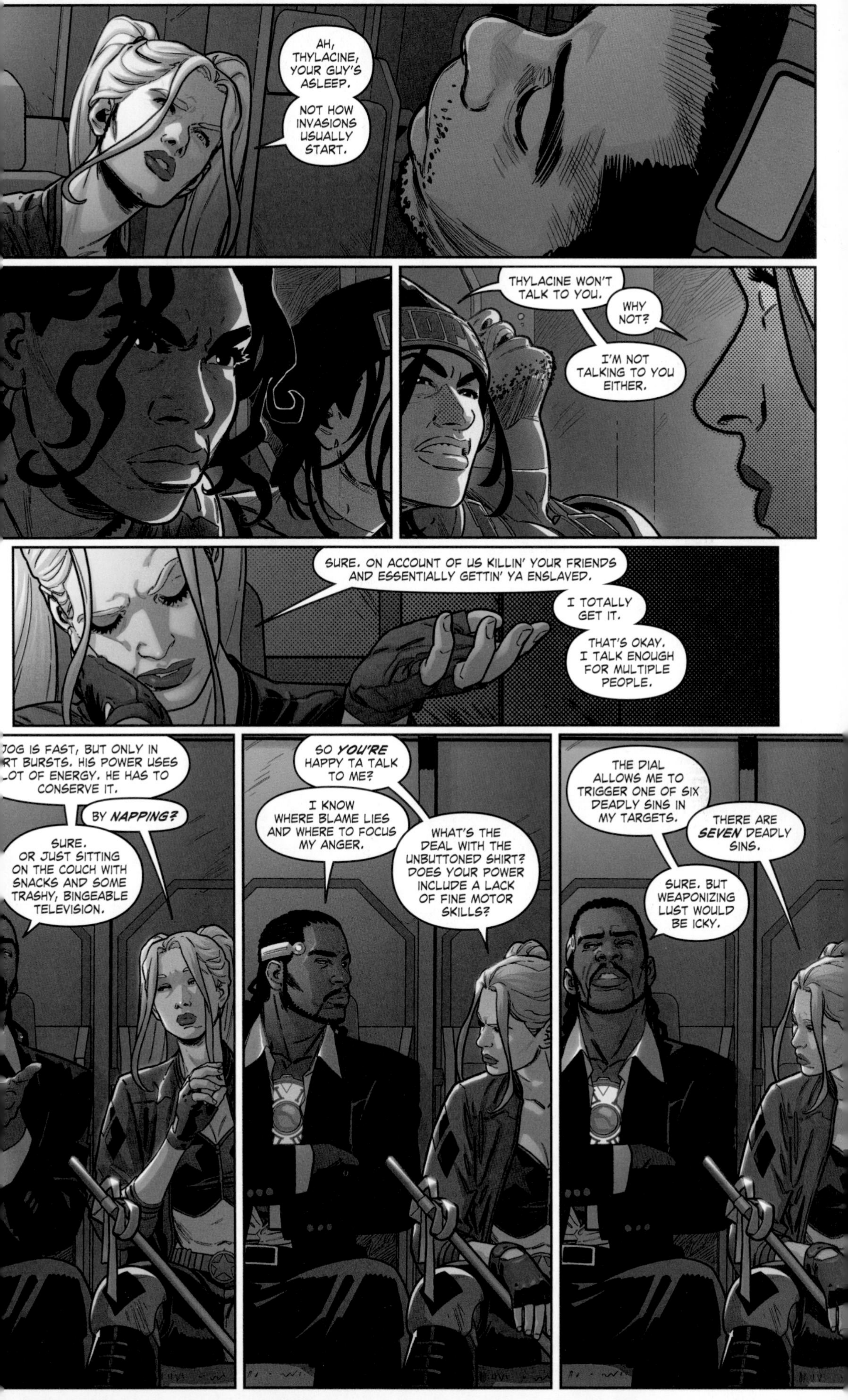
AH, THYLACINE, YOUR GUY'S ASLEEP.
NOT HOW INVASIONS USUALLY START.
THYLACINE WON'T TALK TO YOU.
WHY NOT?
I'M NOT TALKING TO YOU EITHER.
SURE. ON ACCOUNT OF US KILLIN' YOUR FRIENDS AND ESSENTIALLY GETTIN' YA ENSLAVED.
I TOTALLY GET IT.
THAT'S OKAY. I TALK ENOUGH FOR MULTIPLE PEOPLE.
JOG IS FAST, BUT ONLY IN RT BURSTS. HIS POWER USES LOT OF ENERGY. HE HAS TO CONSERVE IT.
BY NAPPING?
SURE. OR JUST SITTING ON THE COUCH WITH SNACKS AND SOME TRASHY, BINGEABLE TELEVISION.
SO YOU'RE HAPPY TA TALK TO ME?
I KNOW WHERE BLAME LIES AND WHERE TO FOCUS MY ANGER.
WHAT'S THE DEAL WITH THE UNBUTTONED SHIRT? DOES YOUR POWER INCLUDE A LACK OF FINE MOTOR SKILLS?
THE DIAL ALLOWS ME TO TRIGGER ONE OF SIX DEADLY SINS IN MY TARGETS.
THERE ARE SEVEN DEADLY SINS.
SURE. BUT WEAPONIZING LUST WOULD BE ICKY.

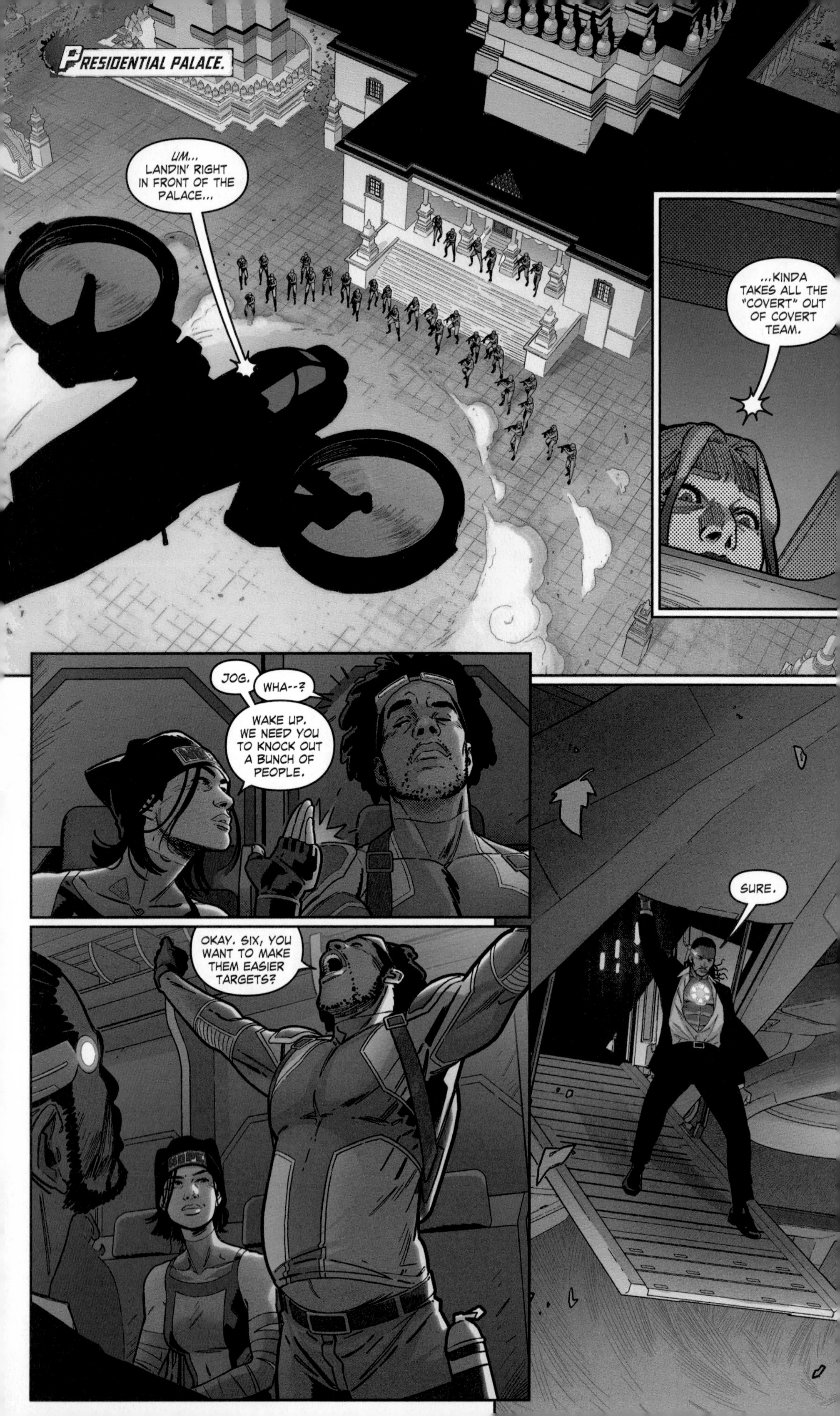
PRESIDENTIAL PALACE.
UM... LANDIN' RIGHT IN FRONT OF THE PALACE...
...KINDA TAKES ALL THE "COVERT" OUT OF COVERT TEAM.
JOG.
WHA--?
WAKE UP. WE NEED YOU TO KNOCK OUT A BUNCH OF PEOPLE.
OKAY. SIX, YOU WANT TO MAKE THEM EASIER TARGETS?
SURE.

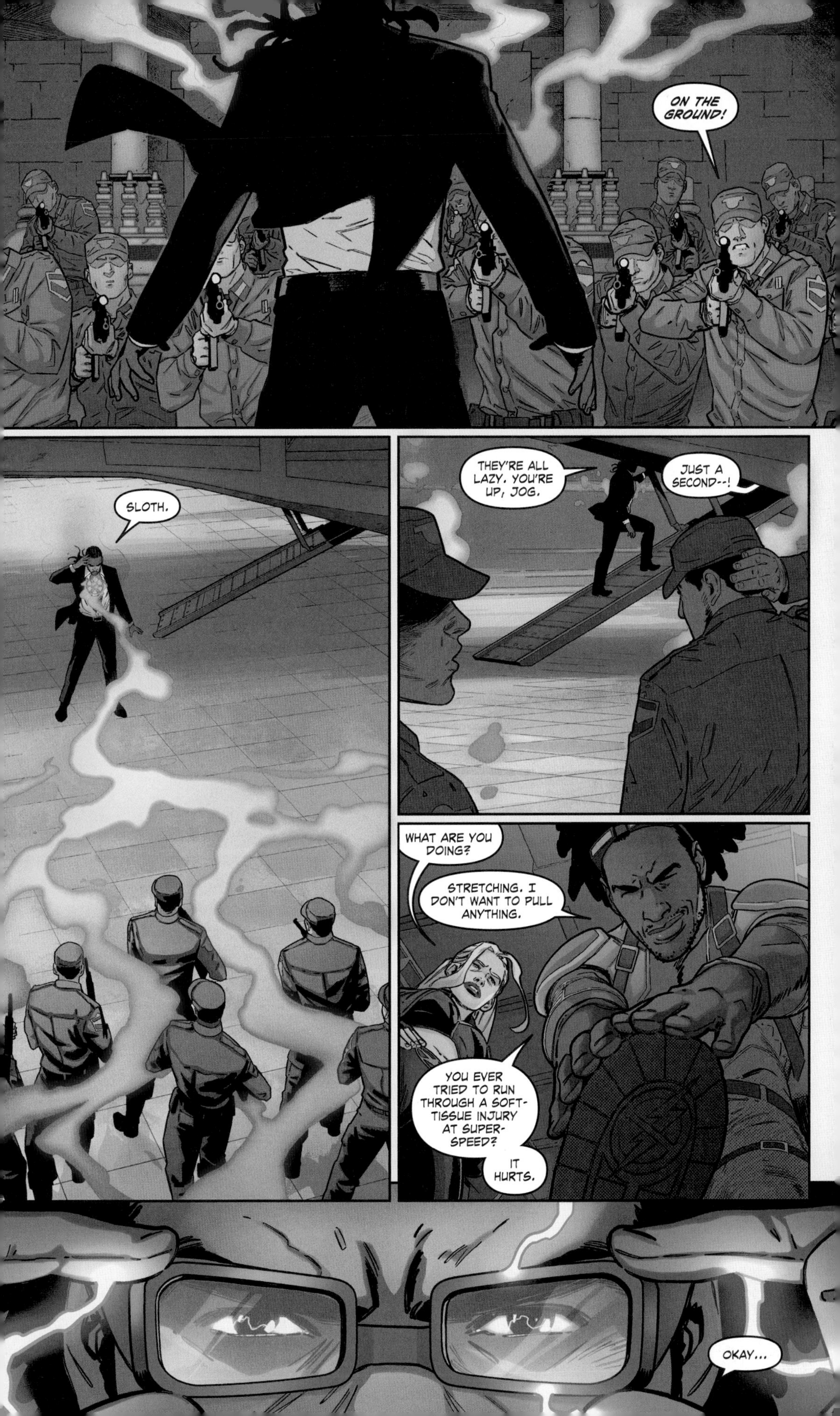
ON THE GROUND!
SLOTH.
THEY'RE ALL LAZY. YOU'RE UP, JOG.
JUST A SECOND--!
WHAT ARE YOU DOING?
STRETCHING. I DON'T WANT TO PULL ANYTHING.
YOU EVER TRIED TO RUN THROUGH A SOFT-TISSUE INJURY AT SUPER-SPEED?
IT HURTS.
OKAY...

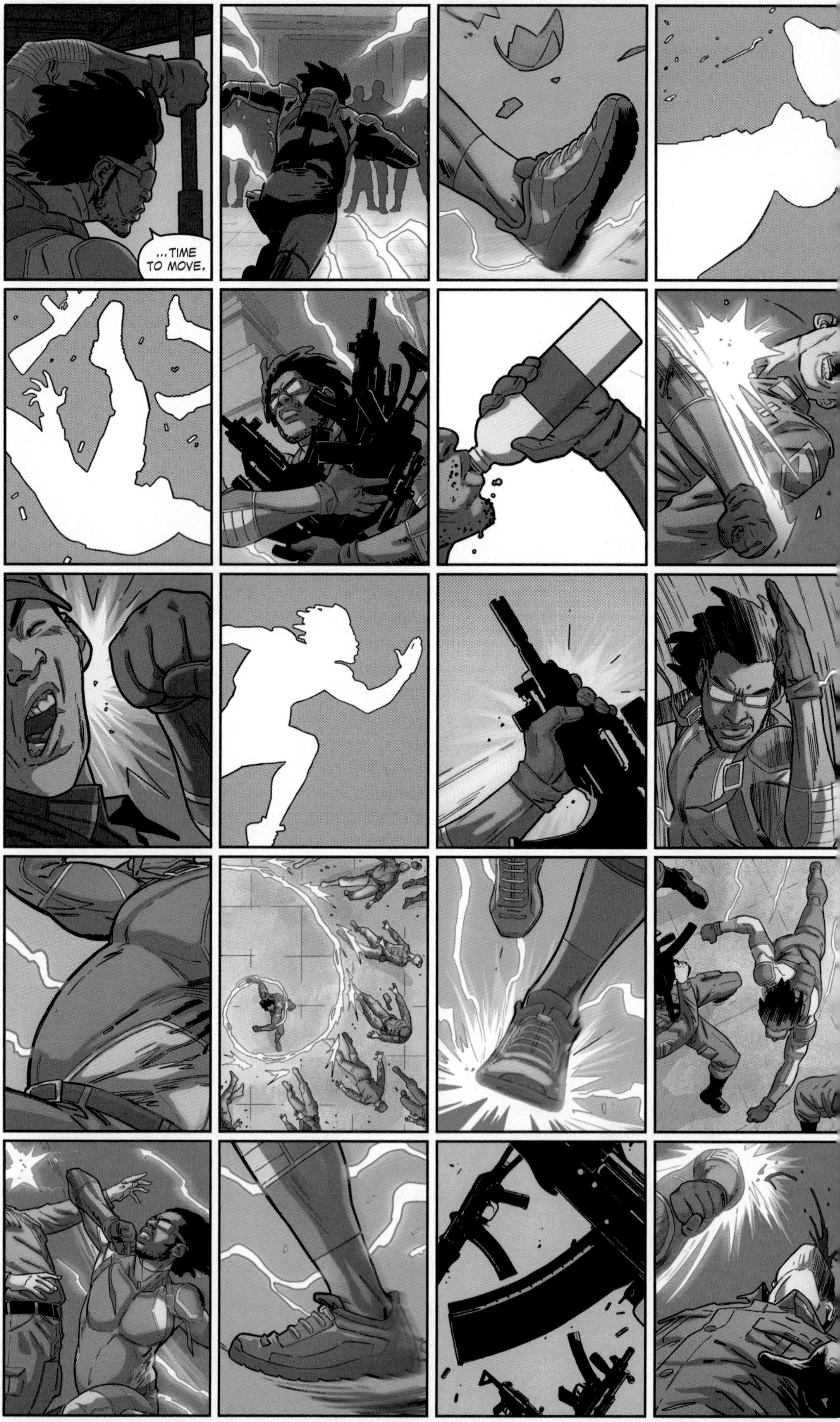
...TIME TO MOVE.

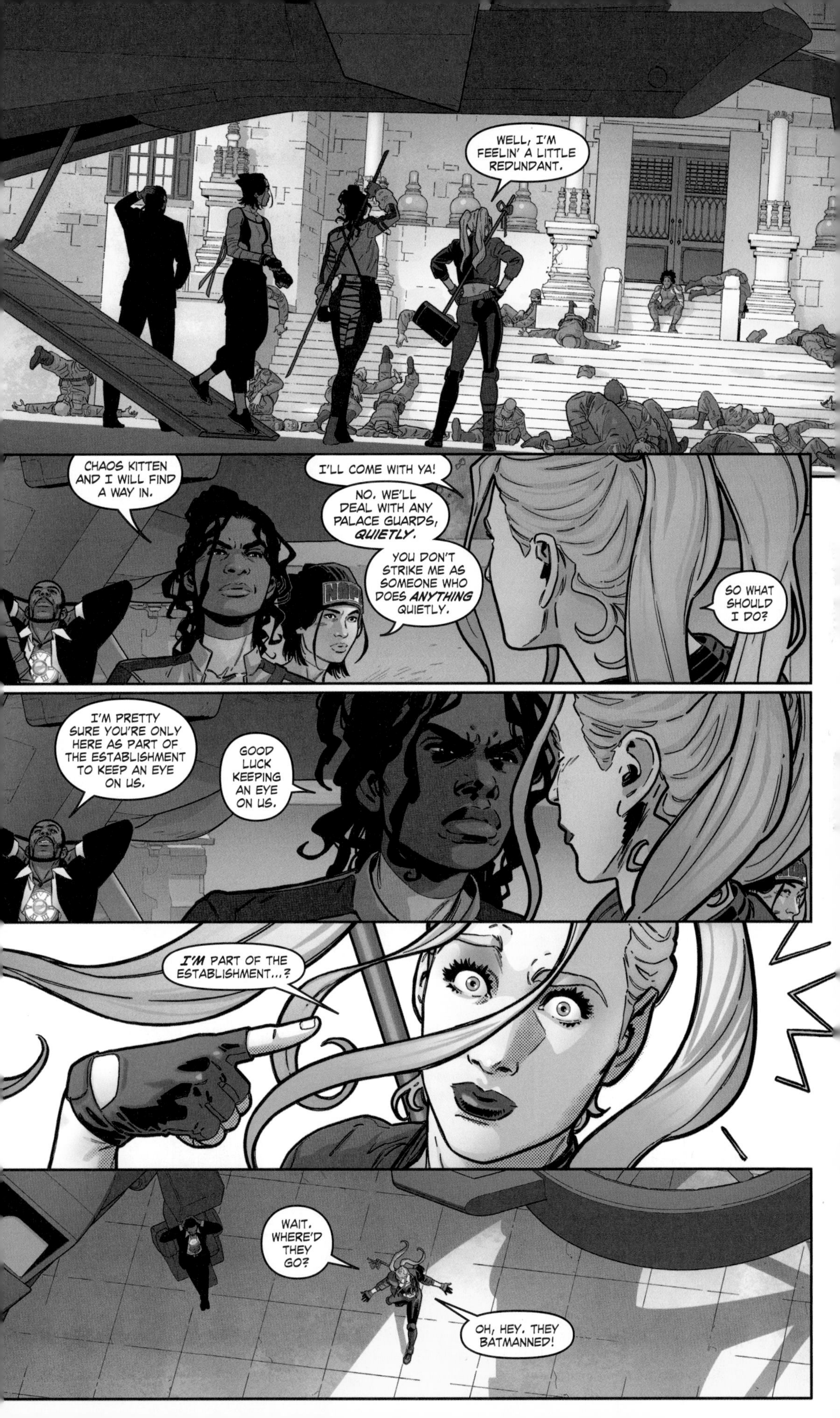
WELL, I'M FEELIN' A LITTLE REDUNDANT.
CHAOS KITTEN AND I WILL FIND A WAY IN.
I'LL COME WITH YA!
NO. WE'LL DEAL WITH ANY PALACE GUARDS, *QUIETLY*.
YOU DON'T STRIKE ME AS SOMEONE WHO DOES *ANYTHING* QUIETLY.
SO WHAT SHOULD I DO?
I'M PRETTY SURE YOU'RE ONLY HERE AS PART OF THE ESTABLISHMENT TO KEEP AN EYE ON US.
GOOD LUCK KEEPING AN EYE ON US.
I'M PART OF THE ESTABLISHMENT...?
WAIT. WHERE'D THEY GO?
OH, HEY. THEY BATMANNED!

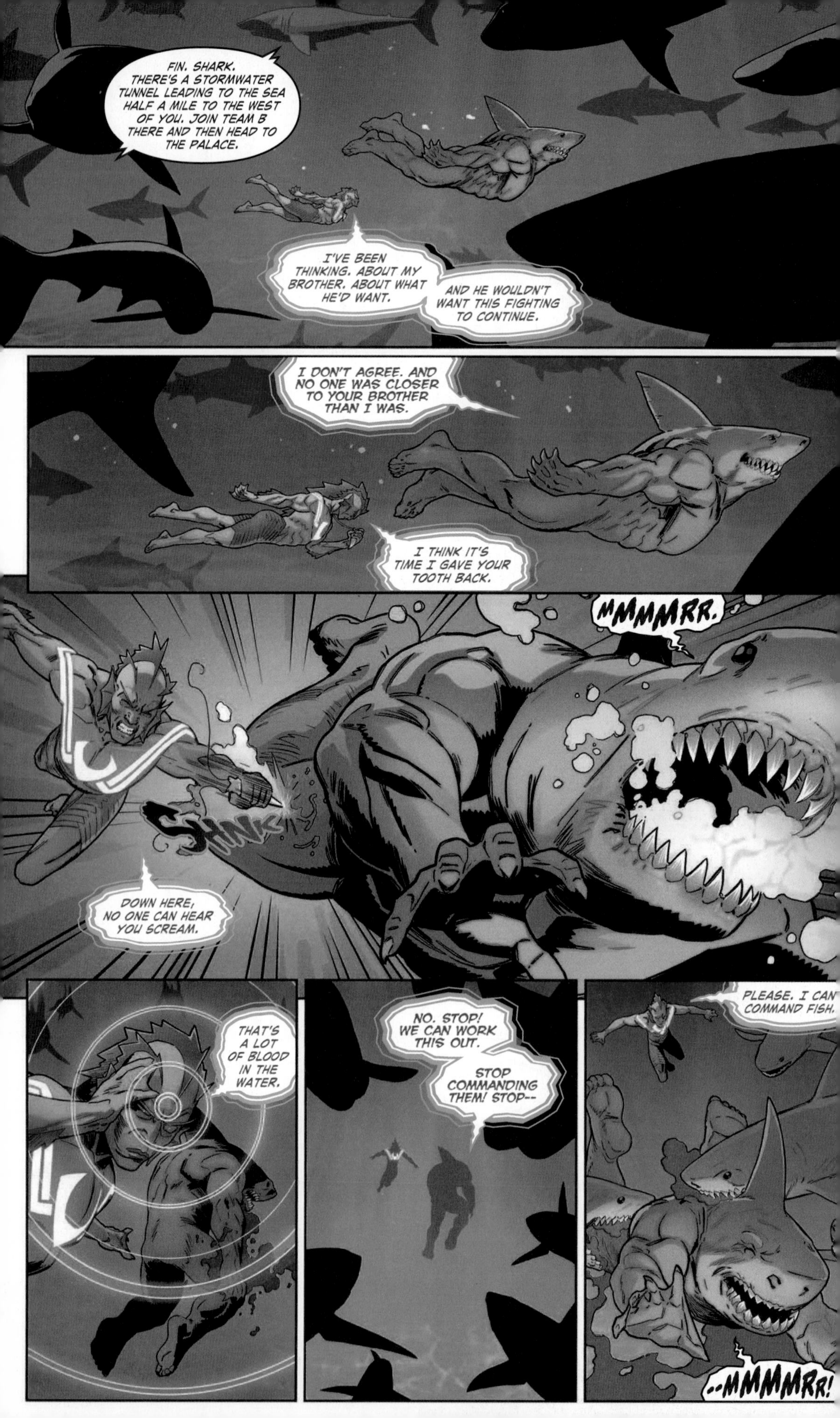
FIN. SHARK. THERE'S A STORMWATER TUNNEL LEADING TO THE SEA HALF A MILE TO THE WEST OF YOU. JOIN TEAM B THERE AND THEN HEAD TO THE PALACE.
I'VE BEEN THINKING. ABOUT MY BROTHER. ABOUT WHAT HE'D WANT.
AND HE WOULDN'T WANT THIS FIGHTING TO CONTINUE.
I DON'T AGREE. AND NO ONE WAS CLOSER TO YOUR BROTHER THAN I WAS.
I THINK IT'S TIME I GAVE YOUR TOOTH BACK.
MMMMRR.
SHINK
DOWN HERE, NO ONE CAN HEAR YOU SCREAM.
THAT'S A LOT OF BLOOD IN THE WATER.
NO. STOP! WE CAN WORK THIS OUT.
STOP COMMANDING THEM! STOP--
PLEASE. I CAN COMMAND FISH.
--MMMMRR!

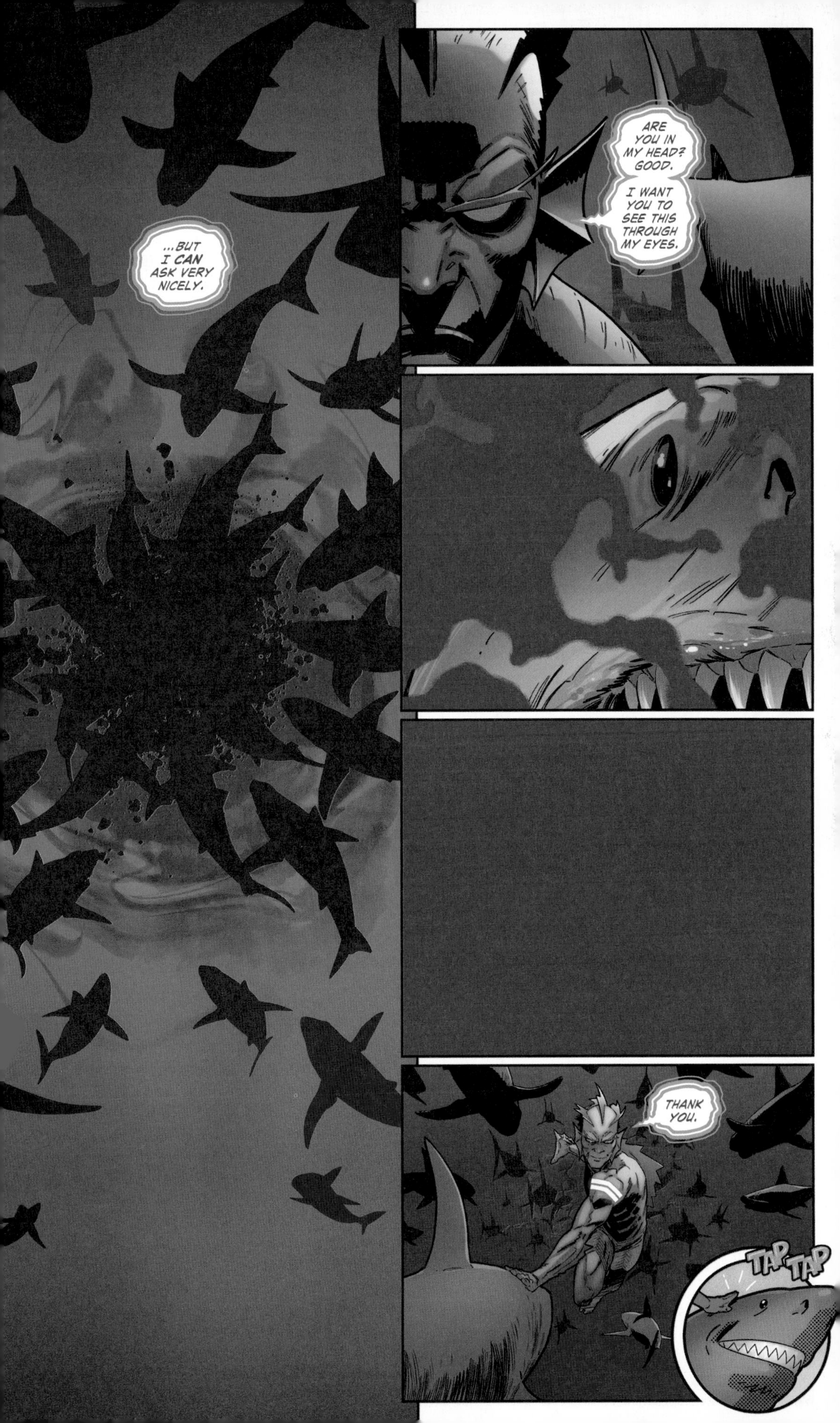
...BUT I CAN ASK VERY NICELY.
ARE YOU IN MY HEAD? GOOD.
I WANT YOU TO SEE THIS THROUGH MY EYES.
THANK YOU.
TAP TAP

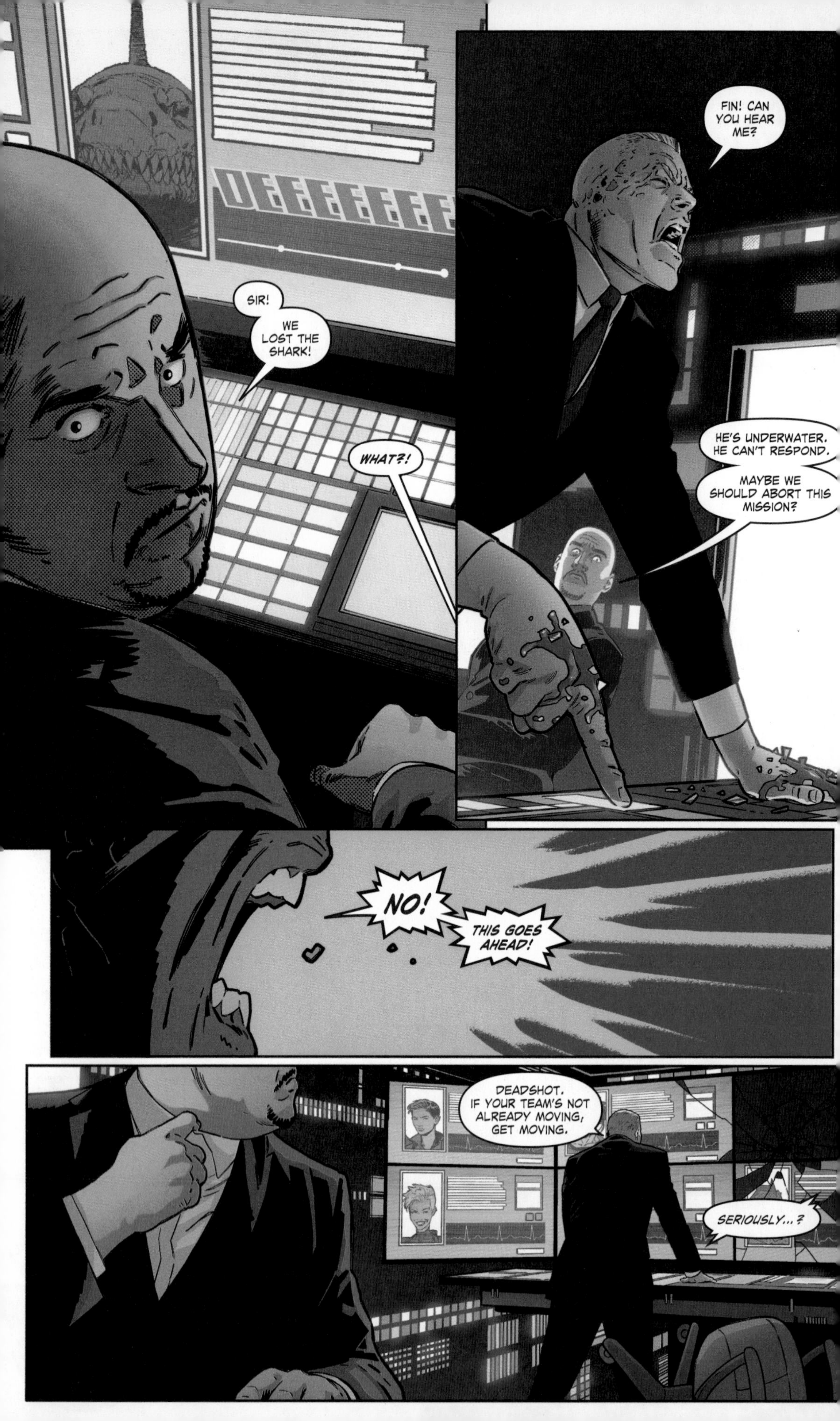
SIR!
WE LOST THE SHARK!
WHAT?!
FIN! CAN YOU HEAR ME?
HE'S UNDERWATER. HE CAN'T RESPOND.
MAYBE WE SHOULD ABORT THIS MISSION?
NO!
THIS GOES AHEAD!
DEADSHOT. IF YOUR TEAM'S NOT ALREADY MOVING, GET MOVING.
SERIOUSLY...?

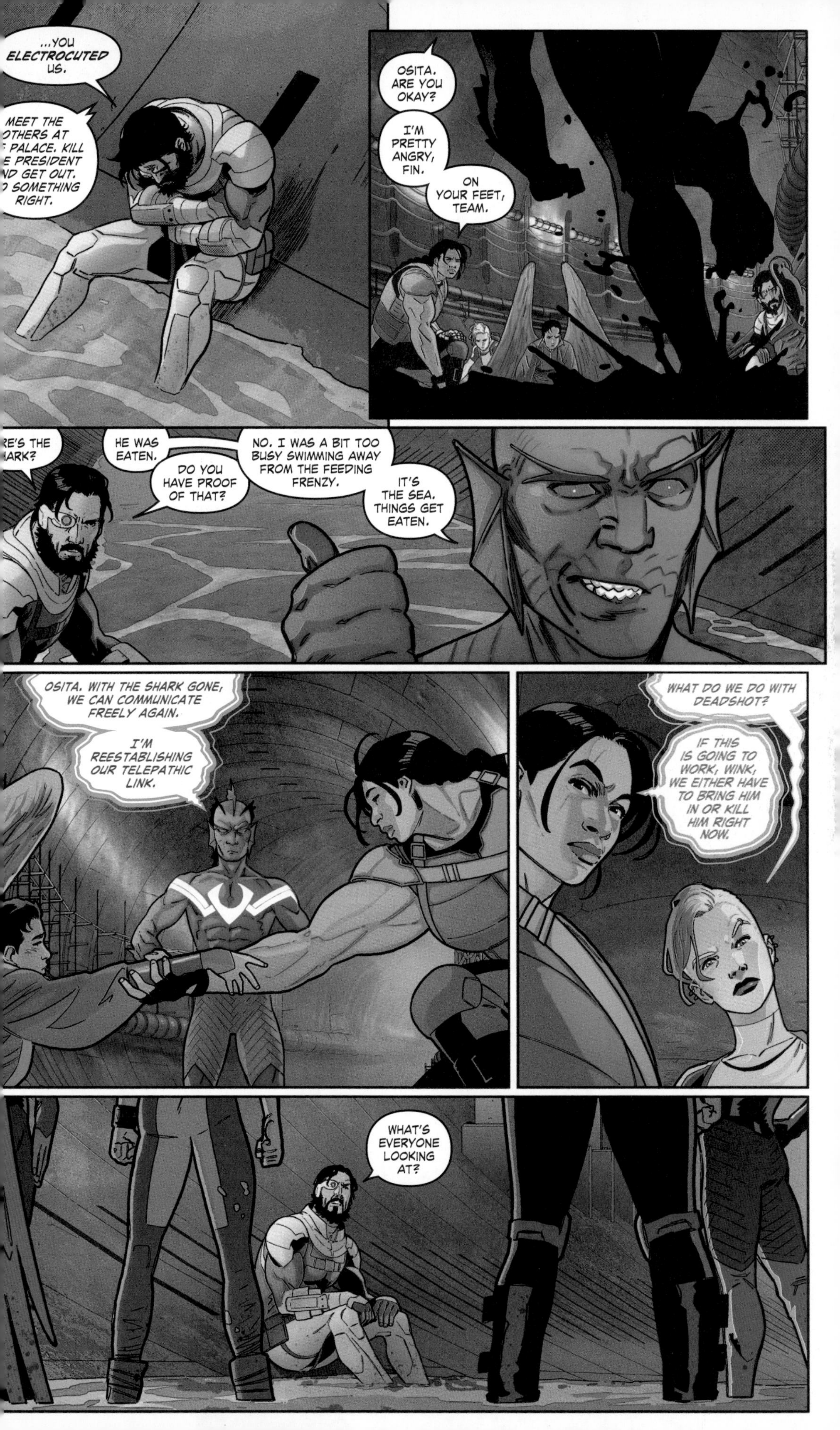

...YOU ELECTROCUTED US.
MEET THE OTHERS AT F PALACE. KILL E PRESIDENT ND GET OUT. O SOMETHING RIGHT.
OSITA. ARE YOU OKAY?
I'M PRETTY ANGRY, FIN.
ON YOUR FEET, TEAM.
RE'S THE ARK?
HE WAS EATEN.
DO YOU HAVE PROOF OF THAT?
NO. I WAS A BIT TOO BUSY SWIMMING AWAY FROM THE FEEDING FRENZY.
IT'S THE SEA. THINGS GET EATEN.
OSITA. WITH THE SHARK GONE, WE CAN COMMUNICATE FREELY AGAIN.
I'M REESTABLISHING OUR TELEPATHIC LINK.
WHAT DO WE DO WITH DEADSHOT?
IF THIS IS GOING TO WORK, WINK, WE EITHER HAVE TO BRING HIM IN OR KILL HIM RIGHT NOW.
WHAT'S EVERYONE LOOKING AT?

HMM.

WHAT?

HE'S SCARED.

OF COURSE HE'S SCARED. HE'S A PRISONER.

HE'S BEEN TRAPPED IN THIS LIFE FOR WHO KNOWS HOW LONG.

HIS FREEDOM AND HUMANITY HAVE BEEN STRIPPED AWAY AND HE'S BEEN USED AS A DISPOSABLE TOOL BY FACELESS, UNCARING MASTERS.

FLOYD'S SPENT YEARS BEING SENT AGAINST NIGHTMARES, AND HE'S PROBABLY EXPECTING TO DIE.

SERIOUSLY, WHAT'S GOING ON?

THE AERIE IS RIGHT.

FIN. BRING DEADSHOT IN.

YOU'RE SURE? IT'S A RISK.

WINK; IF HE TRIES TO ALER LOK, TELEPOR HIS FACE INTO THE WALL.

DONE.

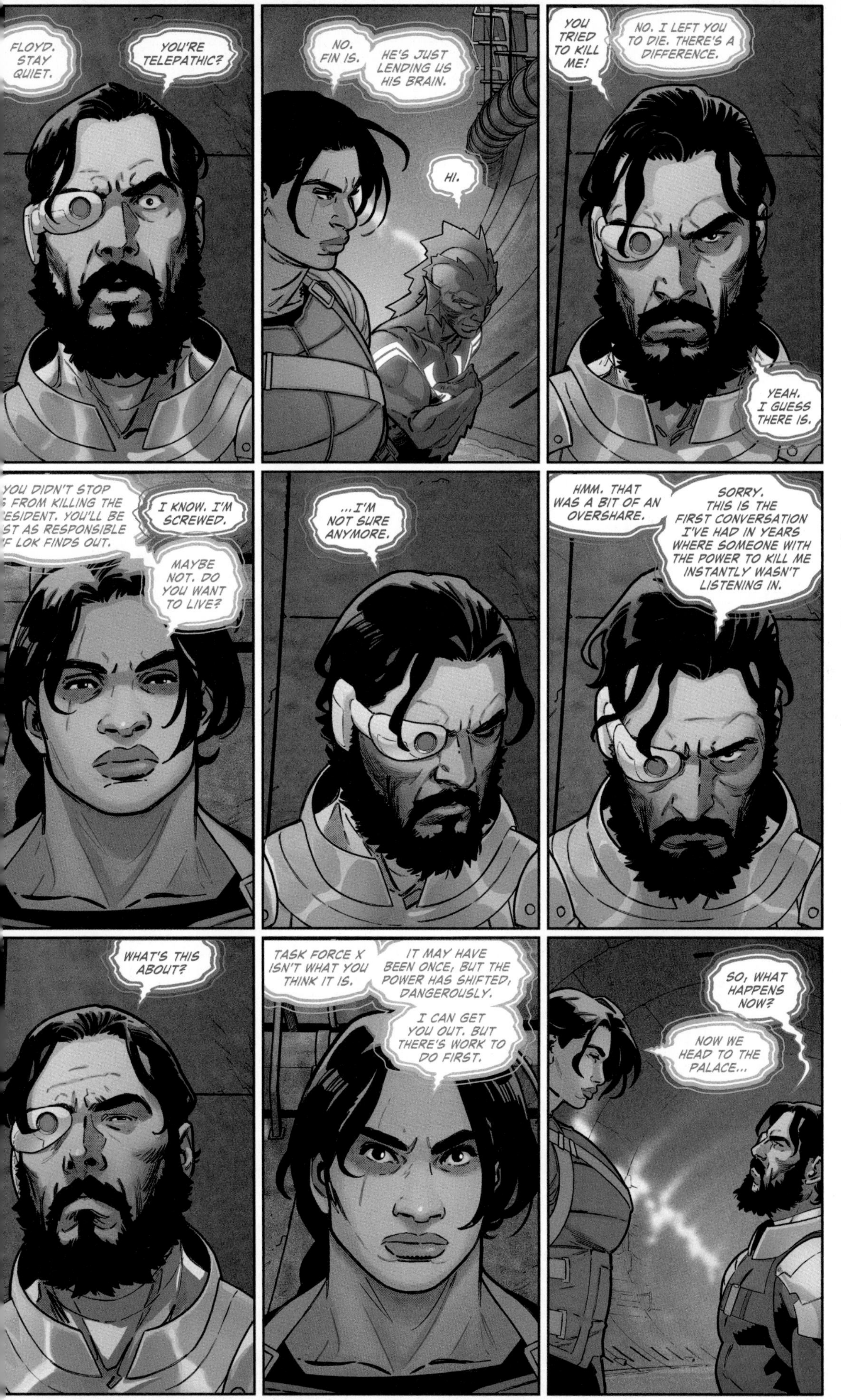
FLOYD. STAY QUIET.
YOU'RE TELEPATHIC?
NO. FIN IS.
HE'S JUST LENDING US HIS BRAIN.
HI.
YOU TRIED TO KILL ME!
NO. I LEFT YOU TO DIE. THERE'S A DIFFERENCE.
YEAH. I GUESS THERE IS.
YOU DIDN'T STOP S FROM KILLING THE ESIDENT. YOU'LL BE ST AS RESPONSIBLE F LOK FINDS OUT.
I KNOW. I'M SCREWED.
MAYBE NOT. DO YOU WANT TO LIVE?
...I'M NOT SURE ANYMORE.
HMM. THAT WAS A BIT OF AN OVERSHARE.
SORRY. THIS IS THE FIRST CONVERSATION I'VE HAD IN YEARS WHERE SOMEONE WITH THE POWER TO KILL ME INSTANTLY WASN'T LISTENING IN.
WHAT'S THIS ABOUT?
TASK FORCE X ISN'T WHAT YOU THINK IT IS.
IT MAY HAVE BEEN ONCE, BUT THE POWER HAS SHIFTED, DANGEROUSLY.
I CAN GET YOU OUT. BUT THERE'S WORK TO DO FIRST.
SO, WHAT HAPPENS NOW?
NOW WE HEAD TO THE PALACE...

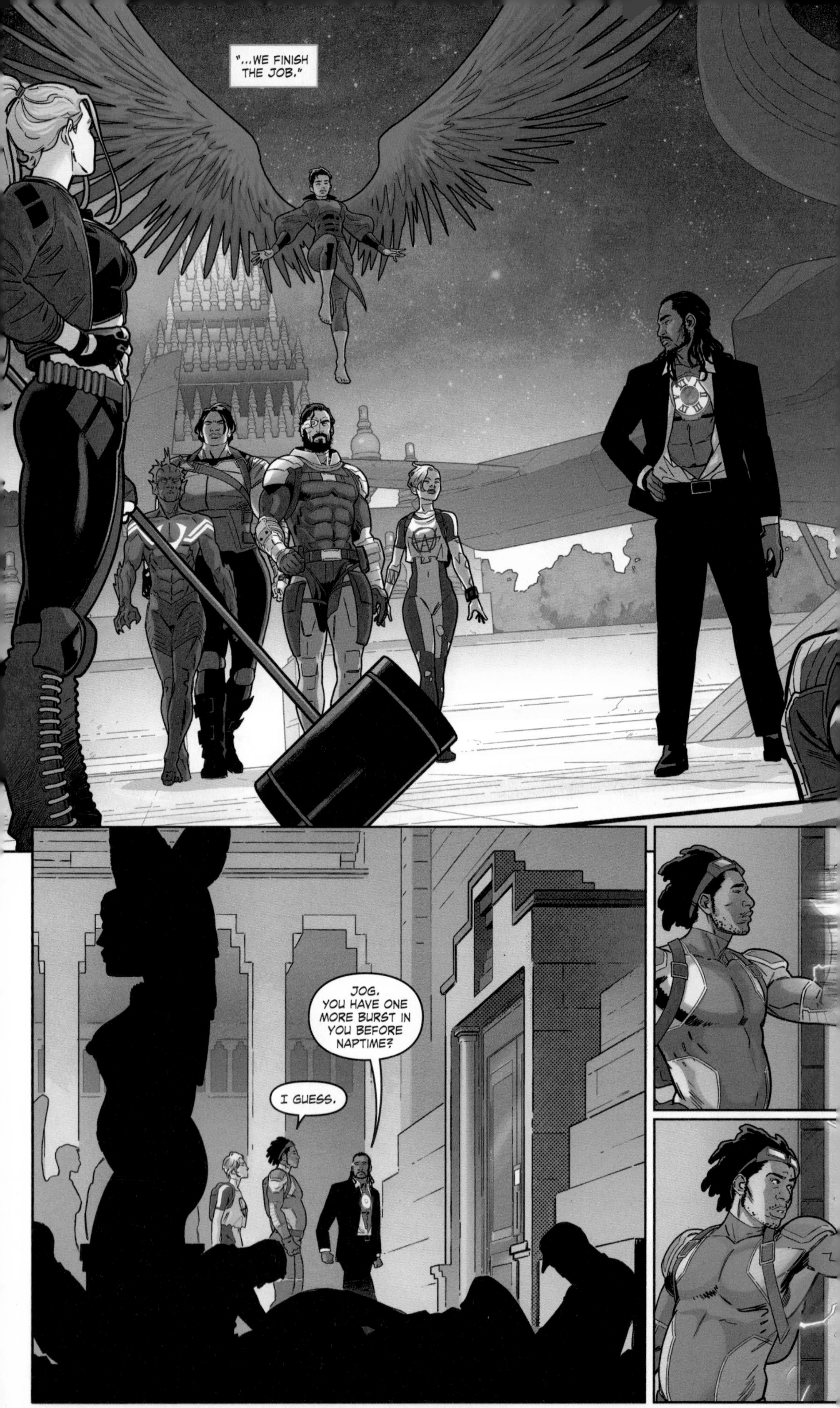

"...WE FINISH THE JOB."
JOG. YOU HAVE ONE MORE BURST IN YOU BEFORE NAPTIME?
I GUESS.

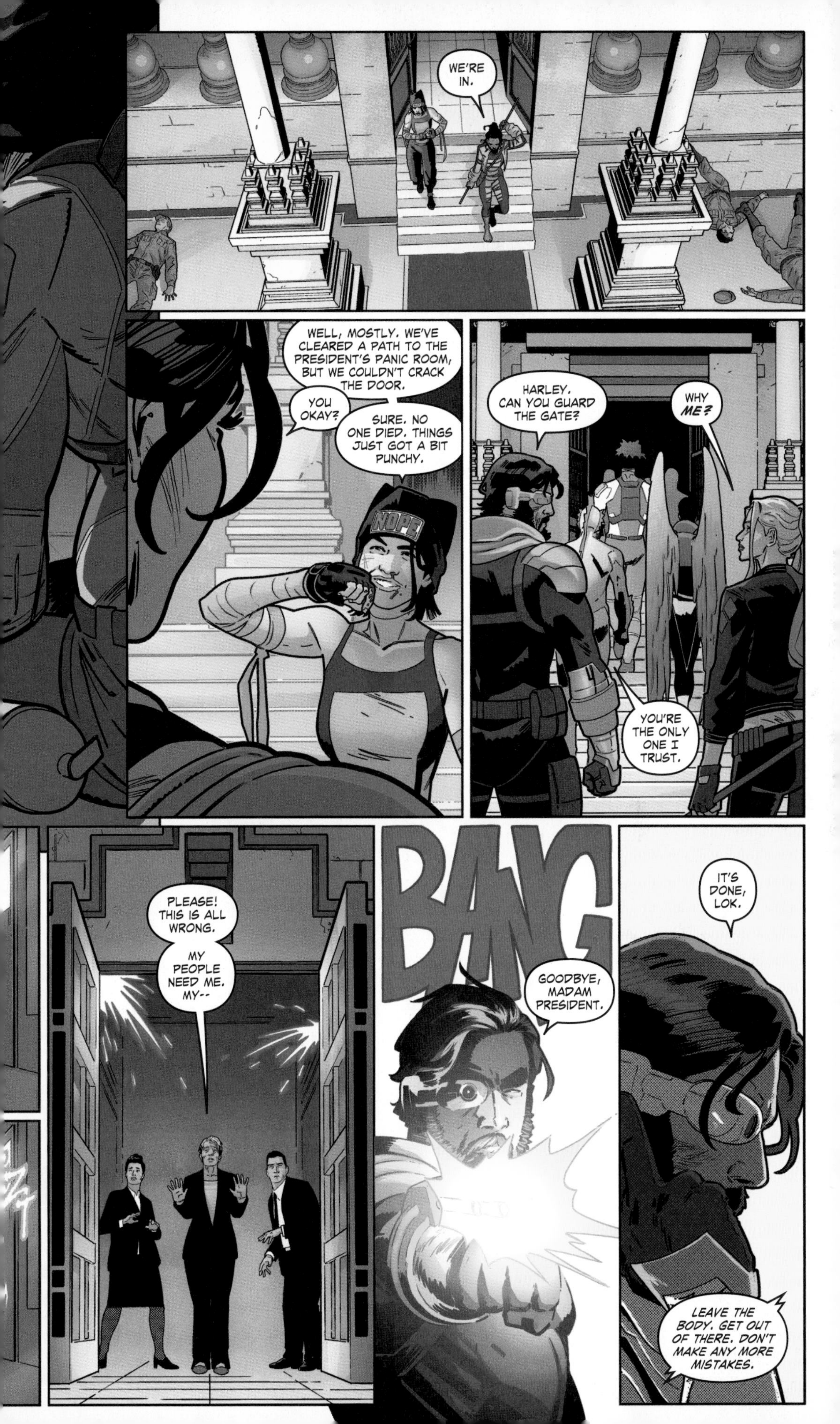
WE'RE IN.
WELL, MOSTLY. WE'VE CLEARED A PATH TO THE PRESIDENT'S PANIC ROOM, BUT WE COULDN'T CRACK THE DOOR.
YOU OKAY?
SURE. NO ONE DIED. THINGS JUST GOT A BIT PUNCHY.
NOPE
HARLEY. CAN YOU GUARD THE GATE?
WHY ME?
YOU'RE THE ONLY ONE I TRUST.
PLEASE! THIS IS ALL WRONG.
MY PEOPLE NEED ME. MY--
BANG
GOODBYE, MADAM PRESIDENT.
IT'S DONE, LOK.
LEAVE THE BODY. GET OUT OF THERE. DON'T MAKE ANY MORE MISTAKES.

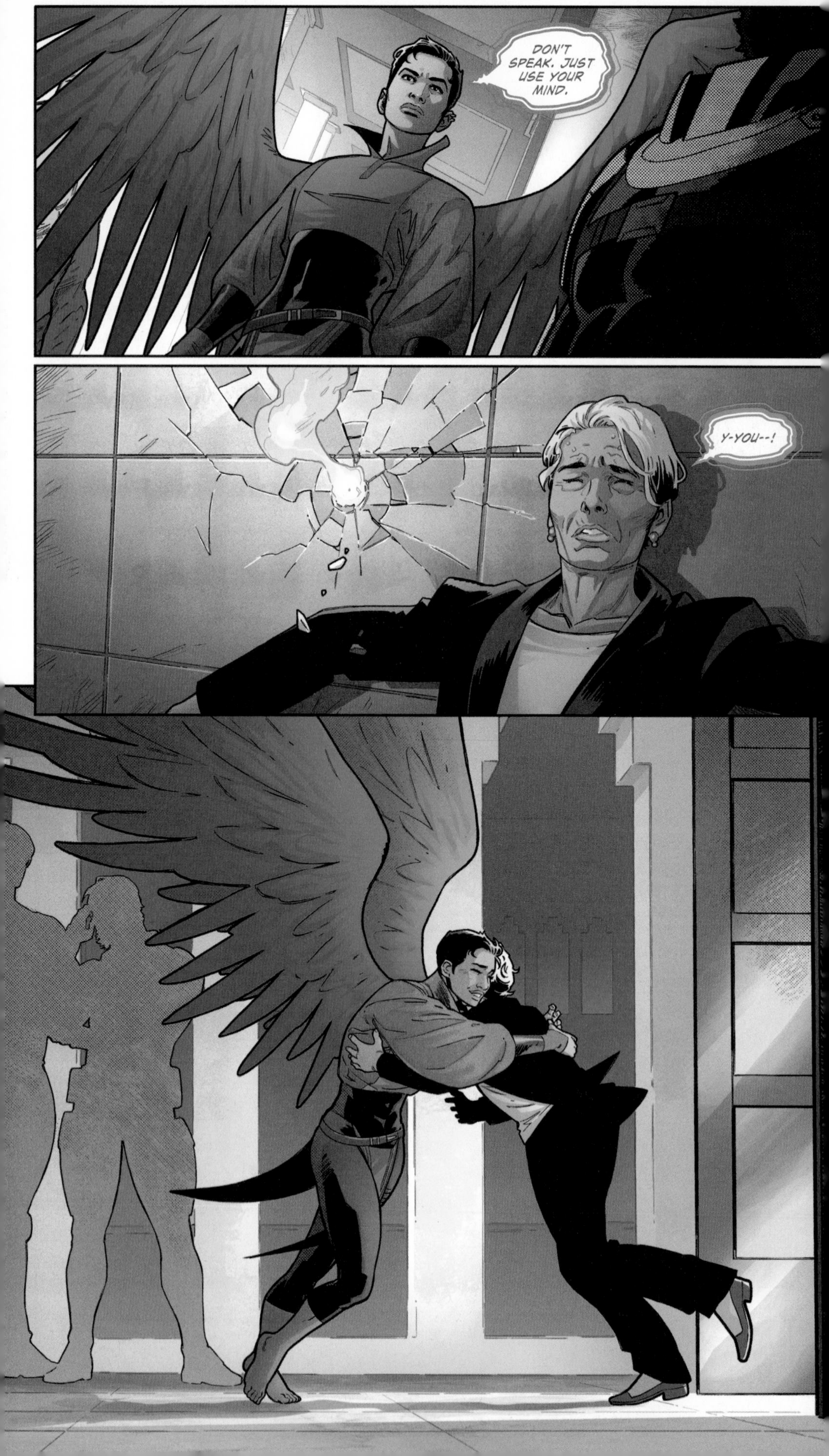
DON'T SPEAK. JUST USE YOUR MIND.
Y-YOU--!

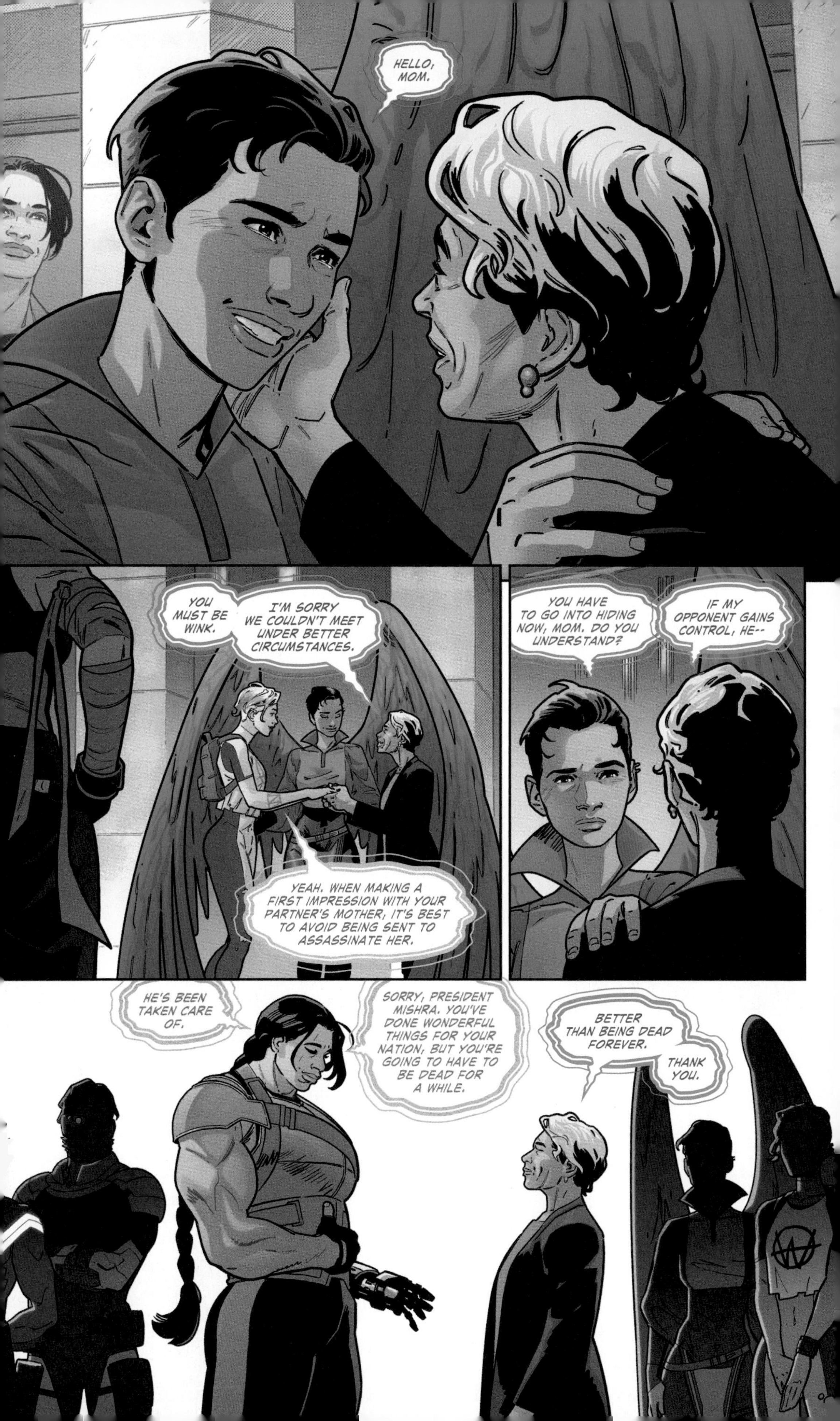
HELLO, MOM.
YOU MUST BE WINK.
I'M SORRY WE COULDN'T MEET UNDER BETTER CIRCUMSTANCES.
YEAH. WHEN MAKING A FIRST IMPRESSION WITH YOUR PARTNER'S MOTHER, IT'S BEST TO AVOID BEING SENT TO ASSASSINATE HER.
YOU HAVE TO GO INTO HIDING NOW, MOM. DO YOU UNDERSTAND?
IF MY OPPONENT GAINS CONTROL, HE--
HE'S BEEN TAKEN CARE OF.
SORRY, PRESIDENT MISHRA. YOU'VE DONE WONDERFUL THINGS FOR YOUR NATION, BUT YOU'RE GOING TO HAVE TO BE DEAD FOR A WHILE.
BETTER THAN BEING DEAD FOREVER.
THANK YOU.

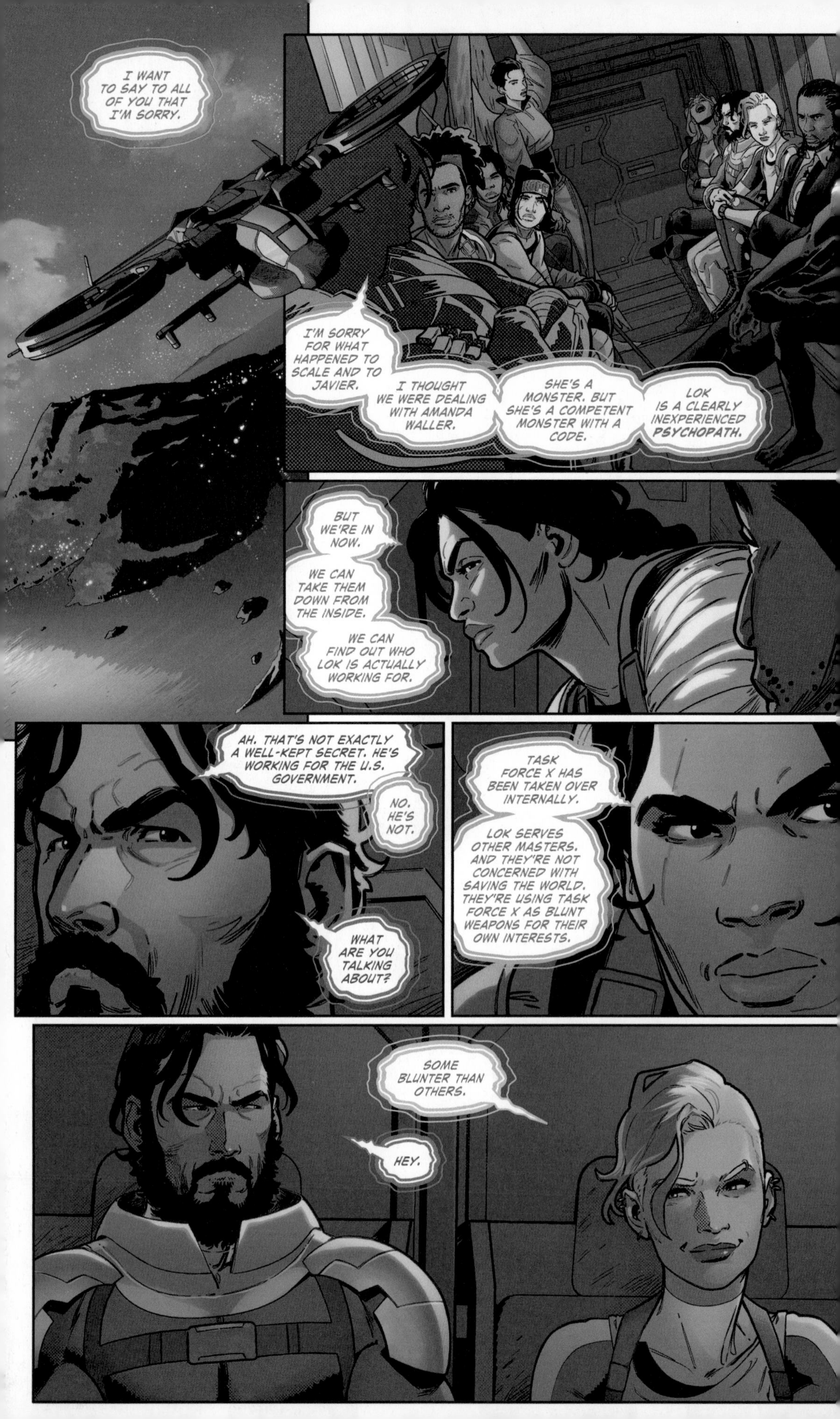
I WANT TO SAY TO ALL OF YOU THAT I'M SORRY.
I'M SORRY FOR WHAT HAPPENED TO SCALE AND TO JAVIER.
I THOUGHT WE WERE DEALING WITH AMANDA WALLER.
SHE'S A MONSTER. BUT SHE'S A COMPETENT MONSTER WITH A CODE.
LOK IS A CLEARLY INEXPERIENCED PSYCHOPATH.
BUT WE'RE IN NOW.
WE CAN TAKE THEM DOWN FROM THE INSIDE.
WE CAN FIND OUT WHO LOK IS ACTUALLY WORKING FOR.
AH. THAT'S NOT EXACTLY A WELL-KEPT SECRET. HE'S WORKING FOR THE U.S. GOVERNMENT.
NO. HE'S NOT.
WHAT ARE YOU TALKING ABOUT?
TASK FORCE X HAS BEEN TAKEN OVER INTERNALLY.
LOK SERVES OTHER MASTERS. AND THEY'RE NOT CONCERNED WITH SAVING THE WORLD. THEY'RE USING TASK FORCE X AS BLUNT WEAPONS FOR THEIR OWN INTERESTS.
SOME BLUNTER THAN OTHERS.
HEY.

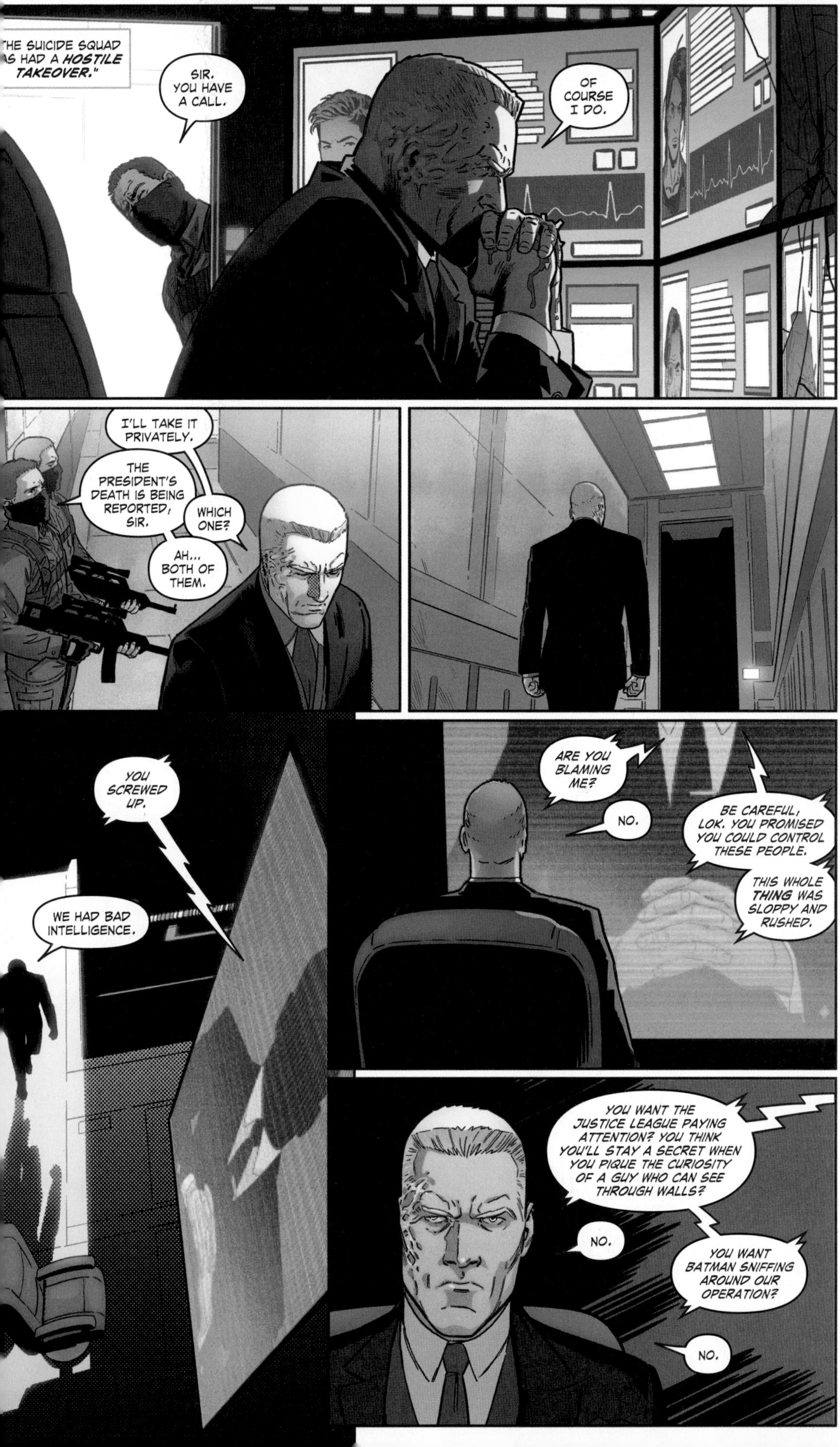
"THE SUICIDE SQUAD HAS HAD A HOSTILE TAKEOVER."
SIR. YOU HAVE A CALL.
OF COURSE I DO.
I'LL TAKE IT PRIVATELY.
THE PRESIDENT'S DEATH IS BEING REPORTED, SIR.
WHICH ONE?
AH... BOTH OF THEM.
YOU SCREWED UP.
WE HAD BAD INTELLIGENCE.
ARE YOU BLAMING ME?
NO.
BE CAREFUL, LOK. YOU PROMISED YOU COULD CONTROL THESE PEOPLE.
THIS WHOLE THING WAS SLOPPY AND RUSHED.
YOU WANT THE JUSTICE LEAGUE PAYING ATTENTION? YOU THINK YOU'LL STAY A SECRET WHEN YOU PIQUE THE CURIOSITY OF A GUY WHO CAN SEE THROUGH WALLS?
NO.
YOU WANT BATMAN SNIFFING AROUND OUR OPERATION?
NO.

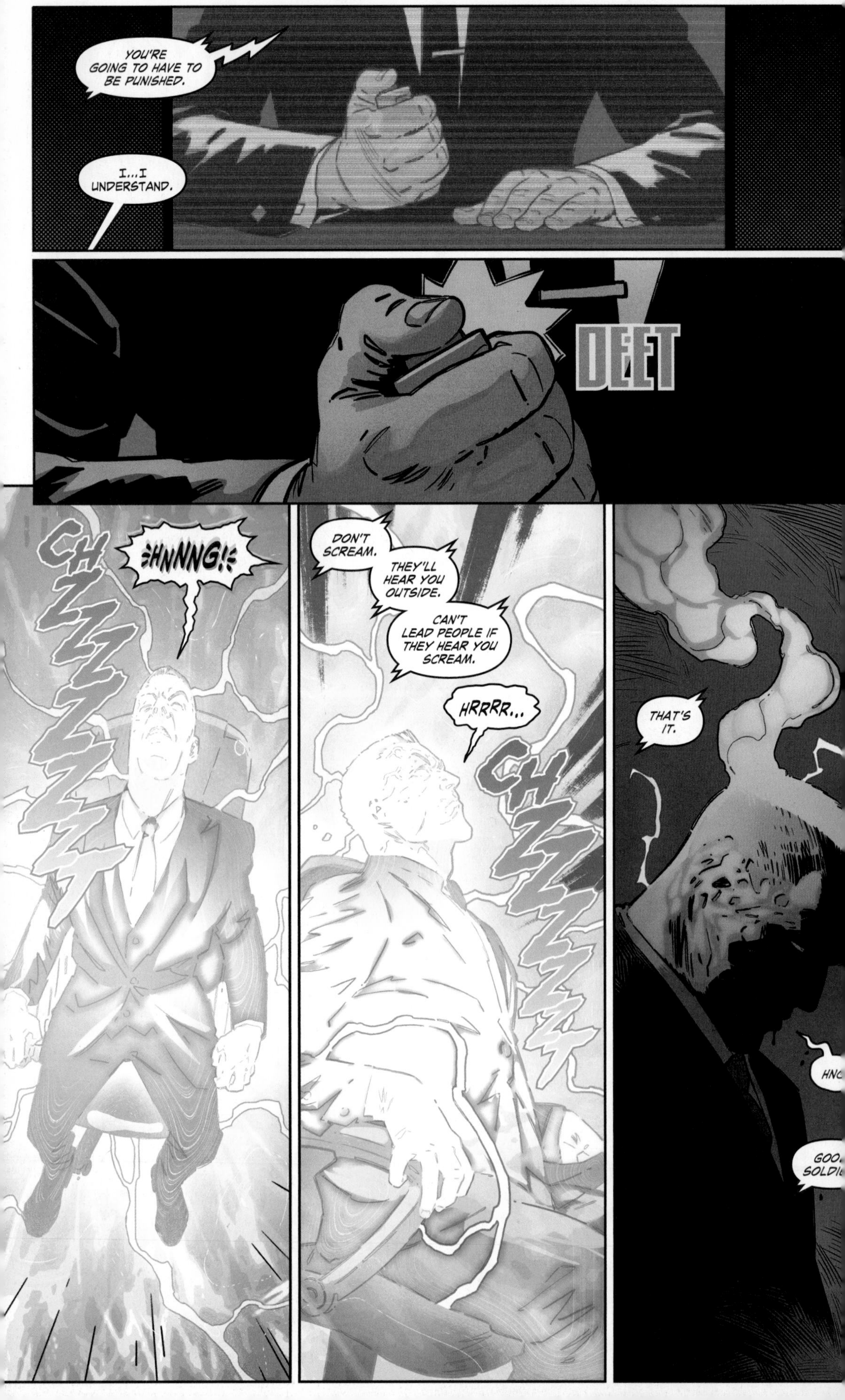
YOU'RE GOING TO HAVE TO BE PUNISHED.
I...I UNDERSTAND.
DEET
CHZZZZZZT
HNNNG!
DON'T SCREAM.
THEY'LL HEAR YOU OUTSIDE.
CAN'T LEAD PEOPLE IF THEY HEAR YOU SCREAM.
HRRRR...
CHZZZZZZT
THAT'S IT.

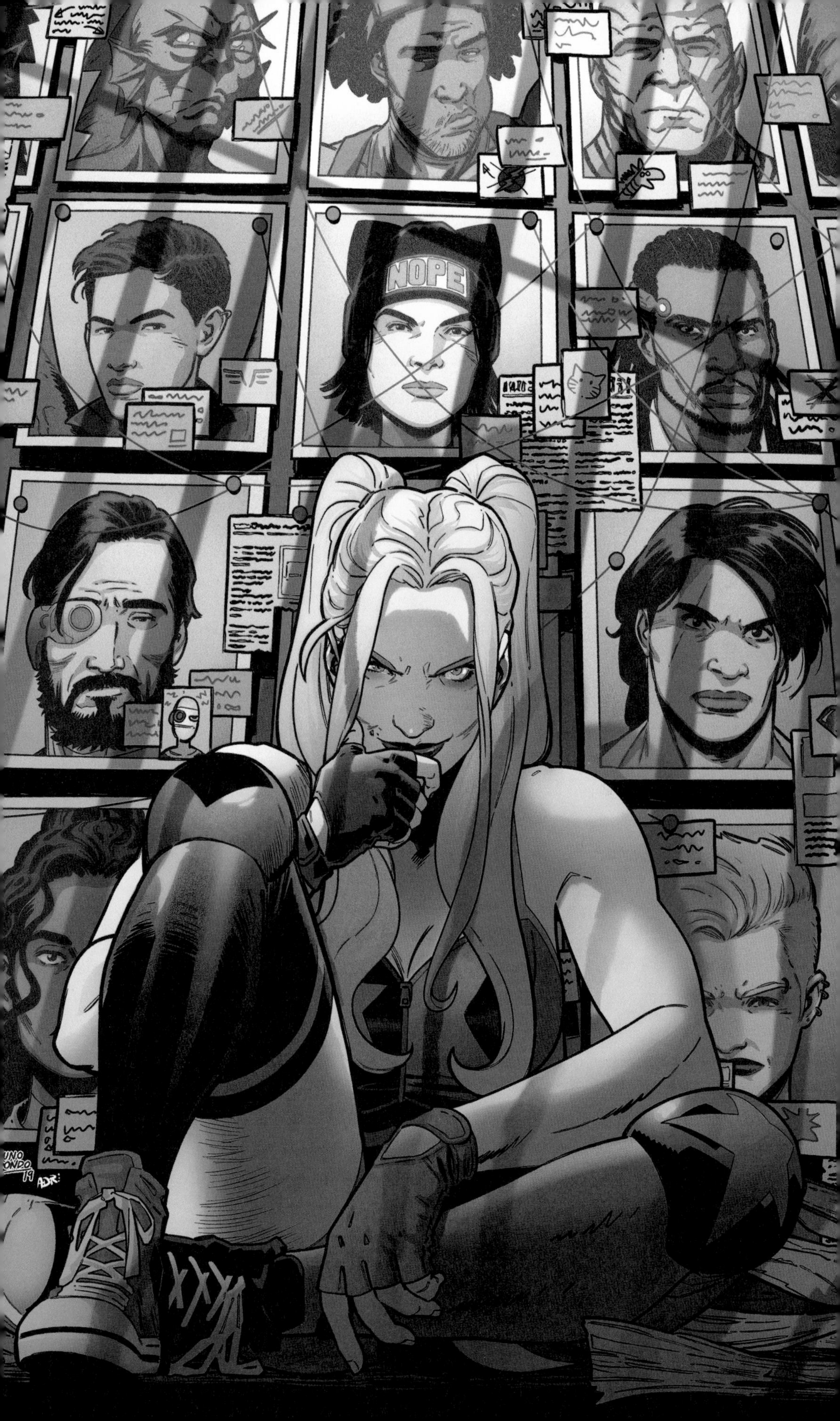
NOPE

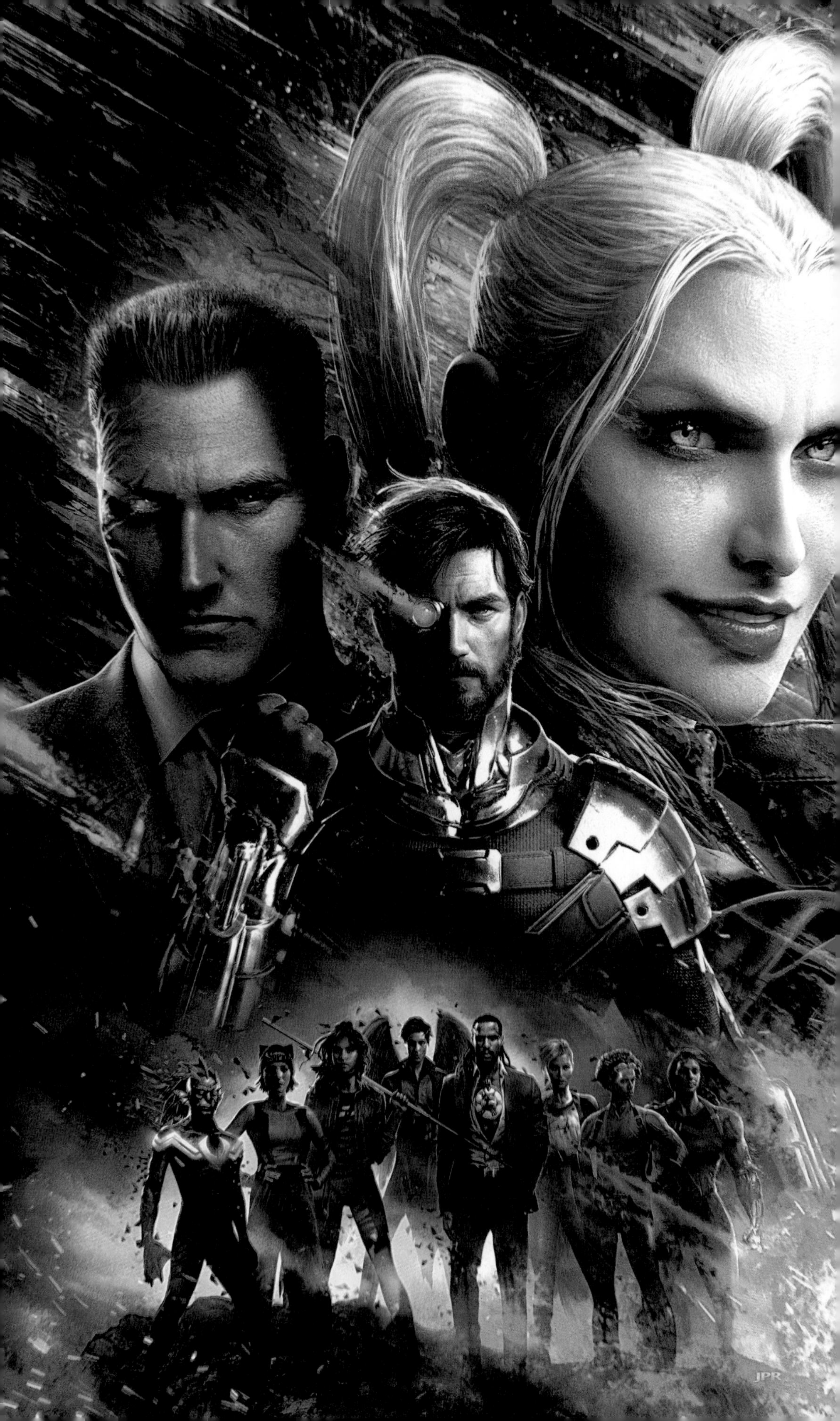
JPR

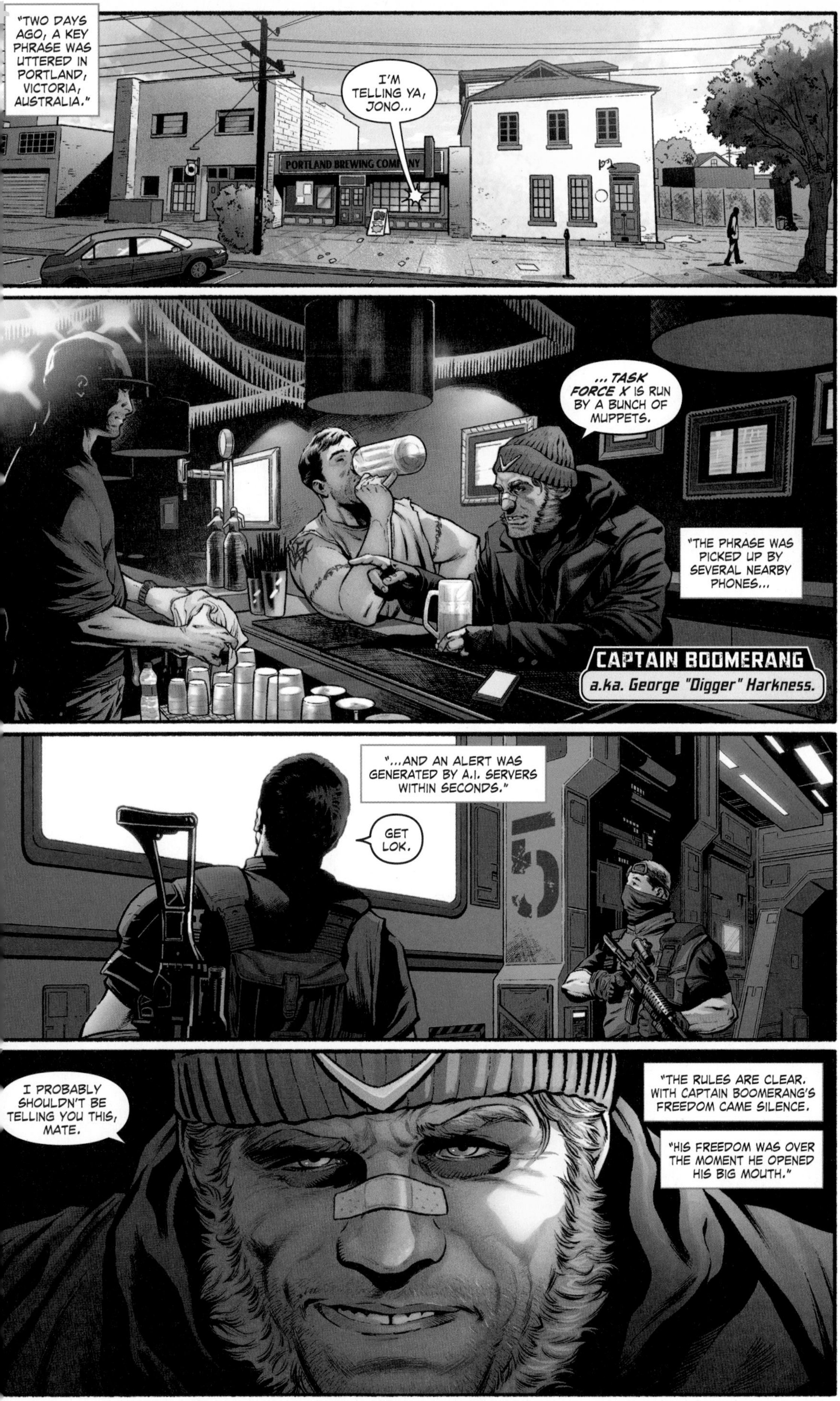
"TWO DAYS AGO, A KEY PHRASE WAS UTTERED IN PORTLAND, VICTORIA, AUSTRALIA."
I'M TELLING YA, JONO...
PORTLAND BREWING COMPANY
...TASK FORCE X IS RUN BY A BUNCH OF MUPPETS.
"THE PHRASE WAS PICKED UP BY SEVERAL NEARBY PHONES...
CAPTAIN BOOMERANG
a.ka. George "Digger" Harkness.
"...AND AN ALERT WAS GENERATED BY A.I. SERVERS WITHIN SECONDS."
GET LOK.
I PROBABLY SHOULDN'T BE TELLING YOU THIS, MATE.
"THE RULES ARE CLEAR. WITH CAPTAIN BOOMERANG'S FREEDOM CAME SILENCE.
"HIS FREEDOM WAS OVER THE MOMENT HE OPENED HIS BIG MOUTH."

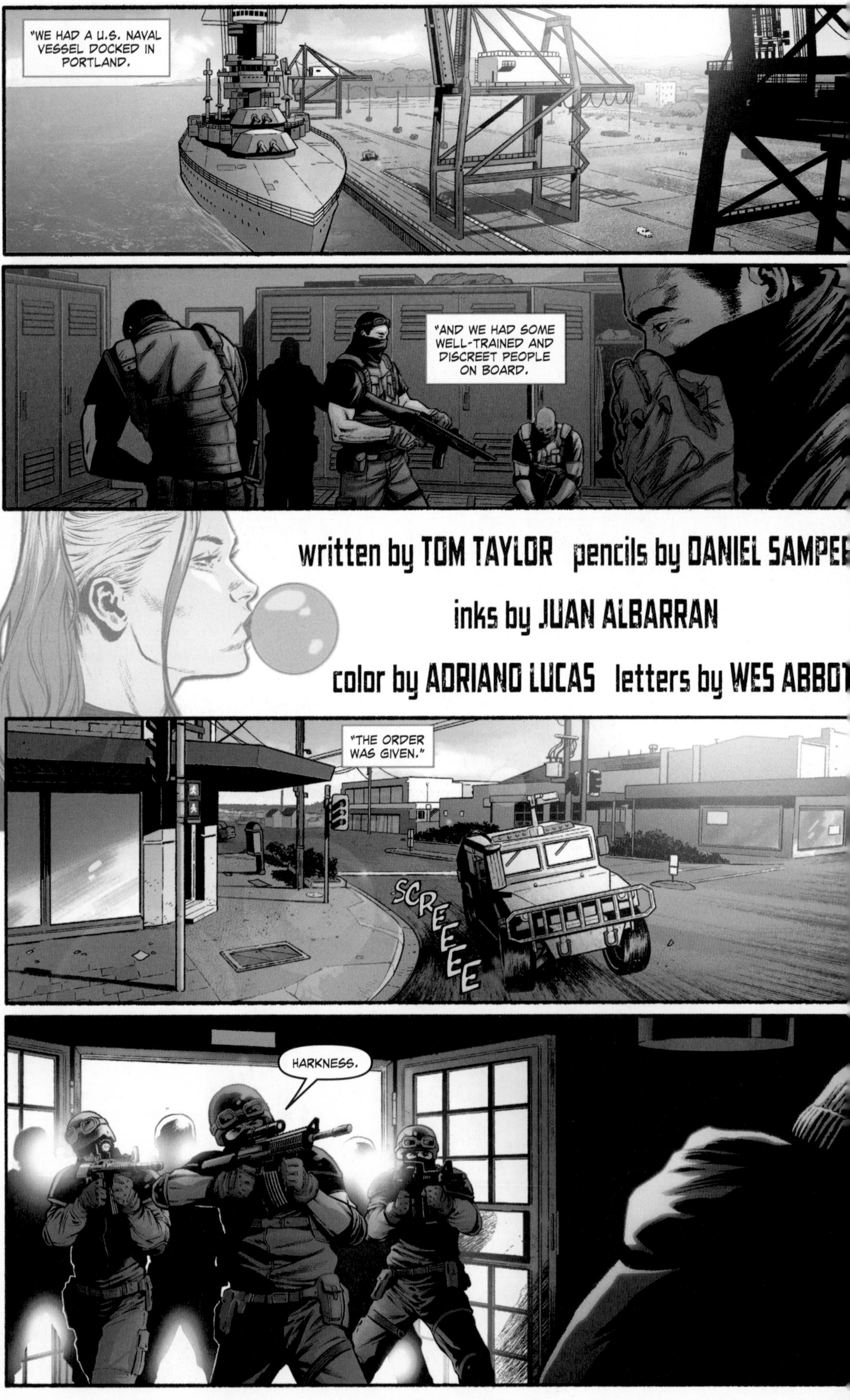
"WE HAD A U.S. NAVAL VESSEL DOCKED IN PORTLAND.
"AND WE HAD SOME WELL-TRAINED AND DISCREET PEOPLE ON BOARD.
written by TOM TAYLOR pencils by DANIEL SAMPE
inks by JUAN ALBARRAN
color by ADRIANO LUCAS letters by WES ABBOT
"THE ORDER WAS GIVEN."
SCREEEEE
HARKNESS.

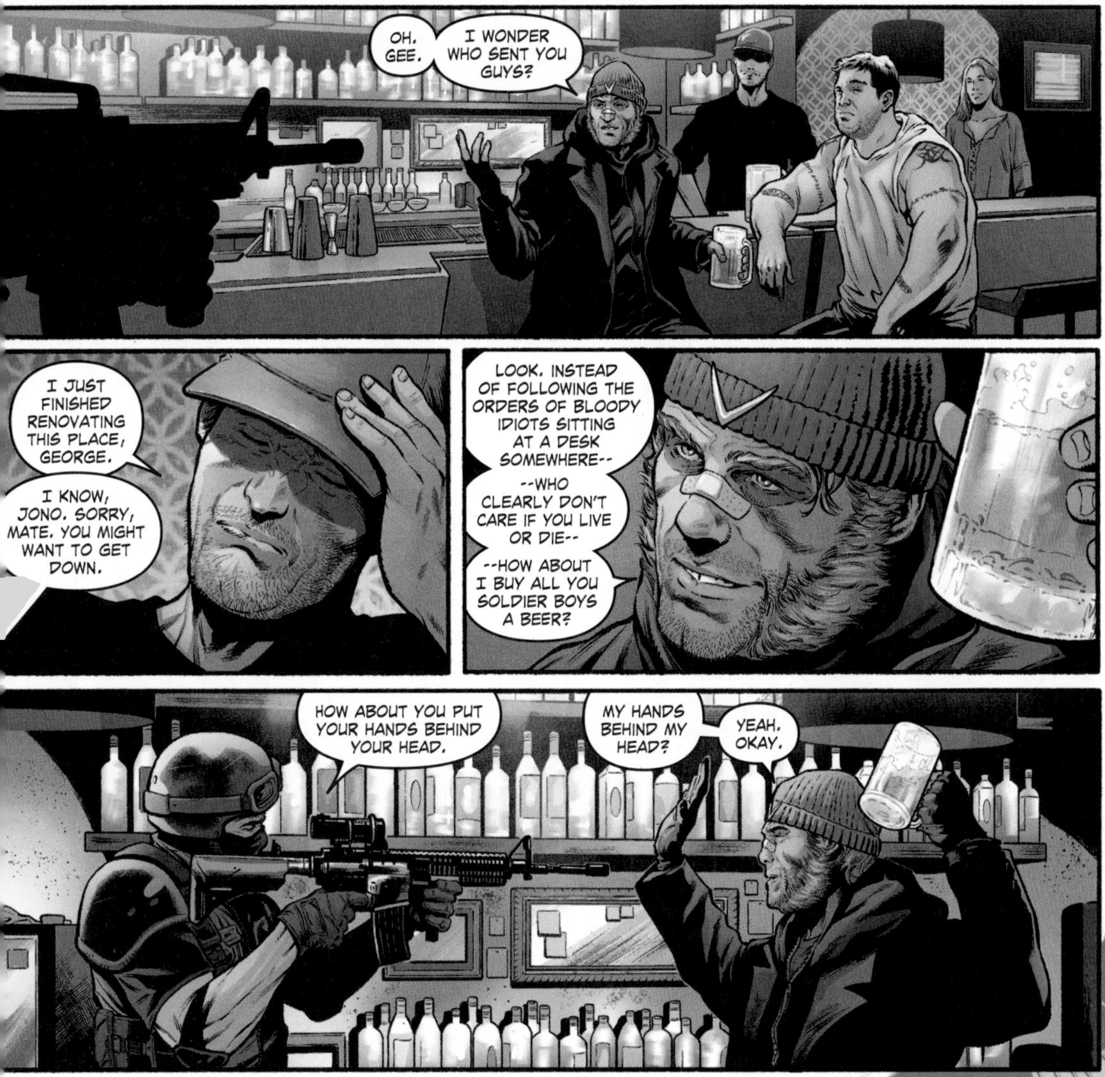
OH. GEE.
I WONDER WHO SENT YOU GUYS?
I JUST FINISHED RENOVATING THIS PLACE, GEORGE.
I KNOW, JONO. SORRY, MATE. YOU MIGHT WANT TO GET DOWN.
LOOK. INSTEAD OF FOLLOWING THE ORDERS OF BLOODY IDIOTS SITTING AT A DESK SOMEWHERE--
--WHO CLEARLY DON'T CARE IF YOU LIVE OR DIE--
--HOW ABOUT I BUY ALL YOU SOLDIER BOYS A BEER?
HOW ABOUT YOU PUT YOUR HANDS BEHIND YOUR HEAD.
MY HANDS BEHIND MY HEAD?
YEAH, OKAY.

ditor ANDREA SHEA group editor ALEX R. CARR

over BRUNO REDONDO and ADRIANO LUCAS

ariant cover JEREMY ROBERTS

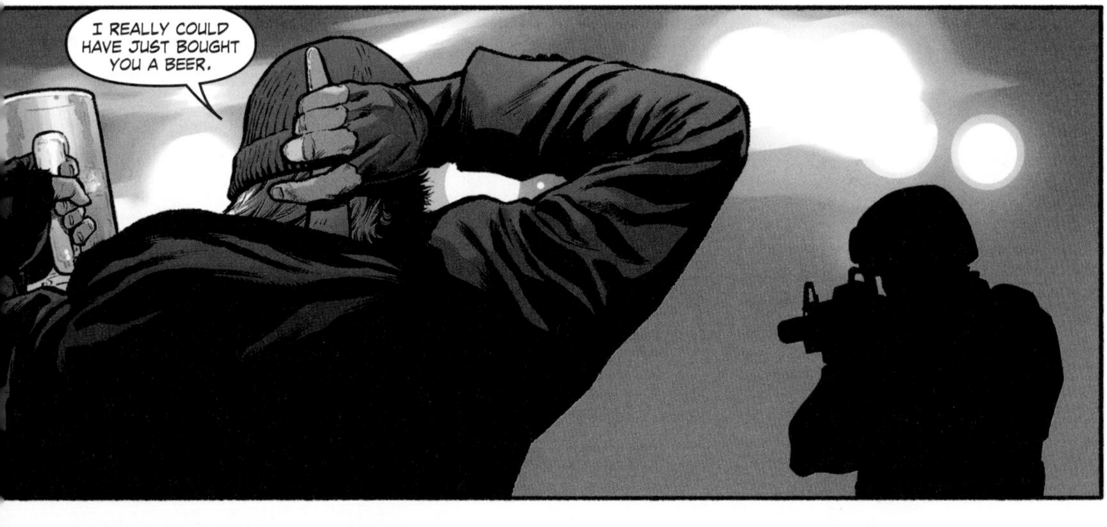
I REALLY COULD HAVE JUST BOUGHT YOU A BEER.

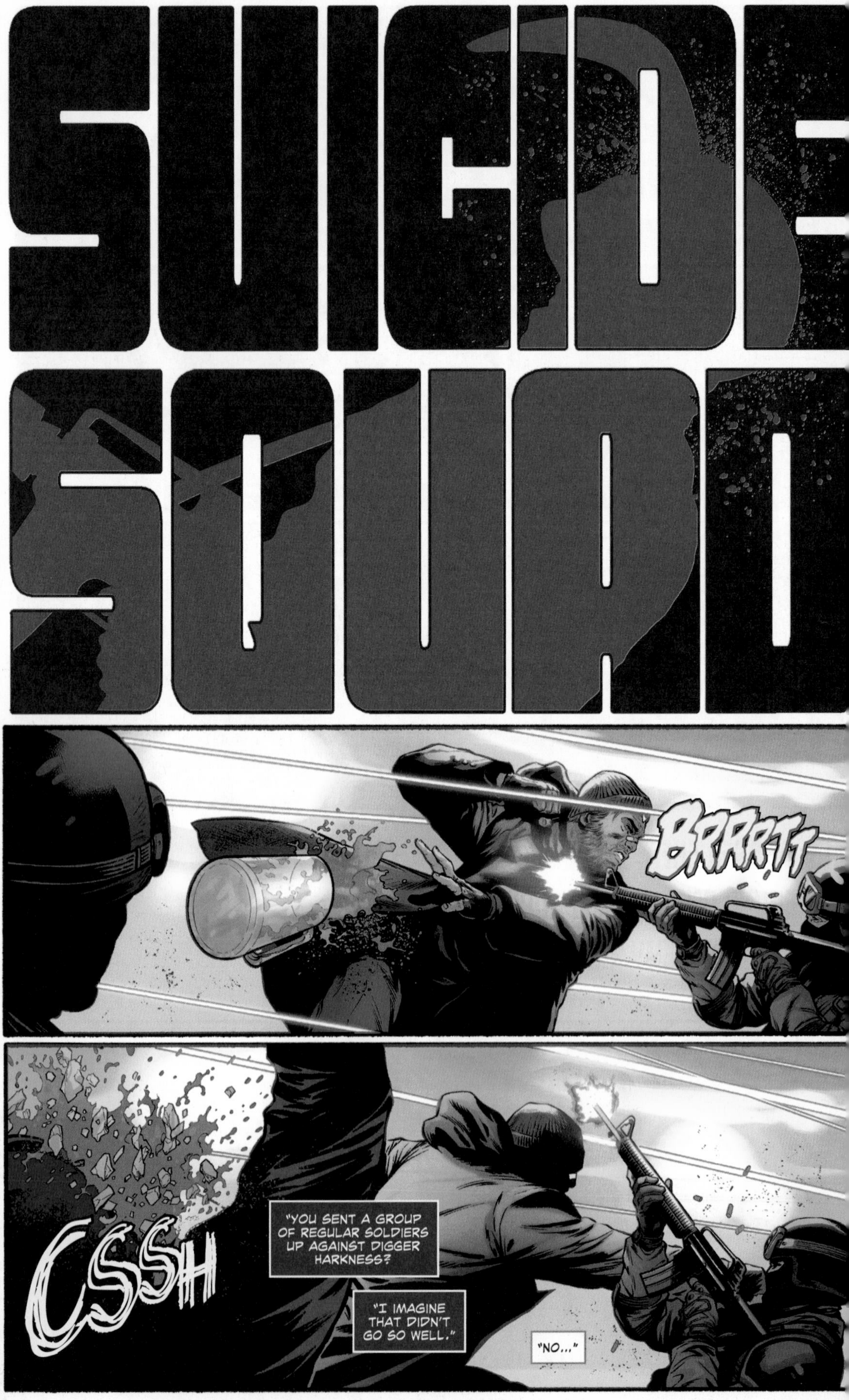
SUICIDE SQUAD
BRRRTT
CSSH
"YOU SENT A GROUP OF REGULAR SOLDIERS UP AGAINST DIGGER HARKNESS?
"I IMAGINE THAT DIDN'T GO SO WELL."
"NO..."

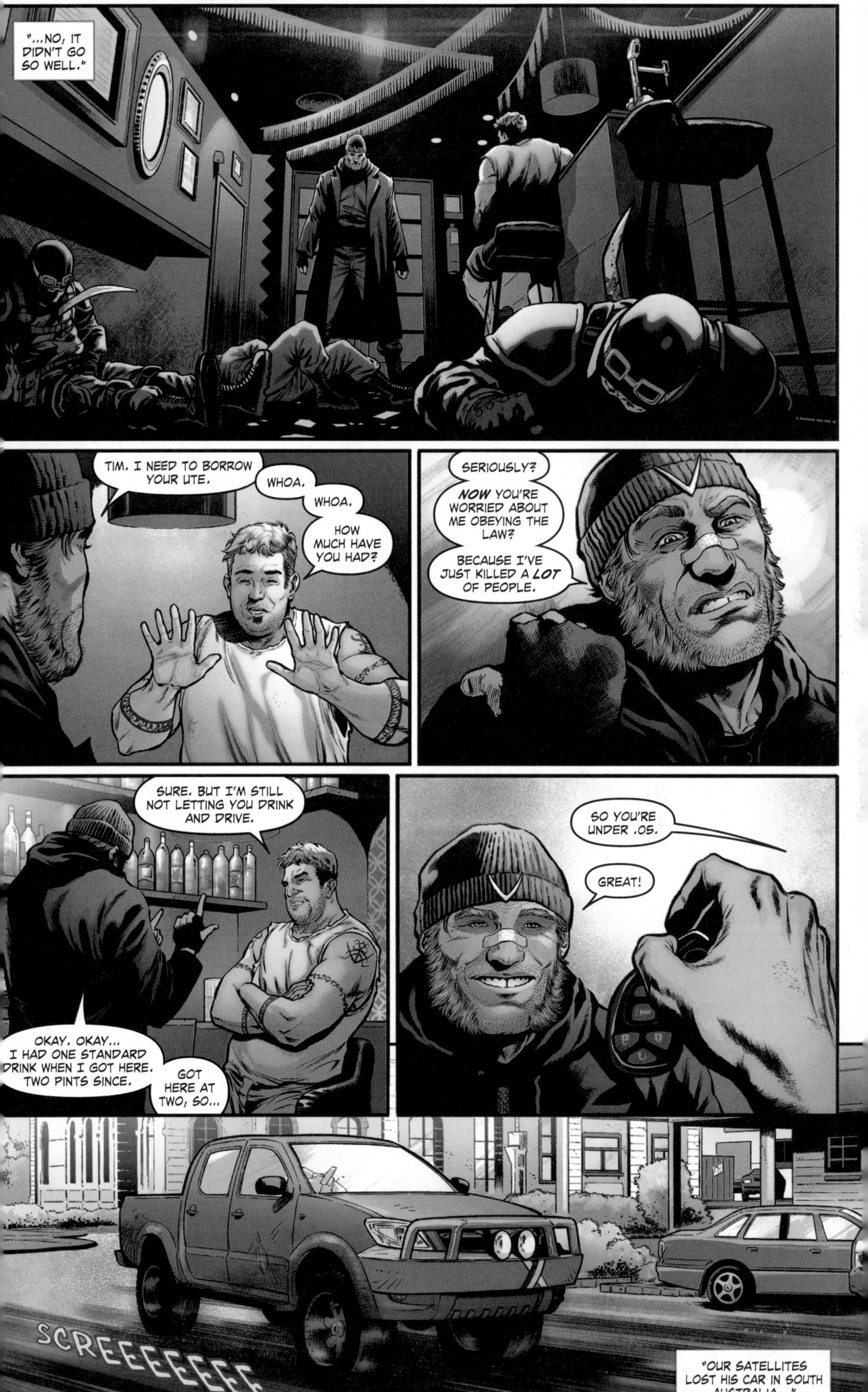
"...NO, IT DIDN'T GO SO WELL."
TIM. I NEED TO BORROW YOUR UTE.
WHOA.
WHOA.
HOW MUCH HAVE YOU HAD?
SERIOUSLY?
NOW YOU'RE WORRIED ABOUT ME OBEYING THE LAW?
BECAUSE I'VE JUST KILLED A LOT OF PEOPLE.
SURE. BUT I'M STILL NOT LETTING YOU DRINK AND DRIVE.
OKAY. OKAY... I HAD ONE STANDARD DRINK WHEN I GOT HERE. TWO PINTS SINCE.
GOT HERE AT TWO, SO...
SO YOU'RE UNDER .05.
GREAT!
SCREEEEEEEEE
"OUR SATELLITES LOST HIS CAR IN SOUTH AUSTRALIA..."

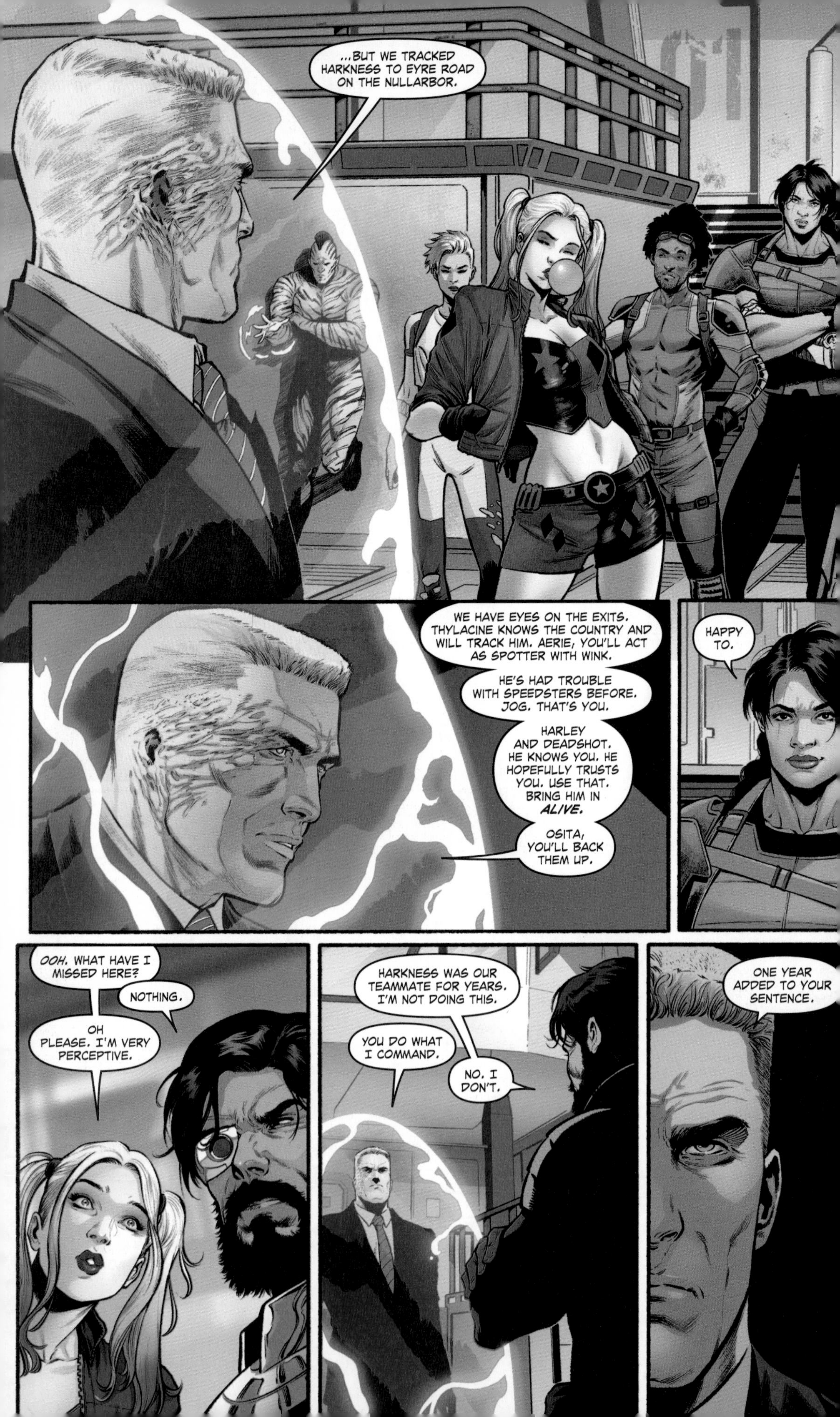
...BUT WE TRACKED HARKNESS TO EYRE ROAD ON THE NULLARBOR.
WE HAVE EYES ON THE EXITS. THYLACINE KNOWS THE COUNTRY AND WILL TRACK HIM. AERIE, YOU'LL ACT AS SPOTTER WITH WINK.
HE'S HAD TROUBLE WITH SPEEDSTERS BEFORE. JOG. THAT'S YOU.
HARLEY AND DEADSHOT. HE KNOWS YOU. HE HOPEFULLY TRUSTS YOU. USE THAT. BRING HIM IN ***ALIVE.***
OSITA, YOU'LL BACK THEM UP.
HAPPY TO.
OOH. WHAT HAVE I MISSED HERE?
NOTHING.
OH PLEASE. I'M VERY PERCEPTIVE.
HARKNESS WAS OUR TEAMMATE FOR YEARS. I'M NOT DOING THIS.
YOU DO WHAT I COMMAND.
NO. I DON'T.
ONE YEAR ADDED TO YOUR SENTENCE.

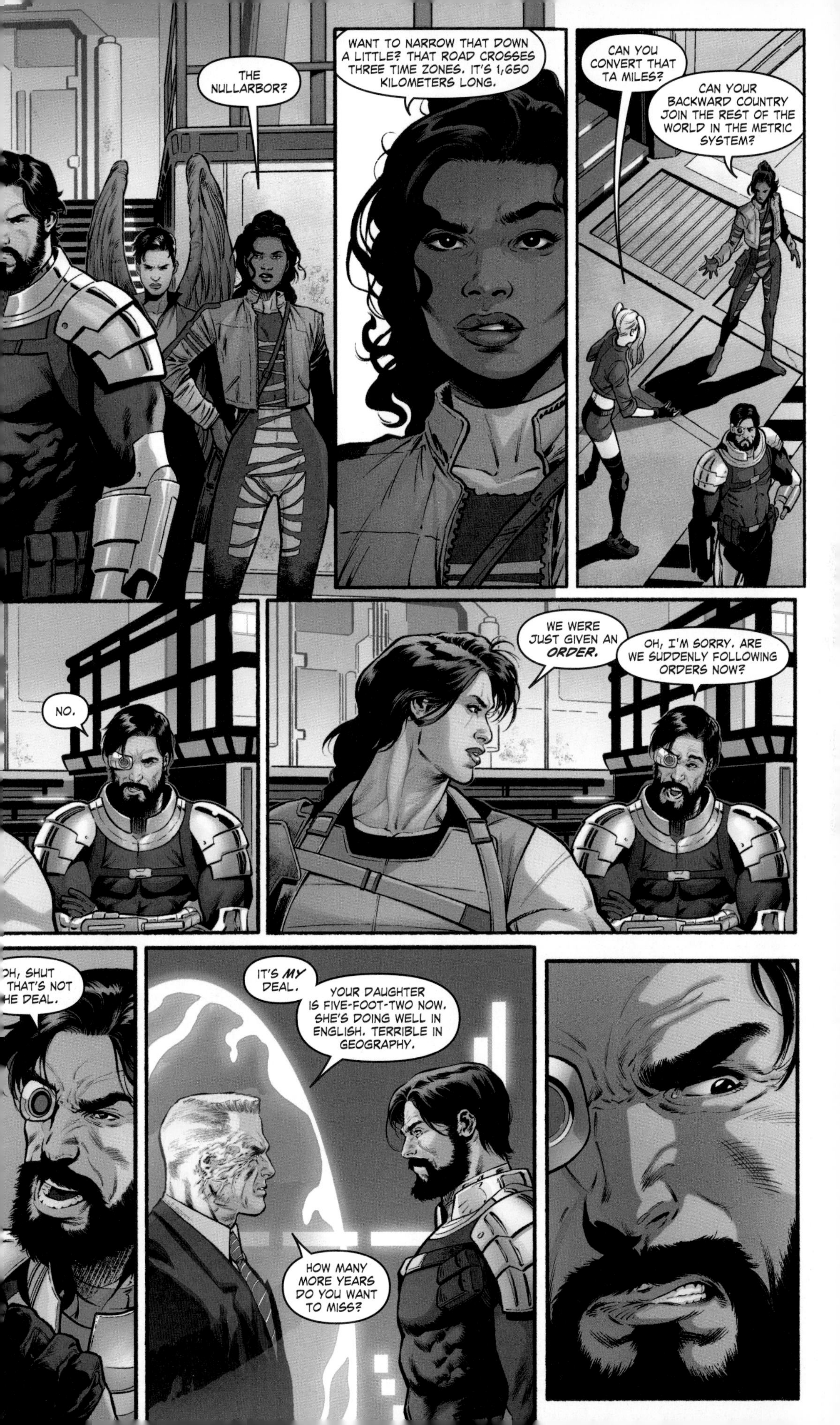
THE NULLARBOR?
WANT TO NARROW THAT DOWN A LITTLE? THAT ROAD CROSSES THREE TIME ZONES. IT'S 1,650 KILOMETERS LONG.
CAN YOU CONVERT THAT TA MILES?
CAN YOUR BACKWARD COUNTRY JOIN THE REST OF THE WORLD IN THE METRIC SYSTEM?
NO.
WE WERE JUST GIVEN AN ORDER.
OH, I'M SORRY. ARE WE SUDDENLY FOLLOWING ORDERS NOW?
THAT'S NOT
IT'S MY DEAL.
YOUR DAUGHTER IS FIVE-FOOT-TWO NOW. SHE'S DOING WELL IN ENGLISH. TERRIBLE IN GEOGRAPHY.
HOW MANY MORE YEARS DO YOU WANT TO MISS?

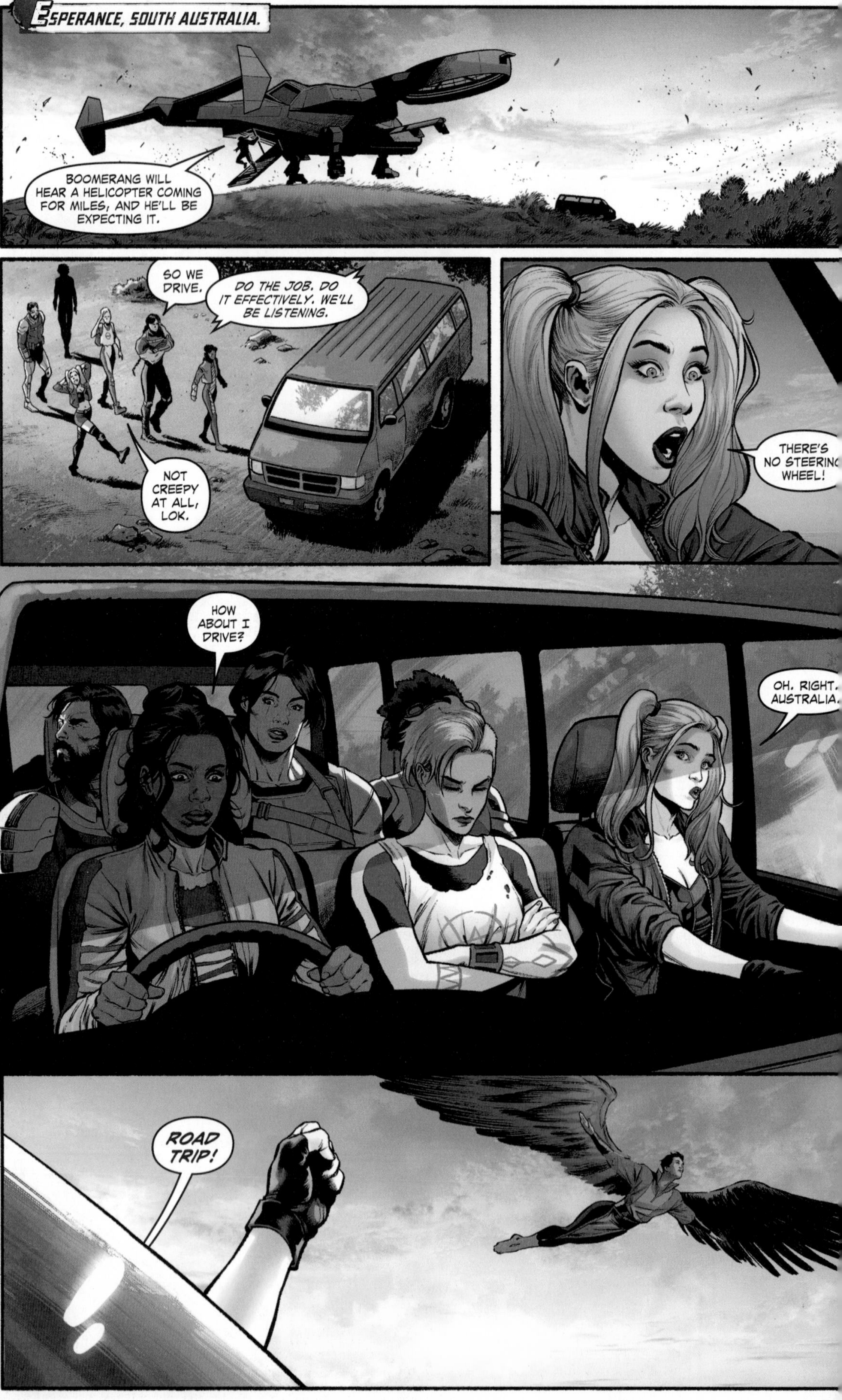
ESPERANCE, SOUTH AUSTRALIA.
BOOMERANG WILL HEAR A HELICOPTER COMING FOR MILES, AND HE'LL BE EXPECTING IT.
SO WE DRIVE.
DO THE JOB. DO IT EFFECTIVELY. WE'LL BE LISTENING.
NOT CREEPY AT ALL, LOK.
THERE'S NO STEERING WHEEL!
HOW ABOUT I DRIVE?
OH. RIGHT. AUSTRALIA.
ROAD TRIP!

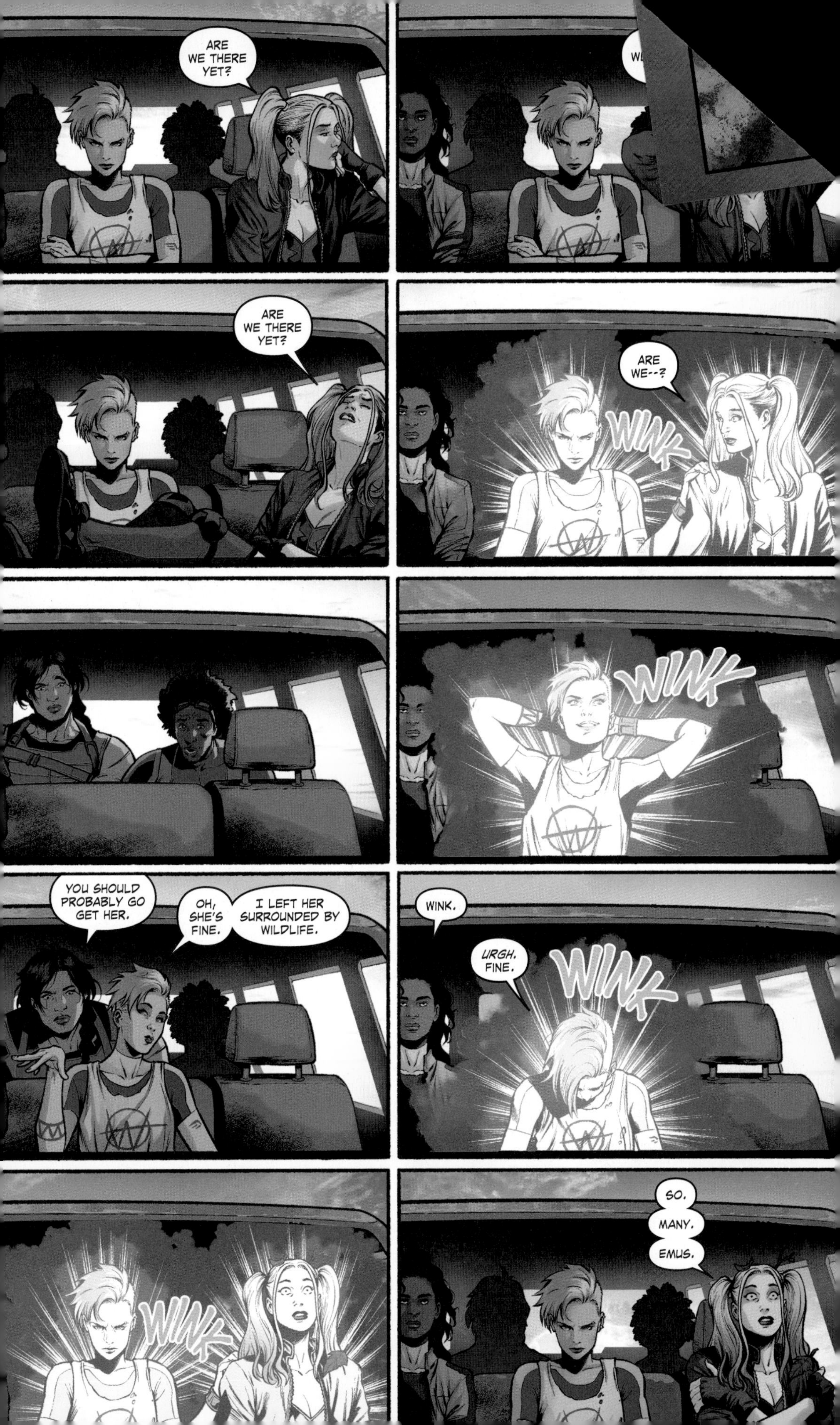
ARE WE THERE YET?
ARE WE THERE YET?
ARE WE--?
WINK
WINK
YOU SHOULD PROBABLY GO GET HER.
OH, SHE'S FINE.
I LEFT HER SURROUNDED BY WILDLIFE.
WINK.
URGH. FINE.
WINK
WINK
SO.
MANY.
EMUS.

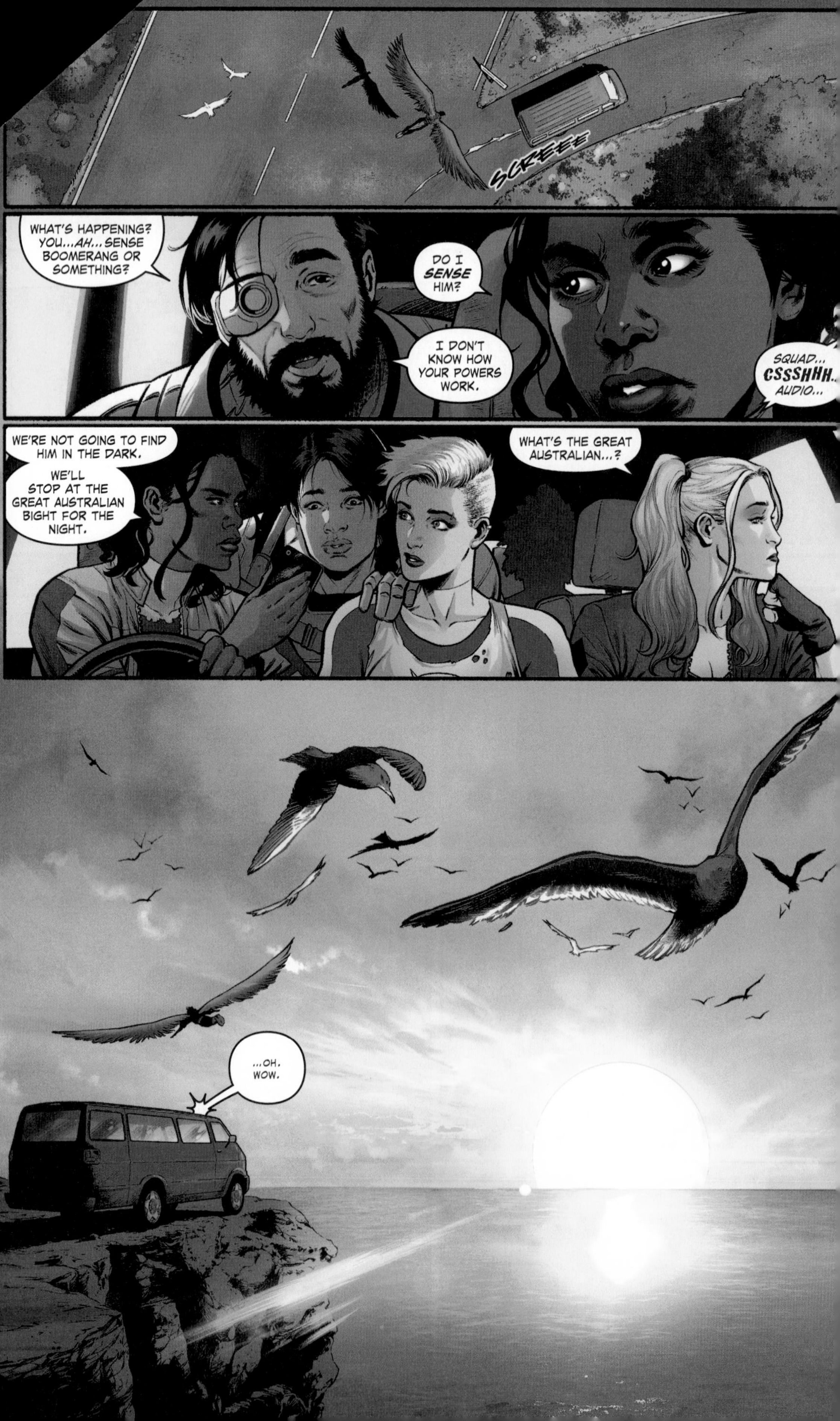
SCREEEE
WHAT'S HAPPENING? YOU...AH...SENSE BOOMERANG OR SOMETHING?
DO I SENSE HIM?
I DON'T KNOW HOW YOUR POWERS WORK.
SQUAD... CSSSHHH... AUDIO...
WE'RE NOT GOING TO FIND HIM IN THE DARK.
WE'LL STOP AT THE GREAT AUSTRALIAN BIGHT FOR THE NIGHT.
WHAT'S THE GREAT AUSTRALIAN...?
...OH, WOW.

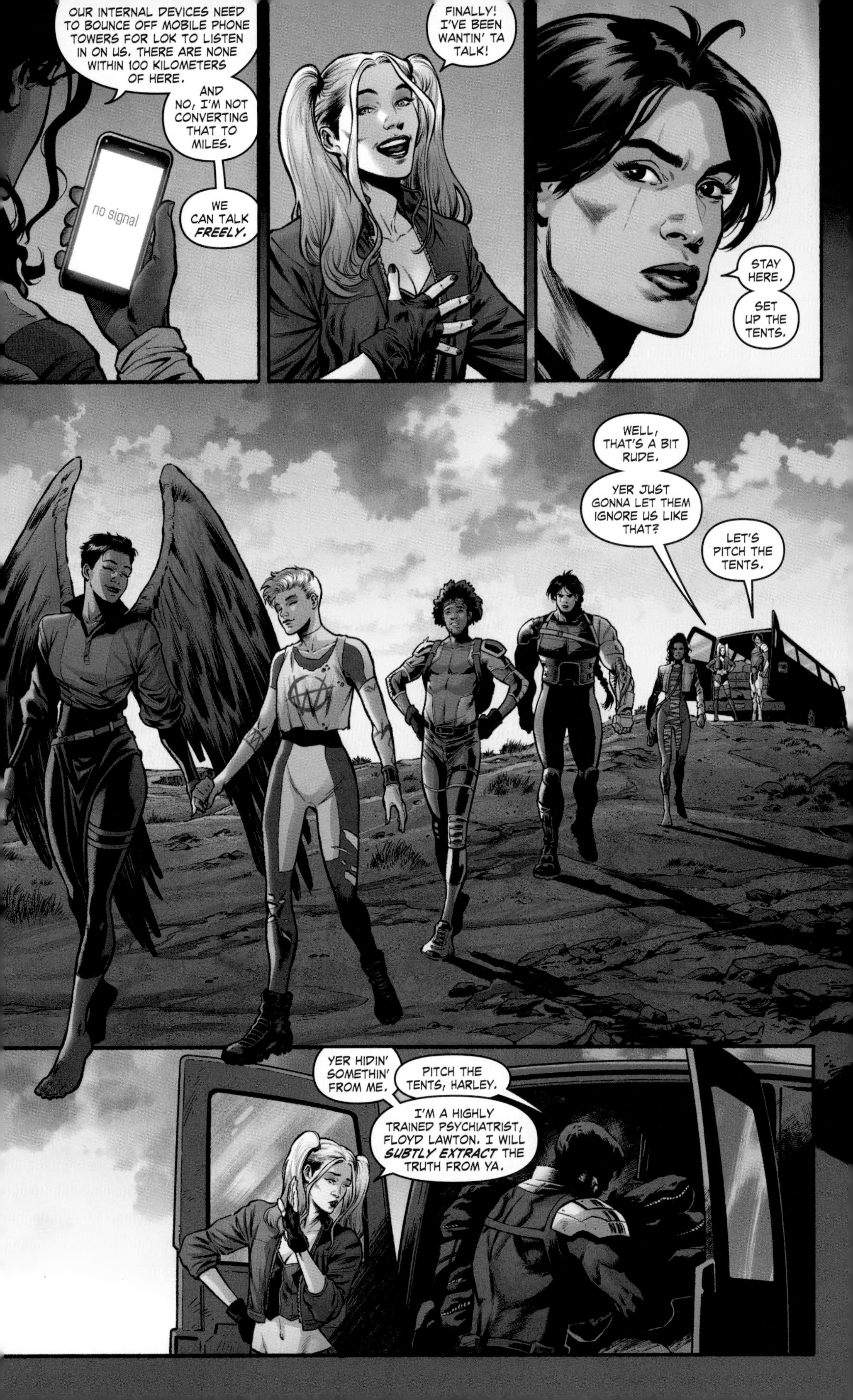

OUR INTERNAL DEVICES NEED TO BOUNCE OFF MOBILE PHONE TOWERS FOR LOK TO LISTEN IN ON US. THERE ARE NONE WITHIN 100 KILOMETERS OF HERE.
AND NO, I'M NOT CONVERTING THAT TO MILES.
WE CAN TALK *FREELY.*
no signal
FINALLY! I'VE BEEN WANTIN' TA TALK!
STAY HERE.
SET UP THE TENTS.
WELL, THAT'S A BIT RUDE.
YER JUST GONNA LET THEM IGNORE US LIKE THAT?
LET'S PITCH THE TENTS.
YER HIDIN' SOMETHIN' FROM ME.
PITCH THE TENTS, HARLEY.
I'M A HIGHLY TRAINED PSYCHIATRIST, FLOYD LAWTON. I WILL *SUBTLY EXTRACT* THE TRUTH FROM YA.

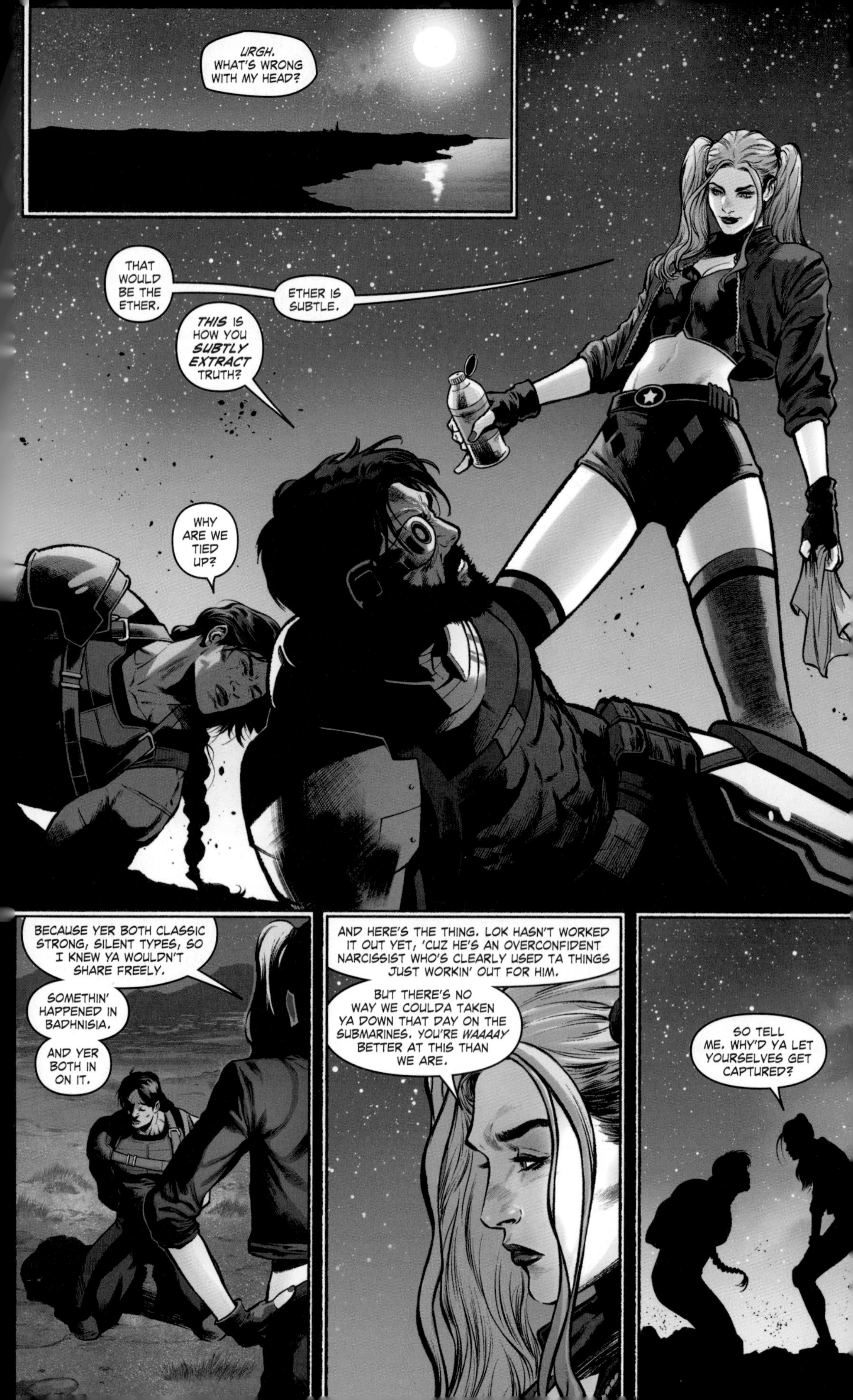

URGH. WHAT'S WRONG WITH MY HEAD?
THAT WOULD BE THE ETHER.
ETHER IS SUBTLE.
THIS IS HOW YOU *SUBTLY EXTRACT* TRUTH?
WHY ARE WE TIED UP?
BECAUSE YER BOTH CLASSIC STRONG, SILENT TYPES, SO I KNEW YA WOULDN'T SHARE FREELY.
SOMETHIN' HAPPENED IN BADHNISIA.
AND YER BOTH IN ON IT.
AND HERE'S THE THING. LOK HASN'T WORKED IT OUT YET, 'CUZ HE'S AN OVERCONFIDENT NARCISSIST WHO'S CLEARLY USED TA THINGS JUST WORKIN' OUT FOR HIM.
BUT THERE'S NO WAY WE COULDA TAKEN YA DOWN THAT DAY ON THE SUBMARINES. YOU'RE *WAAAAY* BETTER AT THIS THAN WE ARE.
SO TELL ME. WHY'D YA LET YOURSELVES GET CAPTURED?

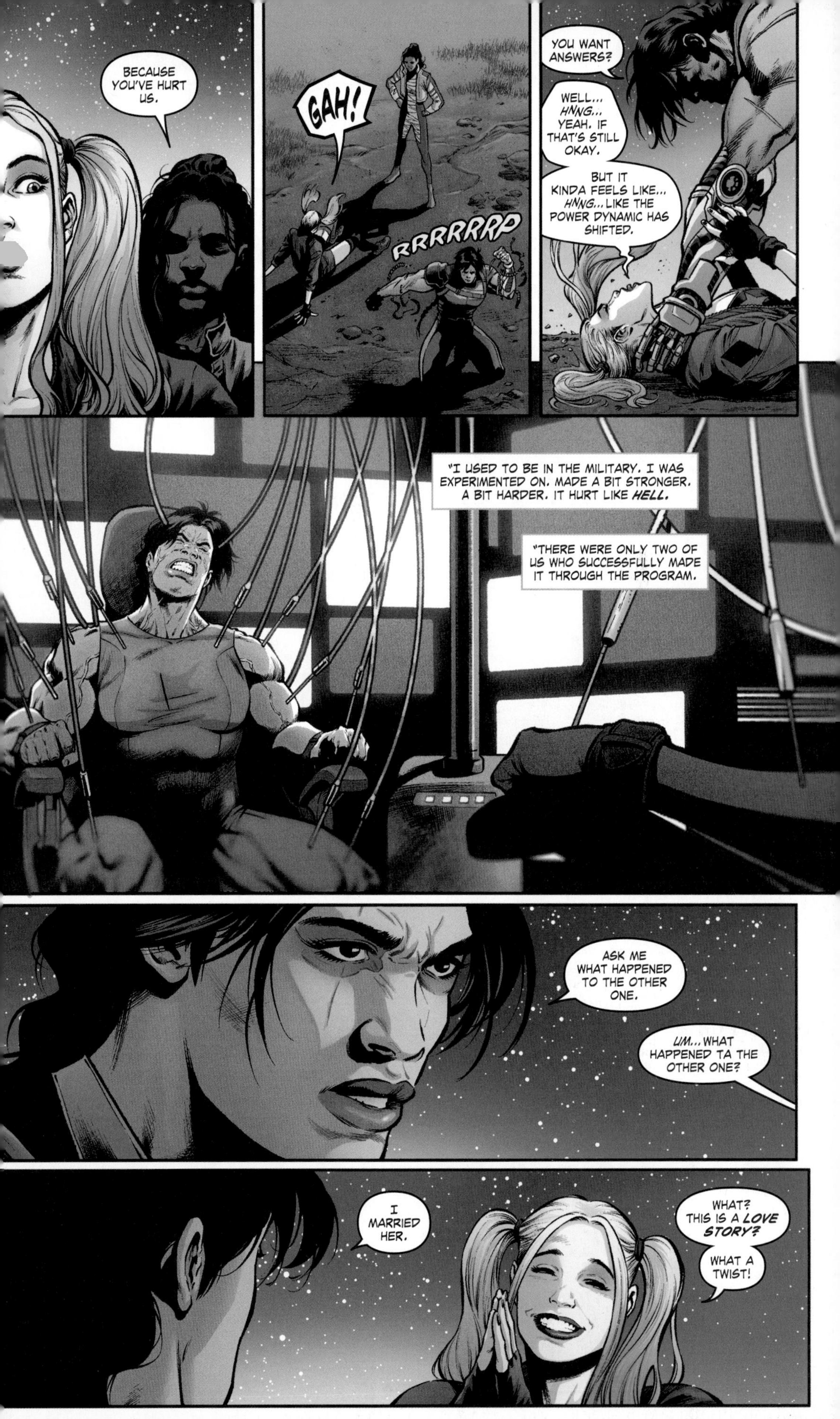
BECAUSE YOU'VE HURT US.
GAH!
RRRRRRP
YOU WANT ANSWERS?
WELL... HNNG... YEAH. IF THAT'S STILL OKAY.
BUT IT KINDA FEELS LIKE... HNNG... LIKE THE POWER DYNAMIC HAS SHIFTED.
"I USED TO BE IN THE MILITARY. I WAS EXPERIMENTED ON. MADE A BIT STRONGER. A BIT HARDER. IT HURT LIKE HELL.
"THERE WERE ONLY TWO OF US WHO SUCCESSFULLY MADE IT THROUGH THE PROGRAM.
ASK ME WHAT HAPPENED TO THE OTHER ONE.
UM... WHAT HAPPENED TA THE OTHER ONE?
I MARRIED HER.
WHAT? THIS IS A LOVE STORY?
WHAT A TWIST!

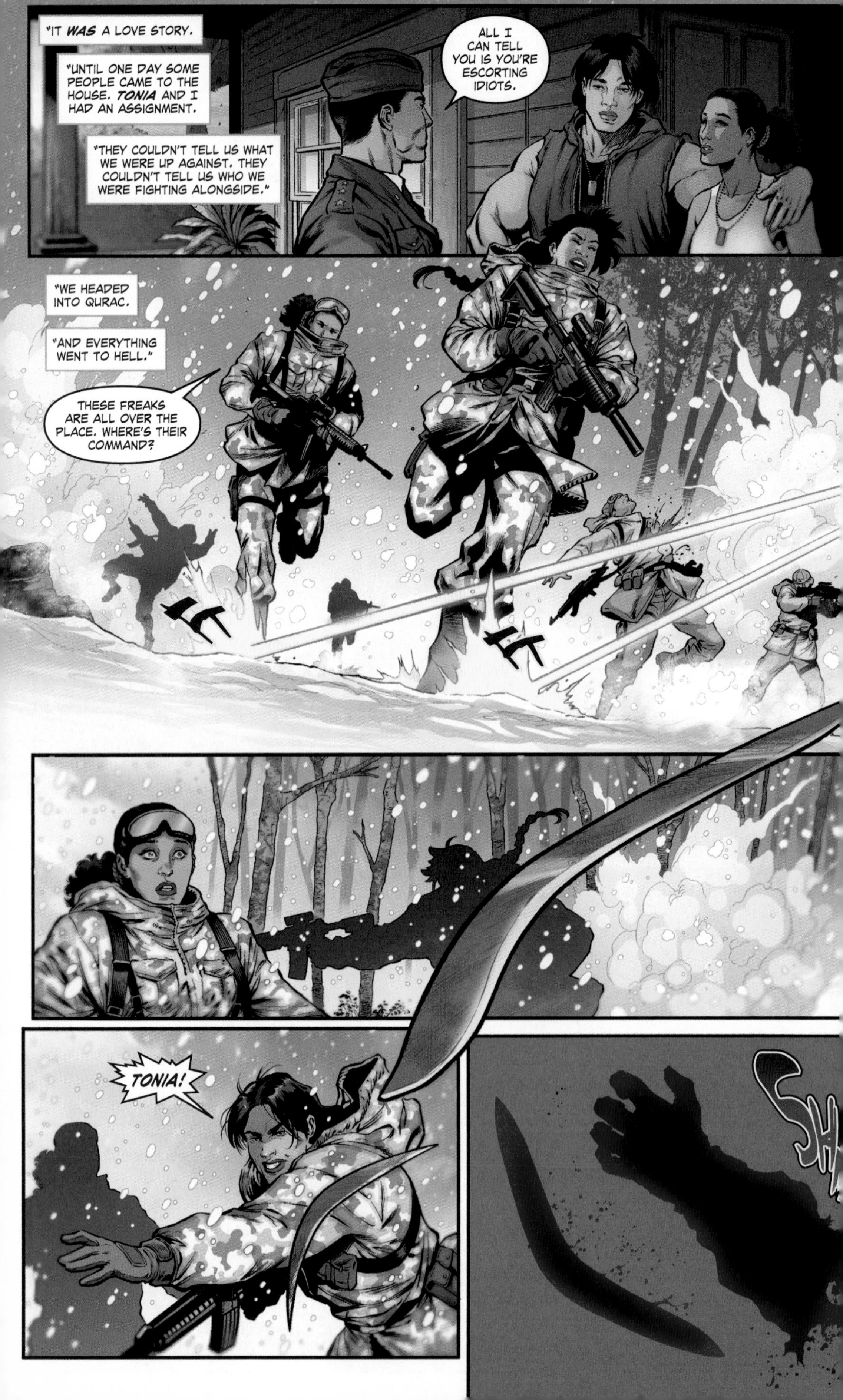
"IT WAS A LOVE STORY.
"UNTIL ONE DAY SOME PEOPLE CAME TO THE HOUSE. TONIA AND I HAD AN ASSIGNMENT.
"THEY COULDN'T TELL US WHAT WE WERE UP AGAINST. THEY COULDN'T TELL US WHO WE WERE FIGHTING ALONGSIDE."
ALL I CAN TELL YOU IS YOU'RE ESCORTING IDIOTS.
"WE HEADED INTO QURAC.
"AND EVERYTHING WENT TO HELL."
THESE FREAKS ARE ALL OVER THE PLACE. WHERE'S THEIR COMMAND?
TONIA!

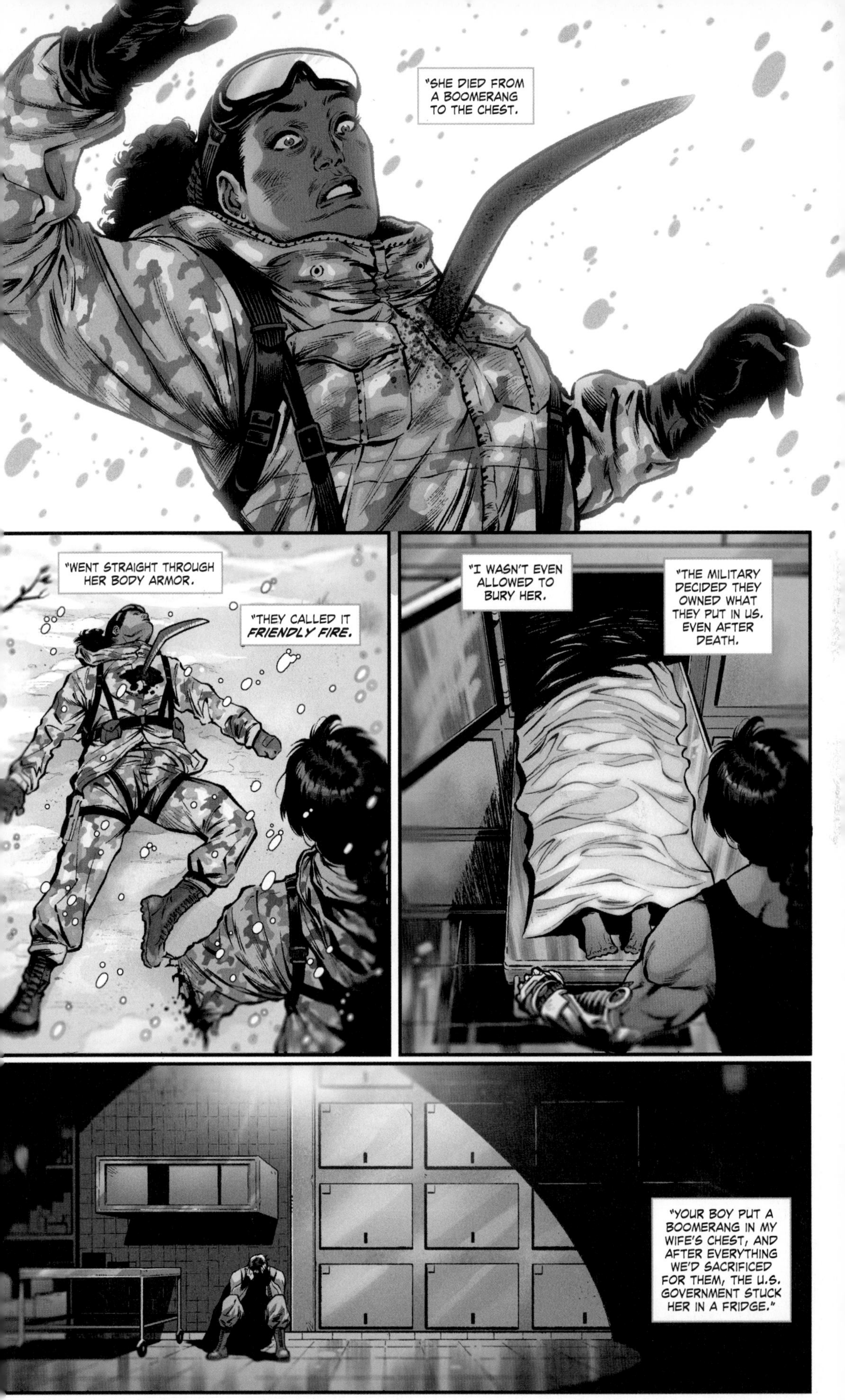
"SHE DIED FROM A BOOMERANG TO THE CHEST.
"WENT STRAIGHT THROUGH HER BODY ARMOR.
"THEY CALLED IT *FRIENDLY FIRE*.
"I WASN'T EVEN ALLOWED TO BURY HER.
"THE MILITARY DECIDED THEY OWNED WHAT THEY PUT IN US. EVEN AFTER DEATH.
"YOUR BOY PUT A BOOMERANG IN MY WIFE'S CHEST, AND AFTER EVERYTHING WE'D SACRIFICED FOR THEM, THE U.S. GOVERNMENT STUCK HER IN A FRIDGE."

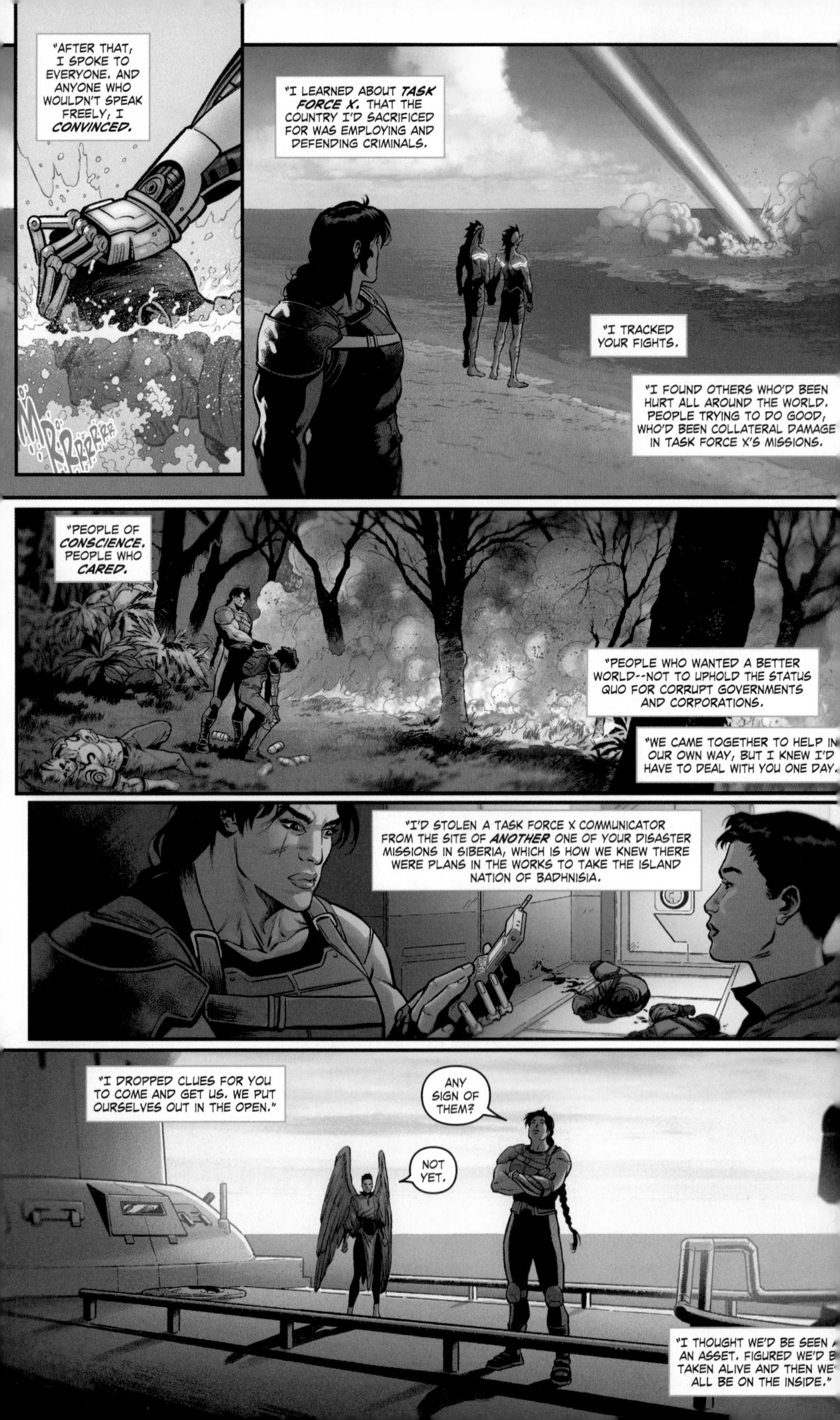
"AFTER THAT, I SPOKE TO EVERYONE. AND ANYONE WHO WOULDN'T SPEAK FREELY, I CONVINCED.
"I LEARNED ABOUT TASK FORCE X. THAT THE COUNTRY I'D SACRIFICED FOR WAS EMPLOYING AND DEFENDING CRIMINALS.
"I TRACKED YOUR FIGHTS.
"I FOUND OTHERS WHO'D BEEN HURT ALL AROUND THE WORLD. PEOPLE TRYING TO DO GOOD, WHO'D BEEN COLLATERAL DAMAGE IN TASK FORCE X'S MISSIONS.
"PEOPLE OF CONSCIENCE. PEOPLE WHO CARED.
"PEOPLE WHO WANTED A BETTER WORLD--NOT TO UPHOLD THE STATUS QUO FOR CORRUPT GOVERNMENTS AND CORPORATIONS.
"WE CAME TOGETHER TO HELP IN OUR OWN WAY, BUT I KNEW I'D HAVE TO DEAL WITH YOU ONE DAY.
"I'D STOLEN A TASK FORCE X COMMUNICATOR FROM THE SITE OF ANOTHER ONE OF YOUR DISASTER MISSIONS IN SIBERIA, WHICH IS HOW WE KNEW THERE WERE PLANS IN THE WORKS TO TAKE THE ISLAND NATION OF BADHNISIA.
"I DROPPED CLUES FOR YOU TO COME AND GET US. WE PUT OURSELVES OUT IN THE OPEN."
ANY SIGN OF THEM?
NOT YET.
"I THOUGHT WE'D BE SEEN A AN ASSET. FIGURED WE'D B TAKEN ALIVE AND THEN WE ALL BE ON THE INSIDE."

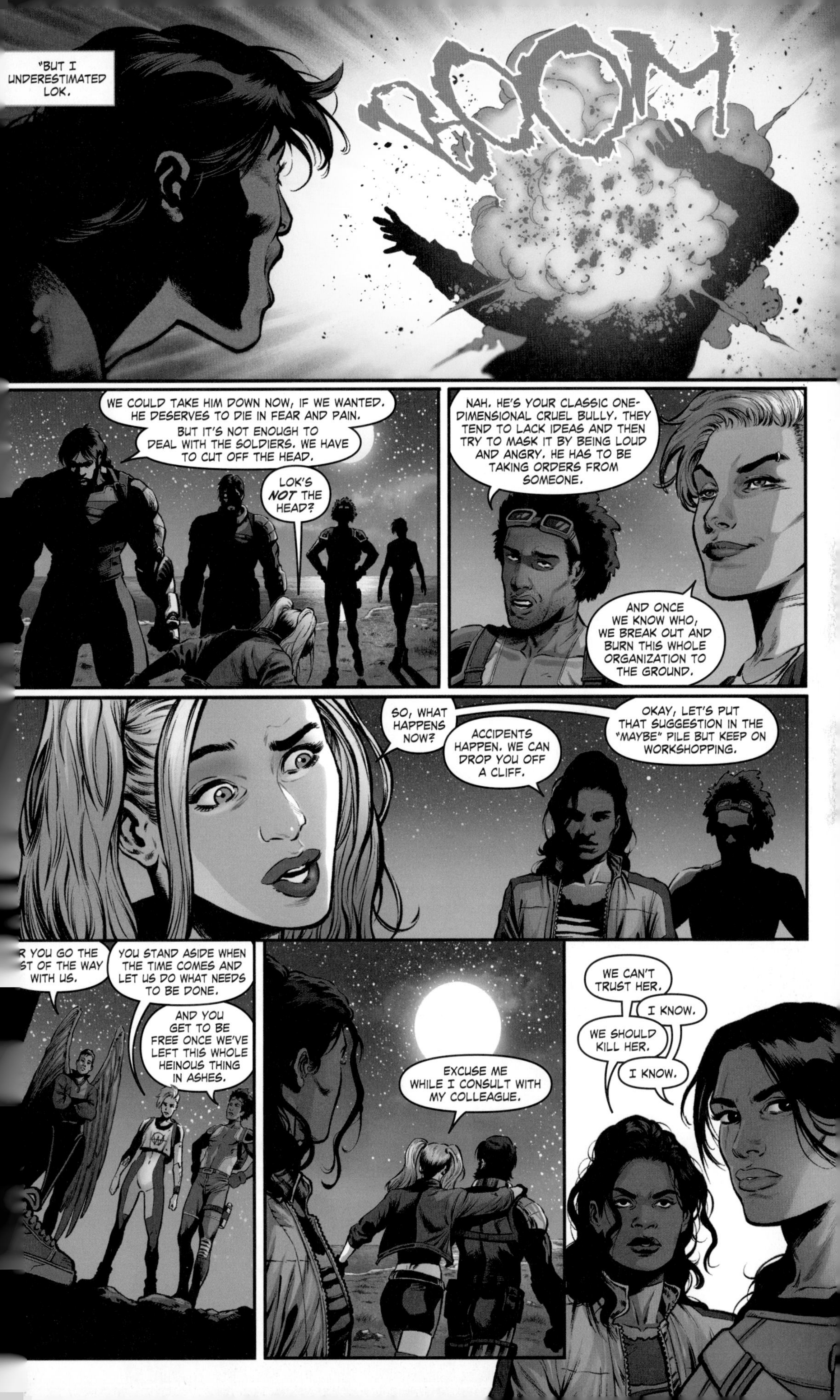

"BUT I UNDERESTIMATED LOK.
BOOM
WE COULD TAKE HIM DOWN NOW, IF WE WANTED. HE DESERVES TO DIE IN FEAR AND PAIN.
BUT IT'S NOT ENOUGH TO DEAL WITH THE SOLDIERS. WE HAVE TO CUT OFF THE HEAD.
LOK'S *NOT* THE HEAD?
NAH. HE'S YOUR CLASSIC ONE-DIMENSIONAL CRUEL BULLY. THEY TEND TO LACK IDEAS AND THEN TRY TO MASK IT BY BEING LOUD AND ANGRY. HE HAS TO BE TAKING ORDERS FROM SOMEONE.
AND ONCE WE KNOW WHO, WE BREAK OUT AND BURN THIS WHOLE ORGANIZATION TO THE GROUND.
SO, WHAT HAPPENS NOW?
ACCIDENTS HAPPEN. WE CAN DROP YOU OFF A CLIFF.
OKAY, LET'S PUT THAT SUGGESTION IN THE "MAYBE" PILE BUT KEEP ON WORKSHOPPING.
R YOU GO THE ST OF THE WAY WITH US.
YOU STAND ASIDE WHEN THE TIME COMES AND LET US DO WHAT NEEDS TO BE DONE.
AND YOU GET TO BE FREE ONCE WE'VE LEFT THIS WHOLE HEINOUS THING IN ASHES.
EXCUSE ME WHILE I CONSULT WITH MY COLLEAGUE.
WE CAN'T TRUST HER.
I KNOW.
WE SHOULD KILL HER.
I KNOW.

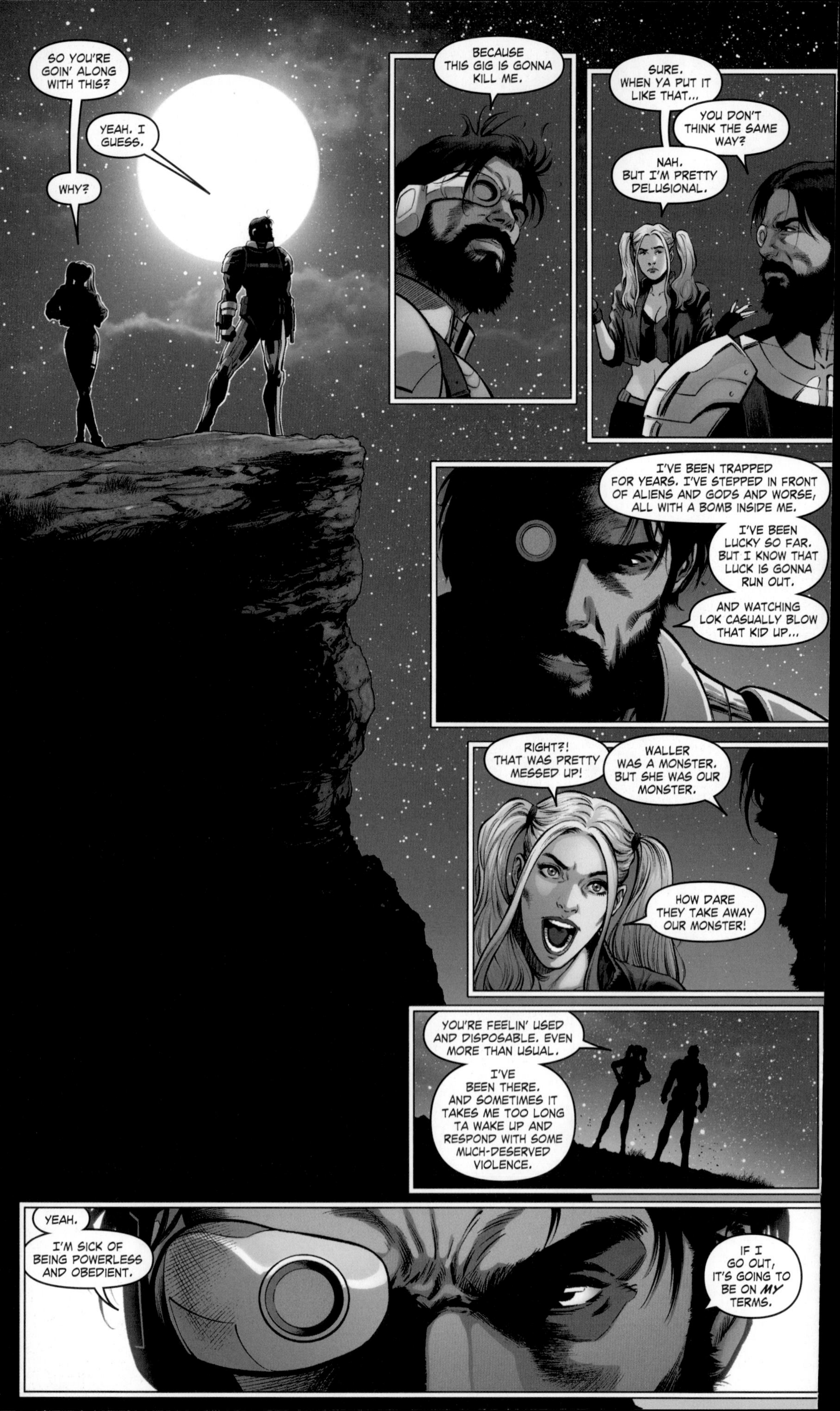
SO YOU'RE GOIN' ALONG WITH THIS?
YEAH. I GUESS.
WHY?
BECAUSE THIS GIG IS GONNA KILL ME.
SURE. WHEN YA PUT IT LIKE THAT...
YOU DON'T THINK THE SAME WAY?
NAH. BUT I'M PRETTY DELUSIONAL.
I'VE BEEN TRAPPED FOR YEARS. I'VE STEPPED IN FRONT OF ALIENS AND GODS AND WORSE, ALL WITH A BOMB INSIDE ME.
I'VE BEEN LUCKY SO FAR. BUT I KNOW THAT LUCK IS GONNA RUN OUT.
AND WATCHING LOK CASUALLY BLOW THAT KID UP...
RIGHT?! THAT WAS PRETTY MESSED UP!
WALLER WAS A MONSTER. BUT SHE WAS OUR MONSTER.
HOW DARE THEY TAKE AWAY OUR MONSTER!
YOU'RE FEELIN' USED AND DISPOSABLE. EVEN MORE THAN USUAL.
I'VE BEEN THERE. AND SOMETIMES IT TAKES ME TOO LONG TA WAKE UP AND RESPOND WITH SOME MUCH-DESERVED VIOLENCE.
YEAH.
I'M SICK OF BEING POWERLESS AND OBEDIENT.
IF I GO OUT, IT'S GOING TO BE ON *MY* TERMS.

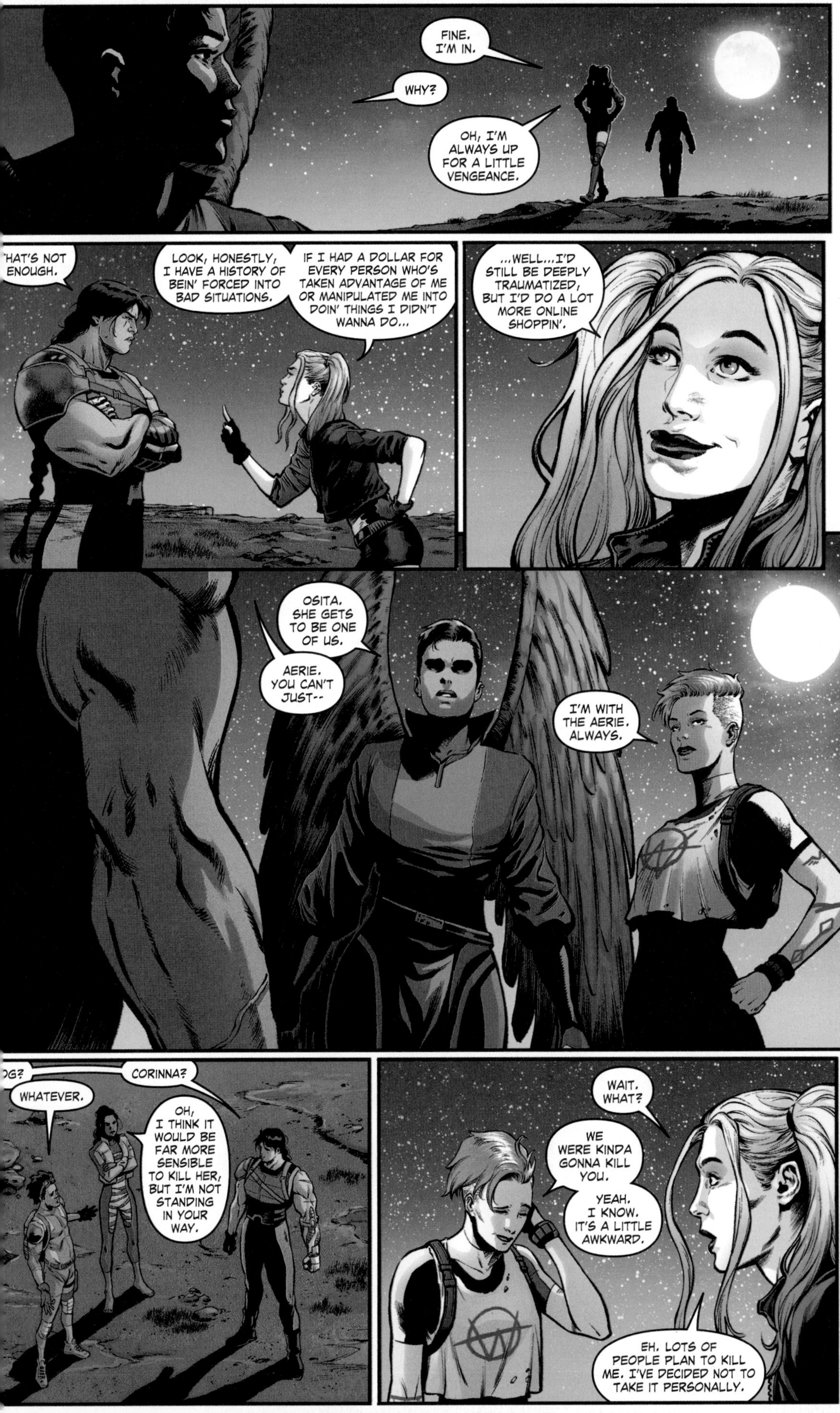
FINE. I'M IN.
WHY?
OH, I'M ALWAYS UP FOR A LITTLE VENGEANCE.
HAT'S NOT ENOUGH.
LOOK, HONESTLY, I HAVE A HISTORY OF BEIN' FORCED INTO BAD SITUATIONS.
IF I HAD A DOLLAR FOR EVERY PERSON WHO'S TAKEN ADVANTAGE OF ME OR MANIPULATED ME INTO DOIN' THINGS I DIDN'T WANNA DO...
...WELL...I'D STILL BE DEEPLY TRAUMATIZED, BUT I'D DO A LOT MORE ONLINE SHOPPIN'.
OSITA. SHE GETS TO BE ONE OF US.
AERIE. YOU CAN'T JUST--
I'M WITH THE AERIE. ALWAYS.
OG?
CORINNA?
WHATEVER.
OH, I THINK IT WOULD BE FAR MORE SENSIBLE TO KILL HER, BUT I'M NOT STANDING IN YOUR WAY.
WAIT. WHAT?
WE WERE KINDA GONNA KILL YOU.
YEAH. I KNOW. IT'S A LITTLE AWKWARD.
EH. LOTS OF PEOPLE PLAN TO KILL ME. I'VE DECIDED NOT TO TAKE IT PERSONALLY.

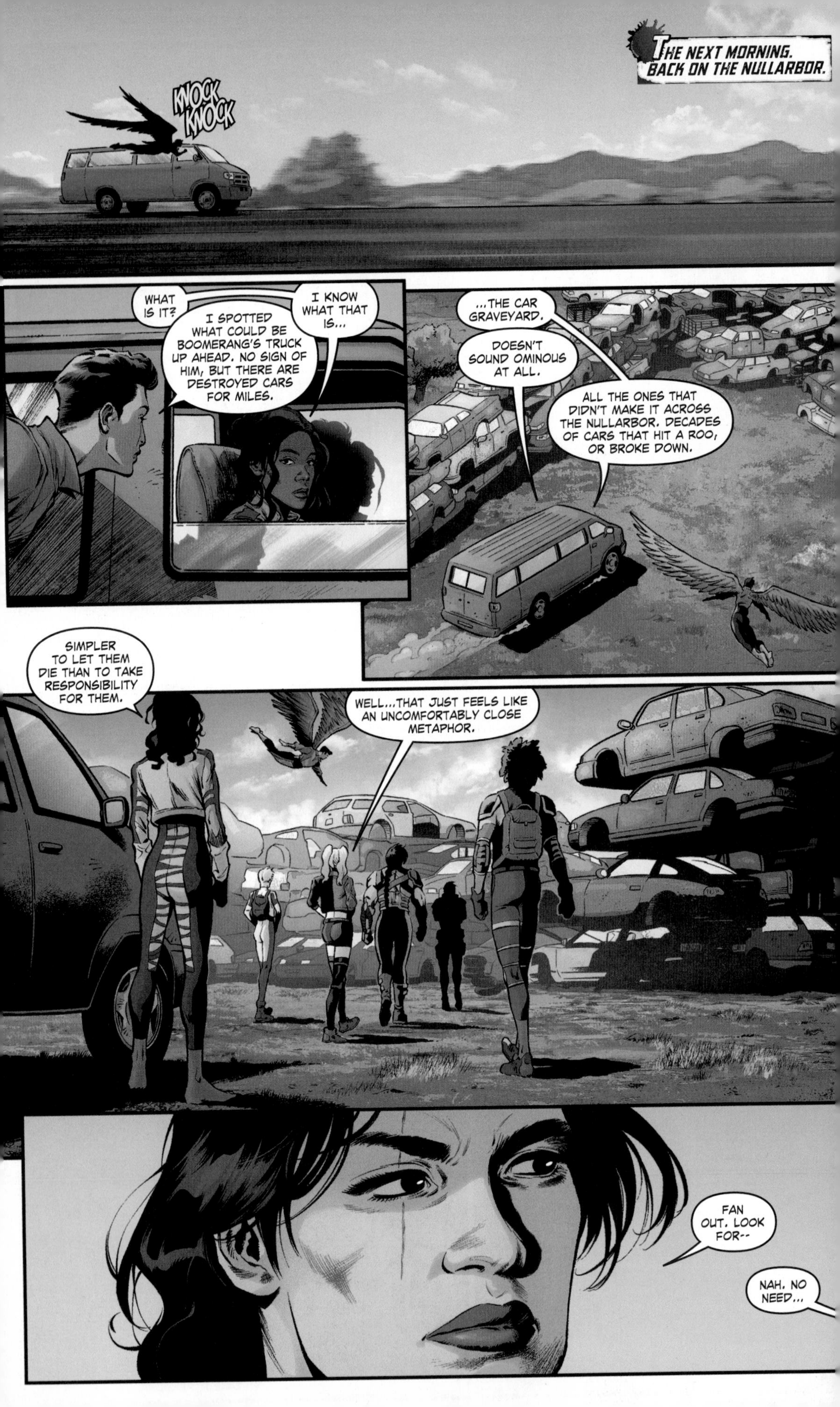
THE NEXT MORNING. BACK ON THE NULLARBOR.
KNOCK KNOCK
WHAT IS IT?
I SPOTTED WHAT COULD BE BOOMERANG'S TRUCK UP AHEAD. NO SIGN OF HIM, BUT THERE ARE DESTROYED CARS FOR MILES.
I KNOW WHAT THAT IS...
...THE CAR GRAVEYARD.
DOESN'T SOUND OMINOUS AT ALL.
ALL THE ONES THAT DIDN'T MAKE IT ACROSS THE NULLARBOR. DECADES OF CARS THAT HIT A ROO, OR BROKE DOWN.
SIMPLER TO LET THEM DIE THAN TO TAKE RESPONSIBILITY FOR THEM.
WELL...THAT JUST FEELS LIKE AN UNCOMFORTABLY CLOSE METAPHOR.
FAN OUT. LOOK FOR--
NAH. NO NEED...

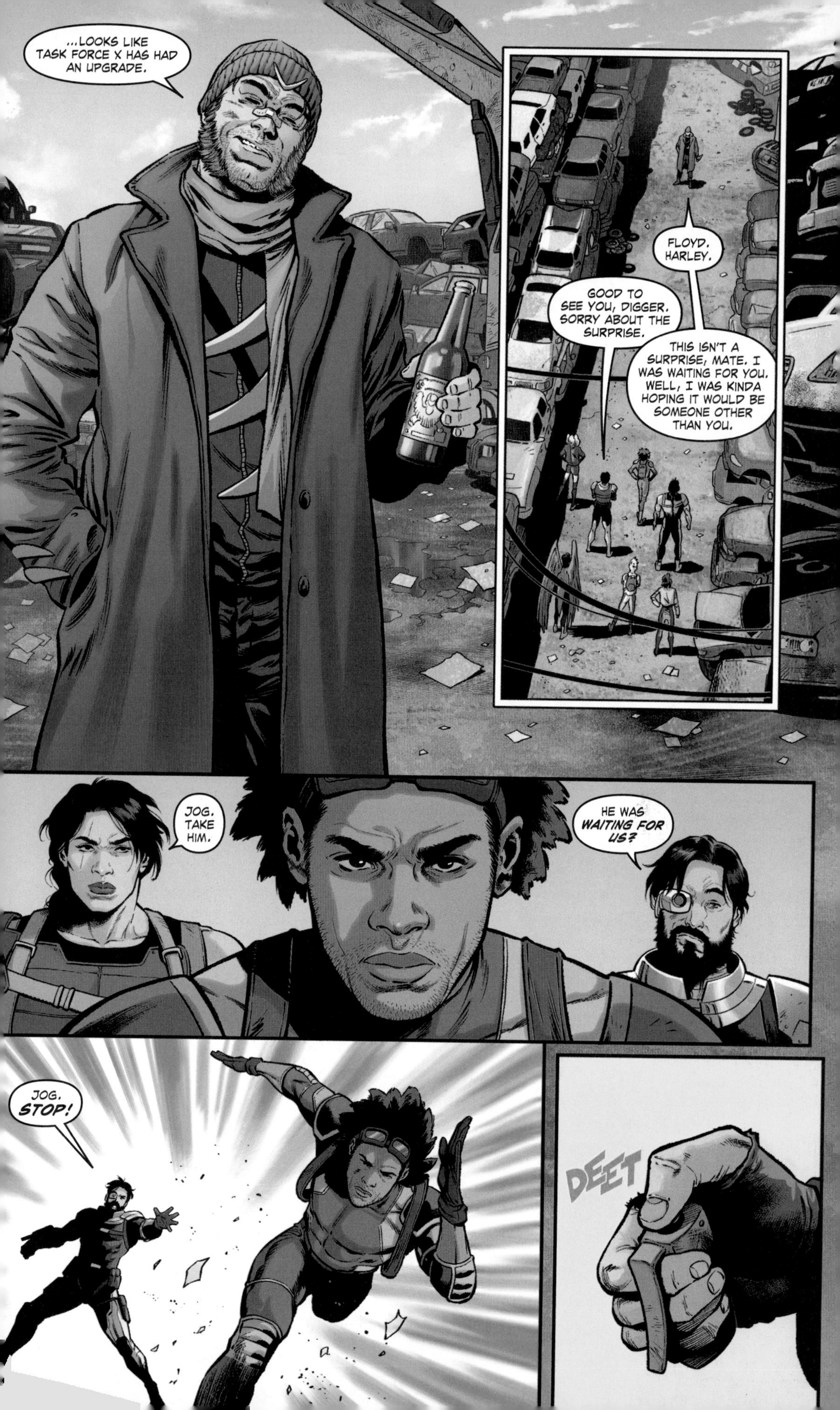
...LOOKS LIKE TASK FORCE X HAS HAD AN UPGRADE.
FLOYD. HARLEY.
GOOD TO SEE YOU, DIGGER. SORRY ABOUT THE SURPRISE.
THIS ISN'T A SURPRISE, MATE. I WAS WAITING FOR YOU. WELL, I WAS KINDA HOPING IT WOULD BE SOMEONE OTHER THAN YOU.
JOG. TAKE HIM.
HE WAS *WAITING FOR US?*
JOG. *STOP!*
DEET

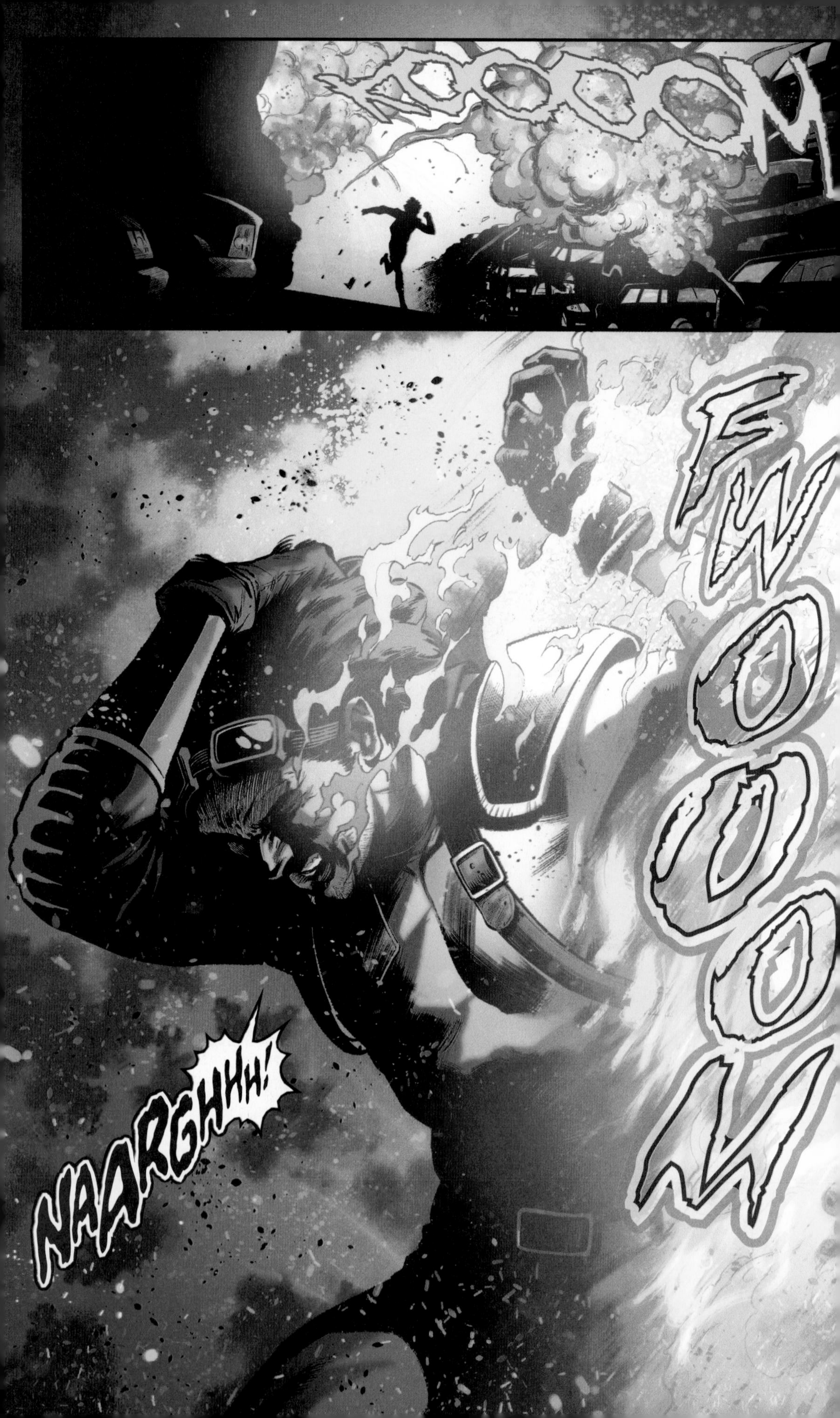
FWOOOOM
NAARGHHH!

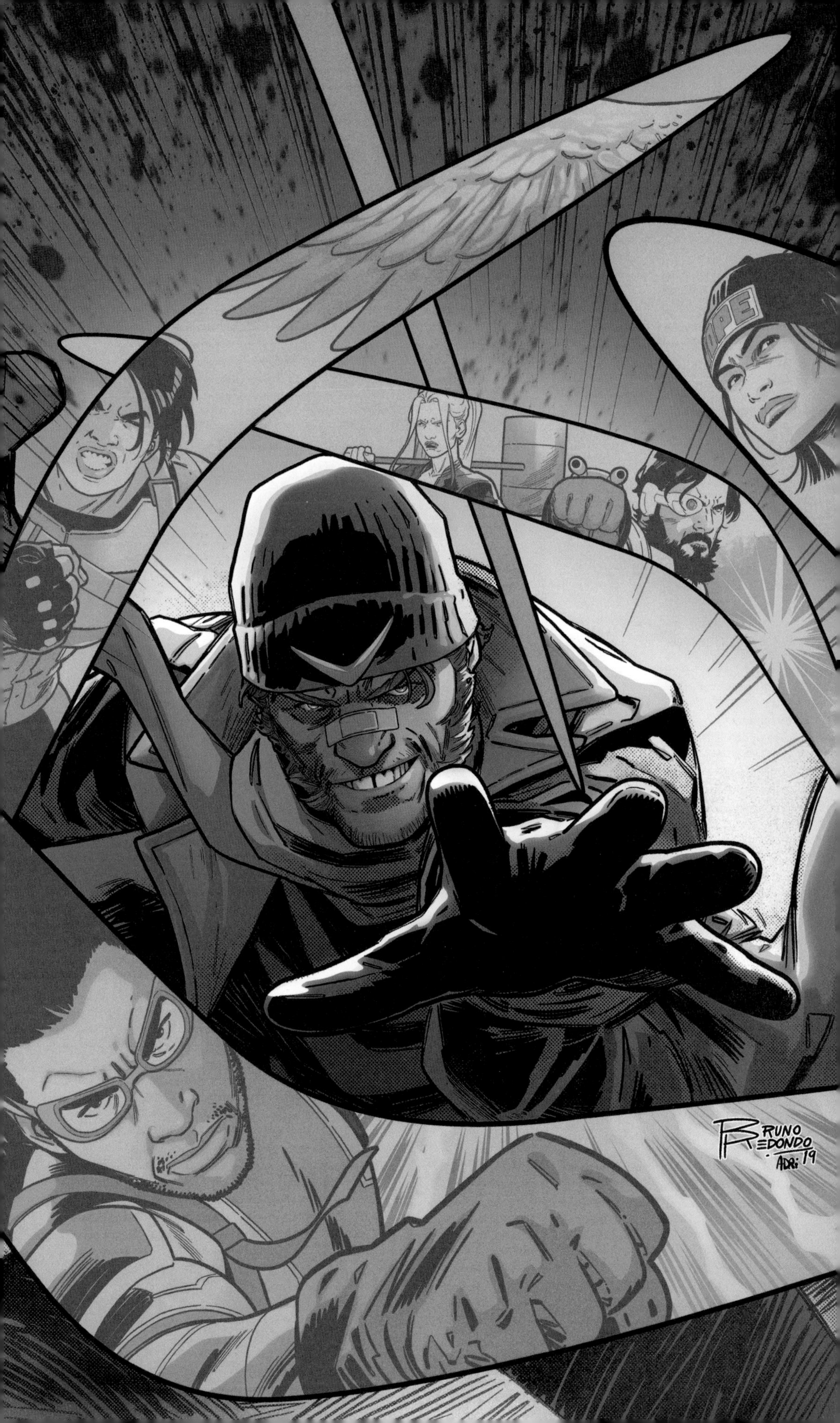
BRUNO REDONDO

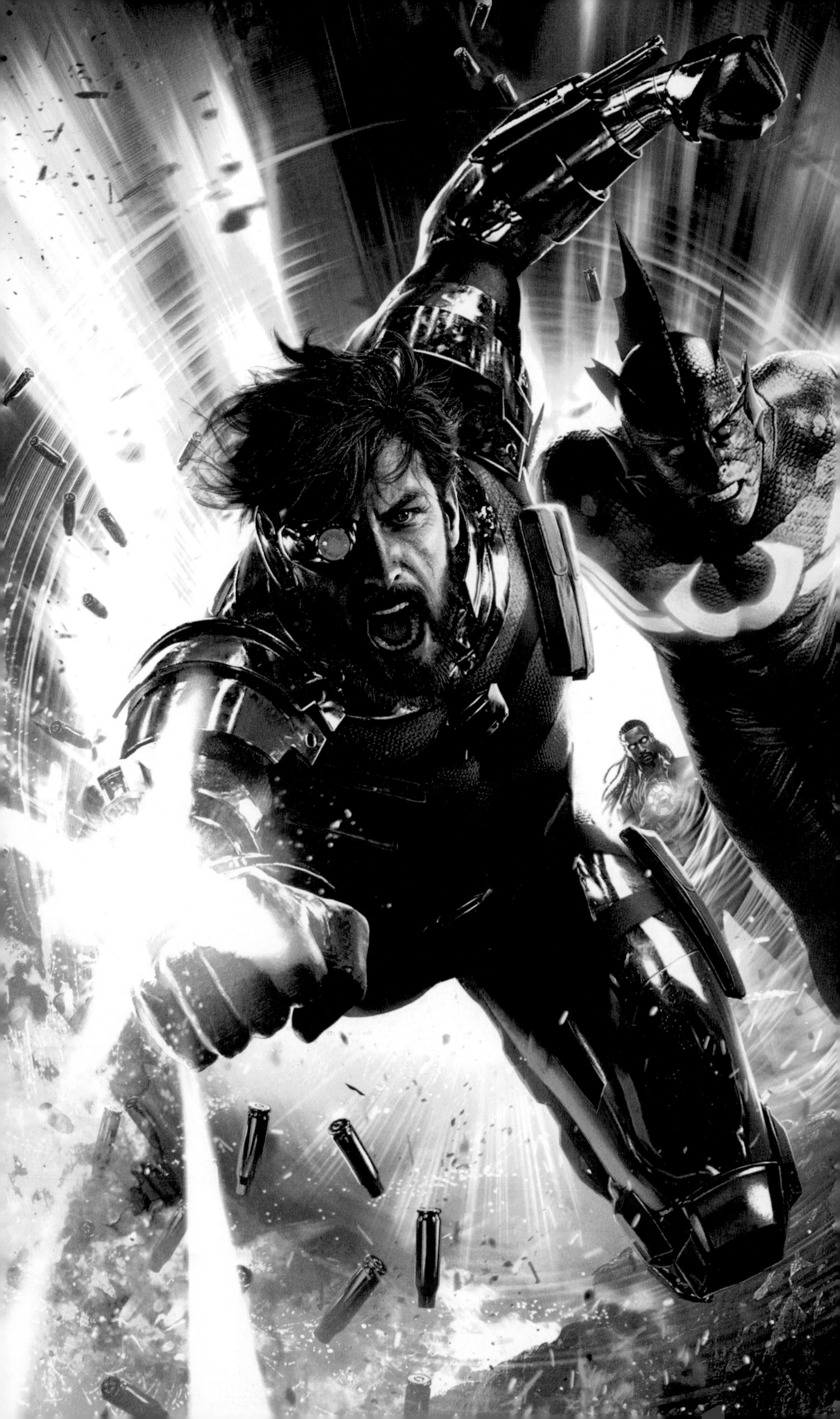

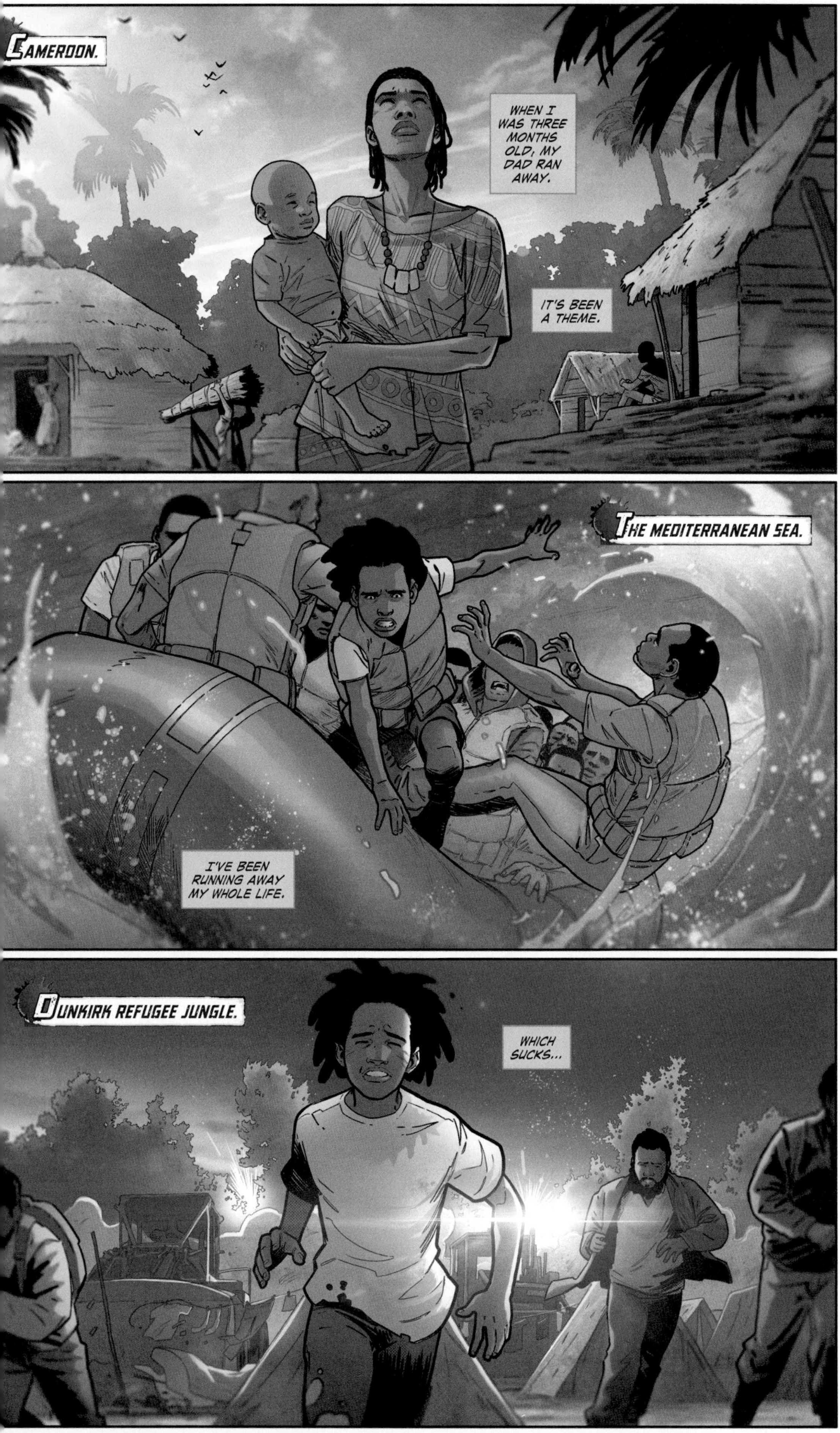
CAMEROON.
WHEN I WAS THREE MONTHS OLD, MY DAD RAN AWAY.
IT'S BEEN A THEME.
THE MEDITERRANEAN SEA.
I'VE BEEN RUNNING AWAY MY WHOLE LIFE.
DUNKIRK REFUGEE JUNGLE.
WHICH SUCKS...

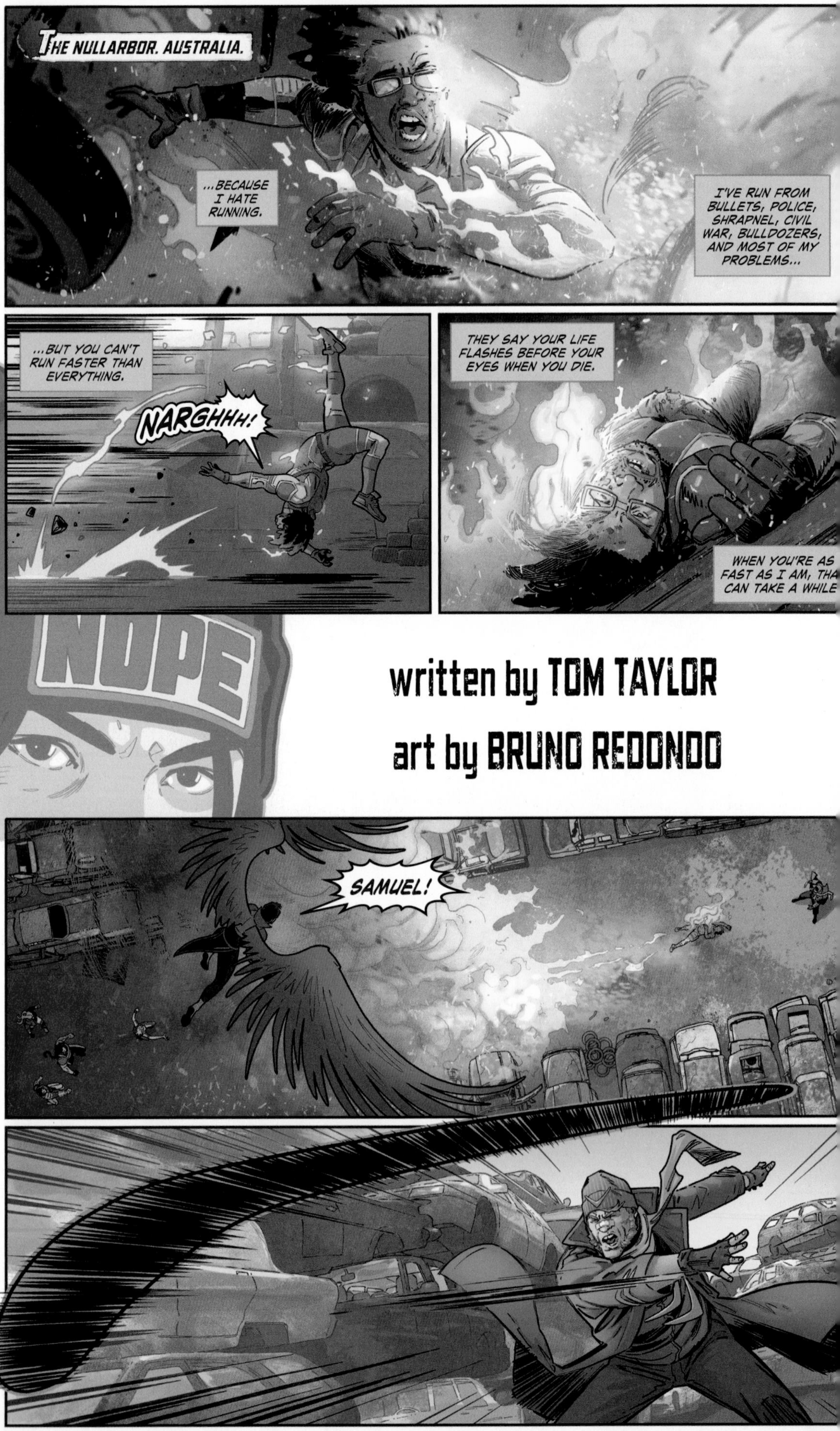
THE NULLARBOR. AUSTRALIA.
...BECAUSE I HATE RUNNING.
I'VE RUN FROM BULLETS, POLICE, SHRAPNEL, CIVIL WAR, BULLDOZERS, AND MOST OF MY PROBLEMS...
...BUT YOU CAN'T RUN FASTER THAN EVERYTHING.
NARGHHH!
THEY SAY YOUR LIFE FLASHES BEFORE YOUR EYES WHEN YOU DIE.
WHEN YOU'RE AS FAST AS I AM, THA CAN TAKE A WHILE
NOPE
written by TOM TAYLOR
art by BRUNO REDONDO
SAMUEL!

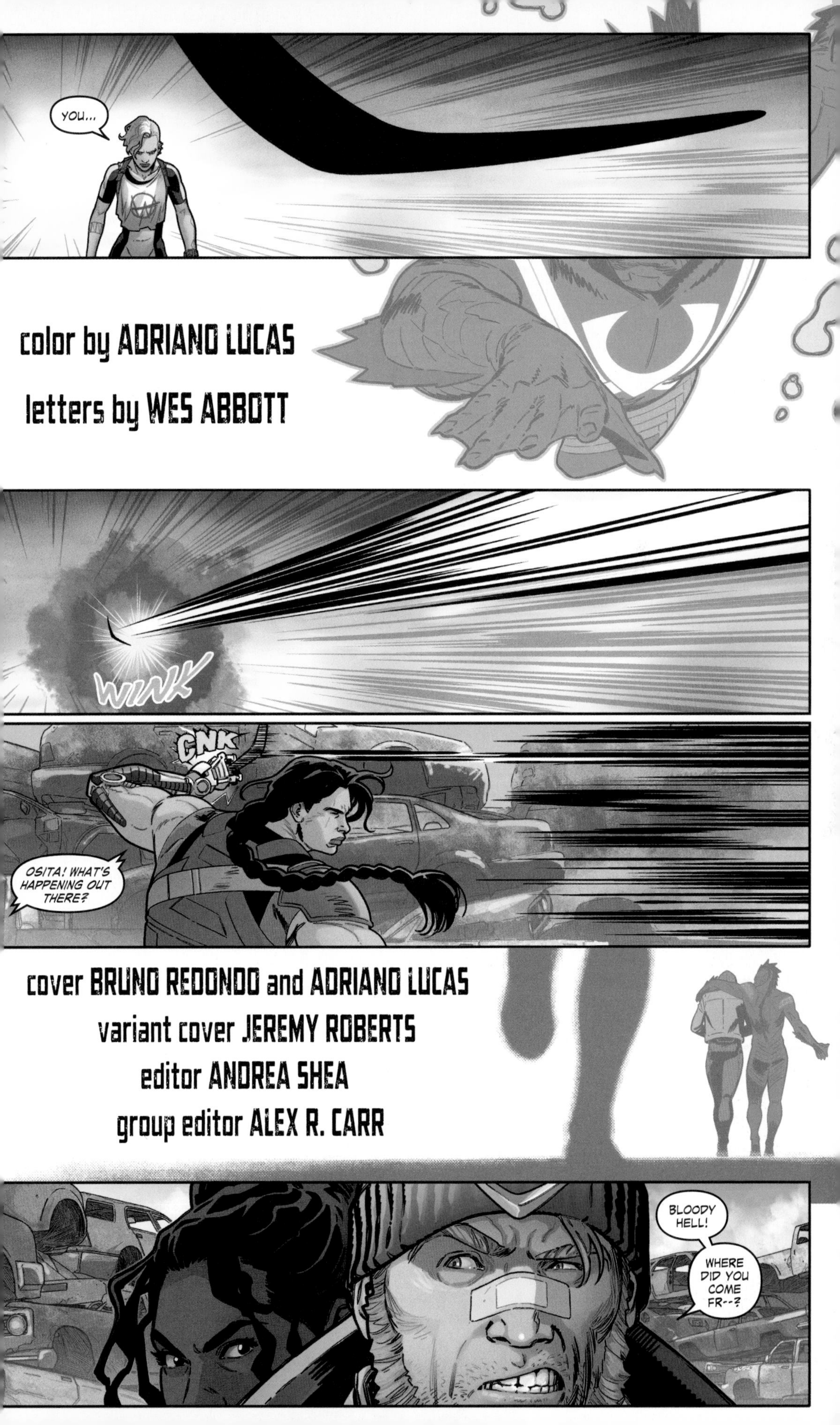
YOU...
WINK
CNK
OSITA! WHAT'S HAPPENING OUT THERE?
BLOODY HELL!
WHERE DID YOU COME FR--?

color by ADRIANO LUCAS
letters by WES ABBOTT
cover BRUNO REDONDO and ADRIANO LUCAS
variant cover JEREMY ROBERTS
editor ANDREA SHEA
group editor ALEX R. CARR

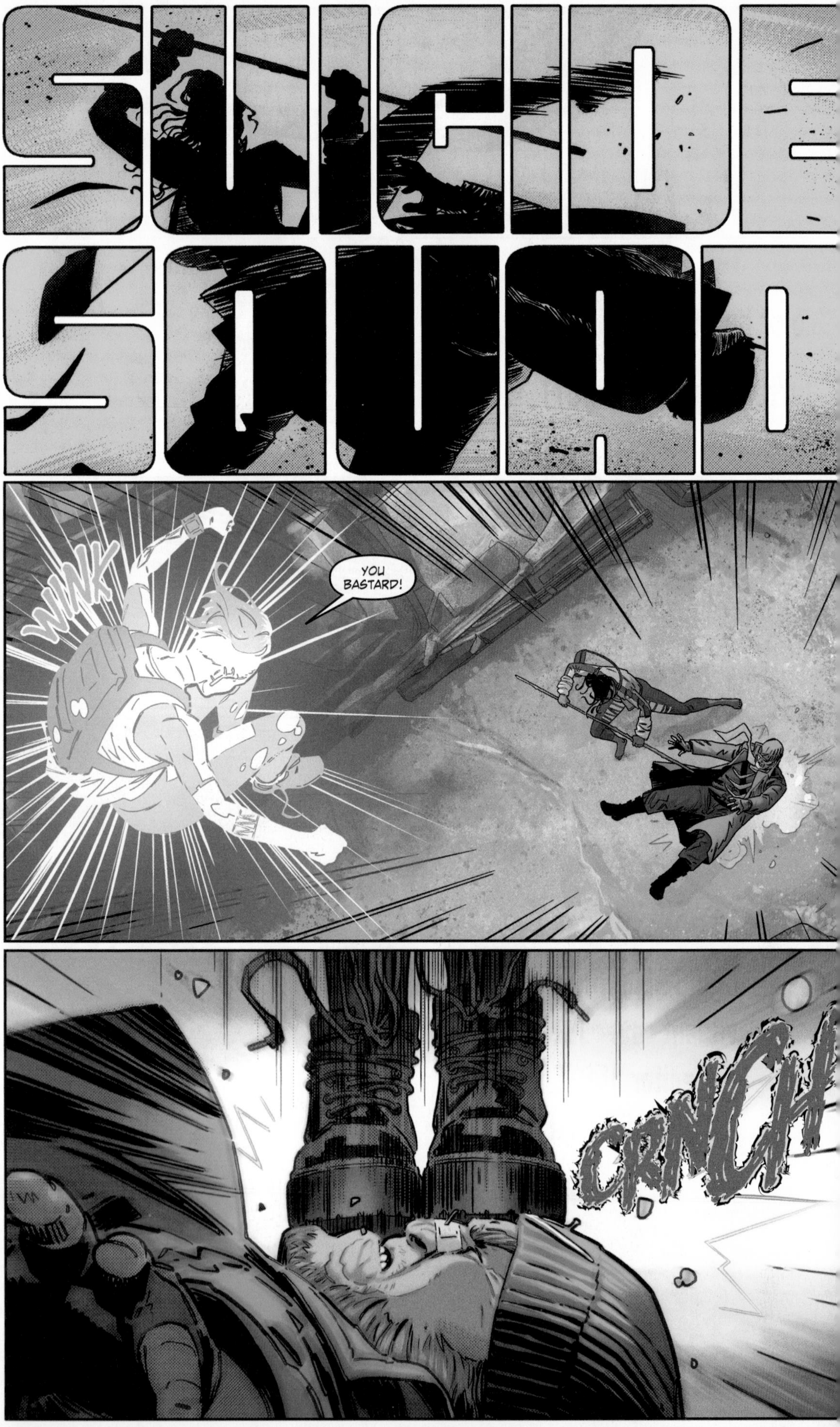
SUICIDE
SQUAD
WINK
YOU BASTARD!
CRNCH

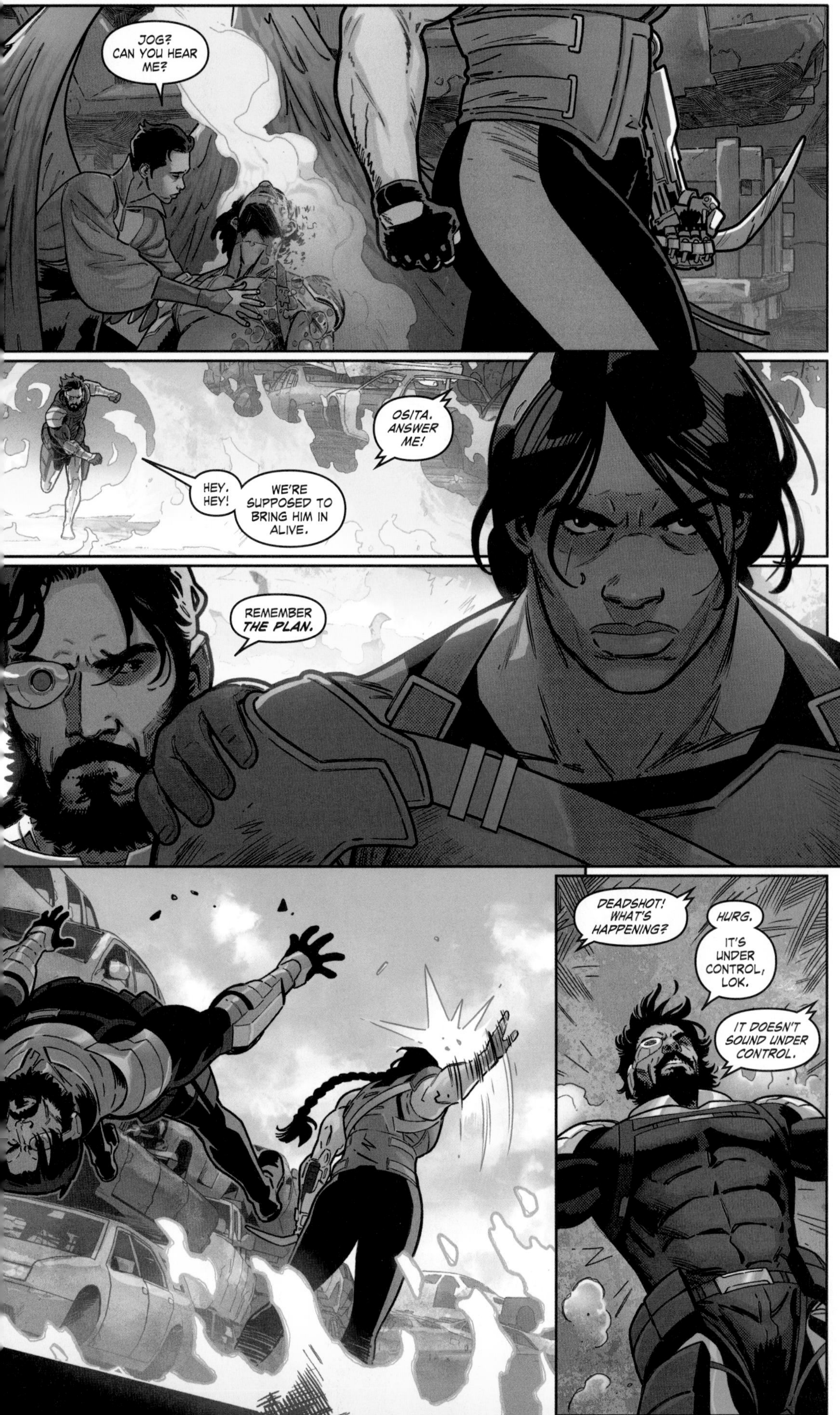
JOG? CAN YOU HEAR ME?
OSITA. ANSWER ME!
HEY. HEY!
WE'RE SUPPOSED TO BRING HIM IN ALIVE.
REMEMBER *THE PLAN.*
DEADSHOT! WHAT'S HAPPENING?
HURG.
IT'S UNDER CONTROL, LOK.
IT DOESN'T SOUND UNDER CONTROL.

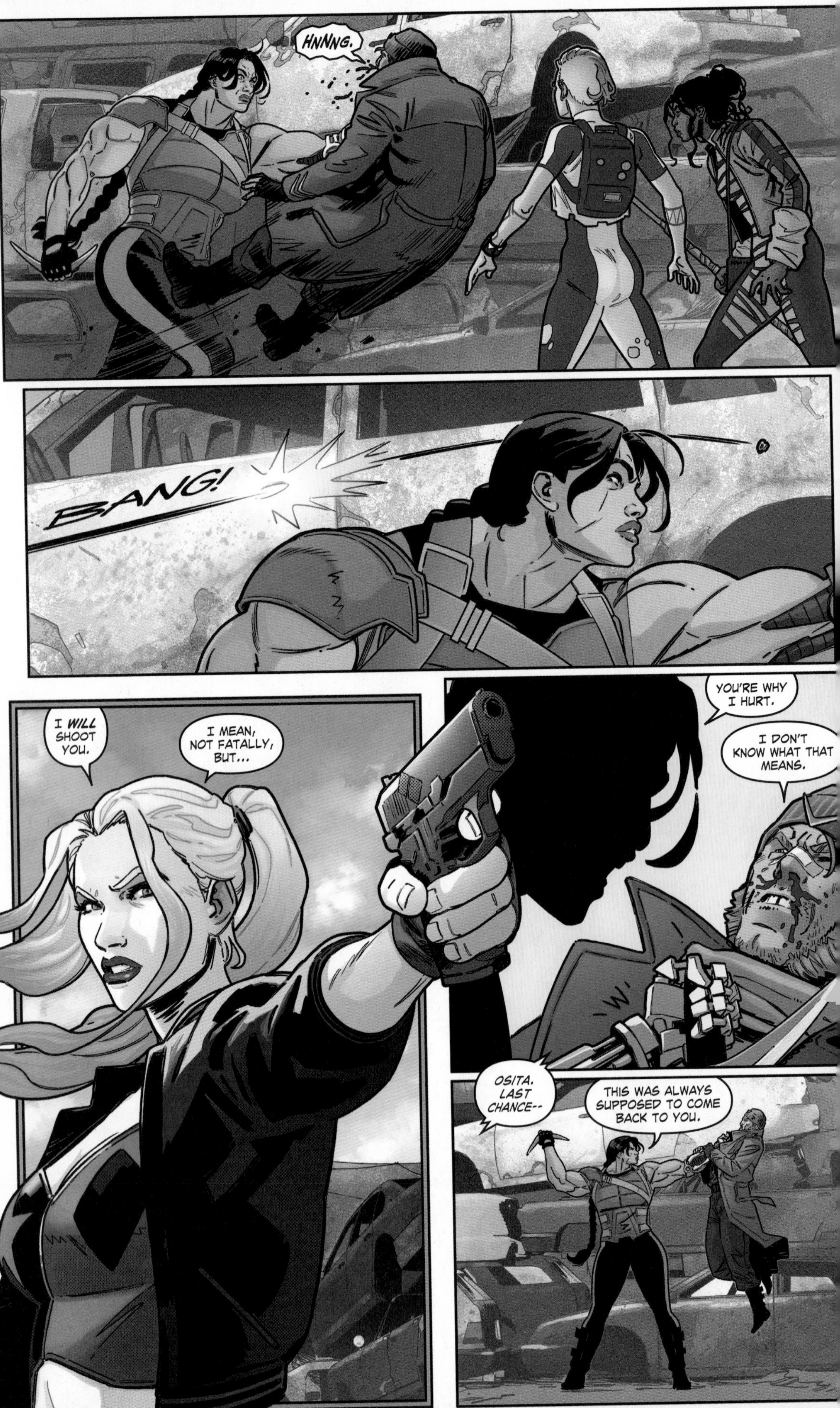
HNNNG.
BANG!
I WILL SHOOT YOU.
I MEAN, NOT FATALLY, BUT...
YOU'RE WHY I HURT.
I DON'T KNOW WHAT THAT MEANS.
OSITA. LAST CHANCE--
THIS WAS ALWAYS SUPPOSED TO COME BACK TO YOU.

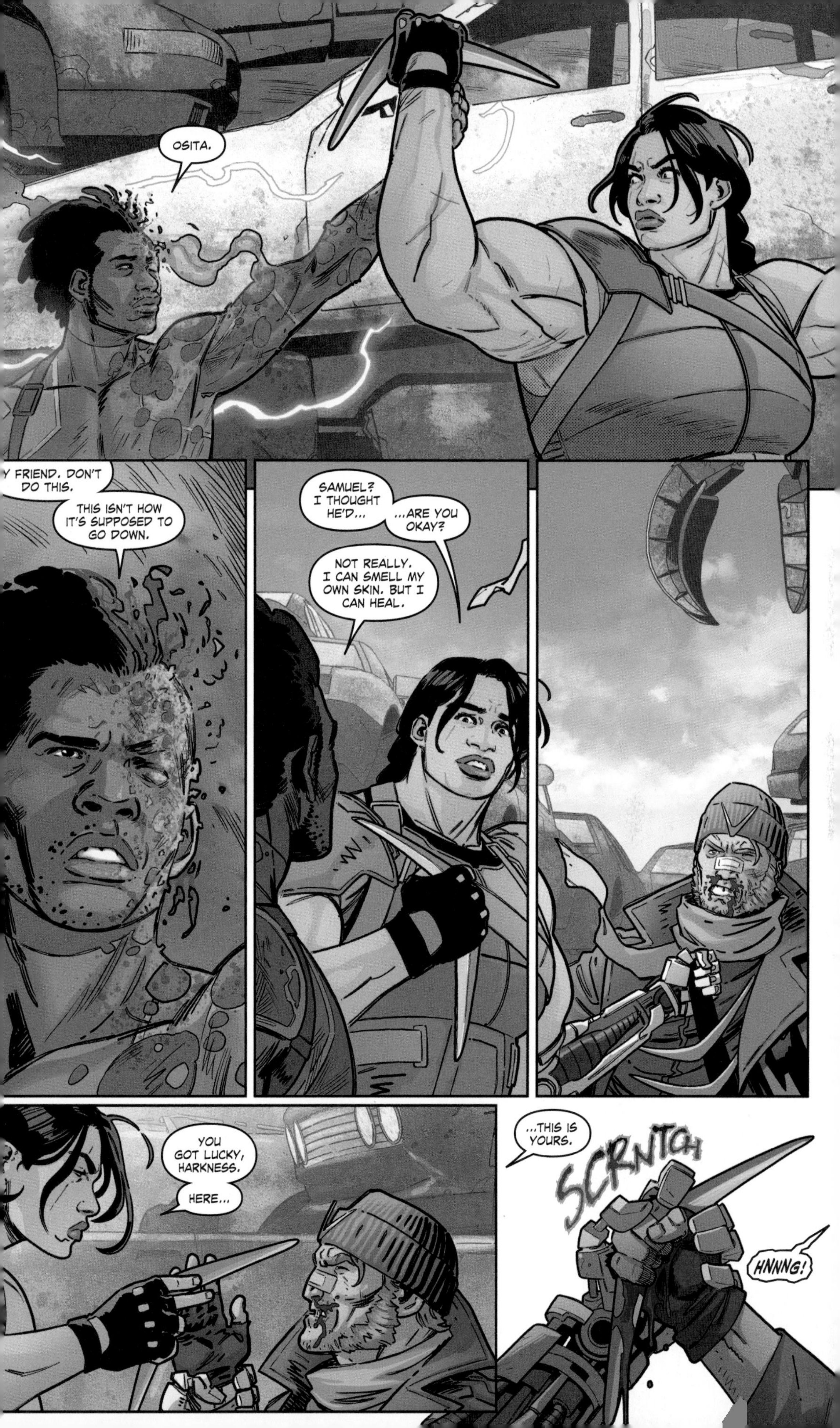
OSITA.
Y FRIEND. DON'T DO THIS.
THIS ISN'T HOW IT'S SUPPOSED TO GO DOWN.
SAMUEL? I THOUGHT HE'D...
...ARE YOU OKAY?
NOT REALLY. I CAN SMELL MY OWN SKIN. BUT I CAN HEAL.
YOU GOT LUCKY, HARKNESS.
HERE...
...THIS IS YOURS.
SCRNTCH
HNNNG!

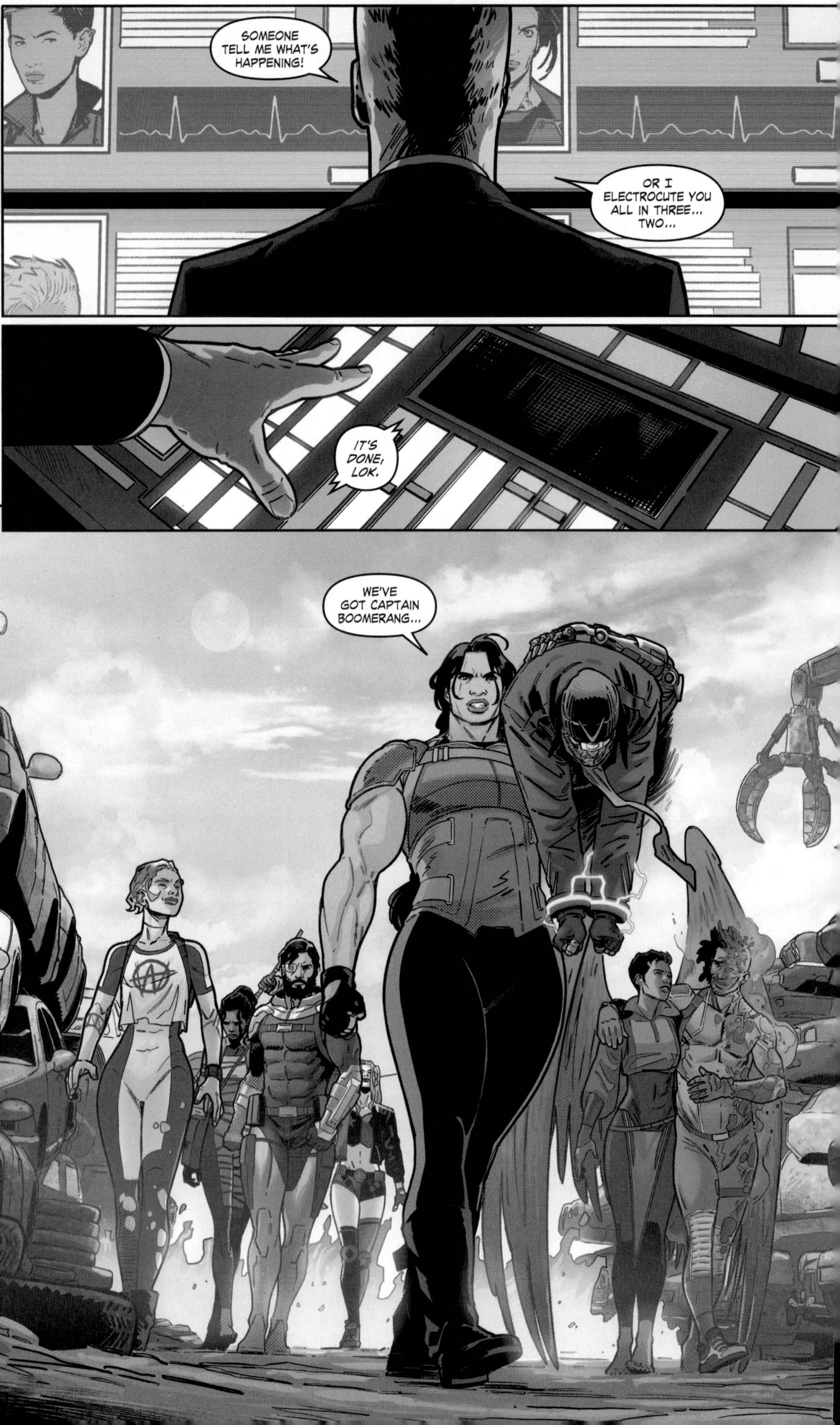
SOMEONE TELL ME WHAT'S HAPPENING!
OR I ELECTROCUTE YOU ALL IN THREE... TWO...
IT'S DONE, LOK.
WE'VE GOT CAPTAIN BOOMERANG...

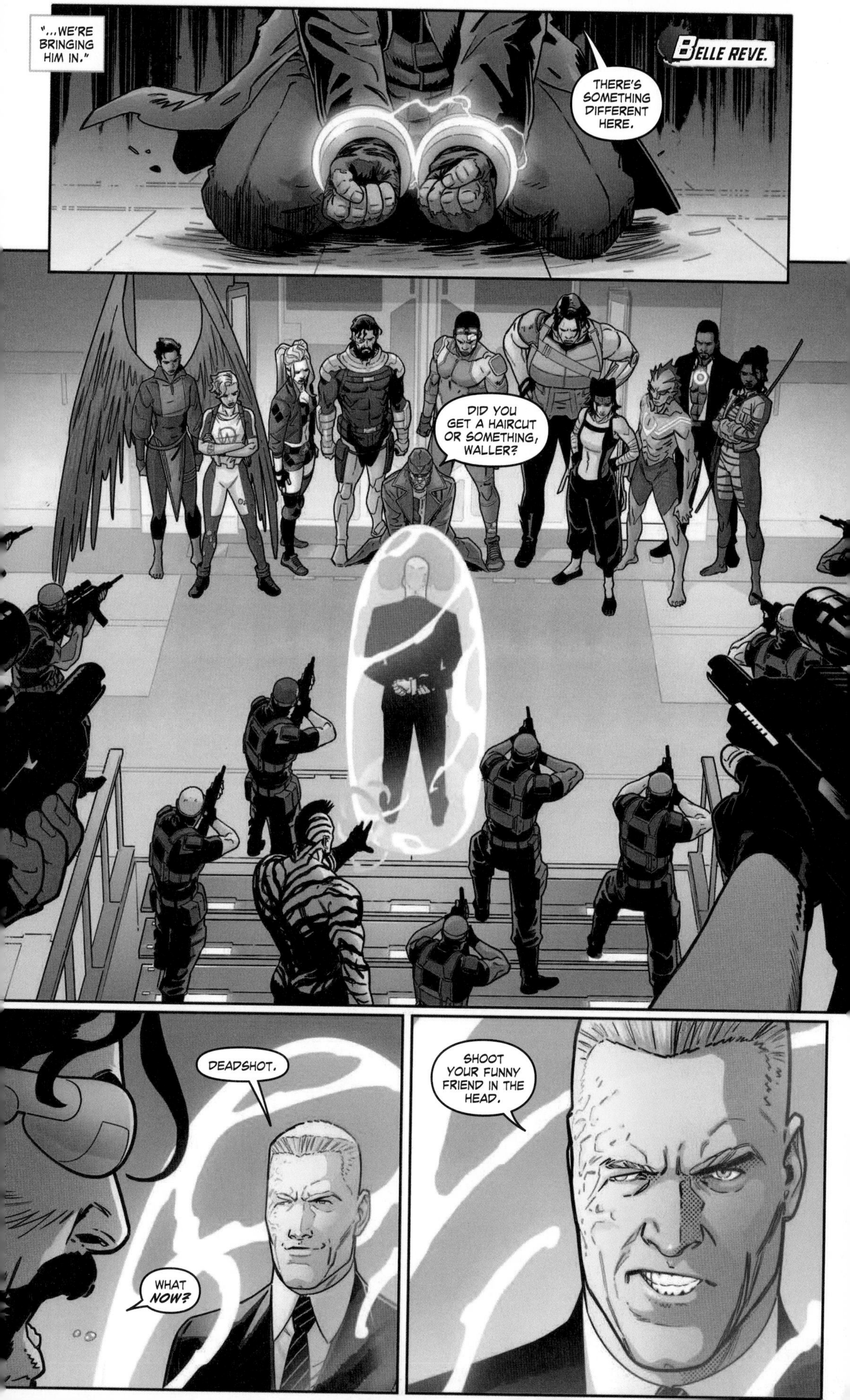
"...WE'RE BRINGING HIM IN."
BELLE REVE.
THERE'S SOMETHING DIFFERENT HERE.
DID YOU GET A HAIRCUT OR SOMETHING, WALLER?
DEADSHOT.
WHAT NOW?
SHOOT YOUR FUNNY FRIEND IN THE HEAD.

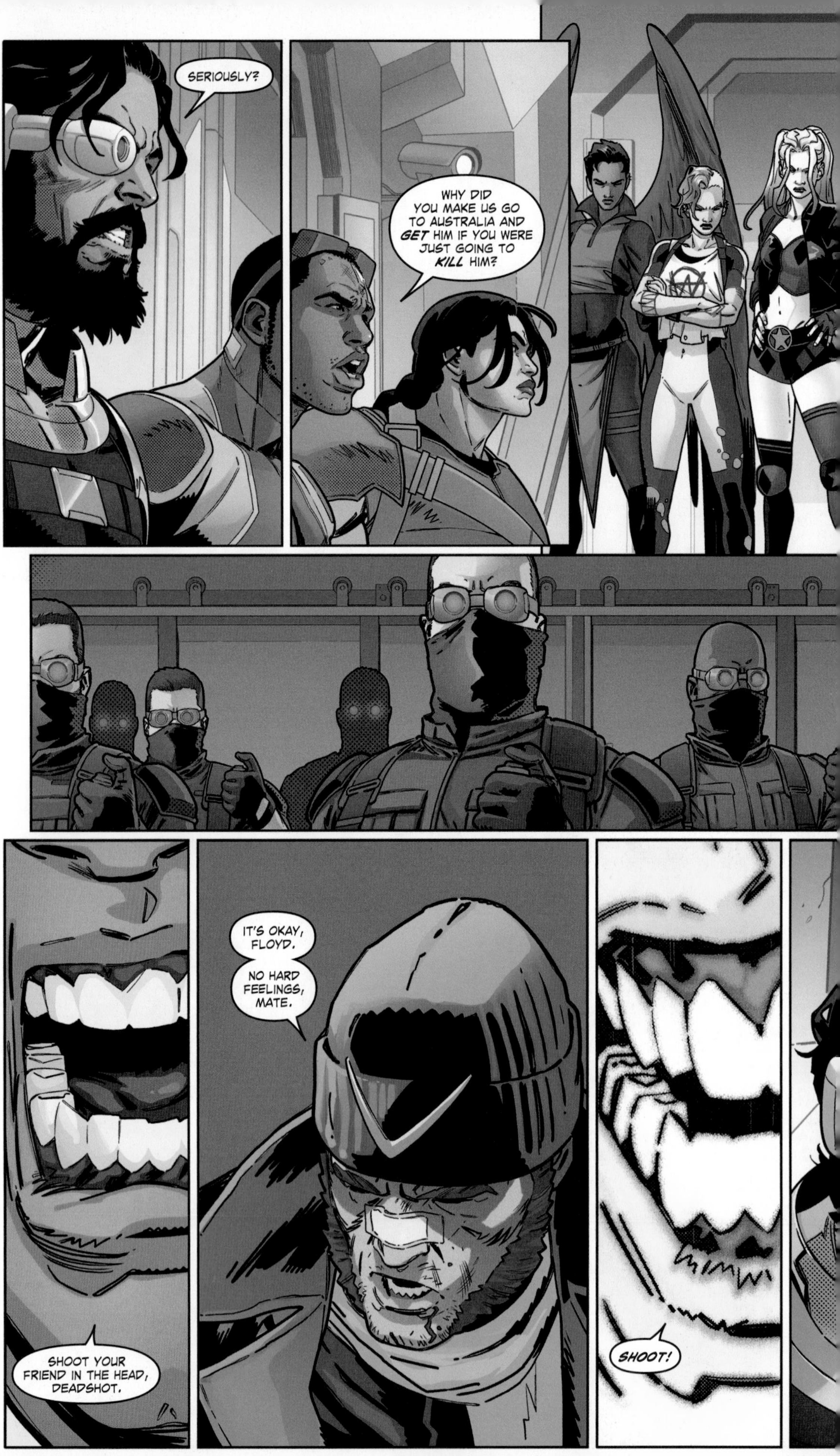
SERIOUSLY?
WHY DID YOU MAKE US GO TO AUSTRALIA AND *GET* HIM IF YOU WERE JUST GOING TO *KILL* HIM?
SHOOT YOUR FRIEND IN THE HEAD, DEADSHOT.
IT'S OKAY, FLOYD.
NO HARD FEELINGS, MATE.
SHOOT!

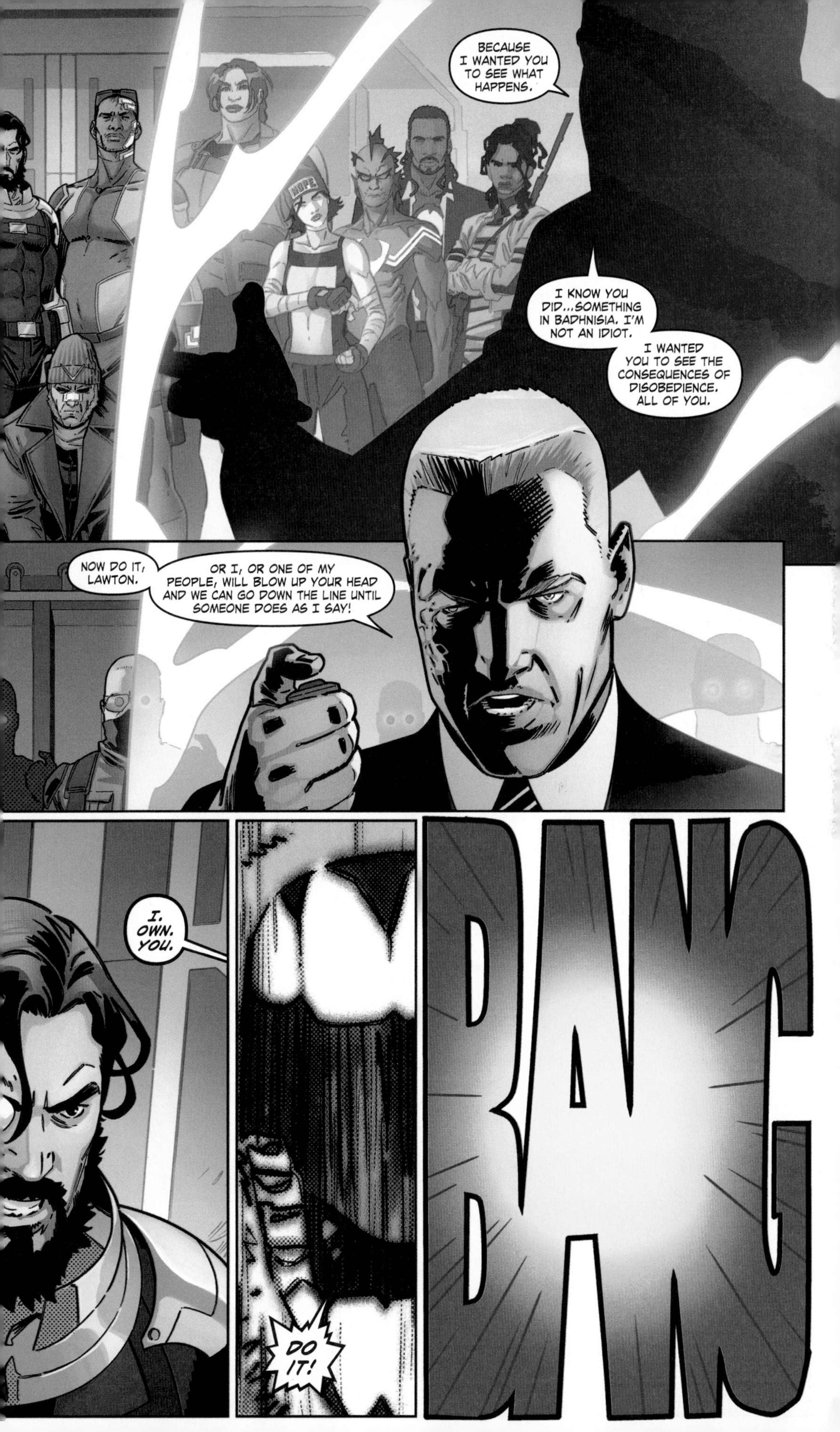

BECAUSE I WANTED YOU TO SEE WHAT HAPPENS.
I KNOW YOU DID...SOMETHING IN BADHNISIA. I'M NOT AN IDIOT.
I WANTED YOU TO SEE THE CONSEQUENCES OF DISOBEDIENCE. ALL OF YOU.
NOW DO IT, LAWTON.
OR I, OR ONE OF MY PEOPLE, WILL BLOW UP YOUR HEAD AND WE CAN GO DOWN THE LINE UNTIL SOMEONE DOES AS I SAY!
I. OWN. YOU.
DO IT!
BANG

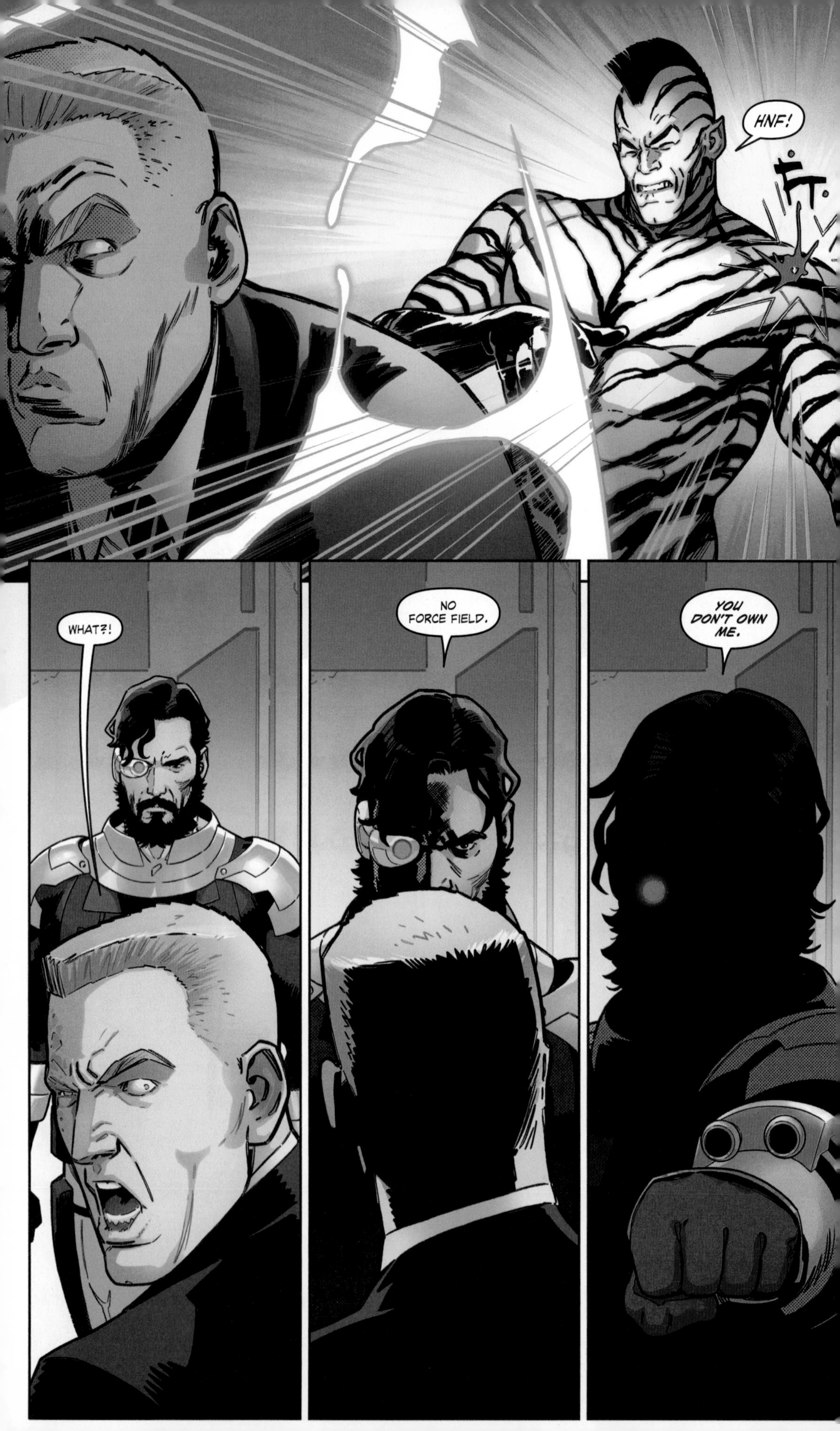
HNF!
FT.
WHAT?!
NO FORCE FIELD.
YOU DON'T OWN ME.

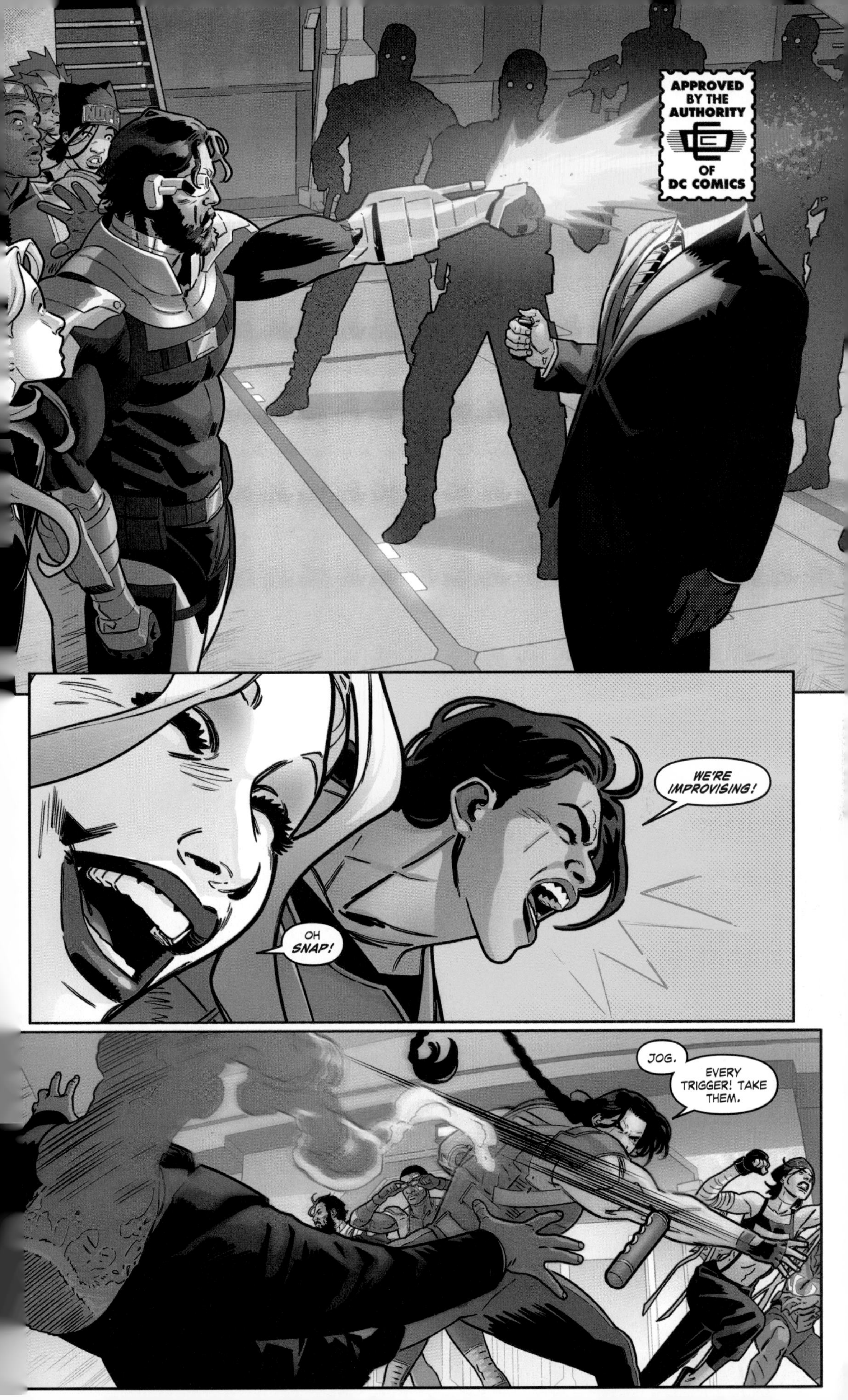
APPROVED BY THE AUTHORITY OF DC COMICS
NDPC
WE'RE IMPROVISING!
OH SNAP!
JOG.
EVERY TRIGGER! TAKE THEM.

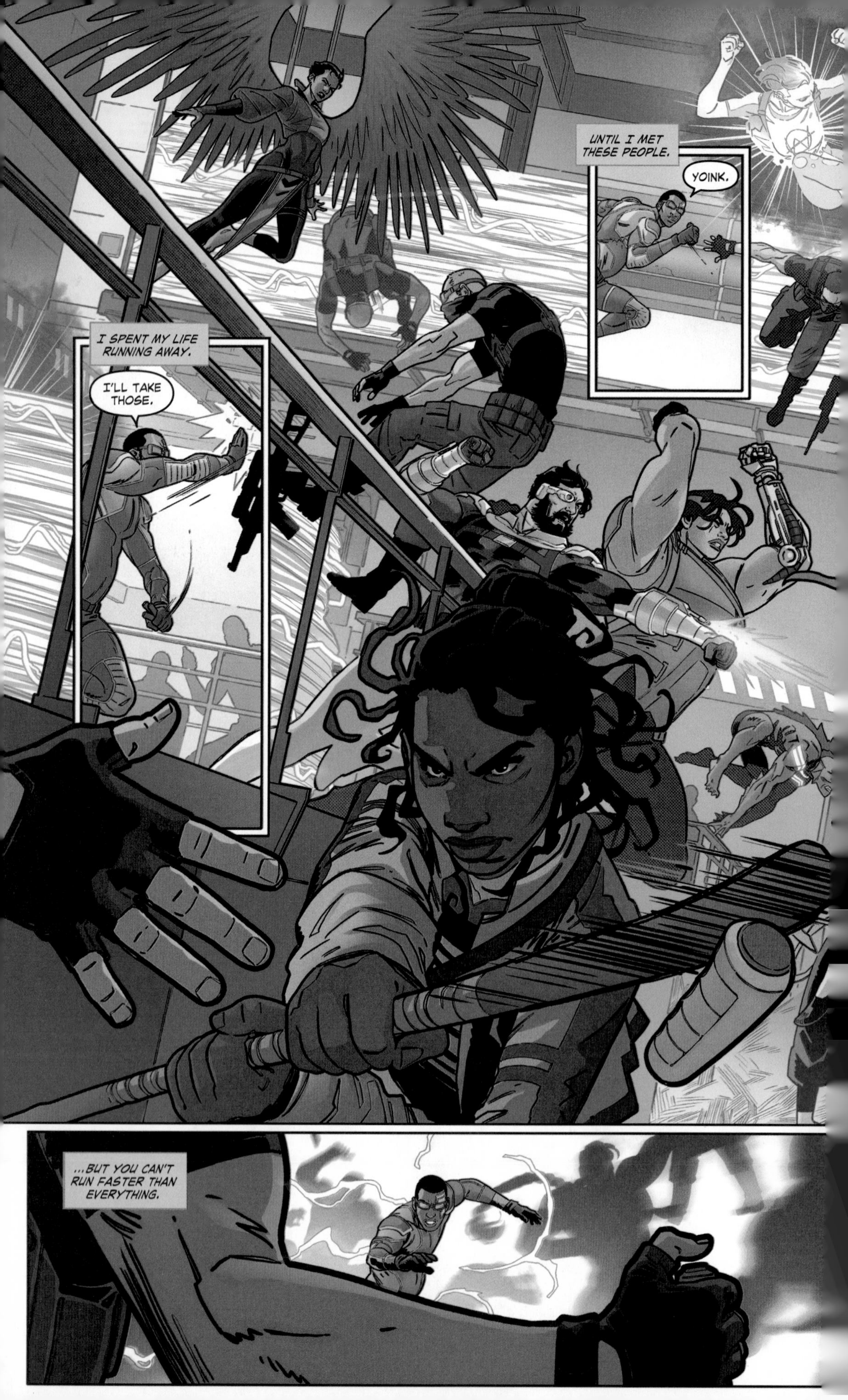
I SPENT MY LIFE RUNNING AWAY.
I'LL TAKE THOSE.
UNTIL I MET THESE PEOPLE.
YOINK.
...BUT YOU CAN'T RUN FASTER THAN EVERYTHING.

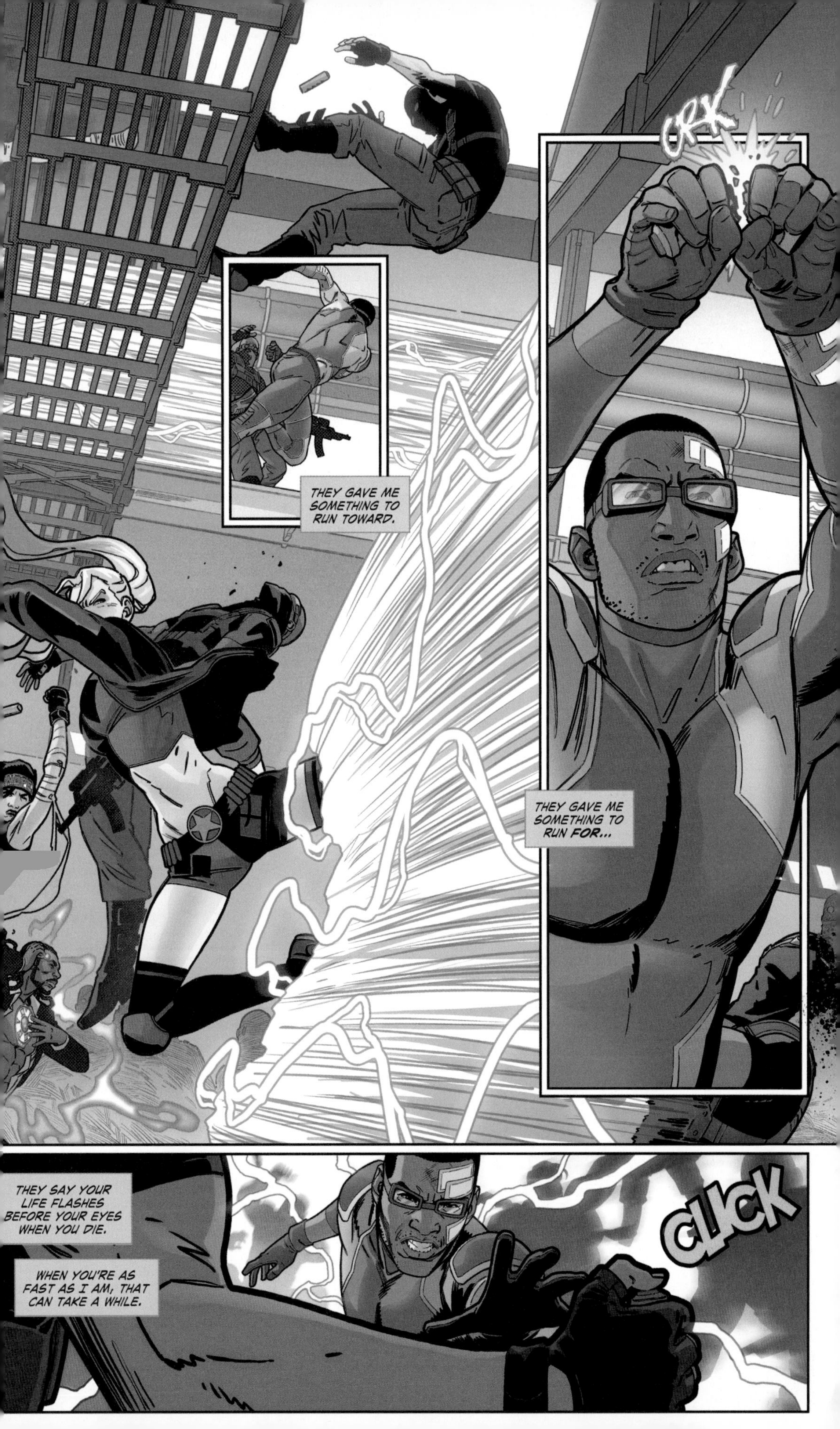
CRK
THEY GAVE ME SOMETHING TO RUN TOWARD.
THEY GAVE ME SOMETHING TO RUN FOR...
THEY SAY YOUR LIFE FLASHES BEFORE YOUR EYES WHEN YOU DIE.
WHEN YOU'RE AS FAST AS I AM, THAT CAN TAKE A WHILE.
CLICK

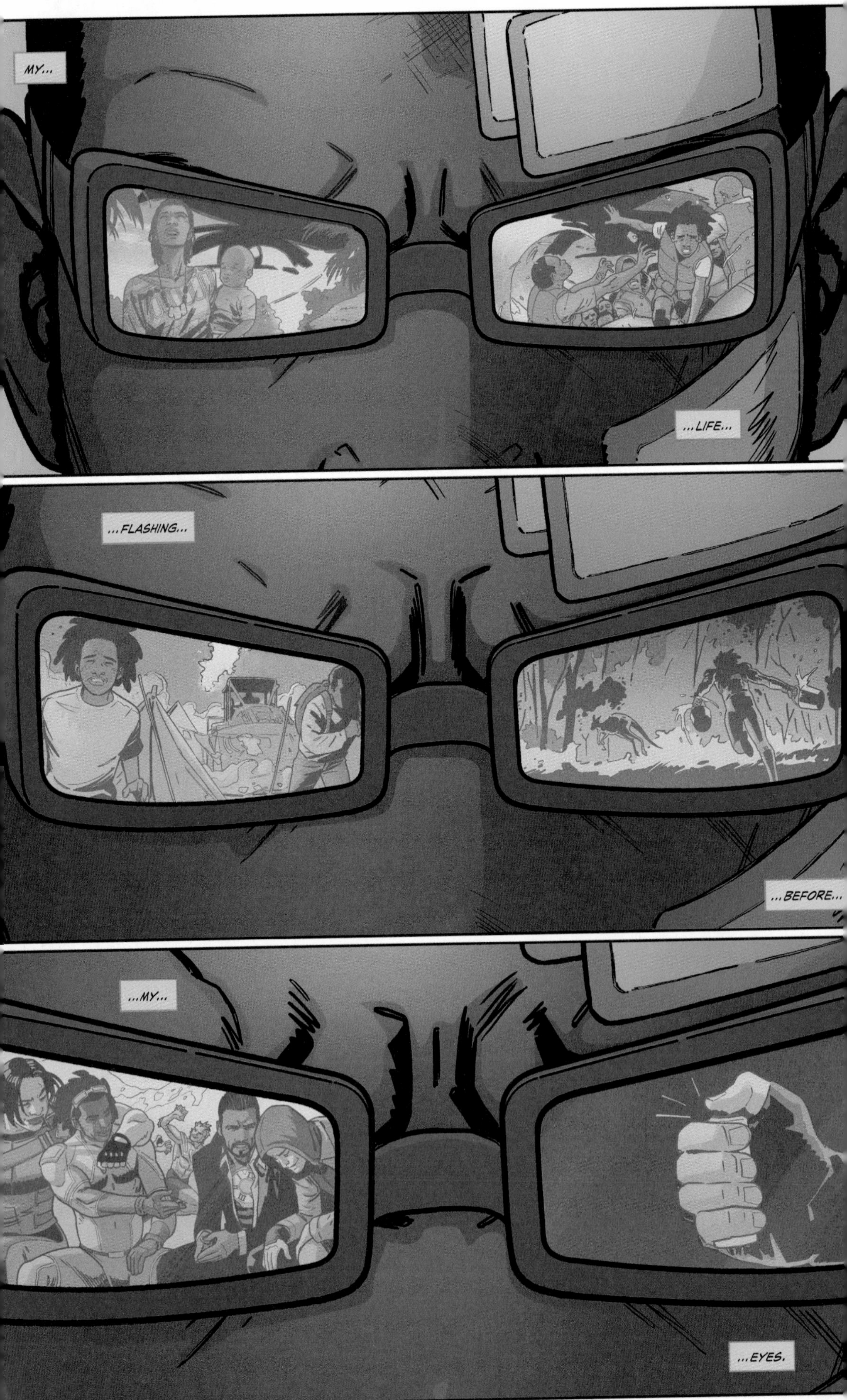
MY...
...LIFE...
...FLASHING...
...BEFORE...
...MY...
...EYES.

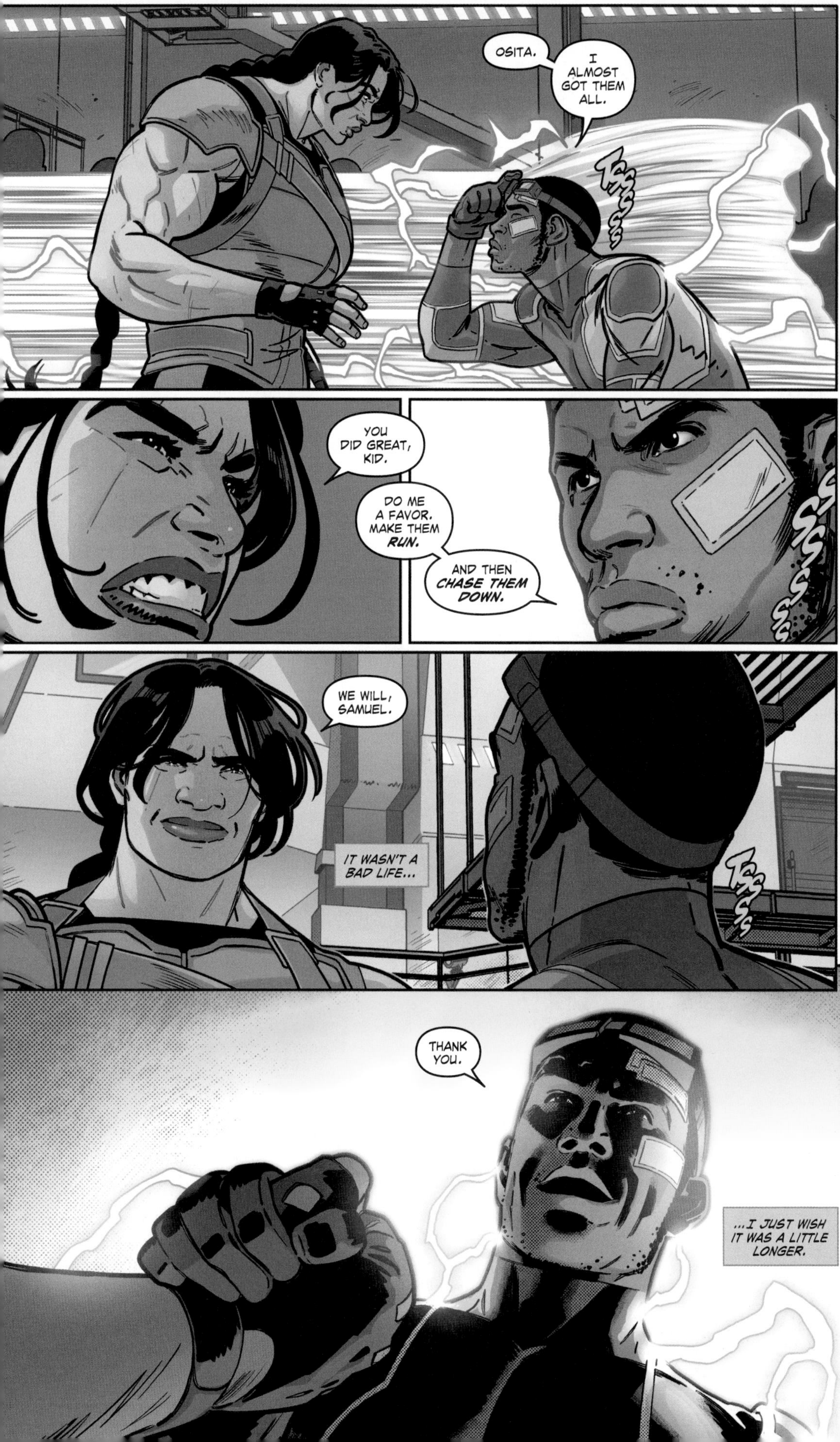
OSITA.
I ALMOST GOT THEM ALL.
TSSSSS
YOU DID GREAT, KID.
DO ME A FAVOR. MAKE THEM RUN.
AND THEN CHASE THEM DOWN.
SSSSSSS
WE WILL, SAMUEL.
IT WASN'T A BAD LIFE...
TSSSS
THANK YOU.
...I JUST WISH IT WAS A LITTLE LONGER.

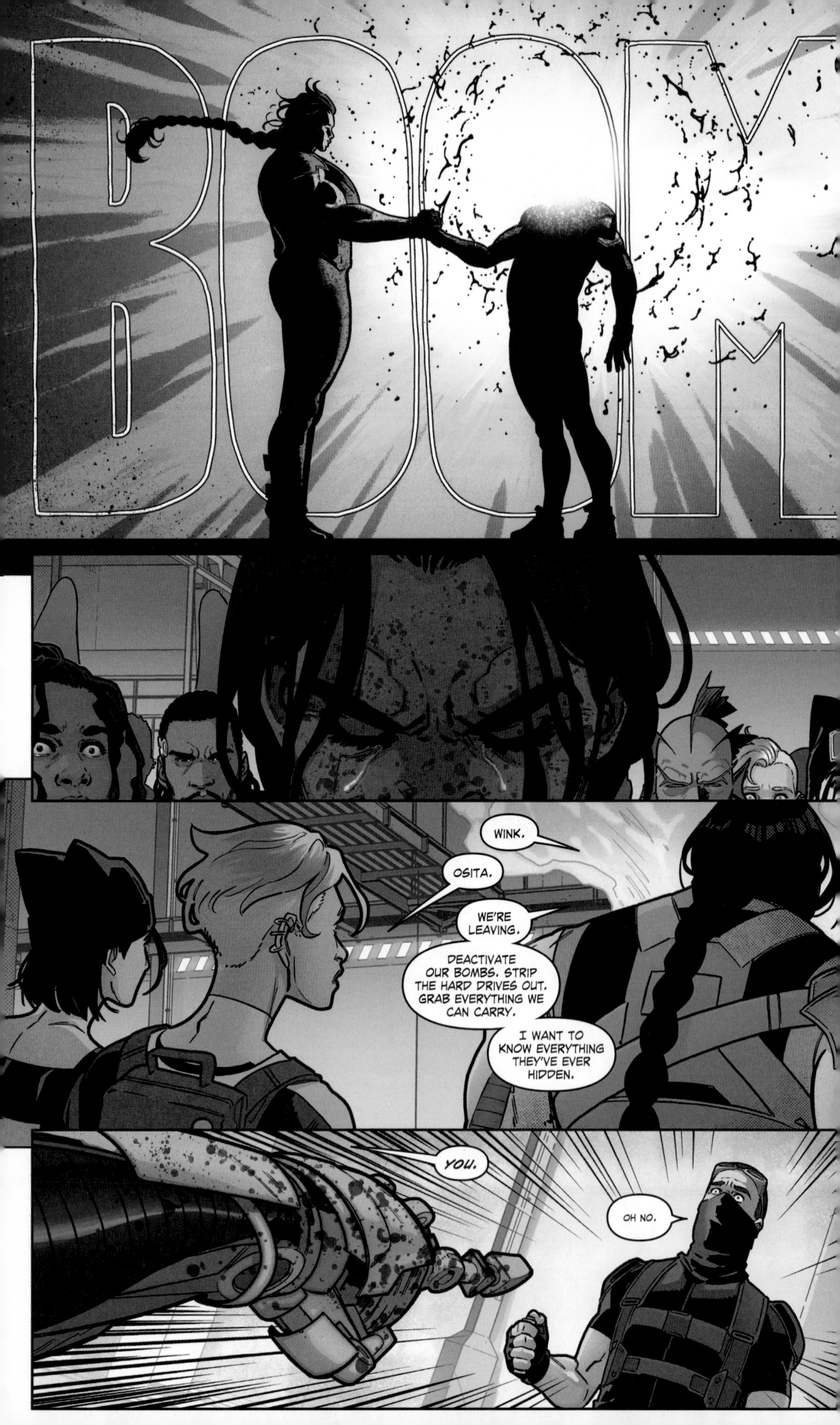
BOOM
WINK.
OSITA.
WE'RE LEAVING.
DEACTIVATE OUR BOMBS. STRIP THE HARD DRIVES OUT. GRAB EVERYTHING WE CAN CARRY.
I WANT TO KNOW EVERYTHING THEY'VE EVER HIDDEN.
YOU.
OH NO.

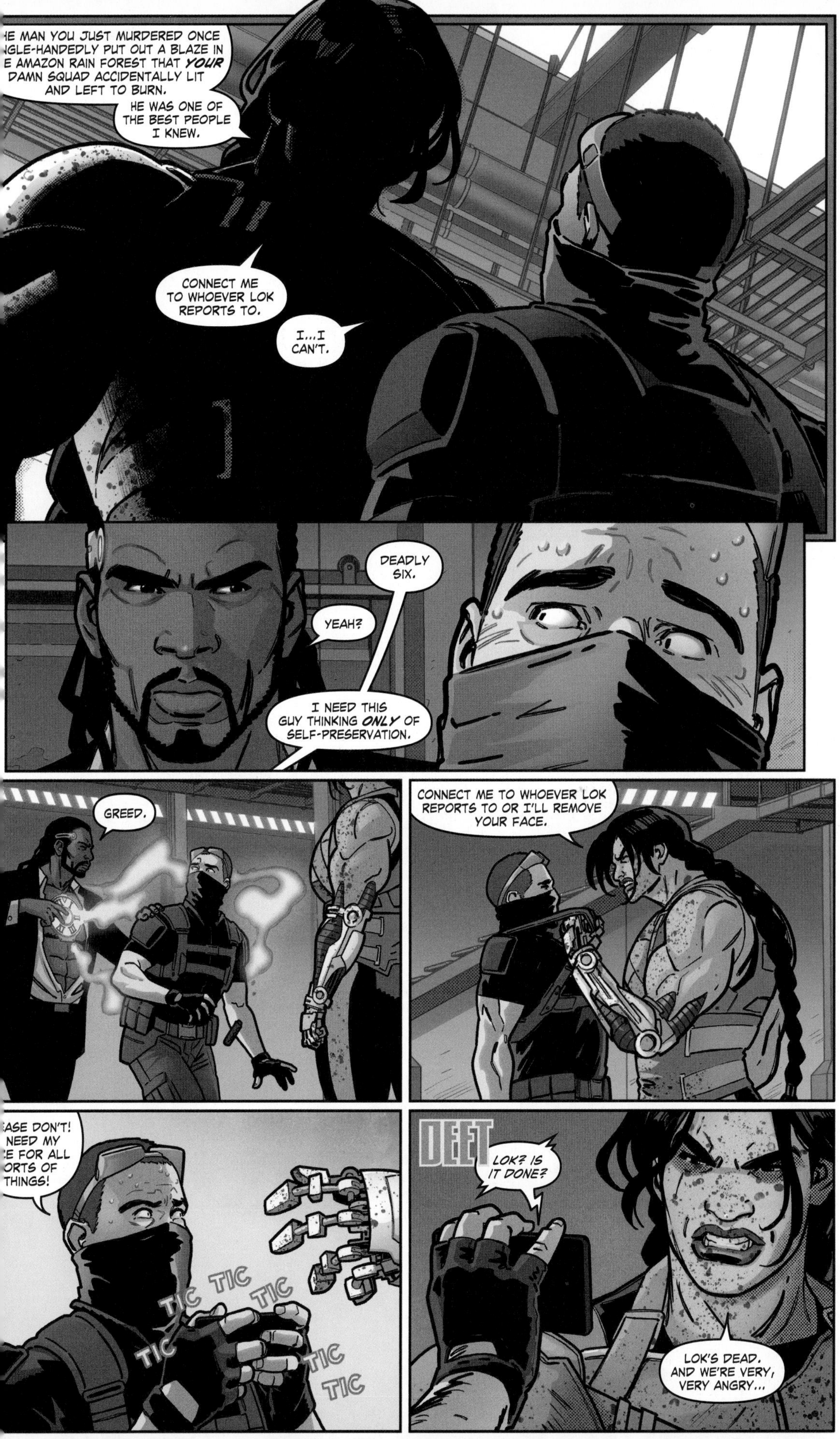
HE MAN YOU JUST MURDERED ONCE NGLE-HANDEDLY PUT OUT A BLAZE IN E AMAZON RAIN FOREST THAT *YOUR* DAMN SQUAD ACCIDENTALLY LIT AND LEFT TO BURN.
HE WAS ONE OF THE BEST PEOPLE I KNEW.
CONNECT ME TO WHOEVER LOK REPORTS TO.
I...I CAN'T.
DEADLY SIX.
YEAH?
I NEED THIS GUY THINKING *ONLY* OF SELF-PRESERVATION.
GREED.
CONNECT ME TO WHOEVER LOK REPORTS TO OR I'LL REMOVE YOUR FACE.
EASE DON'T! NEED MY E FOR ALL ORTS OF THINGS!
TIC TIC TIC
TIC
TIC TIC
DEET
LOK? IS IT DONE?
LOK'S DEAD. AND WE'RE VERY, VERY ANGRY...

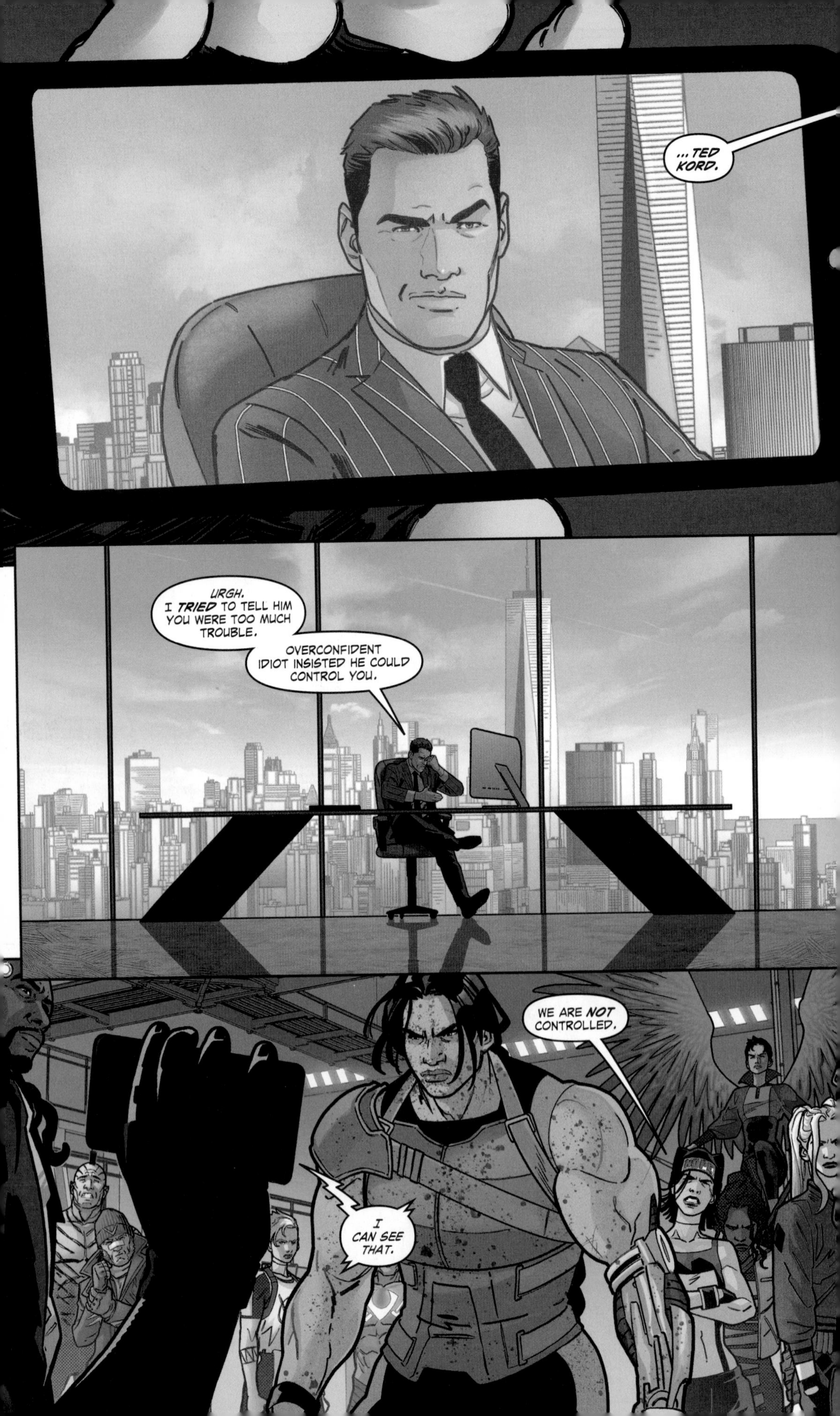
...TED KORD.
URGH. I TRIED TO TELL HIM YOU WERE TOO MUCH TROUBLE.
OVERCONFIDENT IDIOT INSISTED HE COULD CONTROL YOU.
WE ARE NOT CONTROLLED.
I CAN SEE THAT.

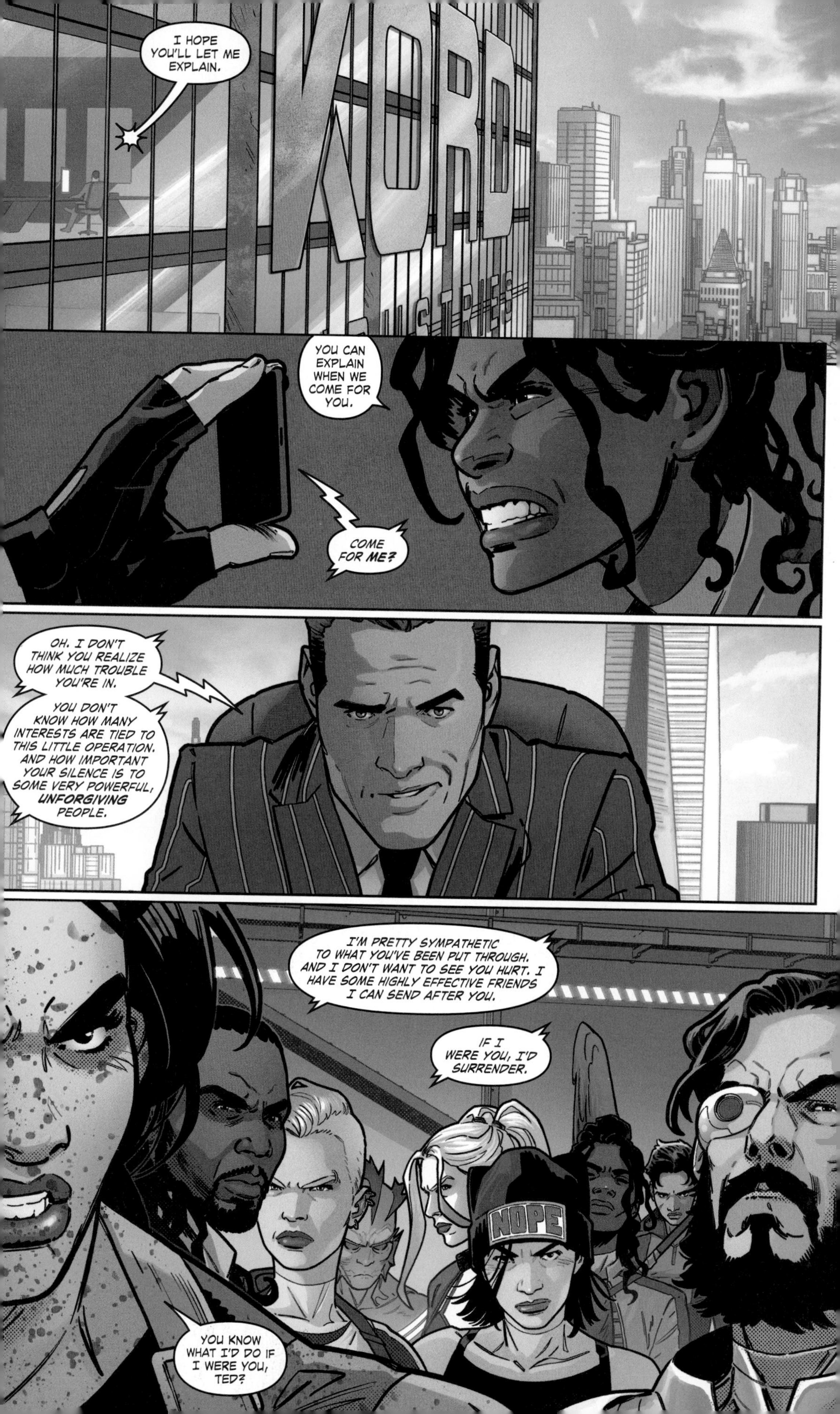
I HOPE YOU'LL LET ME EXPLAIN.
KORD INDUSTRIES
YOU CAN EXPLAIN WHEN WE COME FOR YOU.
COME FOR ME?
OH. I DON'T THINK YOU REALIZE HOW MUCH TROUBLE YOU'RE IN.
YOU DON'T KNOW HOW MANY INTERESTS ARE TIED TO THIS LITTLE OPERATION. AND HOW IMPORTANT YOUR SILENCE IS TO SOME VERY POWERFUL, **UNFORGIVING** PEOPLE.
I'M PRETTY SYMPATHETIC TO WHAT YOU'VE BEEN PUT THROUGH. AND I DON'T WANT TO SEE YOU HURT. I HAVE SOME HIGHLY EFFECTIVE FRIENDS I CAN SEND AFTER YOU.
IF I WERE YOU, I'D SURRENDER.
NOPE
YOU KNOW WHAT I'D DO IF I WERE YOU, TED?

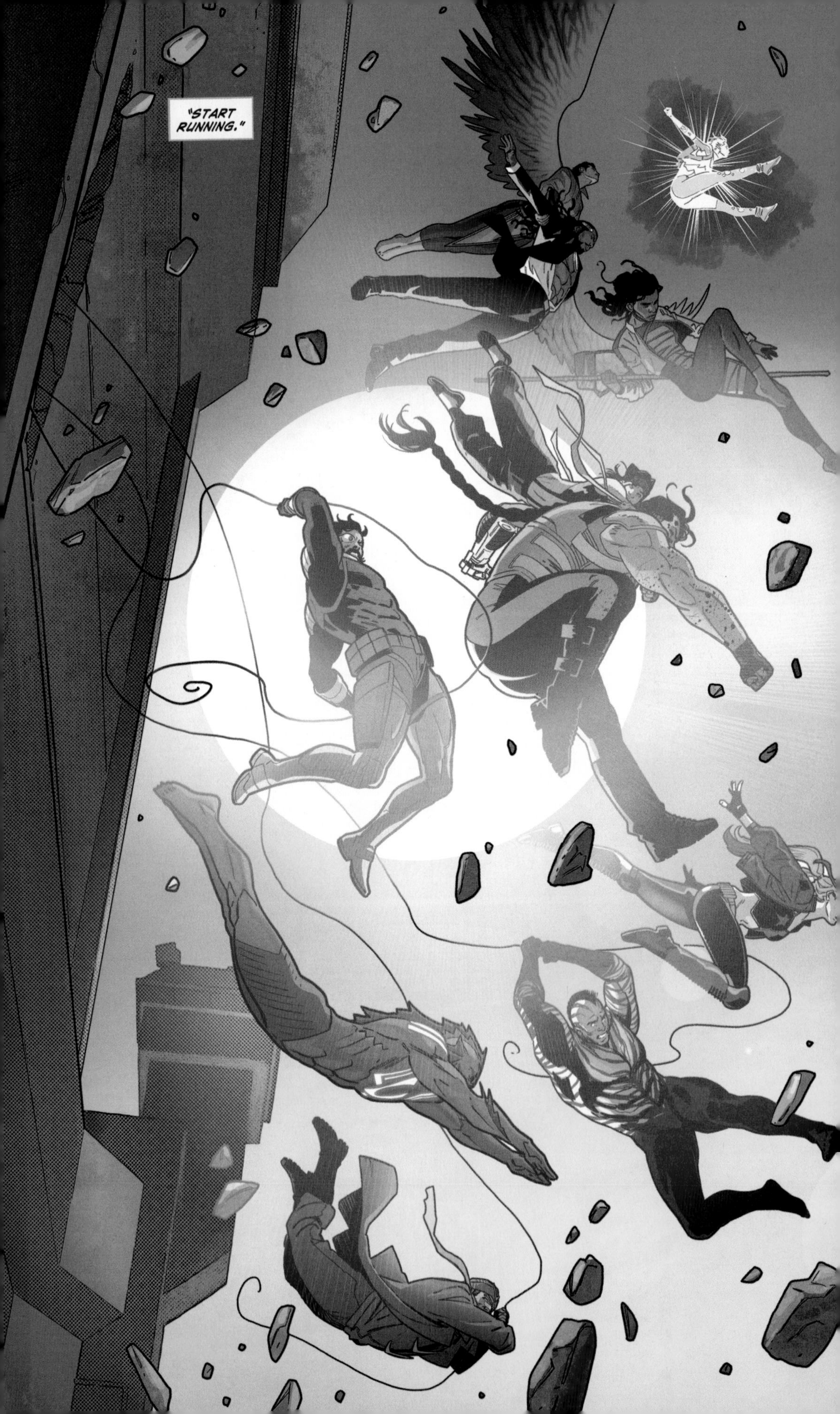
"START RUNNING."

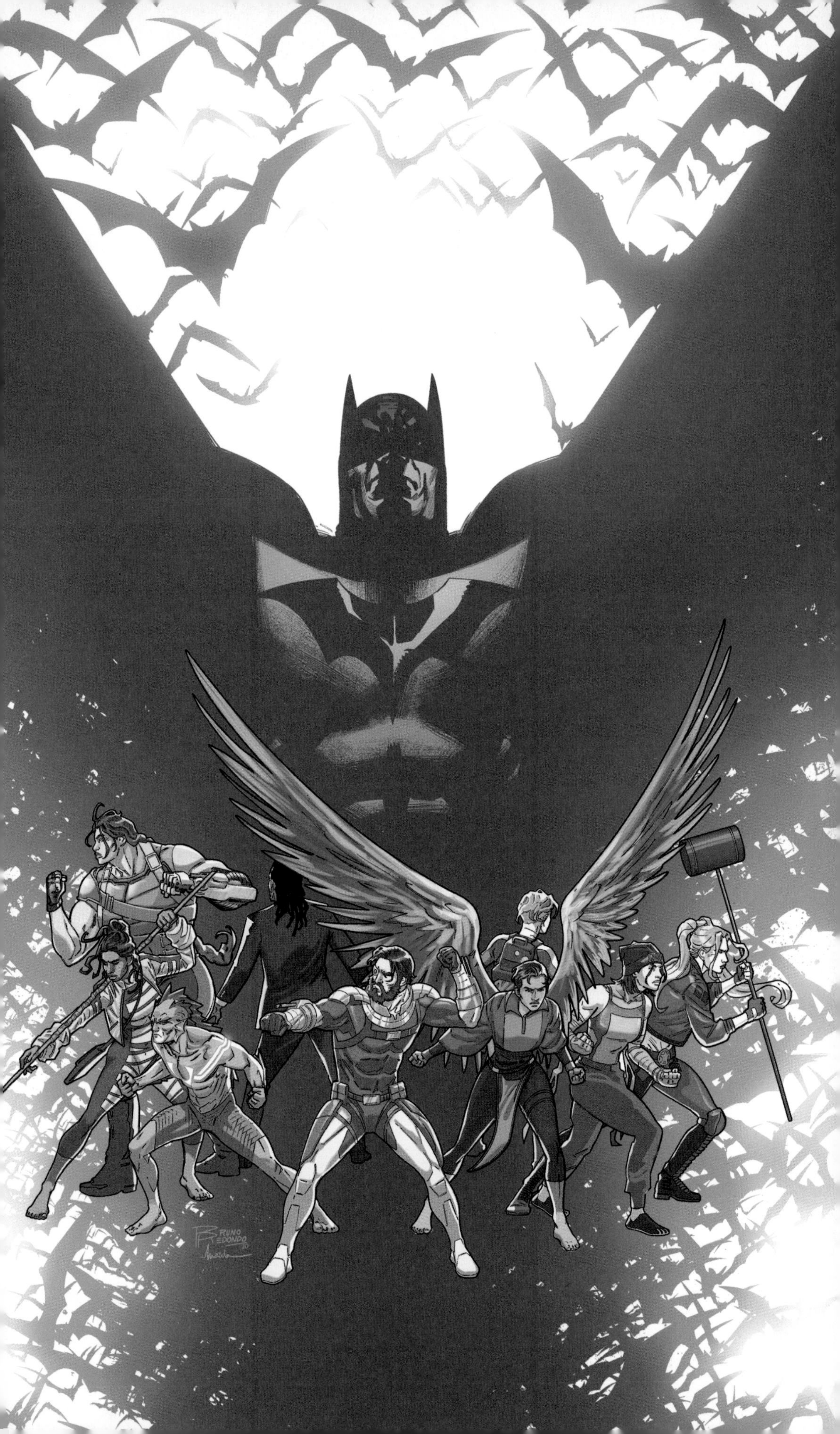
BRUNO REDONDO 20

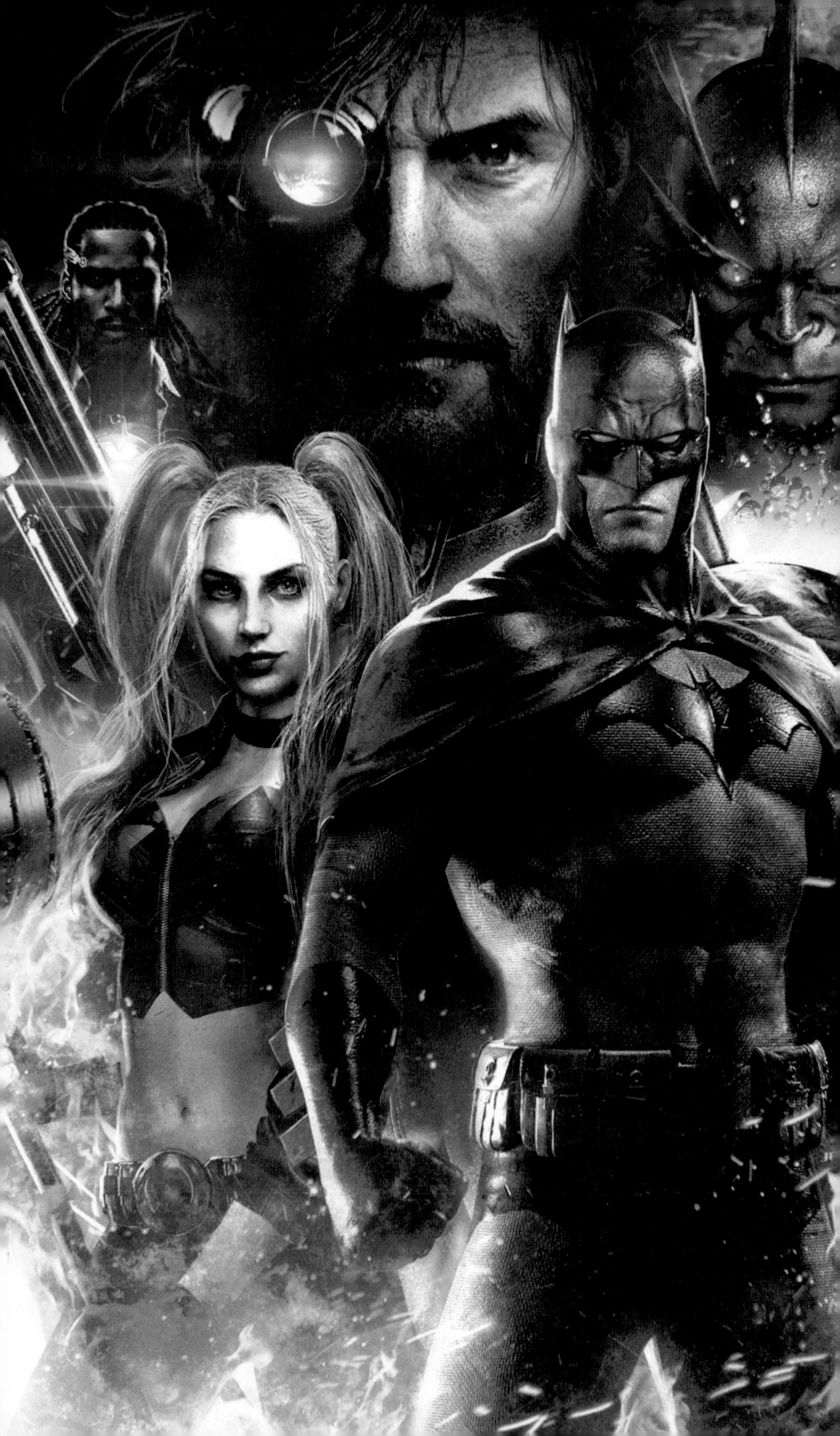

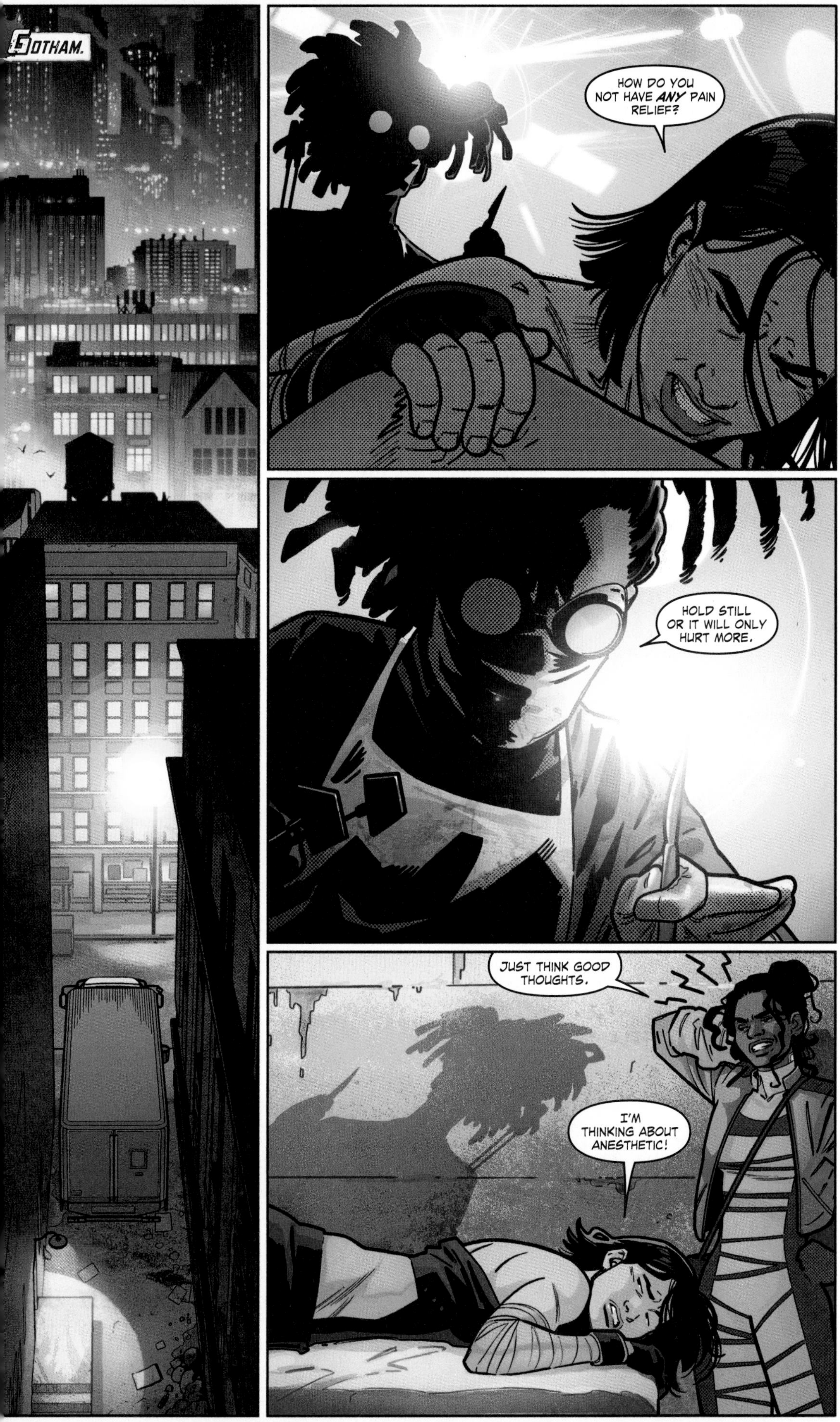
GOTHAM.
HOW DO YOU NOT HAVE ANY PAIN RELIEF?
HOLD STILL OR IT WILL ONLY HURT MORE.
JUST THINK GOOD THOUGHTS.
I'M THINKING ABOUT ANESTHETIC!

SUICIDE SQUAD

written by TOM TAYLOR   art by BRUNO REDONDO

color by ADRIANO LUCAS   letters by WES ABBOTT   cover BRUNO REDONDO and MARCELO MAIOLO

variant cover JEREMY ROBERTS   editor ANDREA SHEA   group editor ALEX R. CARR

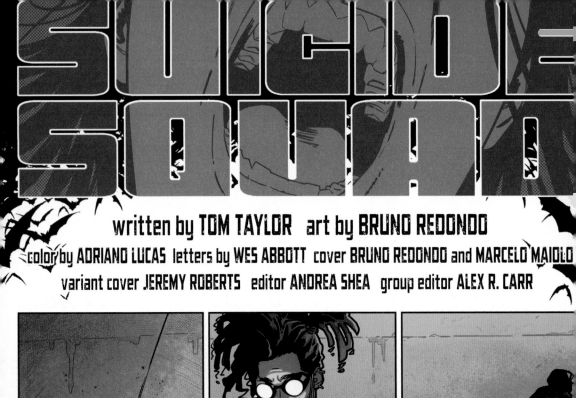

TINK

ding

HMM.

EXCUSE ME.

OH. SURE. WHATEVER TEXT YOU JUST GOT IS *WAY* MORE IMPORTANT THAN THE SURGERY YOU'RE *IN THE MIDDLE OF.*

UH-HUH.

YOU OKAY?

I JUST HAD SURGERY WITH NO PAIN RELIEF.

ABSOLUTE AGONY IS A SMALL PRICE TO PAY FOR NOT HAVING A BOMB INSIDE YOU.

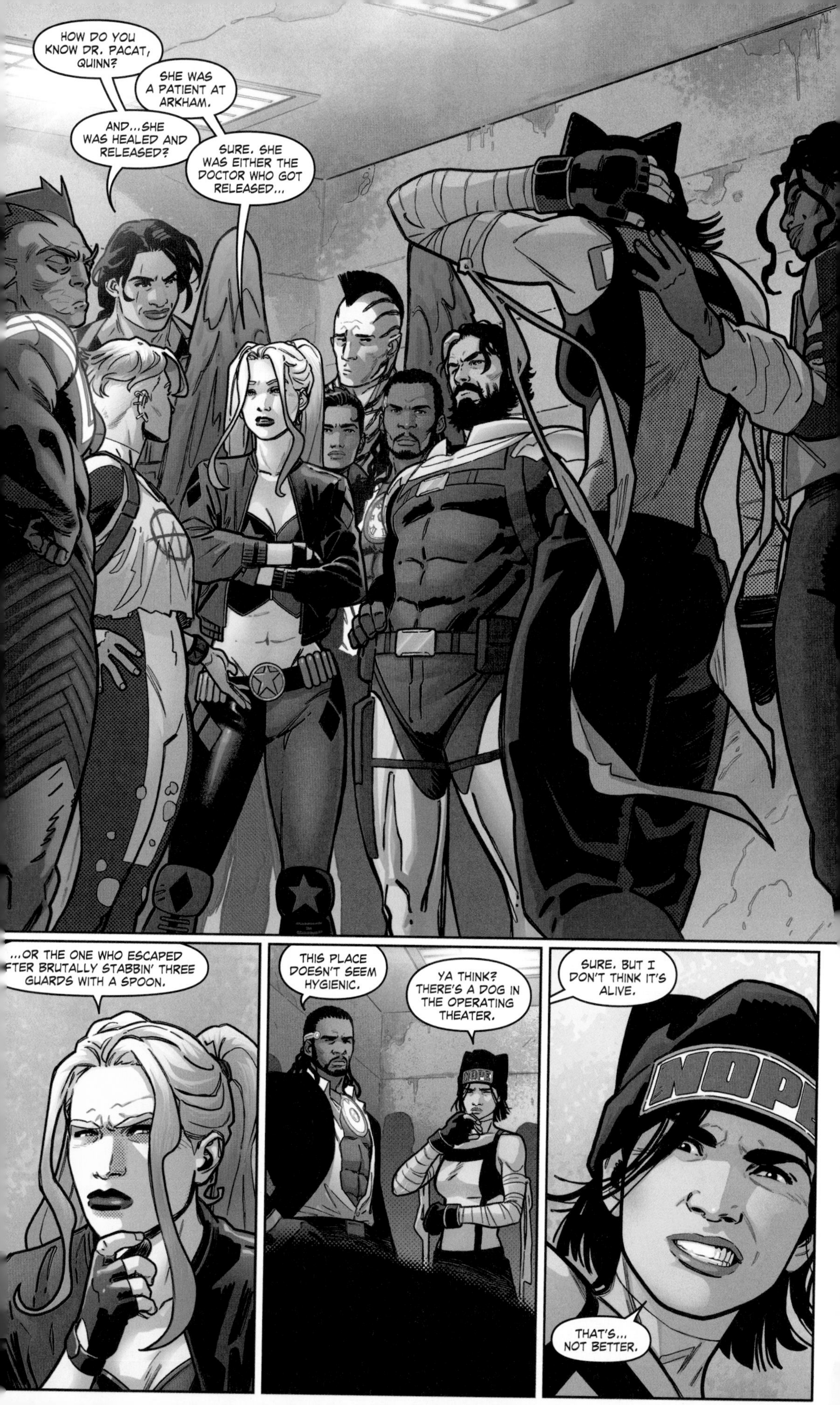
HOW DO YOU KNOW DR. PACAT, QUINN?
SHE WAS A PATIENT AT ARKHAM.
AND...SHE WAS HEALED AND RELEASED?
SURE. SHE WAS EITHER THE DOCTOR WHO GOT RELEASED...
...OR THE ONE WHO ESCAPED FTER BRUTALLY STABBIN' THREE GUARDS WITH A SPOON.
THIS PLACE DOESN'T SEEM HYGIENIC.
YA THINK? THERE'S A DOG IN THE OPERATING THEATER.
NOPE
SURE. BUT I DON'T THINK IT'S ALIVE.
NOPE
THAT'S... NOT BETTER.

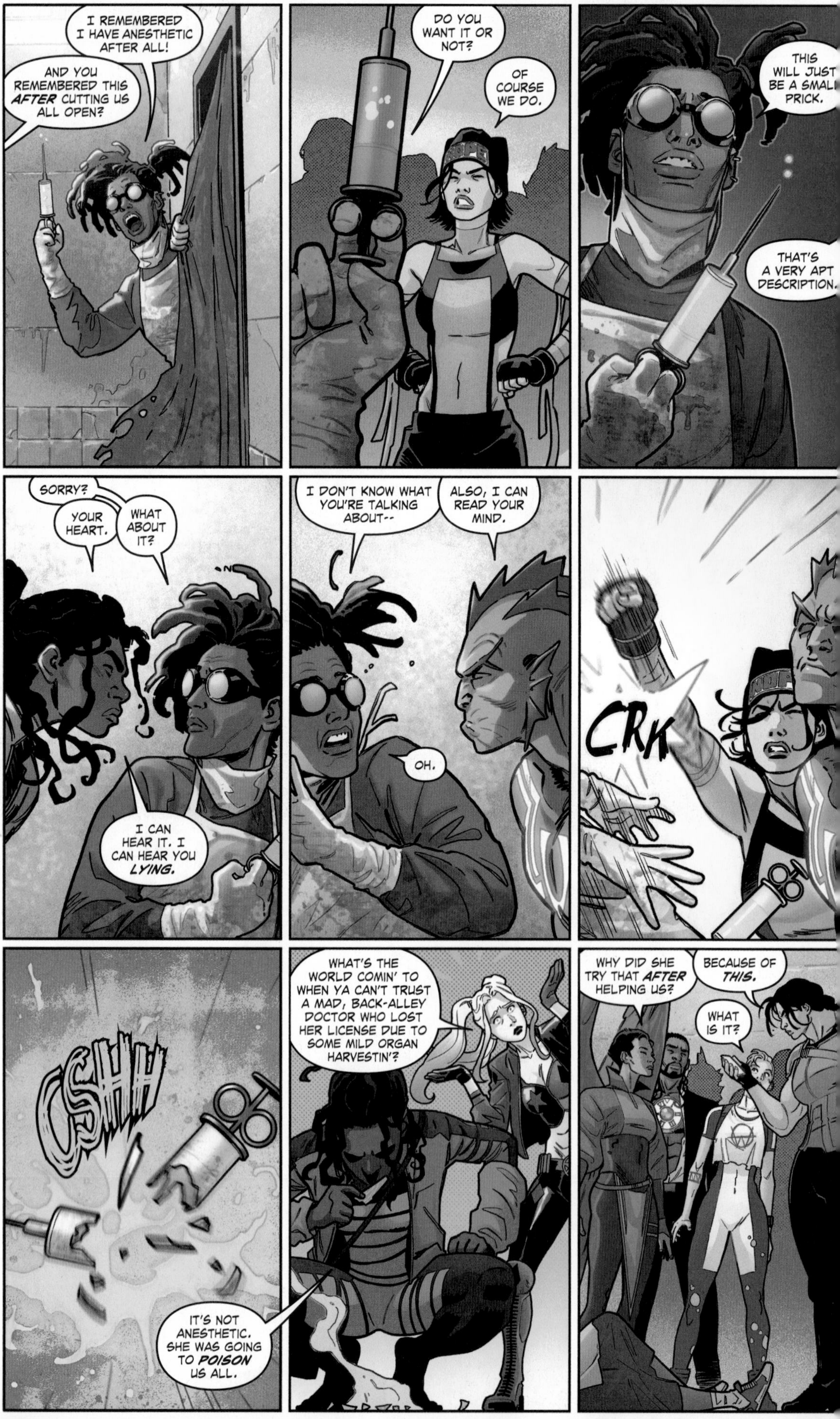

I REMEMBERED I HAVE ANESTHETIC AFTER ALL!
AND YOU REMEMBERED THIS AFTER CUTTING US ALL OPEN?
DO YOU WANT IT OR NOT?
OF COURSE WE DO.
THIS WILL JUST BE A SMALL PRICK.
THAT'S A VERY APT DESCRIPTION.
SORRY?
YOUR HEART.
WHAT ABOUT IT?
I CAN HEAR IT. I CAN HEAR YOU LYING.
I DON'T KNOW WHAT YOU'RE TALKING ABOUT--
ALSO, I CAN READ YOUR MIND.
OH.
CRK
CSHH
IT'S NOT ANESTHETIC. SHE WAS GOING TO POISON US ALL.
WHAT'S THE WORLD COMIN' TO WHEN YA CAN'T TRUST A MAD, BACK-ALLEY DOCTOR WHO LOST HER LICENSE DUE TO SOME MILD ORGAN HARVESTIN'?
WHY DID SHE TRY THAT AFTER HELPING US?
BECAUSE OF THIS.
WHAT IS IT?

"IT'S A BOUNTY.

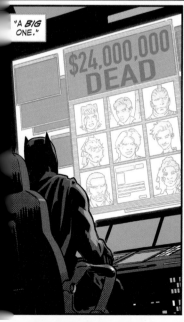

"A *BIG* ONE."

$24,000,000
DEAD

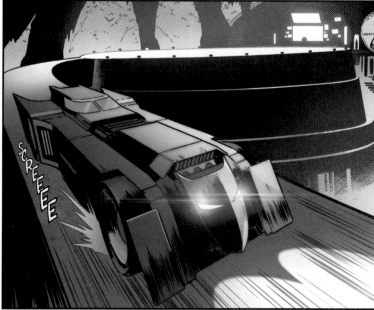

SCREEEE

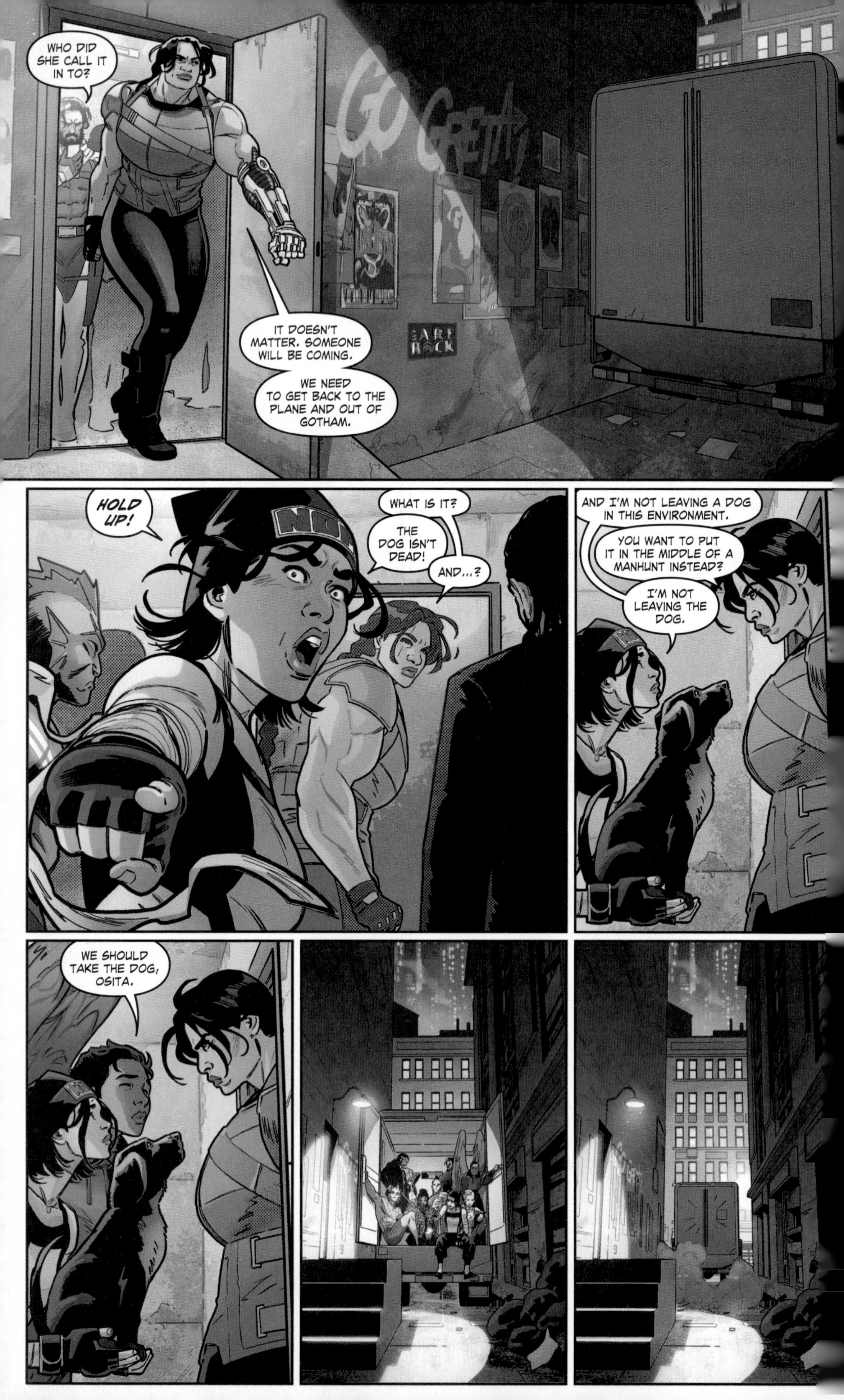
WHO DID SHE CALL IT IN TO?
IT DOESN'T MATTER. SOMEONE WILL BE COMING.
WE NEED TO GET BACK TO THE PLANE AND OUT OF GOTHAM.
GO GRETA!
HOLD UP!
WHAT IS IT?
THE DOG ISN'T DEAD!
AND...?
AND I'M NOT LEAVING A DOG IN THIS ENVIRONMENT.
YOU WANT TO PUT IT IN THE MIDDLE OF A MANHUNT INSTEAD?
I'M NOT LEAVING THE DOG.
WE SHOULD TAKE THE DOG, OSITA.

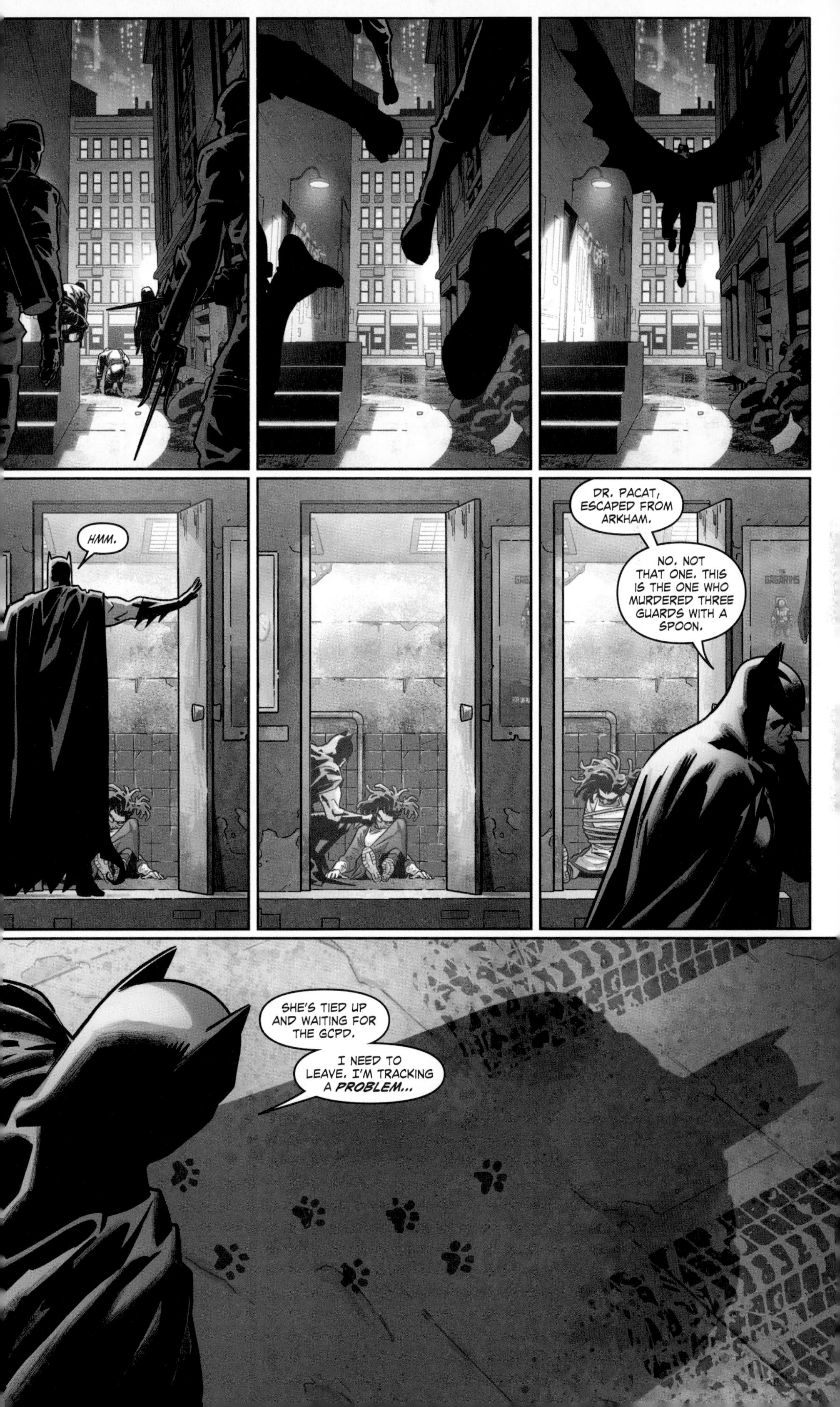
HMM.
DR. PACAT, ESCAPED FROM ARKHAM.
NO. NOT THAT ONE. THIS IS THE ONE WHO MURDERED THREE GUARDS WITH A SPOON.
SHE'S TIED UP AND WAITING FOR THE GCPD.
I NEED TO LEAVE. I'M TRACKING A *PROBLEM...*

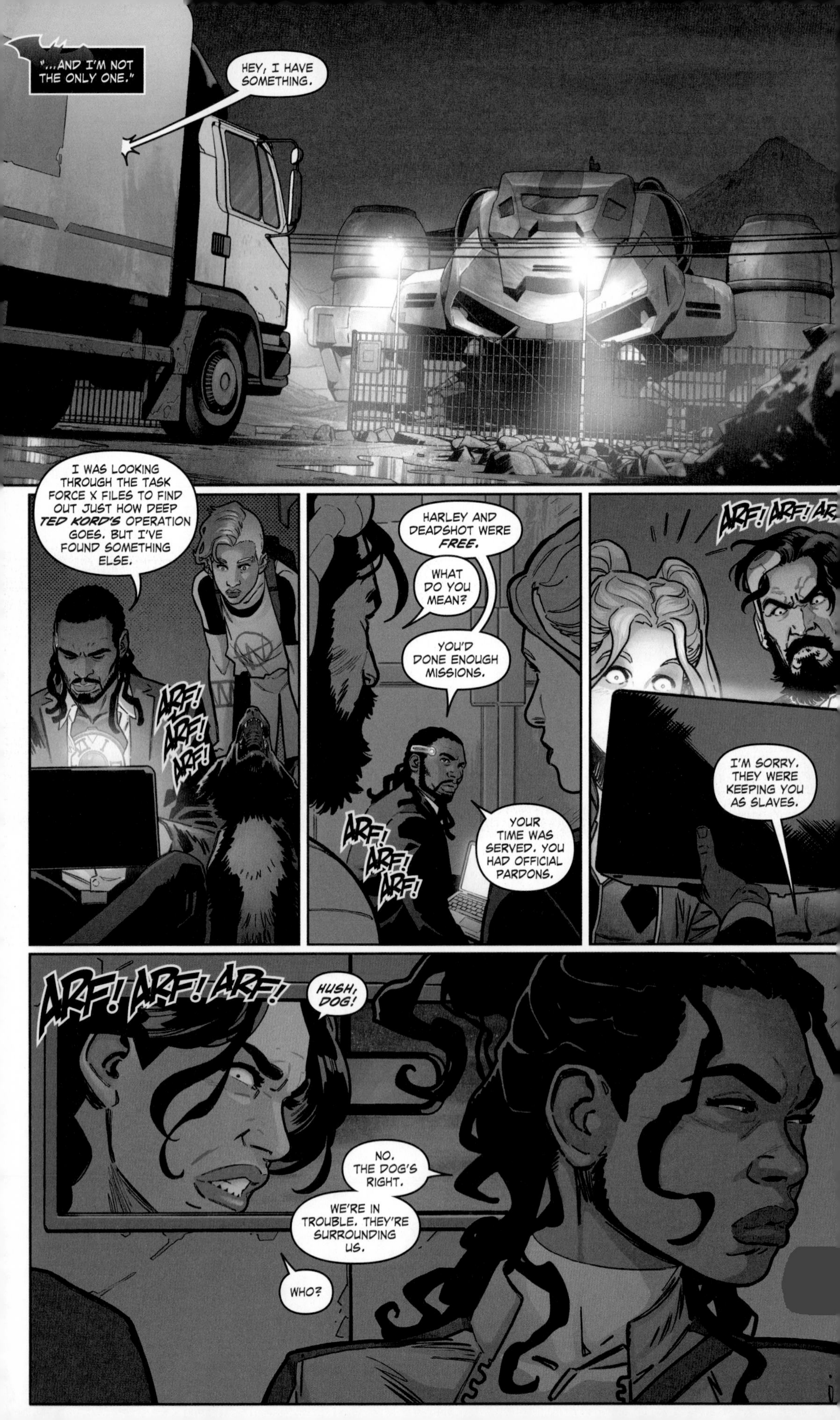
"...AND I'M NOT THE ONLY ONE."
HEY, I HAVE SOMETHING.
I WAS LOOKING THROUGH THE TASK FORCE X FILES TO FIND OUT JUST HOW DEEP TED KORD'S OPERATION GOES. BUT I'VE FOUND SOMETHING ELSE.
ARF! ARF! ARF!
HARLEY AND DEADSHOT WERE FREE.
WHAT DO YOU MEAN?
YOU'D DONE ENOUGH MISSIONS.
YOUR TIME WAS SERVED. YOU HAD OFFICIAL PARDONS.
ARF! ARF! ARF!
I'M SORRY. THEY WERE KEEPING YOU AS SLAVES.
ARF! ARF! ARF!
HUSH, DOG!
NO. THE DOG'S RIGHT.
WE'RE IN TROUBLE. THEY'RE SURROUNDING US.
WHO?

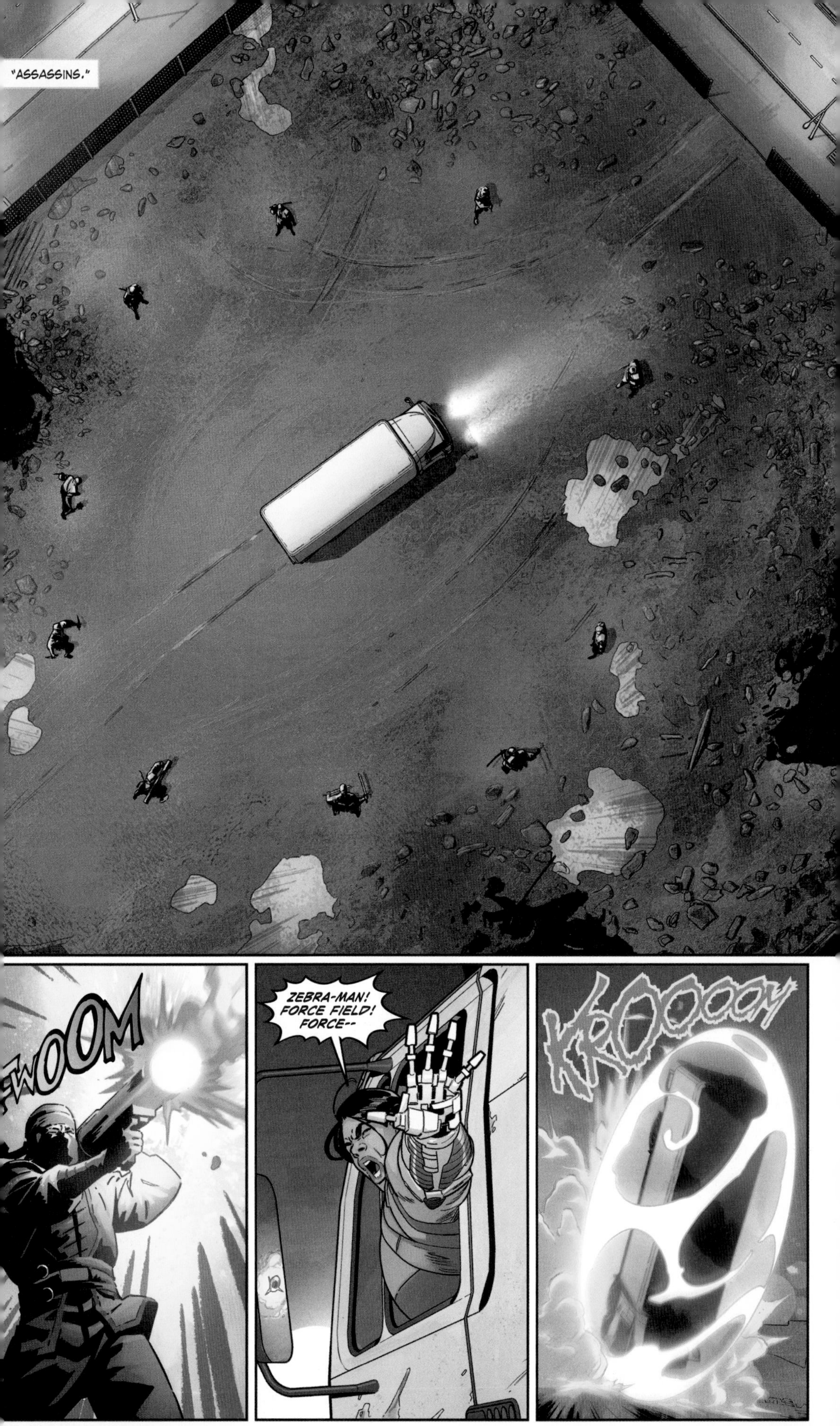
"ASSASSINS."
FWOOM
ZEBRA-MAN! FORCE FIELD! FORCE--
KROOOOOM

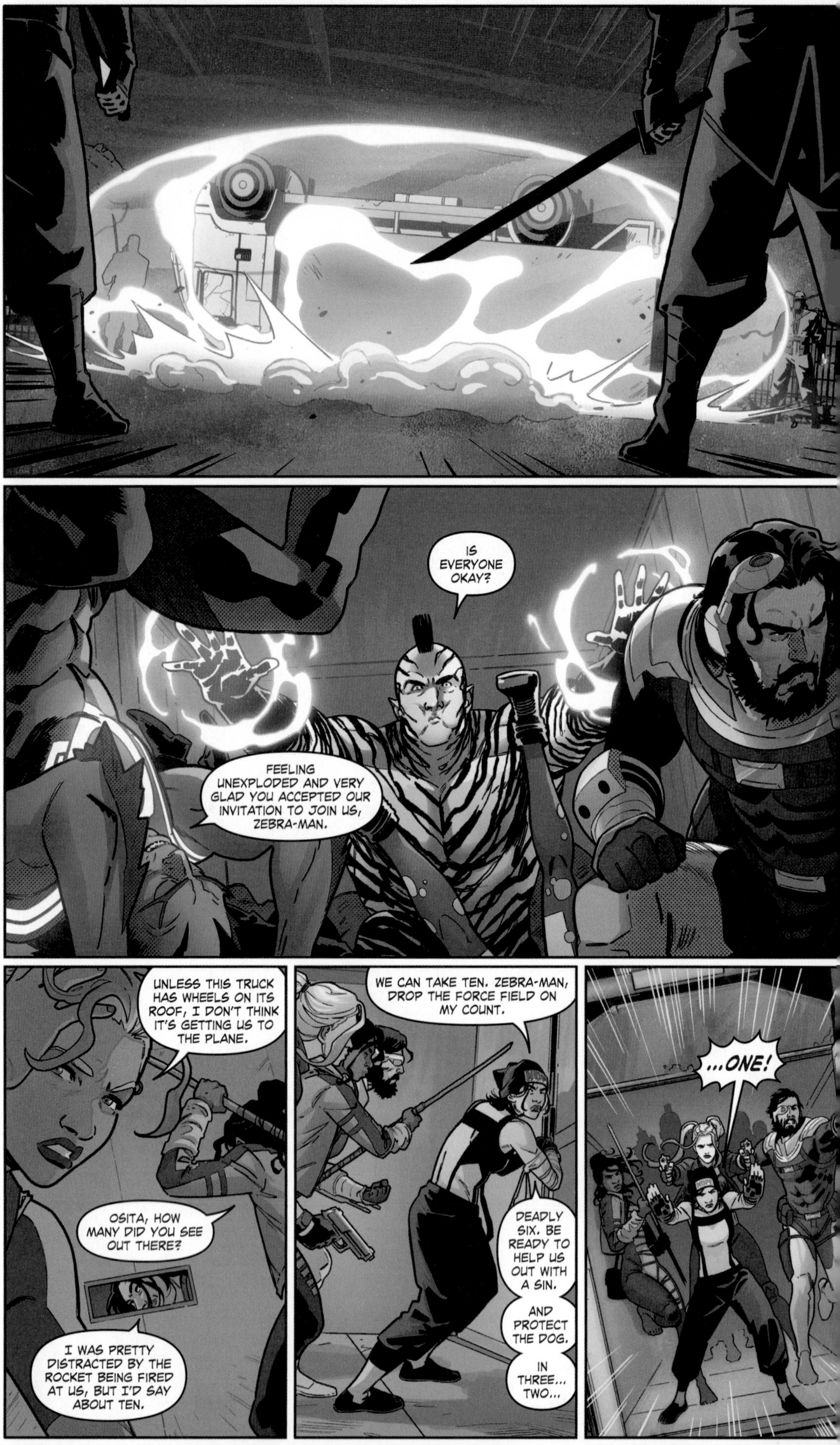
IS EVERYONE OKAY?
FEELING UNEXPLODED AND VERY GLAD YOU ACCEPTED OUR INVITATION TO JOIN US, ZEBRA-MAN.
UNLESS THIS TRUCK HAS WHEELS ON ITS ROOF, I DON'T THINK IT'S GETTING US TO THE PLANE.
OSITA, HOW MANY DID YOU SEE OUT THERE?
I WAS PRETTY DISTRACTED BY THE ROCKET BEING FIRED AT US, BUT I'D SAY ABOUT TEN.
WE CAN TAKE TEN. ZEBRA-MAN, DROP THE FORCE FIELD ON MY COUNT.
DEADLY SIX. BE READY TO HELP US OUT WITH A SIN.
AND PROTECT THE DOG.
IN THREE... TWO...
...ONE!

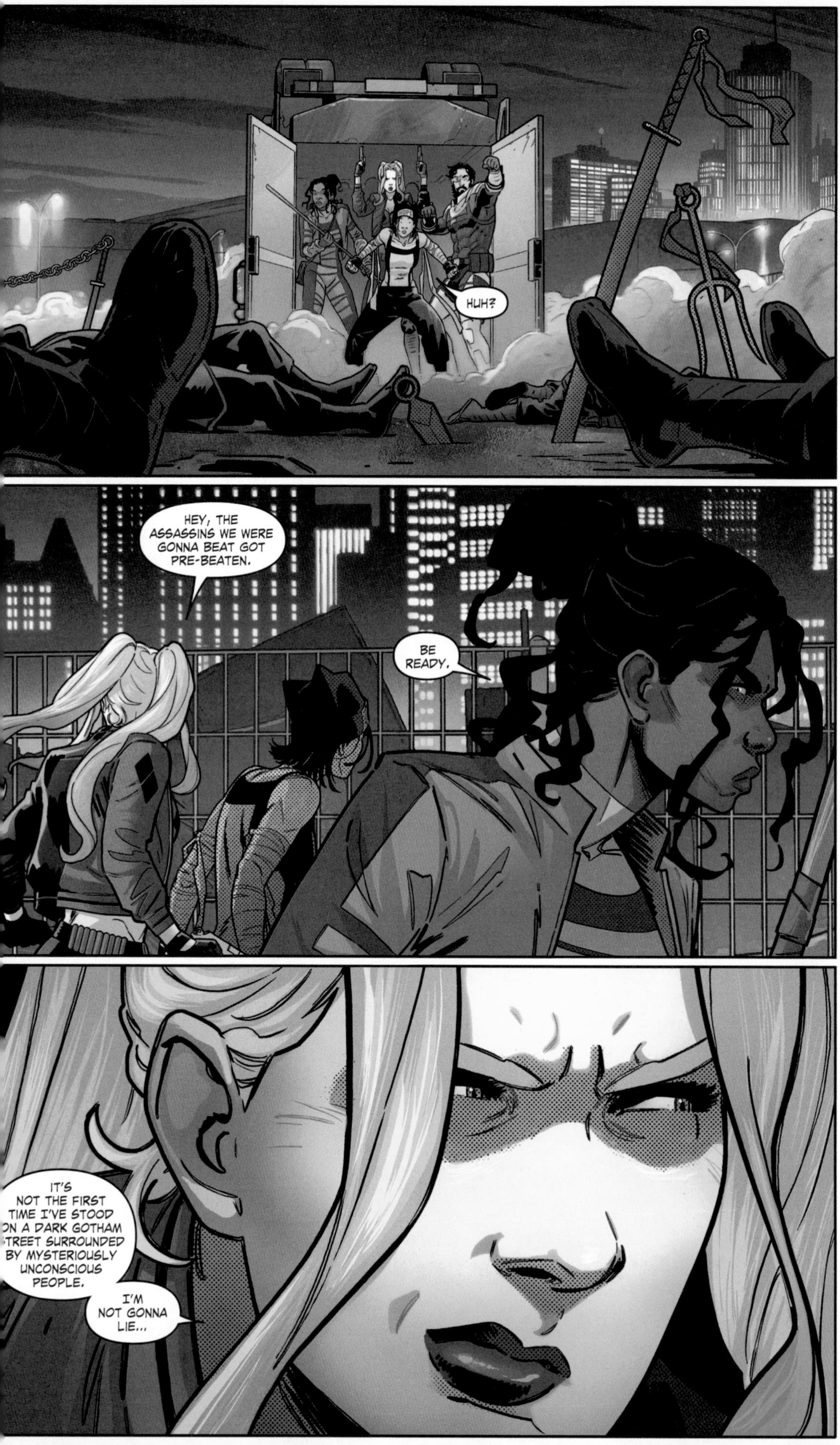
HUH?
HEY, THE ASSASSINS WE WERE GONNA BEAT GOT PRE-BEATEN.
BE READY.
IT'S NOT THE FIRST TIME I'VE STOOD ON A DARK GOTHAM STREET SURROUNDED BY MYSTERIOUSLY UNCONSCIOUS PEOPLE.
I'M NOT GONNA LIE...

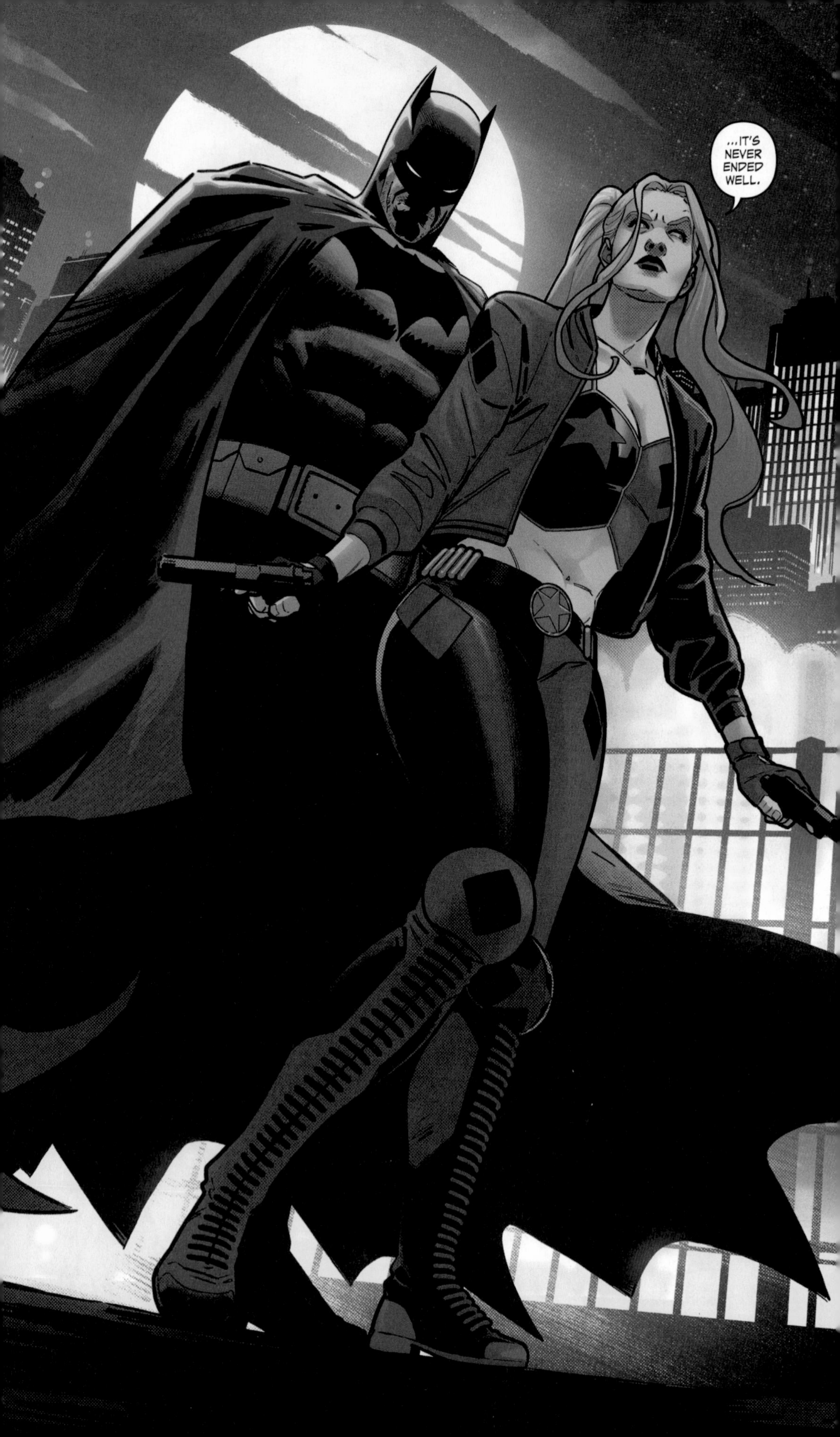
...IT'S NEVER ENDED WELL.

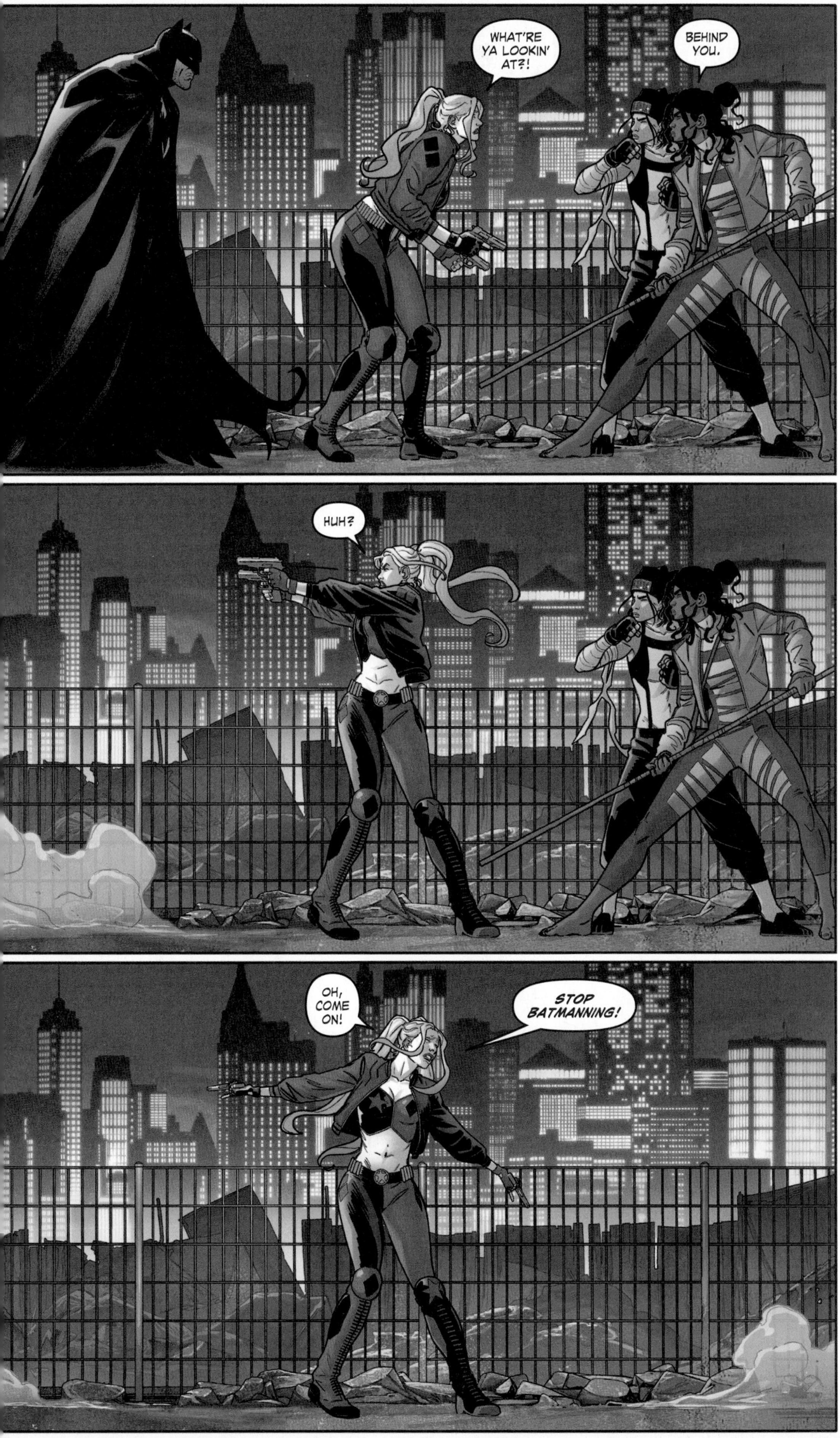
WHAT'RE YA LOOKIN' AT?!
BEHIND YOU.
HUH?
OH, COME ON!
STOP BATMANNING!

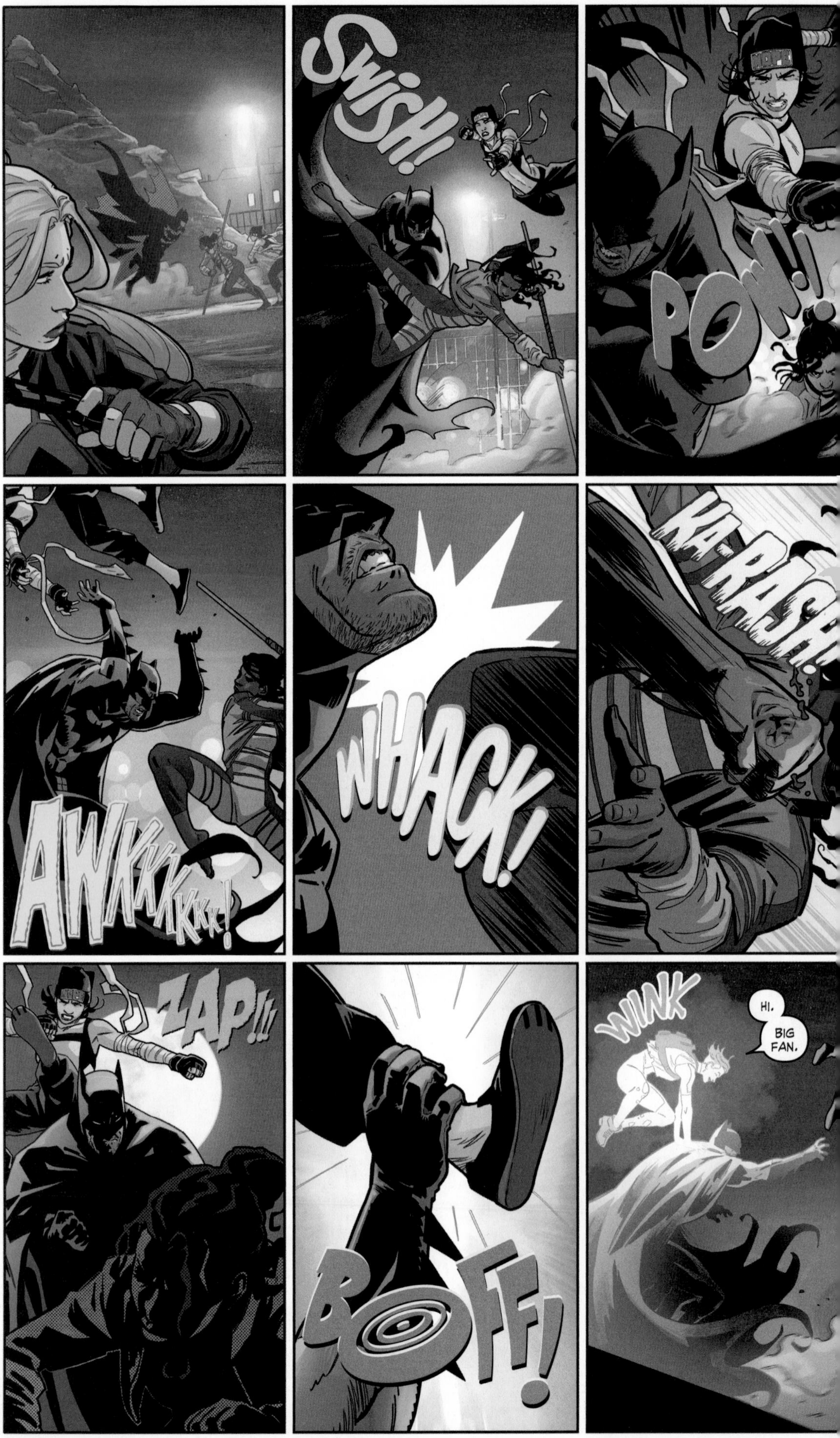
SWISH!
POW!!
AWKKKKKKK!
WHACK!
KA-RASH!
ZAP!!!
BOFF!
WINK
HI.
BIG FAN.

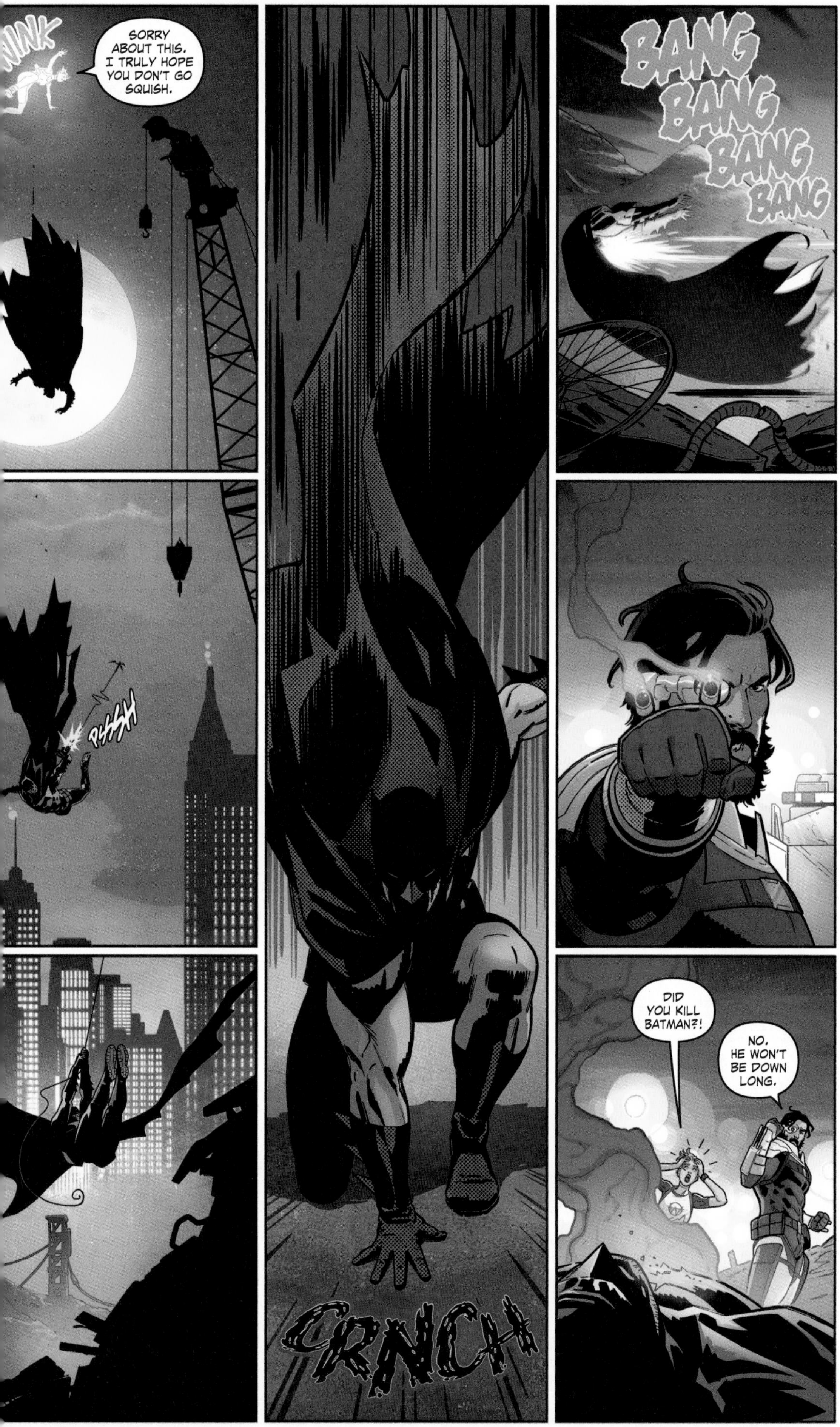

SORRY ABOUT THIS. I TRULY HOPE YOU DON'T GO SQUISH.
BANG
BANG
BANG
BANG
CRNCH
DID YOU KILL BATMAN?!
NO. HE WON'T BE DOWN LONG.

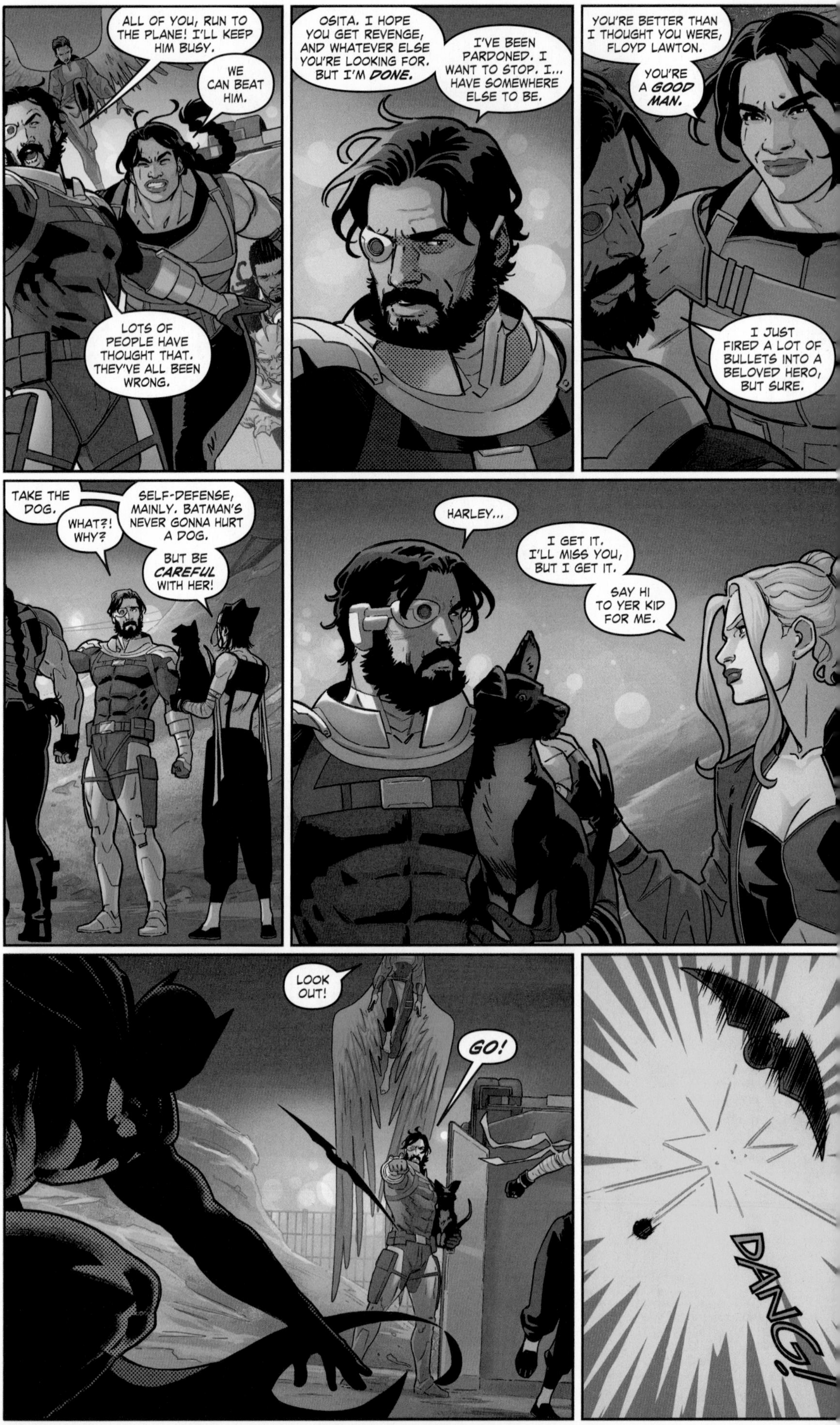
ALL OF YOU, RUN TO THE PLANE! I'LL KEEP HIM BUSY.
WE CAN BEAT HIM.
LOTS OF PEOPLE HAVE THOUGHT THAT. THEY'VE ALL BEEN WRONG.
OSITA. I HOPE YOU GET REVENGE, AND WHATEVER ELSE YOU'RE LOOKING FOR. BUT I'M DONE.
I'VE BEEN PARDONED. I WANT TO STOP. I... HAVE SOMEWHERE ELSE TO BE.
YOU'RE BETTER THAN I THOUGHT YOU WERE, FLOYD LAWTON.
YOU'RE A GOOD MAN.
I JUST FIRED A LOT OF BULLETS INTO A BELOVED HERO, BUT SURE.
TAKE THE DOG.
WHAT?! WHY?
SELF-DEFENSE, MAINLY. BATMAN'S NEVER GONNA HURT A DOG.
BUT BE CAREFUL WITH HER!
HARLEY...
I GET IT. I'LL MISS YOU, BUT I GET IT.
SAY HI TO YER KID FOR ME.
LOOK OUT!
GO!
DANG!

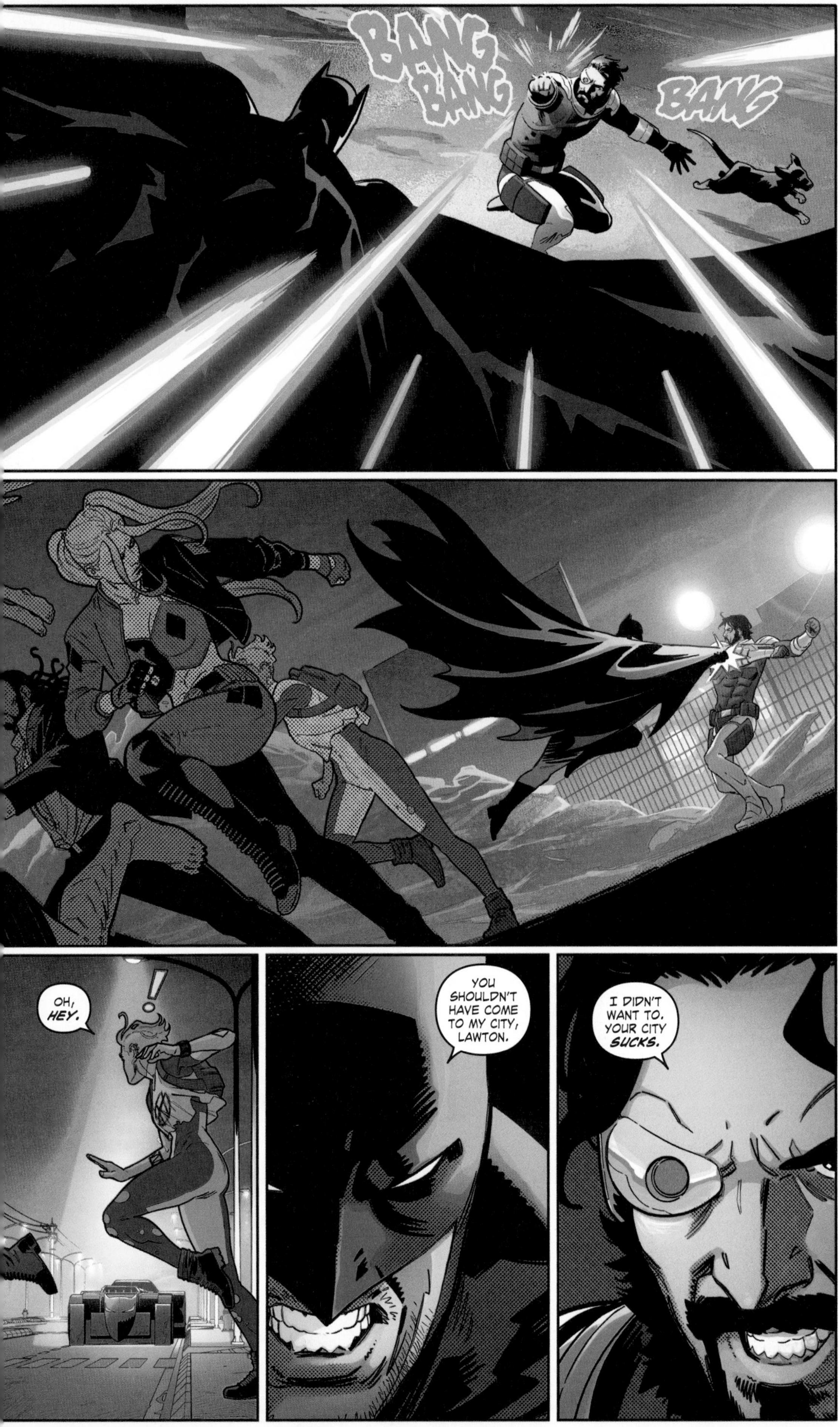
BANG BANG
BANG
OH, HEY.
!
YOU SHOULDN'T HAVE COME TO MY CITY, LAWTON.
I DIDN'T WANT TO. YOUR CITY SUCKS.

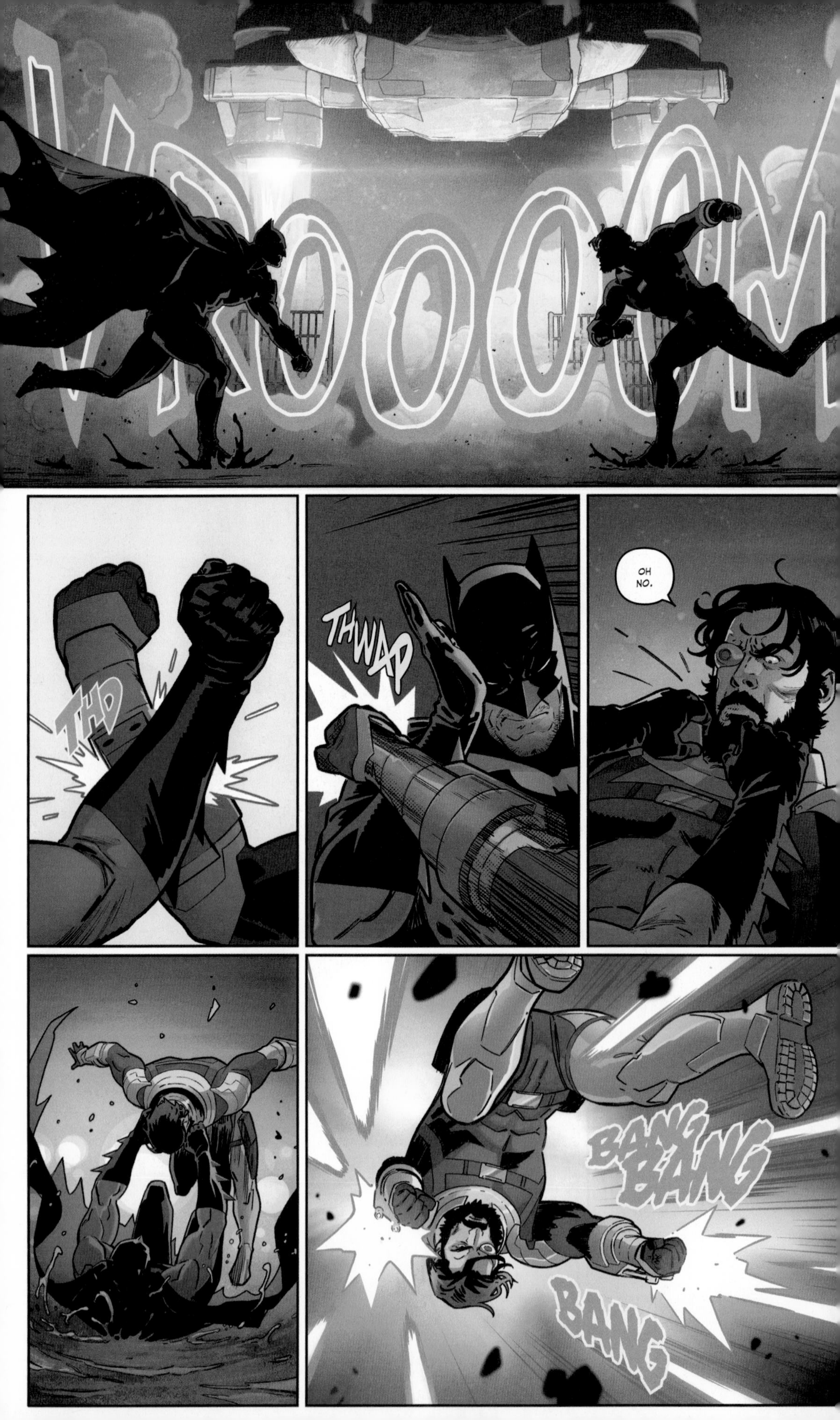
VROOOOOM
THD
THWAP
OH NO.
BANG BANG
BANG

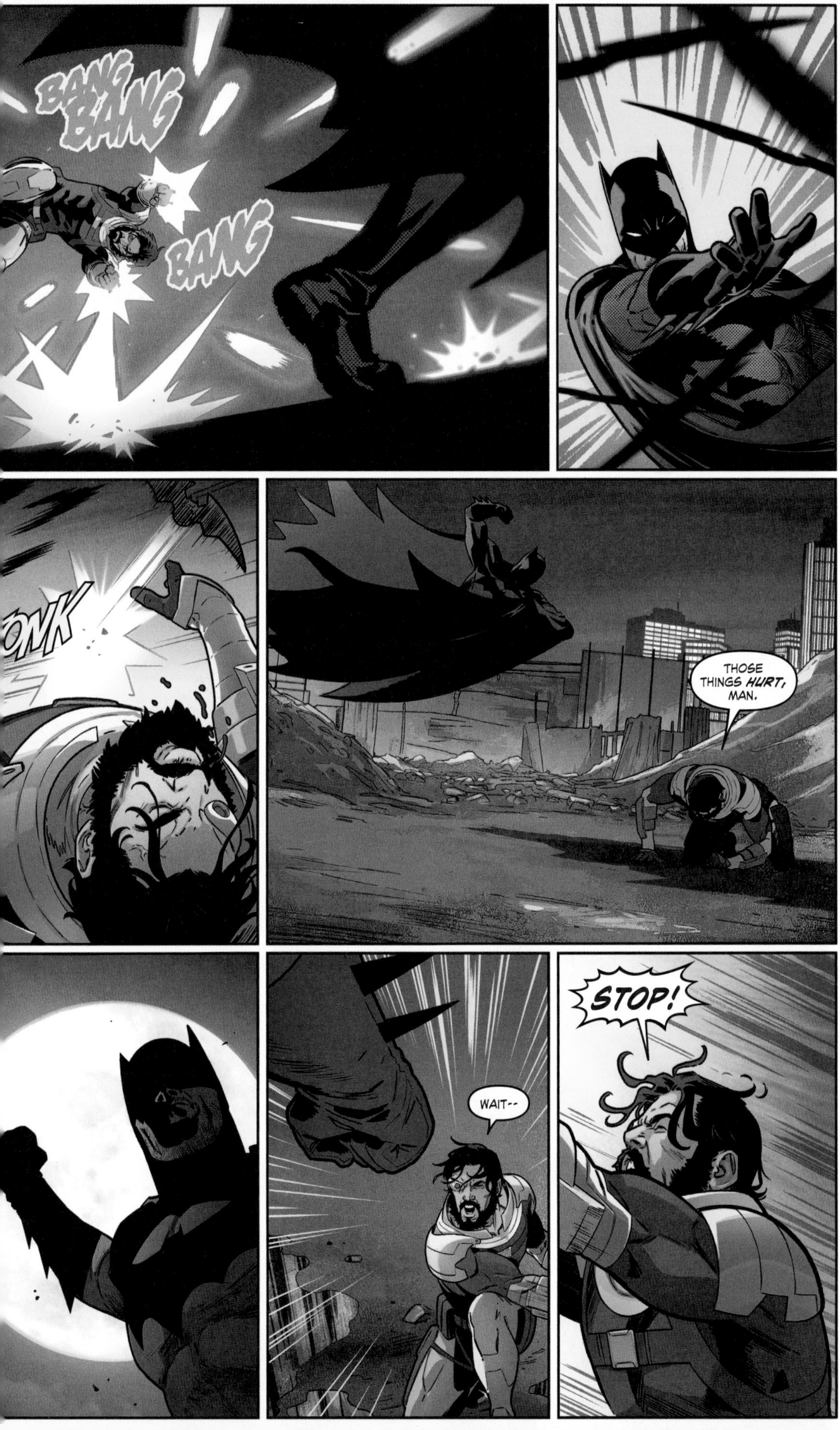
BANG
BANG
BANG
ONK
THOSE THINGS *HURT*, MAN.
WAIT--
STOP!

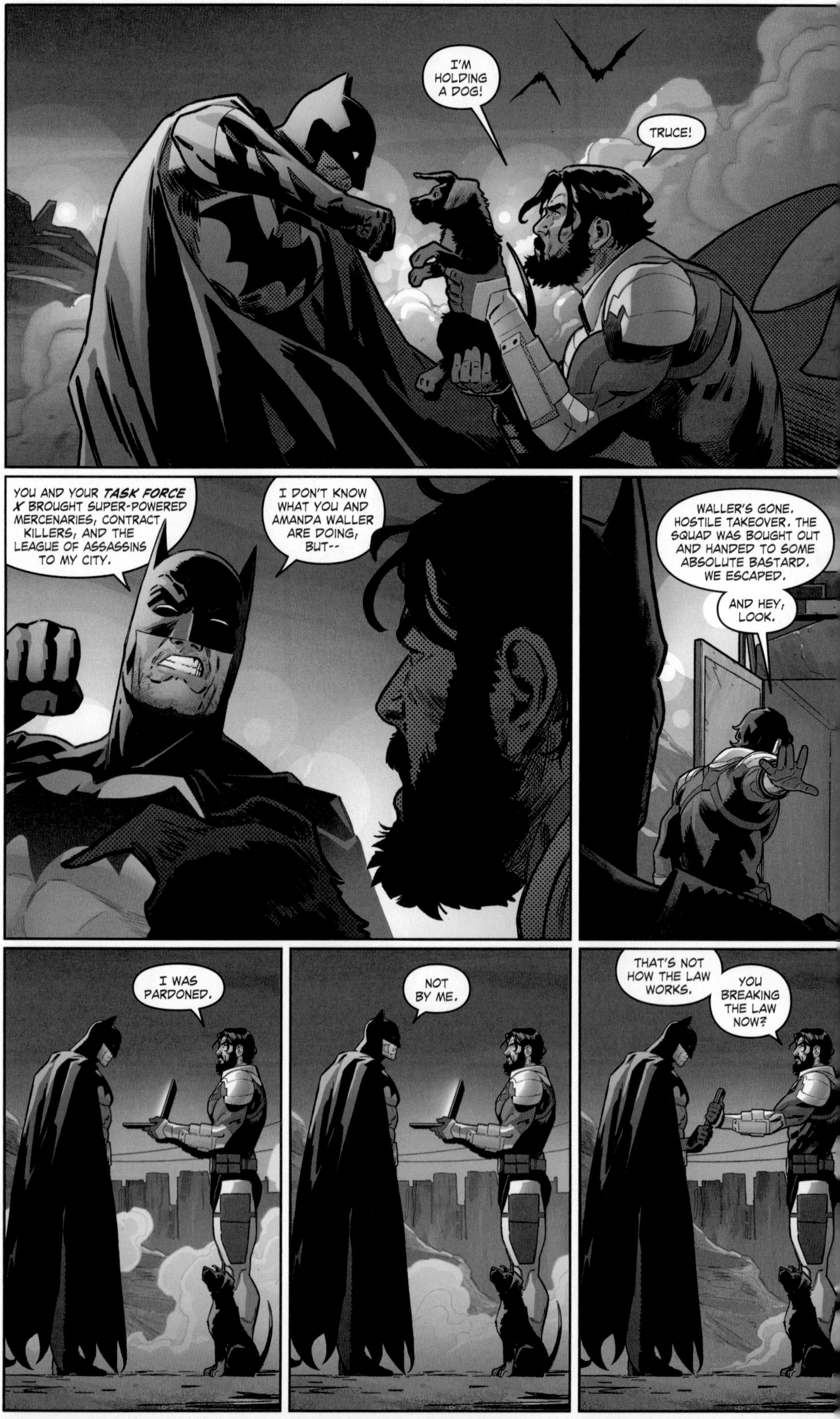
I'M HOLDING A DOG!
TRUCE!
YOU AND YOUR TASK FORCE X BROUGHT SUPER-POWERED MERCENARIES, CONTRACT KILLERS, AND THE LEAGUE OF ASSASSINS TO MY CITY.
I DON'T KNOW WHAT YOU AND AMANDA WALLER ARE DOING, BUT--
WALLER'S GONE. HOSTILE TAKEOVER. THE SQUAD WAS BOUGHT OUT AND HANDED TO SOME ABSOLUTE BASTARD. WE ESCAPED.
AND HEY, LOOK.
I WAS PARDONED.
NOT BY ME.
THAT'S NOT HOW THE LAW WORKS.
YOU BREAKING THE LAW NOW?

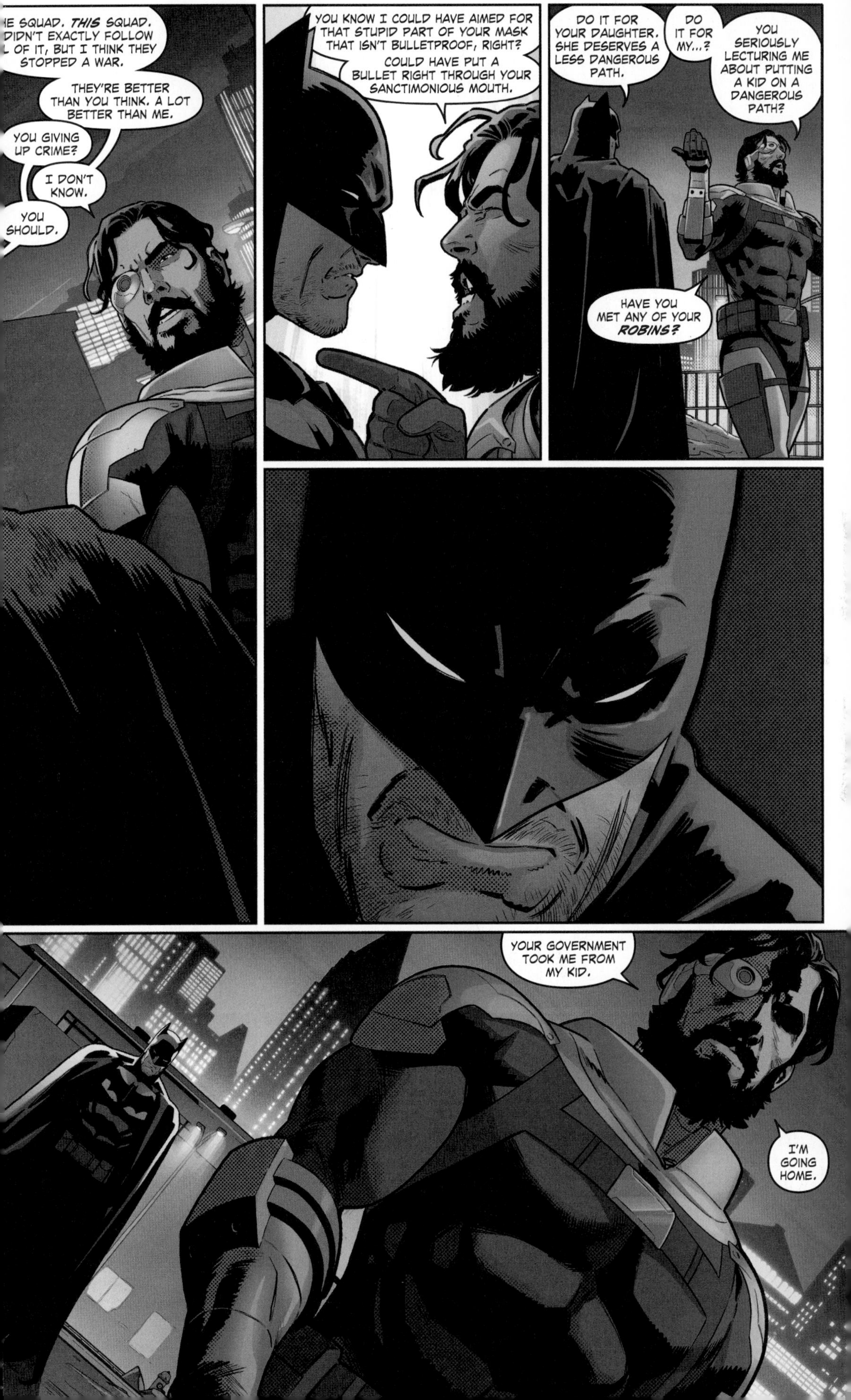

HE SQUAD. THIS SQUAD. DIDN'T EXACTLY FOLLOW L OF IT, BUT I THINK THEY STOPPED A WAR.
THEY'RE BETTER THAN YOU THINK. A LOT BETTER THAN ME.
YOU GIVING UP CRIME?
I DON'T KNOW.
YOU SHOULD.
YOU KNOW I COULD HAVE AIMED FOR THAT STUPID PART OF YOUR MASK THAT ISN'T BULLETPROOF, RIGHT?
COULD HAVE PUT A BULLET RIGHT THROUGH YOUR SANCTIMONIOUS MOUTH.
DO IT FOR YOUR DAUGHTER. SHE DESERVES A LESS DANGEROUS PATH.
DO IT FOR MY...?
YOU SERIOUSLY LECTURING ME ABOUT PUTTING A KID ON A DANGEROUS PATH?
HAVE YOU MET ANY OF YOUR ROBINS?
YOUR GOVERNMENT TOOK ME FROM MY KID.
I'M GOING HOME.

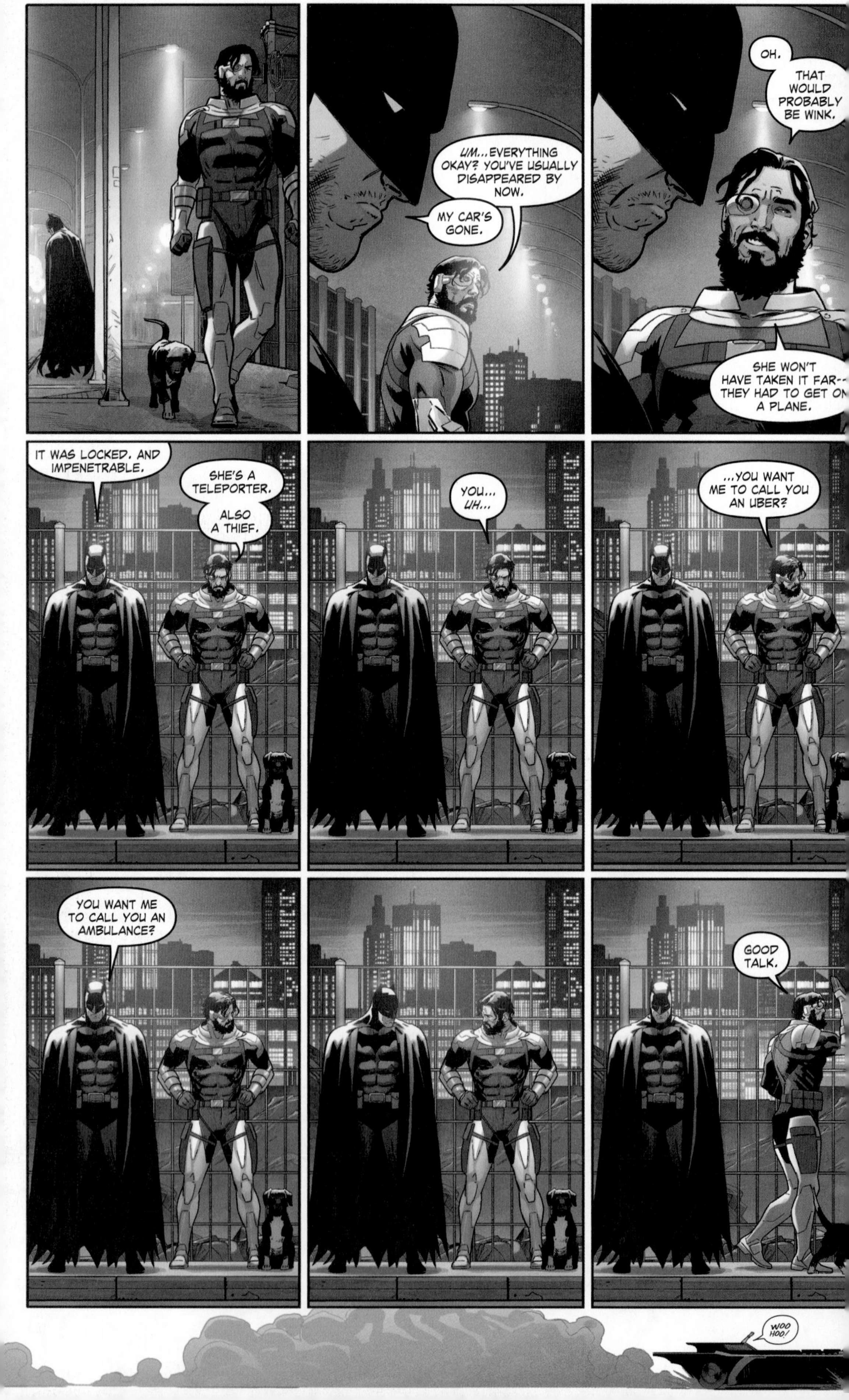
UM...EVERYTHING OKAY? YOU'VE USUALLY DISAPPEARED BY NOW.
MY CAR'S GONE.
OH.
THAT WOULD PROBABLY BE WINK.
SHE WON'T HAVE TAKEN IT FAR-- THEY HAD TO GET ON A PLANE.
IT WAS LOCKED. AND IMPENETRABLE.
SHE'S A TELEPORTER.
ALSO A THIEF.
YOU... UH...
...YOU WANT ME TO CALL YOU AN UBER?
YOU WANT ME TO CALL YOU AN AMBULANCE?
GOOD TALK.
WOO HOO!

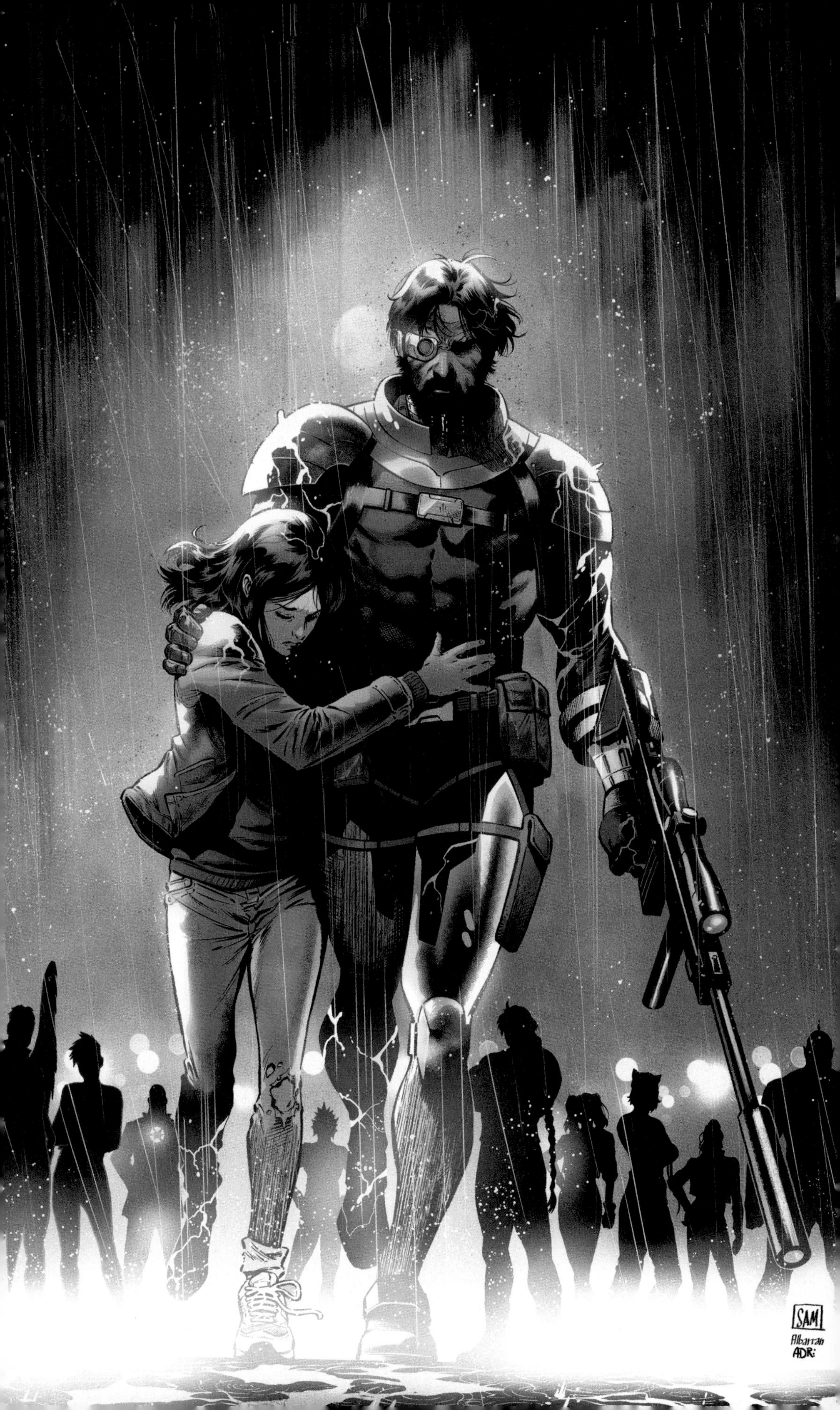
SAM
Albarran
ADR:

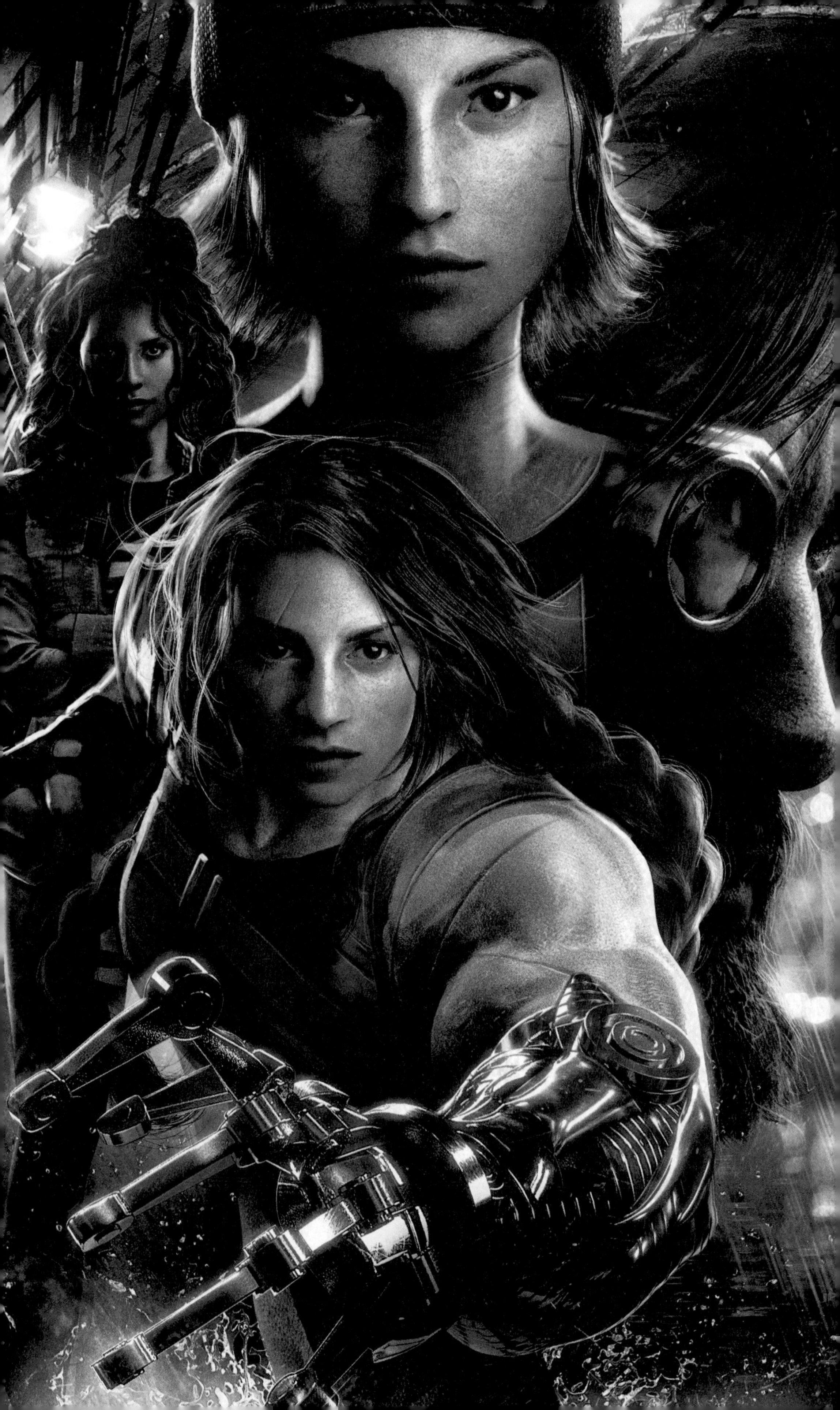

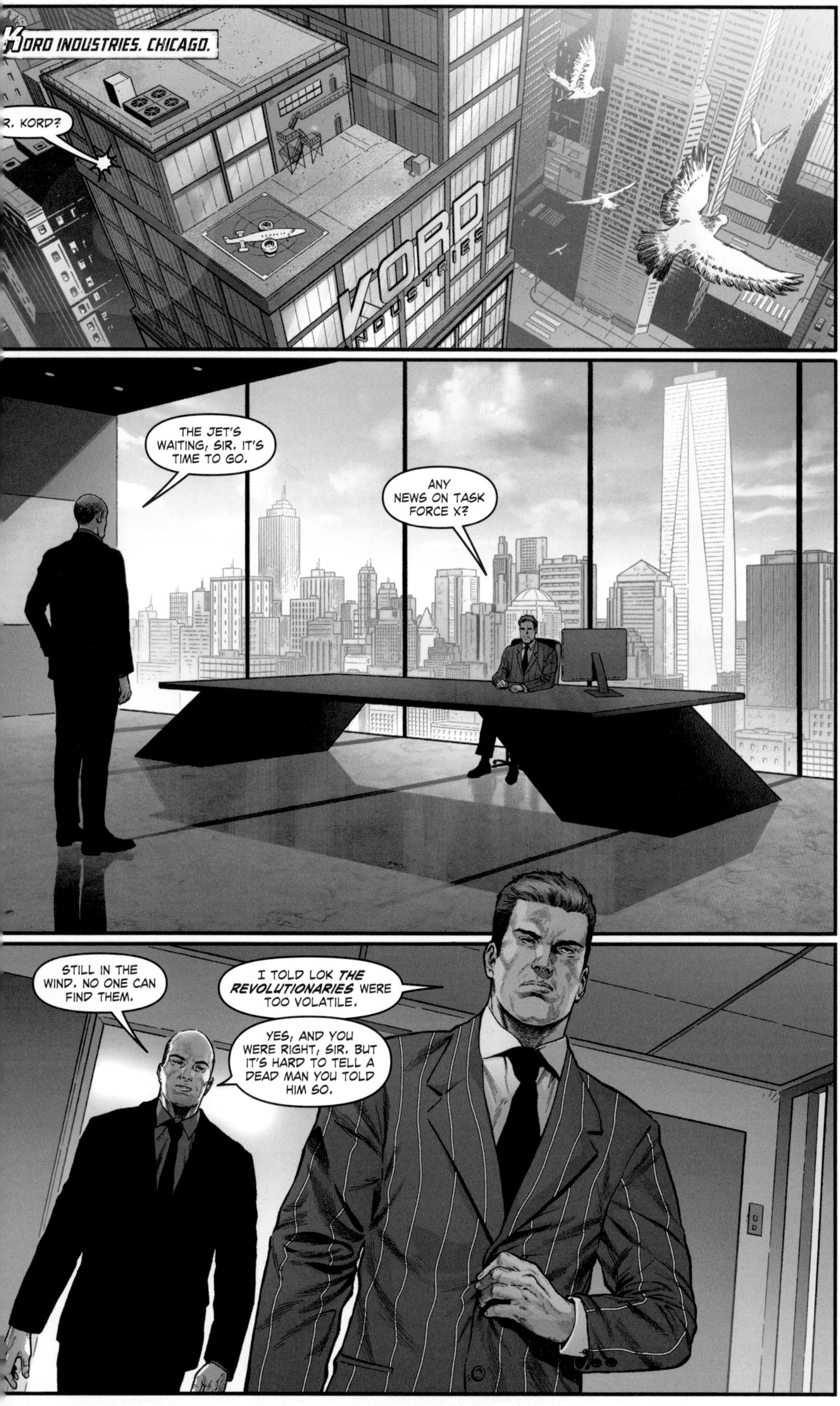
KORD INDUSTRIES. CHICAGO.
R. KORD?
THE JET'S WAITING, SIR. IT'S TIME TO GO.
ANY NEWS ON TASK FORCE X?
STILL IN THE WIND. NO ONE CAN FIND THEM.
I TOLD LOK *THE REVOLUTIONARIES* WERE TOO VOLATILE.
YES, AND YOU WERE RIGHT, SIR. BUT IT'S HARD TO TELL A DEAD MAN YOU TOLD HIM SO.

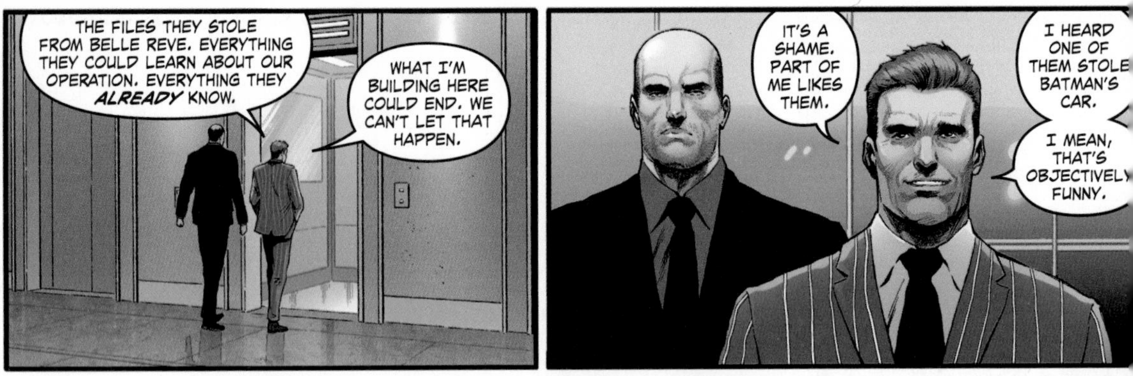
THE FILES THEY STOLE FROM BELLE REVE. EVERYTHING THEY COULD LEARN ABOUT OUR OPERATION. EVERYTHING THEY *ALREADY* KNOW.
WHAT I'M BUILDING HERE COULD END. WE CAN'T LET THAT HAPPEN.
IT'S A SHAME. PART OF ME LIKES THEM.
I HEARD ONE OF THEM STOLE BATMAN'S CAR.
I MEAN, THAT'S OBJECTIVELY FUNNY.

written by TOM TAYLOR pencils by DANIEL SAMPERE inks by JUAN ALBARRA
color by ADRIANO LUCAS letters by WES ABBOTT

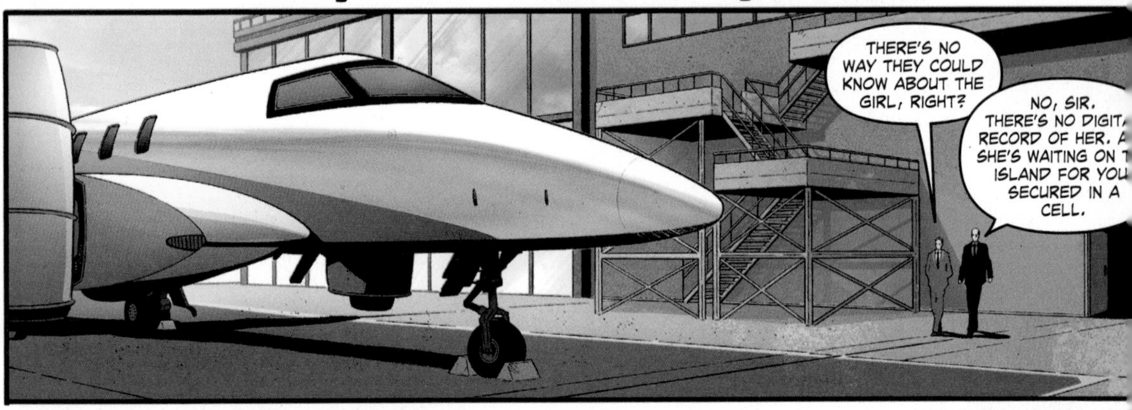
THERE'S NO WAY THEY COULD KNOW ABOUT THE GIRL, RIGHT?
NO, SIR. THERE'S NO DIGIT RECORD OF HER. A SHE'S WAITING ON T ISLAND FOR YOU SECURED IN A CELL.

cover by SAMPERE, ALBARRAN, and LUCAS variant cover by JEREMY ROBERT
editor ANDREA SHEA group editor ALEX R. CARR

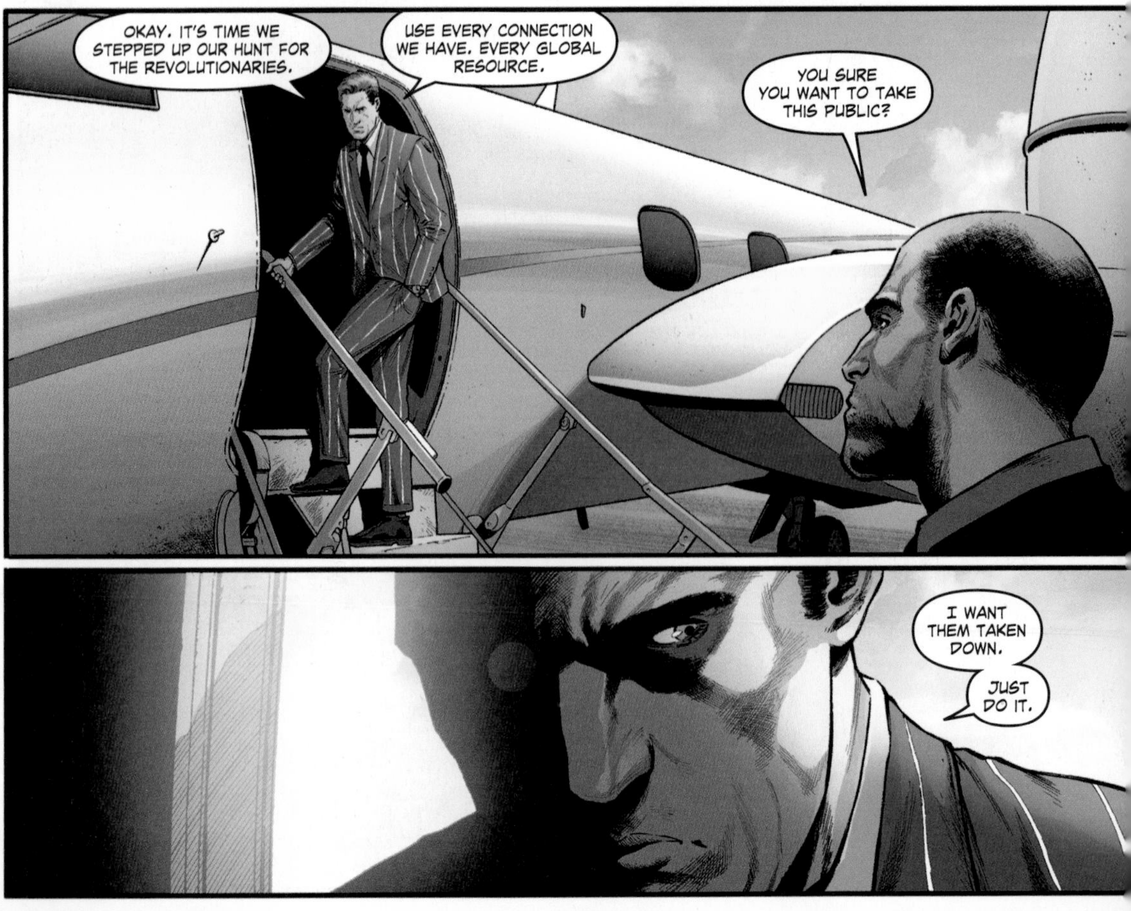
OKAY. IT'S TIME WE STEPPED UP OUR HUNT FOR THE REVOLUTIONARIES.
USE EVERY CONNECTION WE HAVE. EVERY GLOBAL RESOURCE.
YOU SURE YOU WANT TO TAKE THIS PUBLIC?
I WANT THEM TAKEN DOWN.
JUST DO IT.

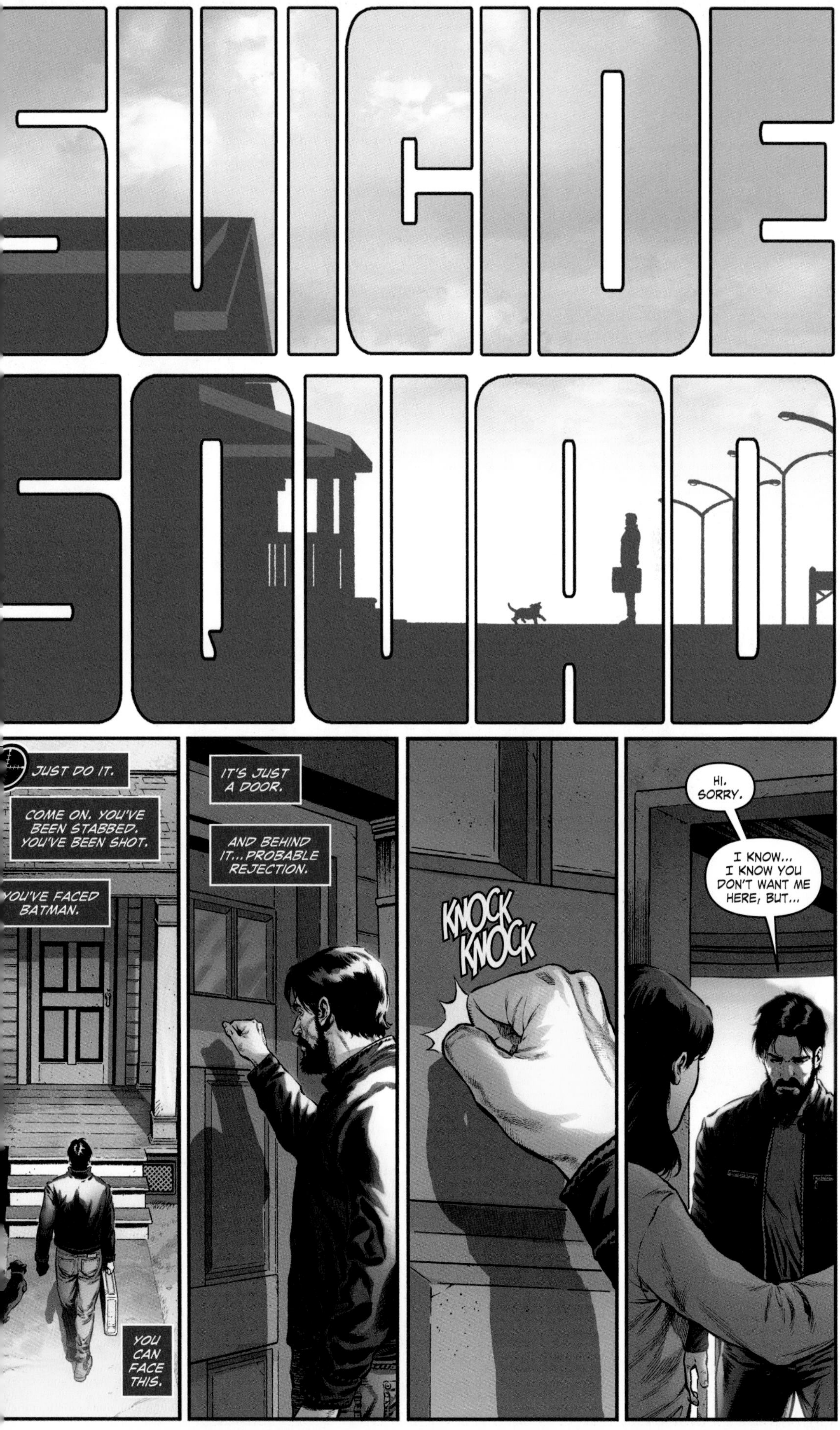
SUICIDE SQUAD
JUST DO IT.
COME ON. YOU'VE BEEN STABBED. YOU'VE BEEN SHOT.
YOU'VE FACED BATMAN.
YOU CAN FACE THIS.
IT'S JUST A DOOR.
AND BEHIND IT...PROBABLE REJECTION.
KNOCK KNOCK
HI. SORRY.
I KNOW... I KNOW YOU DON'T WANT ME HERE, BUT...

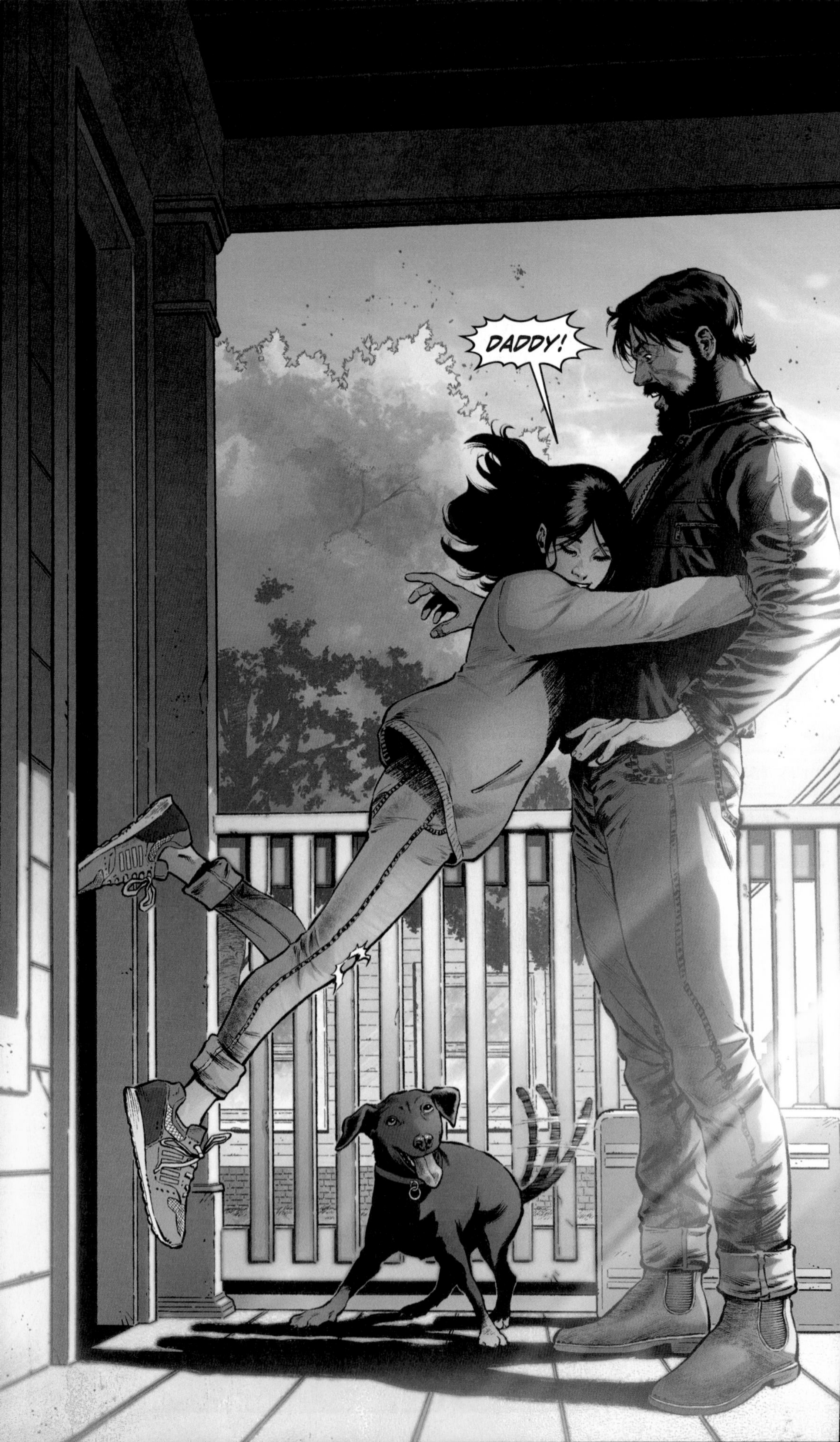
DADDY!

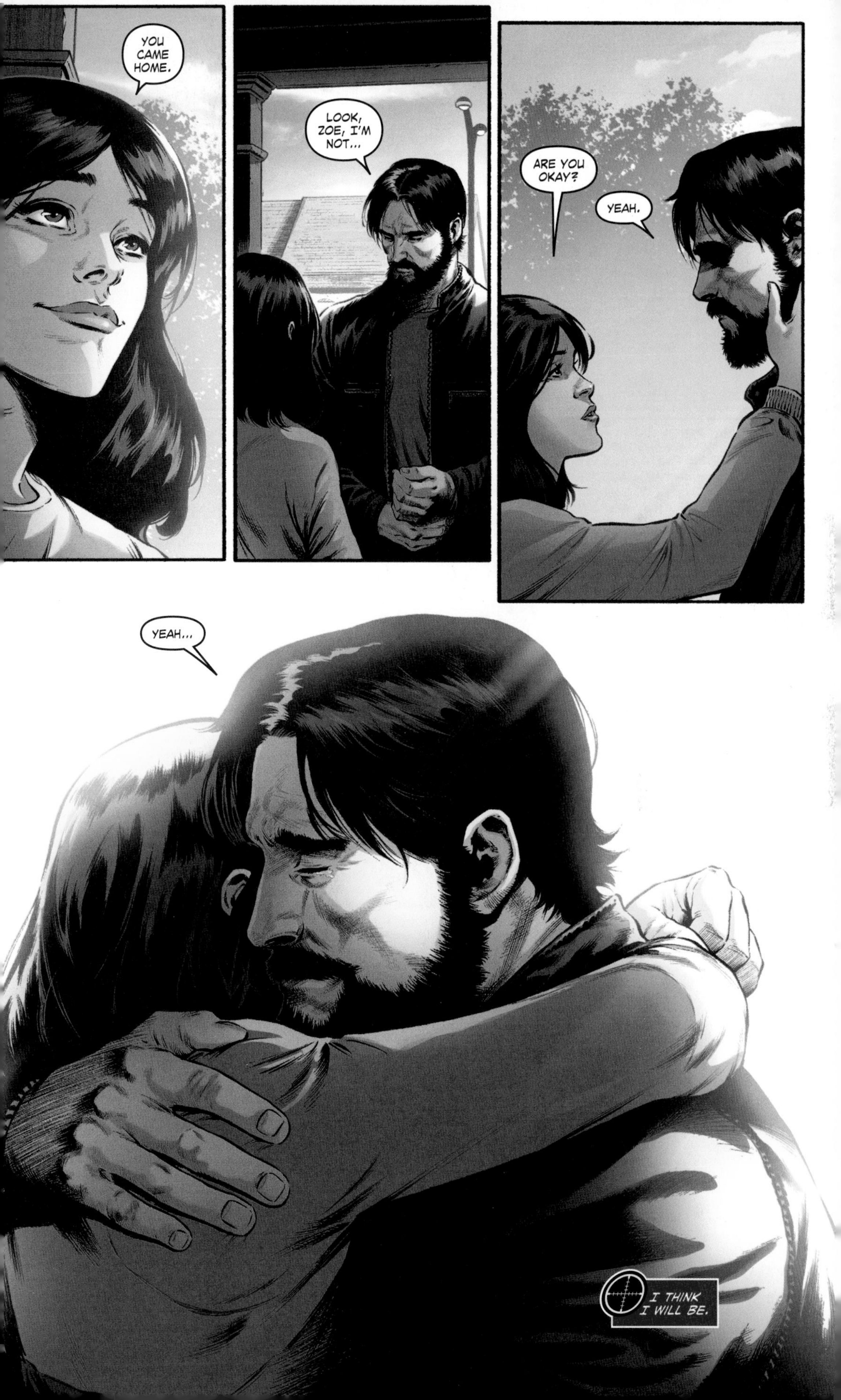
YOU CAME HOME.
LOOK, ZOE, I'M NOT...
ARE YOU OKAY?
YEAH.
YEAH...
I THINK I WILL BE.

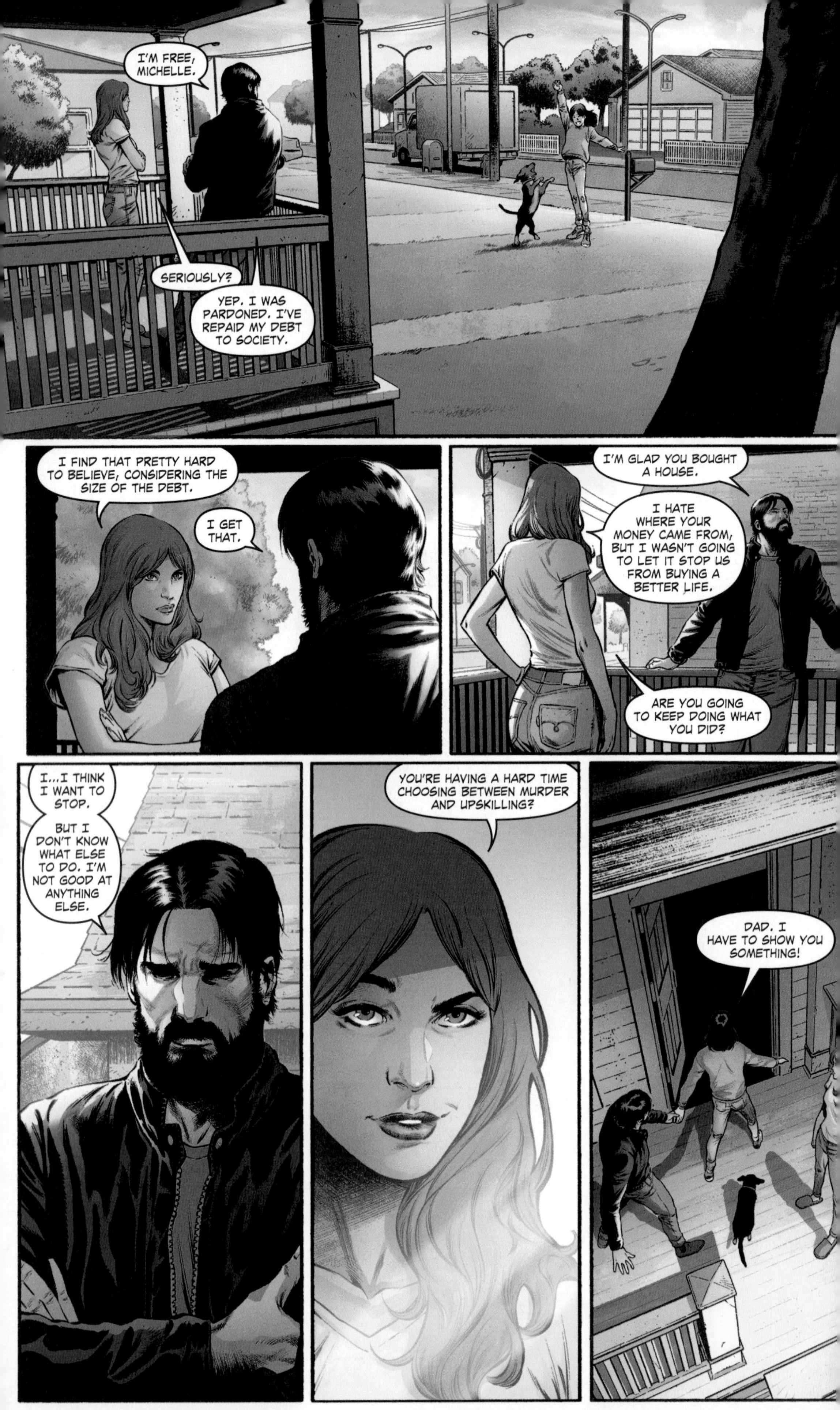
I'M FREE, MICHELLE.
SERIOUSLY?
YEP. I WAS PARDONED. I'VE REPAID MY DEBT TO SOCIETY.
I FIND THAT PRETTY HARD TO BELIEVE, CONSIDERING THE SIZE OF THE DEBT.
I GET THAT.
I'M GLAD YOU BOUGHT A HOUSE.
I HATE WHERE YOUR MONEY CAME FROM, BUT I WASN'T GOING TO LET IT STOP US FROM BUYING A BETTER LIFE.
ARE YOU GOING TO KEEP DOING WHAT YOU DID?
I...I THINK I WANT TO STOP.
BUT I DON'T KNOW WHAT ELSE TO DO. I'M NOT GOOD AT ANYTHING ELSE.
YOU'RE HAVING A HARD TIME CHOOSING BETWEEN MURDER AND UPSKILLING?
DAD. I HAVE TO SHOW YOU SOMETHING!

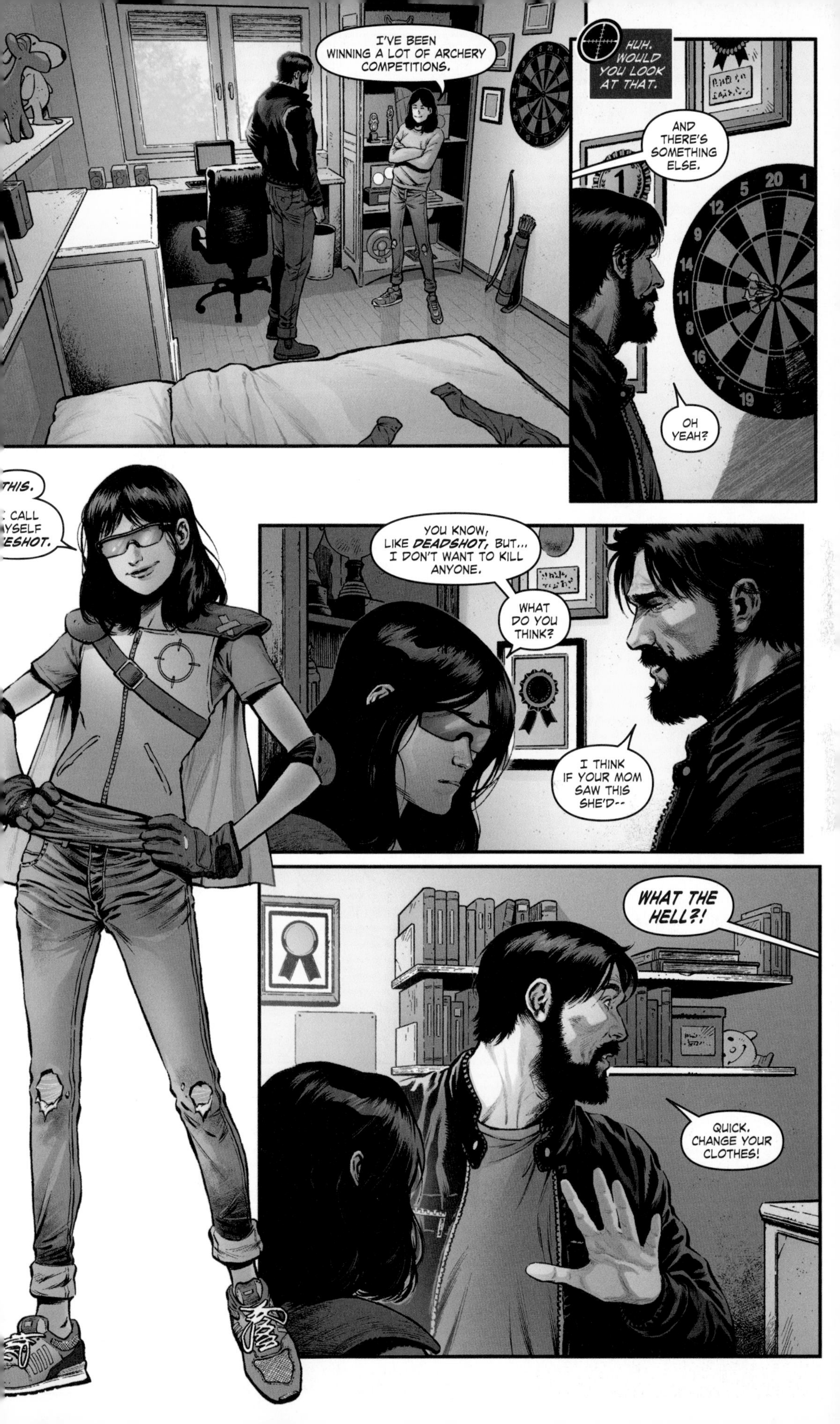
I'VE BEEN WINNING A LOT OF ARCHERY COMPETITIONS.
HUH. WOULD YOU LOOK AT THAT.
AND THERE'S SOMETHING ELSE.
OH YEAH?
THIS.
C CALL YSELF ESHOT.
YOU KNOW, LIKE *DEADSHOT,* BUT... I DON'T WANT TO KILL ANYONE.
WHAT DO YOU THINK?
I THINK IF YOUR MOM SAW THIS SHE'D--
WHAT THE HELL?!
QUICK. CHANGE YOUR CLOTHES!

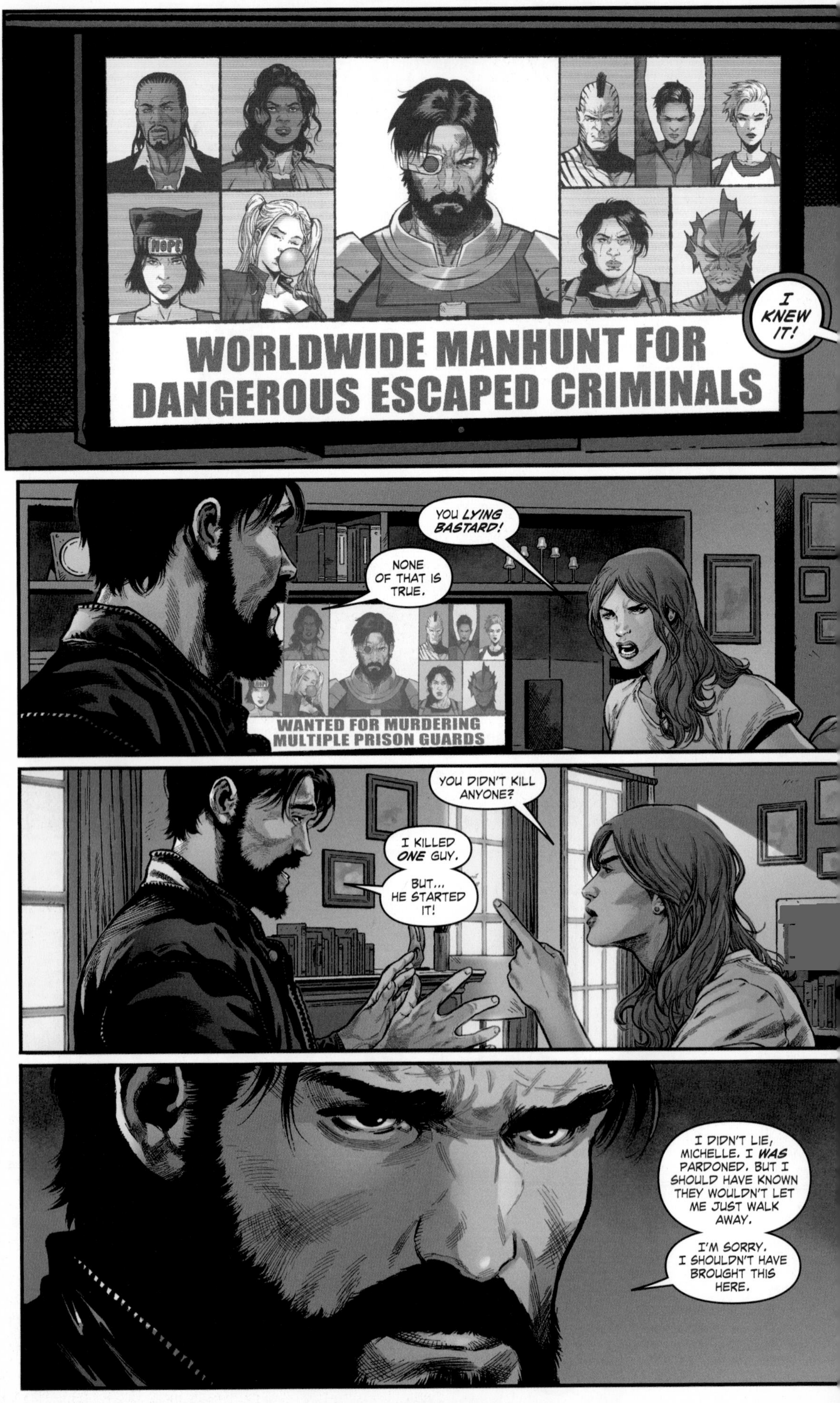
WORLDWIDE MANHUNT FOR DANGEROUS ESCAPED CRIMINALS
I KNEW IT!
YOU LYING BASTARD!
NONE OF THAT IS TRUE.
WANTED FOR MURDERING MULTIPLE PRISON GUARDS
YOU DIDN'T KILL ANYONE?
I KILLED ONE GUY.
BUT... HE STARTED IT!
I DIDN'T LIE, MICHELLE. I WAS PARDONED. BUT I SHOULD HAVE KNOWN THEY WOULDN'T LET ME JUST WALK AWAY.
I'M SORRY. I SHOULDN'T HAVE BROUGHT THIS HERE.

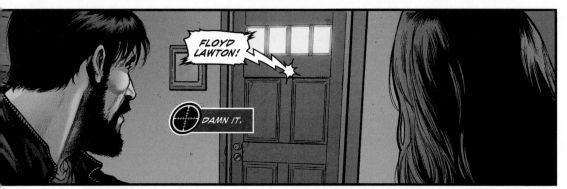

FLOYD LAWTON!

DAMN IT.

THIS IS THE FBI!

COME OUT WITH YOUR HANDS WHERE WE CAN SEE THEM!

DAD?

ZOE, WHAT THE HELL ARE YOU *WEARING*?!

YOU HAVE TO THE COUNT OF FIVE.

ONE... TWO...

DAD? WHAT ARE YOU GOING TO DO?

THREE... FOUR...

DAMN IT.

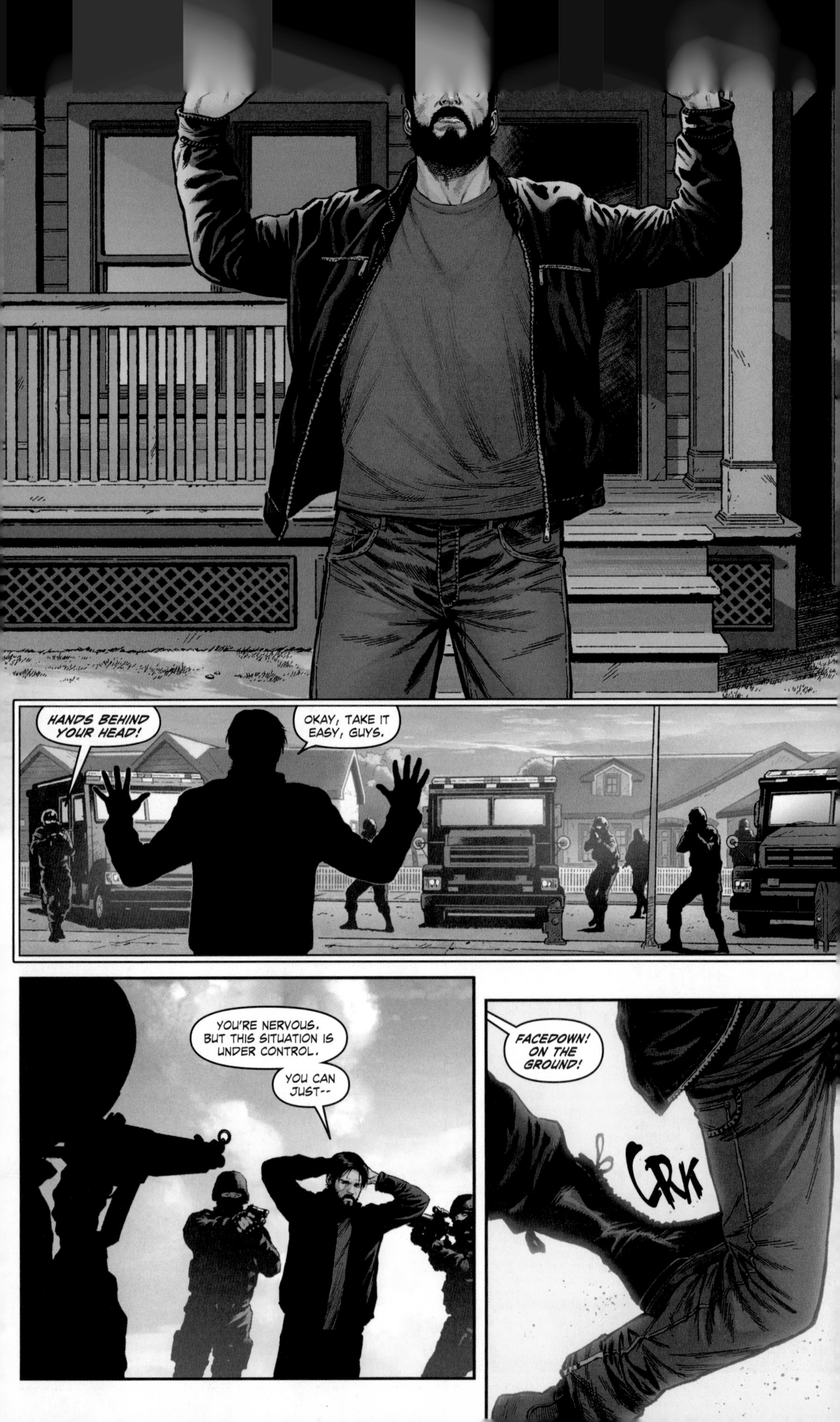
HANDS BEHIND YOUR HEAD!
OKAY, TAKE IT EASY, GUYS.
YOU'RE NERVOUS. BUT THIS SITUATION IS UNDER CONTROL.
YOU CAN JUST--
FACEDOWN! ON THE GROUND!
CRK

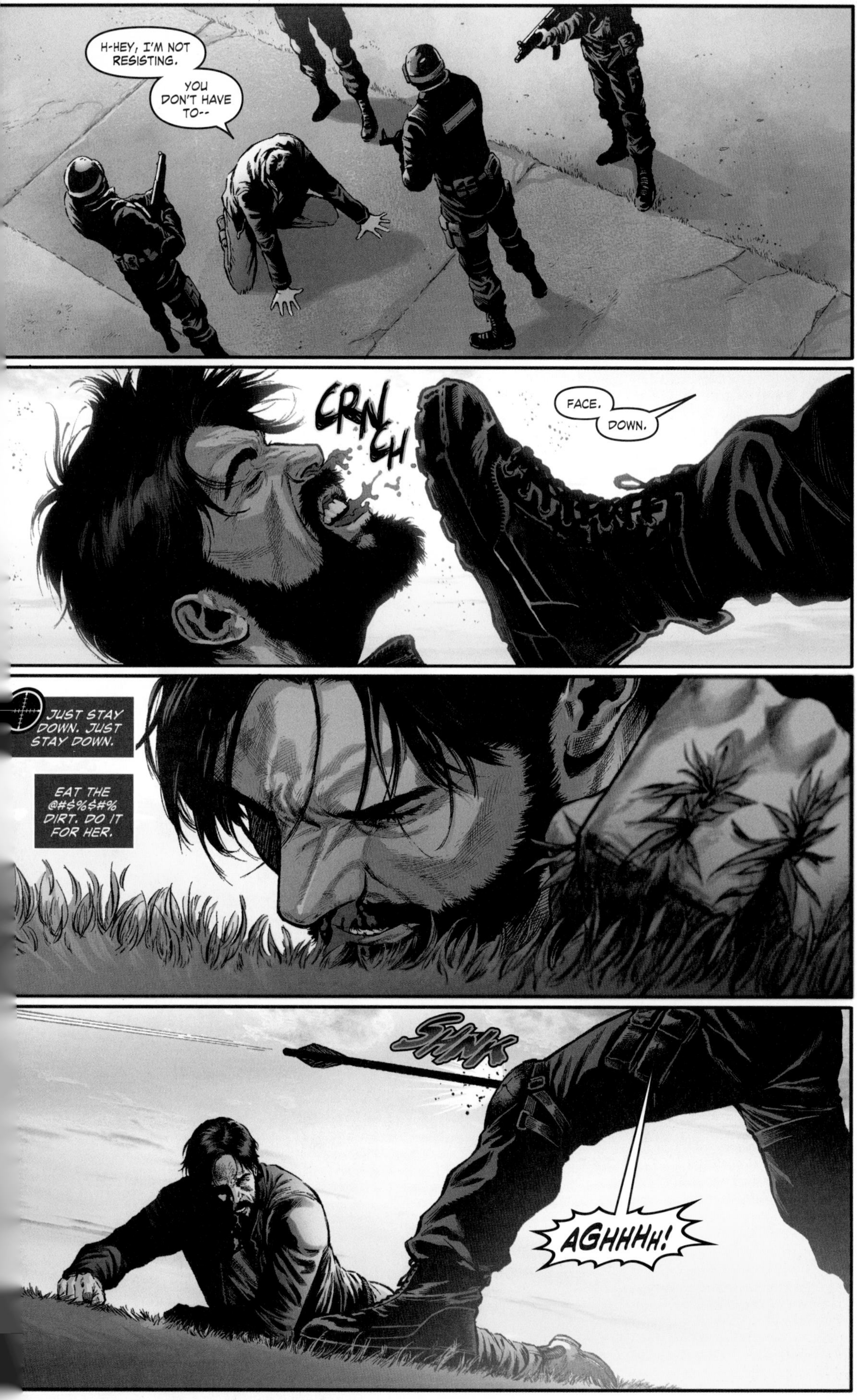
H-HEY, I'M NOT RESISTING.
YOU DON'T HAVE TO--
CRNCH
FACE.
DOWN.
JUST STAY DOWN. JUST STAY DOWN.
EAT THE @#$%$#% DIRT. DO IT FOR HER.
SHNK
AGHHHH!

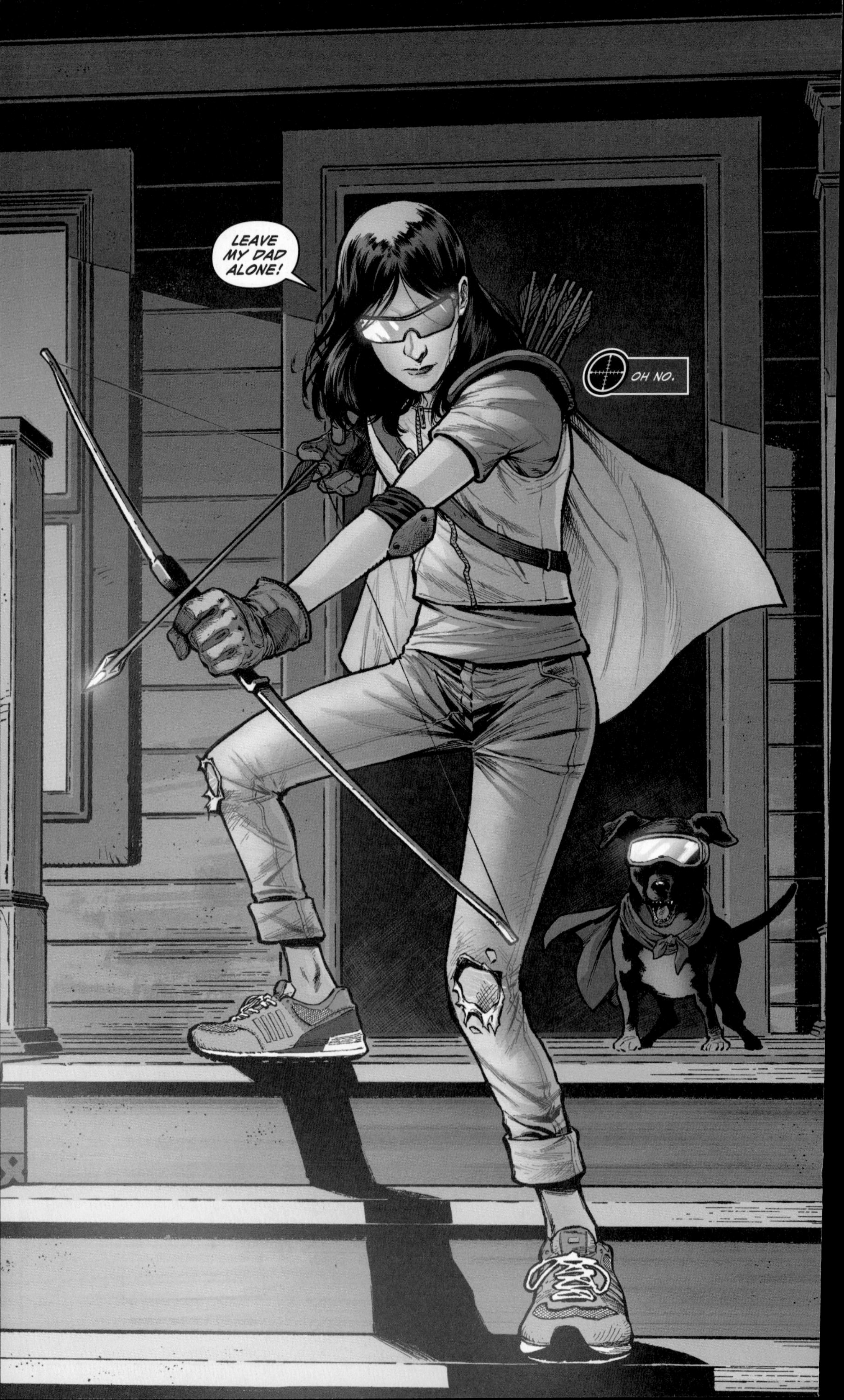
LEAVE MY DAD ALONE!
OH NO.

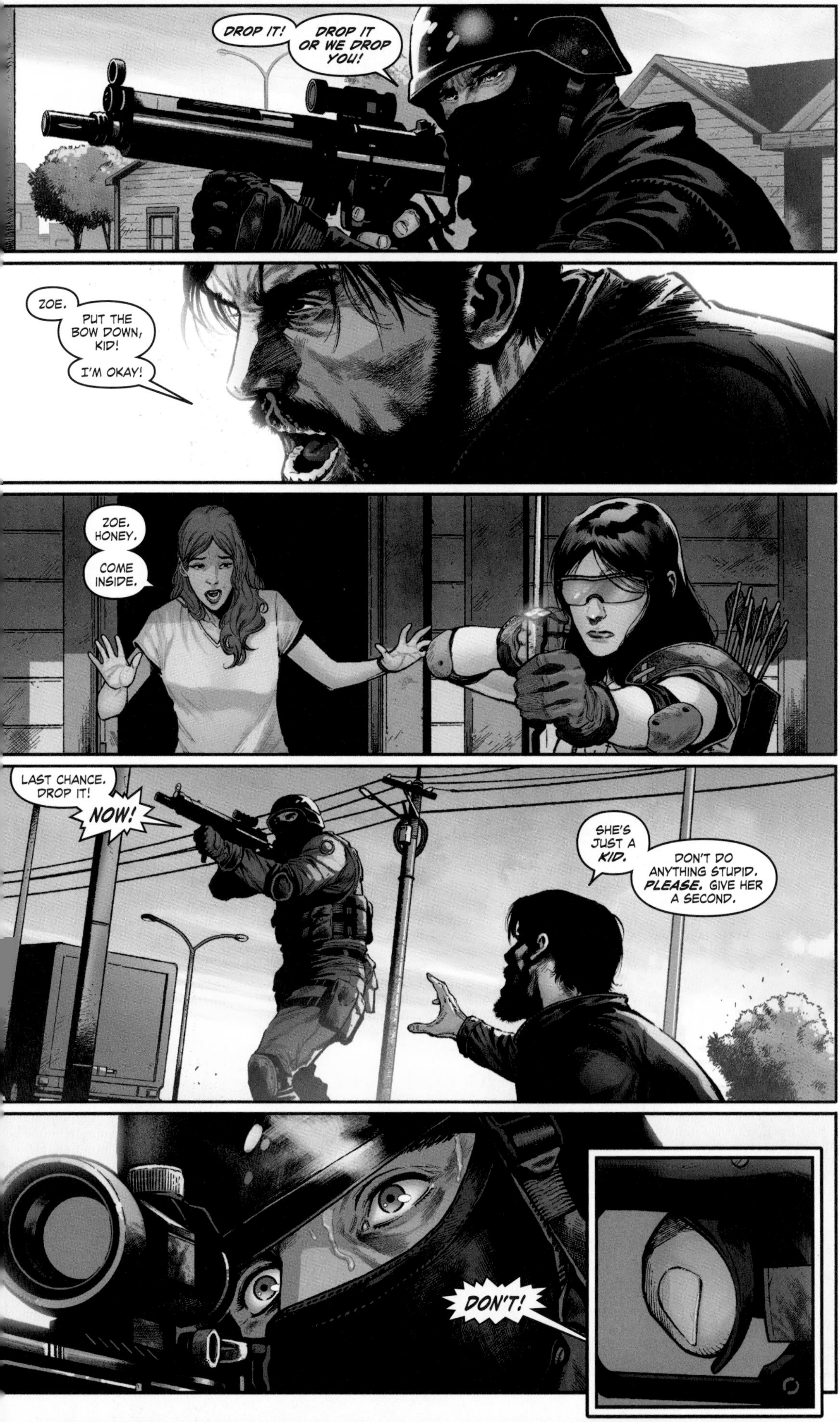
DROP IT!
DROP IT OR WE DROP YOU!
ZOE.
PUT THE BOW DOWN, KID!
I'M OKAY!
ZOE. HONEY.
COME INSIDE.
LAST CHANCE. DROP IT!
NOW!
SHE'S JUST A KID.
DON'T DO ANYTHING STUPID. PLEASE. GIVE HER A SECOND.
DON'T!

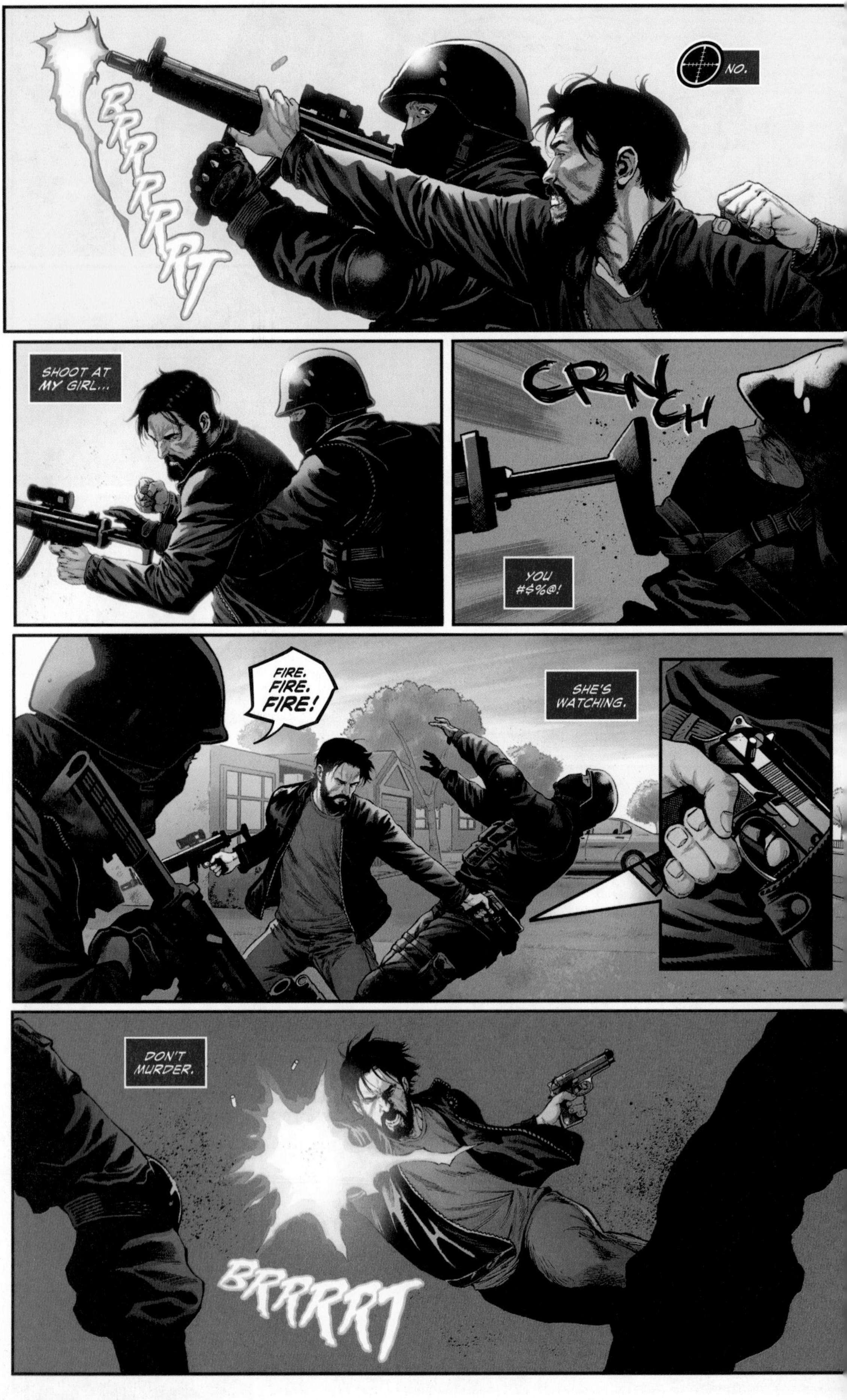
BRRRRRRT
NO.
SHOOT AT MY GIRL...
CRNCH
YOU #$%@!
FIRE. FIRE. FIRE!
SHE'S WATCHING.
DON'T MURDER.
BRRRRRT

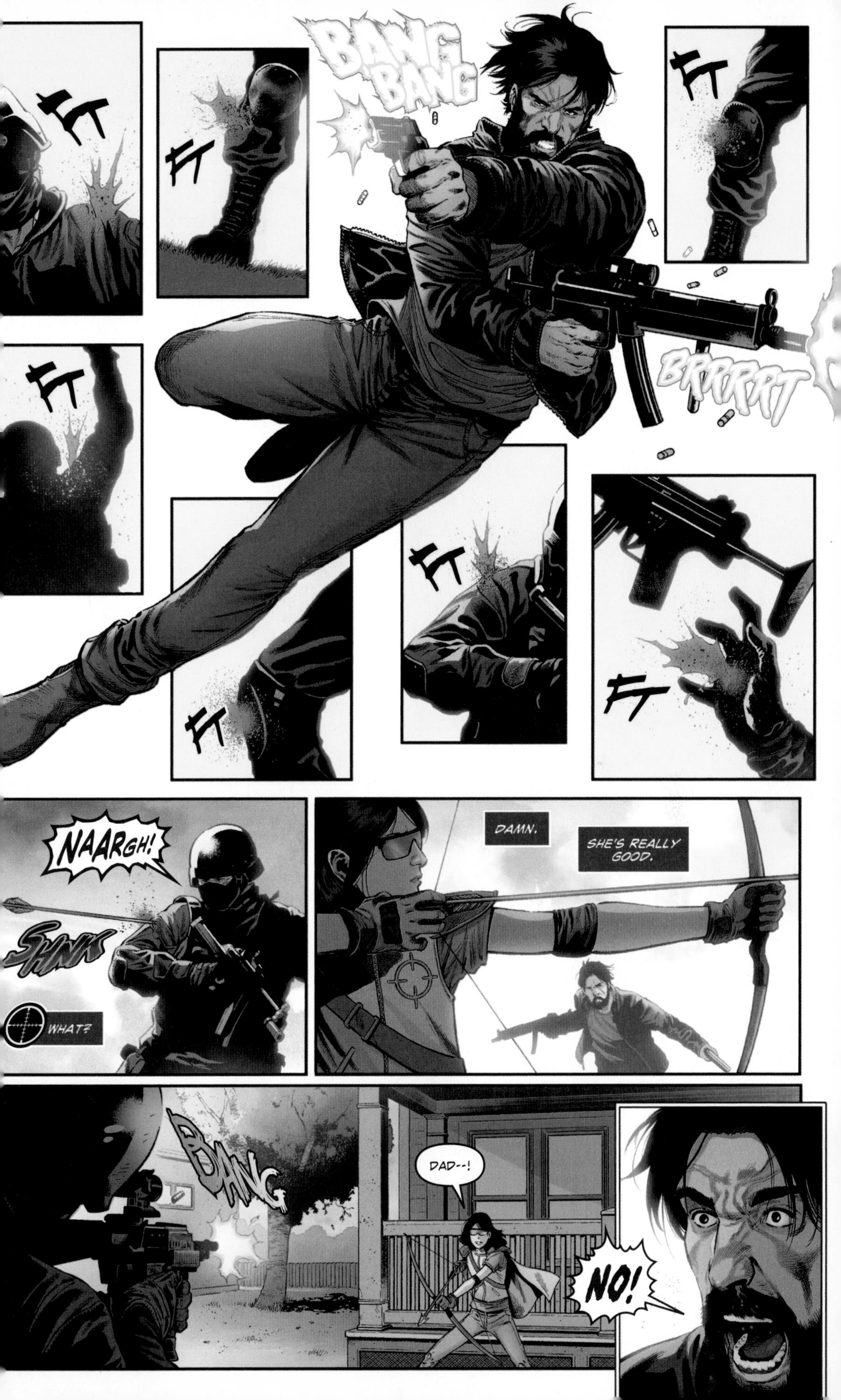
FT
FT
BANG
BANG
FT
FT
BRRRRRT
FT
FT
FT
FT
NAARGH!
SHUNK
WHAT?
DAMN.
SHE'S REALLY GOOD.
BLANG
DAD--!
NO!

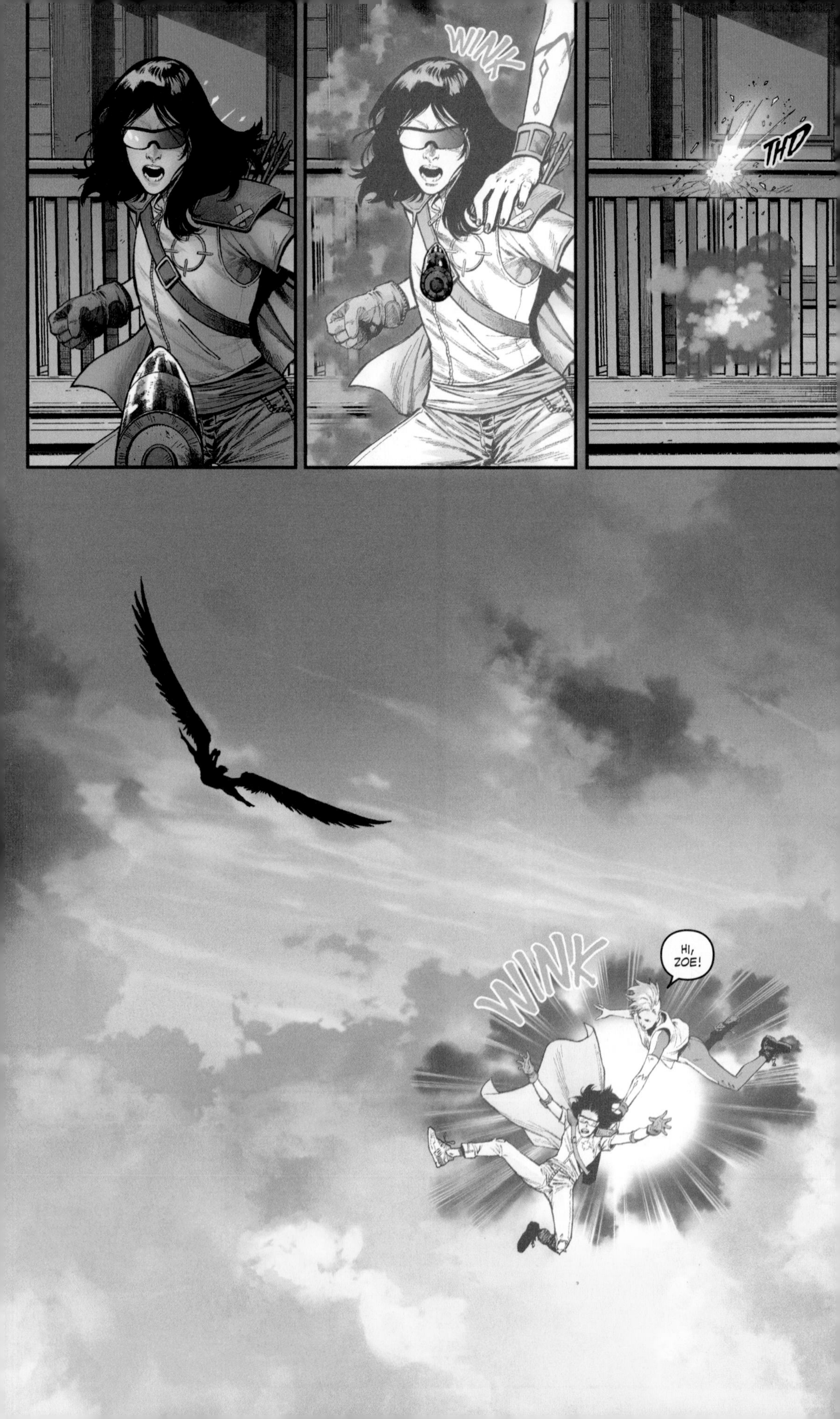
WINK
THD
WINK
HI, ZOE!

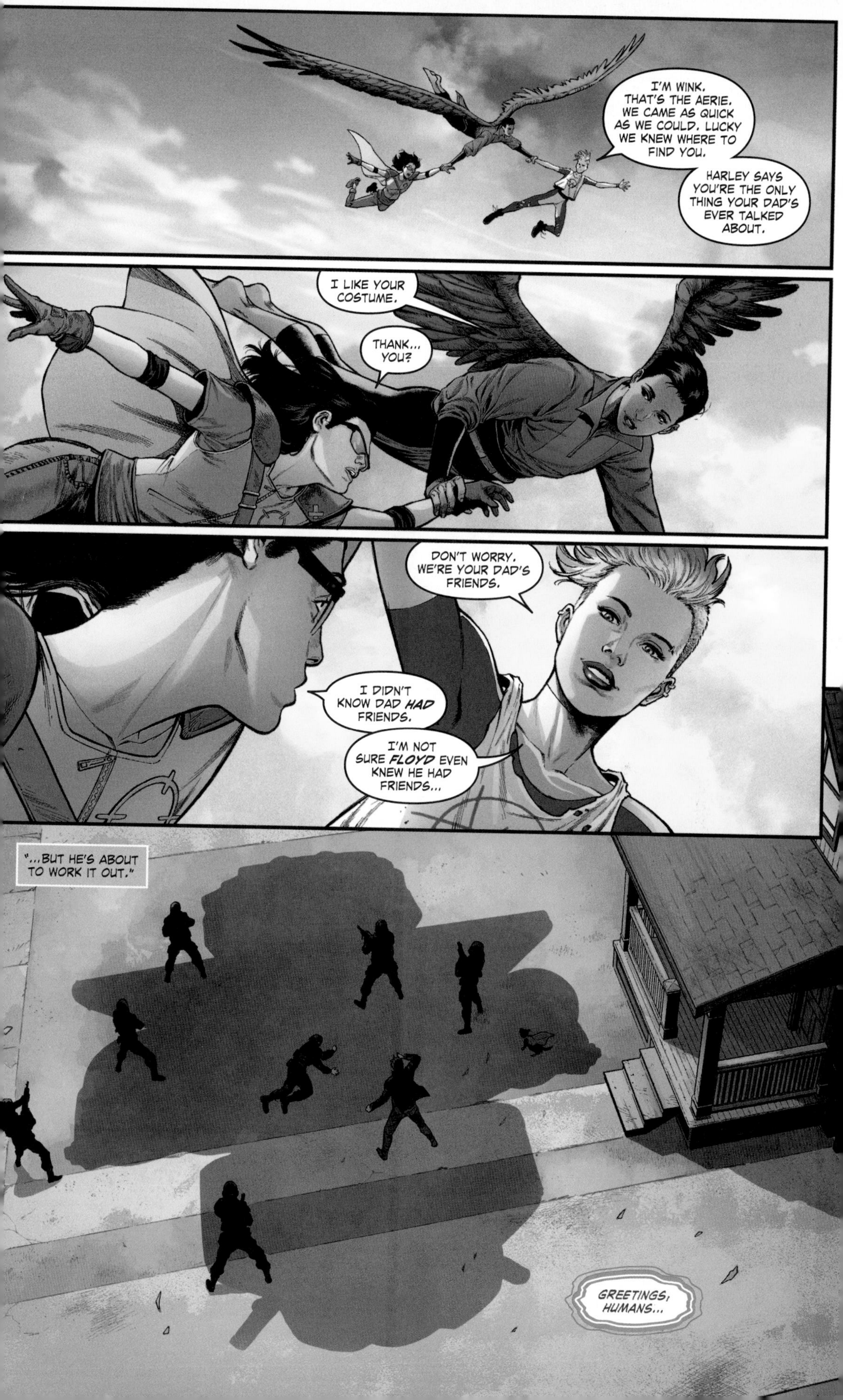
I'M WINK. THAT'S THE AERIE. WE CAME AS QUICK AS WE COULD. LUCKY WE KNEW WHERE TO FIND YOU.
HARLEY SAYS YOU'RE THE ONLY THING YOUR DAD'S EVER TALKED ABOUT.
I LIKE YOUR COSTUME.
THANK... YOU?
DON'T WORRY. WE'RE YOUR DAD'S FRIENDS.
I DIDN'T KNOW DAD HAD FRIENDS.
I'M NOT SURE FLOYD EVEN KNEW HE HAD FRIENDS...
"...BUT HE'S ABOUT TO WORK IT OUT."
GREETINGS, HUMANS...

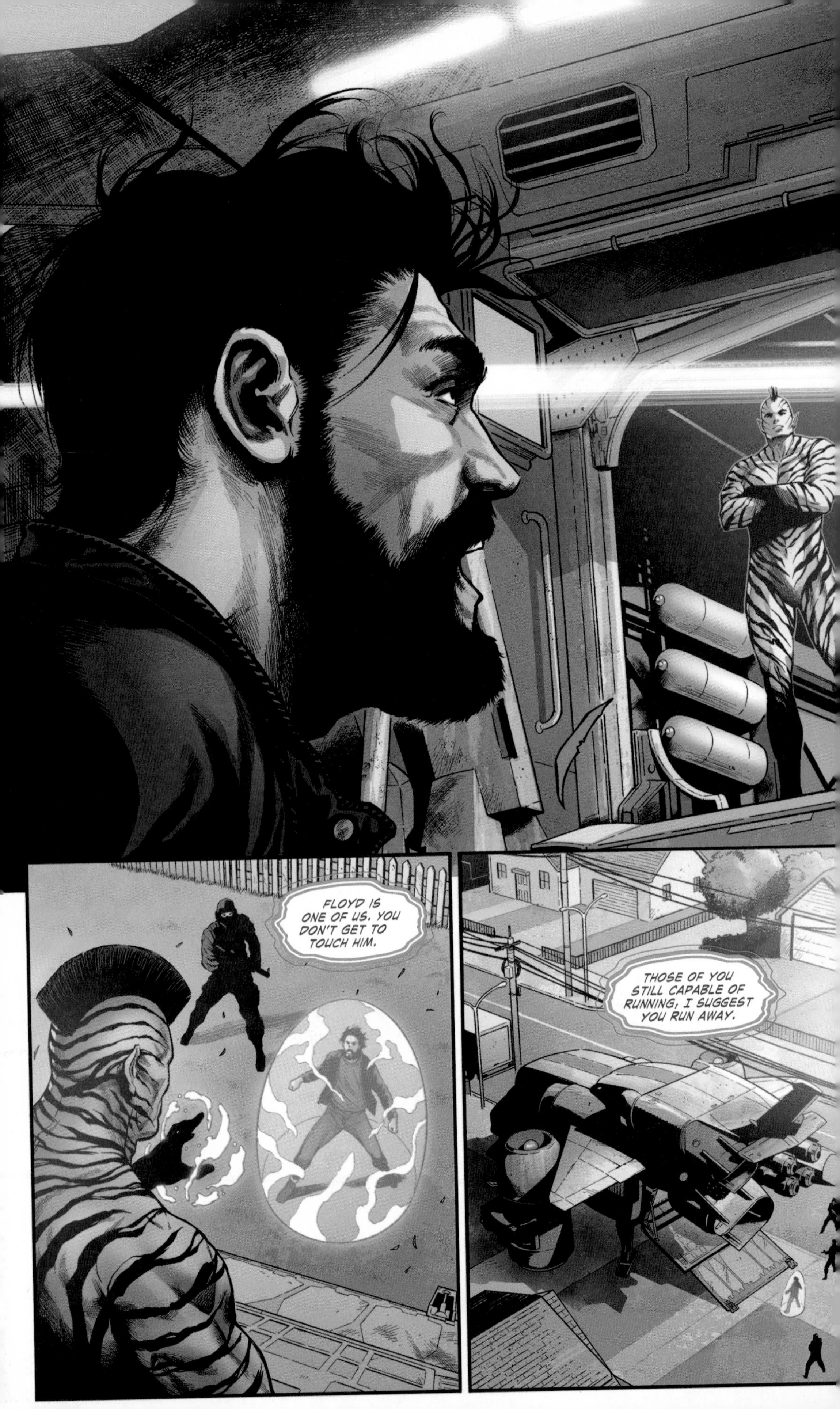
FLOYD IS ONE OF US. YOU DON'T GET TO TOUCH HIM.
THOSE OF YOU STILL CAPABLE OF RUNNING, I SUGGEST YOU RUN AWAY.

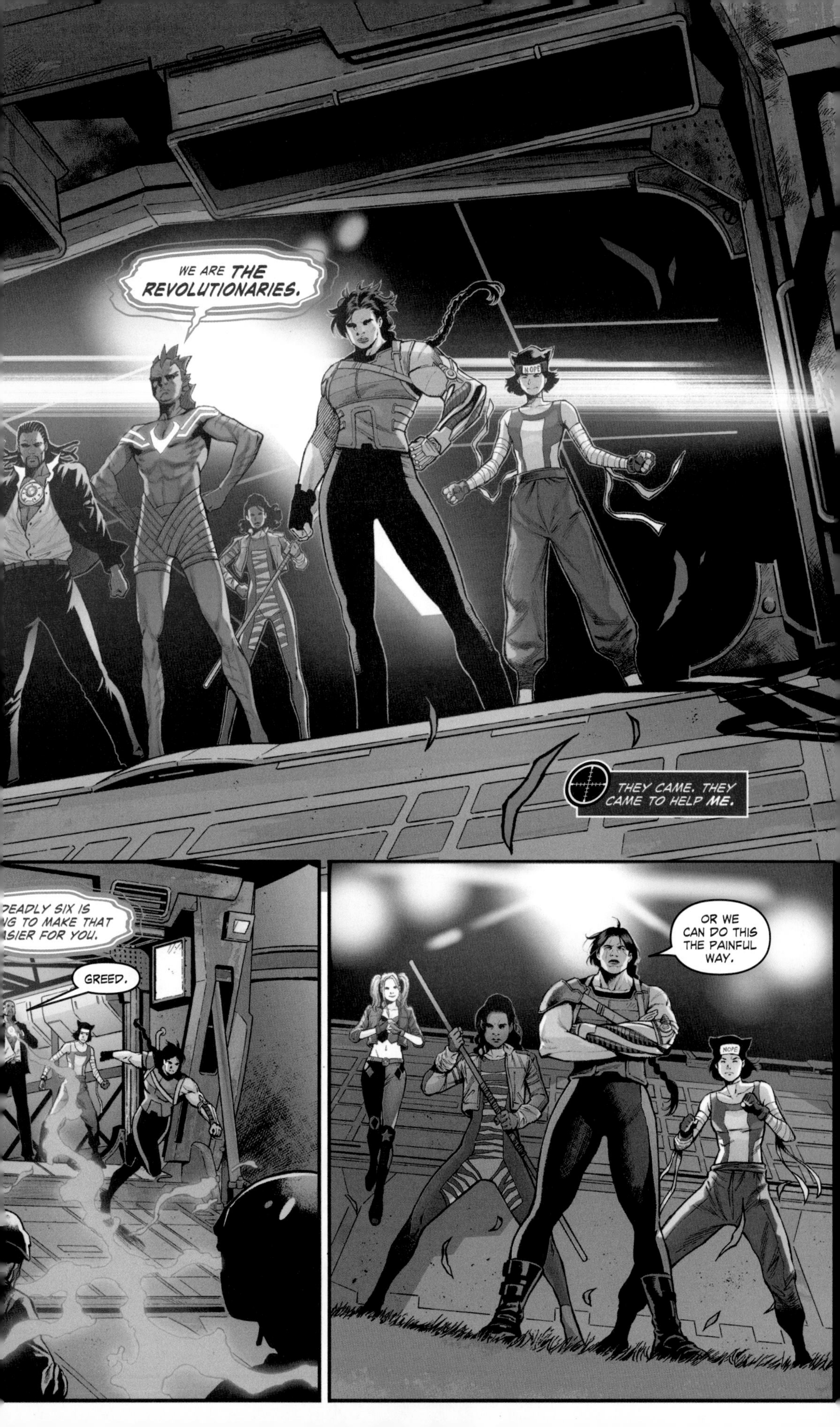

WE ARE THE REVOLUTIONARIES.
NOPE
THEY CAME. THEY CAME TO HELP ME.
DEADLY SIX IS
NG TO MAKE THAT
ASIER FOR YOU.
GREED.
OR WE CAN DO THIS THE PAINFUL WAY.
NOPE

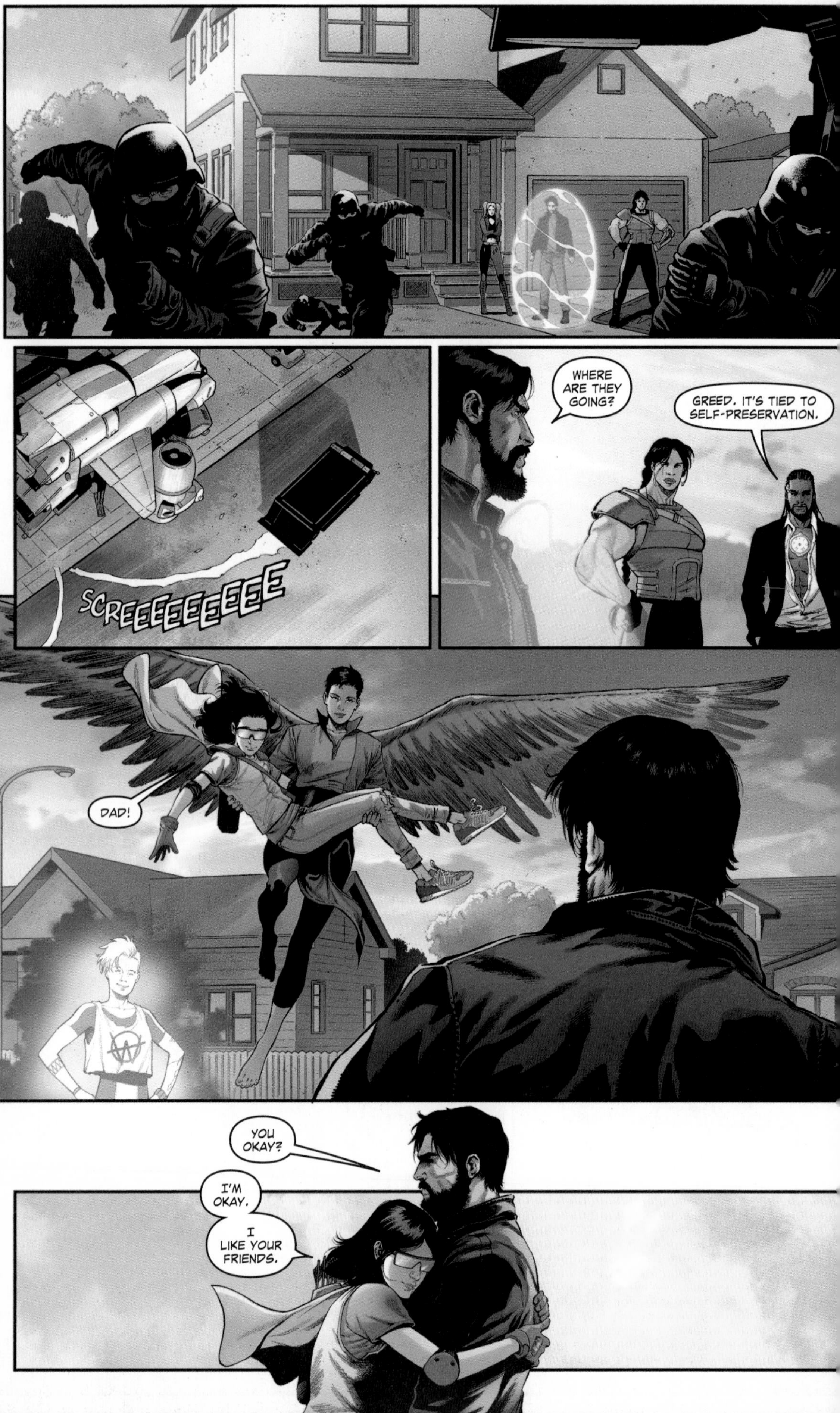
SCREEEEEEEEEE
WHERE ARE THEY GOING?
GREED. IT'S TIED TO SELF-PRESERVATION.
DAD!
YOU OKAY?
I'M OKAY.
I LIKE YOUR FRIENDS.

ARE *YOU* OKAY, DAD?

ZOE!

NO. I'M NOT OKAY.

I TRUSTED THE PARDON.

I LET MY GUARD DOWN.

LAWTON? WHATCHA DOING?

AND IT ALMOST GOT THE ONLY PERSON I CARE ABOUT KILLED.

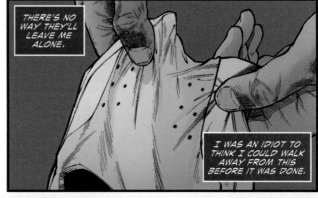

THERE'S NO WAY THEY'LL LEAVE ME ALONE.

I WAS AN IDIOT TO THINK I COULD WALK AWAY FROM THIS BEFORE IT WAS DONE.

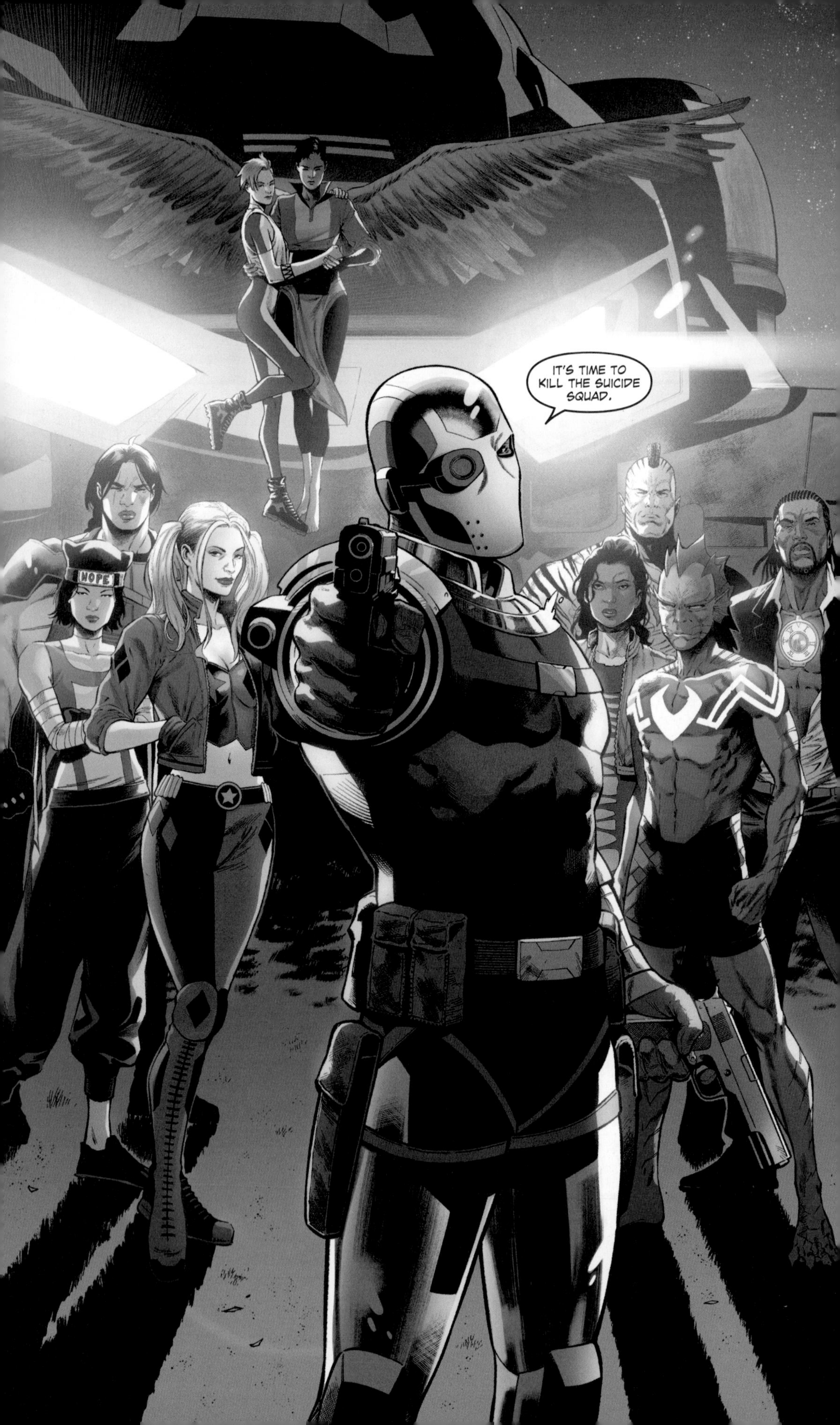
IT'S TIME TO KILL THE SUICIDE SQUAD.

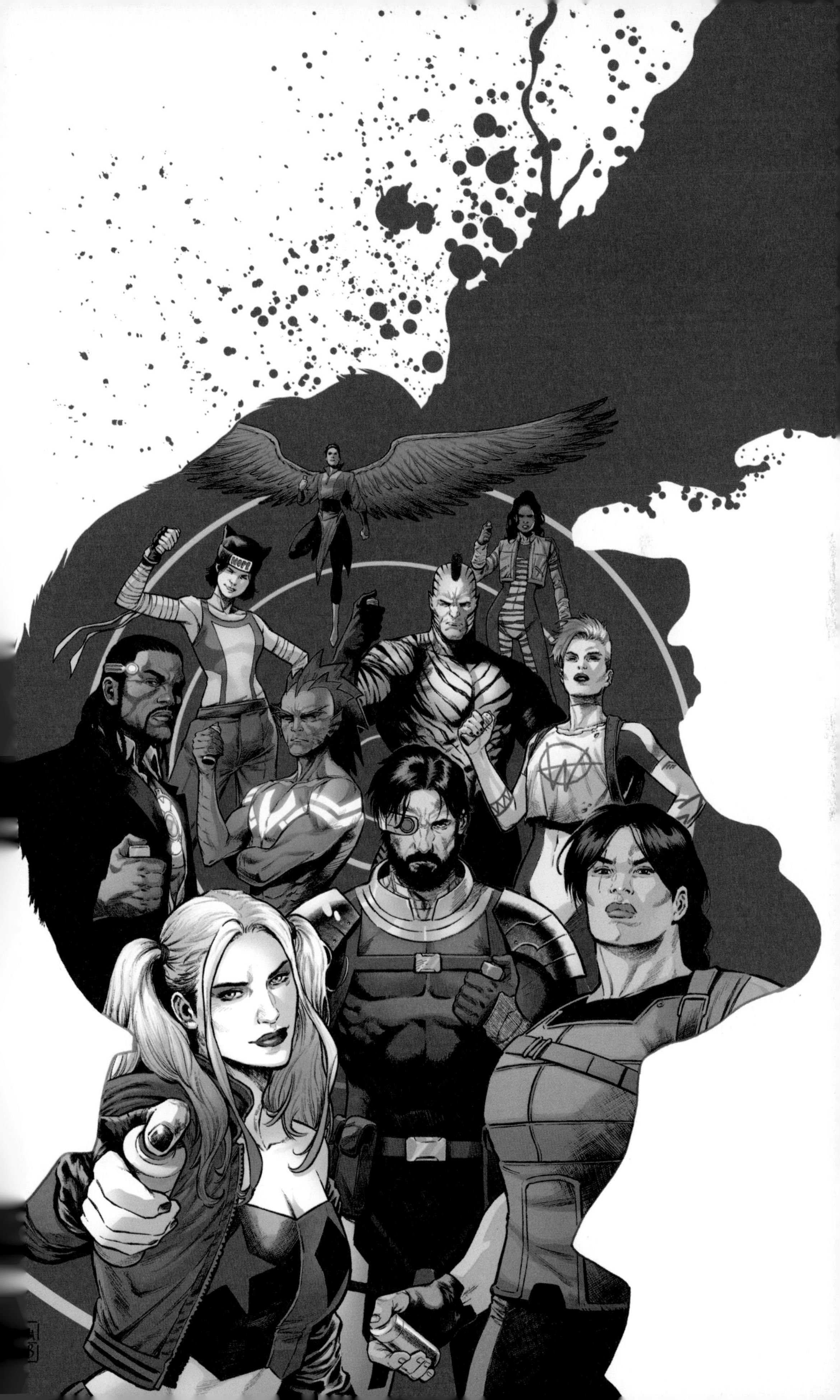

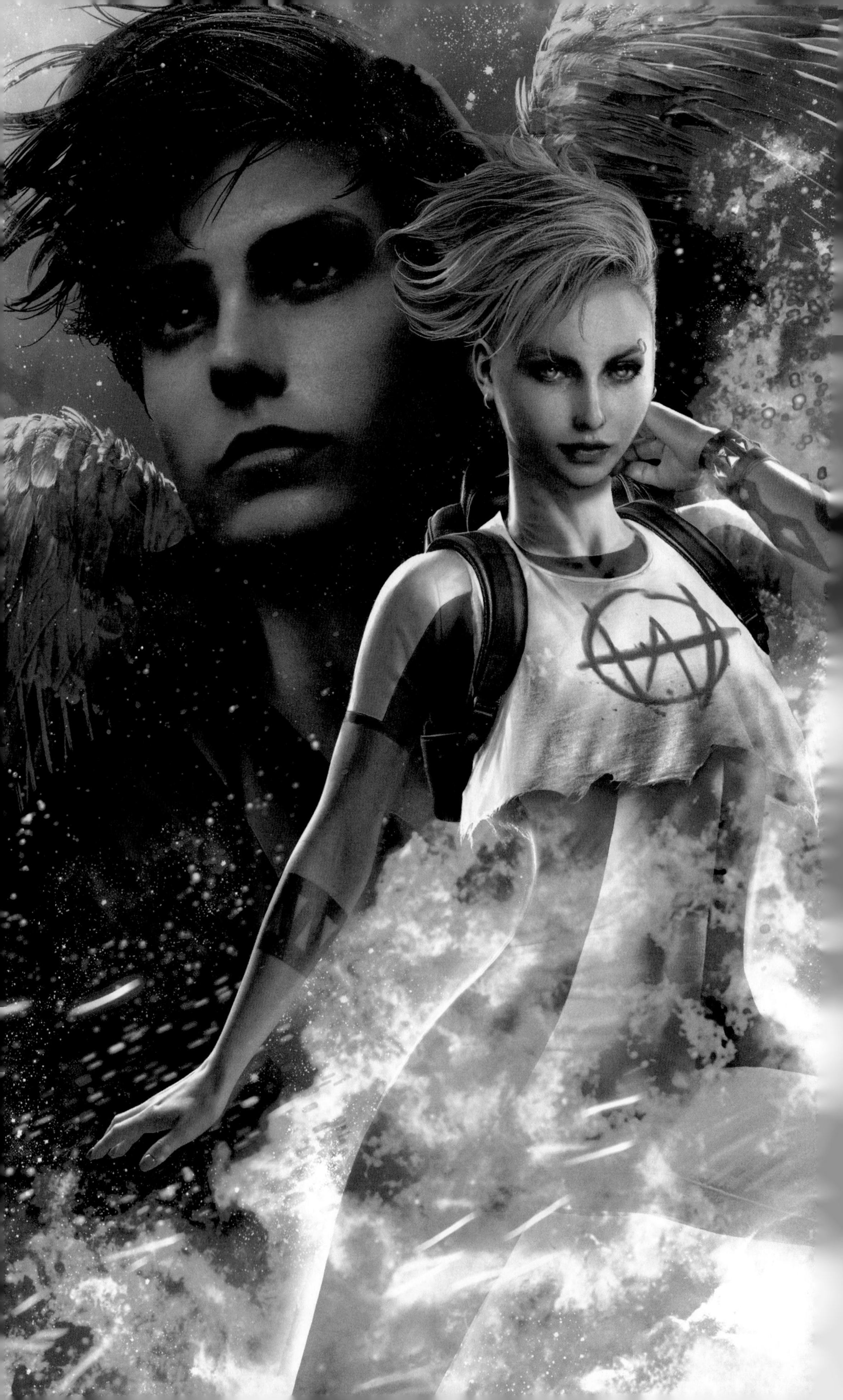

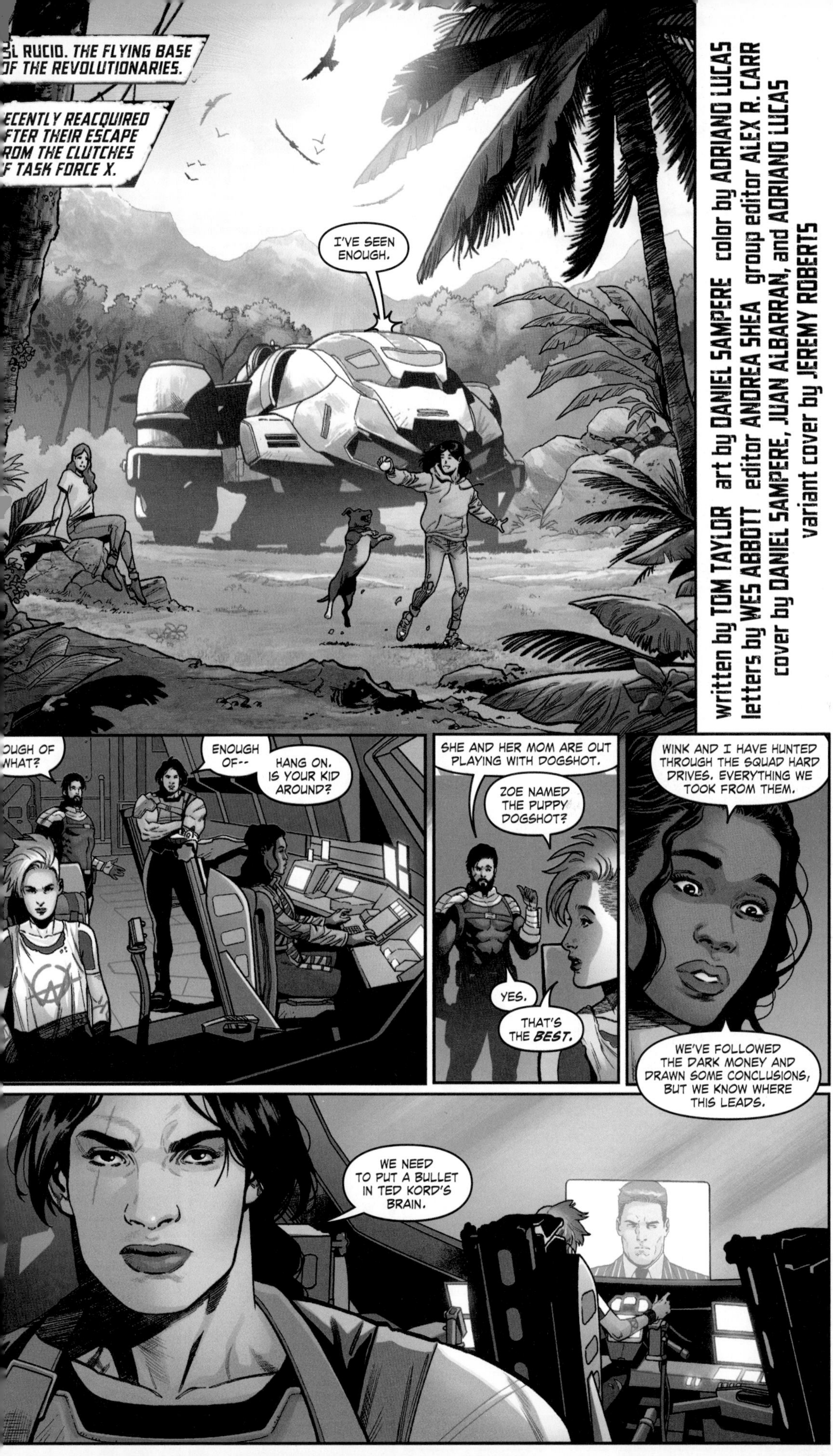

...L RUCIO. THE FLYING BASE OF THE REVOLUTIONARIES.
...ECENTLY REACQUIRED ...FTER THEIR ESCAPE ...ROM THE CLUTCHES ...F TASK FORCE X.
I'VE SEEN ENOUGH.
...OUGH OF WHAT?
ENOUGH OF--
HANG ON. IS YOUR KID AROUND?
SHE AND HER MOM ARE OUT PLAYING WITH DOGSHOT.
ZOE NAMED THE PUPPY DOGSHOT?
YES.
THAT'S THE *BEST*.
WINK AND I HAVE HUNTED THROUGH THE SQUAD HARD DRIVES. EVERYTHING WE TOOK FROM THEM.
WE'VE FOLLOWED THE DARK MONEY AND DRAWN SOME CONCLUSIONS, BUT WE KNOW WHERE THIS LEADS.
WE NEED TO PUT A BULLET IN TED KORD'S BRAIN.

written by TOM TAYLOR art by DANIEL SAMPERE color by ADRIANO LUCAS
letters by WES ABBOTT editor ANDREA SHEA group editor ALEX R. CARR
cover by DANIEL SAMPERE, JUAN ALBARRAN, and ADRIANO LUCAS
variant cover by JEREMY ROBERTS

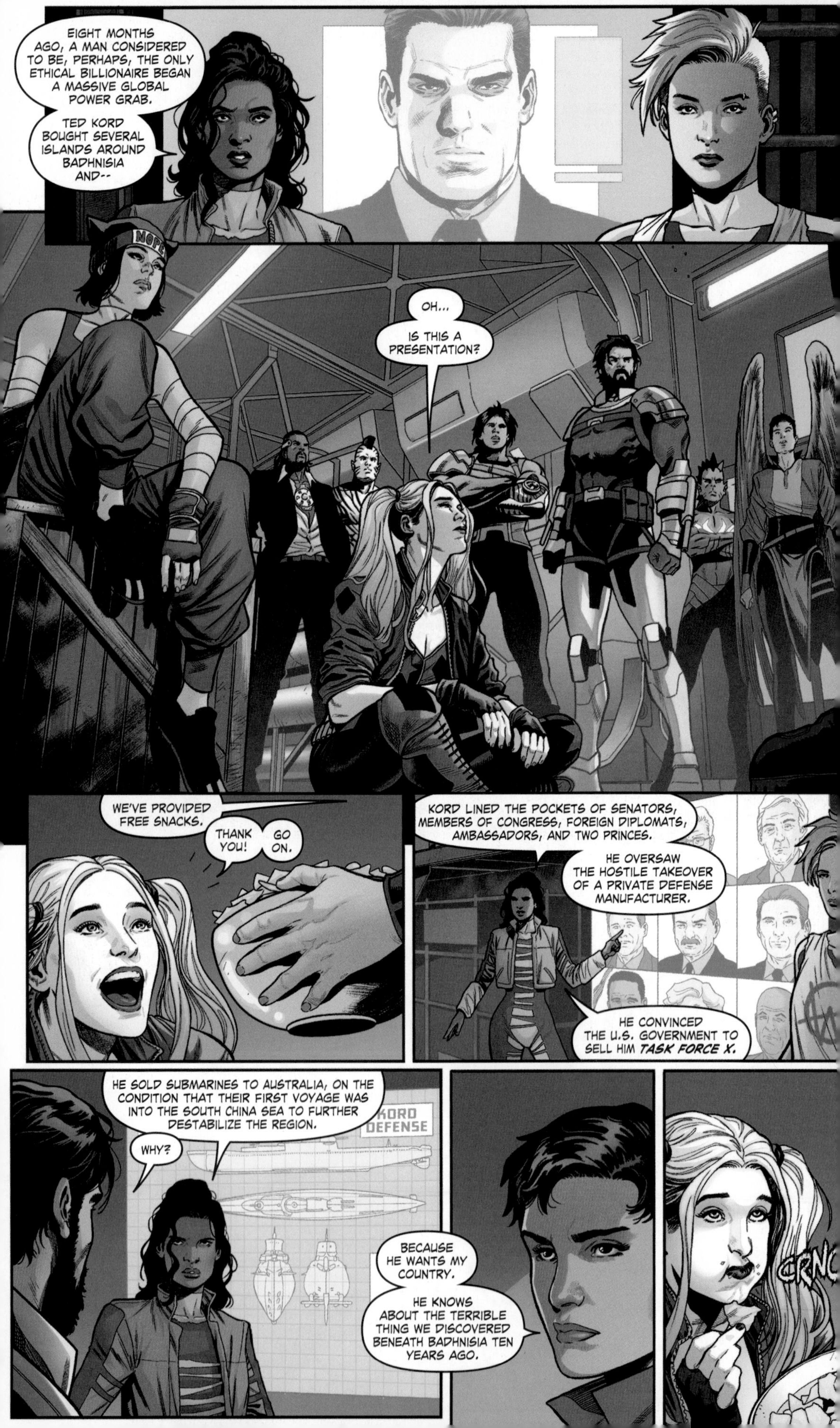
EIGHT MONTHS AGO, A MAN CONSIDERED TO BE, PERHAPS, THE ONLY ETHICAL BILLIONAIRE BEGAN A MASSIVE GLOBAL POWER GRAB.
TED KORD BOUGHT SEVERAL ISLANDS AROUND BADHNISIA AND--
NOPE
OH...
IS THIS A PRESENTATION?
WE'VE PROVIDED FREE SNACKS.
THANK YOU!
GO ON.
KORD LINED THE POCKETS OF SENATORS, MEMBERS OF CONGRESS, FOREIGN DIPLOMATS, AMBASSADORS, AND TWO PRINCES.
HE OVERSAW THE HOSTILE TAKEOVER OF A PRIVATE DEFENSE MANUFACTURER.
HE CONVINCED THE U.S. GOVERNMENT TO SELL HIM *TASK FORCE X.*
HE SOLD SUBMARINES TO AUSTRALIA, ON THE CONDITION THAT THEIR FIRST VOYAGE WAS INTO THE SOUTH CHINA SEA TO FURTHER DESTABILIZE THE REGION.
KORD DEFENSE
WHY?
BECAUSE HE WANTS MY COUNTRY.
HE KNOWS ABOUT THE TERRIBLE THING WE DISCOVERED BENEATH BADHNISIA TEN YEARS AGO.
CRNC

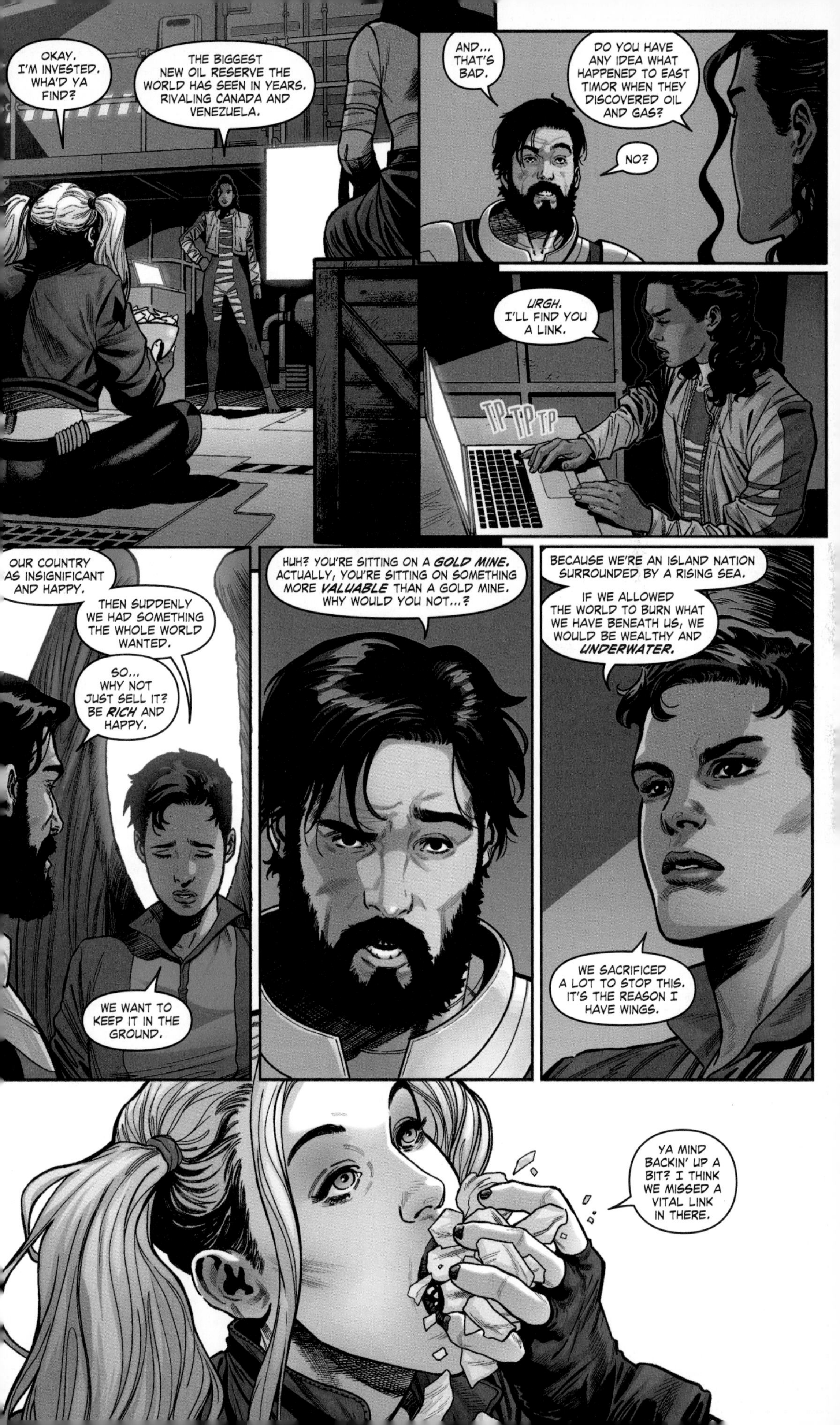

OKAY. I'M INVESTED. WHA'D YA FIND?
THE BIGGEST NEW OIL RESERVE THE WORLD HAS SEEN IN YEARS. RIVALING CANADA AND VENEZUELA.
AND... THAT'S BAD.
DO YOU HAVE ANY IDEA WHAT HAPPENED TO EAST TIMOR WHEN THEY DISCOVERED OIL AND GAS?
NO?
URGH. I'LL FIND YOU A LINK.
TP TP TP
OUR COUNTRY AS INSIGNIFICANT AND HAPPY.
THEN SUDDENLY WE HAD SOMETHING THE WHOLE WORLD WANTED.
SO... WHY NOT JUST SELL IT? BE RICH AND HAPPY.
WE WANT TO KEEP IT IN THE GROUND.
HUH? YOU'RE SITTING ON A GOLD MINE. ACTUALLY, YOU'RE SITTING ON SOMETHING MORE VALUABLE THAN A GOLD MINE. WHY WOULD YOU NOT...?
BECAUSE WE'RE AN ISLAND NATION SURROUNDED BY A RISING SEA.
IF WE ALLOWED THE WORLD TO BURN WHAT WE HAVE BENEATH US, WE WOULD BE WEALTHY AND UNDERWATER.
WE SACRIFICED A LOT TO STOP THIS. IT'S THE REASON I HAVE WINGS.
YA MIND BACKIN' UP A BIT? I THINK WE MISSED A VITAL LINK IN THERE.

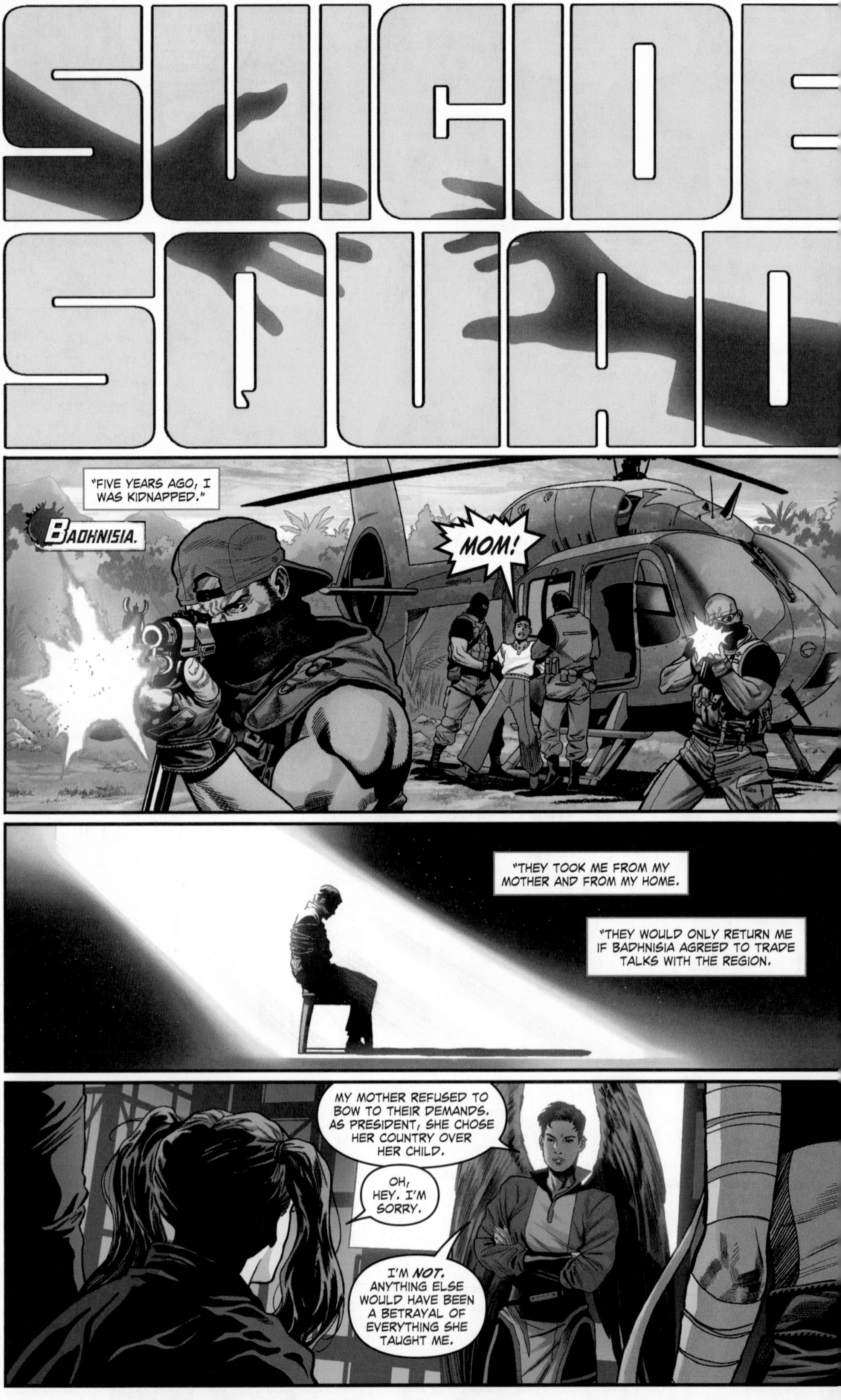
SUICIDE SQUAD
"FIVE YEARS AGO, I WAS KIDNAPPED."
BADHNISIA.
MOM!
"THEY TOOK ME FROM MY MOTHER AND FROM MY HOME.
"THEY WOULD ONLY RETURN ME IF BADHNISIA AGREED TO TRADE TALKS WITH THE REGION.
MY MOTHER REFUSED TO BOW TO THEIR DEMANDS. AS PRESIDENT, SHE CHOSE HER COUNTRY OVER HER CHILD.
OH, HEY. I'M SORRY.
I'M NOT. ANYTHING ELSE WOULD HAVE BEEN A BETRAYAL OF EVERYTHING SHE TAUGHT ME.

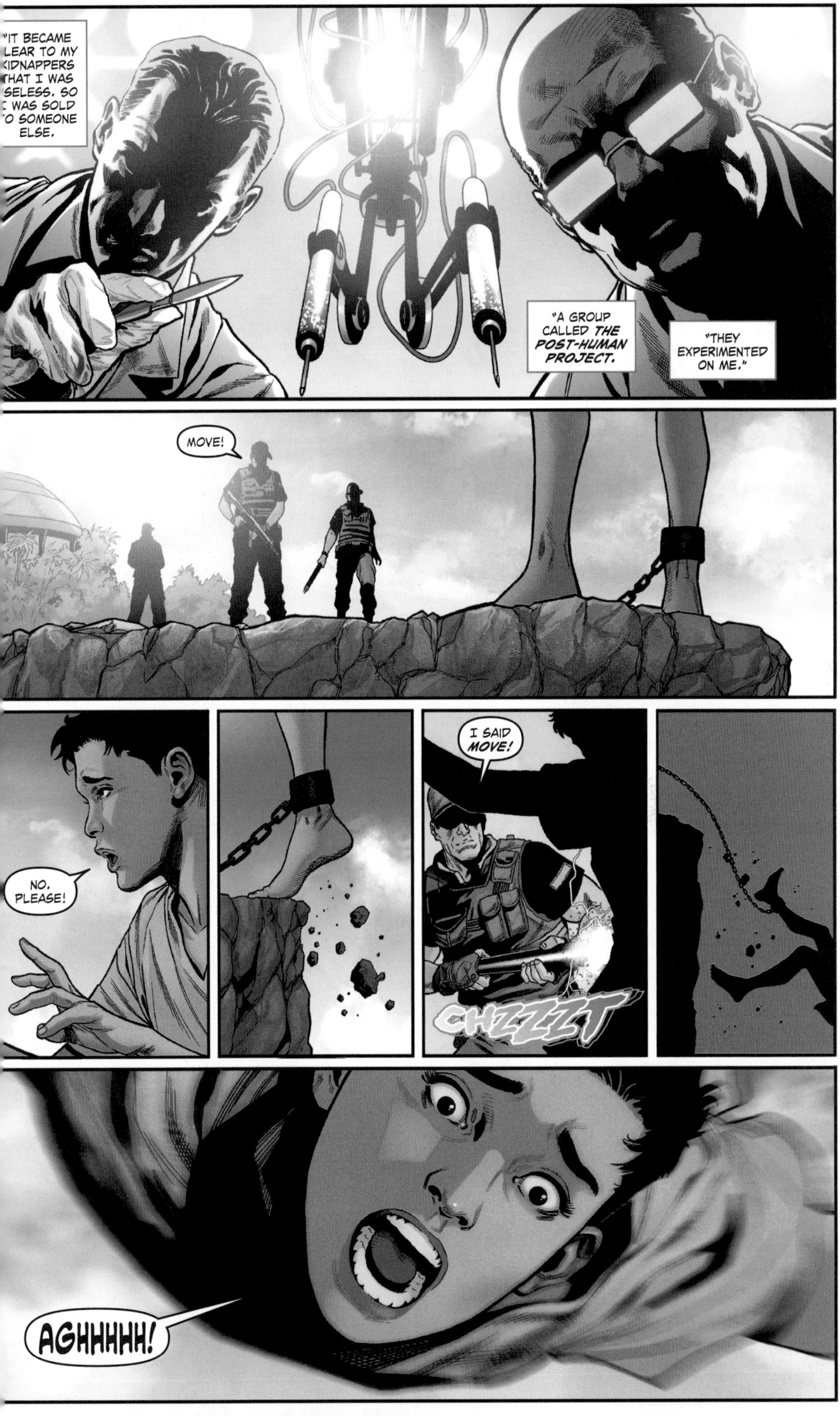
"IT BECAME LEAR TO MY KIDNAPPERS THAT I WAS SELESS. SO I WAS SOLD TO SOMEONE ELSE.
"A GROUP CALLED THE POST-HUMAN PROJECT.
"THEY EXPERIMENTED ON ME."
MOVE!
NO. PLEASE!
I SAID MOVE!
CHZZZT
AGHHHHH!

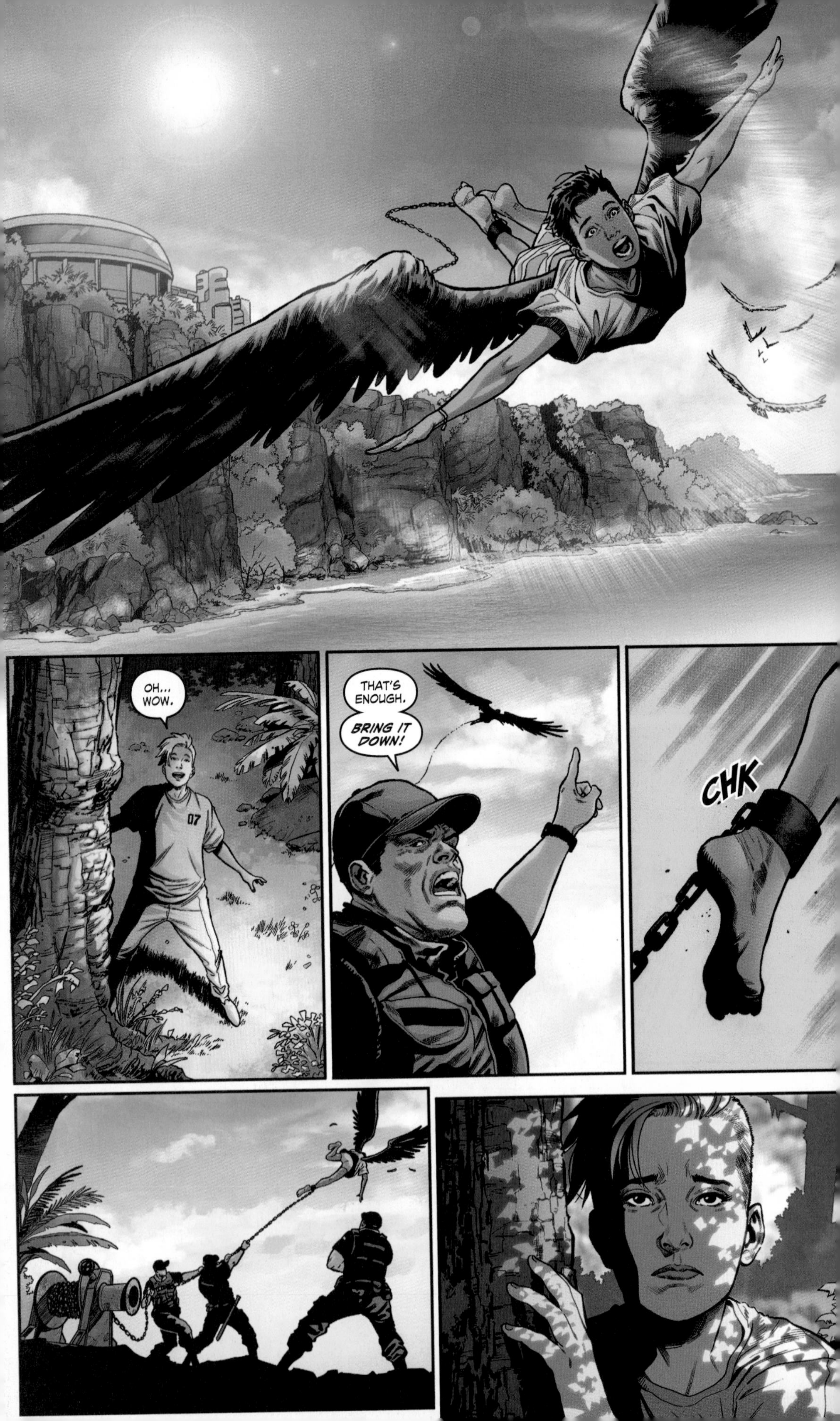
OH... WOW.
THAT'S ENOUGH.
BRING IT DOWN!
CHK
07

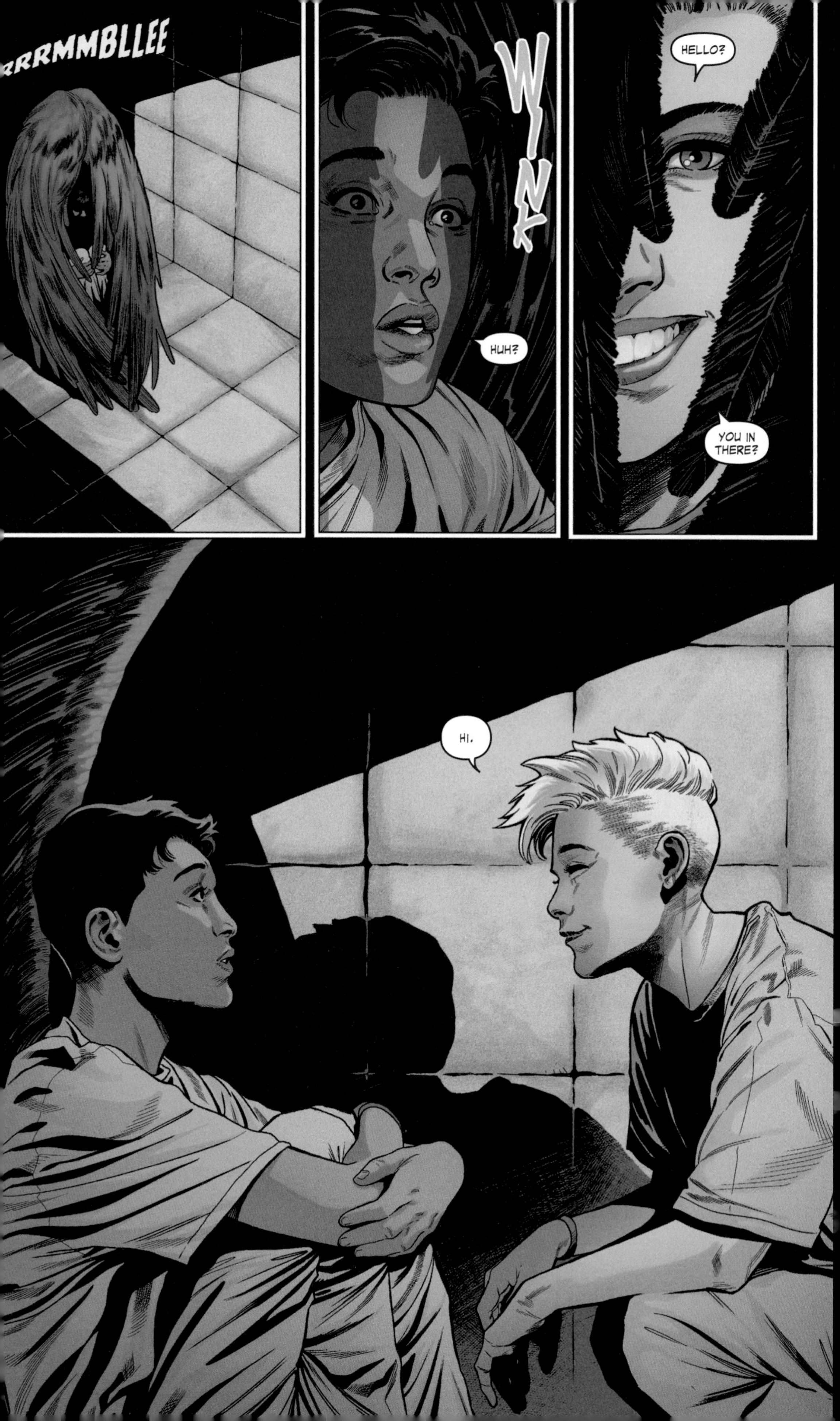
RRRMMBLLEE
WZNK
HUH?
HELLO?
YOU IN THERE?
HI.

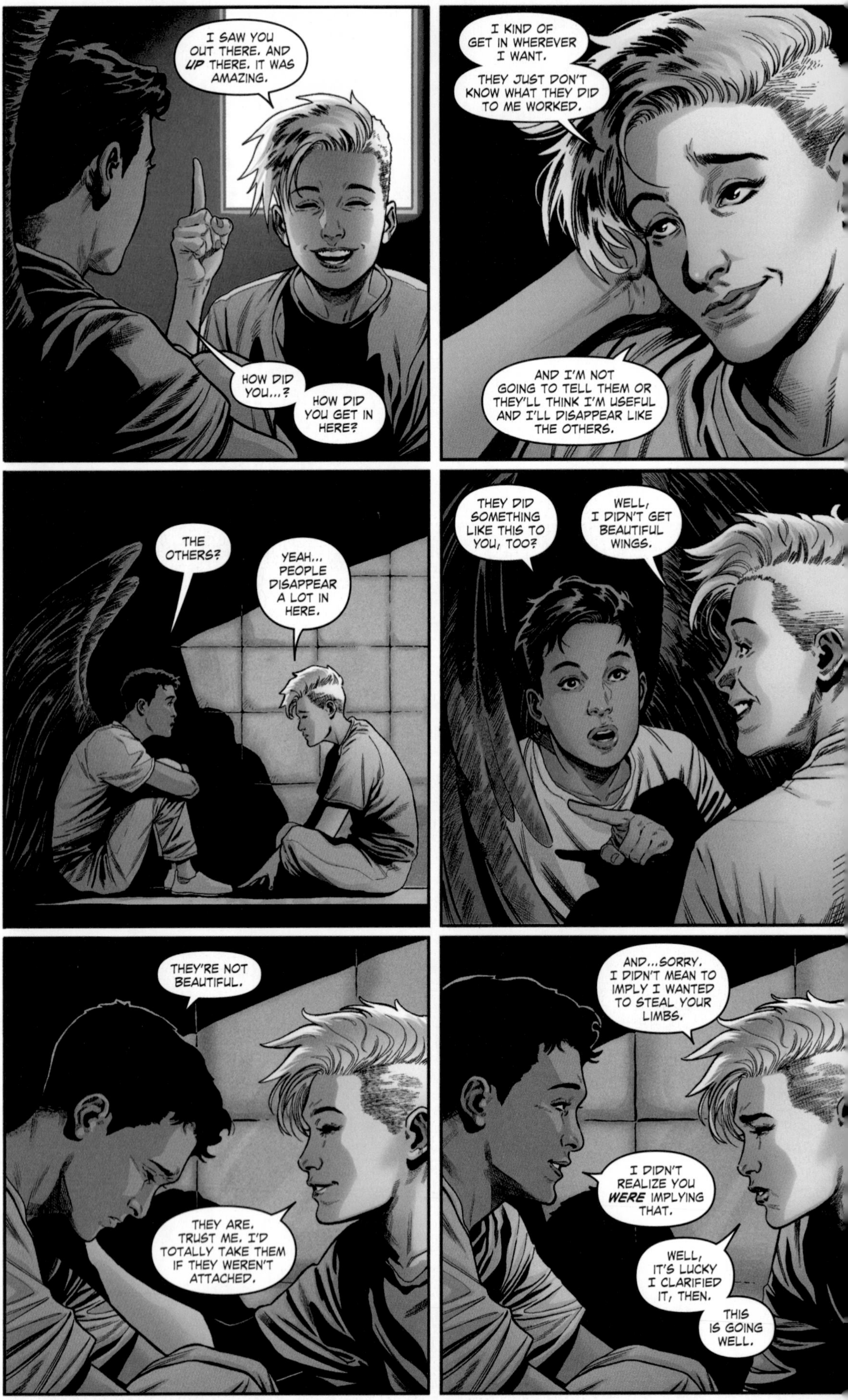
I SAW YOU OUT THERE. AND *UP* THERE. IT WAS AMAZING.
HOW DID YOU...?
HOW DID YOU GET IN HERE?
I KIND OF GET IN WHEREVER I WANT.
THEY JUST DON'T KNOW WHAT THEY DID TO ME WORKED.
AND I'M NOT GOING TO TELL THEM OR THEY'LL THINK I'M USEFUL AND I'LL DISAPPEAR LIKE THE OTHERS.
THE OTHERS?
YEAH... PEOPLE DISAPPEAR A LOT IN HERE.
THEY DID SOMETHING LIKE THIS TO YOU, TOO?
WELL, I DIDN'T GET BEAUTIFUL WINGS.
THEY'RE NOT BEAUTIFUL.
THEY ARE. TRUST ME. I'D TOTALLY TAKE THEM IF THEY WEREN'T ATTACHED.
AND...SORRY. I DIDN'T MEAN TO IMPLY I WANTED TO STEAL YOUR LIMBS.
I DIDN'T REALIZE YOU *WERE* IMPLYING THAT.
WELL, IT'S LUCKY I CLARIFIED IT, THEN.
THIS IS GOING WELL.

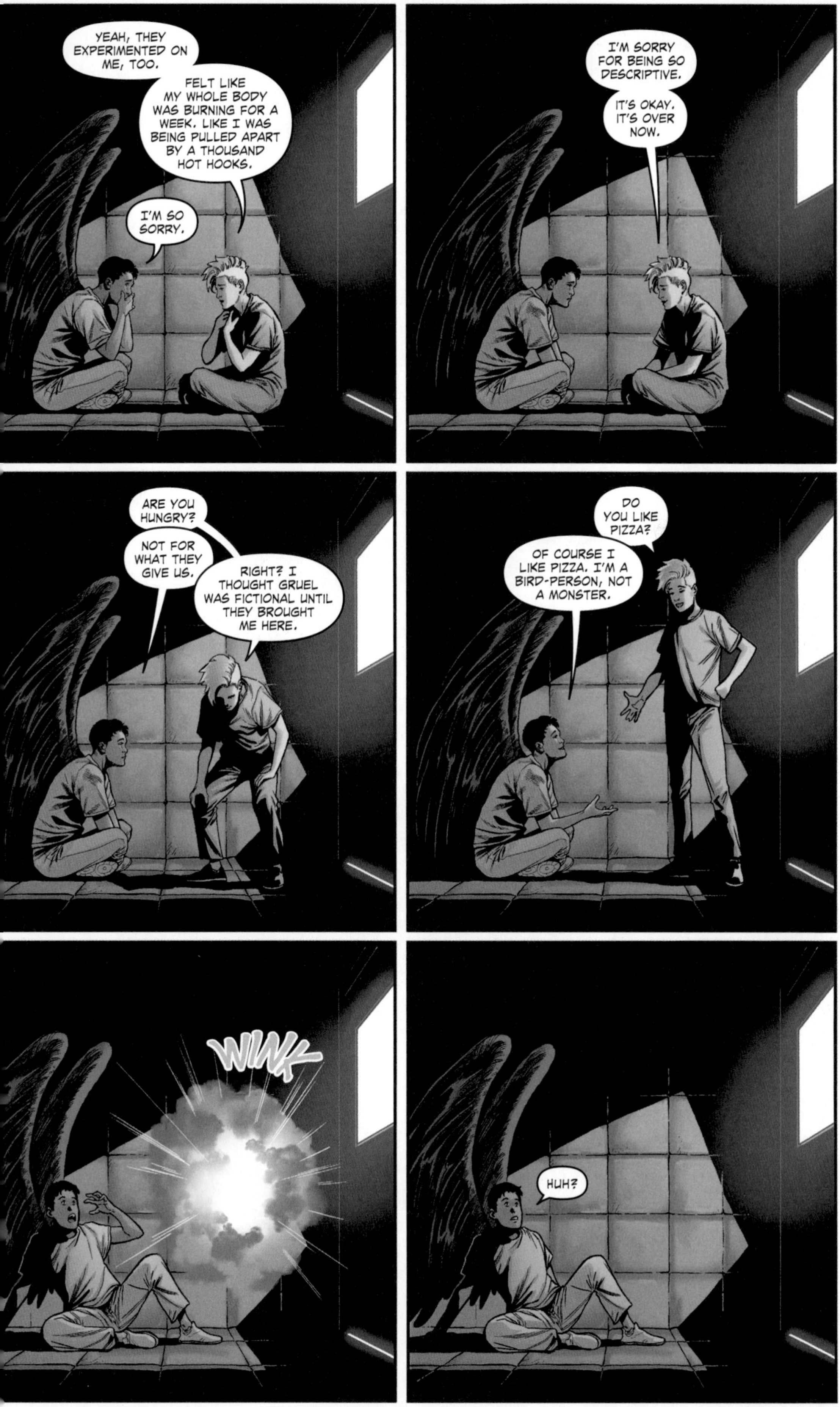
YEAH, THEY EXPERIMENTED ON ME, TOO.
FELT LIKE MY WHOLE BODY WAS BURNING FOR A WEEK. LIKE I WAS BEING PULLED APART BY A THOUSAND HOT HOOKS.
I'M SO SORRY.
I'M SORRY FOR BEING SO DESCRIPTIVE.
IT'S OKAY. IT'S OVER NOW.
ARE YOU HUNGRY?
NOT FOR WHAT THEY GIVE US.
RIGHT? I THOUGHT GRUEL WAS FICTIONAL UNTIL THEY BROUGHT ME HERE.
DO YOU LIKE PIZZA?
OF COURSE I LIKE PIZZA. I'M A BIRD-PERSON, NOT A MONSTER.
WINK
HUH?

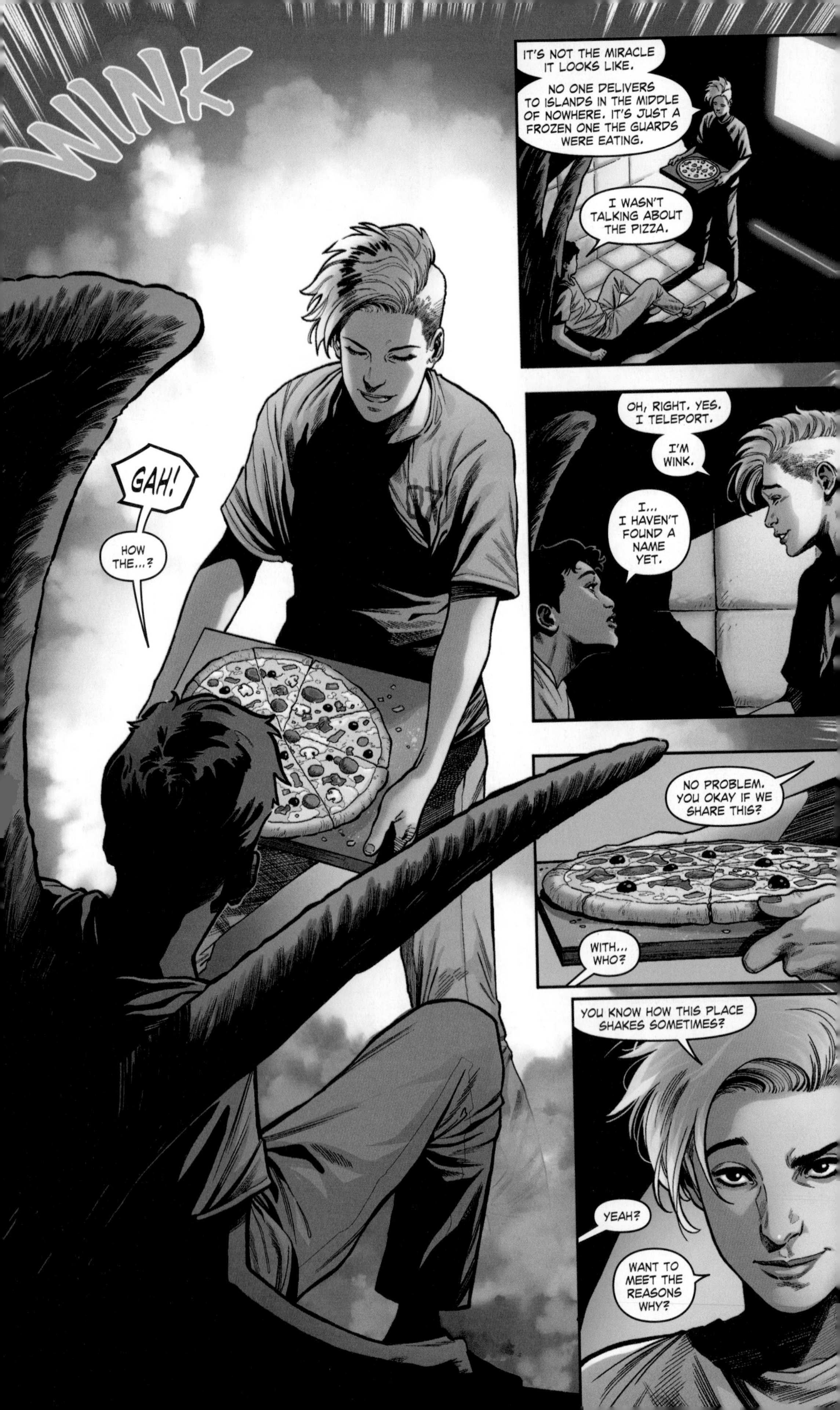
WINK
GAH!
HOW THE...?
IT'S NOT THE MIRACLE IT LOOKS LIKE.
NO ONE DELIVERS TO ISLANDS IN THE MIDDLE OF NOWHERE. IT'S JUST A FROZEN ONE THE GUARDS WERE EATING.
I WASN'T TALKING ABOUT THE PIZZA.
OH, RIGHT. YES. I TELEPORT.
I'M WINK.
I... I HAVEN'T FOUND A NAME YET.
NO PROBLEM. YOU OKAY IF WE SHARE THIS?
WITH... WHO?
YOU KNOW HOW THIS PLACE SHAKES SOMETIMES?
YEAH?
WANT TO MEET THE REASONS WHY?

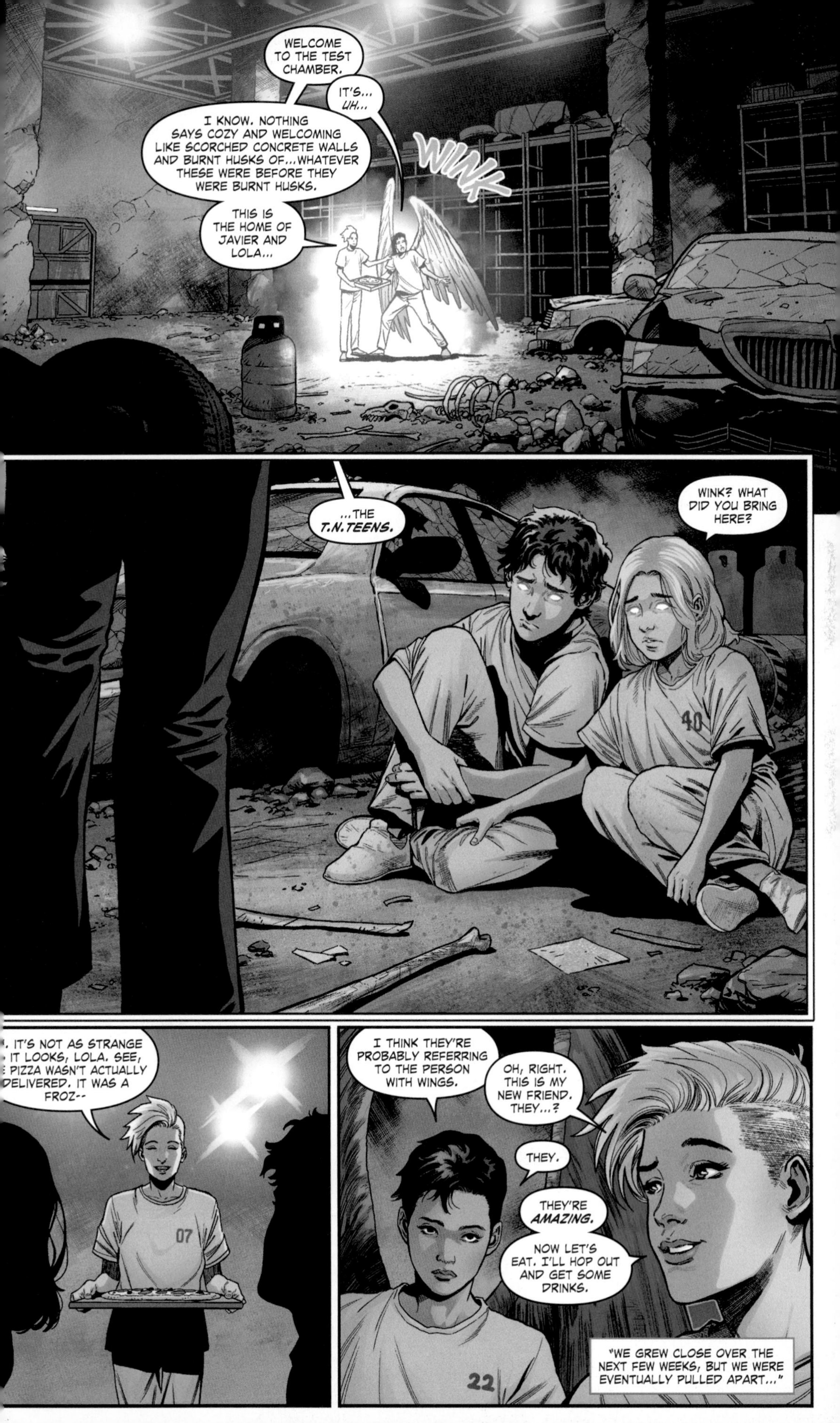

WELCOME TO THE TEST CHAMBER.
IT'S... UH...
I KNOW. NOTHING SAYS COZY AND WELCOMING LIKE SCORCHED CONCRETE WALLS AND BURNT HUSKS OF... WHATEVER THESE WERE BEFORE THEY WERE BURNT HUSKS.
WINK
THIS IS THE HOME OF JAVIER AND LOLA...
...THE T.N.TEENS.
WINK? WHAT DID YOU BRING HERE?
IT'S NOT AS STRANGE IT LOOKS, LOLA. SEE, PIZZA WASN'T ACTUALLY DELIVERED. IT WAS A FROZ--
I THINK THEY'RE PROBABLY REFERRING TO THE PERSON WITH WINGS.
OH, RIGHT. THIS IS MY NEW FRIEND. THEY...?
THEY.
THEY'RE AMAZING.
NOW LET'S EAT. I'LL HOP OUT AND GET SOME DRINKS.
"WE GREW CLOSE OVER THE NEXT FEW WEEKS, BUT WE WERE EVENTUALLY PULLED APART..."

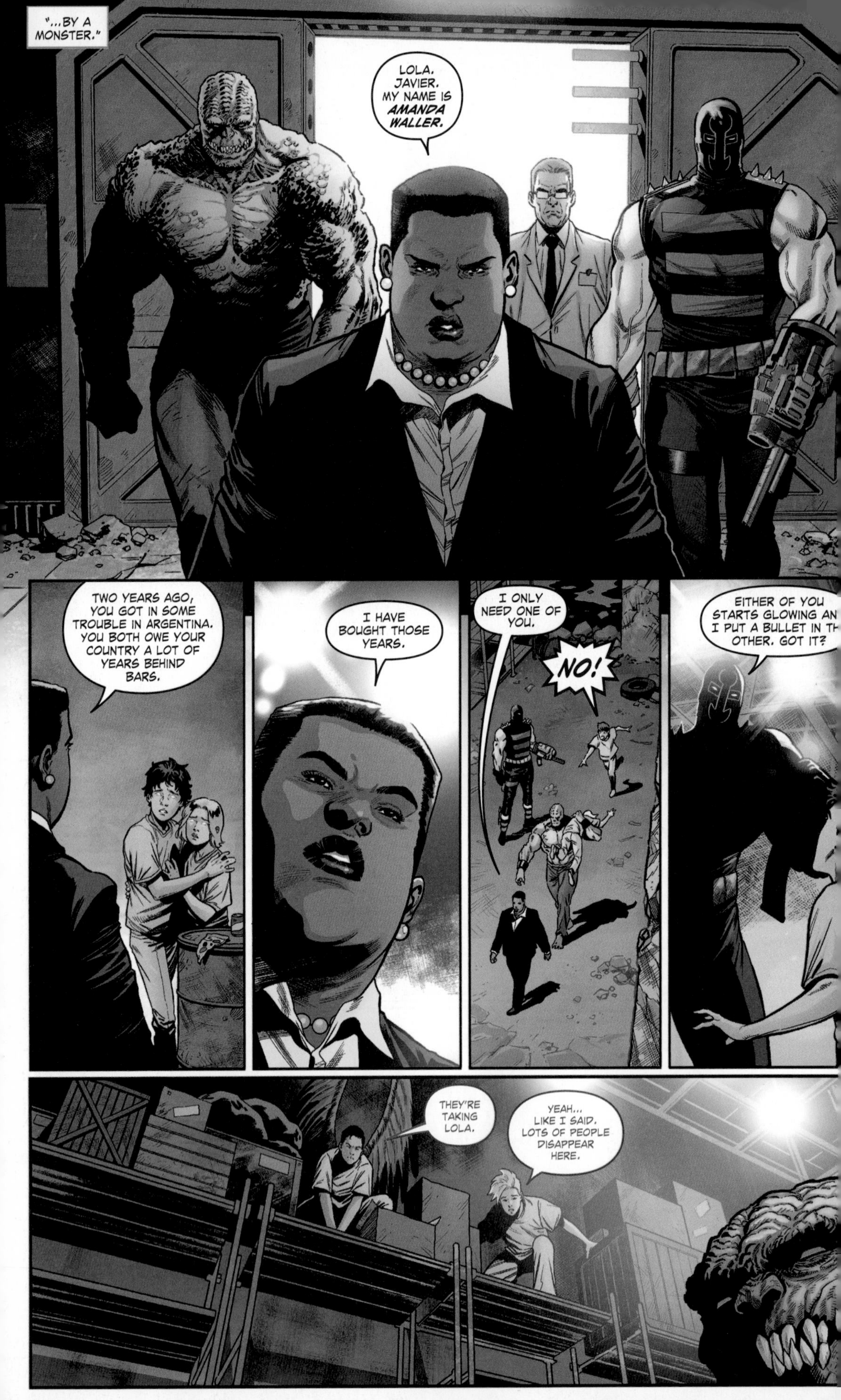
"...BY A MONSTER."
LOLA. JAVIER. MY NAME IS AMANDA WALLER.
TWO YEARS AGO, YOU GOT IN SOME TROUBLE IN ARGENTINA. YOU BOTH OWE YOUR COUNTRY A LOT OF YEARS BEHIND BARS.
I HAVE BOUGHT THOSE YEARS.
I ONLY NEED ONE OF YOU.
NO!
EITHER OF YOU STARTS GLOWING AN I PUT A BULLET IN TH OTHER. GOT IT?
THEY'RE TAKING LOLA.
YEAH... LIKE I SAID. LOTS OF PEOPLE DISAPPEAR HERE.

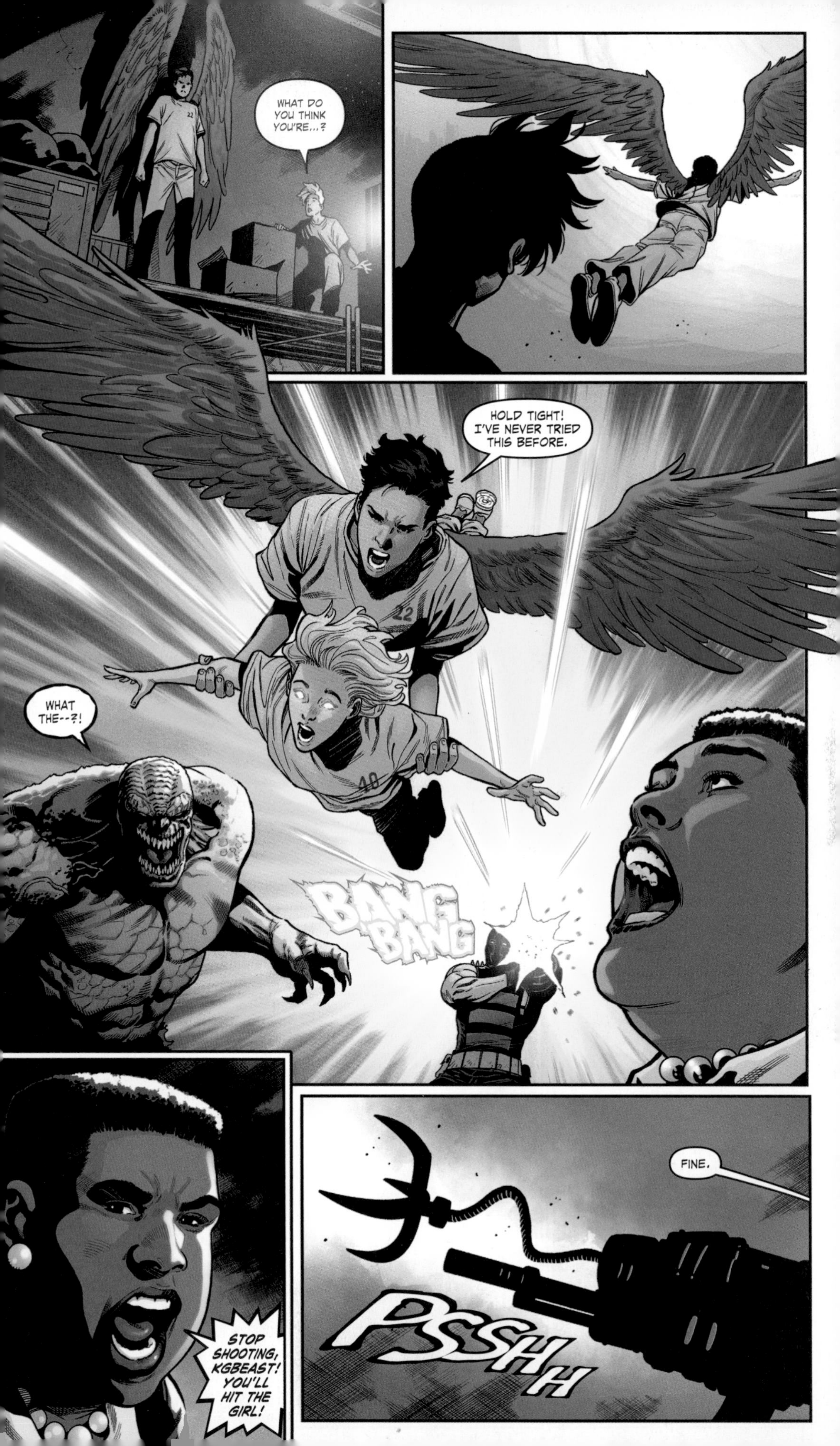
WHAT DO YOU THINK YOU'RE...?
HOLD TIGHT! I'VE NEVER TRIED THIS BEFORE.
WHAT THE--?!
BANG BANG
STOP SHOOTING, KGBEAST! YOU'LL HIT THE GIRL!
FINE.
PSSHH

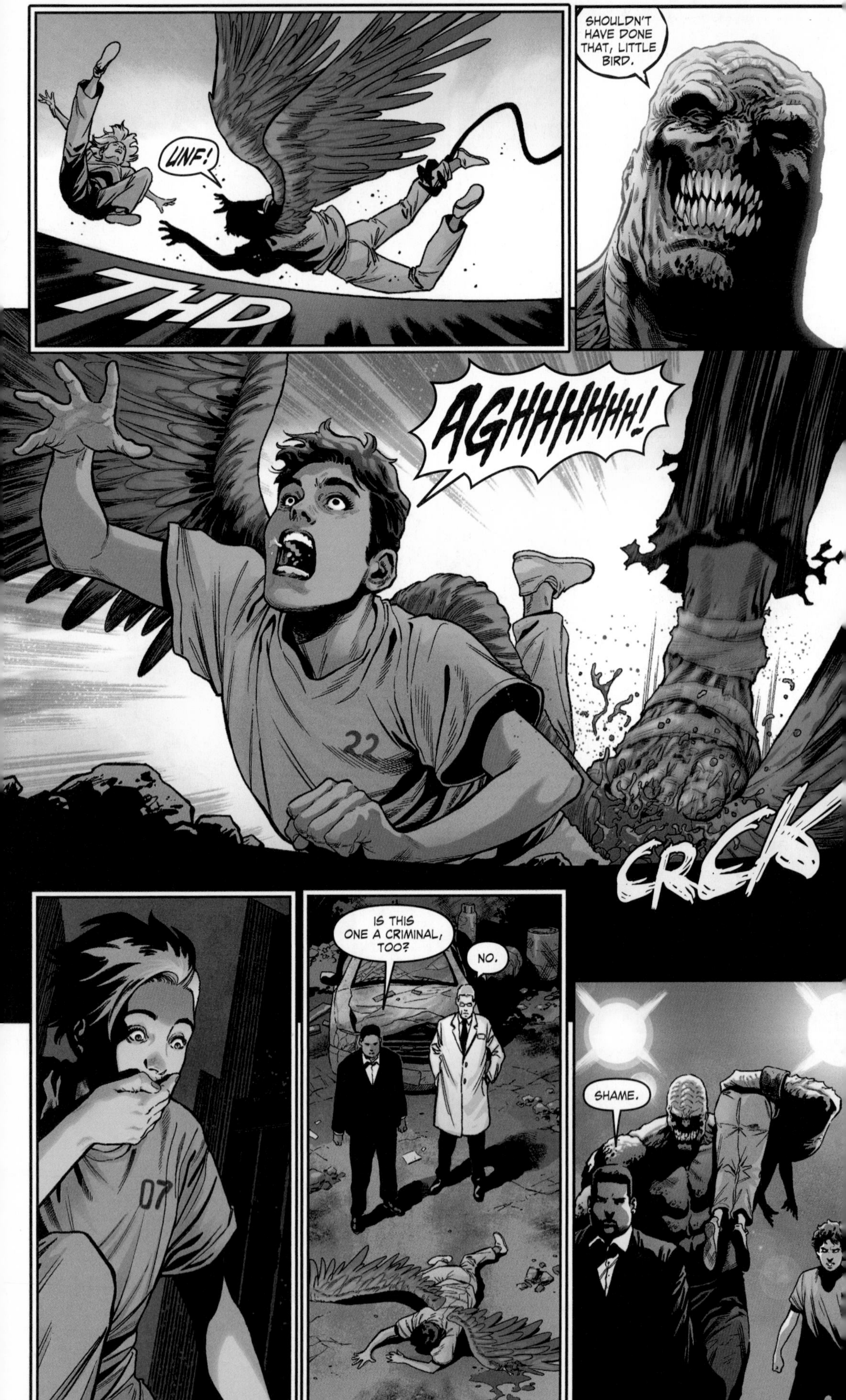
UNF!
THD
SHOULDN'T HAVE DONE THAT, LITTLE BIRD.
AGHHHHHH!
22
CRCK
07
IS THIS ONE A CRIMINAL, TOO?
NO.
SHAME.

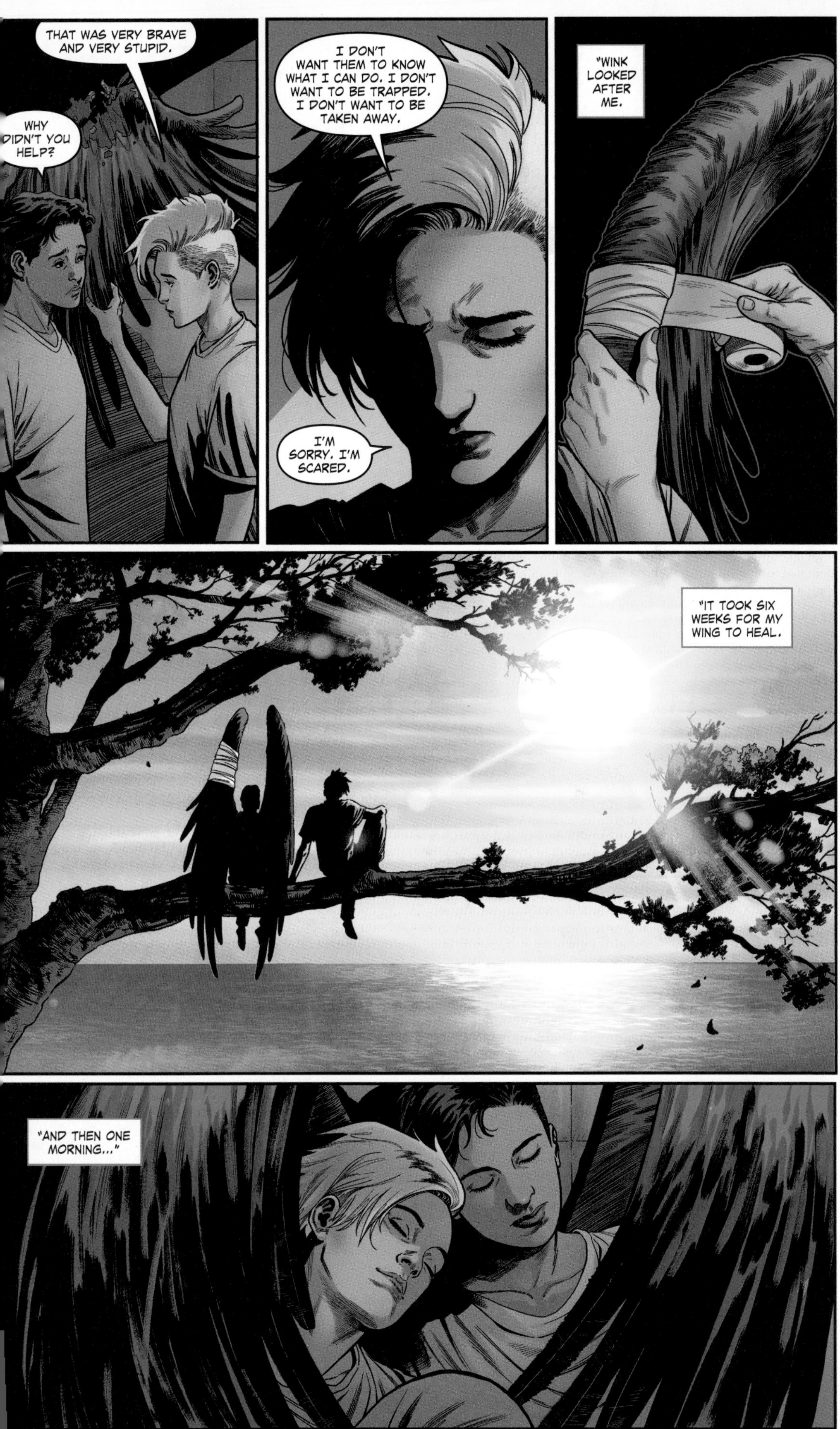
THAT WAS VERY BRAVE AND VERY STUPID.
WHY DIDN'T YOU HELP?
I DON'T WANT THEM TO KNOW WHAT I CAN DO. I DON'T WANT TO BE TRAPPED. I DON'T WANT TO BE TAKEN AWAY.
I'M SORRY. I'M SCARED.
"WINK LOOKED AFTER ME.
"IT TOOK SIX WEEKS FOR MY WING TO HEAL.
"AND THEN ONE MORNING..."

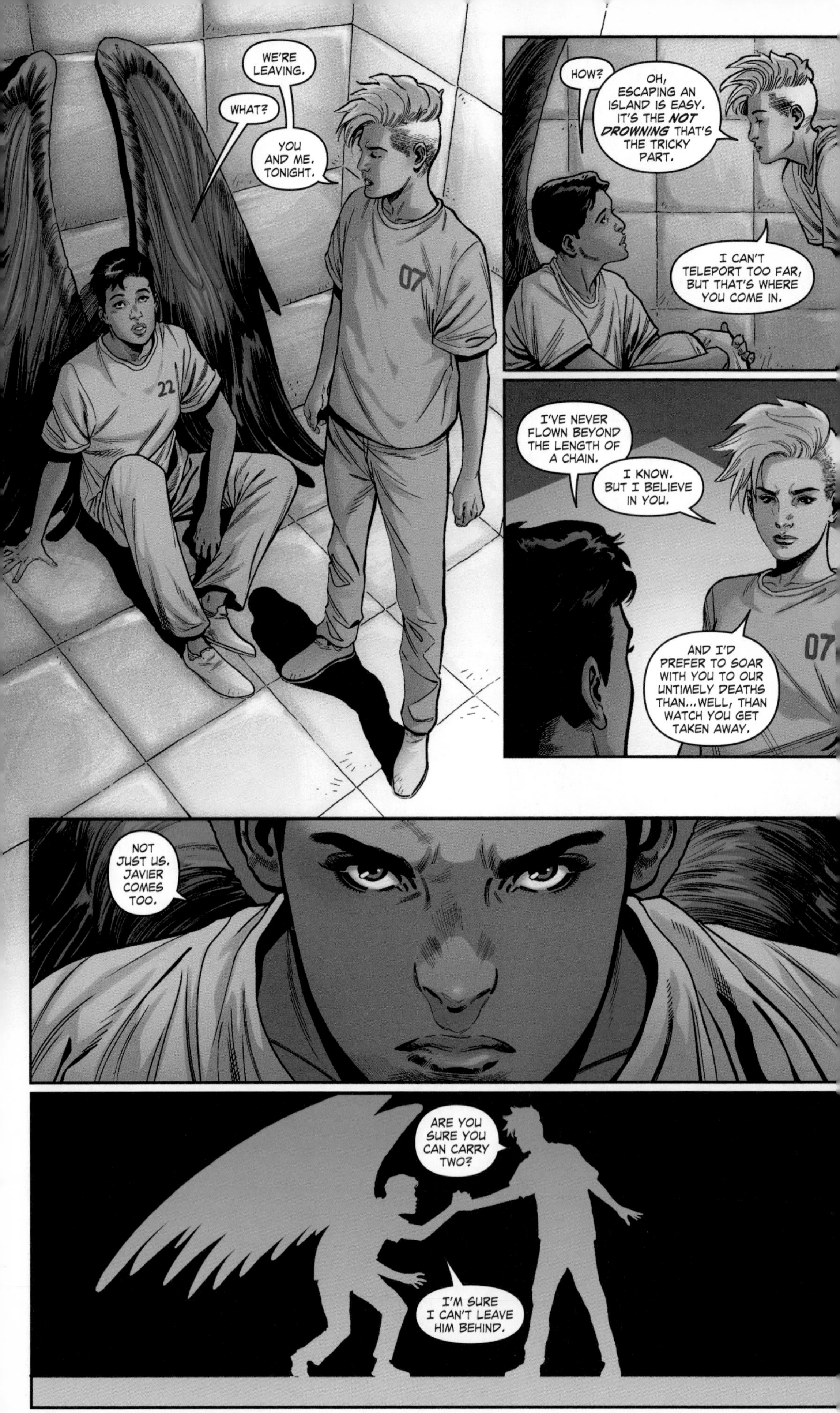
WE'RE LEAVING.
WHAT?
YOU AND ME. TONIGHT.
HOW?
OH, ESCAPING AN ISLAND IS EASY. IT'S THE ***NOT DROWNING*** THAT'S THE TRICKY PART.
I CAN'T TELEPORT TOO FAR, BUT THAT'S WHERE YOU COME IN.
I'VE NEVER FLOWN BEYOND THE LENGTH OF A CHAIN.
I KNOW. BUT I BELIEVE IN YOU.
AND I'D PREFER TO SOAR WITH YOU TO OUR UNTIMELY DEATHS THAN...WELL, THAN WATCH YOU GET TAKEN AWAY.
NOT JUST US. JAVIER COMES TOO.
ARE YOU SURE YOU CAN CARRY TWO?
I'M SURE I CAN'T LEAVE HIM BEHIND.

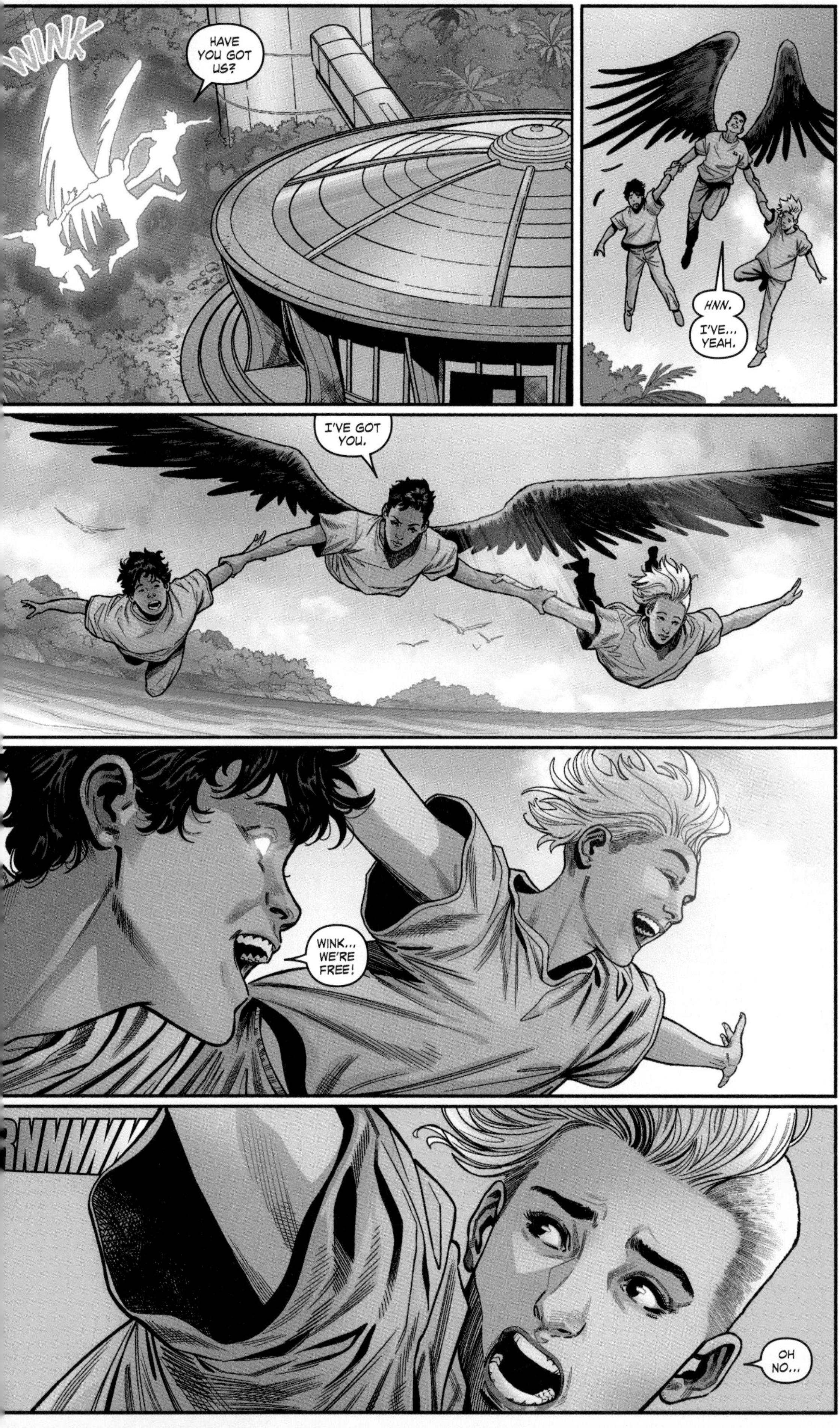
WINK
HAVE YOU GOT US?
HNN. I'VE... YEAH.
I'VE GOT YOU.
WINK... WE'RE FREE!
RNNNNN
OH NO...

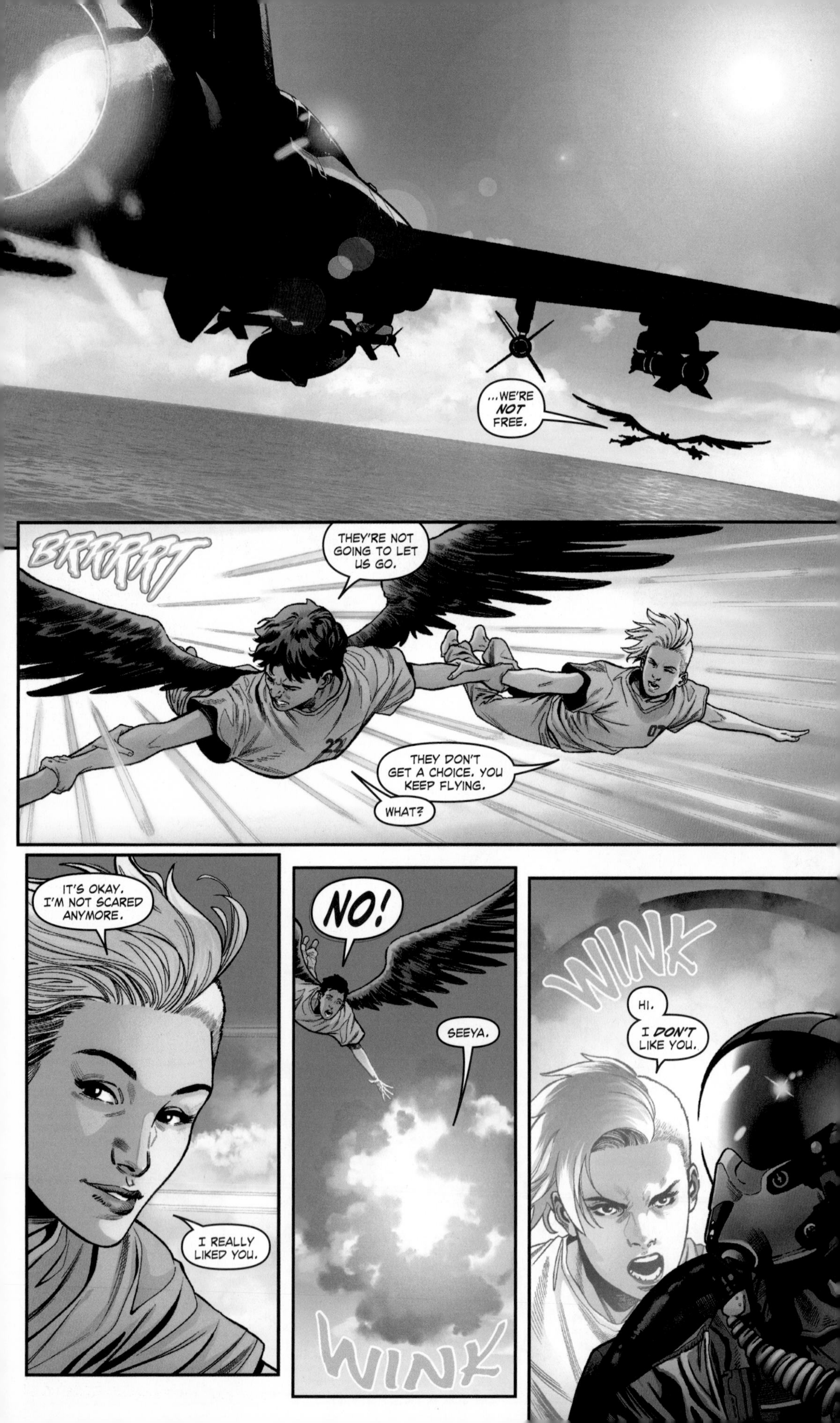
...WE'RE NOT FREE.
BRRRRAT
THEY'RE NOT GOING TO LET US GO.
THEY DON'T GET A CHOICE. YOU KEEP FLYING.
WHAT?
IT'S OKAY. I'M NOT SCARED ANYMORE.
I REALLY LIKED YOU.
NO!
SEEYA.
WINK
WINK
HI.
I DON'T LIKE YOU.

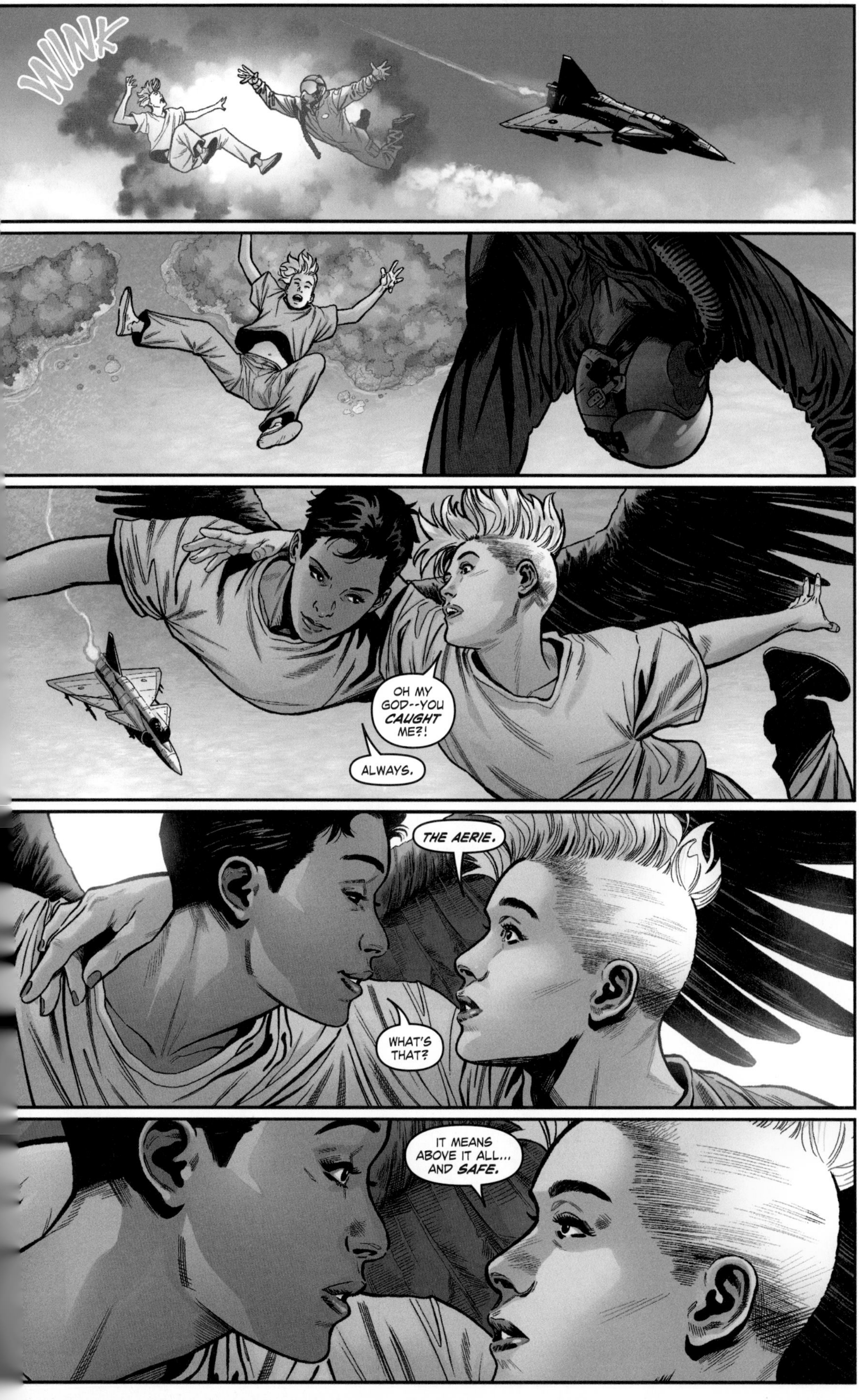
WINK
OH MY GOD--YOU CAUGHT ME?!
ALWAYS.
THE AERIE.
WHAT'S THAT?
IT MEANS ABOVE IT ALL... AND SAFE.

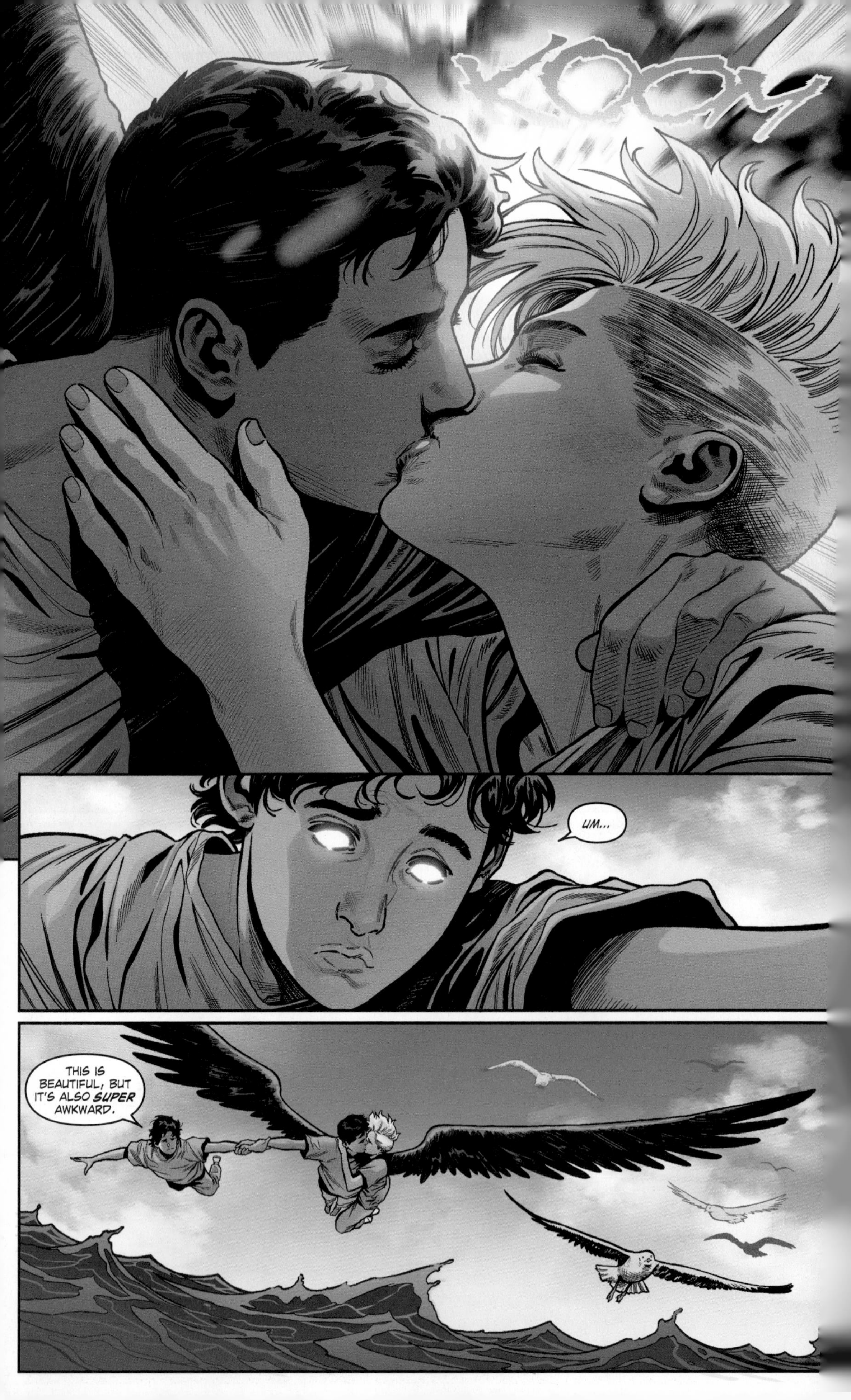
KOOM
UM...
THIS IS BEAUTIFUL, BUT IT'S ALSO SUPER AWKWARD.

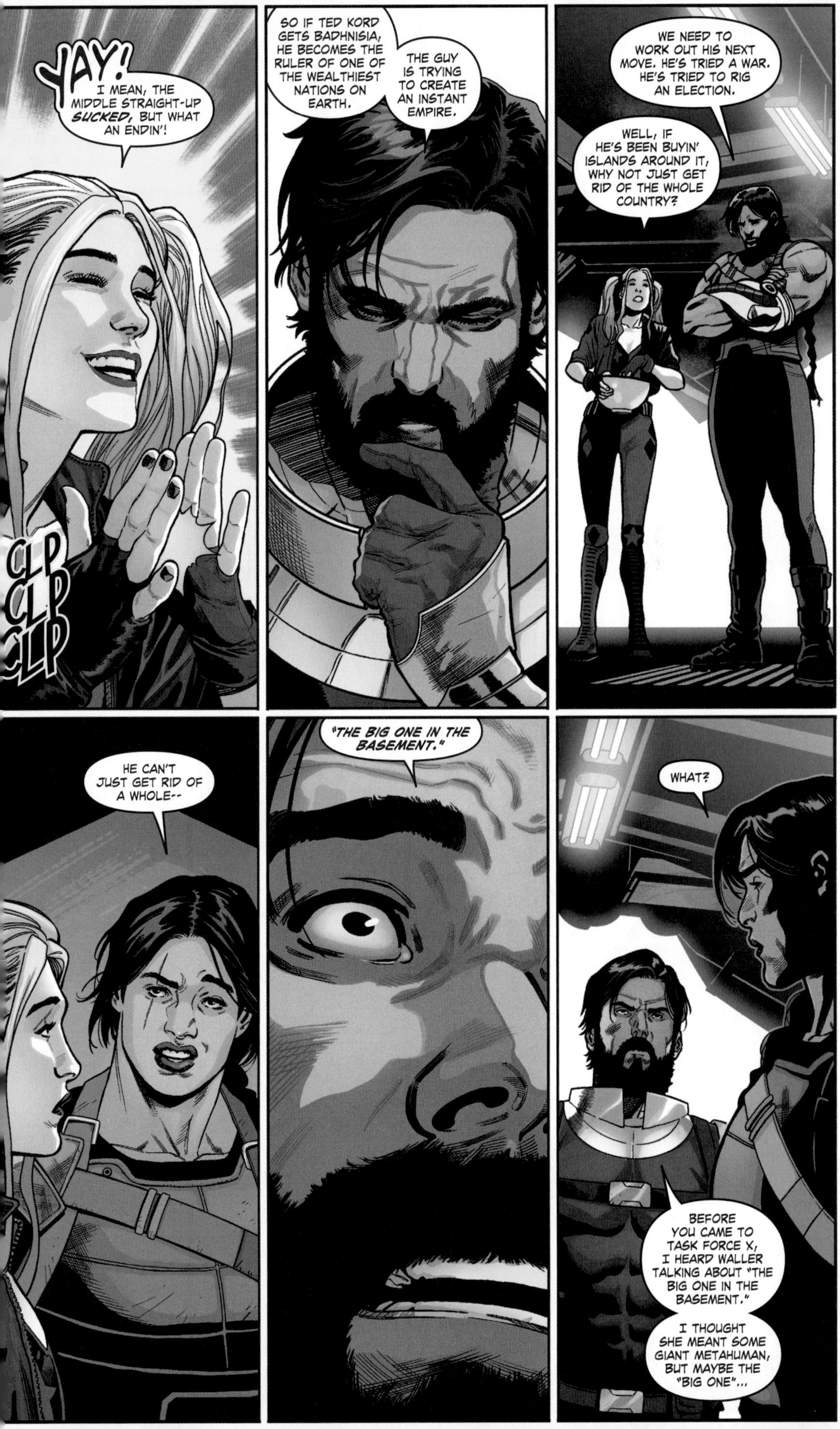
YAY!
I MEAN, THE MIDDLE STRAIGHT-UP *SUCKED,* BUT WHAT AN ENDIN'!
CLP CLP CLP
SO IF TED KORD GETS BADHNISIA, HE BECOMES THE RULER OF ONE OF THE WEALTHIEST NATIONS ON EARTH.
THE GUY IS TRYING TO CREATE AN INSTANT EMPIRE.
WE NEED TO WORK OUT HIS NEXT MOVE. HE'S TRIED A WAR. HE'S TRIED TO RIG AN ELECTION.
WELL, IF HE'S BEEN BUYIN' ISLANDS AROUND IT, WHY NOT JUST GET RID OF THE WHOLE COUNTRY?
HE CAN'T JUST GET RID OF A WHOLE--
"THE BIG ONE IN THE BASEMENT."
WHAT?
BEFORE YOU CAME TO TASK FORCE X, I HEARD WALLER TALKING ABOUT "THE BIG ONE IN THE BASEMENT."
I THOUGHT SHE MEANT SOME GIANT METAHUMAN, BUT MAYBE THE "BIG ONE"...

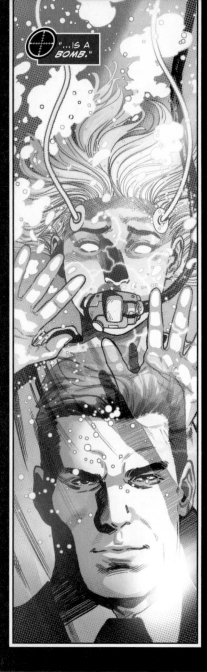

"...IS A *BOMB*."

HOW ARE YOU FEELING, LOLA?

IT'LL ALL BE OVER SOON.

ALMOST THE BIG DAY.

SOMEONE *WILL* STOP YOU. IT'S ONLY A MATTER OF TIME.

SOMEONE, HEY? YOU COULDN'T COME UP WITH A MORE SPECIFIC THREAT?

IT'S OKAY. I'M ALMOST DONE WITH YOU, TOO.

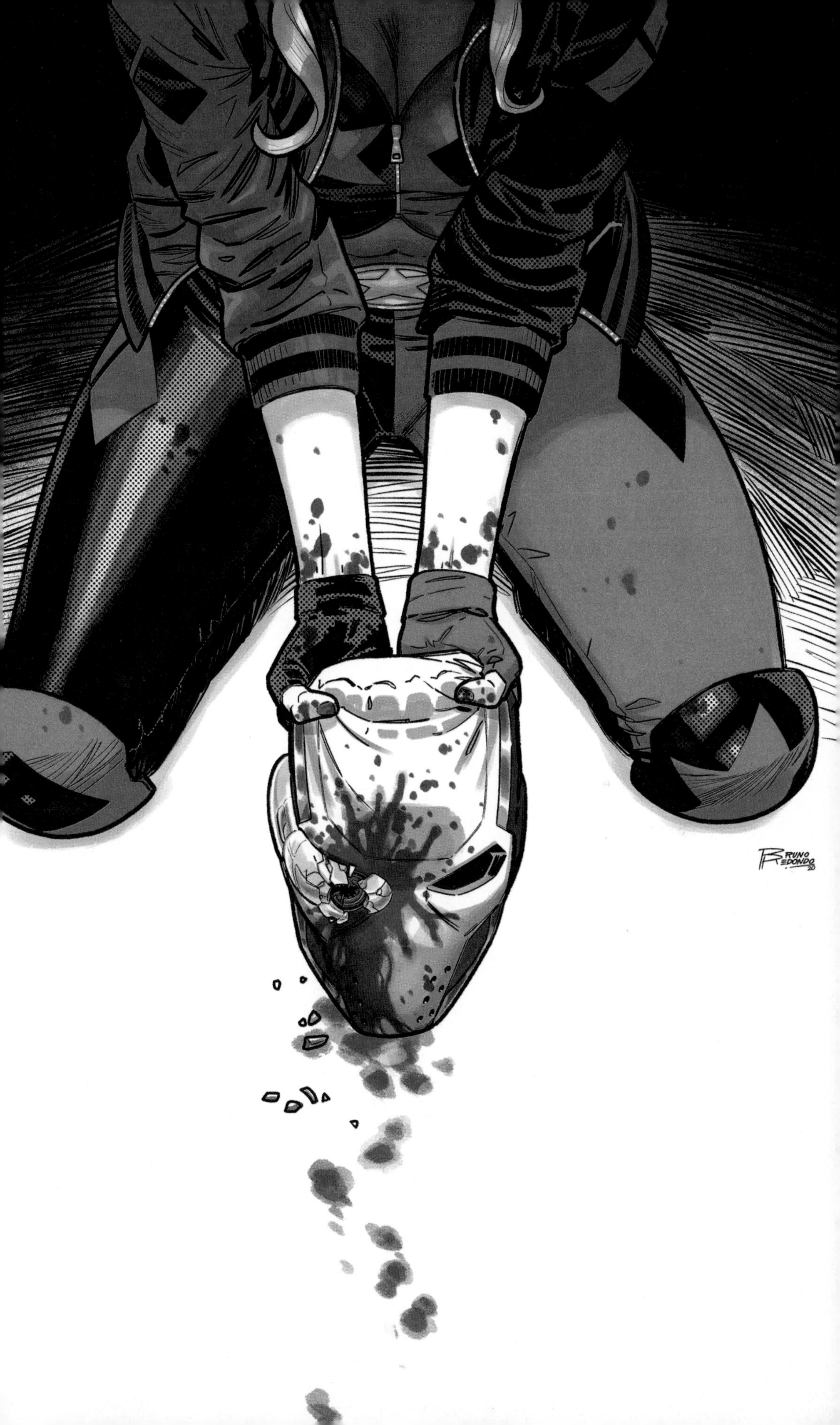
BRUNO
REDONDO
20

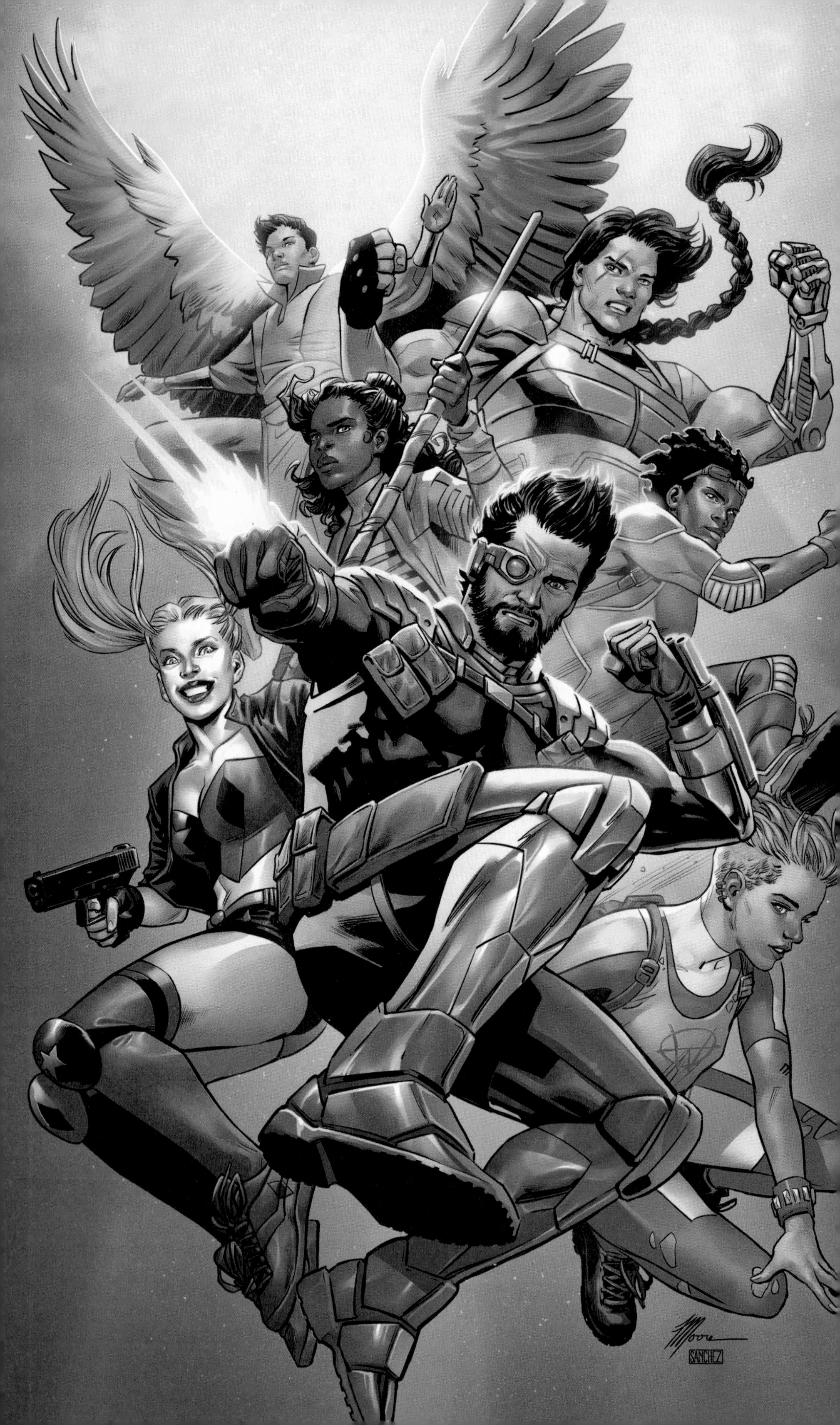
Moore
SANCHEZ

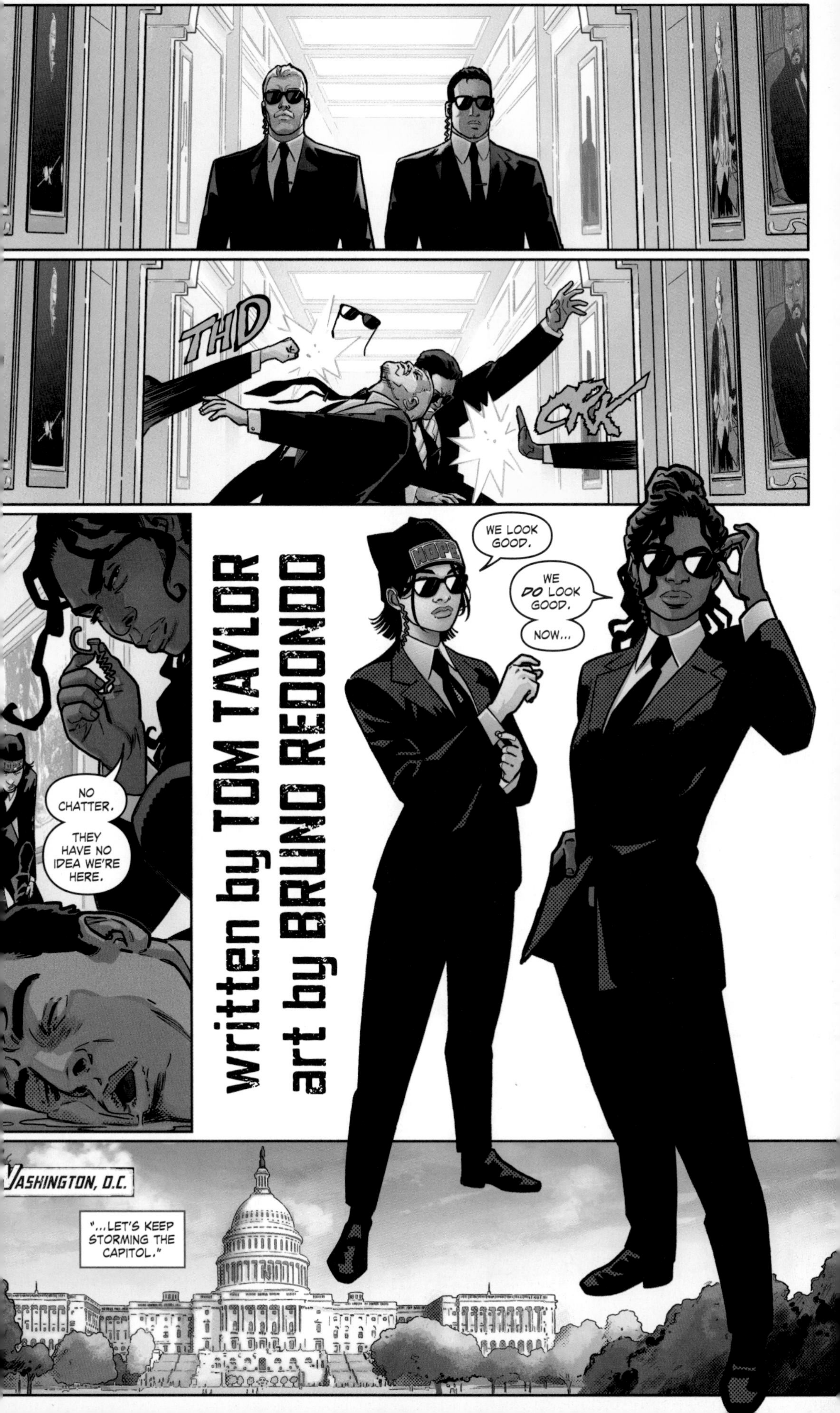
THD
CRK
written by TOM TAYLOR
art by BRUNO REDONDO
NO CHATTER.
THEY HAVE NO IDEA WE'RE HERE.
WE LOOK GOOD.
WE DO LOOK GOOD.
NOW...
WASHINGTON, D.C.
"...LET'S KEEP STORMING THE CAPITOL."

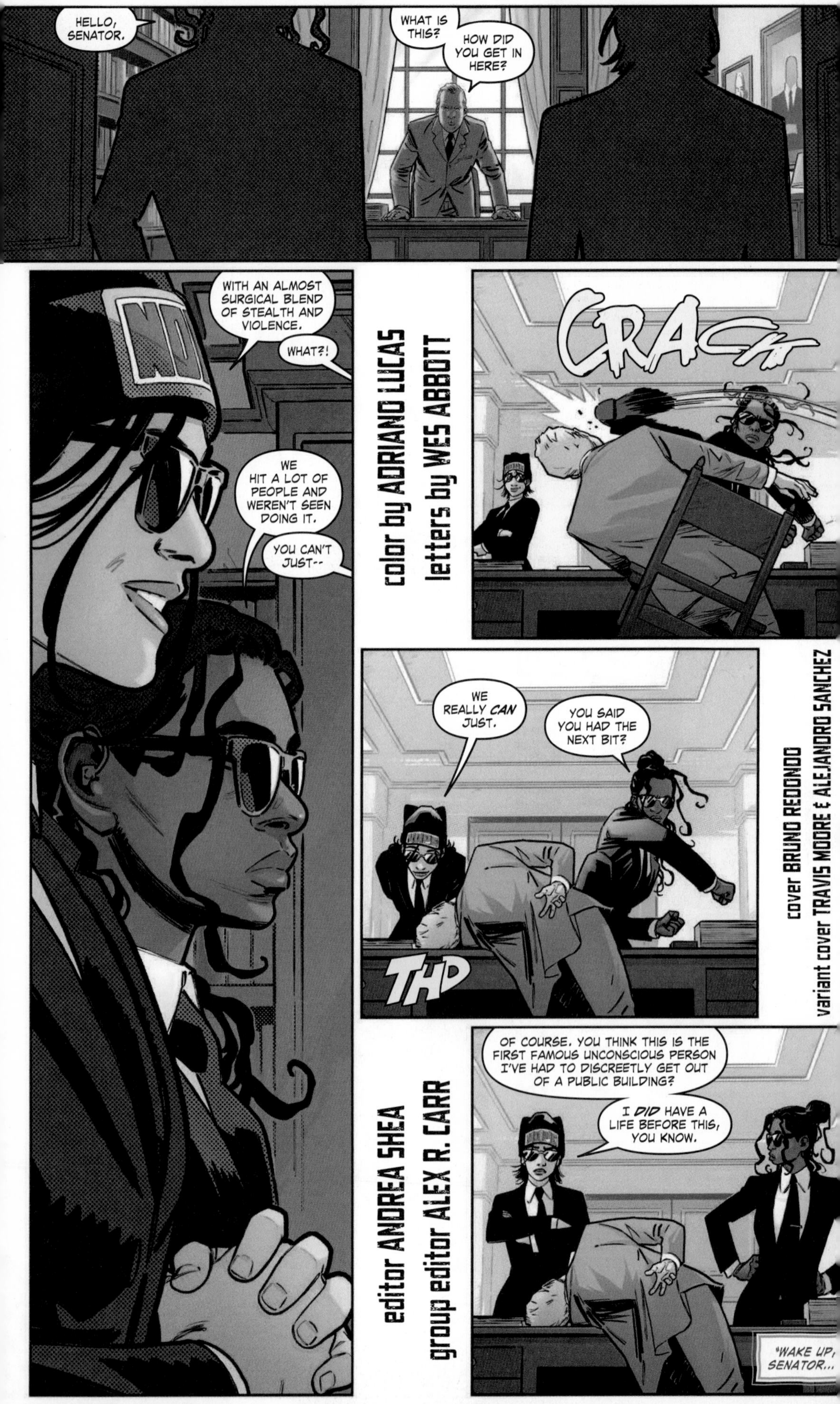
HELLO, SENATOR.
WHAT IS THIS?
HOW DID YOU GET IN HERE?
WITH AN ALMOST SURGICAL BLEND OF STEALTH AND VIOLENCE.
WHAT?!
WE HIT A LOT OF PEOPLE AND WEREN'T SEEN DOING IT.
YOU CAN'T JUST--
color by ADRIANO LUCAS
letters by WES ABBOTT
CRACK
WE REALLY *CAN* JUST.
YOU SAID YOU HAD THE NEXT BIT?
THD
cover BRUNO REDONDO
variant cover TRAVIS MOORE & ALEJANDRO SANCHEZ
editor ANDREA SHEA
group editor ALEX R. CARR
OF COURSE. YOU THINK THIS IS THE FIRST FAMOUS UNCONSCIOUS PERSON I'VE HAD TO DISCREETLY GET OUT OF A PUBLIC BUILDING?
I *DID* HAVE A LIFE BEFORE THIS, YOU KNOW.
"WAKE UP, SENATOR...

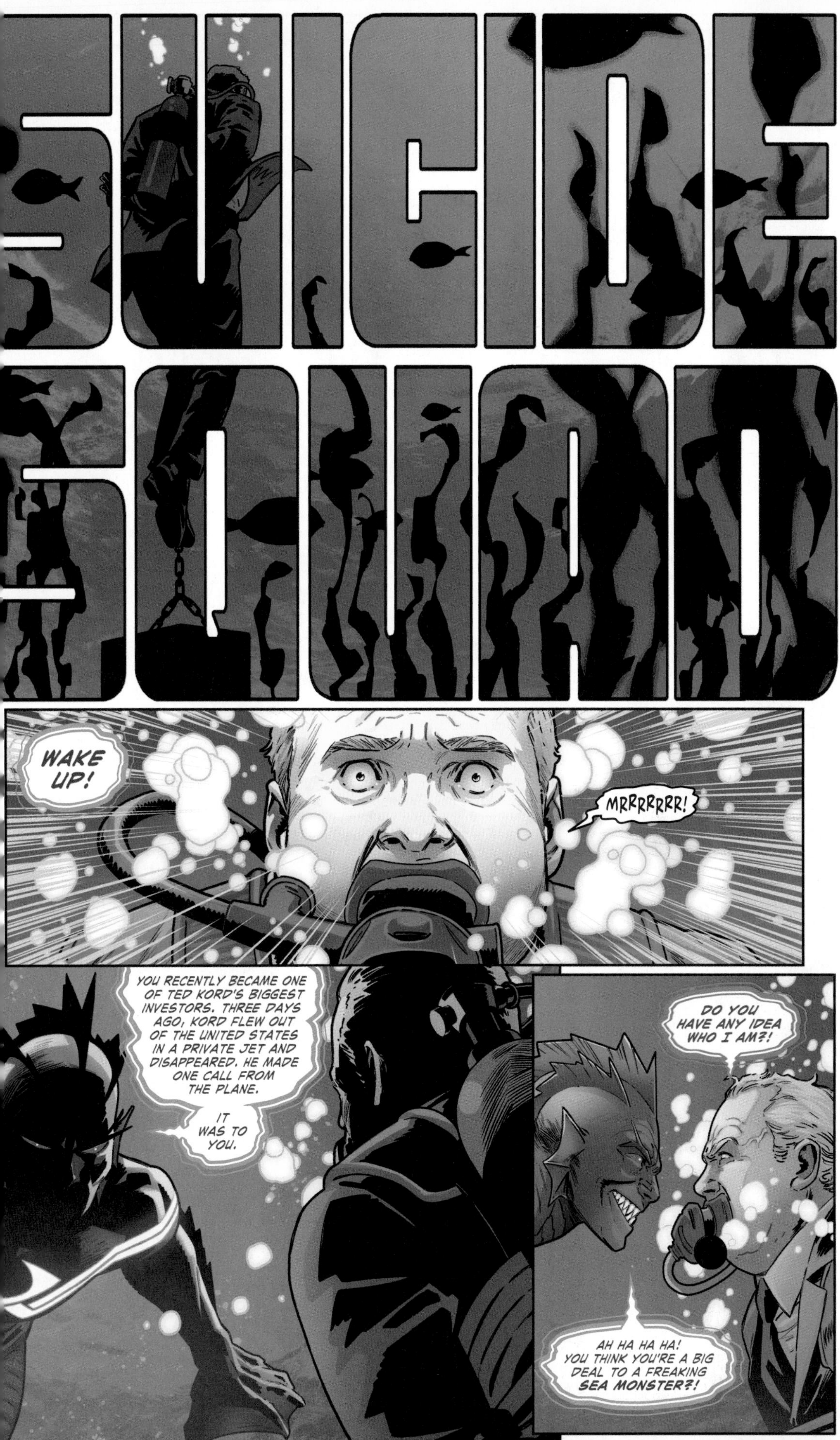
SUICIDE SQUAD
WAKE UP!
MRRRRRRR!
YOU RECENTLY BECAME ONE OF TED KORD'S BIGGEST INVESTORS. THREE DAYS AGO, KORD FLEW OUT OF THE UNITED STATES IN A PRIVATE JET AND DISAPPEARED. HE MADE ONE CALL FROM THE PLANE.
IT WAS TO YOU.
DO YOU HAVE ANY IDEA WHO I AM?!
AH HA HA HA! YOU THINK YOU'RE A BIG DEAL TO A FREAKING SEA MONSTER?!

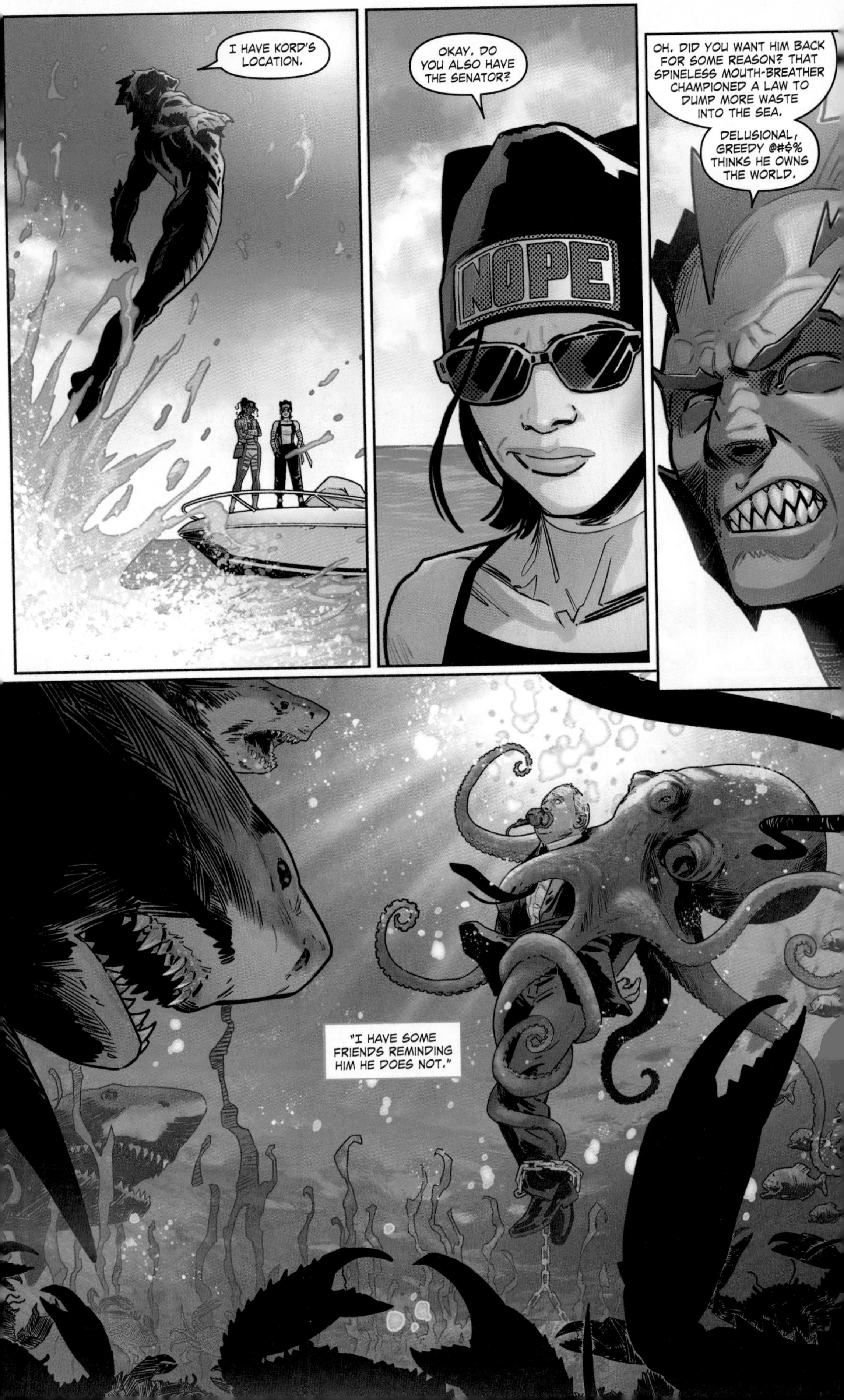
I HAVE KORD'S LOCATION.
OKAY. DO YOU ALSO HAVE THE SENATOR?
OH. DID YOU WANT HIM BACK FOR SOME REASON? THAT SPINELESS MOUTH-BREATHER CHAMPIONED A LAW TO DUMP MORE WASTE INTO THE SEA.
DELUSIONAL, GREEDY @#$% THINKS HE OWNS THE WORLD.
NOPE
"I HAVE SOME FRIENDS REMINDING HIM HE DOES NOT."

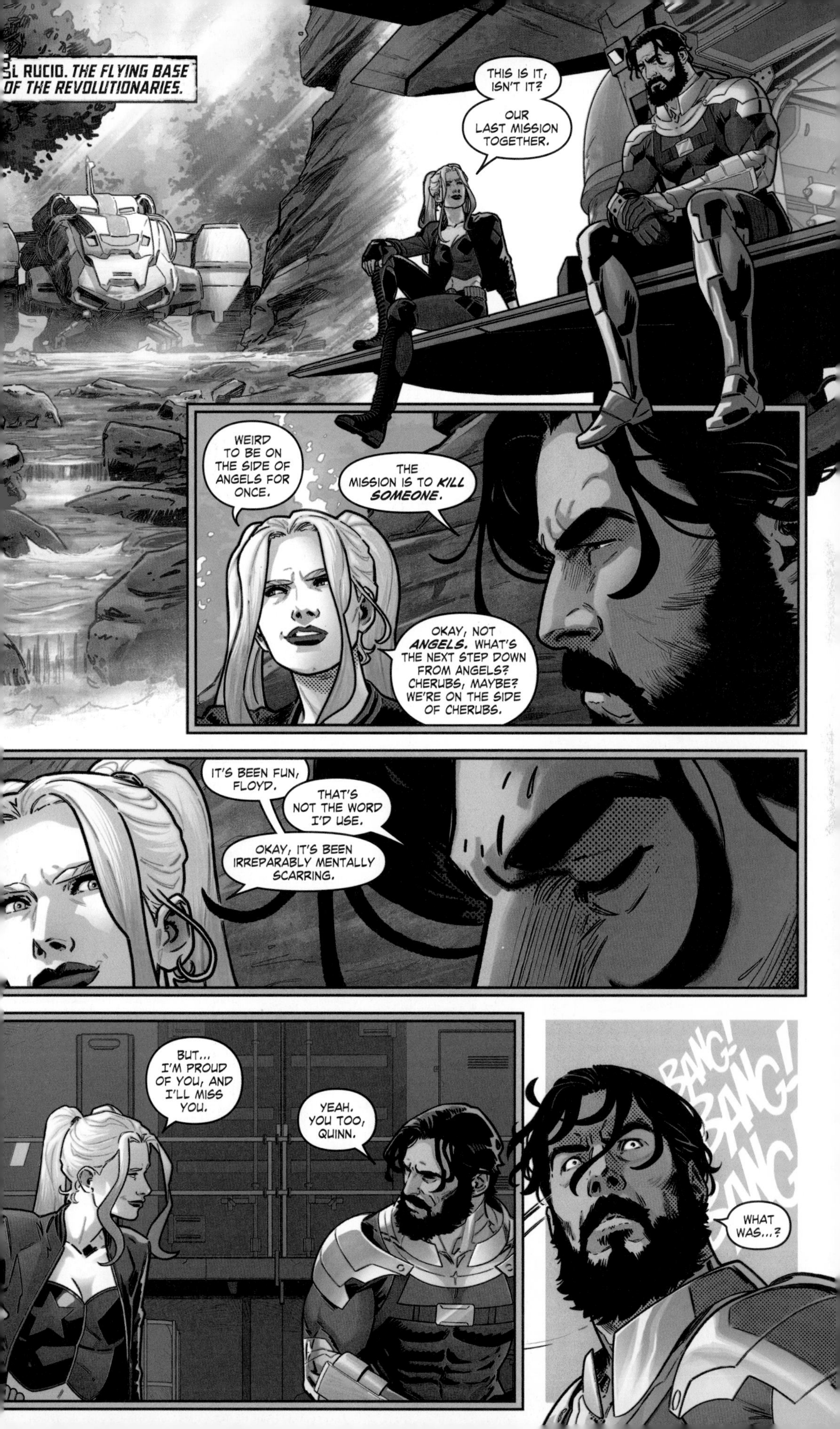

ΞL RUCIO. THE FLYING BASE OF THE REVOLUTIONARIES.
THIS IS IT, ISN'T IT?
OUR LAST MISSION TOGETHER.
WEIRD TO BE ON THE SIDE OF ANGELS FOR ONCE.
THE MISSION IS TO KILL SOMEONE.
OKAY, NOT ANGELS. WHAT'S THE NEXT STEP DOWN FROM ANGELS? CHERUBS, MAYBE? WE'RE ON THE SIDE OF CHERUBS.
IT'S BEEN FUN, FLOYD.
THAT'S NOT THE WORD I'D USE.
OKAY, IT'S BEEN IRREPARABLY MENTALLY SCARRING.
BUT... I'M PROUD OF YOU, AND I'LL MISS YOU.
YEAH. YOU TOO, QUINN.
BANG! BANG!
WHAT WAS...?

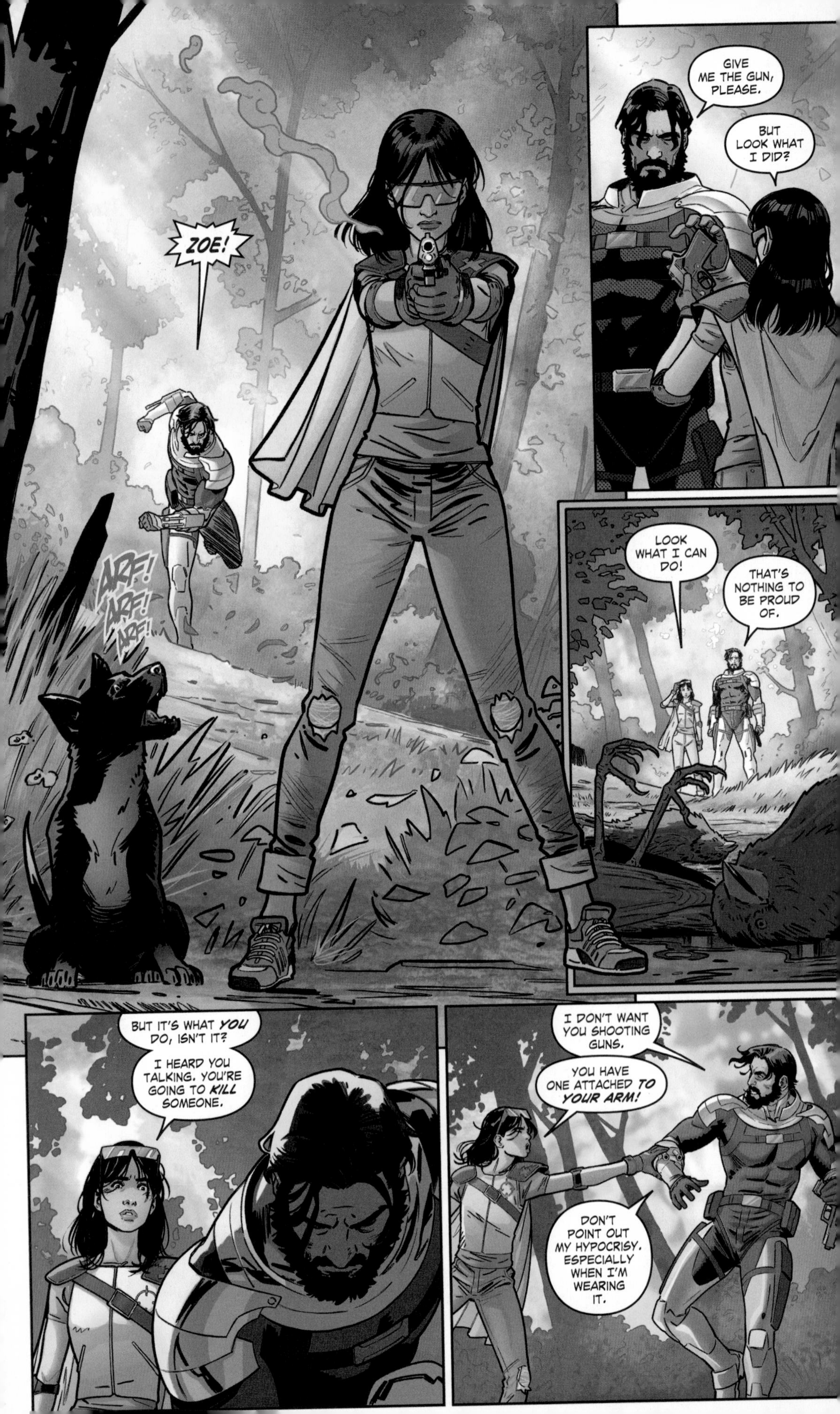
ZOE!
ARF! ARF! ARF!
GIVE ME THE GUN, PLEASE.
BUT LOOK WHAT I DID?
LOOK WHAT I CAN DO!
THAT'S NOTHING TO BE PROUD OF.
BUT IT'S WHAT *YOU* DO, ISN'T IT?
I HEARD YOU TALKING. YOU'RE GOING TO *KILL* SOMEONE.
I DON'T WANT YOU SHOOTING GUNS.
YOU HAVE ONE ATTACHED *TO YOUR ARM!*
DON'T POINT OUT MY HYPOCRISY. ESPECIALLY WHEN I'M WEARING IT.

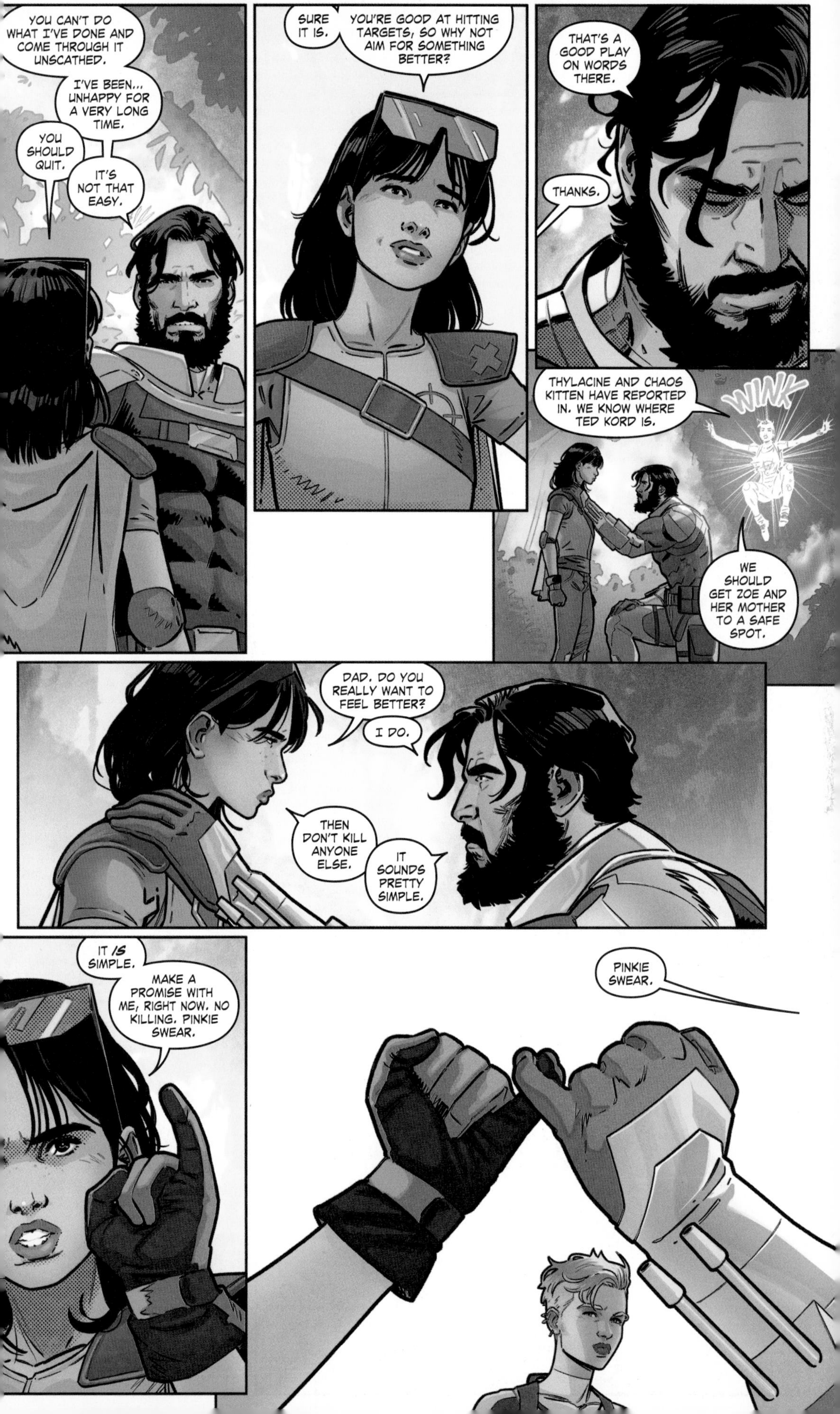

YOU CAN'T DO WHAT I'VE DONE AND COME THROUGH IT UNSCATHED.
I'VE BEEN... UNHAPPY FOR A VERY LONG TIME.
YOU SHOULD QUIT.
IT'S NOT THAT EASY.
SURE IT IS.
YOU'RE GOOD AT HITTING TARGETS, SO WHY NOT AIM FOR SOMETHING BETTER?
THAT'S A GOOD PLAY ON WORDS THERE.
THANKS.
THYLACINE AND CHAOS KITTEN HAVE REPORTED IN. WE KNOW WHERE TED KORD IS.
WINK
WE SHOULD GET ZOE AND HER MOTHER TO A SAFE SPOT.
DAD. DO YOU REALLY WANT TO FEEL BETTER?
I DO.
THEN DON'T KILL ANYONE ELSE.
IT SOUNDS PRETTY SIMPLE.
IT *IS* SIMPLE.
MAKE A PROMISE WITH ME, RIGHT NOW. NO KILLING. PINKIE SWEAR.
PINKIE SWEAR.

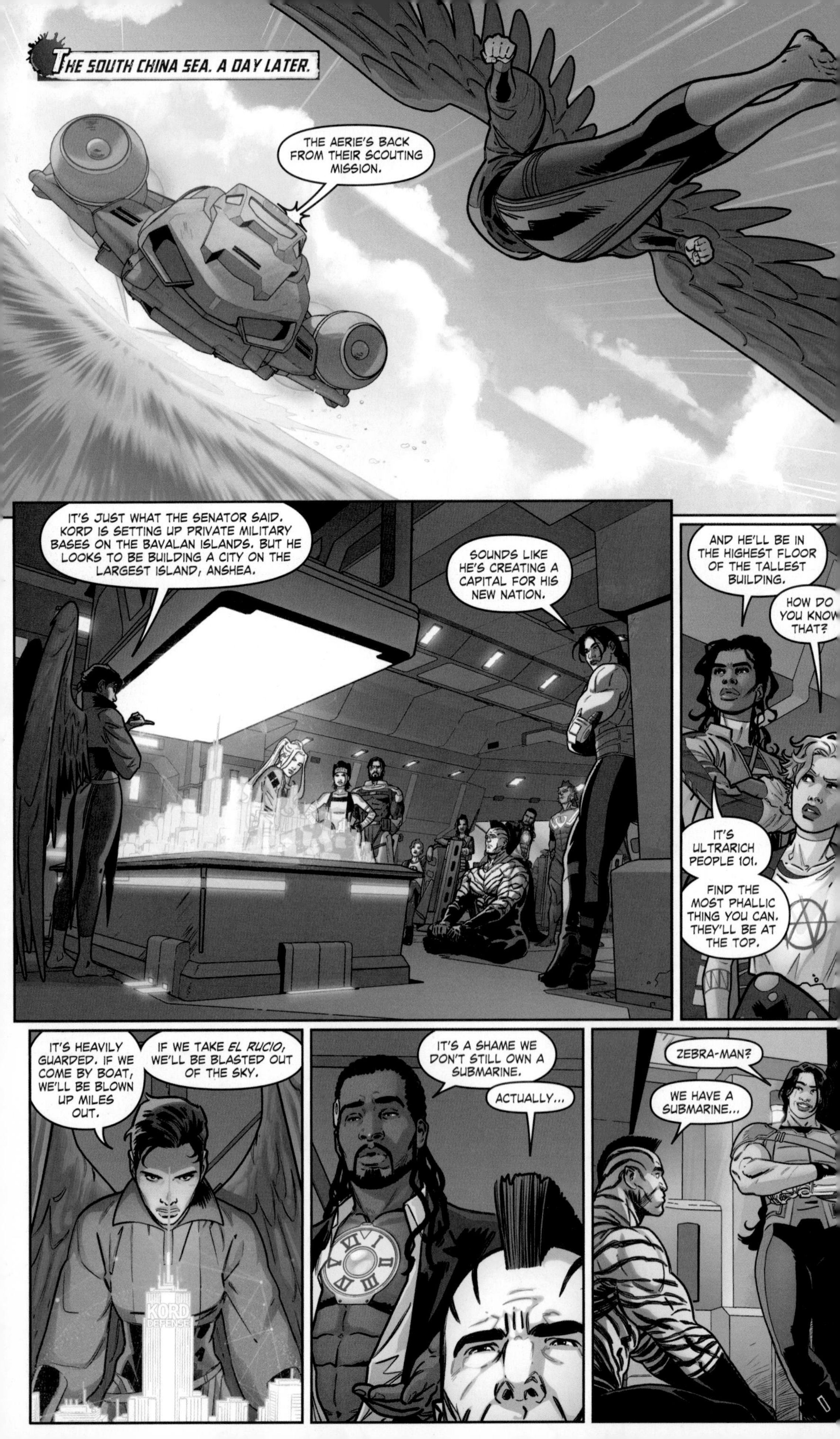
THE SOUTH CHINA SEA. A DAY LATER.
THE AERIE'S BACK FROM THEIR SCOUTING MISSION.
IT'S JUST WHAT THE SENATOR SAID. KORD IS SETTING UP PRIVATE MILITARY BASES ON THE BAVALAN ISLANDS. BUT HE LOOKS TO BE BUILDING A CITY ON THE LARGEST ISLAND, ANSHEA.
SOUNDS LIKE HE'S CREATING A CAPITAL FOR HIS NEW NATION.
AND HE'LL BE IN THE HIGHEST FLOOR OF THE TALLEST BUILDING.
HOW DO YOU KNOW THAT?
IT'S ULTRARICH PEOPLE 101.
FIND THE MOST PHALLIC THING YOU CAN. THEY'LL BE AT THE TOP.
IT'S HEAVILY GUARDED. IF WE COME BY BOAT, WE'LL BE BLOWN UP MILES OUT.
IF WE TAKE *EL RUCIO*, WE'LL BE BLASTED OUT OF THE SKY.
KORD DEFENSE
IT'S A SHAME WE DON'T STILL OWN A SUBMARINE.
ACTUALLY...
ZEBRA-MAN?
WE HAVE A SUBMARINE...

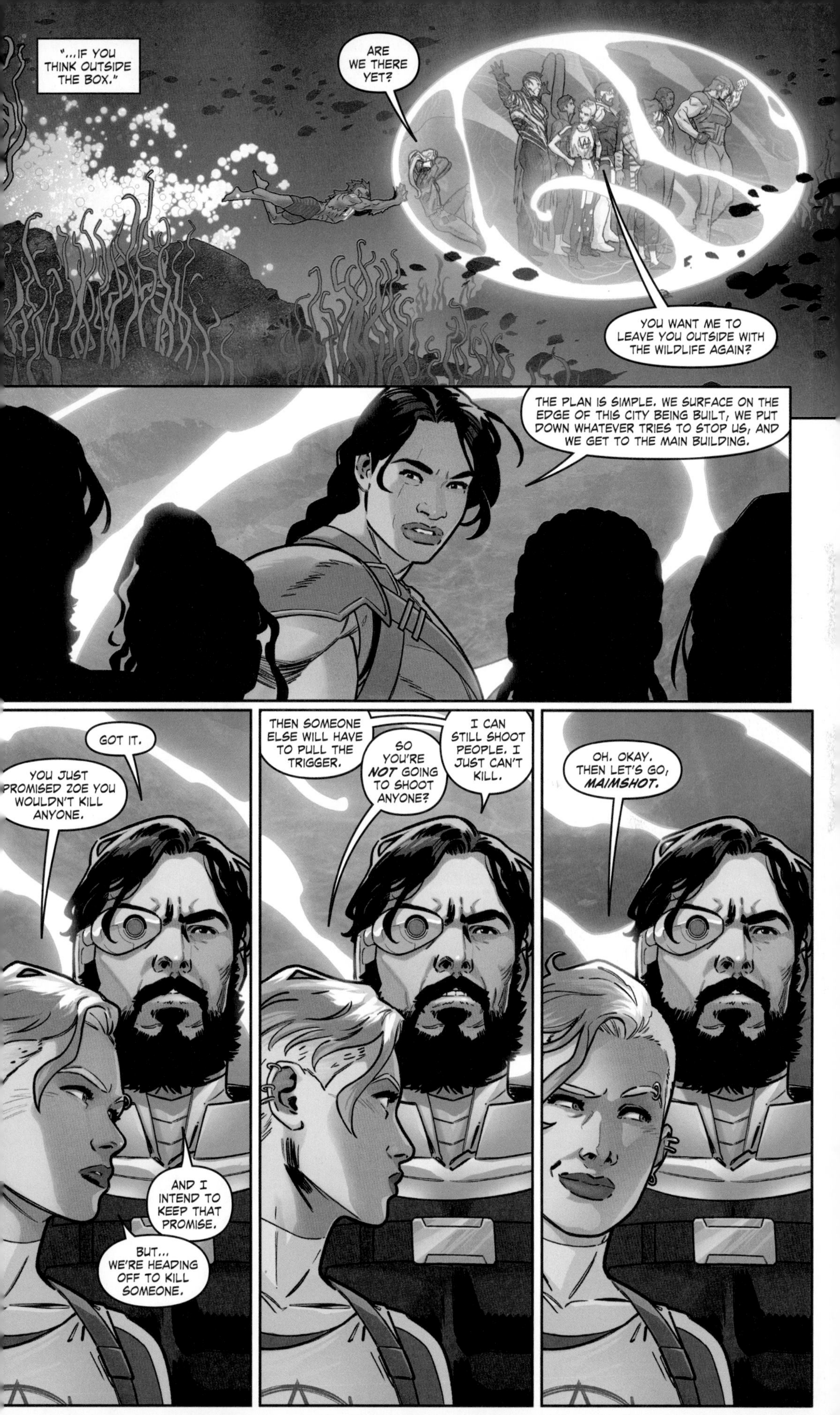
"...IF YOU THINK OUTSIDE THE BOX."
ARE WE THERE YET?
YOU WANT ME TO LEAVE YOU OUTSIDE WITH THE WILDLIFE AGAIN?
THE PLAN IS SIMPLE. WE SURFACE ON THE EDGE OF THIS CITY BEING BUILT, WE PUT DOWN WHATEVER TRIES TO STOP US, AND WE GET TO THE MAIN BUILDING.
GOT IT.
YOU JUST PROMISED ZOE YOU WOULDN'T KILL ANYONE.
AND I INTEND TO KEEP THAT PROMISE.
BUT... WE'RE HEADING OFF TO KILL SOMEONE.
THEN SOMEONE ELSE WILL HAVE TO PULL THE TRIGGER.
SO YOU'RE ***NOT*** GOING TO SHOOT ANYONE?
I CAN STILL SHOOT PEOPLE. I JUST CAN'T KILL.
OH. OKAY. THEN LET'S GO, ***MAIMSHOT.***

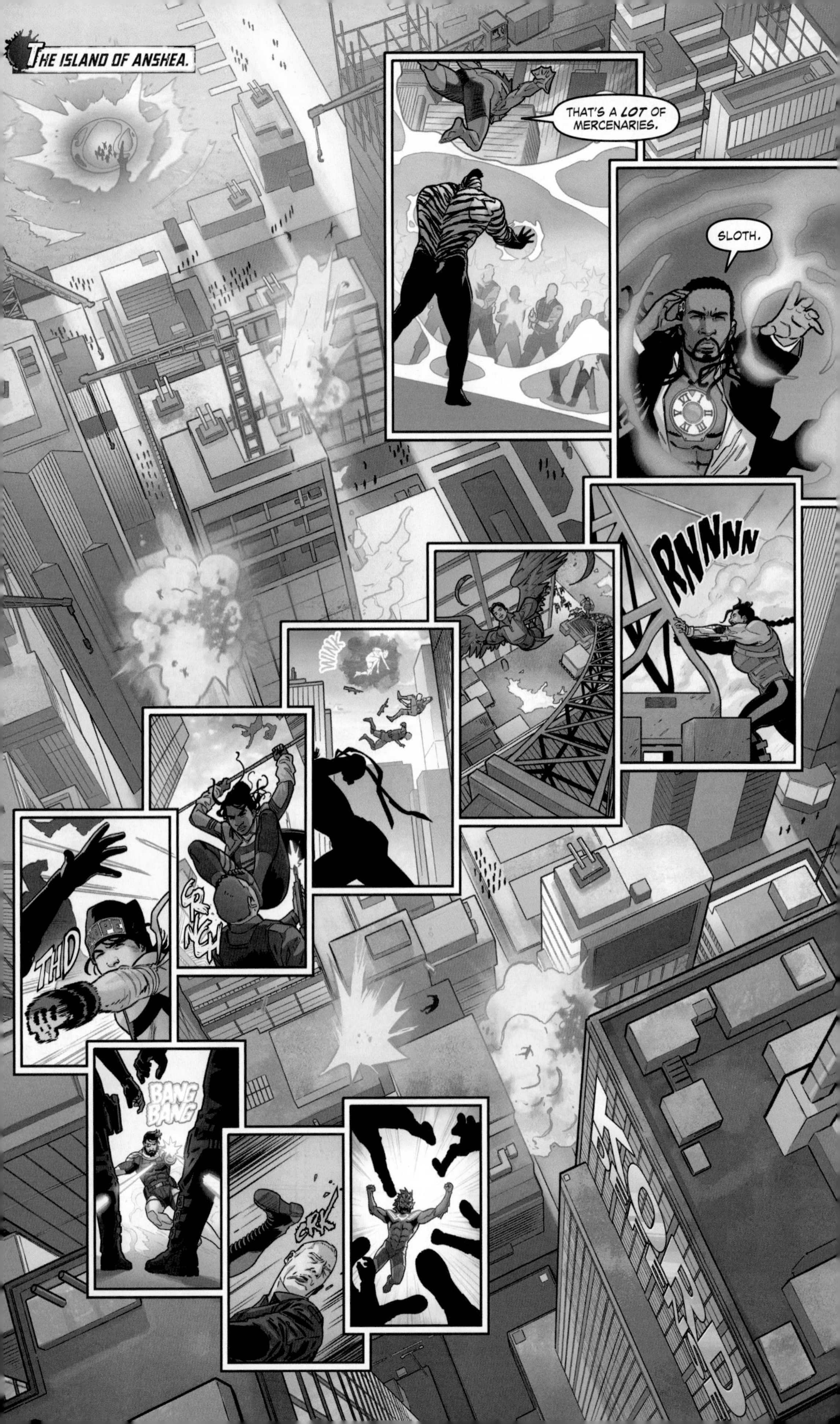

THE ISLAND OF ANSHEA.
THAT'S A LOT OF MERCENARIES.
SLOTH.
RNNNN
WINK
CRUNCH
THD
BANG BANG
CRK

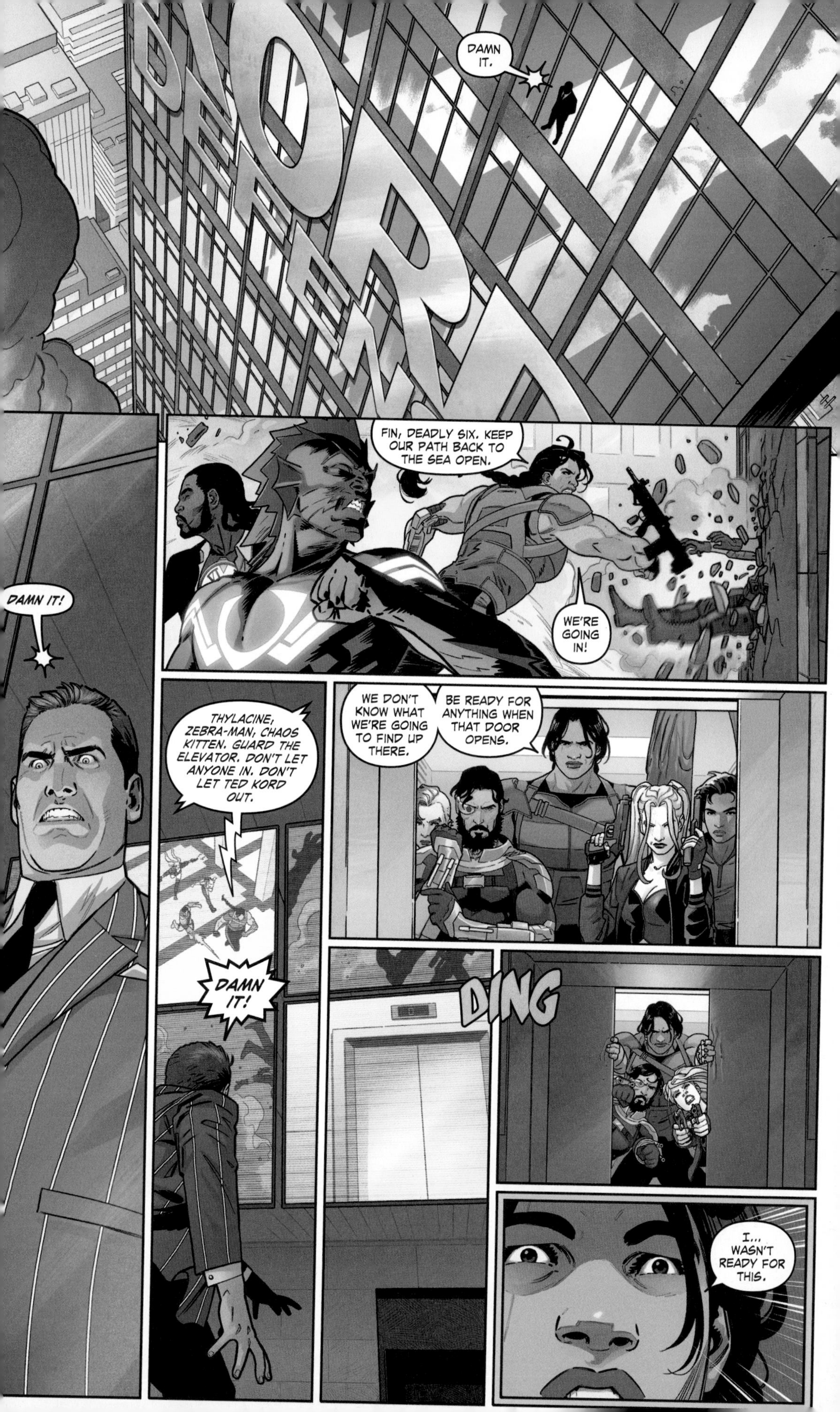
DAMN IT.
FIN, DEADLY SIX. KEEP OUR PATH BACK TO THE SEA OPEN.
WE'RE GOING IN!
DAMN IT!
THYLACINE, ZEBRA-MAN, CHAOS KITTEN. GUARD THE ELEVATOR. DON'T LET ANYONE IN. DON'T LET TED KORD OUT.
DAMN IT!
WE DON'T KNOW WHAT WE'RE GOING TO FIND UP THERE.
BE READY FOR ANYTHING WHEN THAT DOOR OPENS.
DING
I... WASN'T READY FOR THIS.

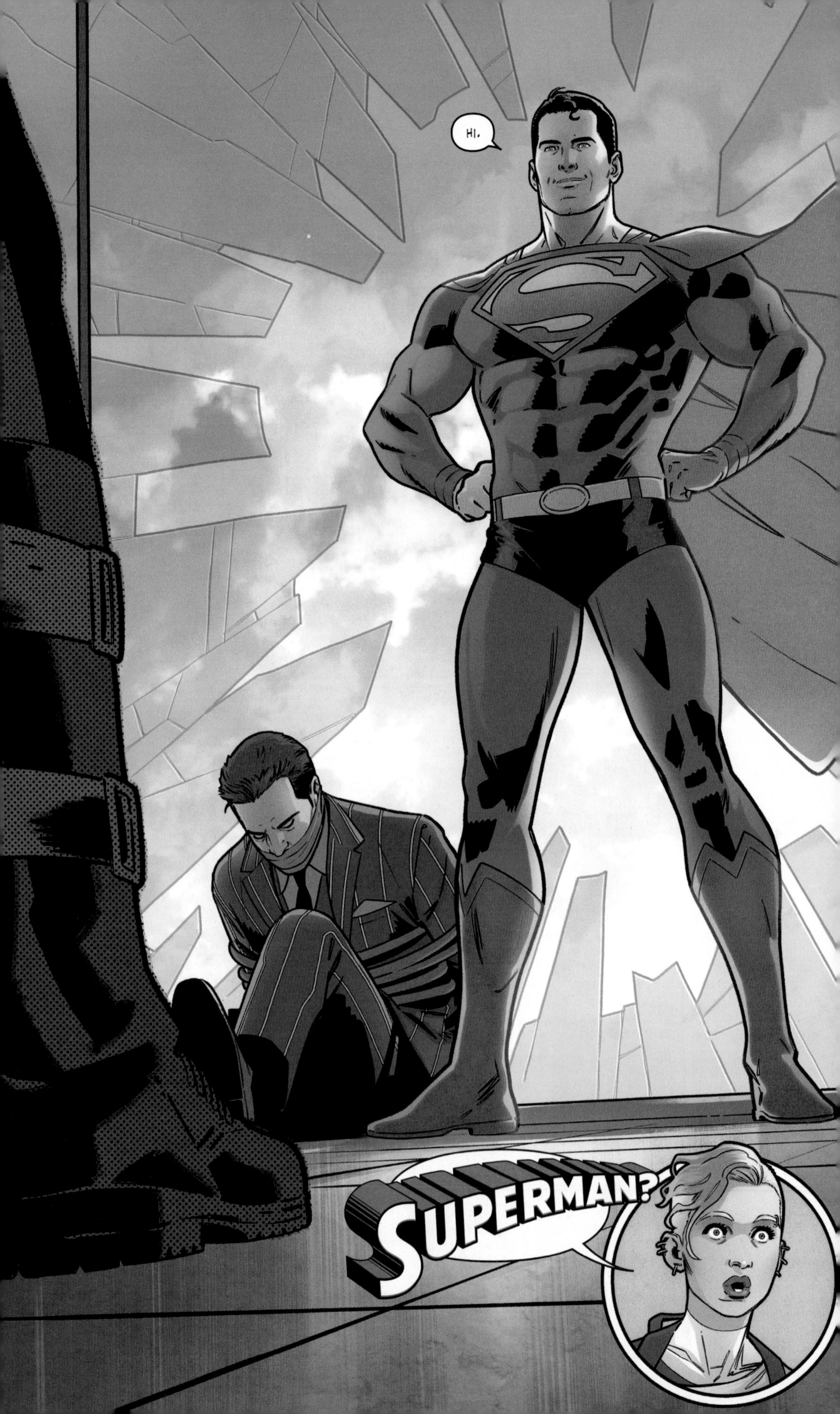
HI.
SUPERMAN?!

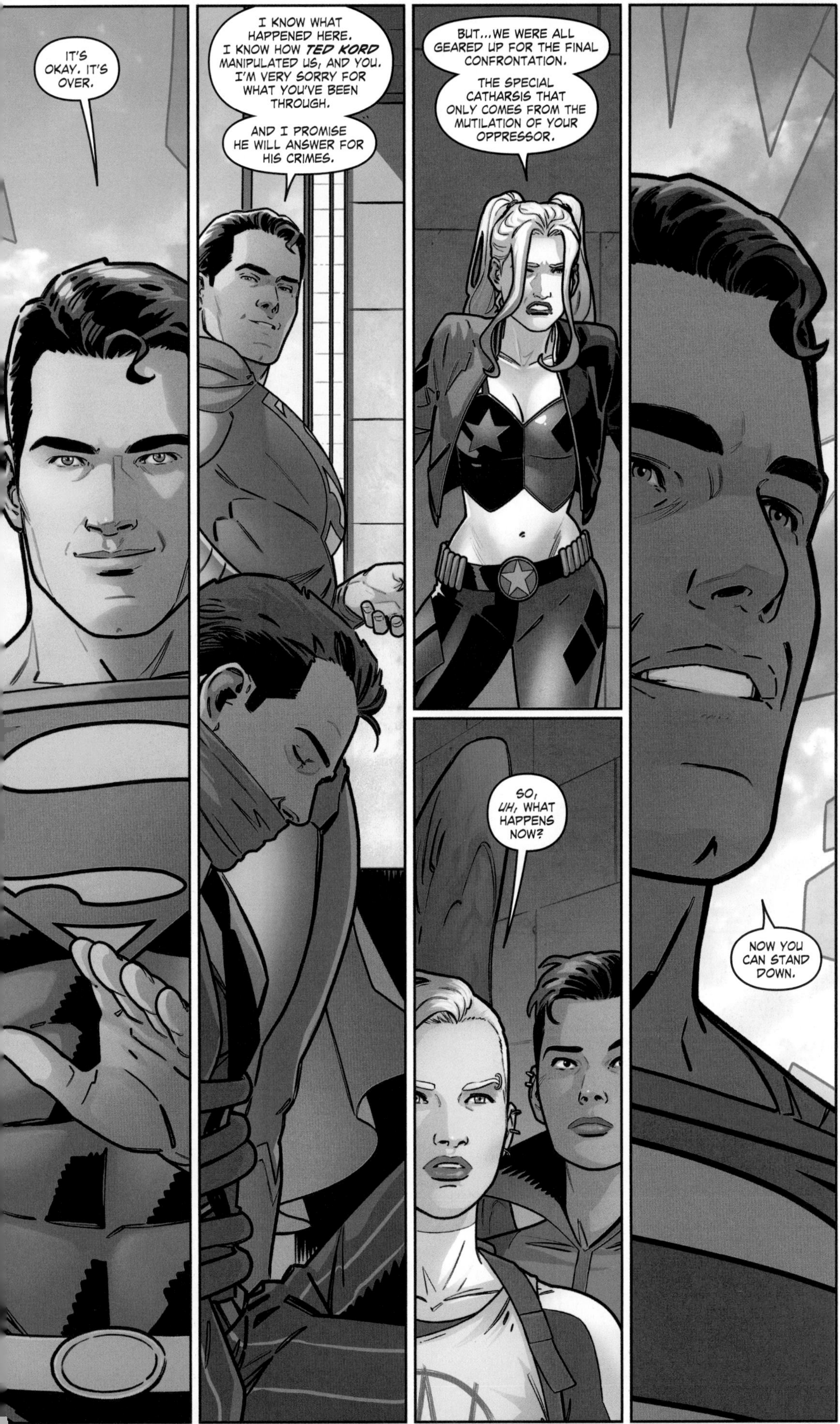
IT'S OKAY. IT'S OVER.
I KNOW WHAT HAPPENED HERE. I KNOW HOW TED KORD MANIPULATED US, AND YOU. I'M VERY SORRY FOR WHAT YOU'VE BEEN THROUGH.
AND I PROMISE HE WILL ANSWER FOR HIS CRIMES.
BUT...WE WERE ALL GEARED UP FOR THE FINAL CONFRONTATION.
THE SPECIAL CATHARSIS THAT ONLY COMES FROM THE MUTILATION OF YOUR OPPRESSOR.
SO, UH, WHAT HAPPENS NOW?
NOW YOU CAN STAND DOWN.

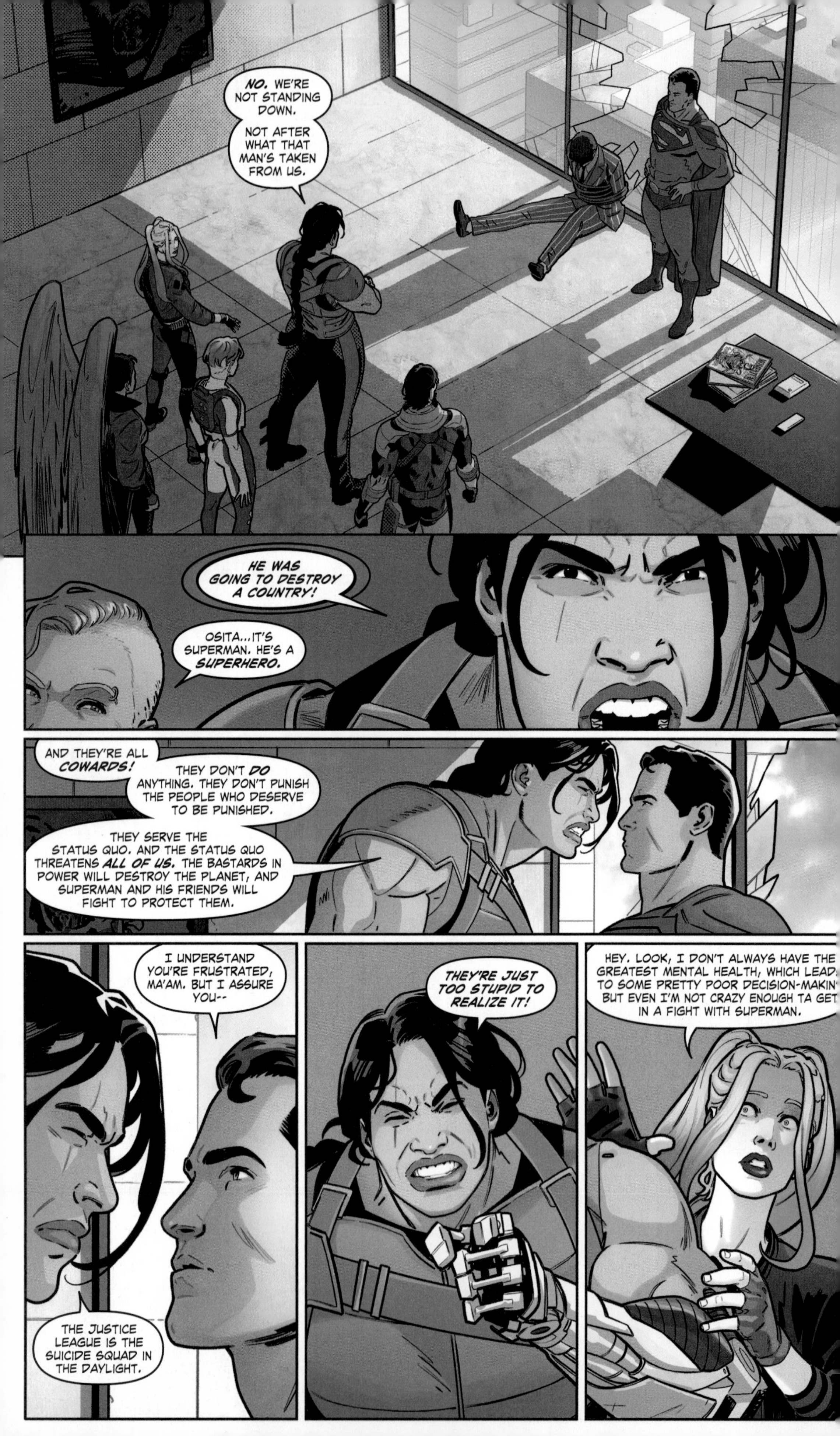
NO. WE'RE NOT STANDING DOWN.
NOT AFTER WHAT THAT MAN'S TAKEN FROM US.
HE WAS GOING TO DESTROY A COUNTRY!
OSITA...IT'S SUPERMAN. HE'S A SUPERHERO.
AND THEY'RE ALL COWARDS!
THEY DON'T DO ANYTHING. THEY DON'T PUNISH THE PEOPLE WHO DESERVE TO BE PUNISHED.
THEY SERVE THE STATUS QUO. AND THE STATUS QUO THREATENS ALL OF US. THE BASTARDS IN POWER WILL DESTROY THE PLANET, AND SUPERMAN AND HIS FRIENDS WILL FIGHT TO PROTECT THEM.
I UNDERSTAND YOU'RE FRUSTRATED, MA'AM. BUT I ASSURE YOU--
THE JUSTICE LEAGUE IS THE SUICIDE SQUAD IN THE DAYLIGHT.
THEY'RE JUST TOO STUPID TO REALIZE IT!
HEY. LOOK, I DON'T ALWAYS HAVE THE GREATEST MENTAL HEALTH, WHICH LEAD TO SOME PRETTY POOR DECISION-MAKIN BUT EVEN I'M NOT CRAZY ENOUGH TA GET IN A FIGHT WITH SUPERMAN.

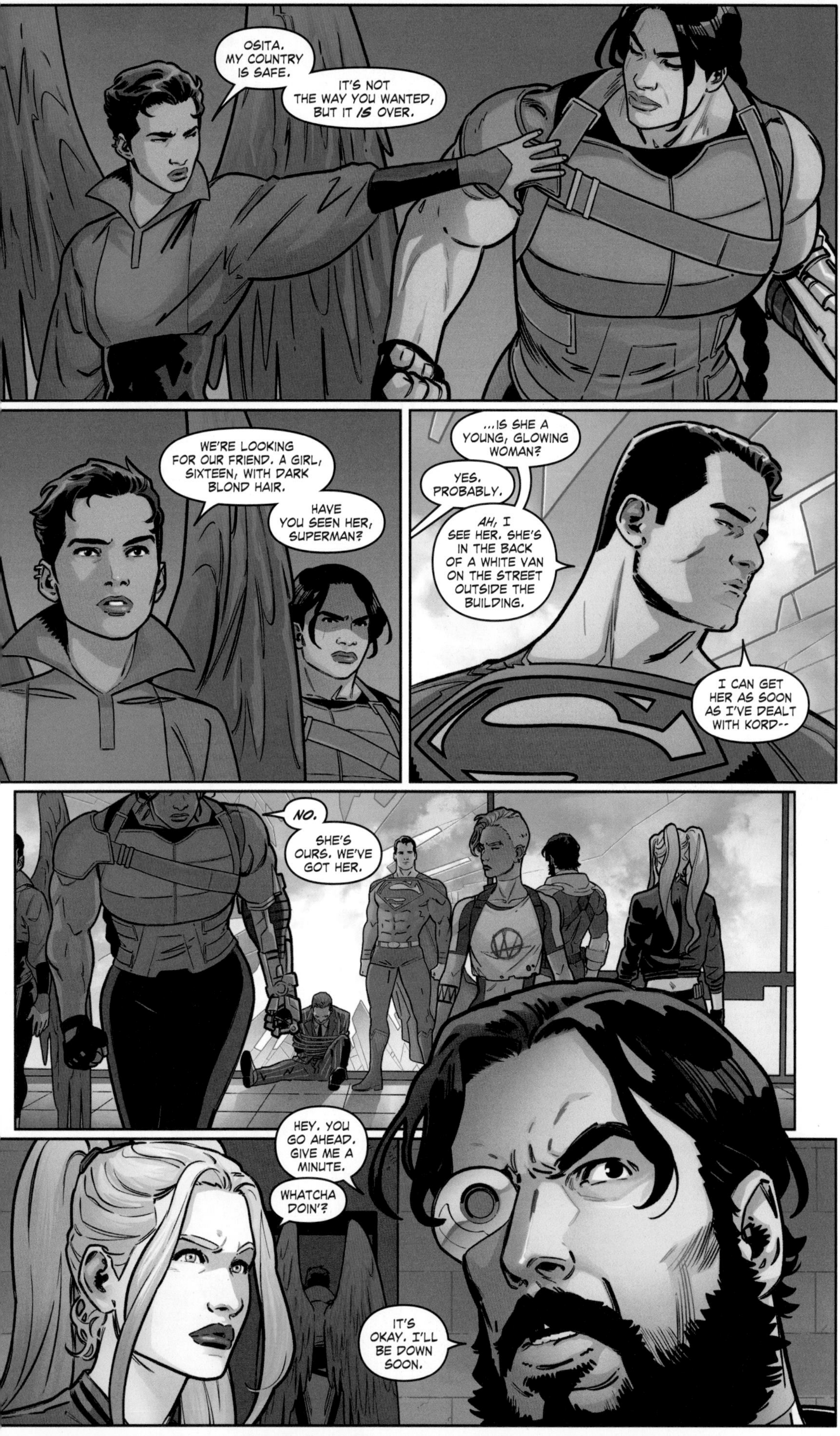
OSITA. MY COUNTRY IS SAFE.
IT'S NOT THE WAY YOU WANTED, BUT IT *IS* OVER.
WE'RE LOOKING FOR OUR FRIEND. A GIRL, SIXTEEN, WITH DARK BLOND HAIR.
HAVE YOU SEEN HER, SUPERMAN?
...IS SHE A YOUNG, GLOWING WOMAN?
YES. PROBABLY.
AH, I SEE HER. SHE'S IN THE BACK OF A WHITE VAN ON THE STREET OUTSIDE THE BUILDING.
I CAN GET HER AS SOON AS I'VE DEALT WITH KORD--
NO.
SHE'S OURS. WE'VE GOT HER.
HEY. YOU GO AHEAD. GIVE ME A MINUTE.
WHATCHA DOIN'?
IT'S OKAY. I'LL BE DOWN SOON.

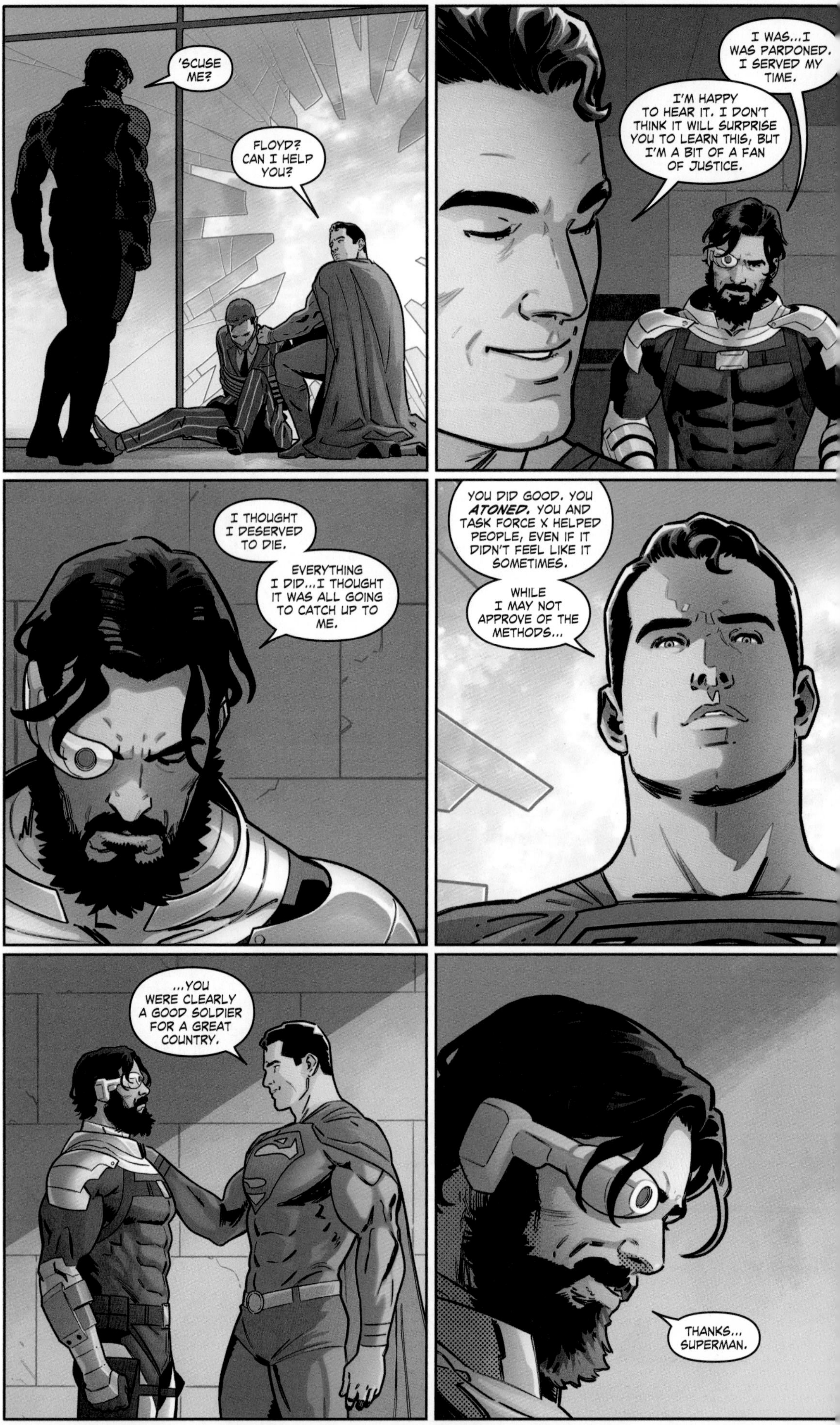
'SCUSE ME?
FLOYD? CAN I HELP YOU?
I WAS...I WAS PARDONED. I SERVED MY TIME.
I'M HAPPY TO HEAR IT. I DON'T THINK IT WILL SURPRISE YOU TO LEARN THIS, BUT I'M A BIT OF A FAN OF JUSTICE.
I THOUGHT I DESERVED TO DIE.
EVERYTHING I DID...I THOUGHT IT WAS ALL GOING TO CATCH UP TO ME.
YOU DID GOOD. YOU *ATONED.* YOU AND TASK FORCE X HELPED PEOPLE, EVEN IF IT DIDN'T FEEL LIKE IT SOMETIMES.
WHILE I MAY NOT APPROVE OF THE METHODS...
...YOU WERE CLEARLY A GOOD SOLDIER FOR A GREAT COUNTRY.
THANKS... SUPERMAN.

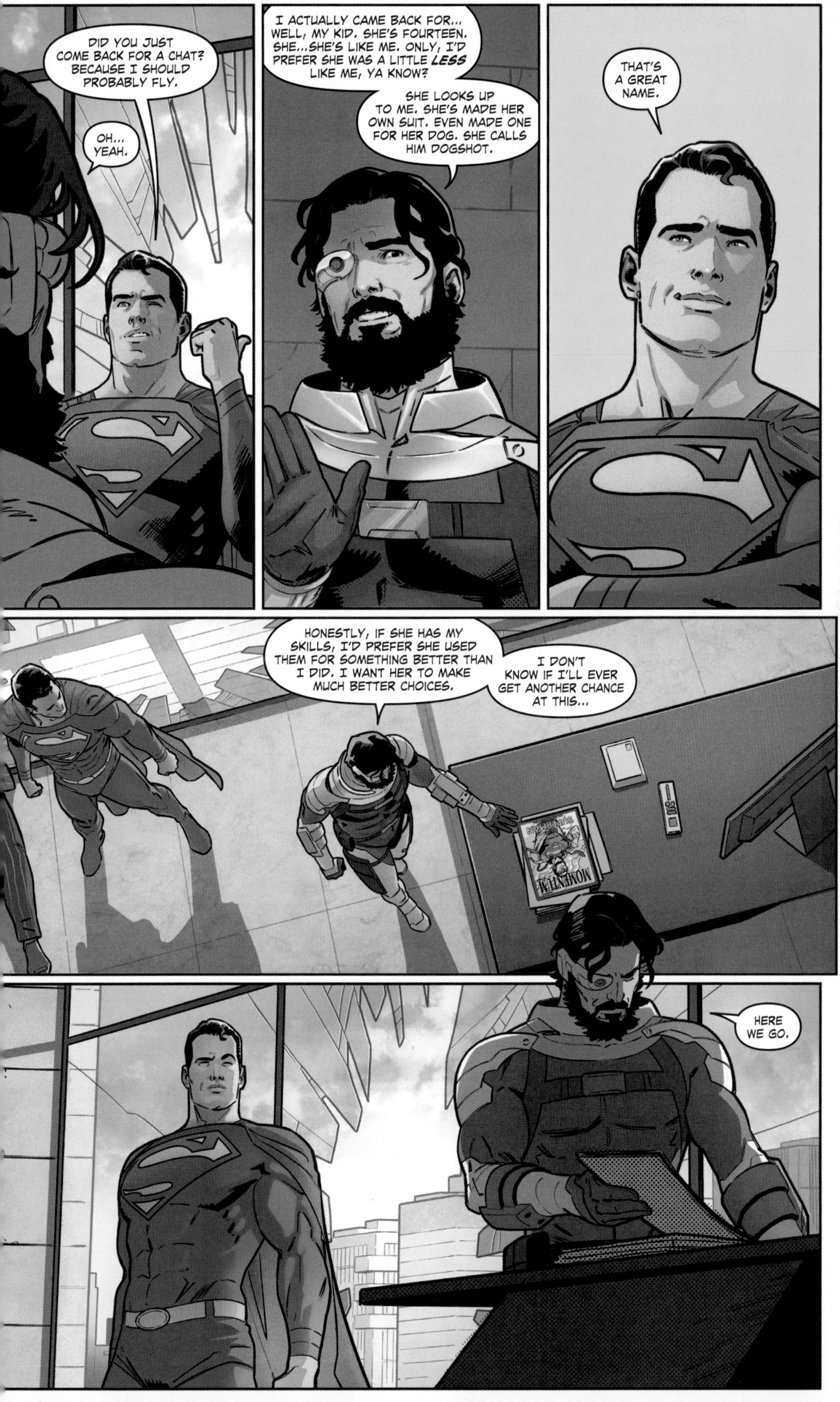
DID YOU JUST COME BACK FOR A CHAT? BECAUSE I SHOULD PROBABLY FLY.
OH... YEAH.
I ACTUALLY CAME BACK FOR... WELL, MY KID. SHE'S FOURTEEN. SHE...SHE'S LIKE ME. ONLY, I'D PREFER SHE WAS A LITTLE *LESS* LIKE ME, YA KNOW?
SHE LOOKS UP TO ME. SHE'S MADE HER OWN SUIT. EVEN MADE ONE FOR HER DOG. SHE CALLS HIM DOGSHOT.
THAT'S A GREAT NAME.
HONESTLY, IF SHE HAS MY SKILLS, I'D PREFER SHE USED THEM FOR SOMETHING BETTER THAN I DID. I WANT HER TO MAKE MUCH BETTER CHOICES.
I DON'T KNOW IF I'LL EVER GET ANOTHER CHANCE AT THIS...
HERE WE GO.

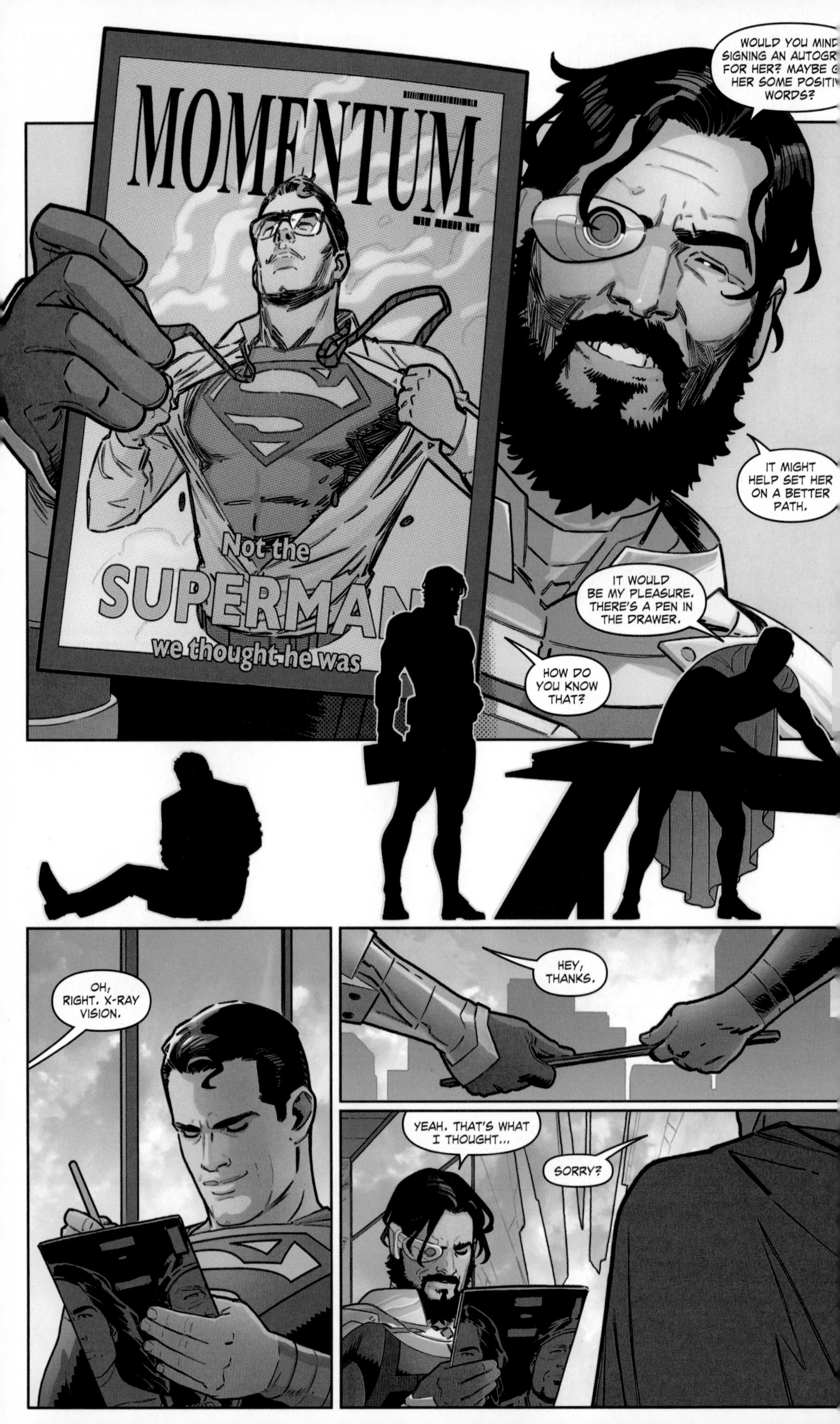
MOMENTUM
Not the
SUPERMAN
we thought he was
WOULD YOU MIND SIGNING AN AUTOGR FOR HER? MAYBE G HER SOME POSITIV WORDS?
IT MIGHT HELP SET HER ON A BETTER PATH.
IT WOULD BE MY PLEASURE. THERE'S A PEN IN THE DRAWER.
HOW DO YOU KNOW THAT?
OH, RIGHT. X-RAY VISION.
HEY, THANKS.
YEAH. THAT'S WHAT I THOUGHT...
SORRY?

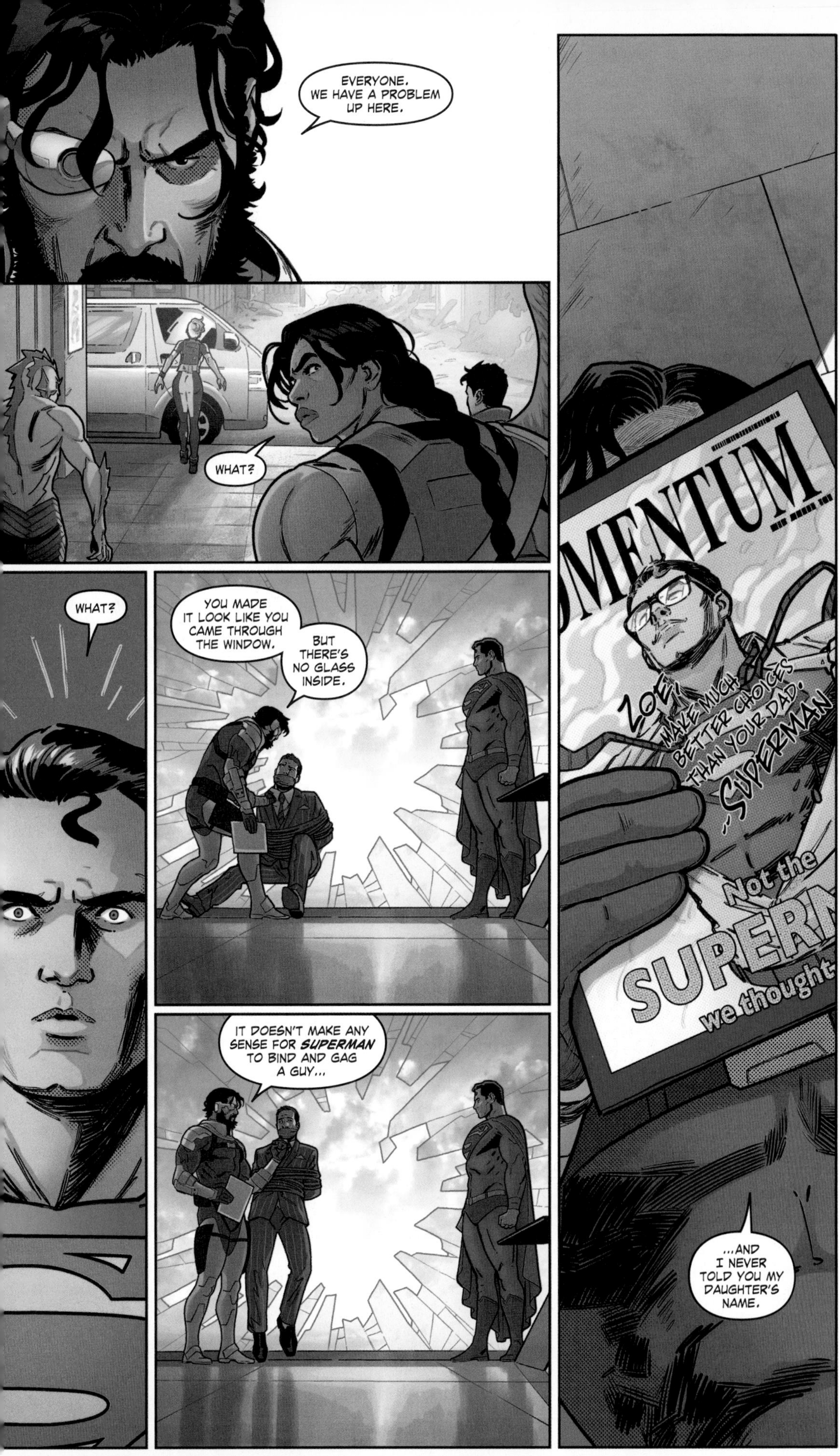
EVERYONE. WE HAVE A PROBLEM UP HERE.
WHAT?
WHAT?
YOU MADE IT LOOK LIKE YOU CAME THROUGH THE WINDOW.
BUT THERE'S NO GLASS INSIDE.
IT DOESN'T MAKE ANY SENSE FOR *SUPERMAN* TO BIND AND GAG A GUY...
MENTUM
ZOE! MAKE MUCH BETTER CHOICES THAN YOUR DAD. -SUPERMAN
Not the
SUPERM
we thought
...AND I NEVER TOLD YOU MY DAUGHTER'S NAME.

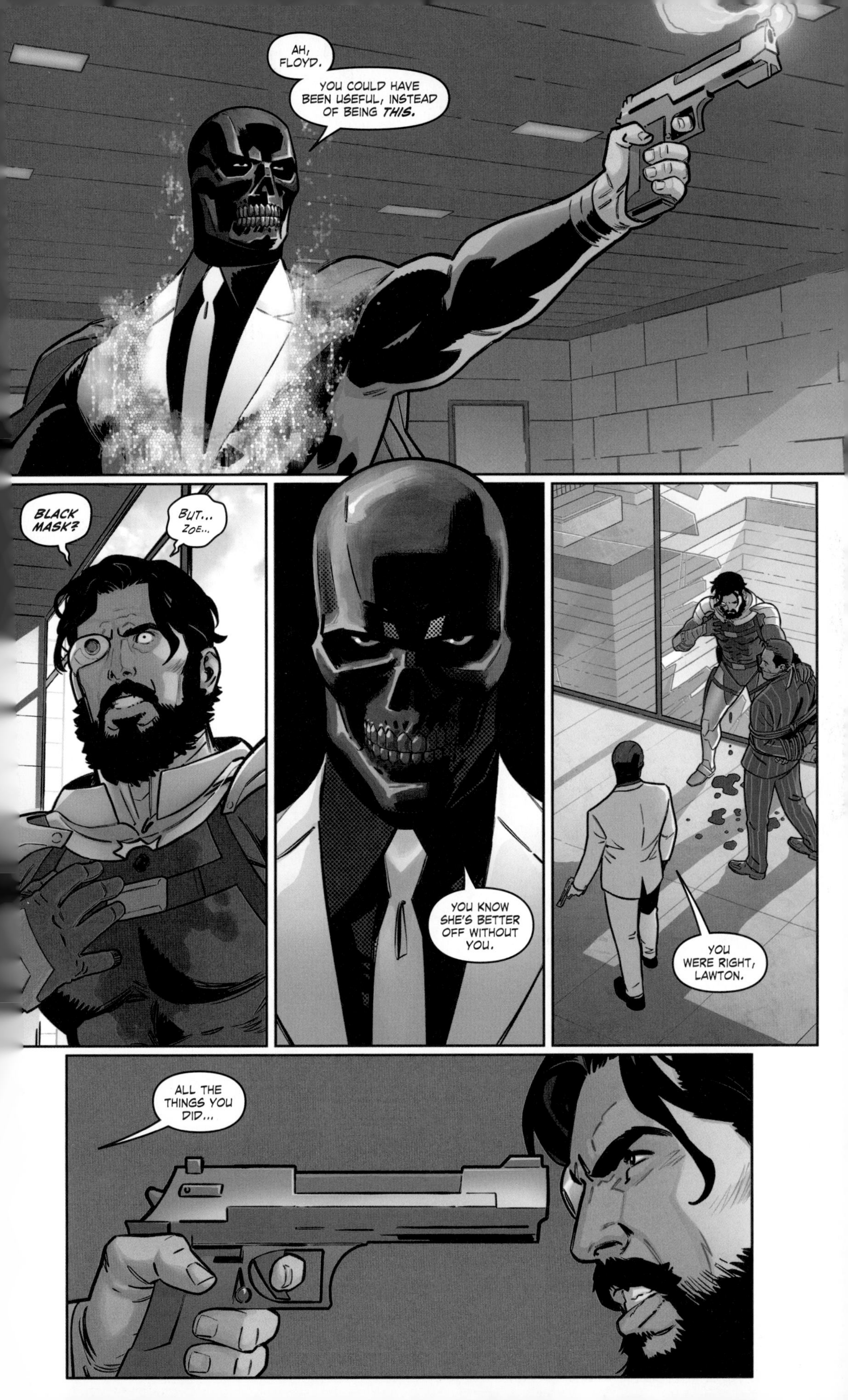
AH, FLOYD.
YOU COULD HAVE BEEN USEFUL, INSTEAD OF BEING *THIS.*
BLACK MASK?
BUT... ZOE...
YOU KNOW SHE'S BETTER OFF WITHOUT YOU.
YOU WERE RIGHT, LAWTON.
ALL THE THINGS YOU DID...

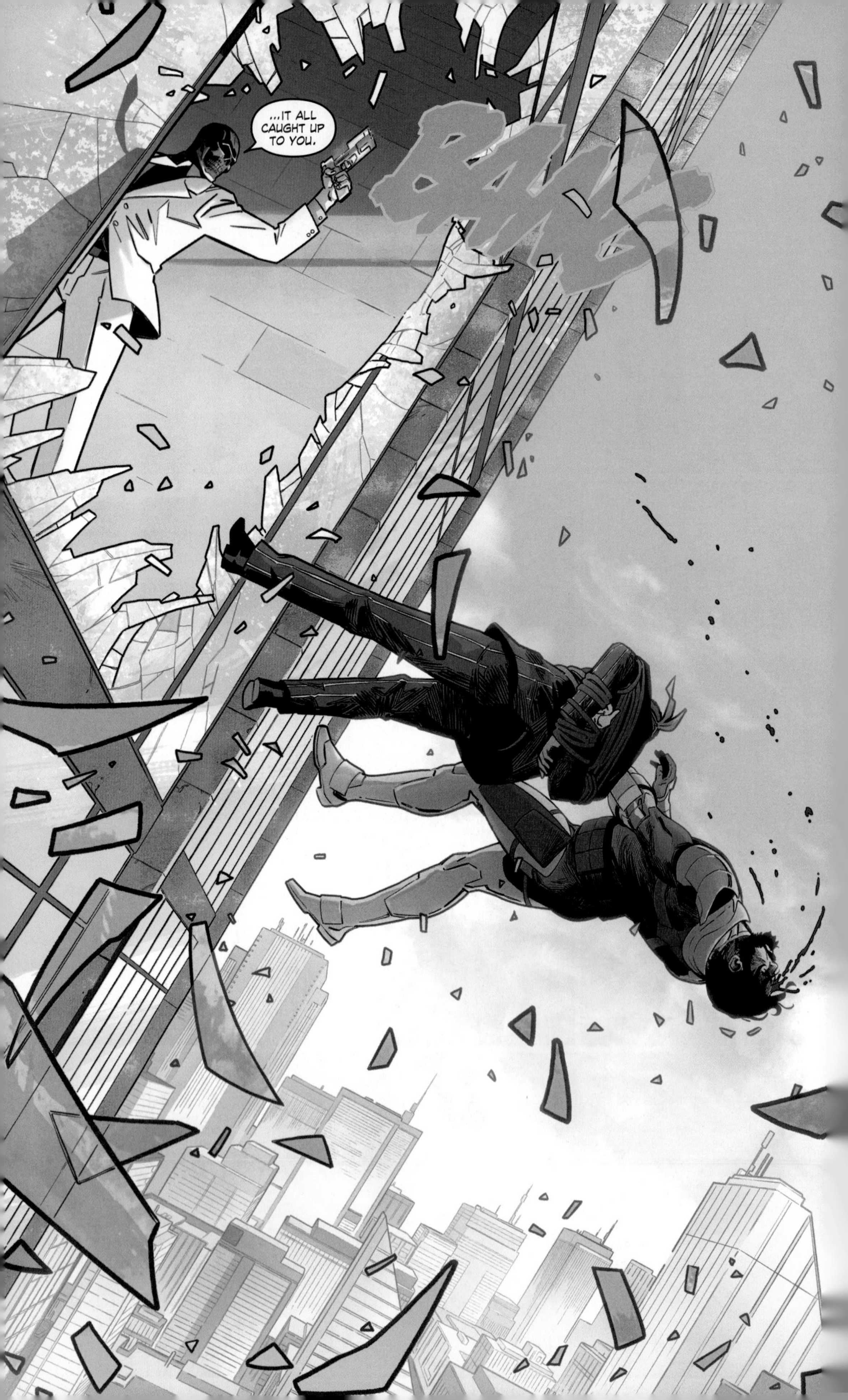
...IT ALL
CAUGHT UP
TO YOU.

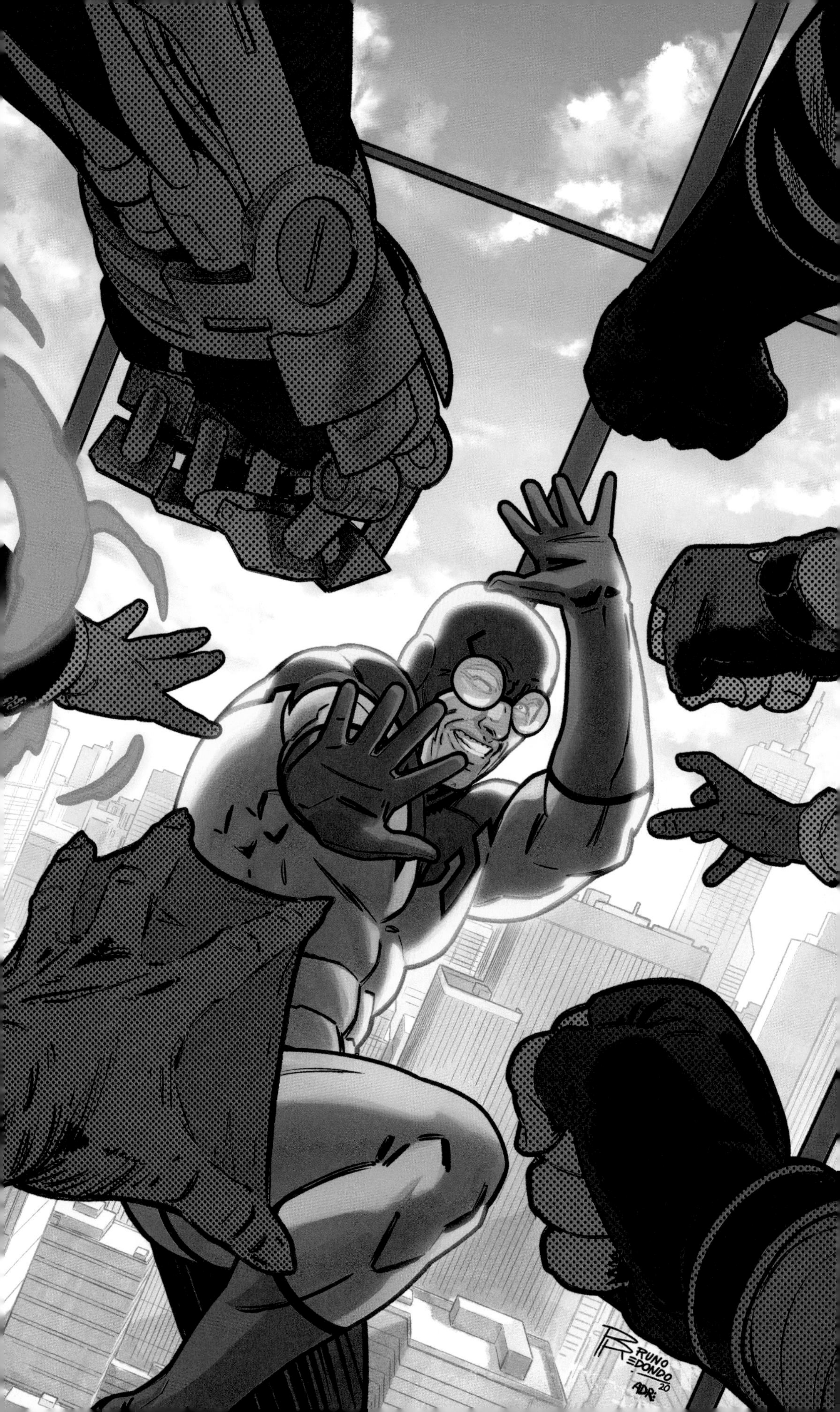

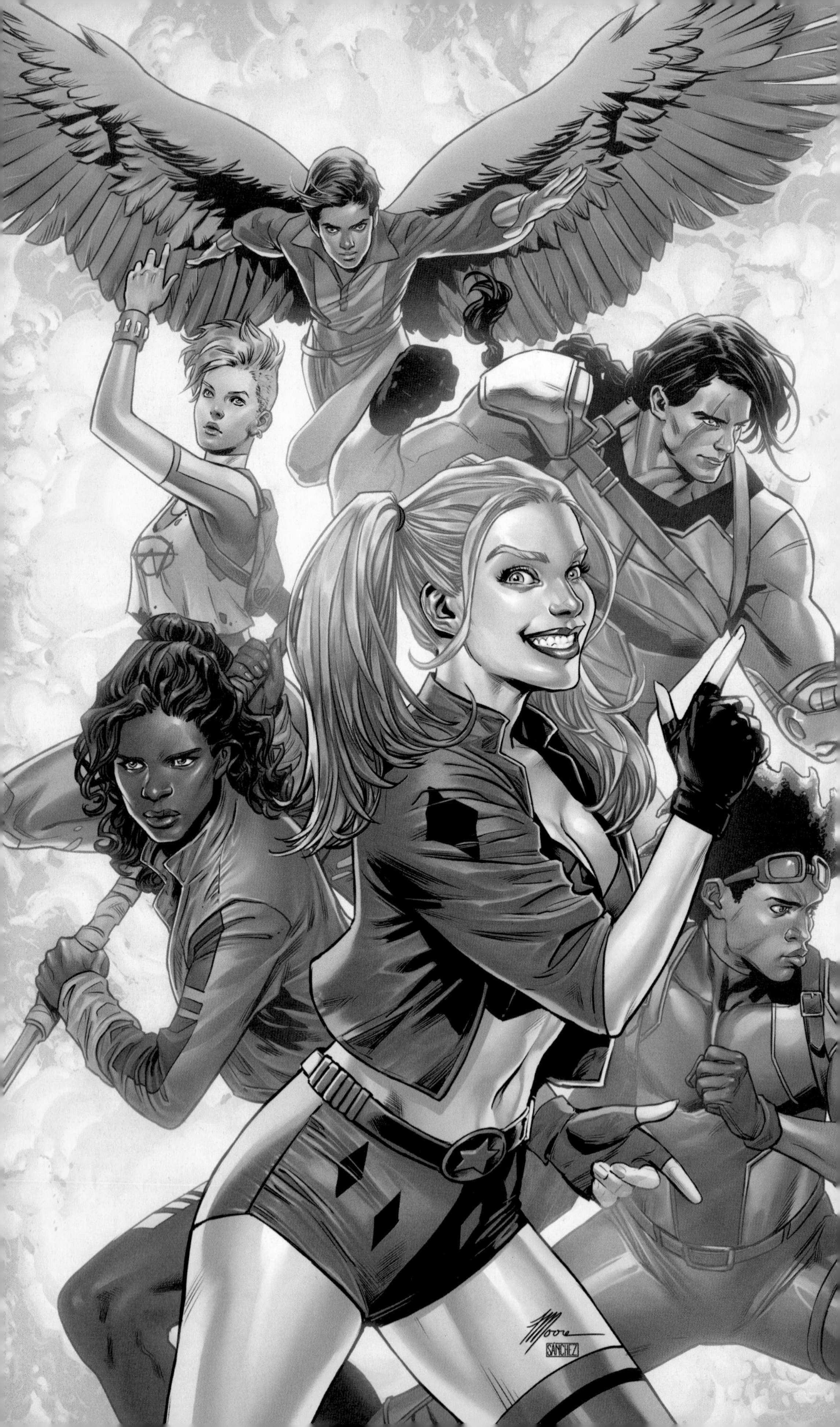

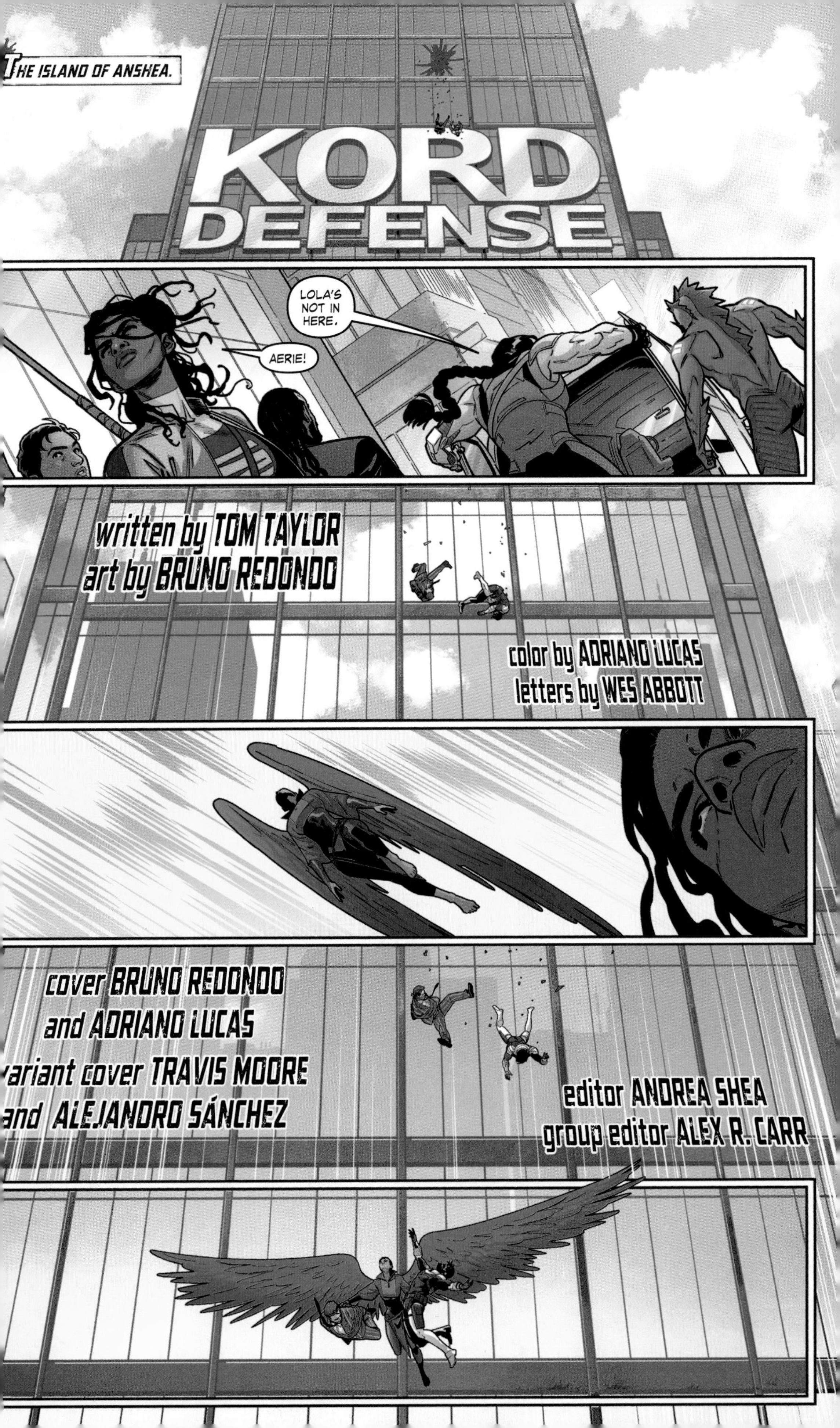
THE ISLAND OF ANSHEA.
KORD DEFENSE
LOLA'S NOT IN HERE.
AERIE!
written by TOM TAYLOR
art by BRUNO REDONDO
color by ADRIANO LUCAS
letters by WES ABBOTT
cover BRUNO REDONDO
and ADRIANO LUCAS
variant cover TRAVIS MOORE
and ALEJANDRO SÁNCHEZ
editor ANDREA SHEA
group editor ALEX R. CARR

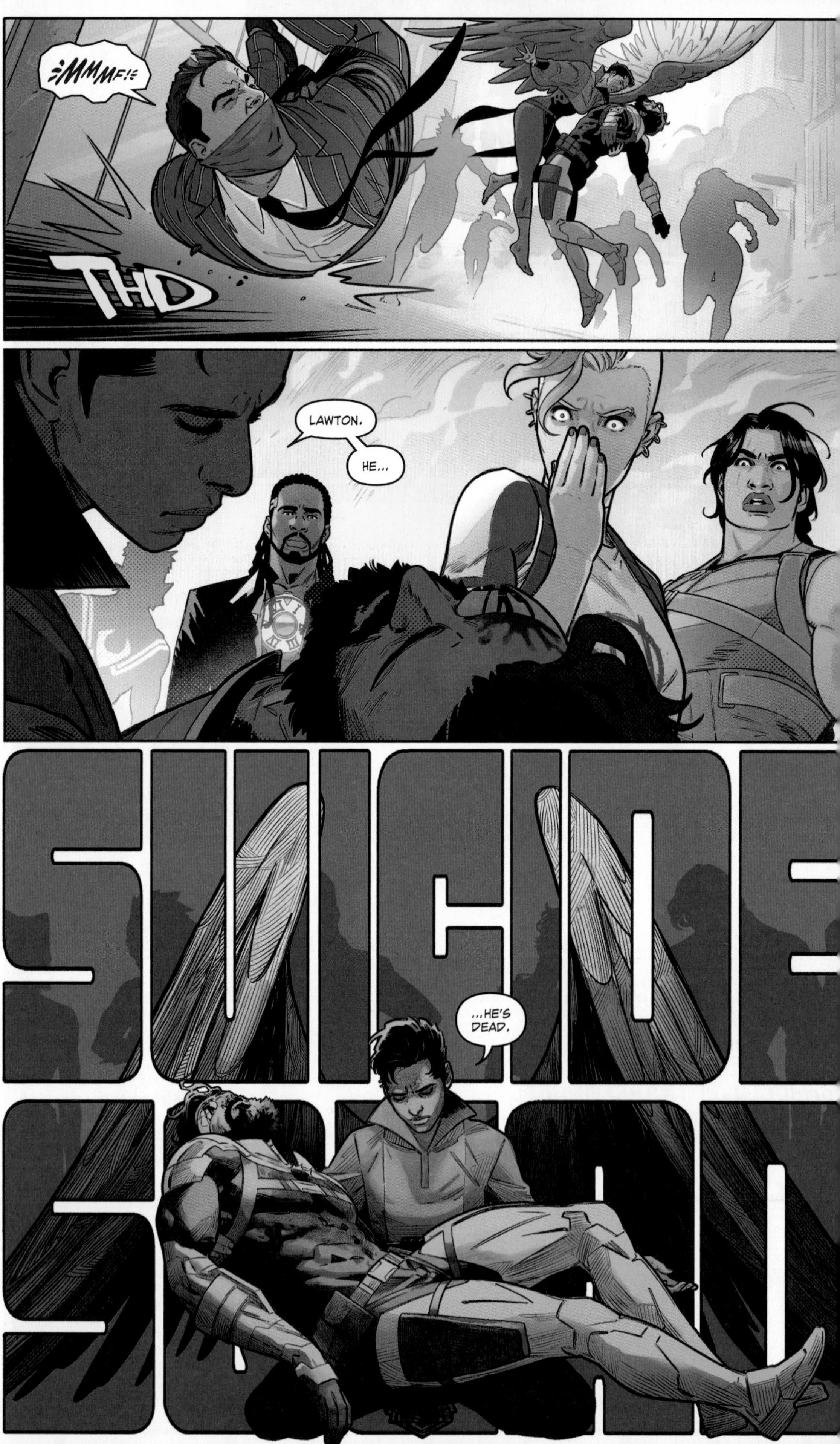

MMMMF!
THD
LAWTON.
HE...
SUICIDE SQUAD
...HE'S DEAD.

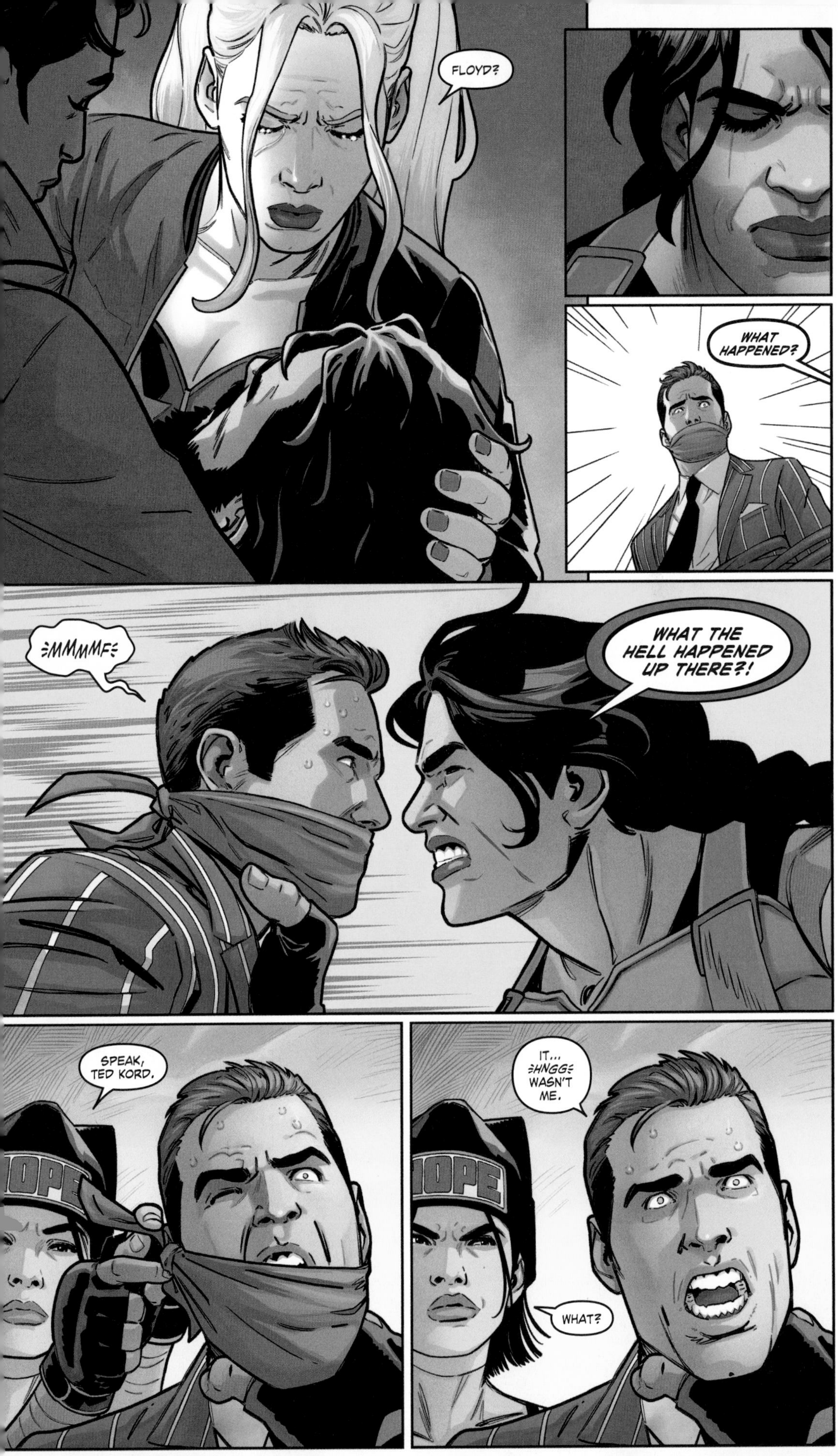
FLOYD?
WHAT HAPPENED?
MMMMF
WHAT THE HELL HAPPENED UP THERE?!
SPEAK, TED KORD.
IT... HNGG WASN'T ME.
WHAT?

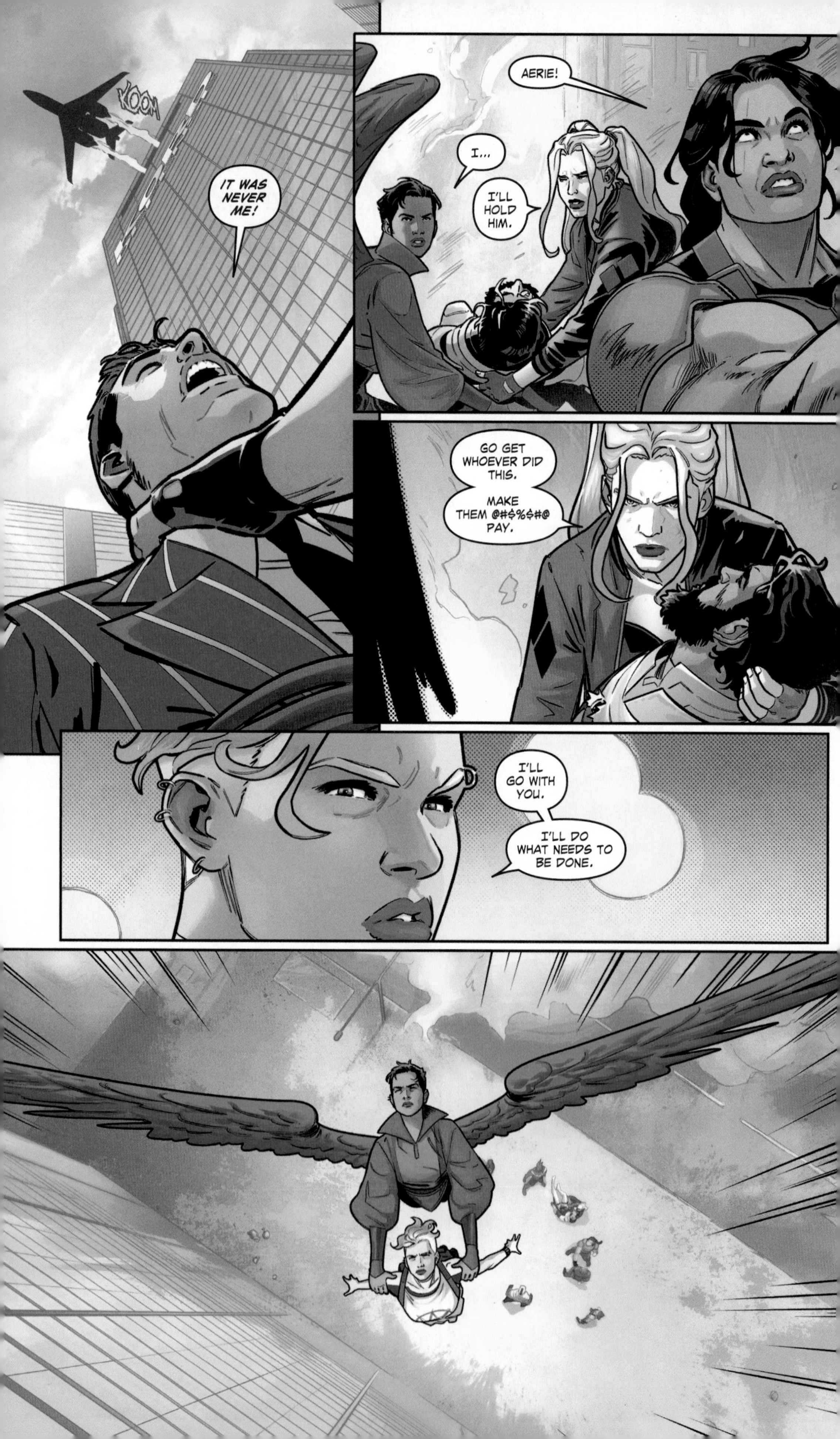
KOOM
IT WAS NEVER ME!
AERIE!
I...
I'LL HOLD HIM.
GO GET WHOEVER DID THIS.
MAKE THEM @#$%$#@ PAY.
I'LL GO WITH YOU.
I'LL DO WHAT NEEDS TO BE DONE.

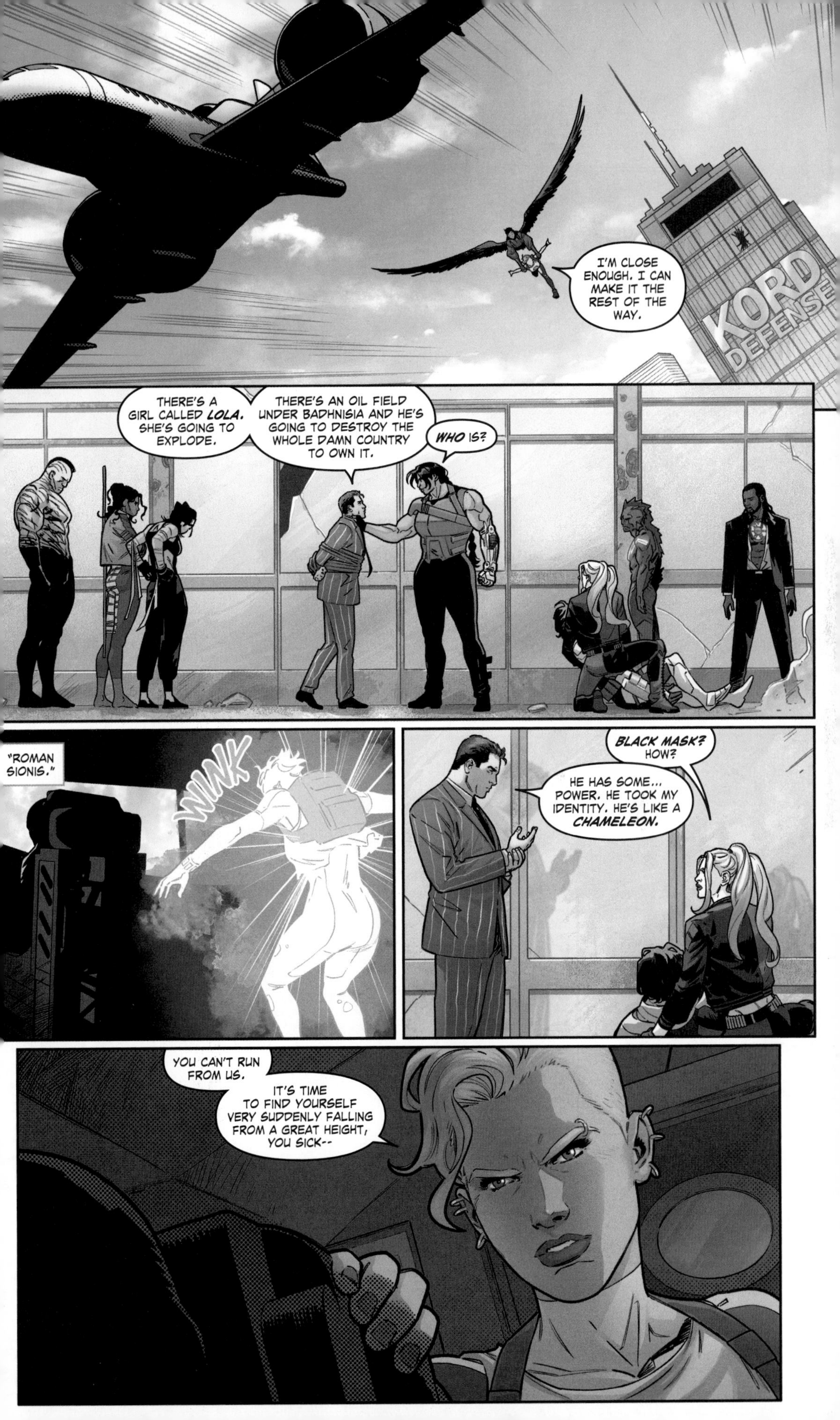
I'M CLOSE ENOUGH. I CAN MAKE IT THE REST OF THE WAY.
KORD DEFENSE
THERE'S A GIRL CALLED LOLA. SHE'S GOING TO EXPLODE.
THERE'S AN OIL FIELD UNDER BADHNISIA AND HE'S GOING TO DESTROY THE WHOLE DAMN COUNTRY TO OWN IT.
WHO IS?
"ROMAN SIONIS."
WINK
BLACK MASK? HOW?
HE HAS SOME... POWER. HE TOOK MY IDENTITY. HE'S LIKE A CHAMELEON.
YOU CAN'T RUN FROM US.
IT'S TIME TO FIND YOURSELF VERY SUDDENLY FALLING FROM A GREAT HEIGHT, YOU SICK--

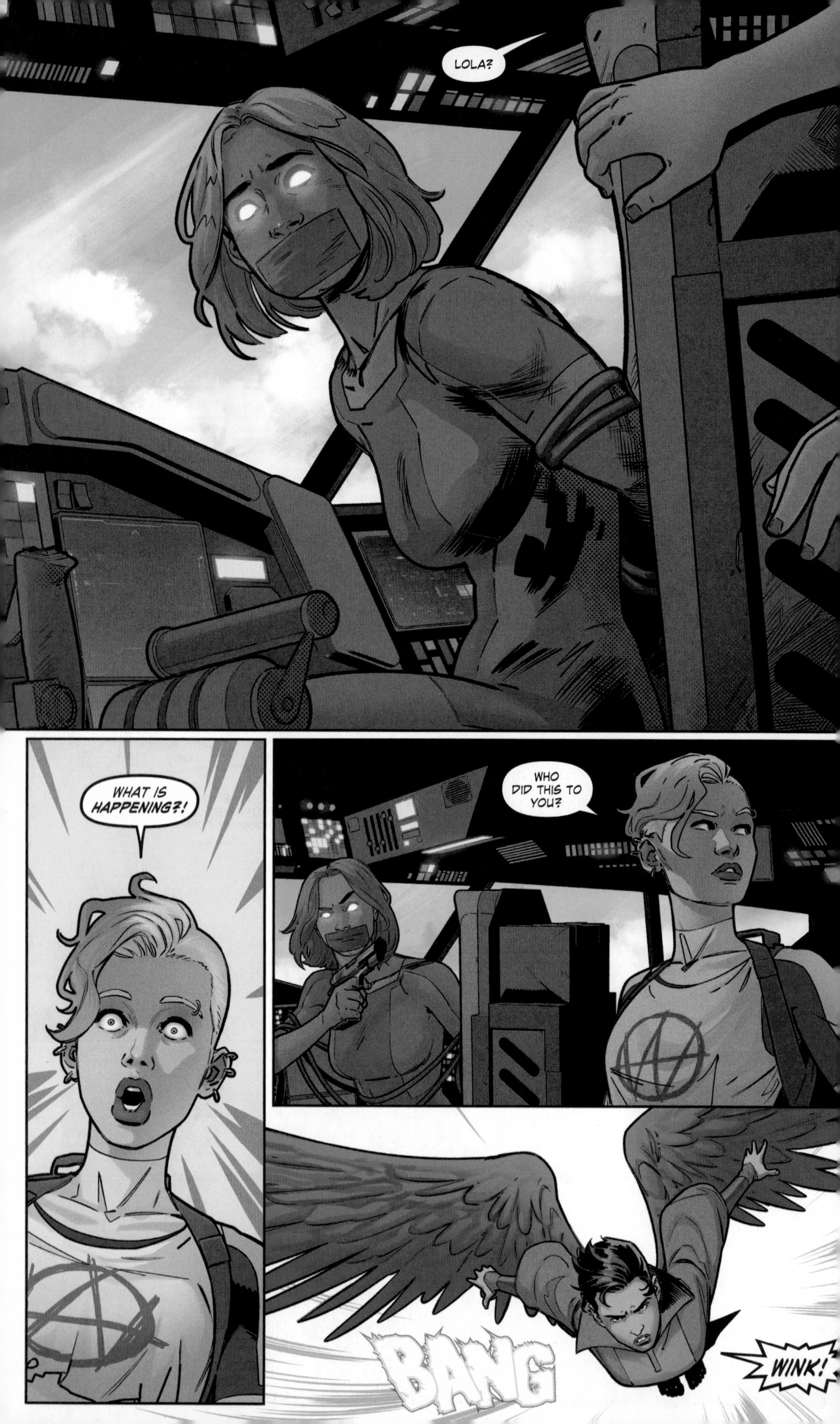
LOLA?
WHAT IS HAPPENING?!
WHO DID THIS TO YOU?
BANG
WINK!

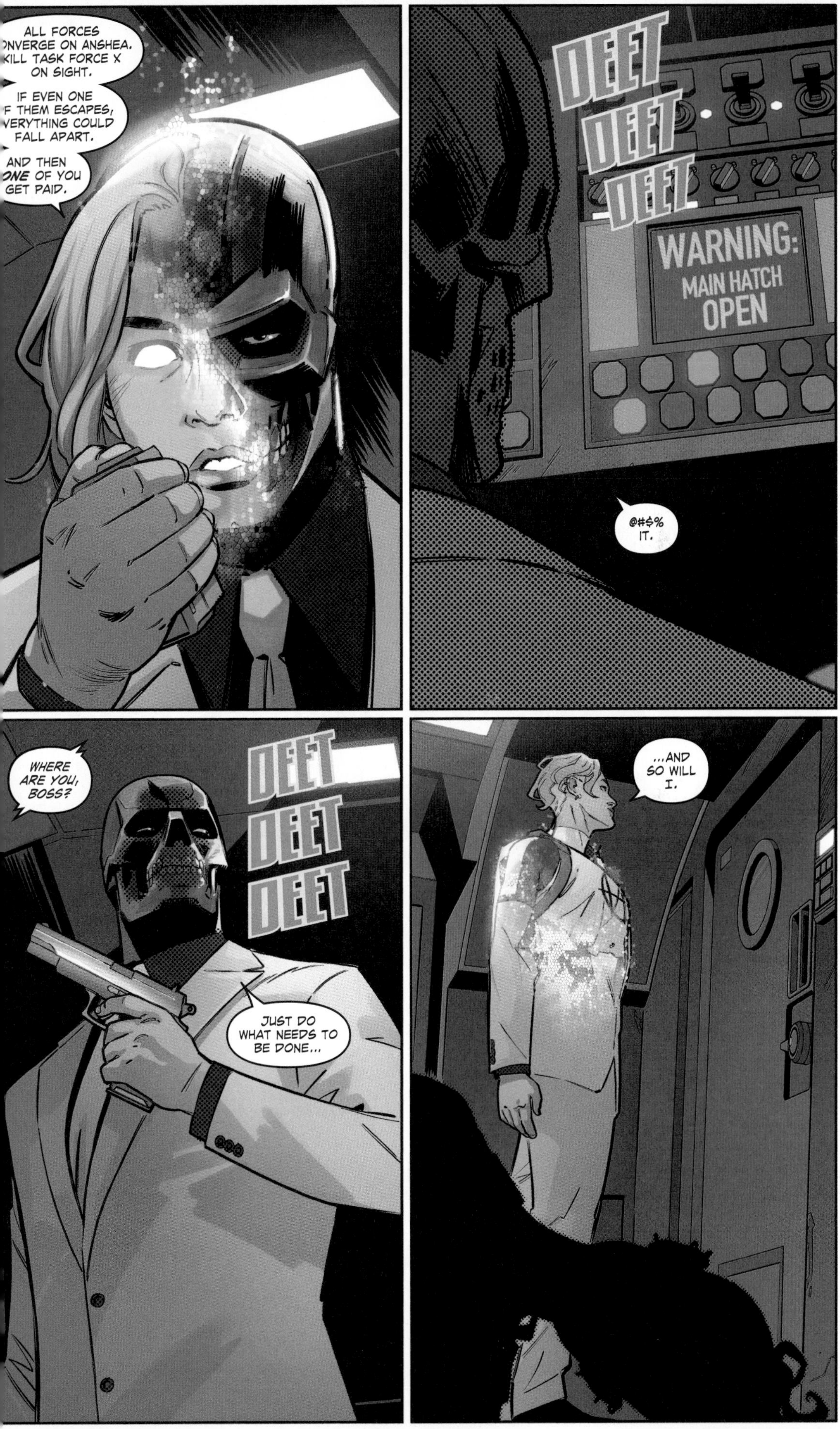
ALL FORCES
ONVERGE ON ANSHEA.
KILL TASK FORCE X
ON SIGHT.
IF EVEN ONE
F THEM ESCAPES,
VERYTHING COULD
FALL APART.
AND THEN
ONE OF YOU
GET PAID.
DEET
DEET
DEET
WARNING:
MAIN HATCH
OPEN
@#$%
IT.
WHERE
ARE YOU,
BOSS?
DEET
DEET
DEET
JUST DO
WHAT NEEDS TO
BE DONE...
...AND
SO WILL
I.

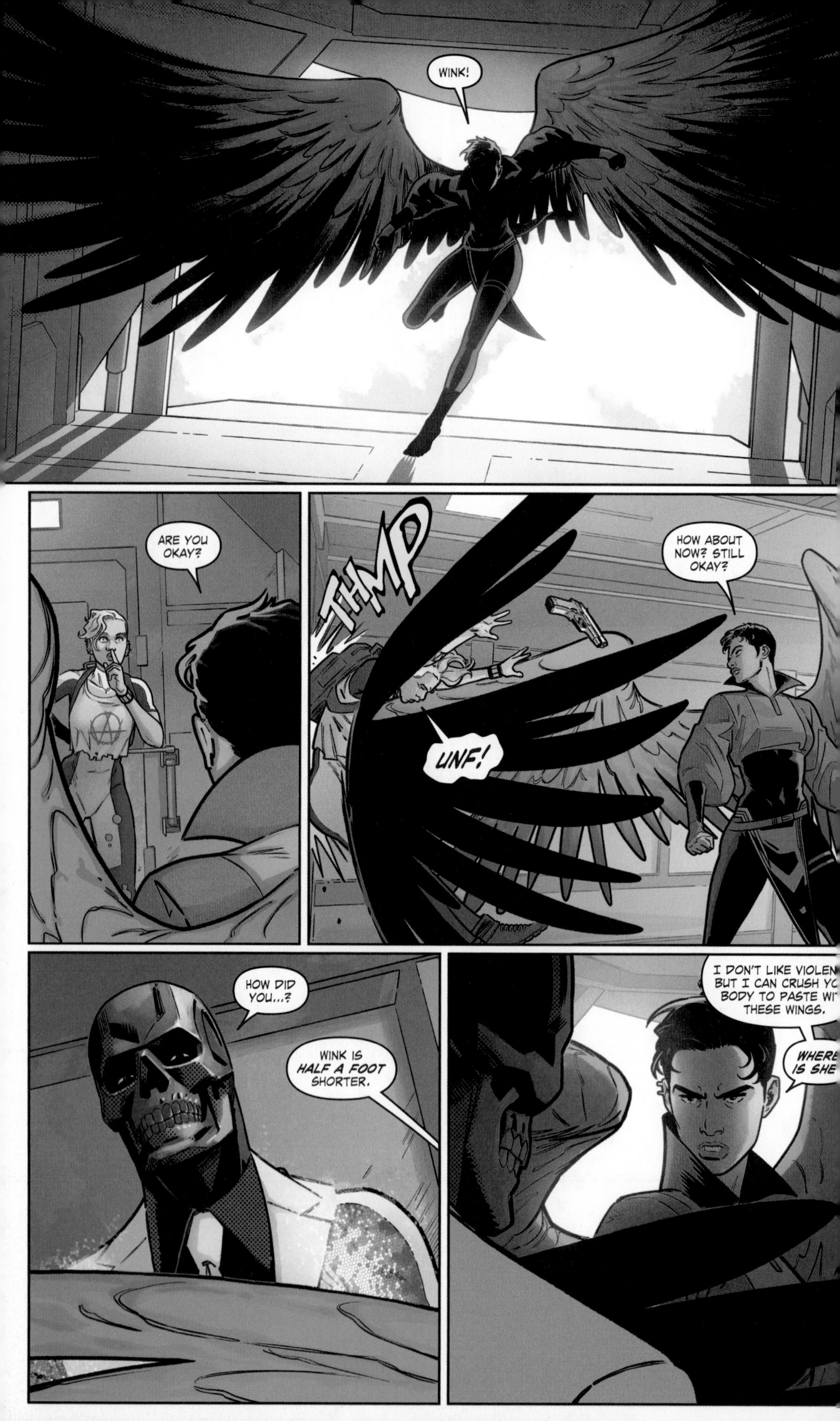
WINK!
ARE YOU OKAY?
THMP
HOW ABOUT NOW? STILL OKAY?
UNF!
HOW DID YOU...?
WINK IS *HALF A FOOT* SHORTER.
I DON'T LIKE VIOLEN
BUT I CAN CRUSH YO
BODY TO PASTE WI
THESE WINGS.
WHERE
IS SHE

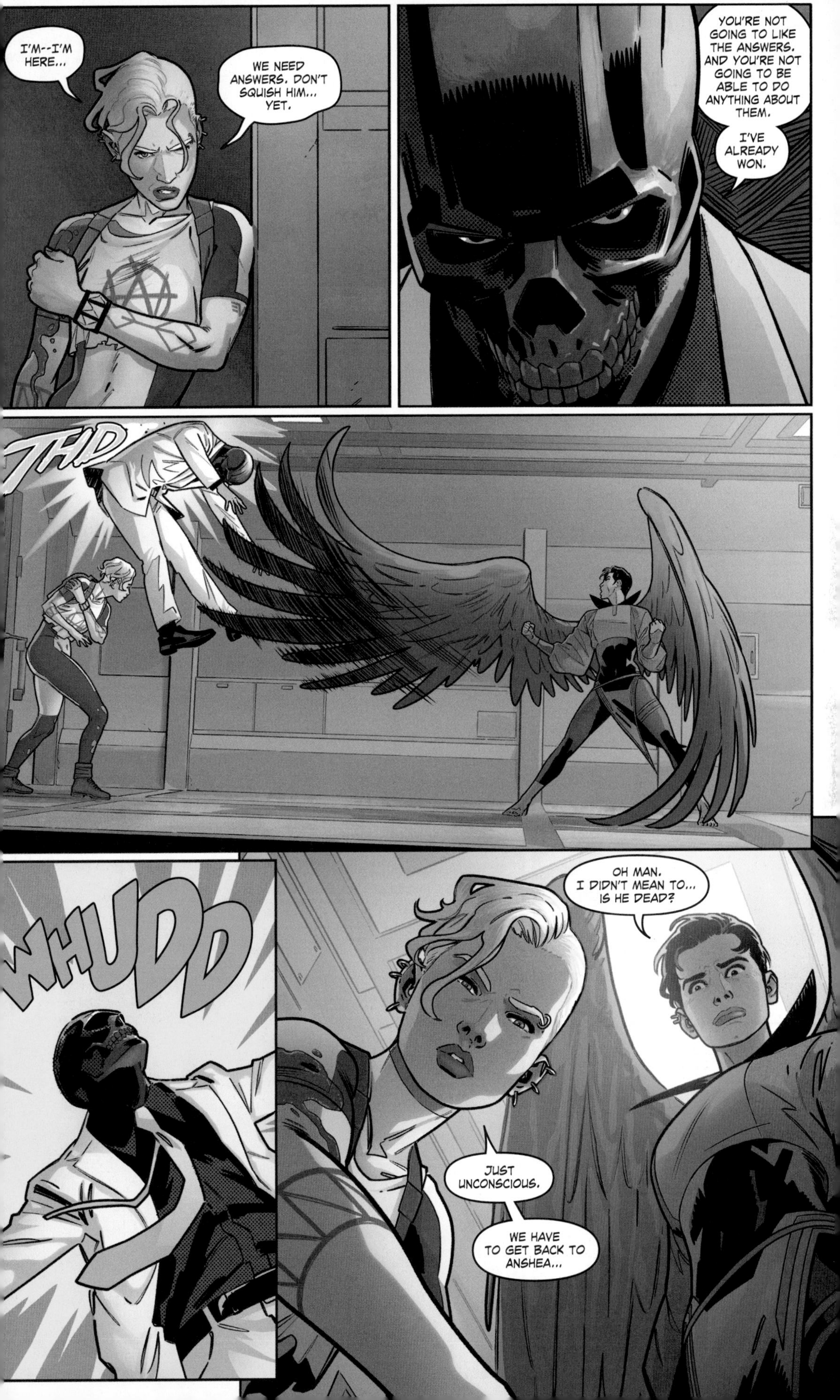
I'M--I'M HERE...
WE NEED ANSWERS. DON'T SQUISH HIM... YET.
YOU'RE NOT GOING TO LIKE THE ANSWERS. AND YOU'RE NOT GOING TO BE ABLE TO DO ANYTHING ABOUT THEM.
I'VE ALREADY WON.
THD
WHUDD
OH MAN. I DIDN'T MEAN TO... IS HE DEAD?
JUST UNCONSCIOUS.
WE HAVE TO GET BACK TO ANSHEA...

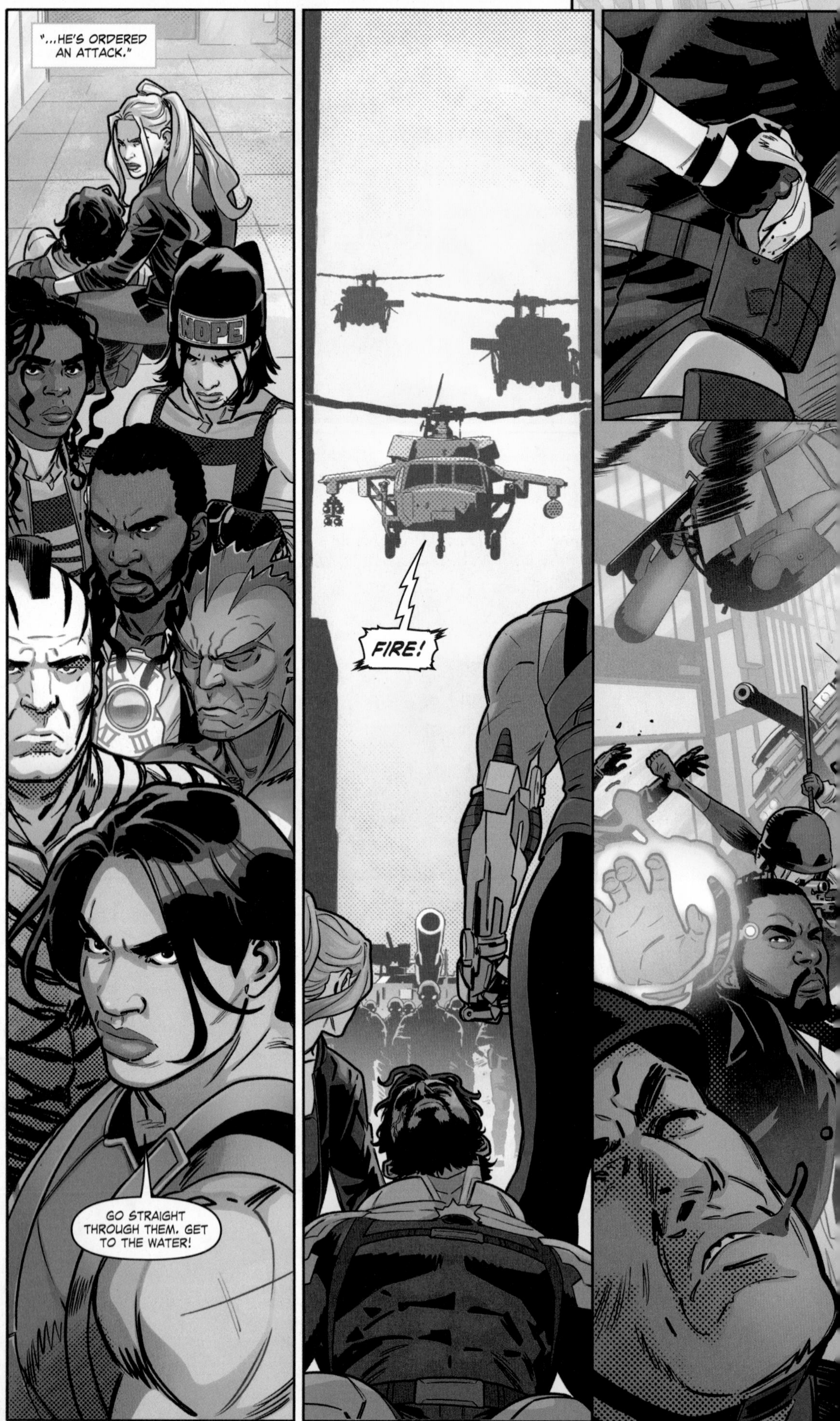
"...HE'S ORDERED AN ATTACK."
GO STRAIGHT THROUGH THEM. GET TO THE WATER!
FIRE!

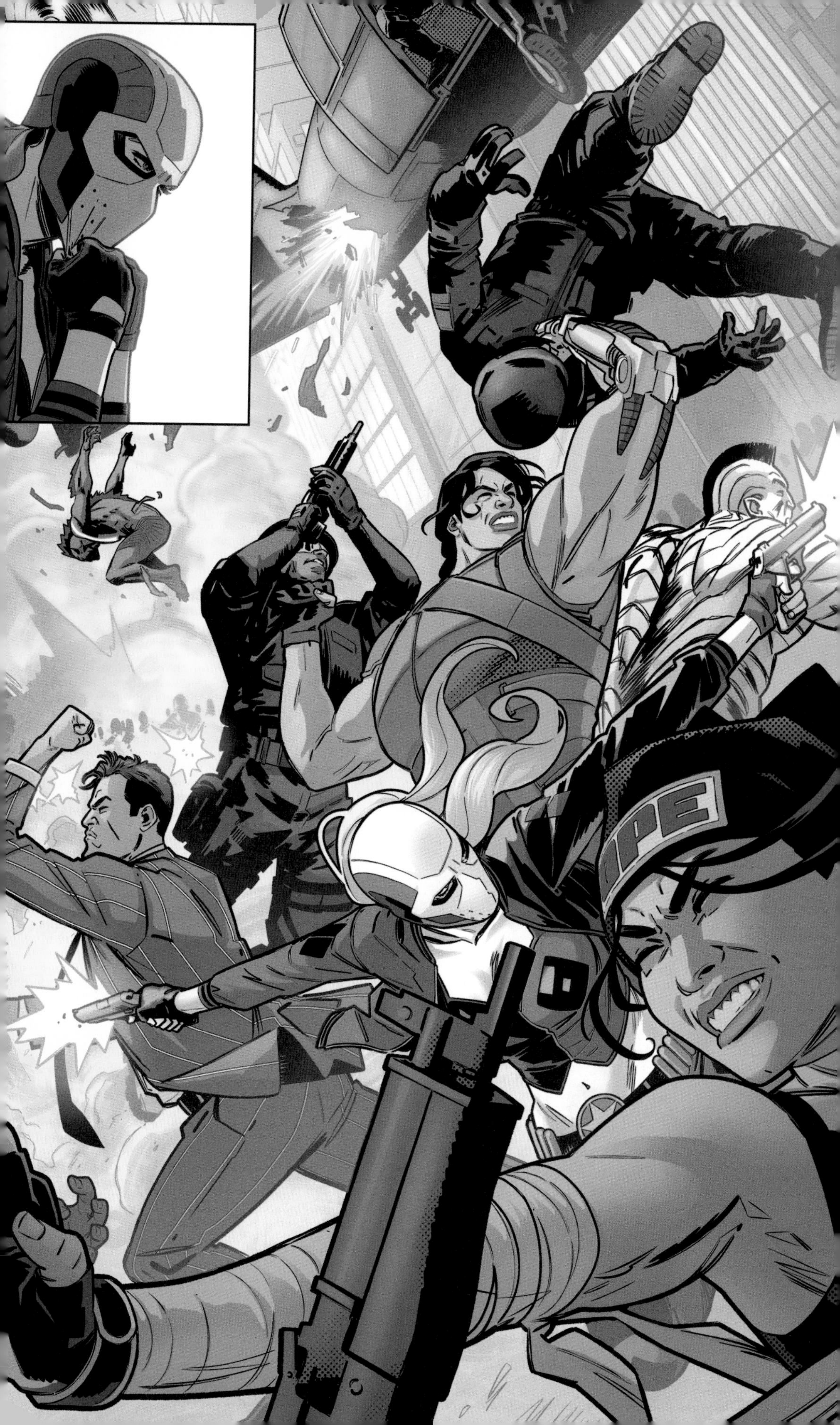

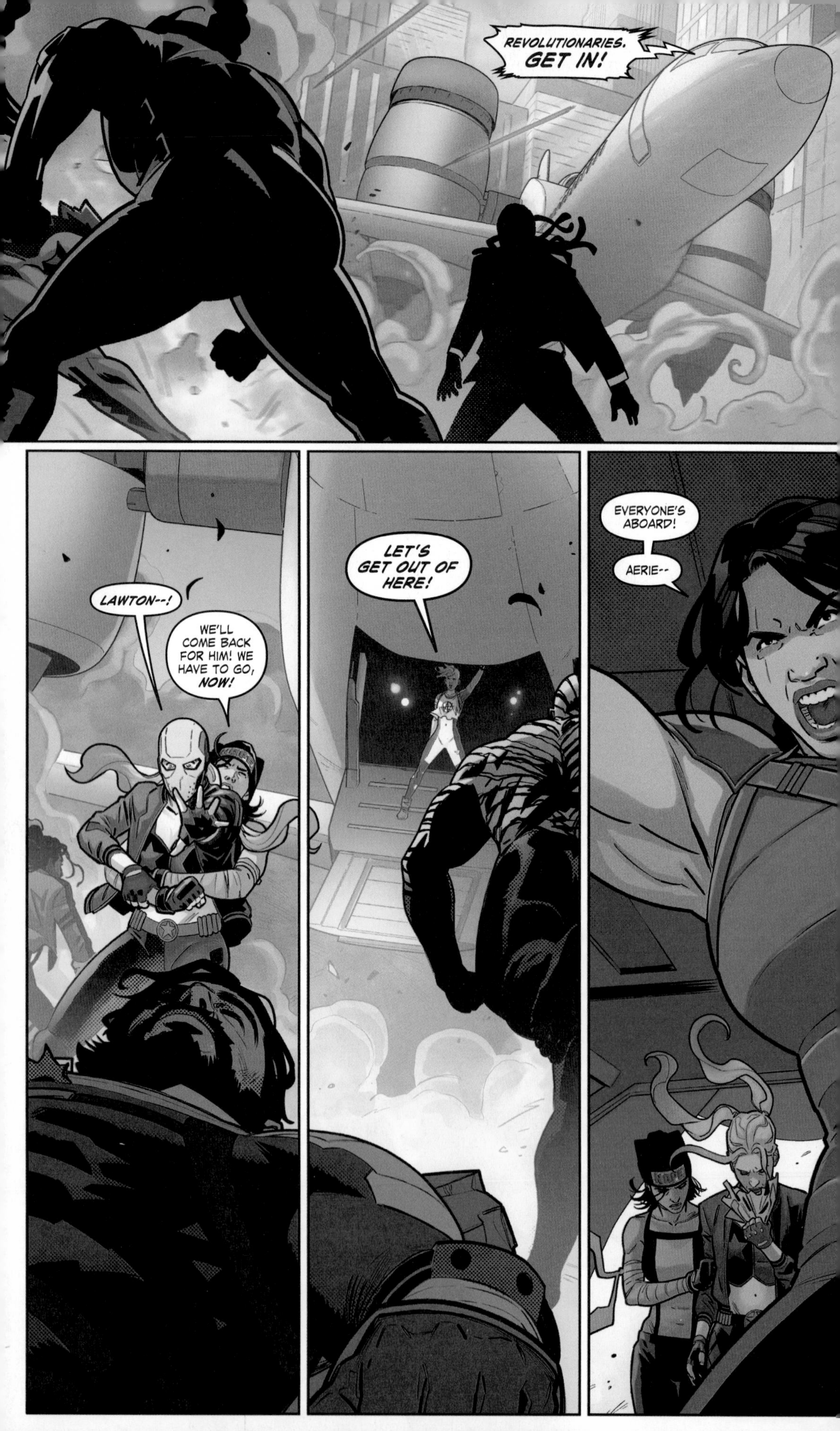
REVOLUTIONARIES. GET IN!
LAWTON--!
WE'LL COME BACK FOR HIM! WE HAVE TO GO, NOW!
LET'S GET OUT OF HERE!
EVERYONE'S ABOARD!
AERIE--

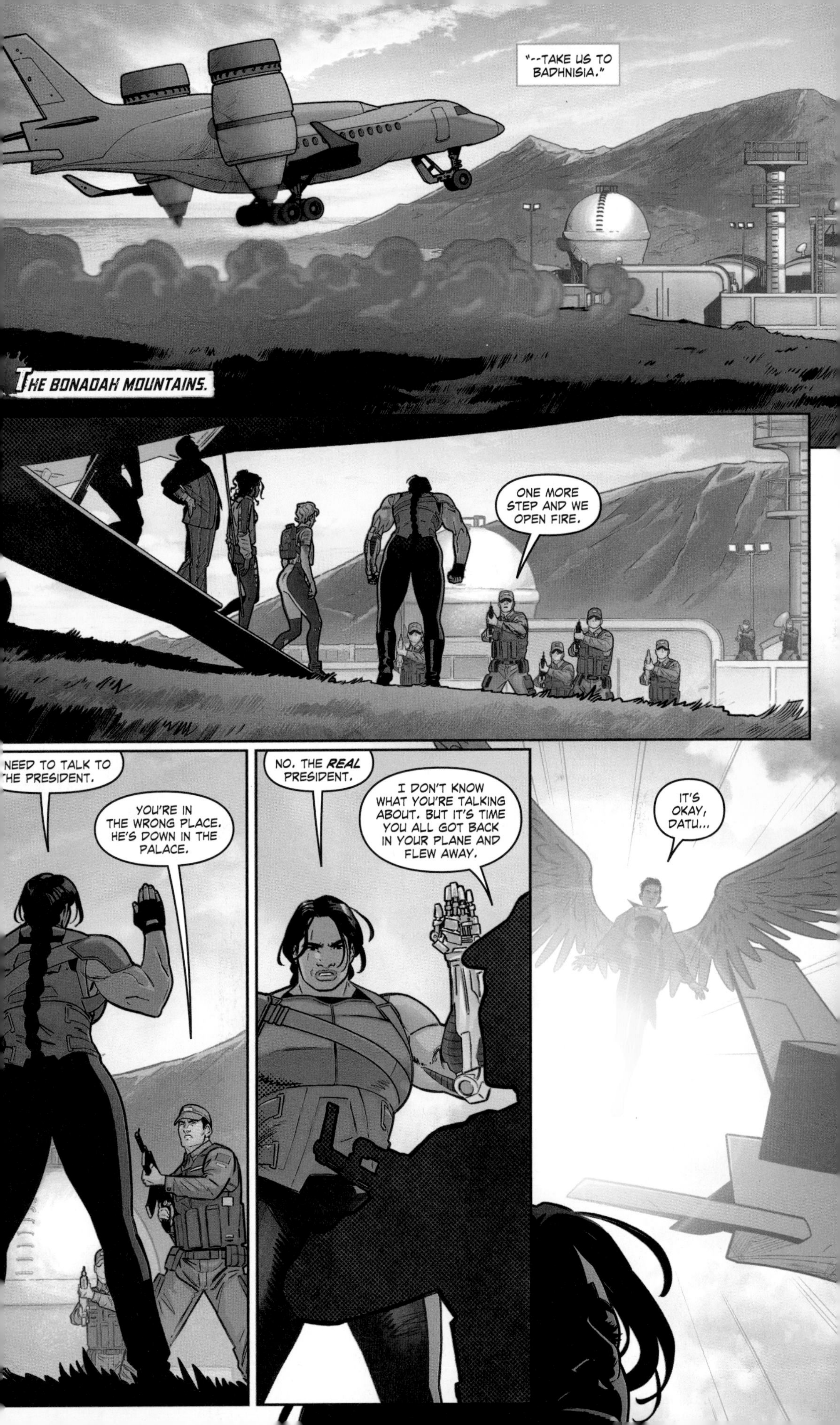
"--TAKE US TO BADHNISIA."
THE BONADAH MOUNTAINS.
ONE MORE STEP AND WE OPEN FIRE.
NEED TO TALK TO THE PRESIDENT.
YOU'RE IN THE WRONG PLACE. HE'S DOWN IN THE PALACE.
NO. THE REAL PRESIDENT.
I DON'T KNOW WHAT YOU'RE TALKING ABOUT. BUT IT'S TIME YOU ALL GOT BACK IN YOUR PLANE AND FLEW AWAY.
IT'S OKAY, DATU...

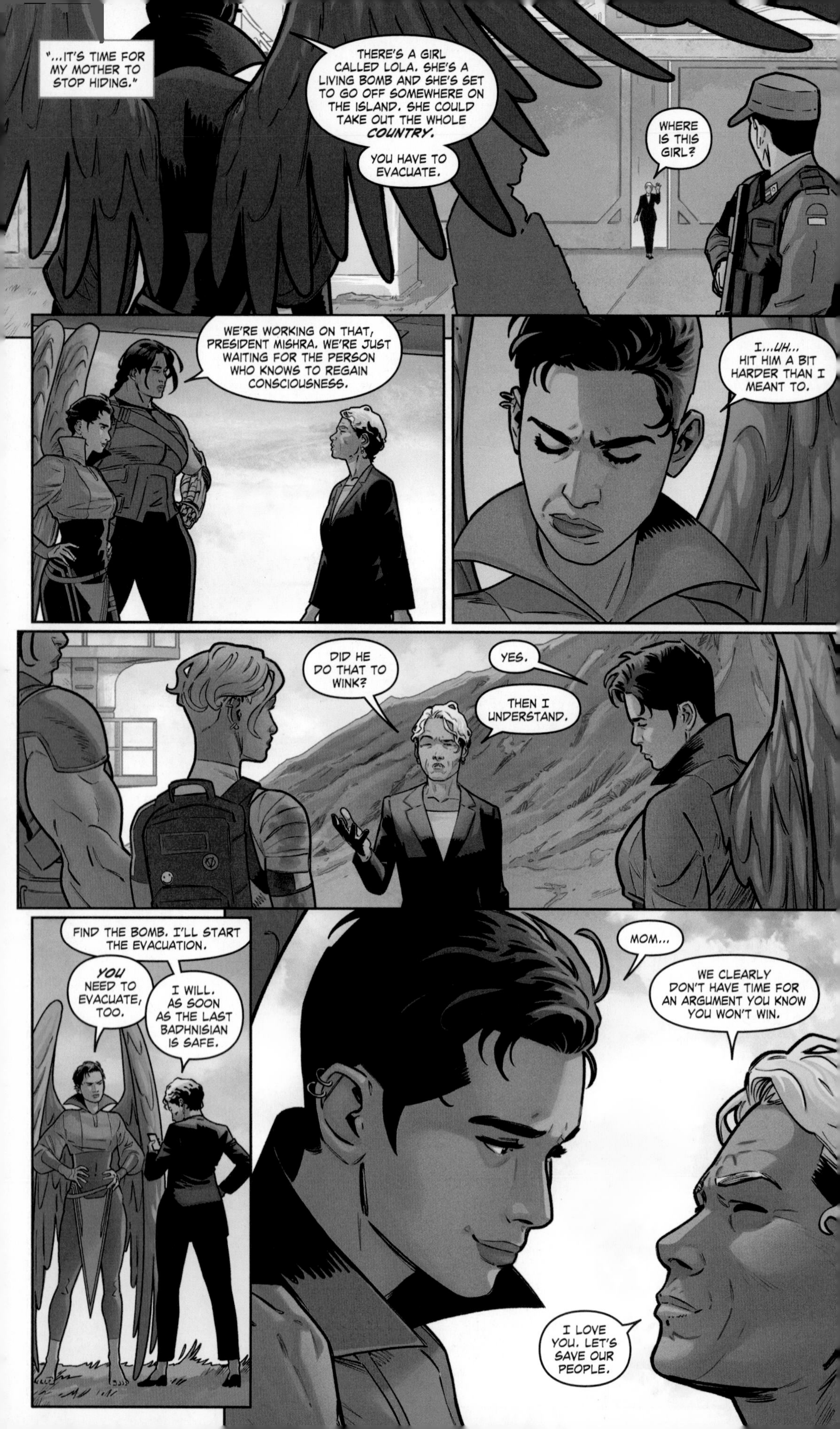
"...IT'S TIME FOR MY MOTHER TO STOP HIDING."
THERE'S A GIRL CALLED LOLA. SHE'S A LIVING BOMB AND SHE'S SET TO GO OFF SOMEWHERE ON THE ISLAND. SHE COULD TAKE OUT THE WHOLE ***COUNTRY.***
YOU HAVE TO EVACUATE.
WHERE IS THIS GIRL?
WE'RE WORKING ON THAT, PRESIDENT MISHRA. WE'RE JUST WAITING FOR THE PERSON WHO KNOWS TO REGAIN CONSCIOUSNESS.
I...*UH*... HIT HIM A BIT HARDER THAN I MEANT TO.
DID HE DO THAT TO WINK?
YES.
THEN I UNDERSTAND.
FIND THE BOMB. I'LL START THE EVACUATION.
YOU NEED TO EVACUATE, TOO.
I WILL. AS SOON AS THE LAST BADHNISIAN IS SAFE.
MOM...
WE CLEARLY DON'T HAVE TIME FOR AN ARGUMENT YOU KNOW YOU WON'T WIN.
I LOVE YOU. LET'S SAVE OUR PEOPLE.

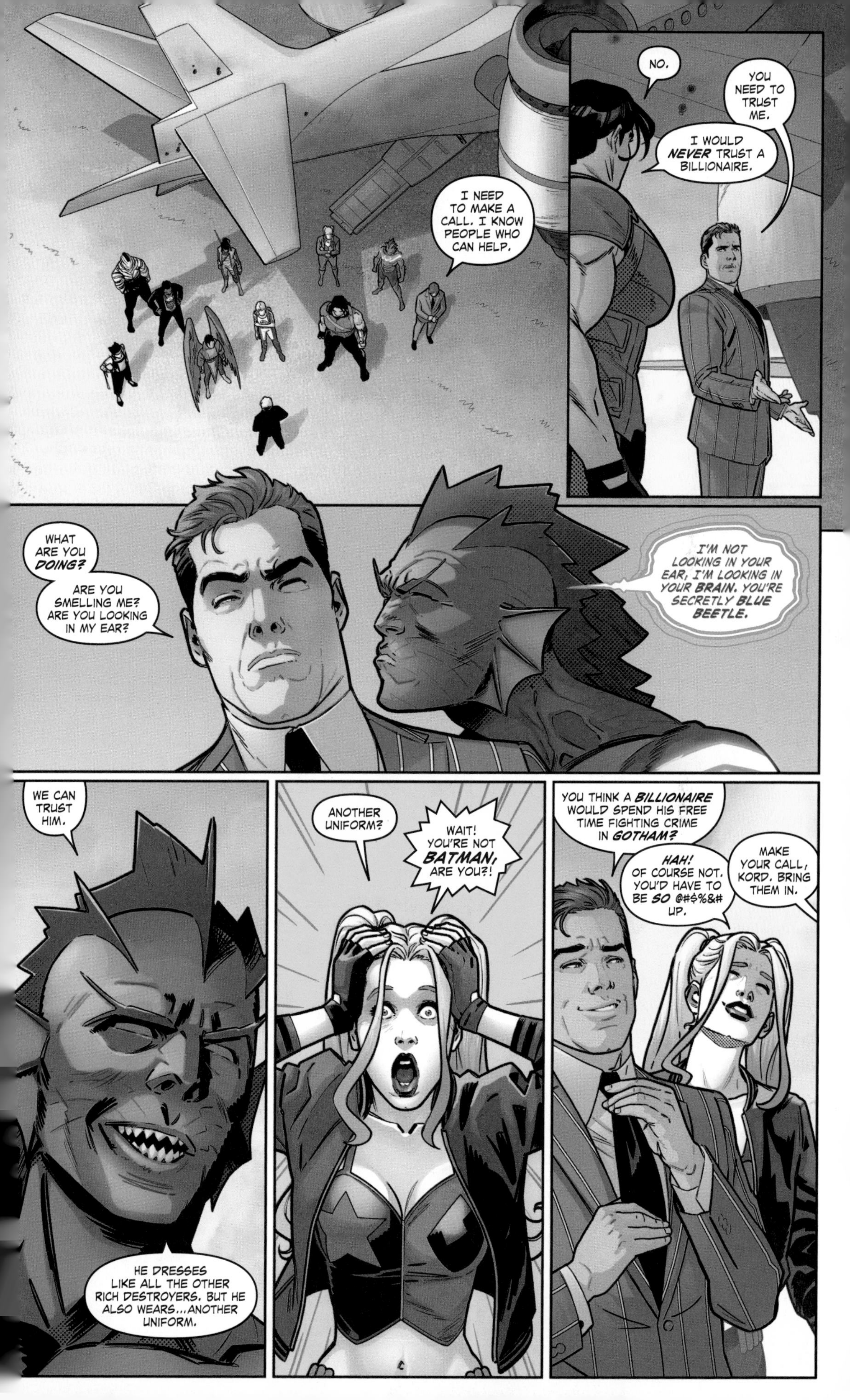
I NEED TO MAKE A CALL. I KNOW PEOPLE WHO CAN HELP.
NO.
YOU NEED TO TRUST ME.
I WOULD NEVER TRUST A BILLIONAIRE.
WHAT ARE YOU DOING?
ARE YOU SMELLING ME? ARE YOU LOOKING IN MY EAR?
I'M NOT LOOKING IN YOUR EAR, I'M LOOKING IN YOUR BRAIN. YOU'RE SECRETLY BLUE BEETLE.
WE CAN TRUST HIM.
HE DRESSES LIKE ALL THE OTHER RICH DESTROYERS. BUT HE ALSO WEARS...ANOTHER UNIFORM.
ANOTHER UNIFORM?
WAIT! YOU'RE NOT BATMAN, ARE YOU?!
YOU THINK A BILLIONAIRE WOULD SPEND HIS FREE TIME FIGHTING CRIME IN GOTHAM?
HAH! OF COURSE NOT. YOU'D HAVE TO BE SO @#$%&# UP.
MAKE YOUR CALL, KORD. BRING THEM IN.

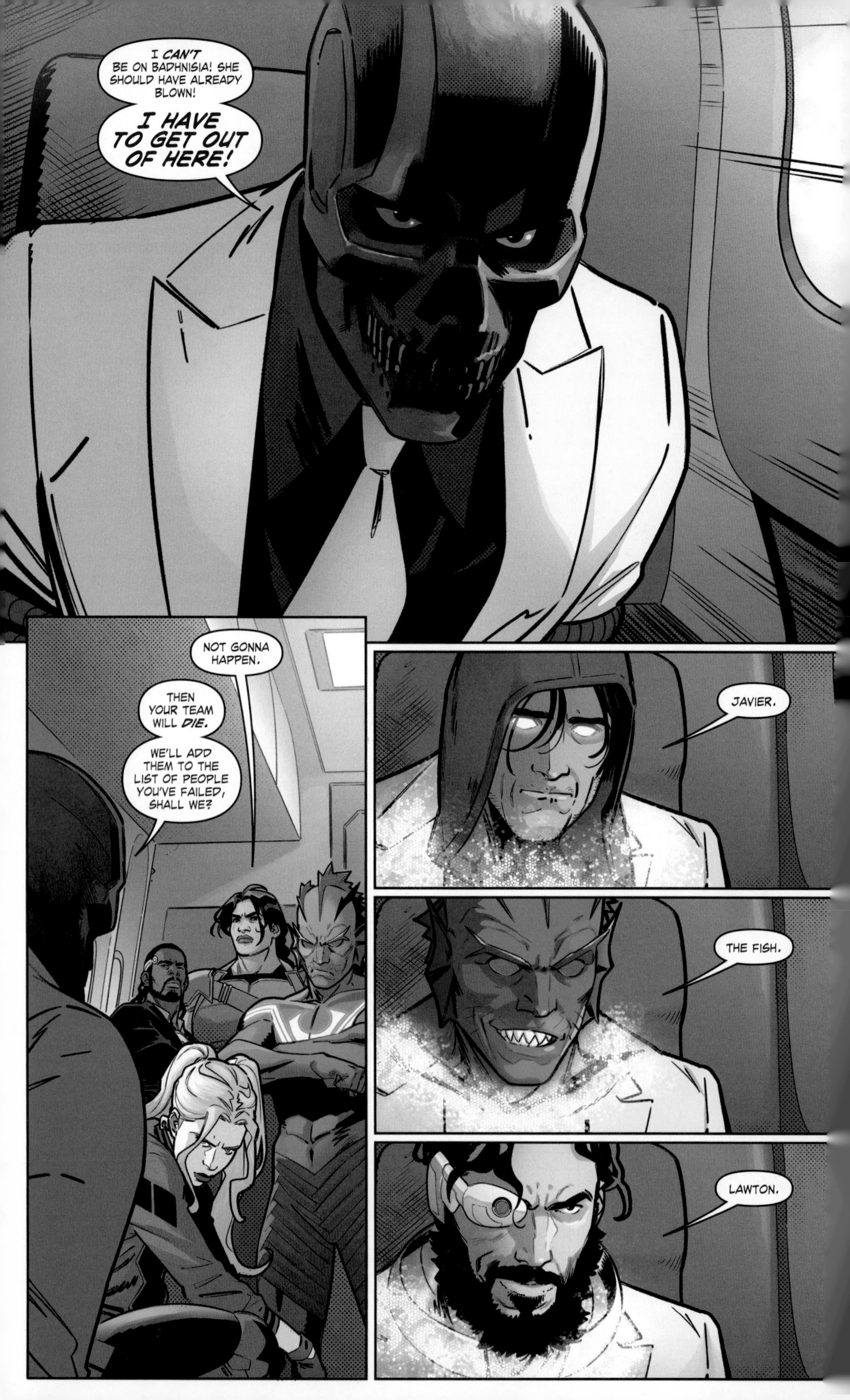
I *CAN'T* BE ON BADHNISIA! SHE SHOULD HAVE ALREADY BLOWN!
I HAVE TO GET OUT OF HERE!
NOT GONNA HAPPEN.
THEN YOUR TEAM WILL *DIE*.
WE'LL ADD THEM TO THE LIST OF PEOPLE YOU'VE FAILED, SHALL WE?
JAVIER.
THE FISH.
LAWTON.

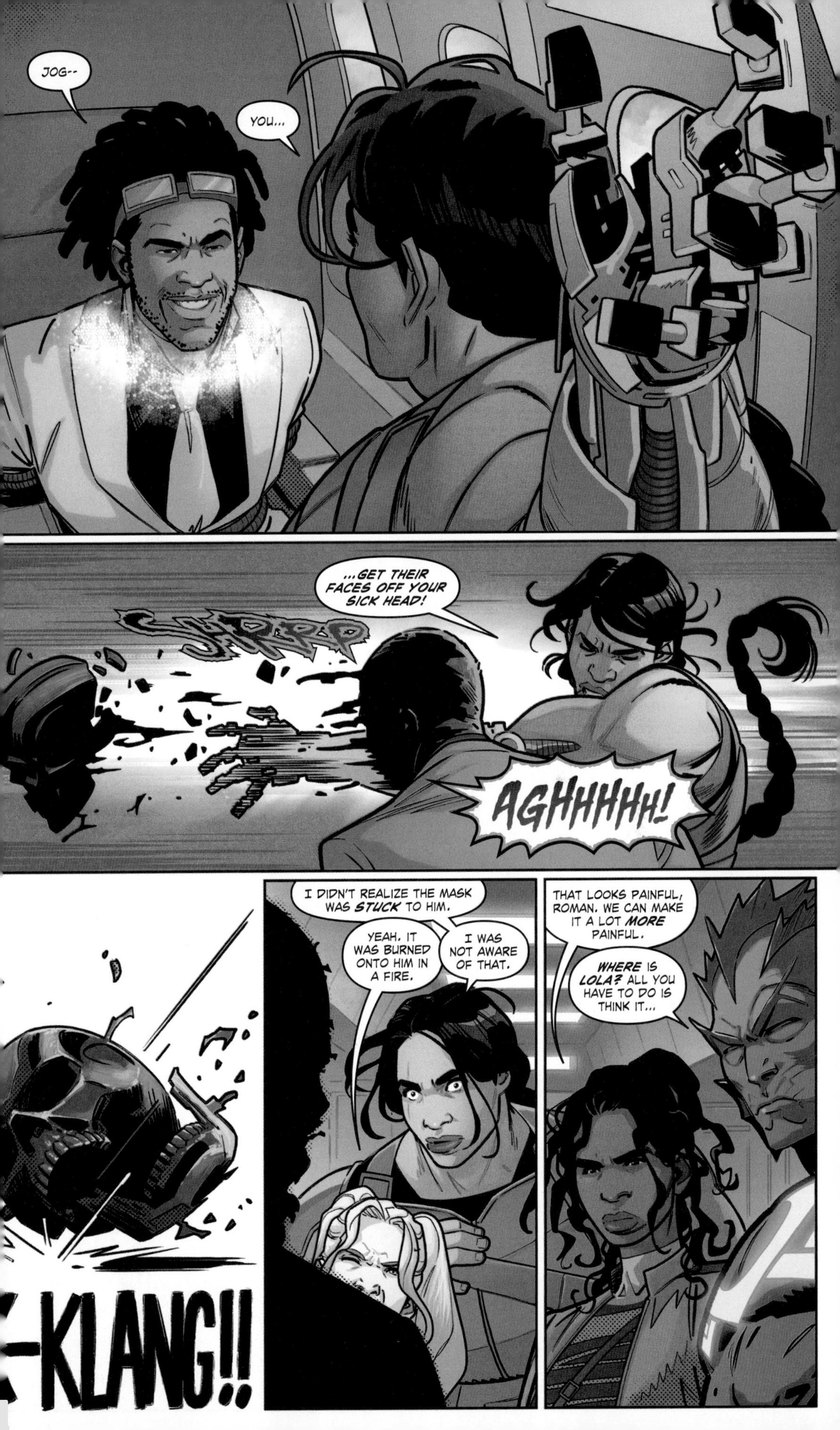

JOG--
YOU...
...GET THEIR FACES OFF YOUR SICK HEAD!
SHRRRP
AGHHHHH!
K-KLANG!!
I DIDN'T REALIZE THE MASK WAS STUCK TO HIM.
YEAH. IT WAS BURNED ONTO HIM IN A FIRE.
I WAS NOT AWARE OF THAT.
THAT LOOKS PAINFUL, ROMAN. WE CAN MAKE IT A LOT MORE PAINFUL.
WHERE IS LOLA? ALL YOU HAVE TO DO IS THINK IT...

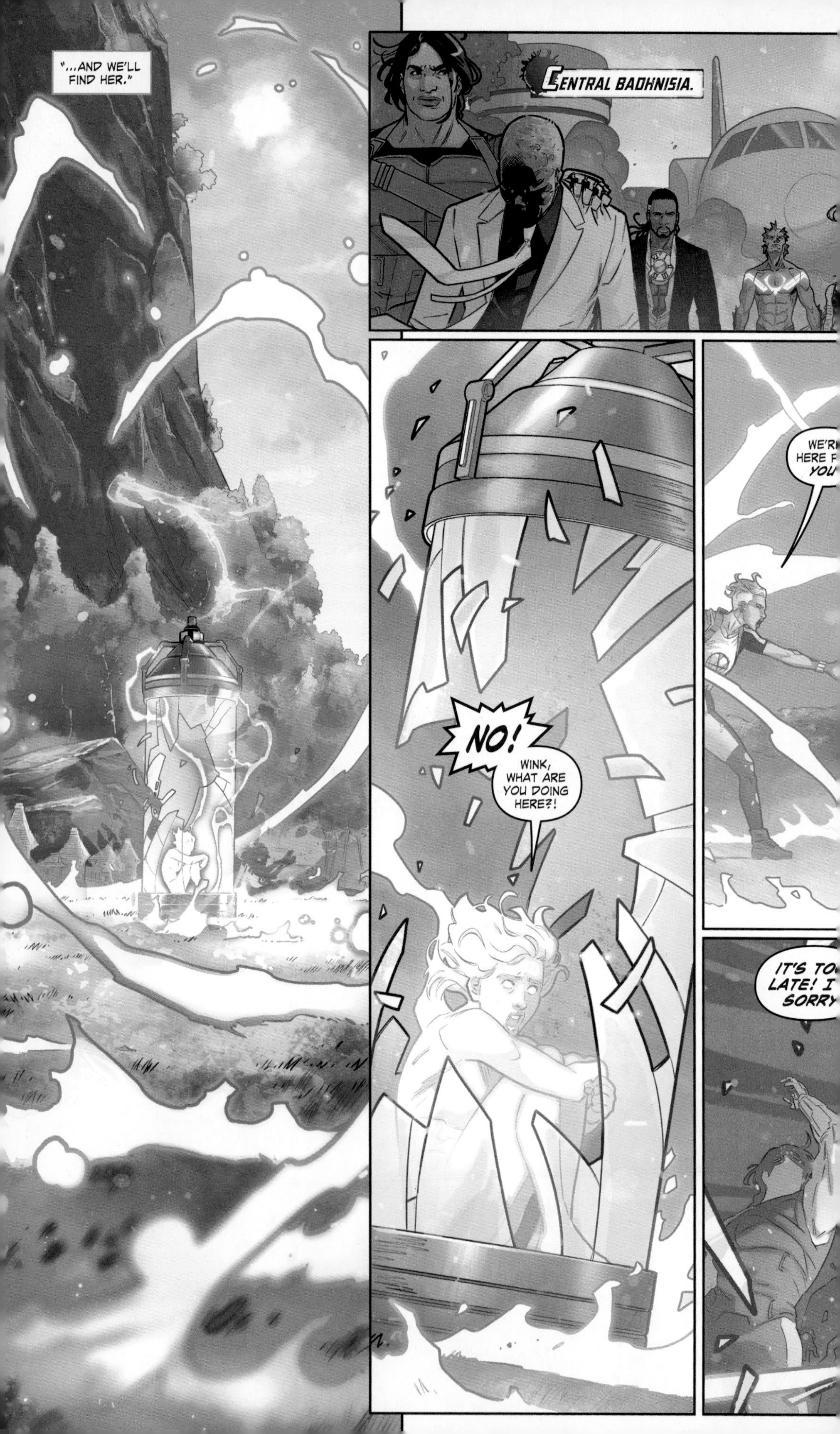
"...AND WE'LL FIND HER."
CENTRAL BADHNISIA.
NO!
WINK, WHAT ARE YOU DOING HERE?!
WE'R HERE F YOU
IT'S TO LATE! I SORRY

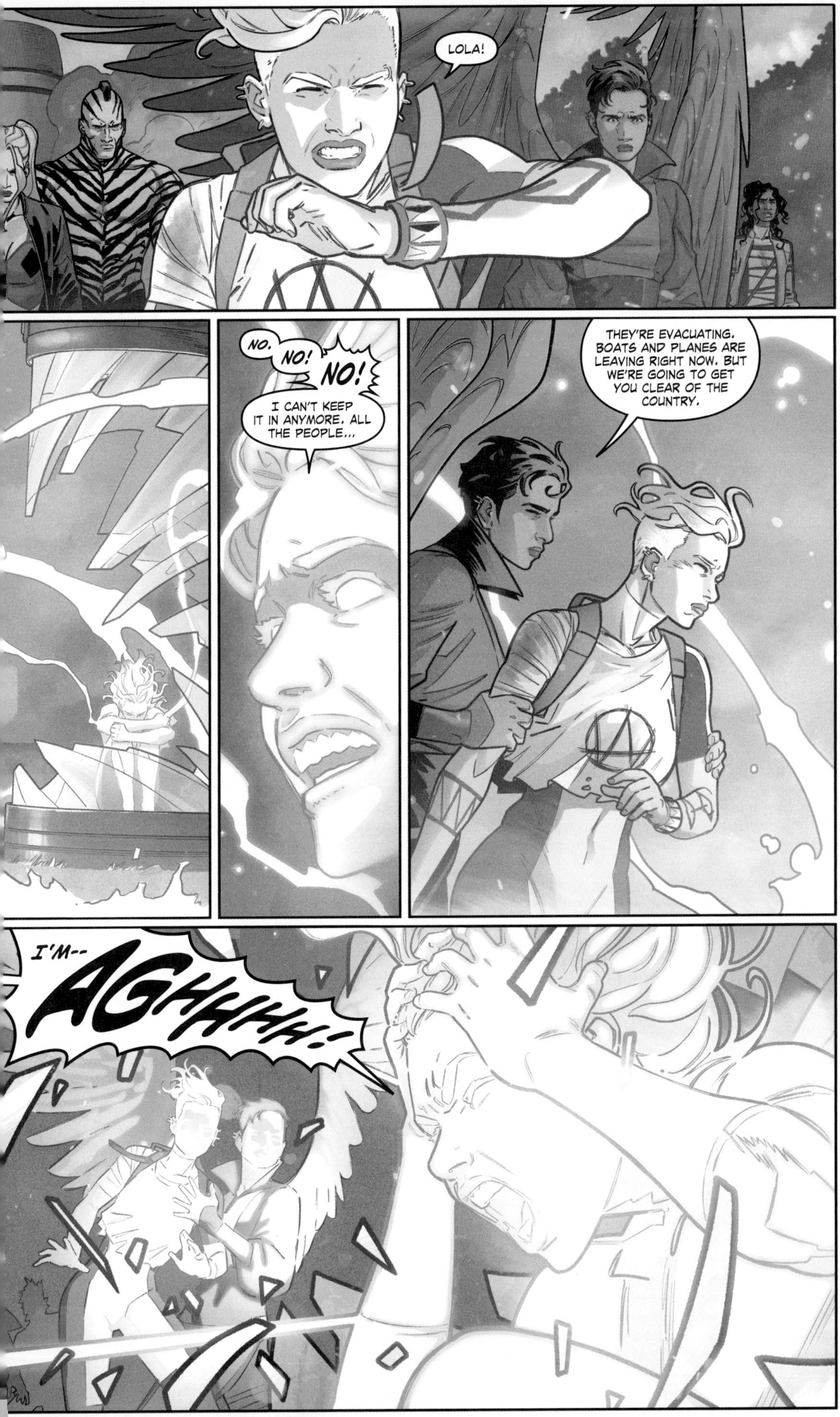
LOLA!
NO.
NO!
NO!
I CAN'T KEEP IT IN ANYMORE. ALL THE PEOPLE...
THEY'RE EVACUATING. BOATS AND PLANES ARE LEAVING RIGHT NOW. BUT WE'RE GOING TO GET YOU CLEAR OF THE COUNTRY.
I'M--
AGHHHH!!

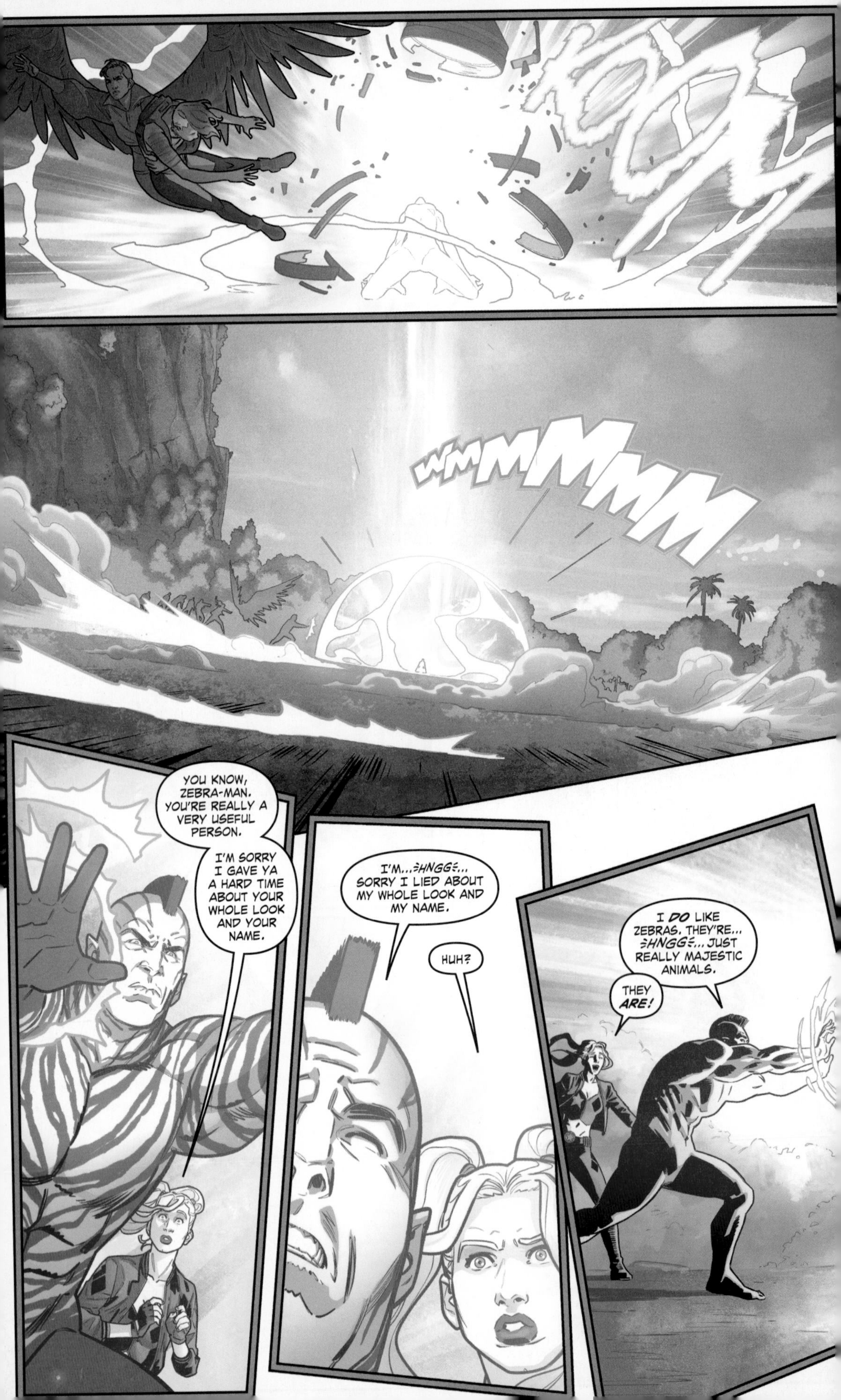
KOOOM
WMMMMMM
YOU KNOW, ZEBRA-MAN. YOU'RE REALLY A VERY USEFUL PERSON.
I'M SORRY I GAVE YA A HARD TIME ABOUT YOUR WHOLE LOOK AND YOUR NAME.
I'M... HNGG... SORRY I LIED ABOUT MY WHOLE LOOK AND MY NAME.
HUH?
I DO LIKE ZEBRAS. THEY'RE... HNGG... JUST REALLY MAJESTIC ANIMALS.
THEY ARE!

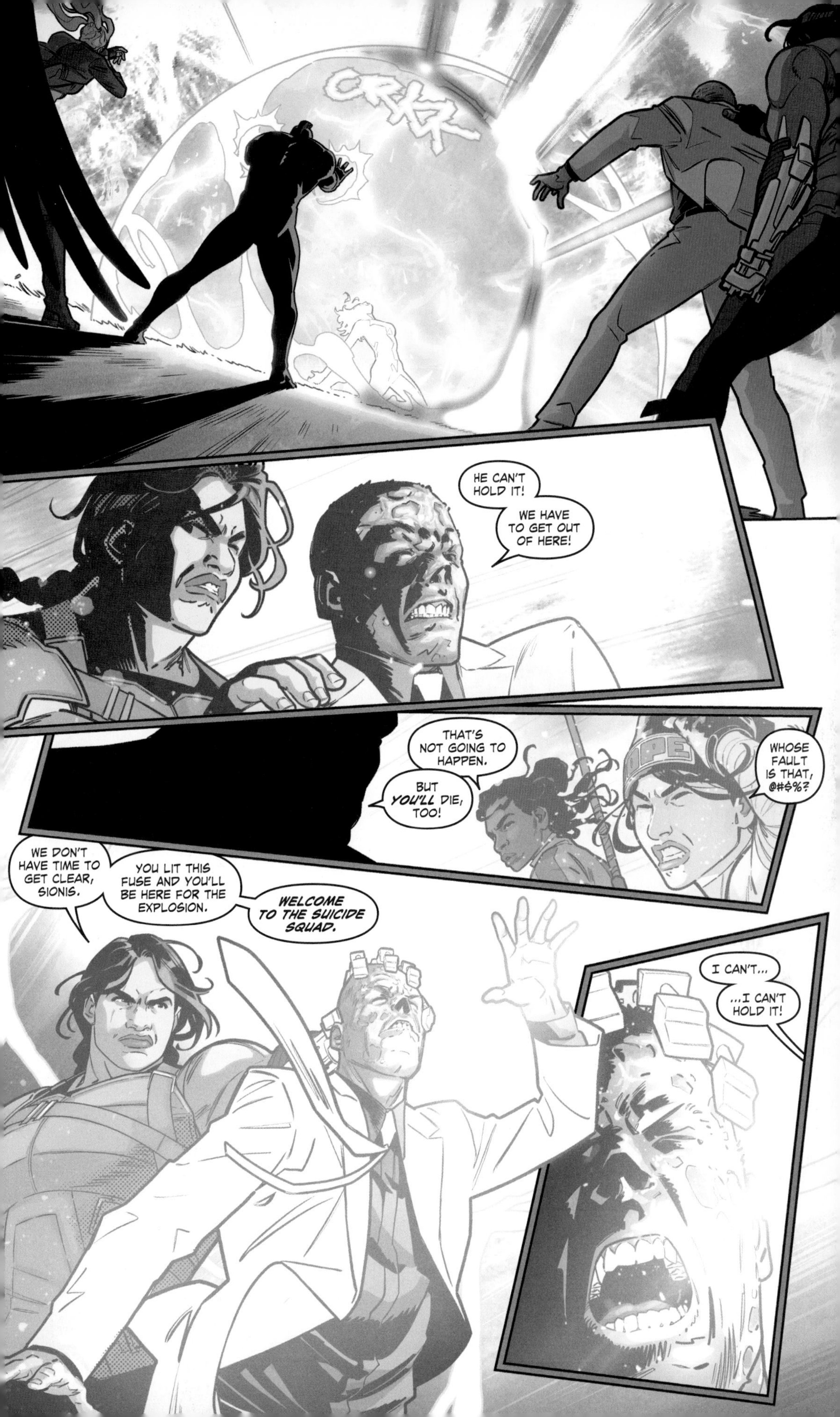
CRXR
HE CAN'T HOLD IT!
WE HAVE TO GET OUT OF HERE!
THAT'S NOT GOING TO HAPPEN.
BUT YOU'LL DIE, TOO!
WHOSE FAULT IS THAT, @#$%?
WE DON'T HAVE TIME TO GET CLEAR, SIONIS.
YOU LIT THIS FUSE AND YOU'LL BE HERE FOR THE EXPLOSION.
WELCOME TO THE SUICIDE SQUAD.
I CAN'T...
...I CAN'T HOLD IT!

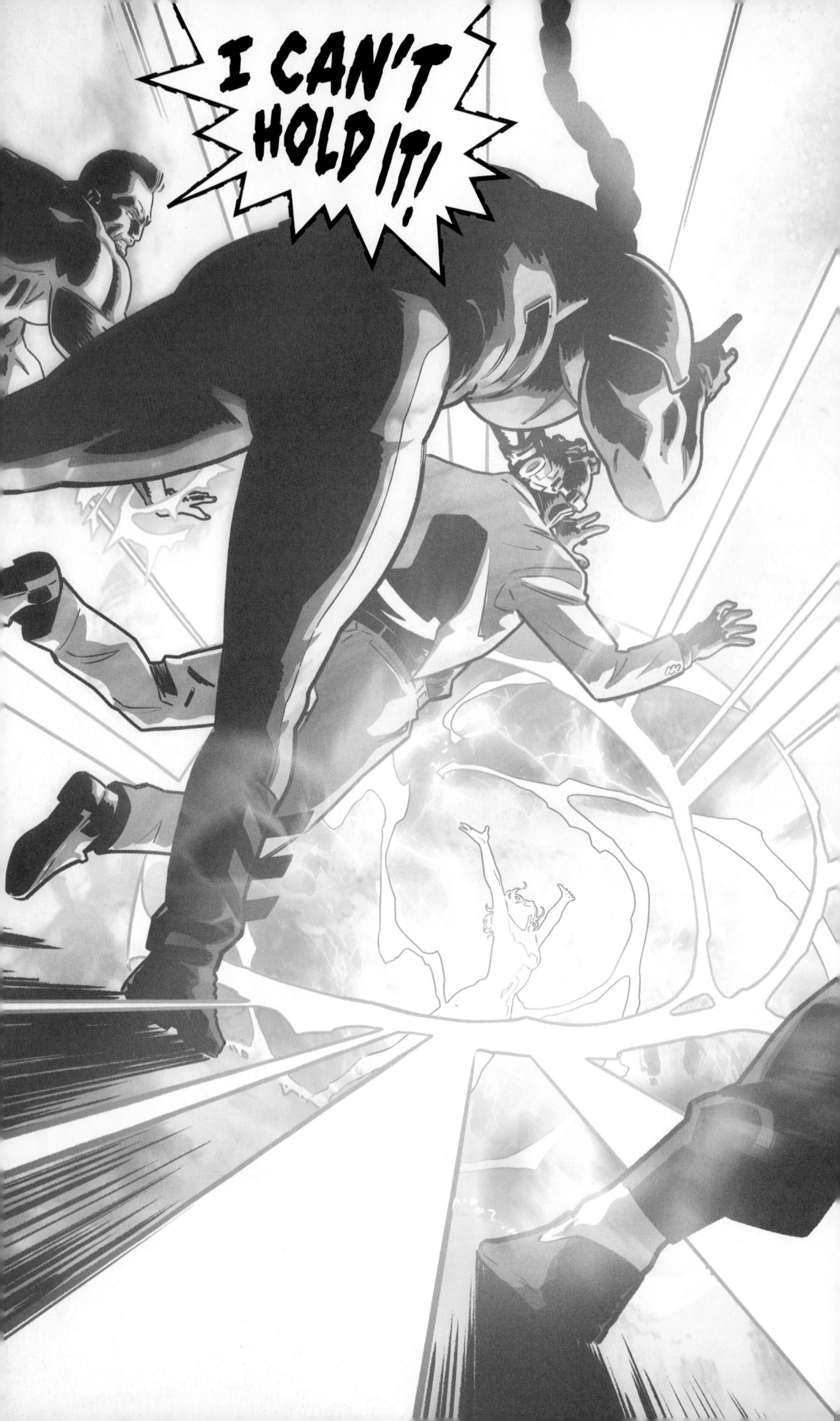
I CAN'T HOLD IT!

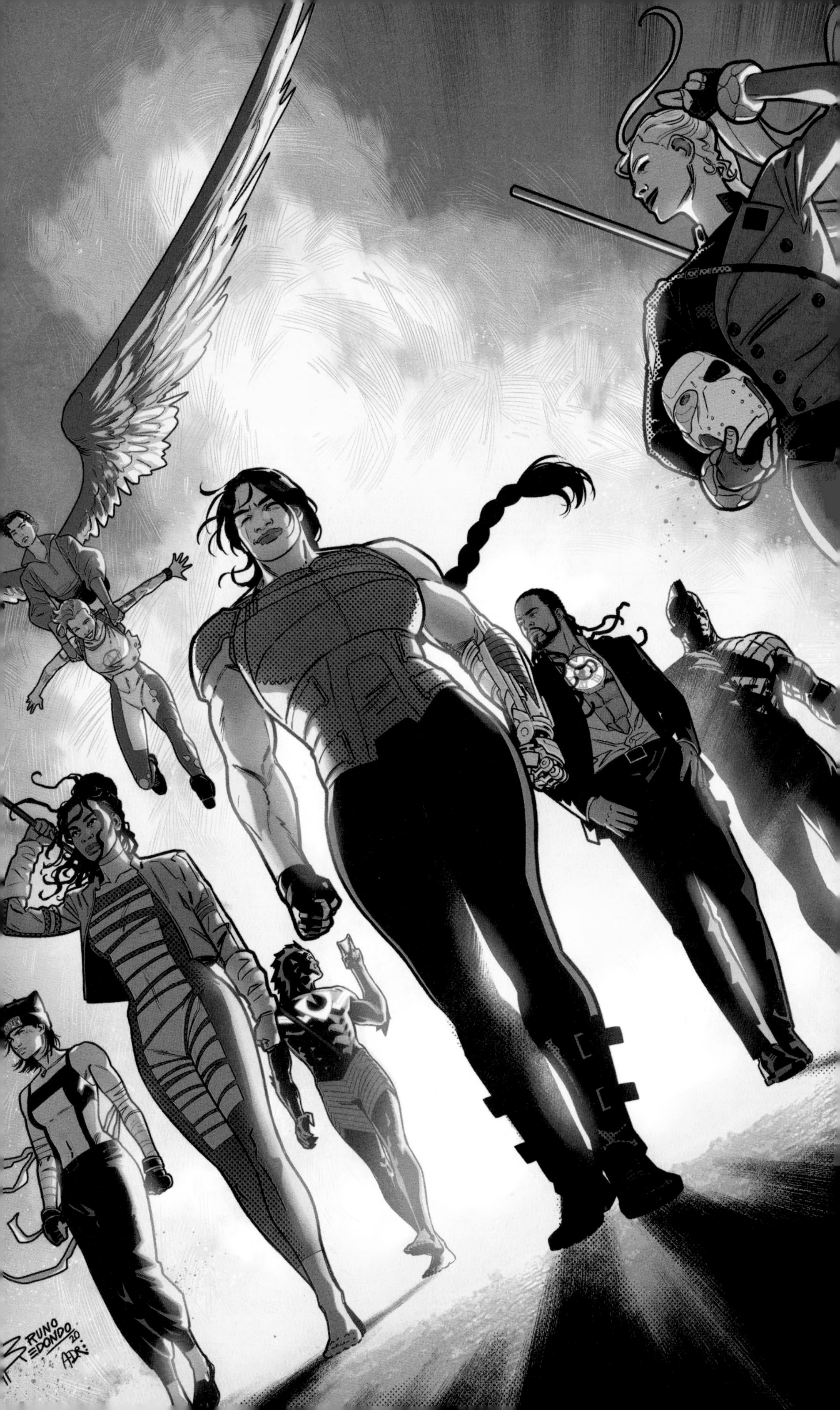
BRUNO REDONDO 20
ADR

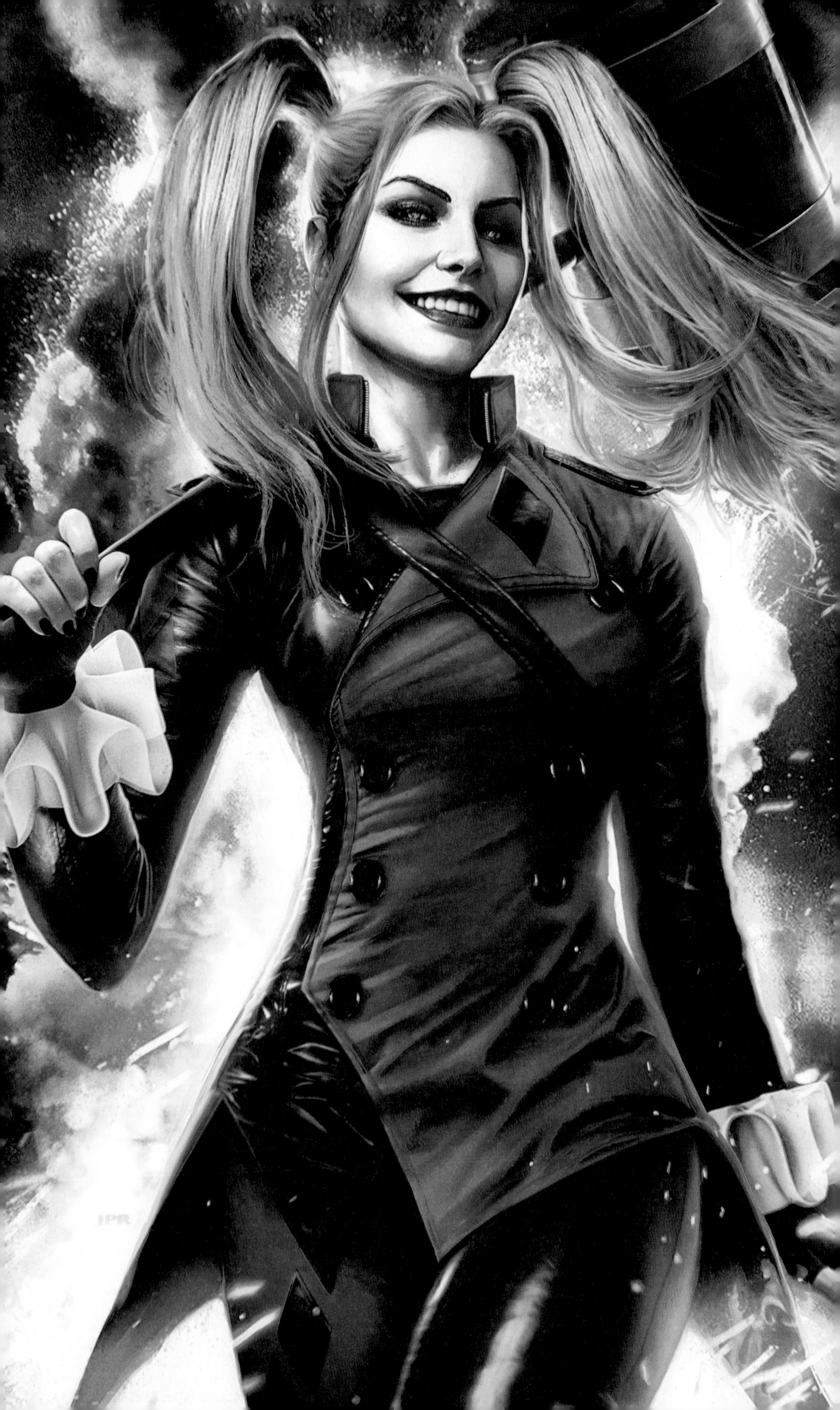

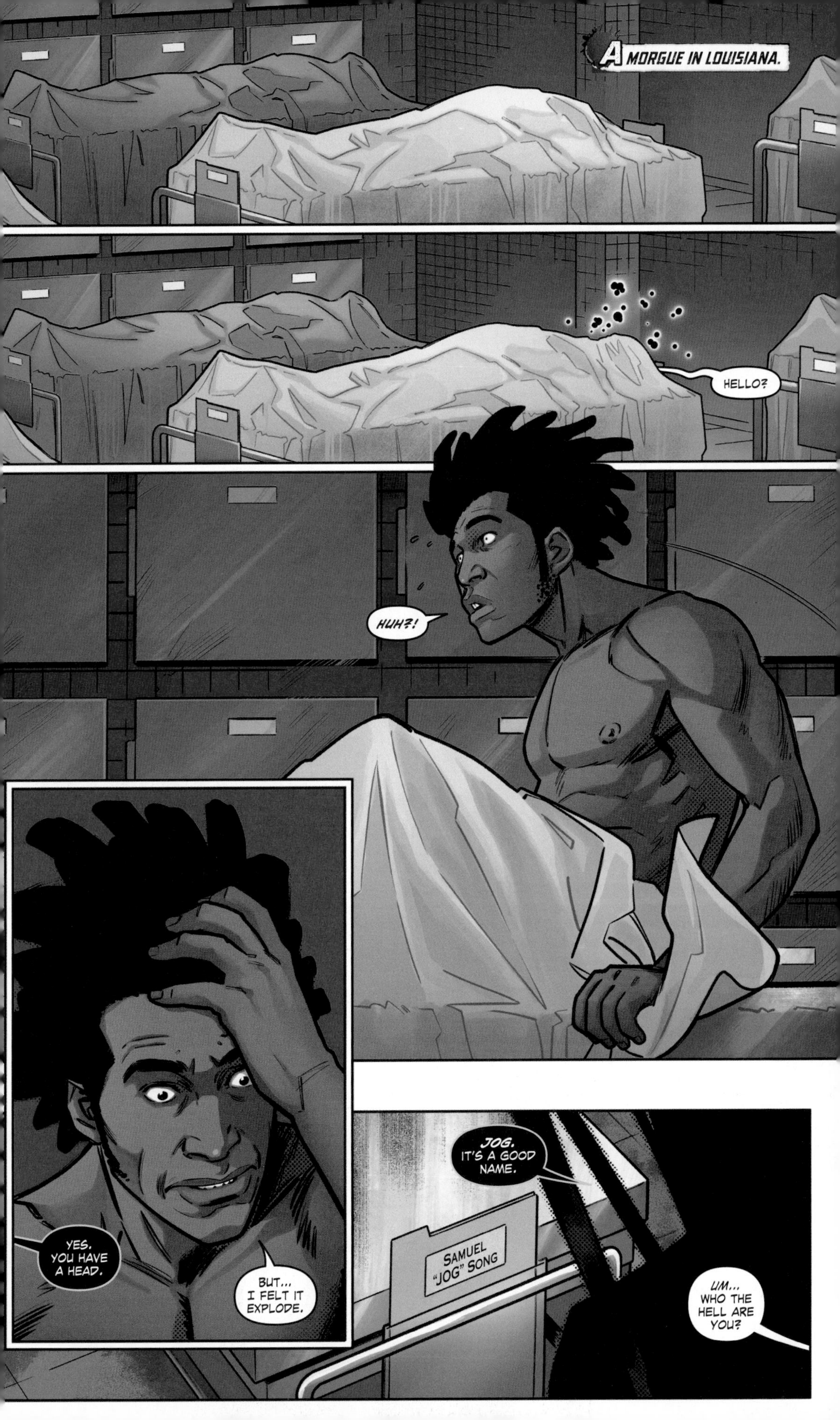
A MORGUE IN LOUISIANA.
HELLO?
HUH?!
JOG. IT'S A GOOD NAME.
SAMUEL "JOG" SONG
UM... WHO THE HELL ARE YOU?
BUT... I FELT IT EXPLODE.
YES. YOU HAVE A HEAD.

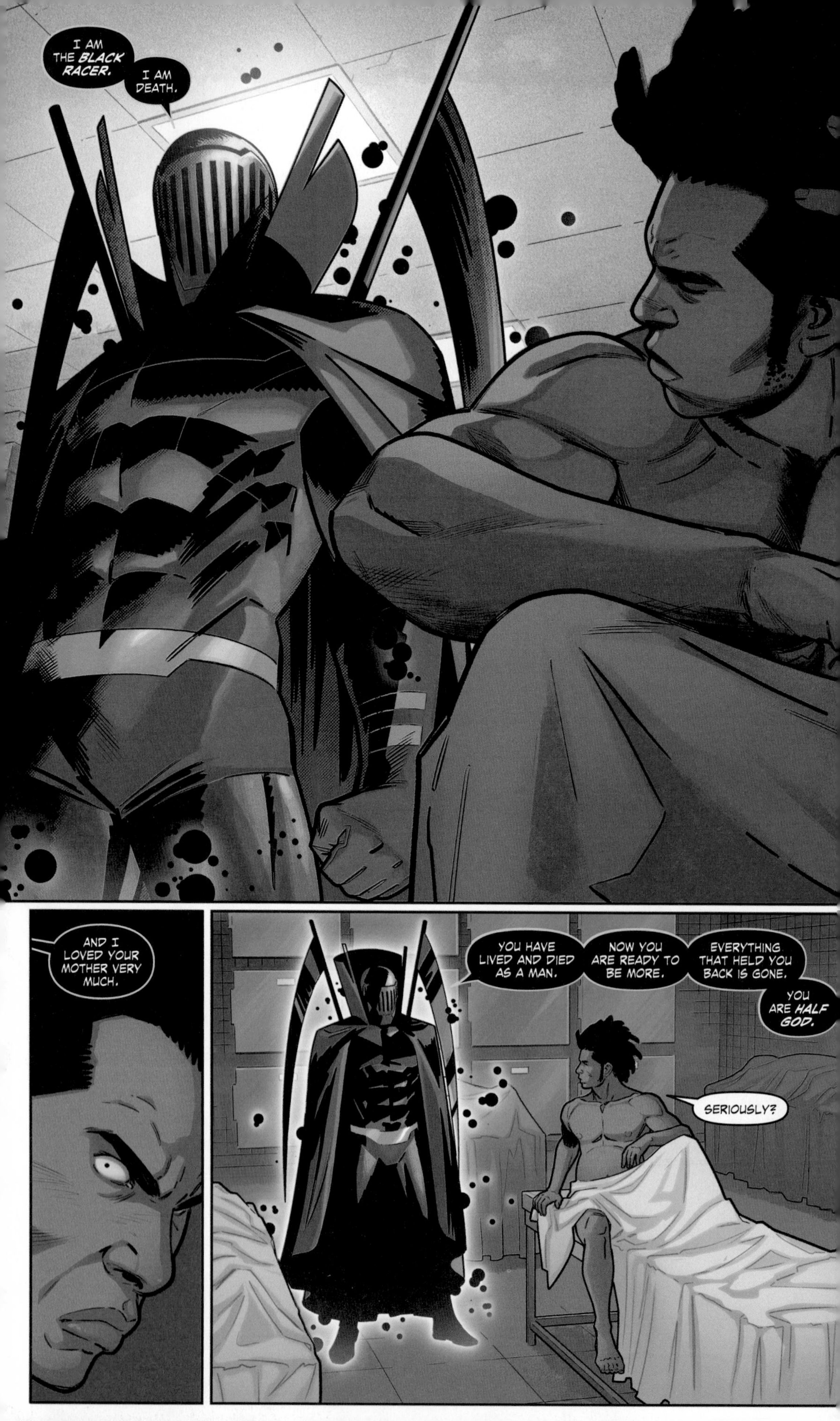

I AM THE *BLACK RACER.*
I AM DEATH.
AND I LOVED YOUR MOTHER VERY MUCH.
YOU HAVE LIVED AND DIED AS A MAN.
NOW YOU ARE READY TO BE MORE.
EVERYTHING THAT HELD YOU BACK IS GONE.
YOU ARE *HALF GOD.*
SERIOUSLY?

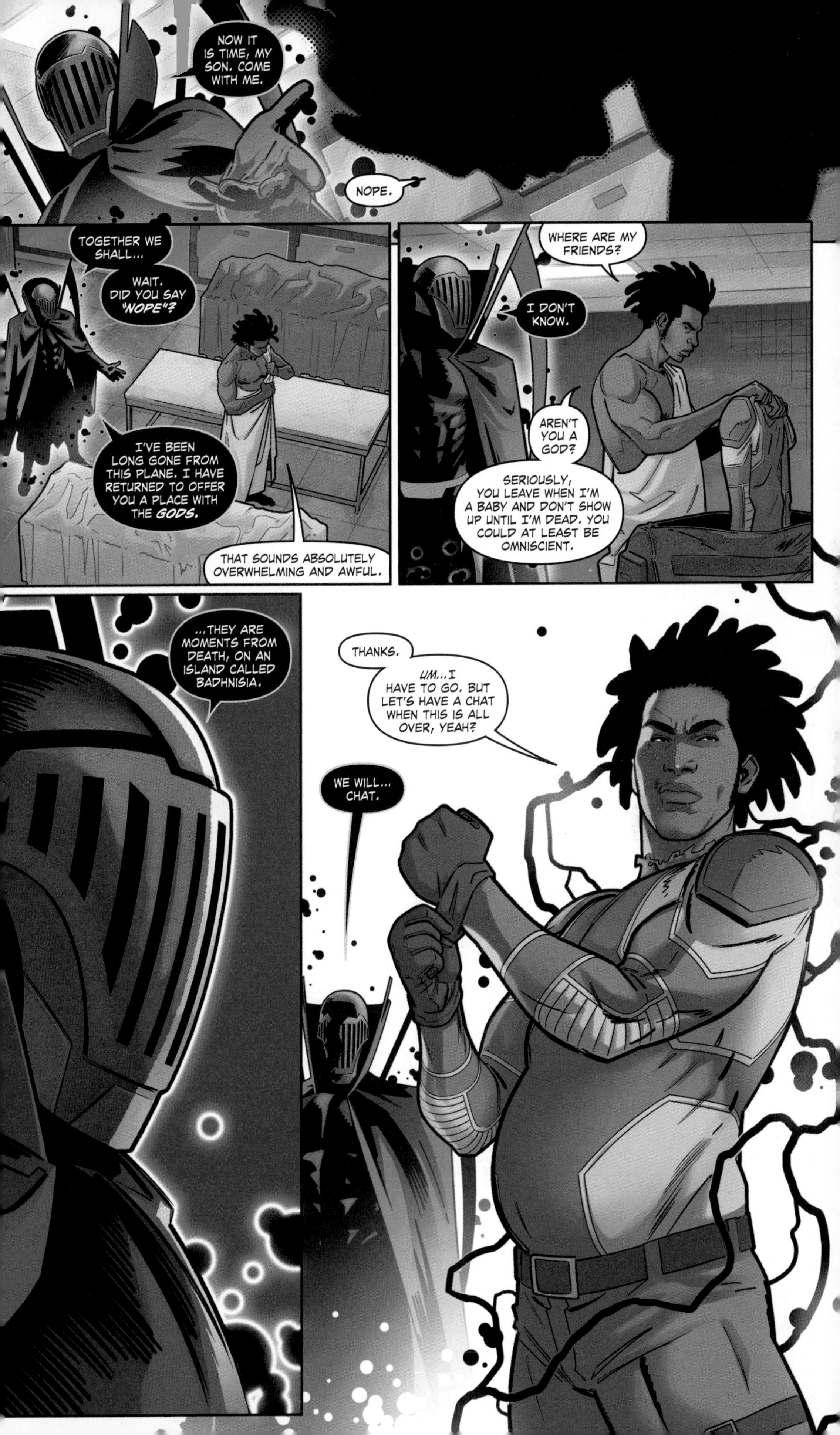
NOW IT IS TIME, MY SON. COME WITH ME.
NOPE.
TOGETHER WE SHALL...
WAIT. DID YOU SAY "NOPE"?
I'VE BEEN LONG GONE FROM THIS PLANE. I HAVE RETURNED TO OFFER YOU A PLACE WITH THE GODS.
THAT SOUNDS ABSOLUTELY OVERWHELMING AND AWFUL.
WHERE ARE MY FRIENDS?
I DON'T KNOW.
AREN'T YOU A GOD?
SERIOUSLY, YOU LEAVE WHEN I'M A BABY AND DON'T SHOW UP UNTIL I'M DEAD. YOU COULD AT LEAST BE OMNISCIENT.
...THEY ARE MOMENTS FROM DEATH, ON AN ISLAND CALLED BADHNISIA.
THANKS.
UM...I HAVE TO GO. BUT LET'S HAVE A CHAT WHEN THIS IS ALL OVER, YEAH?
WE WILL... CHAT.

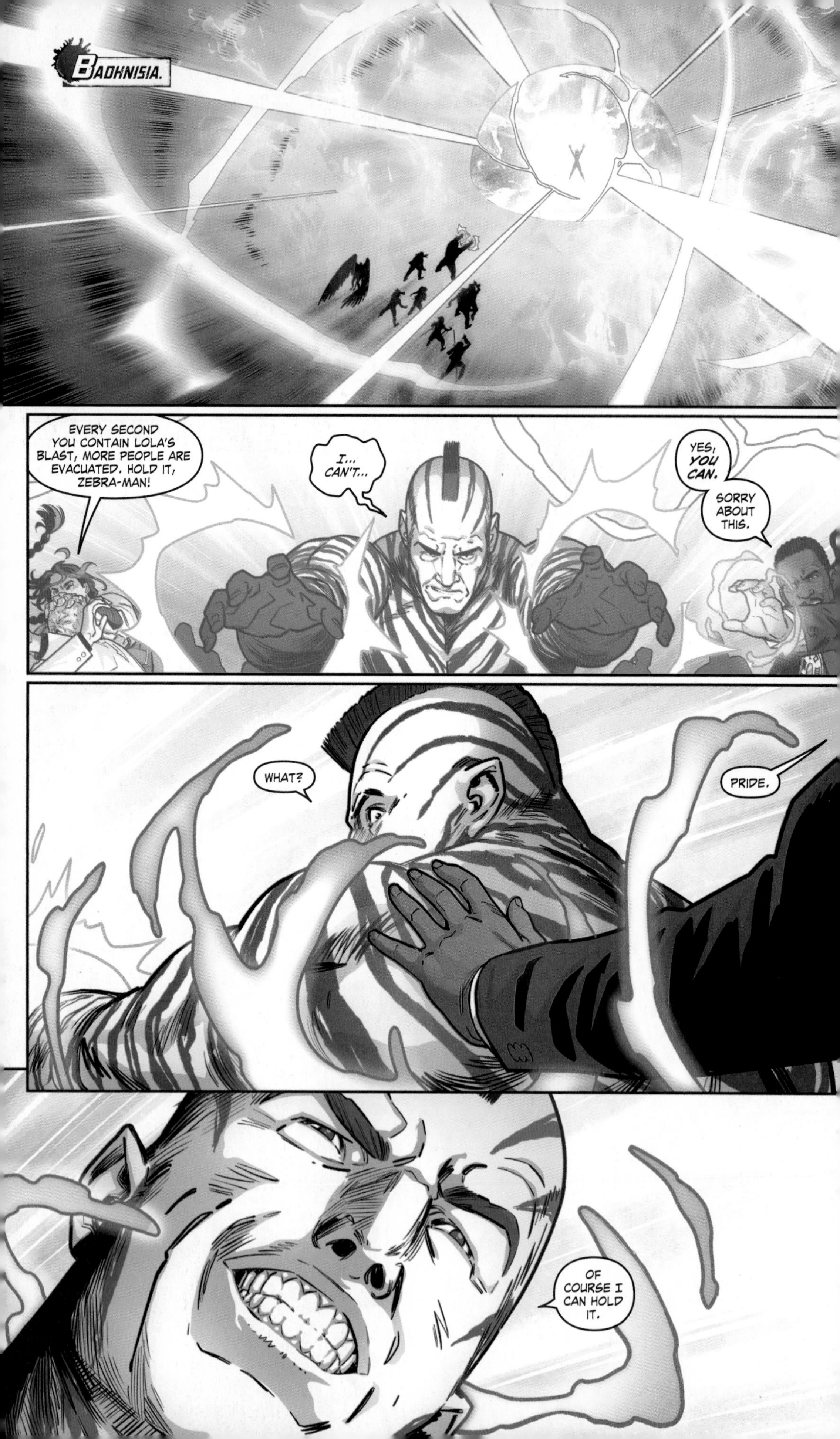
BADHNISIA.
EVERY SECOND YOU CONTAIN LOLA'S BLAST, MORE PEOPLE ARE EVACUATED. HOLD IT, ZEBRA-MAN!
I... CAN'T...
YES, YOU CAN.
SORRY ABOUT THIS.
WHAT?
PRIDE.
OF COURSE I CAN HOLD IT.

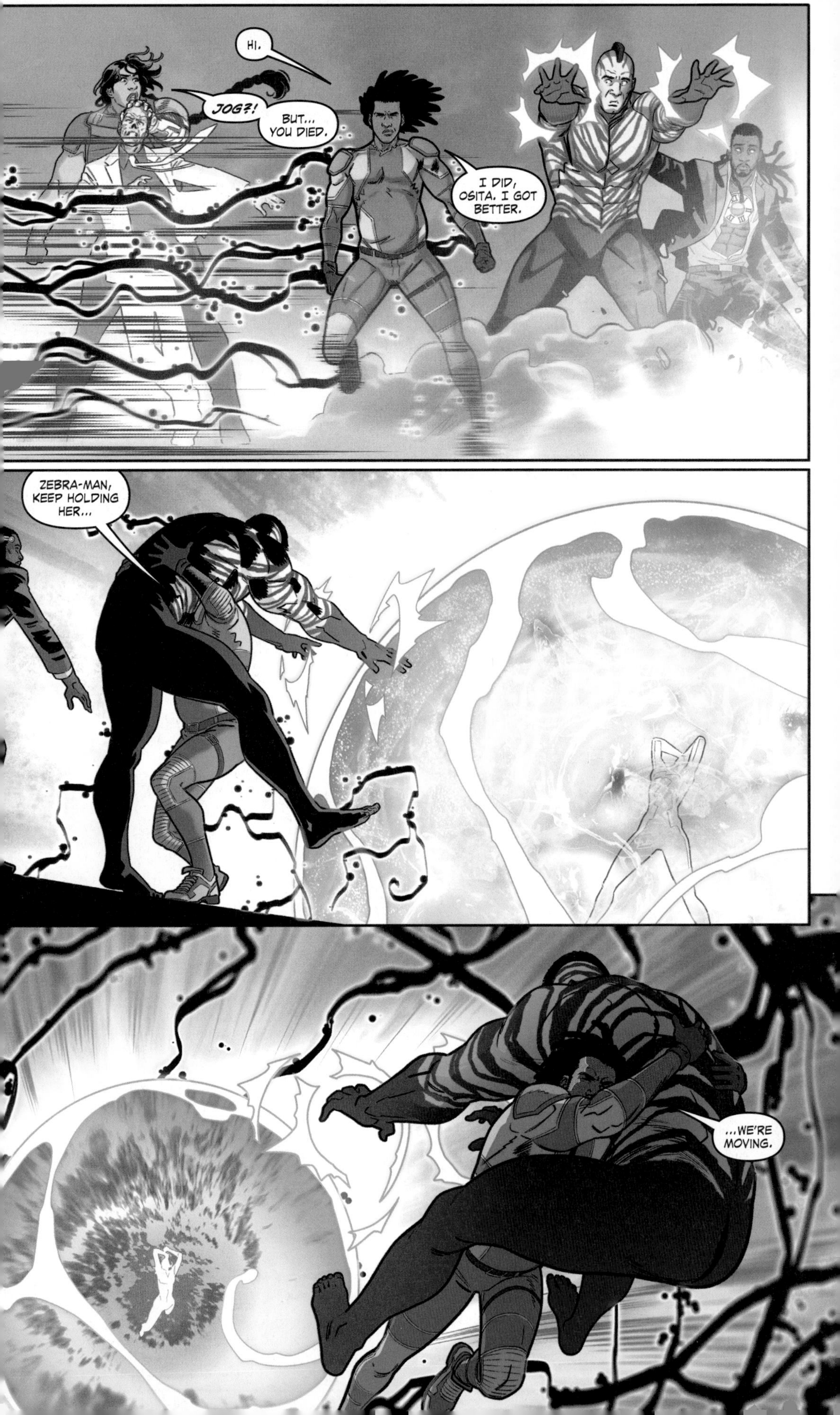
HI.
JOG?!
BUT... YOU DIED.
I DID, OSITA. I GOT BETTER.
ZEBRA-MAN, KEEP HOLDING HER...
...WE'RE MOVING.

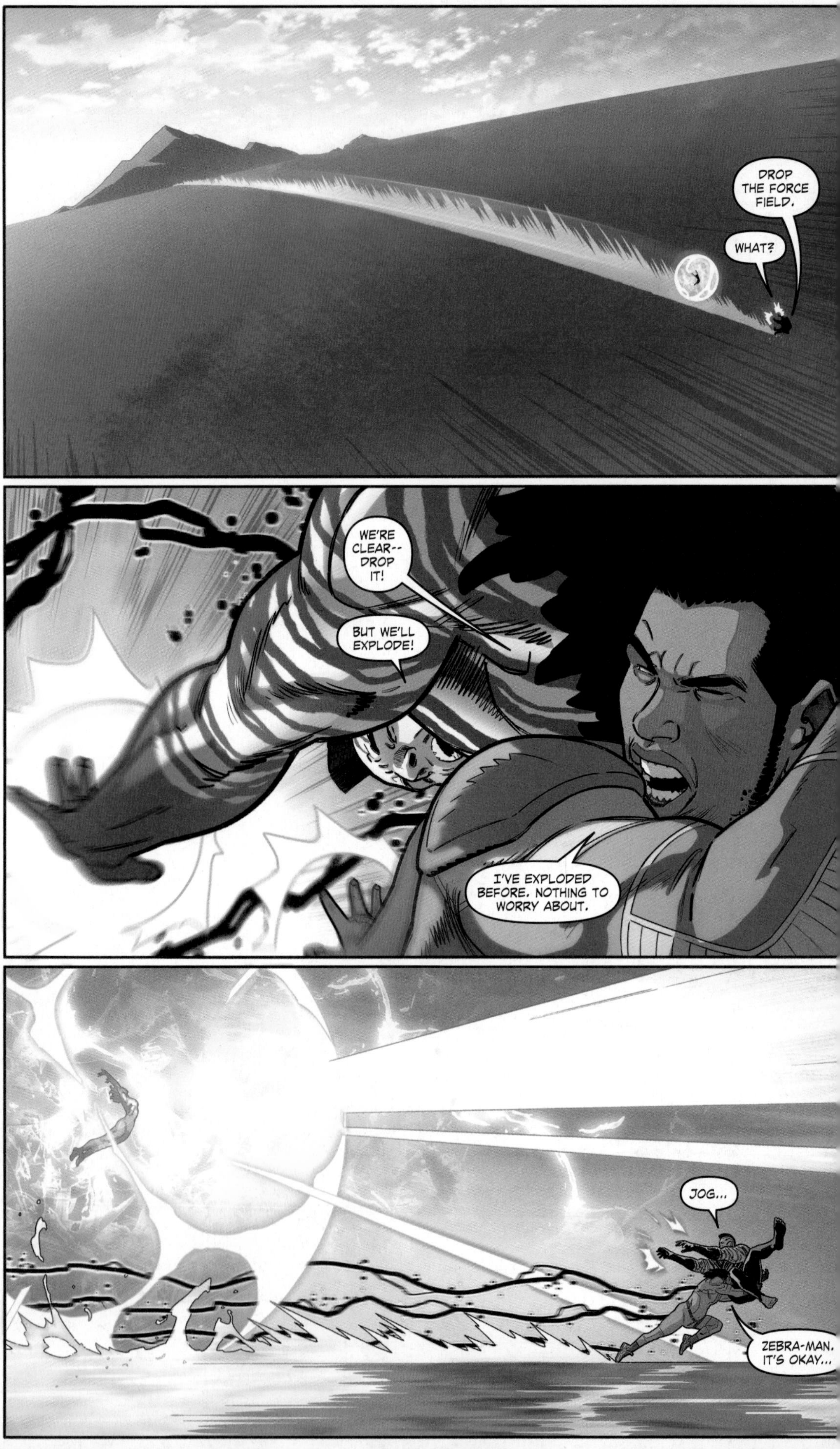
DROP THE FORCE FIELD.
WHAT?
WE'RE CLEAR-- DROP IT!
BUT WE'LL EXPLODE!
I'VE EXPLODED BEFORE. NOTHING TO WORRY ABOUT.
JOG...
ZEBRA-MAN. IT'S OKAY...

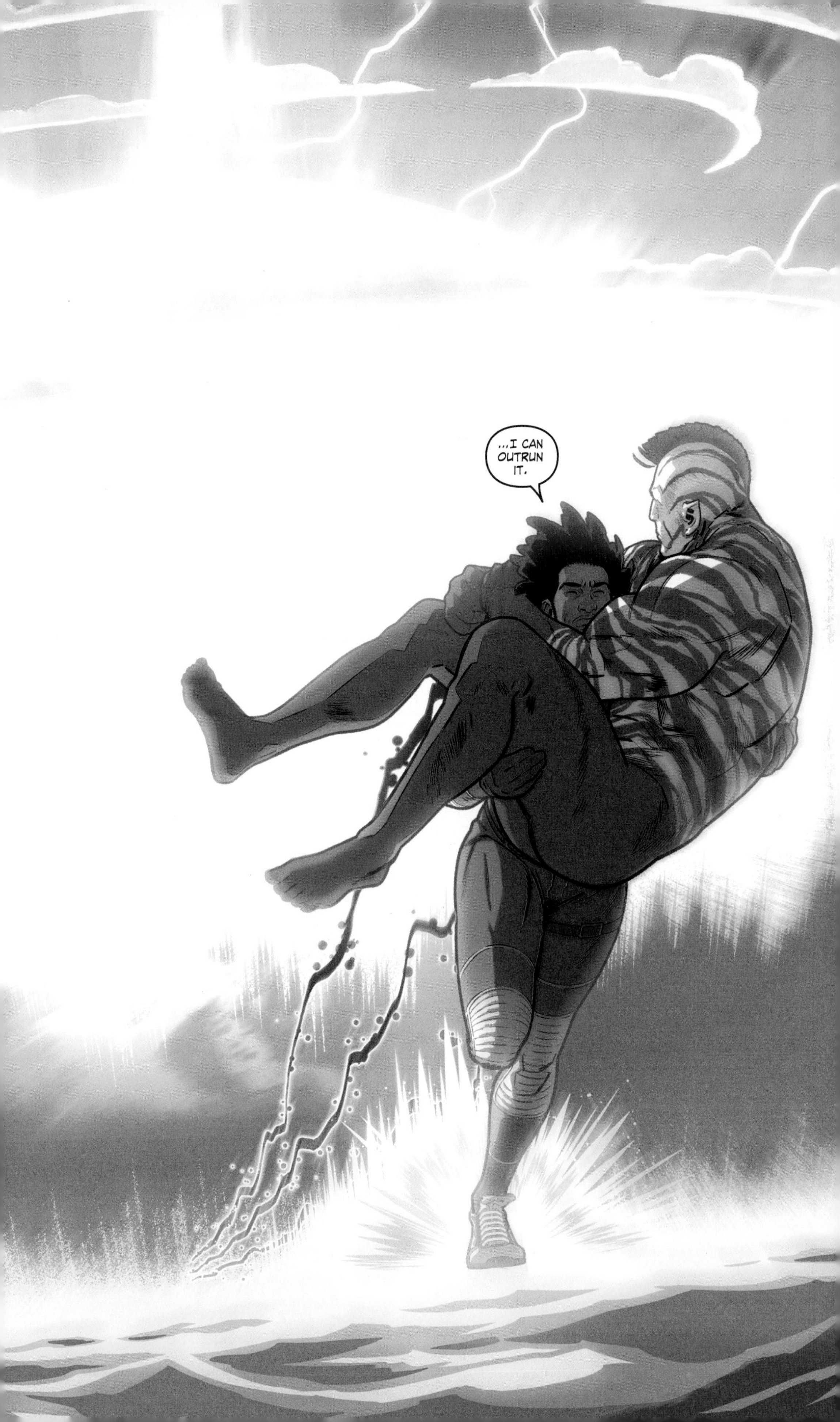
...I CAN OUTRUN IT.

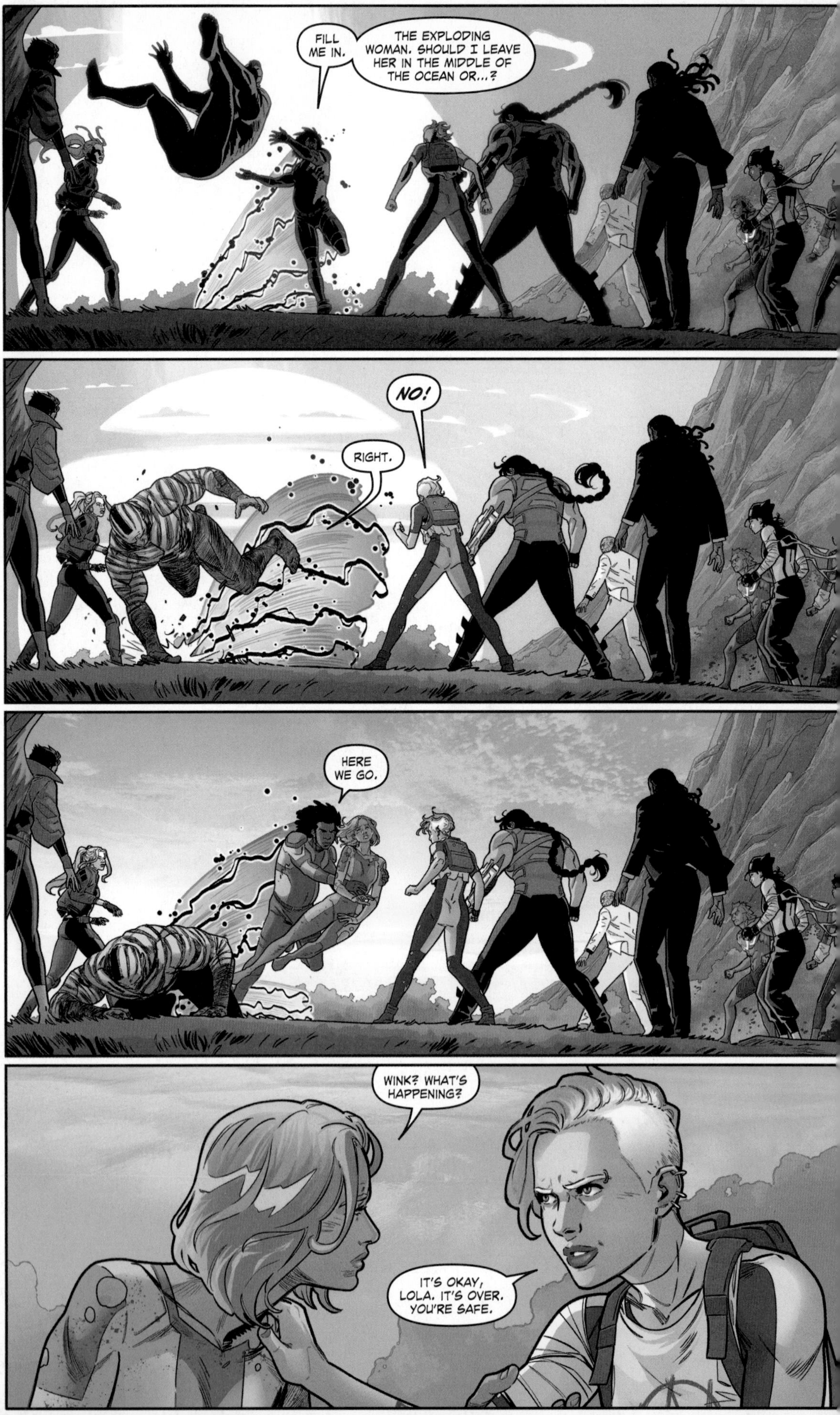
FILL ME IN.
THE EXPLODING WOMAN. SHOULD I LEAVE HER IN THE MIDDLE OF THE OCEAN OR...?
NO!
RIGHT.
HERE WE GO.
WINK? WHAT'S HAPPENING?
IT'S OKAY, LOLA. IT'S OVER. YOU'RE SAFE.

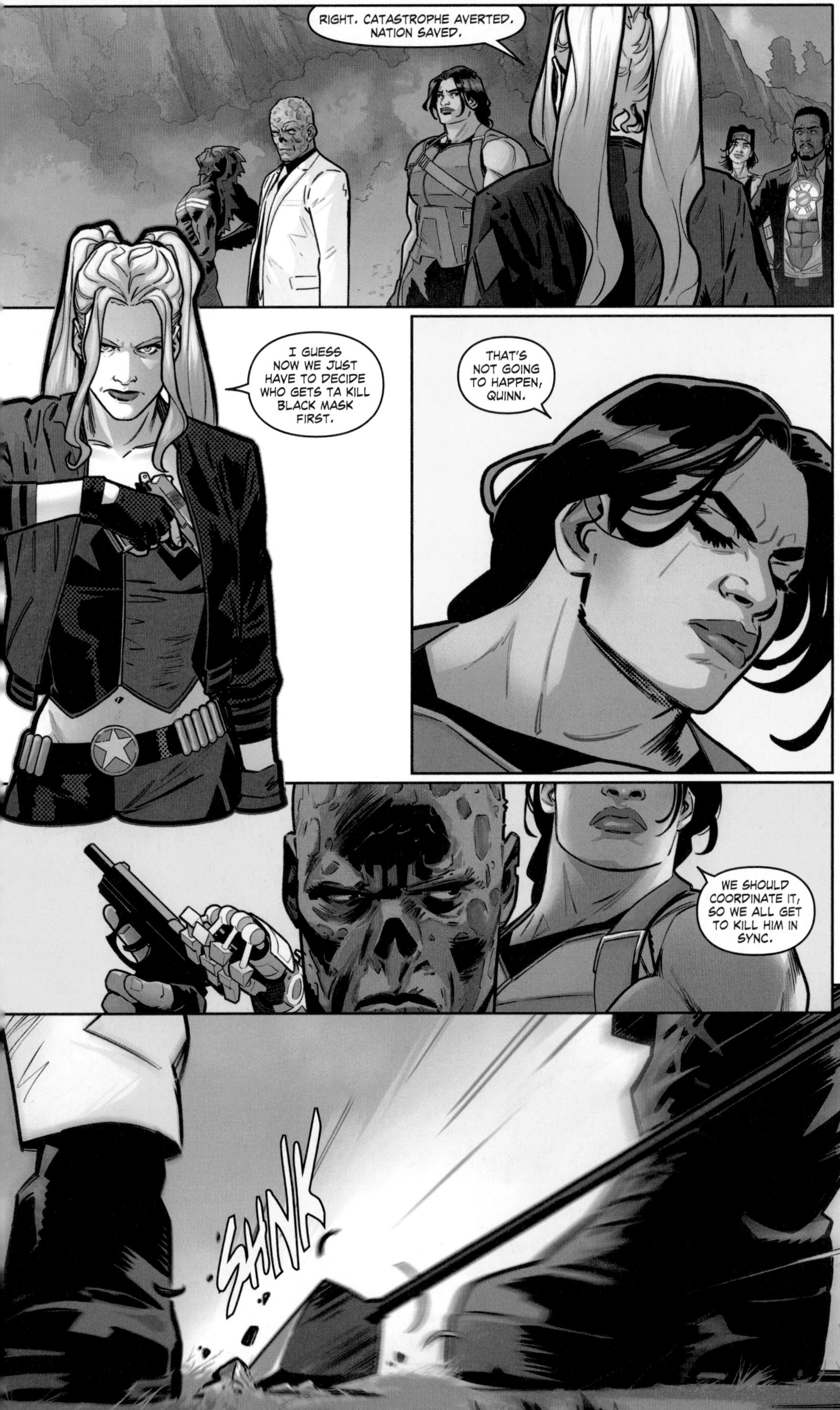
RIGHT. CATASTROPHE AVERTED. NATION SAVED.
I GUESS NOW WE JUST HAVE TO DECIDE WHO GETS TA KILL BLACK MASK FIRST.
THAT'S NOT GOING TO HAPPEN, QUINN.
WE SHOULD COORDINATE IT, SO WE ALL GET TO KILL HIM IN SYNC.
SHNK

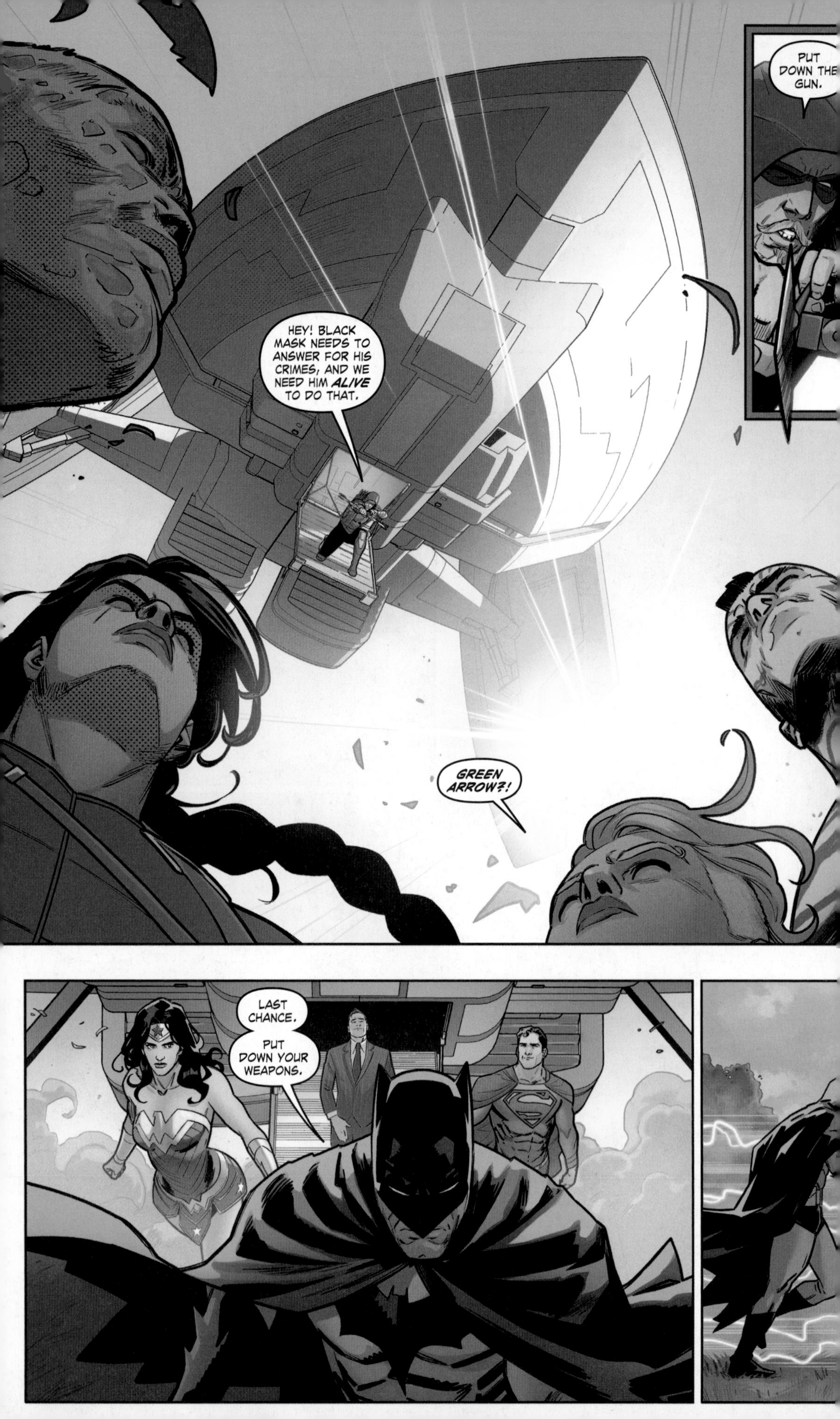
PUT DOWN THE GUN.
HEY! BLACK MASK NEEDS TO ANSWER FOR HIS CRIMES, AND WE NEED HIM ALIVE TO DO THAT.
GREEN ARROW?!
LAST CHANCE.
PUT DOWN YOUR WEAPONS.

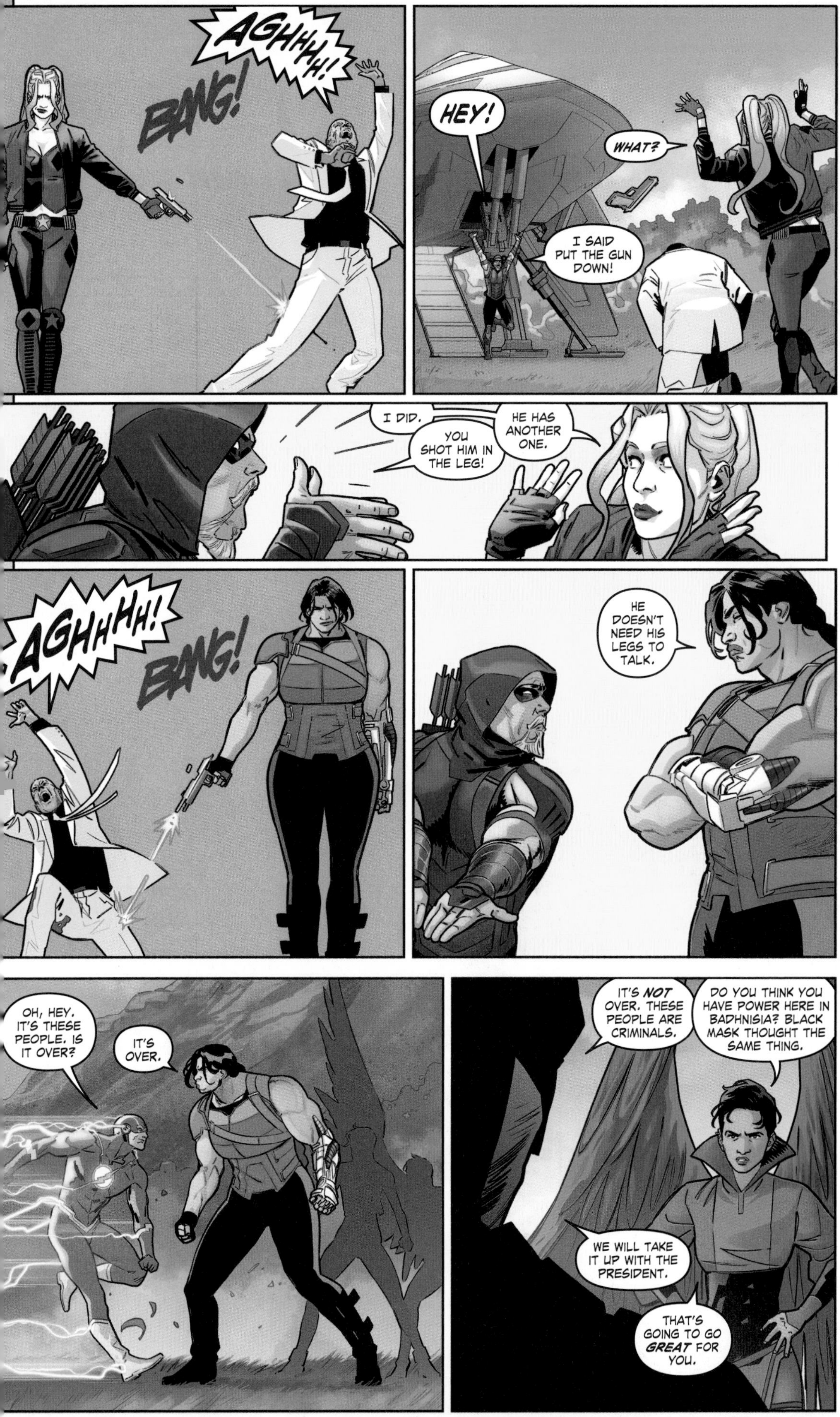
AGHHHH!
BANG!
HEY!
WHAT?
I SAID PUT THE GUN DOWN!
I DID.
YOU SHOT HIM IN THE LEG!
HE HAS ANOTHER ONE.
AGHHHH!
BANG!
HE DOESN'T NEED HIS LEGS TO TALK.
OH, HEY. IT'S THESE PEOPLE. IS IT OVER?
IT'S OVER.
IT'S NOT OVER. THESE PEOPLE ARE CRIMINALS.
DO YOU THINK YOU HAVE POWER HERE IN BADHNISIA? BLACK MASK THOUGHT THE SAME THING.
WE WILL TAKE IT UP WITH THE PRESIDENT.
THAT'S GOING TO GO GREAT FOR YOU.

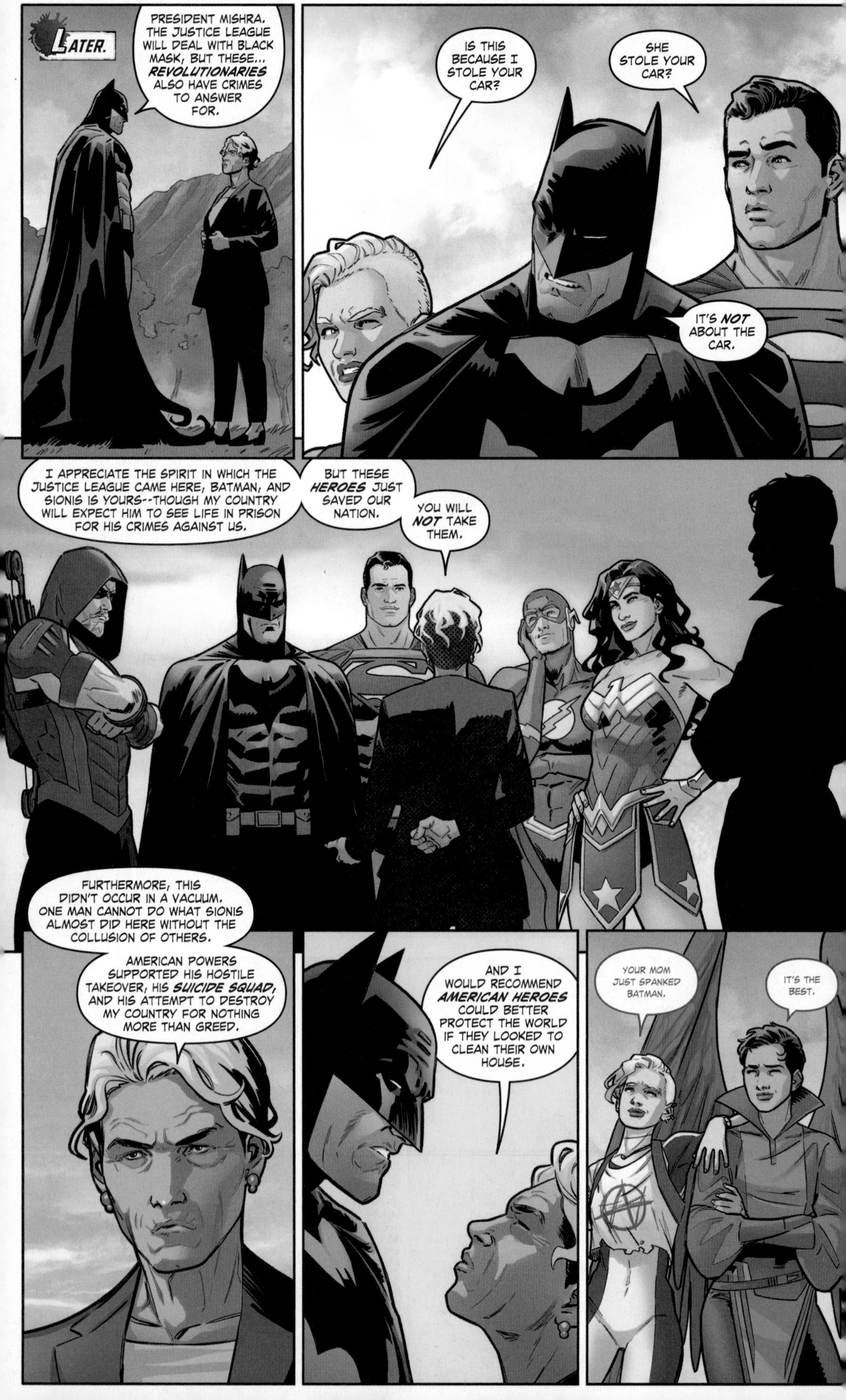
LATER.
PRESIDENT MISHRA. THE JUSTICE LEAGUE WILL DEAL WITH BLACK MASK, BUT THESE... REVOLUTIONARIES ALSO HAVE CRIMES TO ANSWER FOR.
IS THIS BECAUSE I STOLE YOUR CAR?
SHE STOLE YOUR CAR?
IT'S NOT ABOUT THE CAR.
I APPRECIATE THE SPIRIT IN WHICH THE JUSTICE LEAGUE CAME HERE, BATMAN, AND SIONIS IS YOURS--THOUGH MY COUNTRY WILL EXPECT HIM TO SEE LIFE IN PRISON FOR HIS CRIMES AGAINST US.
BUT THESE HEROES JUST SAVED OUR NATION.
YOU WILL NOT TAKE THEM.
FURTHERMORE, THIS DIDN'T OCCUR IN A VACUUM. ONE MAN CANNOT DO WHAT SIONIS ALMOST DID HERE WITHOUT THE COLLUSION OF OTHERS.
AMERICAN POWERS SUPPORTED HIS HOSTILE TAKEOVER, HIS SUICIDE SQUAD, AND HIS ATTEMPT TO DESTROY MY COUNTRY FOR NOTHING MORE THAN GREED.
AND I WOULD RECOMMEND AMERICAN HEROES COULD BETTER PROTECT THE WORLD IF THEY LOOKED TO CLEAN THEIR OWN HOUSE.
YOUR MOM JUST SPANKED BATMAN.
IT'S THE BEST.

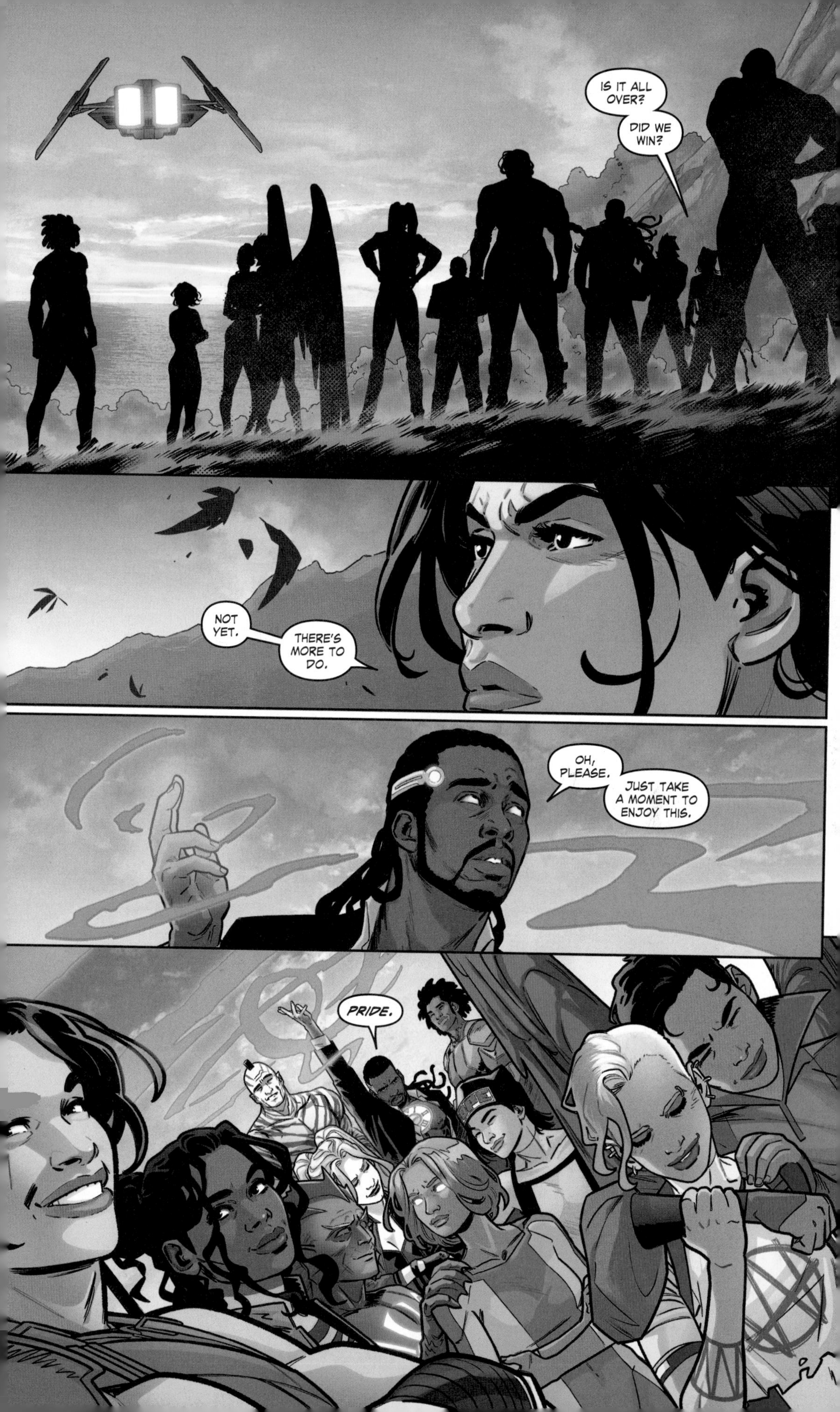
IS IT ALL OVER?
DID WE WIN?
NOT YET.
THERE'S MORE TO DO.
OH, PLEASE.
JUST TAKE A MOMENT TO ENJOY THIS.
PRIDE.

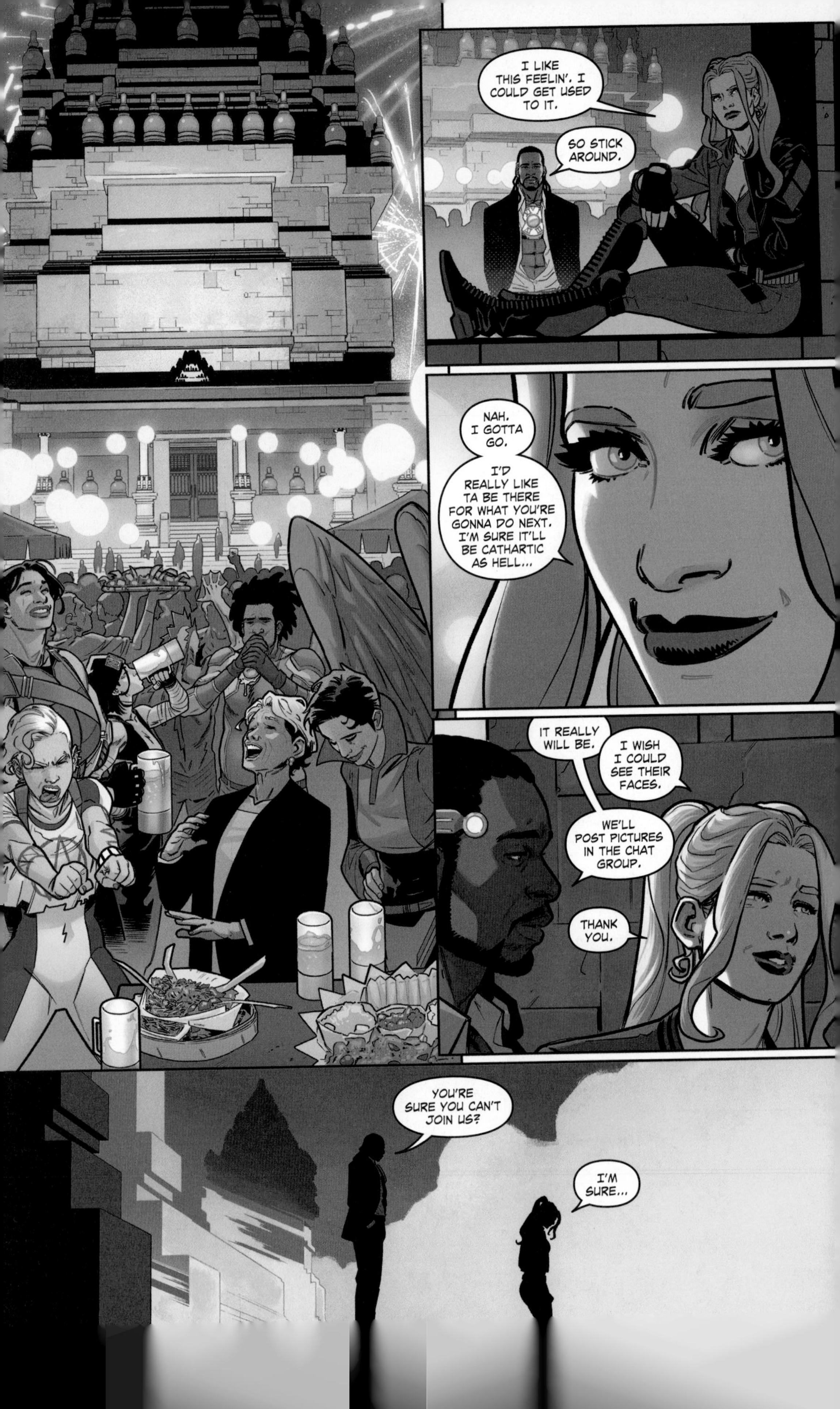
I LIKE THIS FEELIN'. I COULD GET USED TO IT.
SO STICK AROUND.
NAH. I GOTTA GO.
I'D REALLY LIKE TA BE THERE FOR WHAT YOU'RE GONNA DO NEXT. I'M SURE IT'LL BE CATHARTIC AS HELL...
IT REALLY WILL BE.
I WISH I COULD SEE THEIR FACES.
WE'LL POST PICTURES IN THE CHAT GROUP.
THANK YOU.
YOU'RE SURE YOU CAN'T JOIN US?
I'M SURE...

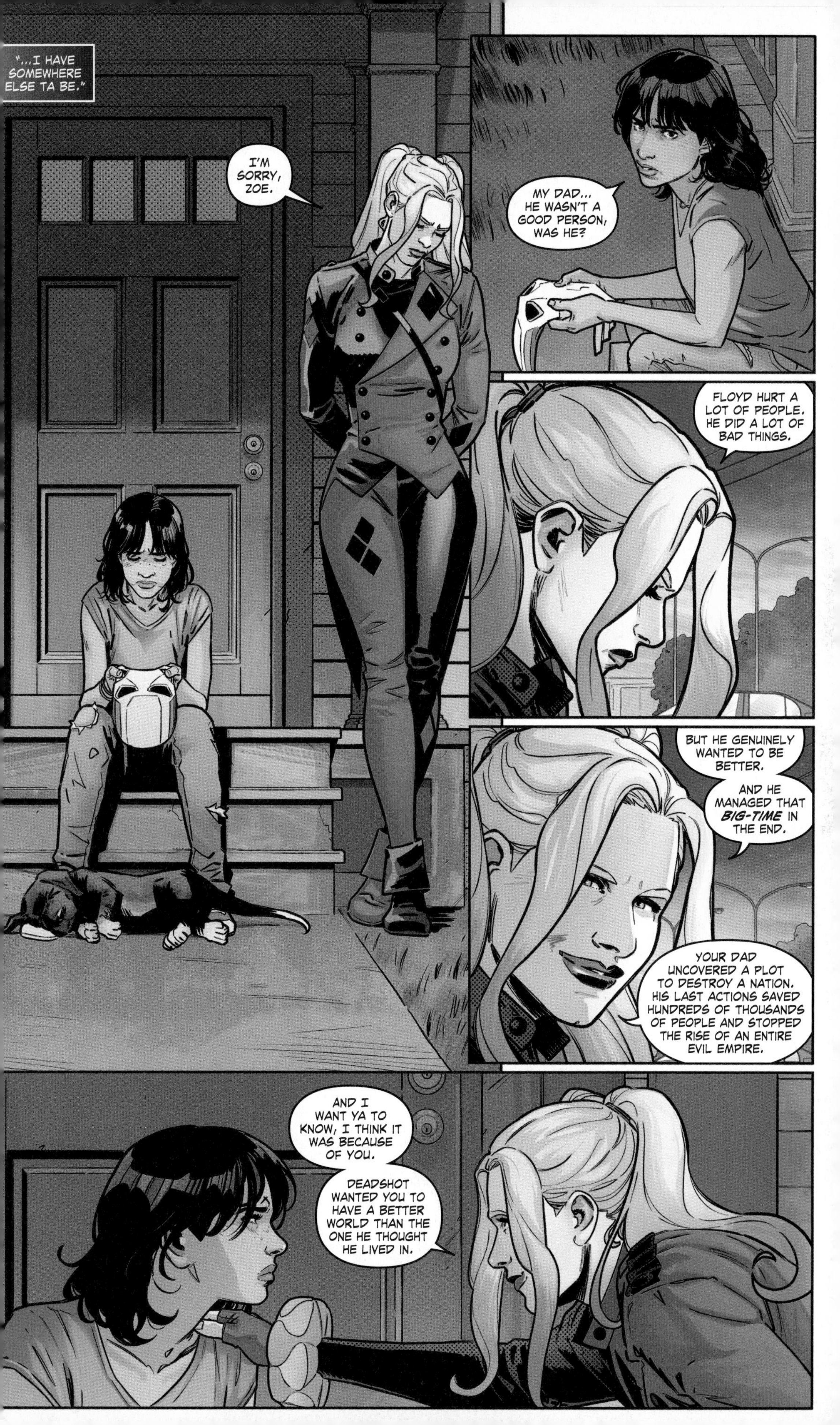
"...I HAVE SOMEWHERE ELSE TA BE."
I'M SORRY, ZOE.
MY DAD... HE WASN'T A GOOD PERSON, WAS HE?
FLOYD HURT A LOT OF PEOPLE. HE DID A LOT OF BAD THINGS.
BUT HE GENUINELY WANTED TO BE BETTER.
AND HE MANAGED THAT *BIG-TIME* IN THE END.
YOUR DAD UNCOVERED A PLOT TO DESTROY A NATION. HIS LAST ACTIONS SAVED HUNDREDS OF THOUSANDS OF PEOPLE AND STOPPED THE RISE OF AN ENTIRE EVIL EMPIRE.
AND I WANT YA TO KNOW, I THINK IT WAS BECAUSE OF YOU.
DEADSHOT WANTED YOU TO HAVE A BETTER WORLD THAN THE ONE HE THOUGHT HE LIVED IN.

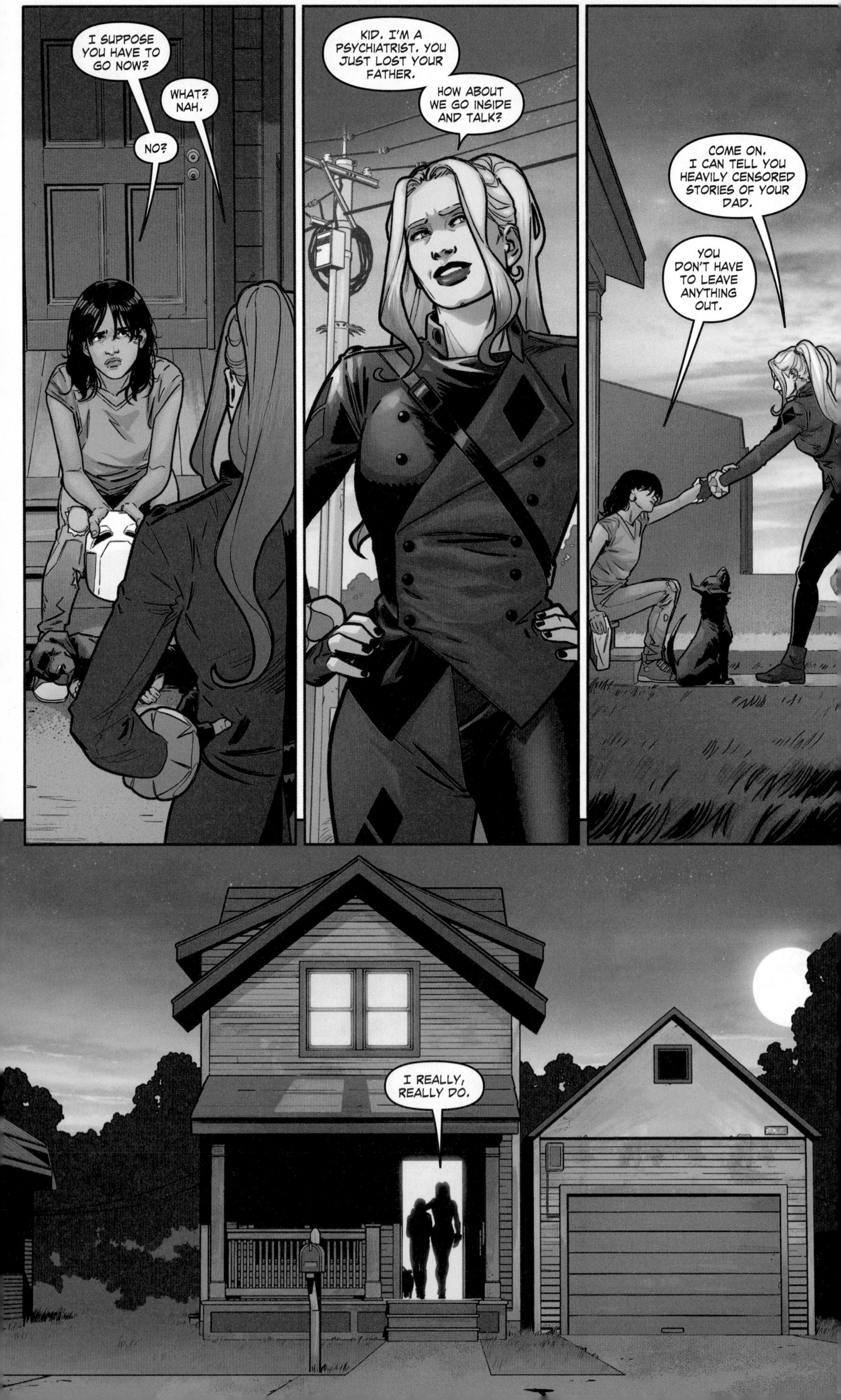
I SUPPOSE YOU HAVE TO GO NOW?
WHAT? NAH.
NO?
KID. I'M A PSYCHIATRIST. YOU JUST LOST YOUR FATHER.
HOW ABOUT WE GO INSIDE AND TALK?
COME ON. I CAN TELL YOU HEAVILY CENSORED STORIES OF YOUR DAD.
YOU DON'T HAVE TO LEAVE ANYTHING OUT.
I REALLY, REALLY DO.

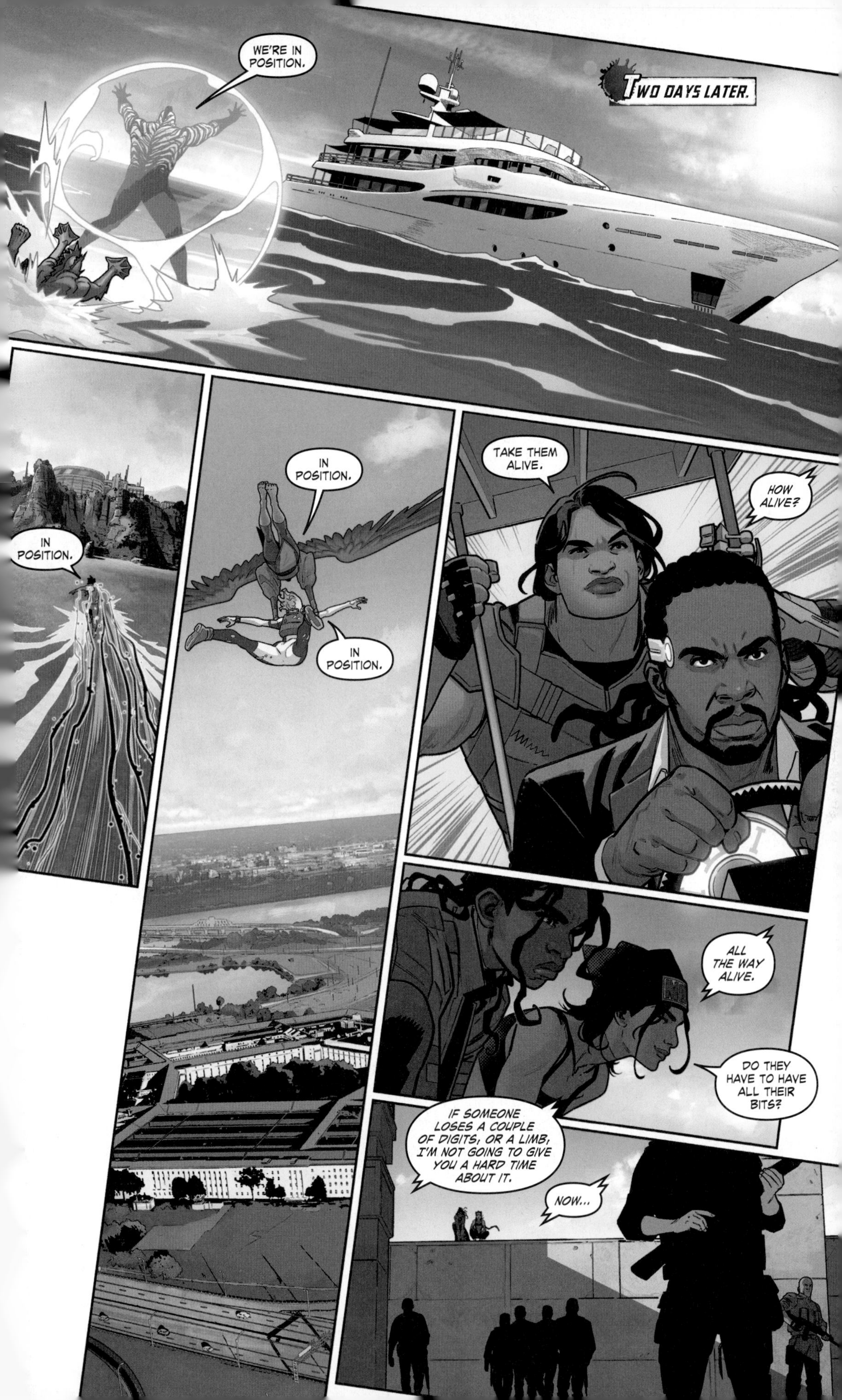
TWO DAYS LATER.
WE'RE IN POSITION.
IN POSITION.
IN POSITION.
IN POSITION.
TAKE THEM ALIVE.
HOW ALIVE?
ALL THE WAY ALIVE.
DO THEY HAVE TO HAVE ALL THEIR BITS?
IF SOMEONE LOSES A COUPLE OF DIGITS, OR A LIMB, I'M NOT GOING TO GIVE YOU A HARD TIME ABOUT IT.
NOW...

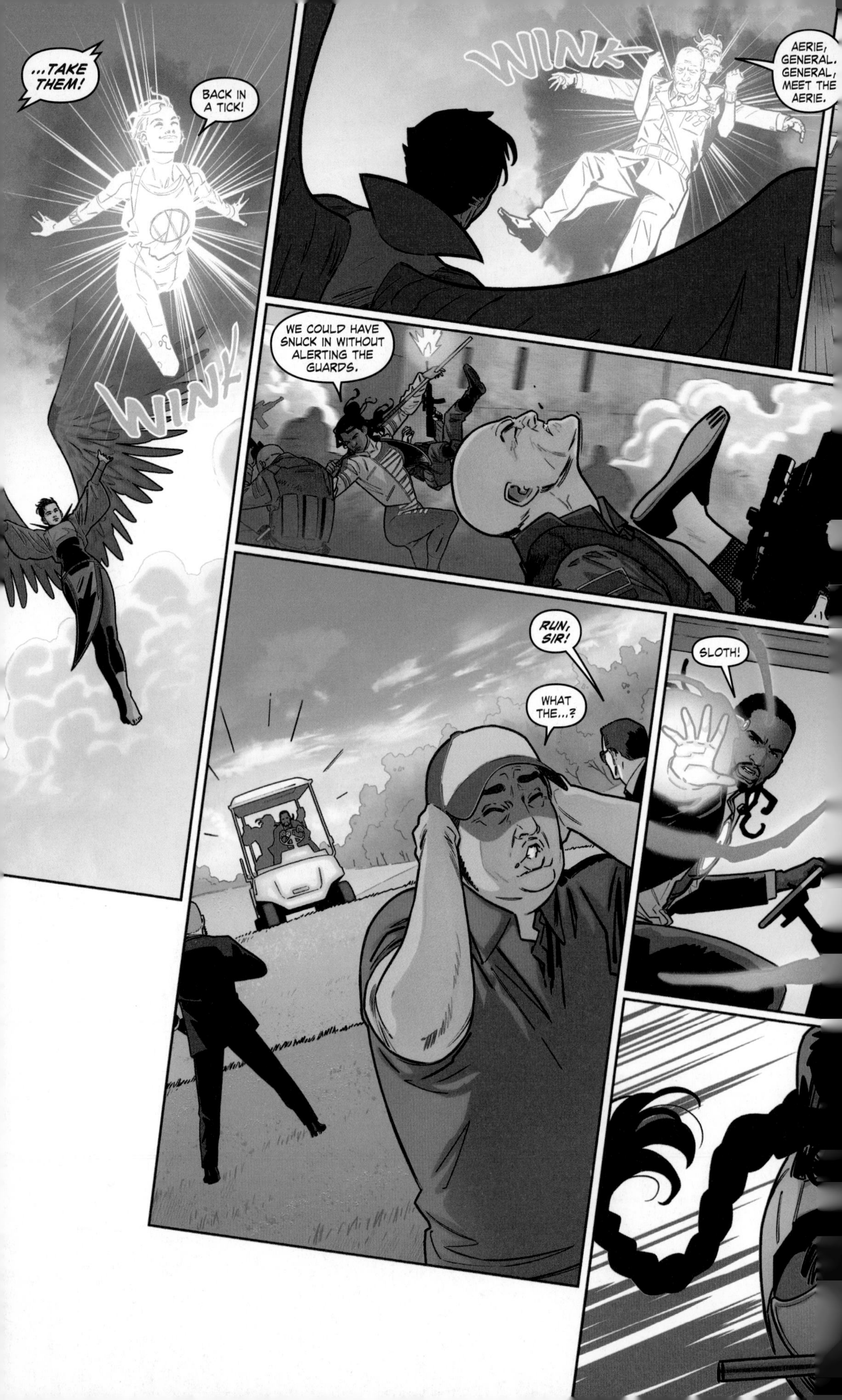
...TAKE THEM!
BACK IN A TICK!
WINK
WINK
AERIE, GENERAL. GENERAL, MEET THE AERIE.
WE COULD HAVE SNUCK IN WITHOUT ALERTING THE GUARDS.
RUN, SIR!
WHAT THE...?
SLOTH!

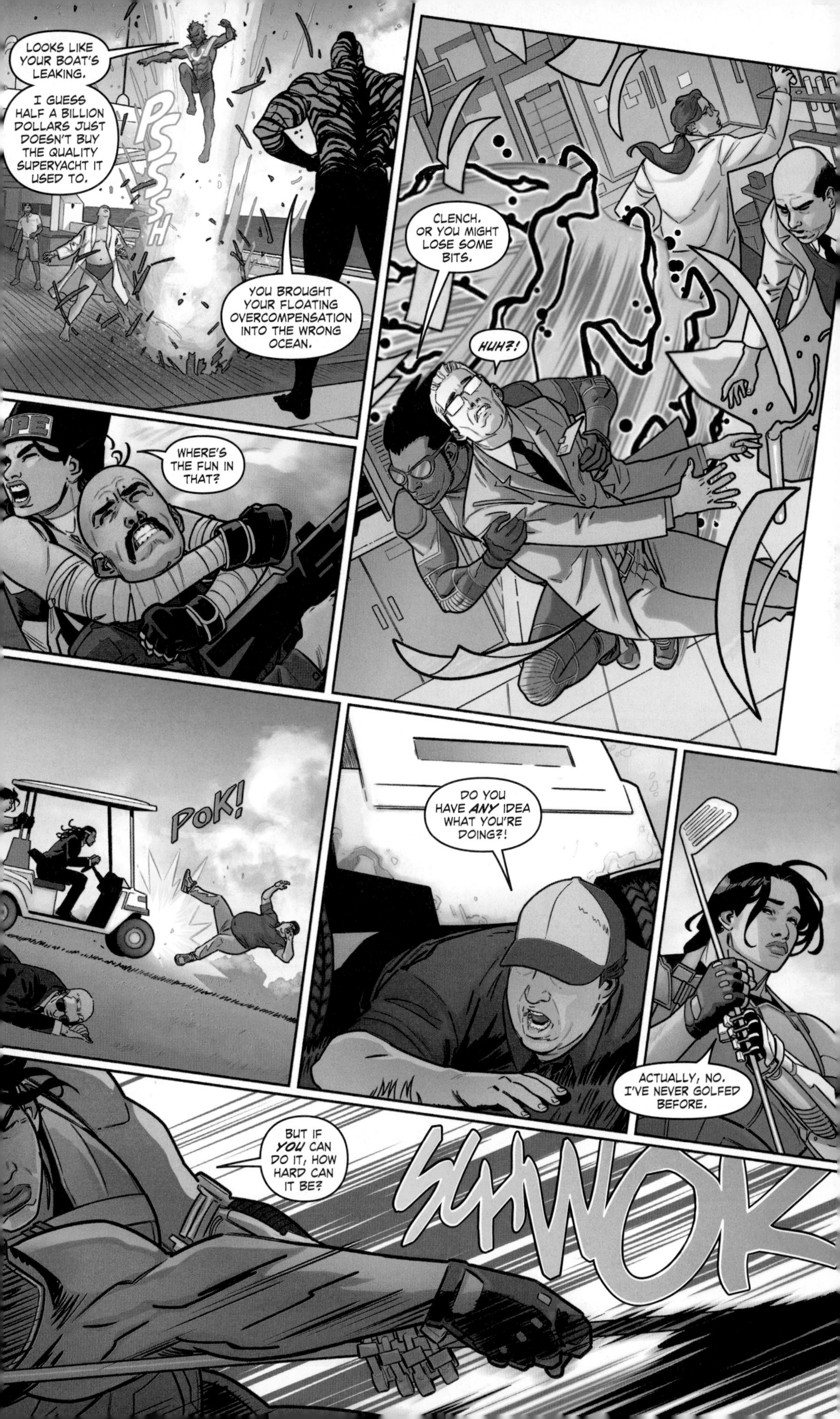
LOOKS LIKE YOUR BOAT'S LEAKING.
I GUESS HALF A BILLION DOLLARS JUST DOESN'T BUY THE QUALITY SUPERYACHT IT USED TO.
PSSSH
YOU BROUGHT YOUR FLOATING OVERCOMPENSATION INTO THE WRONG OCEAN.
WHERE'S THE FUN IN THAT?
CLENCH. OR YOU MIGHT LOSE SOME BITS.
HUH?!
POK!
DO YOU HAVE ANY IDEA WHAT YOU'RE DOING?!
ACTUALLY, NO. I'VE NEVER GOLFED BEFORE.
BUT IF YOU CAN DO IT, HOW HARD CAN IT BE?
SWWOK

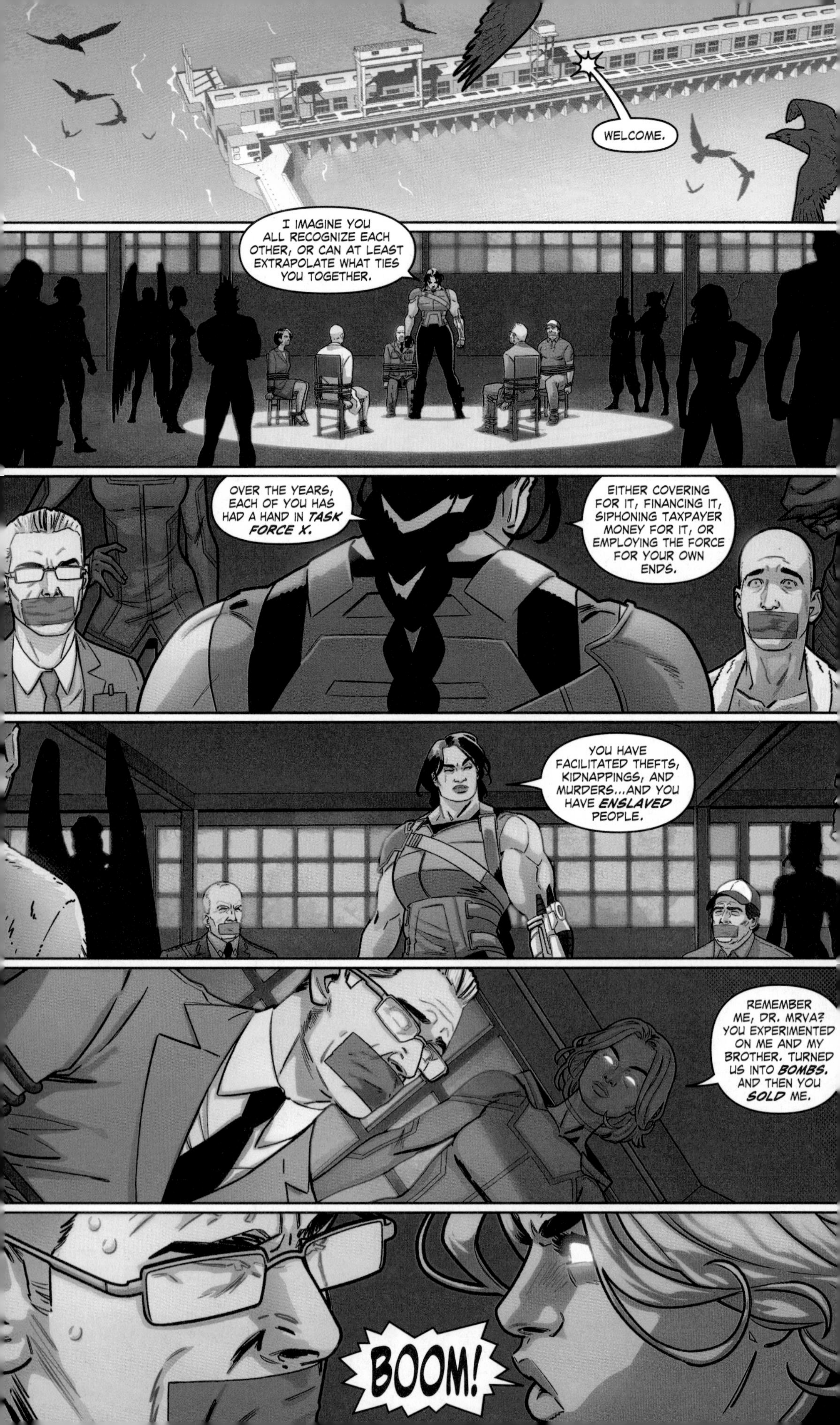
WELCOME.
I IMAGINE YOU ALL RECOGNIZE EACH OTHER, OR CAN AT LEAST EXTRAPOLATE WHAT TIES YOU TOGETHER.
OVER THE YEARS, EACH OF YOU HAS HAD A HAND IN *TASK FORCE X.*
EITHER COVERING FOR IT, FINANCING IT, SIPHONING TAXPAYER MONEY FOR IT, OR EMPLOYING THE FORCE FOR YOUR OWN ENDS.
YOU HAVE FACILITATED THEFTS, KIDNAPPINGS, AND MURDERS...AND YOU HAVE ***ENSLAVED*** PEOPLE.
REMEMBER ME, DR. MRVA? YOU EXPERIMENTED ON ME AND MY BROTHER. TURNED US INTO ***BOMBS.*** AND THEN YOU ***SOLD*** ME.
BOOM!

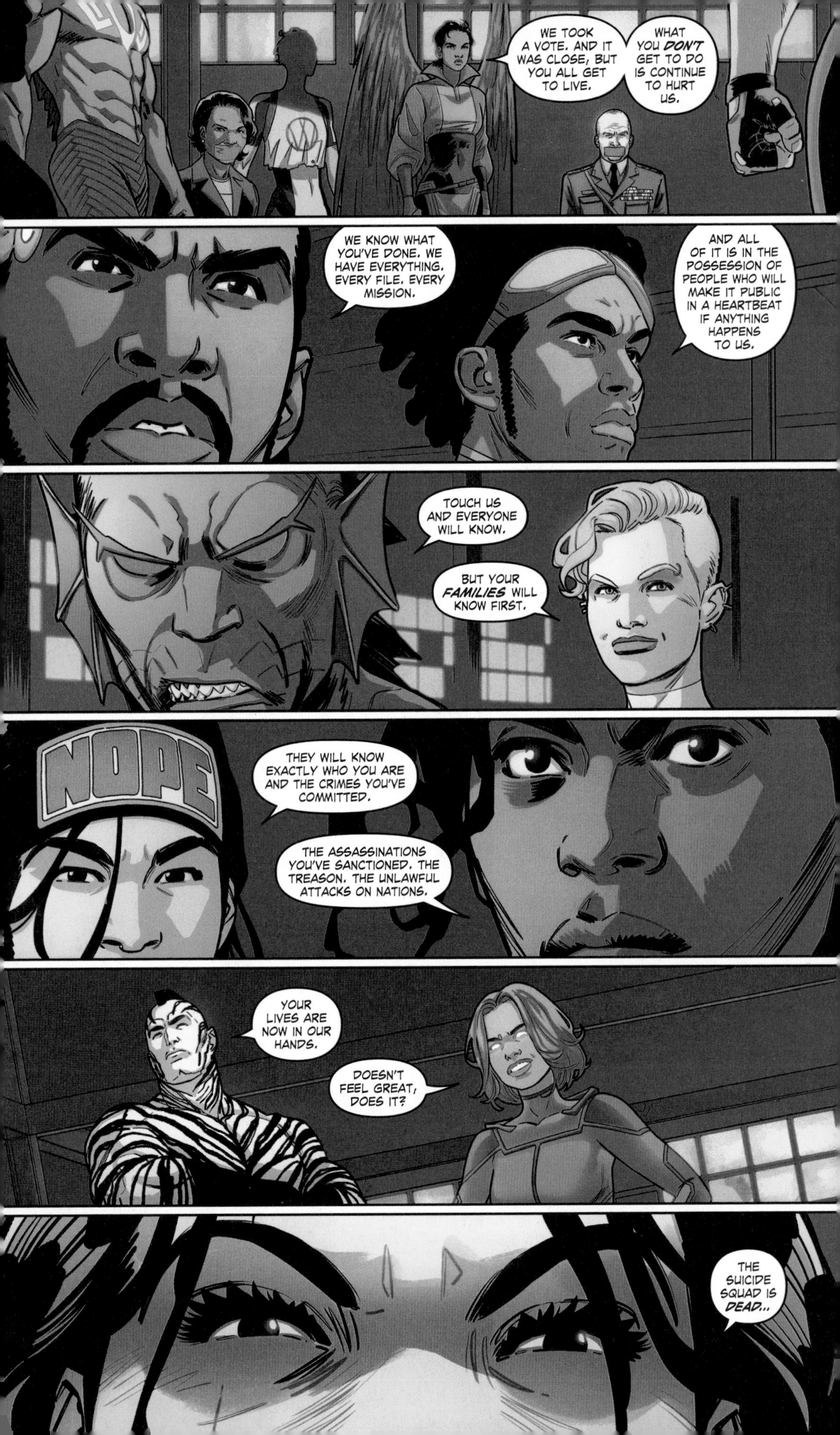
WE TOOK A VOTE. AND IT WAS CLOSE, BUT YOU ALL GET TO LIVE.
WHAT YOU ***DON'T*** GET TO DO IS CONTINUE TO HURT US.
WE KNOW WHAT YOU'VE DONE. WE HAVE EVERYTHING. EVERY FILE. EVERY MISSION.
AND ALL OF IT IS IN THE POSSESSION OF PEOPLE WHO WILL MAKE IT PUBLIC IN A HEARTBEAT IF ANYTHING HAPPENS TO US.
TOUCH US AND EVERYONE WILL KNOW.
BUT YOUR ***FAMILIES*** WILL KNOW FIRST.
NOPE
THEY WILL KNOW EXACTLY WHO YOU ARE AND THE CRIMES YOU'VE COMMITTED.
THE ASSASSINATIONS YOU'VE SANCTIONED. THE TREASON. THE UNLAWFUL ATTACKS ON NATIONS.
YOUR LIVES ARE NOW IN OUR HANDS.
DOESN'T FEEL GREAT, DOES IT?
THE SUICIDE SQUAD IS ***DEAD...***

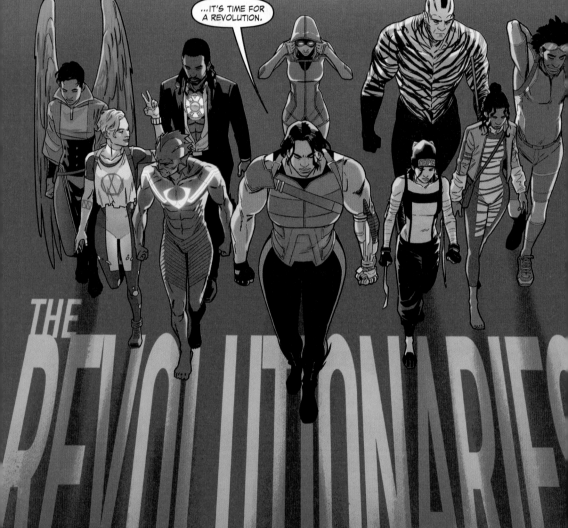

...IT'S TIME FOR A REVOLUTION.

THE REVOLUTIONARIES

written by TOM TAYLOR   art by BRUNO REDONDO

color by ADRIANO LUCAS   letters by WES ABBOTT   cover BRUNO REDONDO and ADRIANO LUC.

variant cover JEREMY ROBERTS   editor ANDREA SHEA   group editor ALEX R. CARR

TASK FORCE X: DECLASSIFIED

Designs by Bruno Redondo

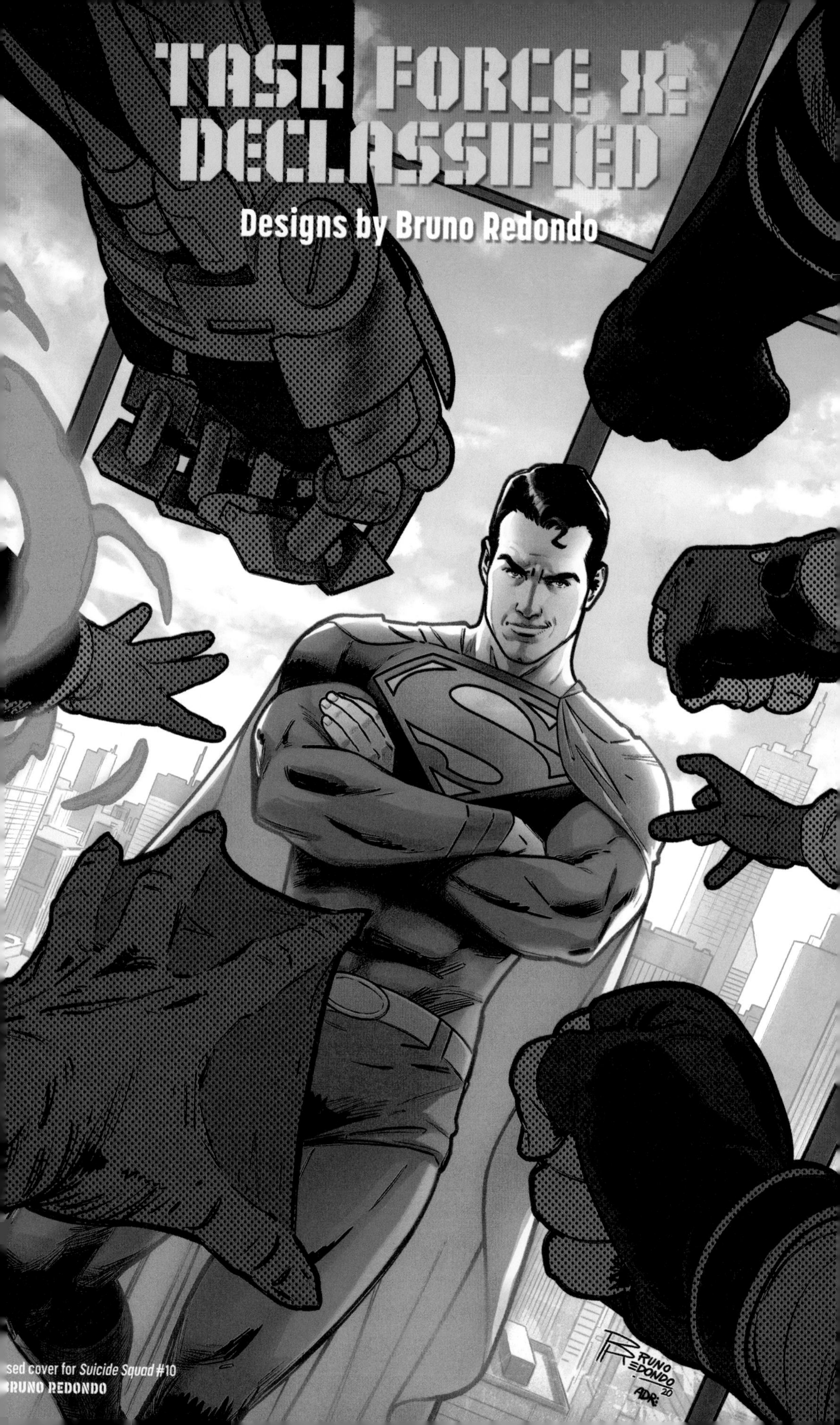

sed cover for *Suicide Squad* #10
BRUNO REDONDO

HARLEY QUINN

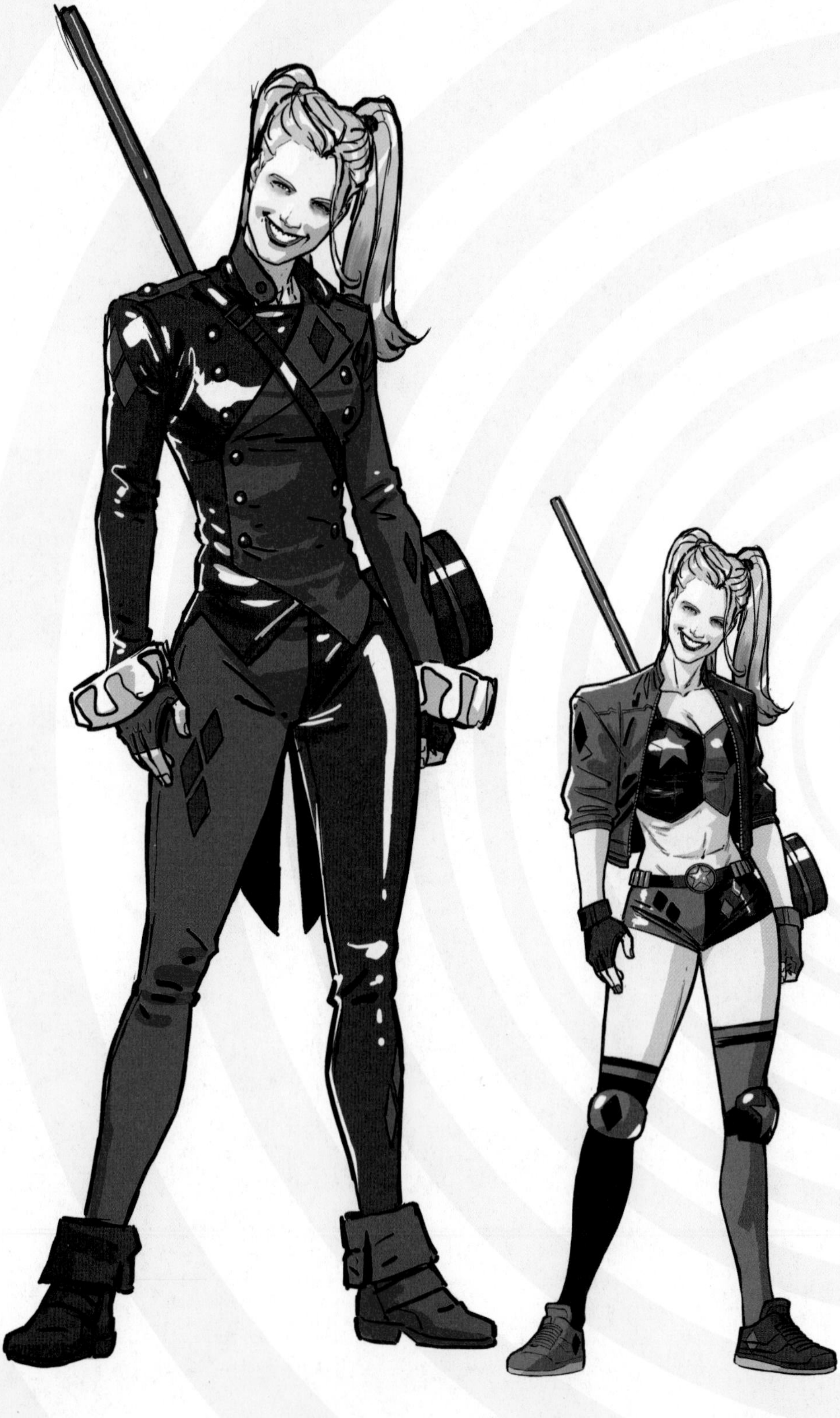

DEADSHOT

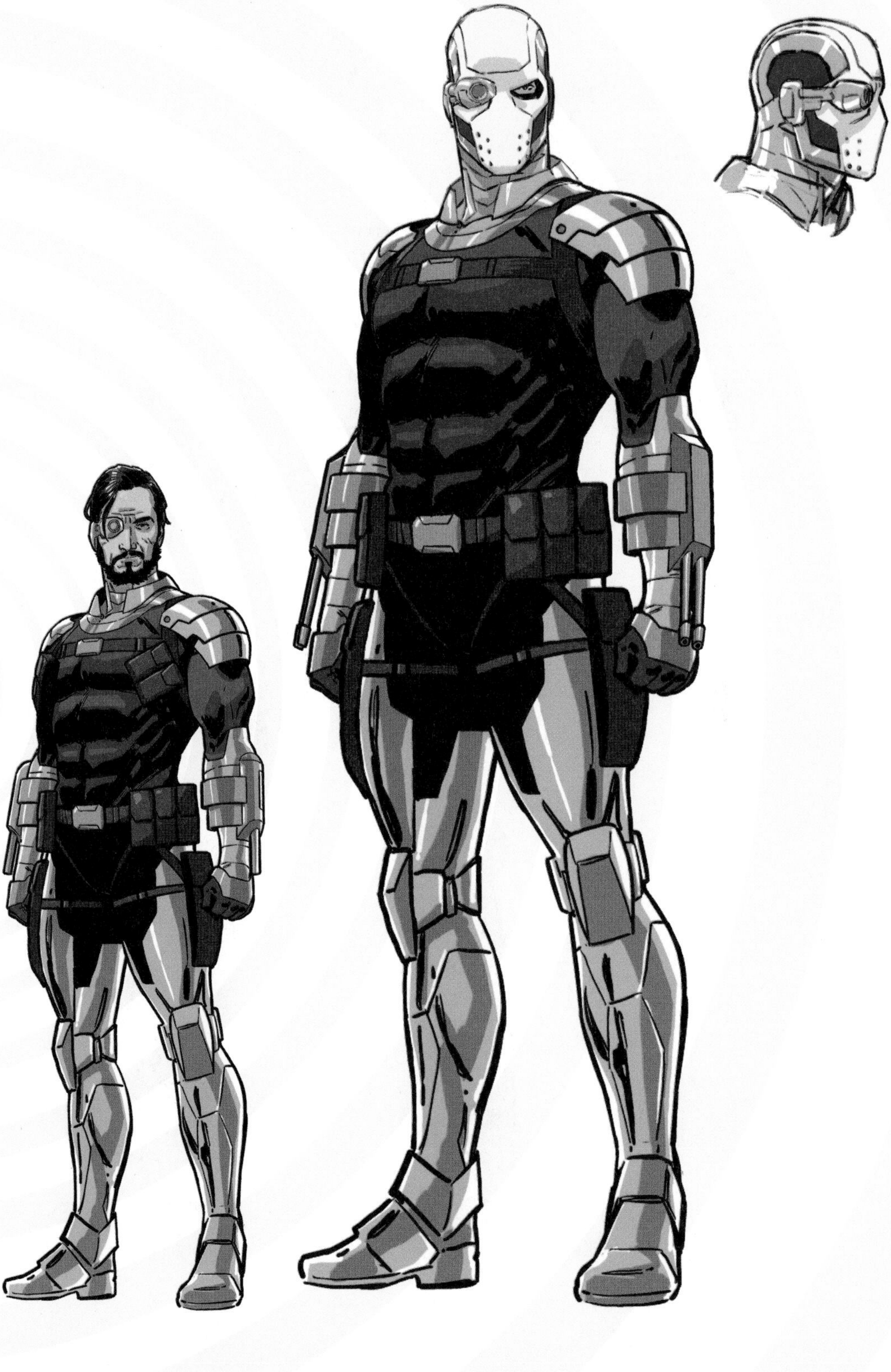

OSITA

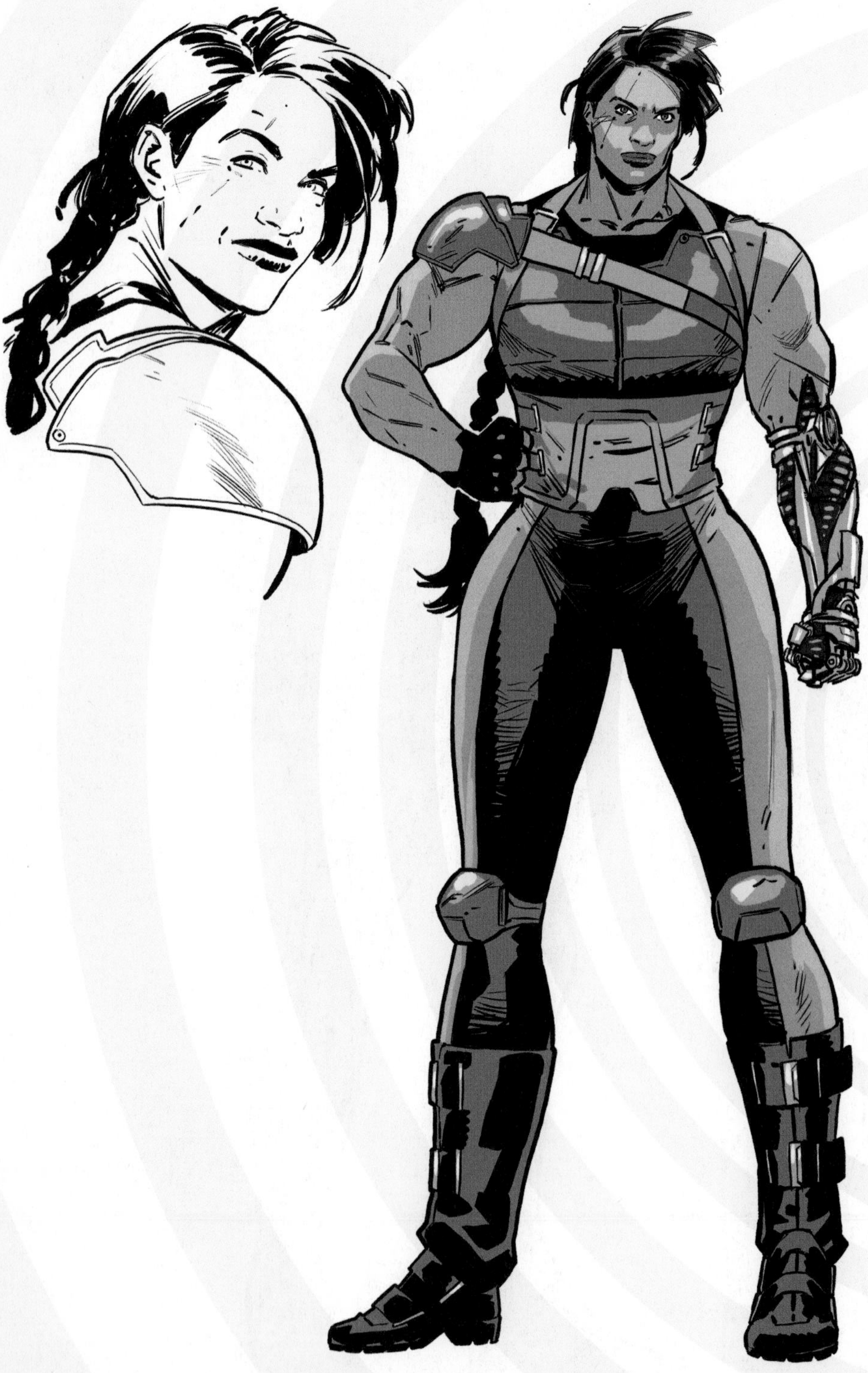

JOG

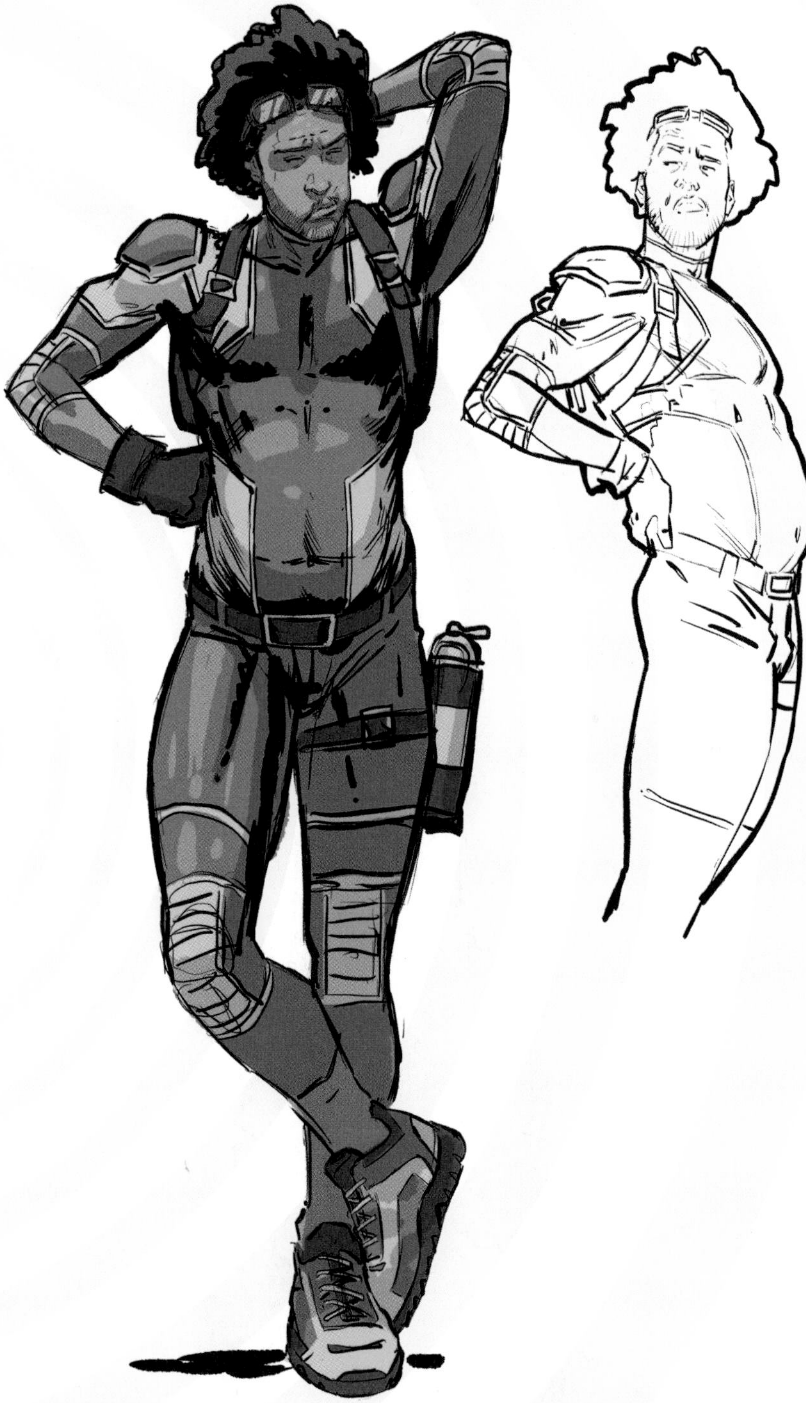

WINK

THE AERIE

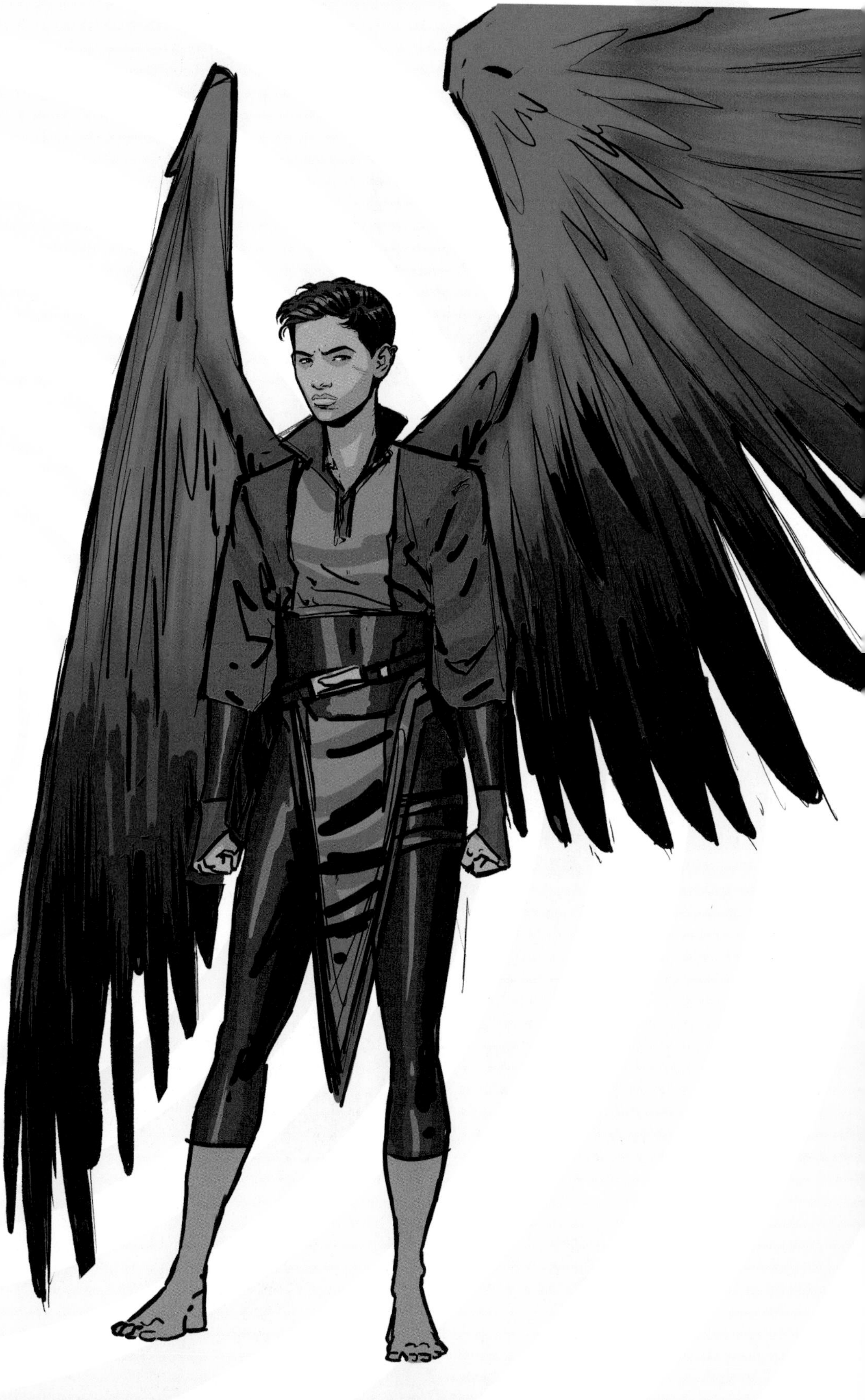

CHAOS KITTEN

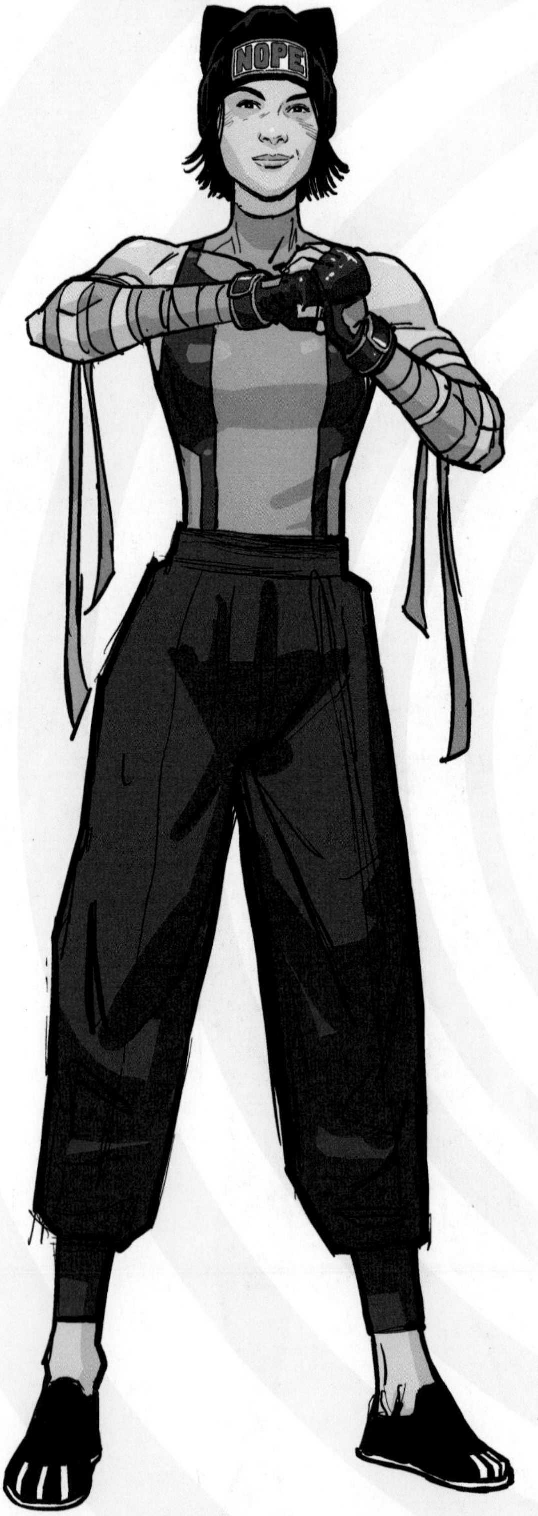
NOPE

THYLACINE

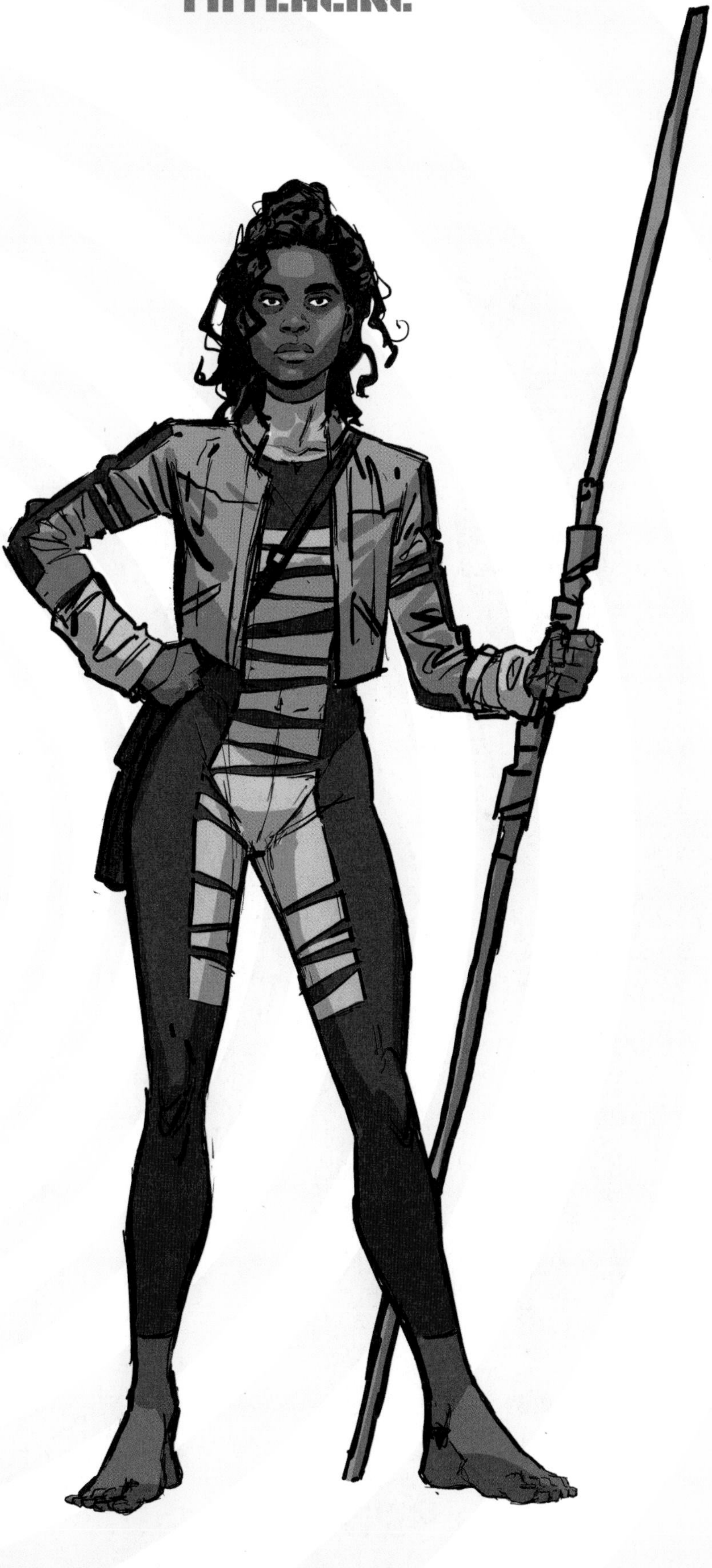

SCALE & FIN

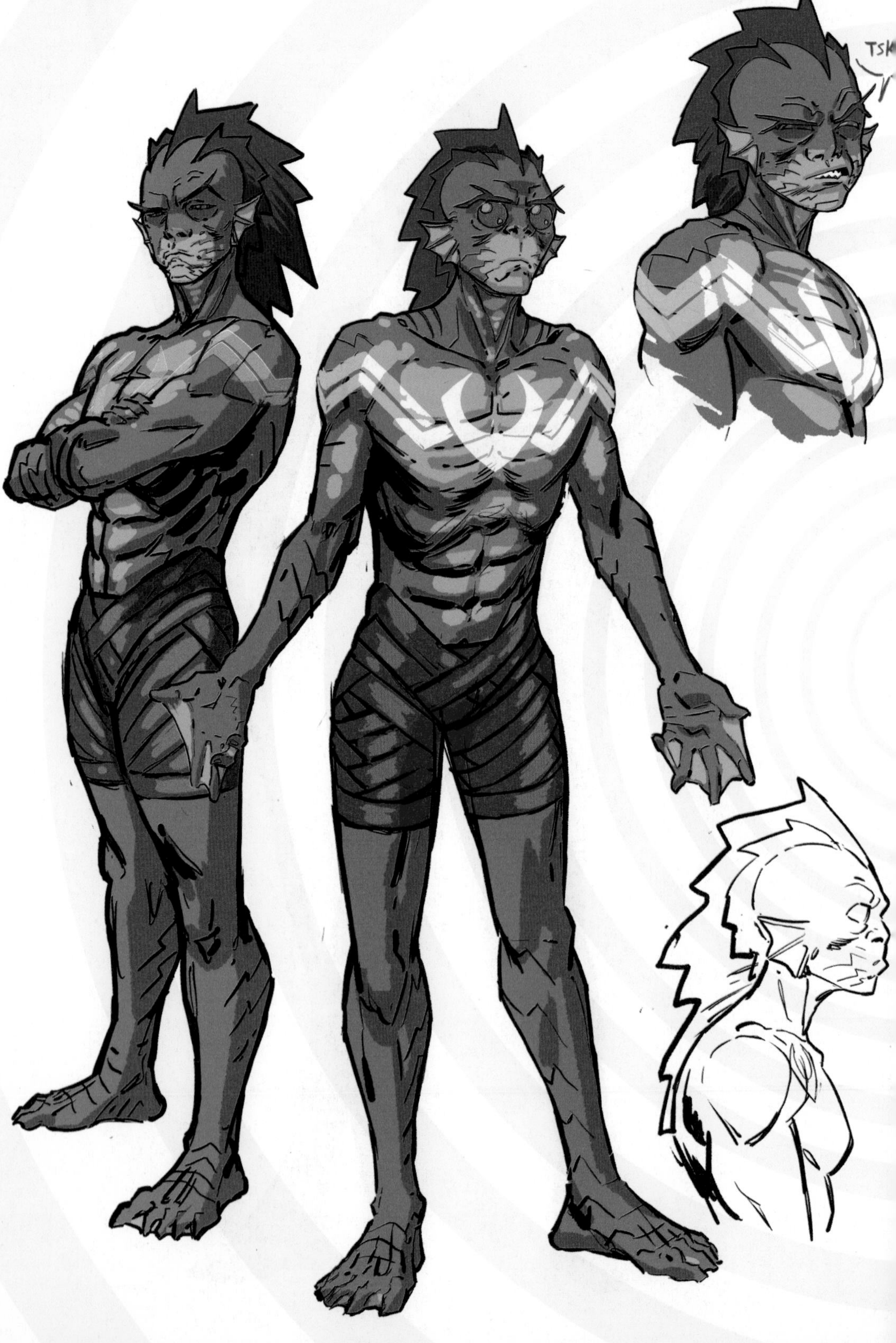
TSK

DEADLY SIX

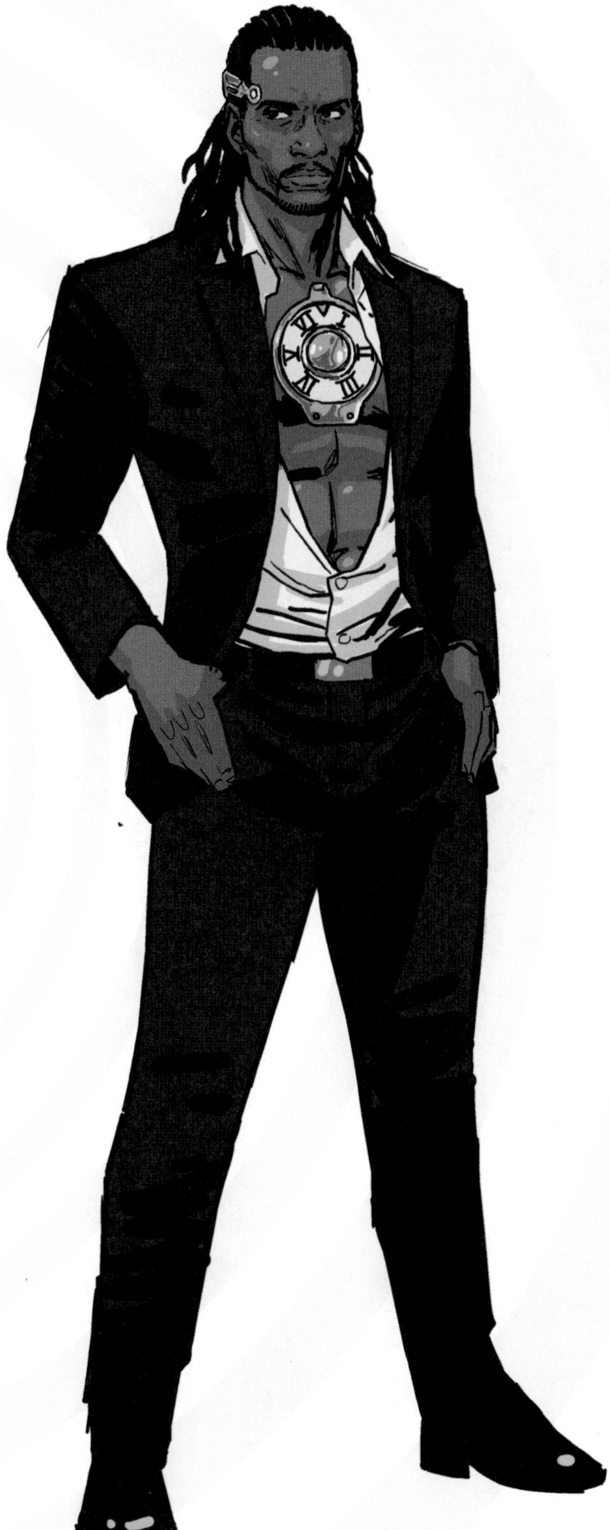

THE T.N.TEENS

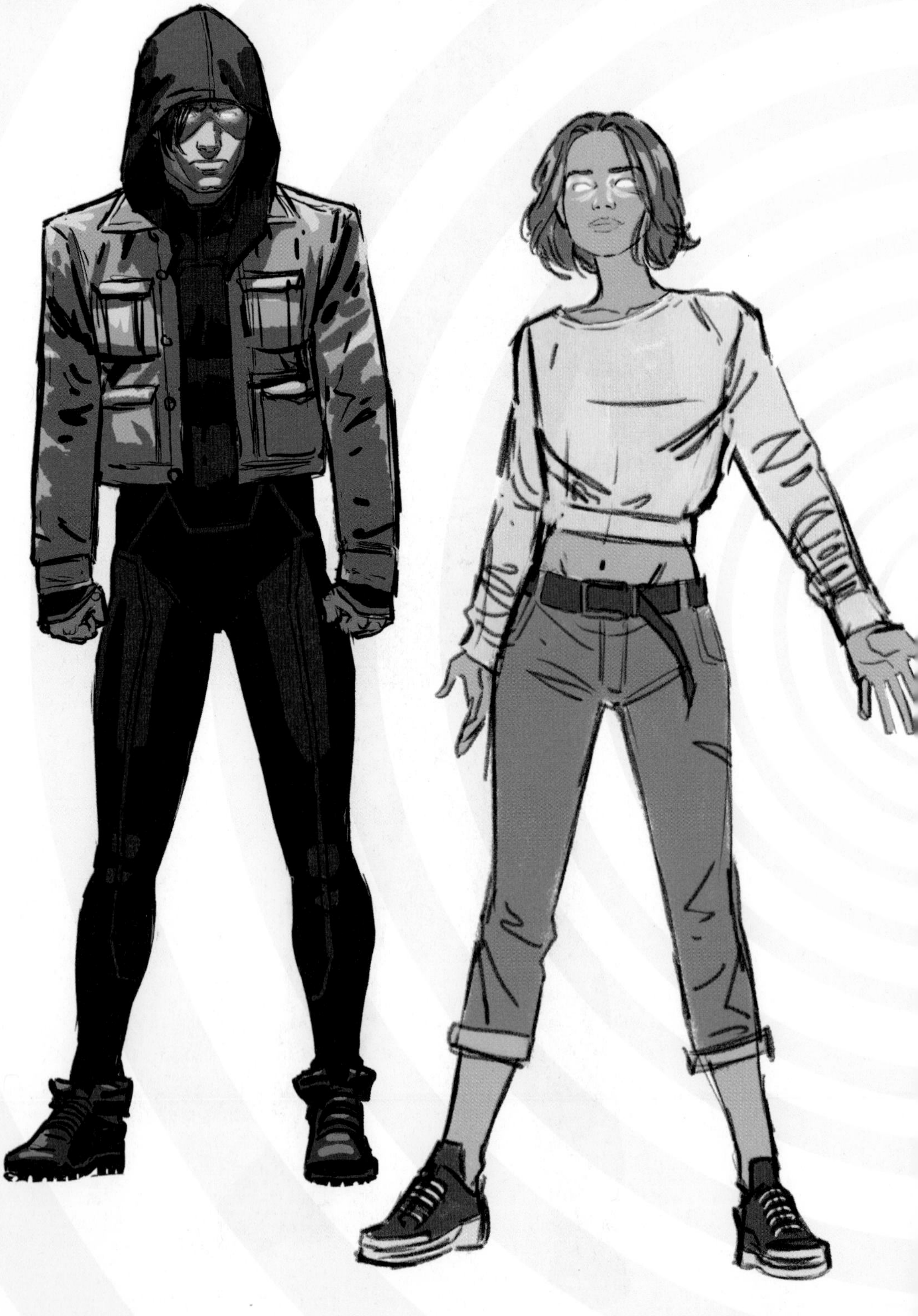

LOK

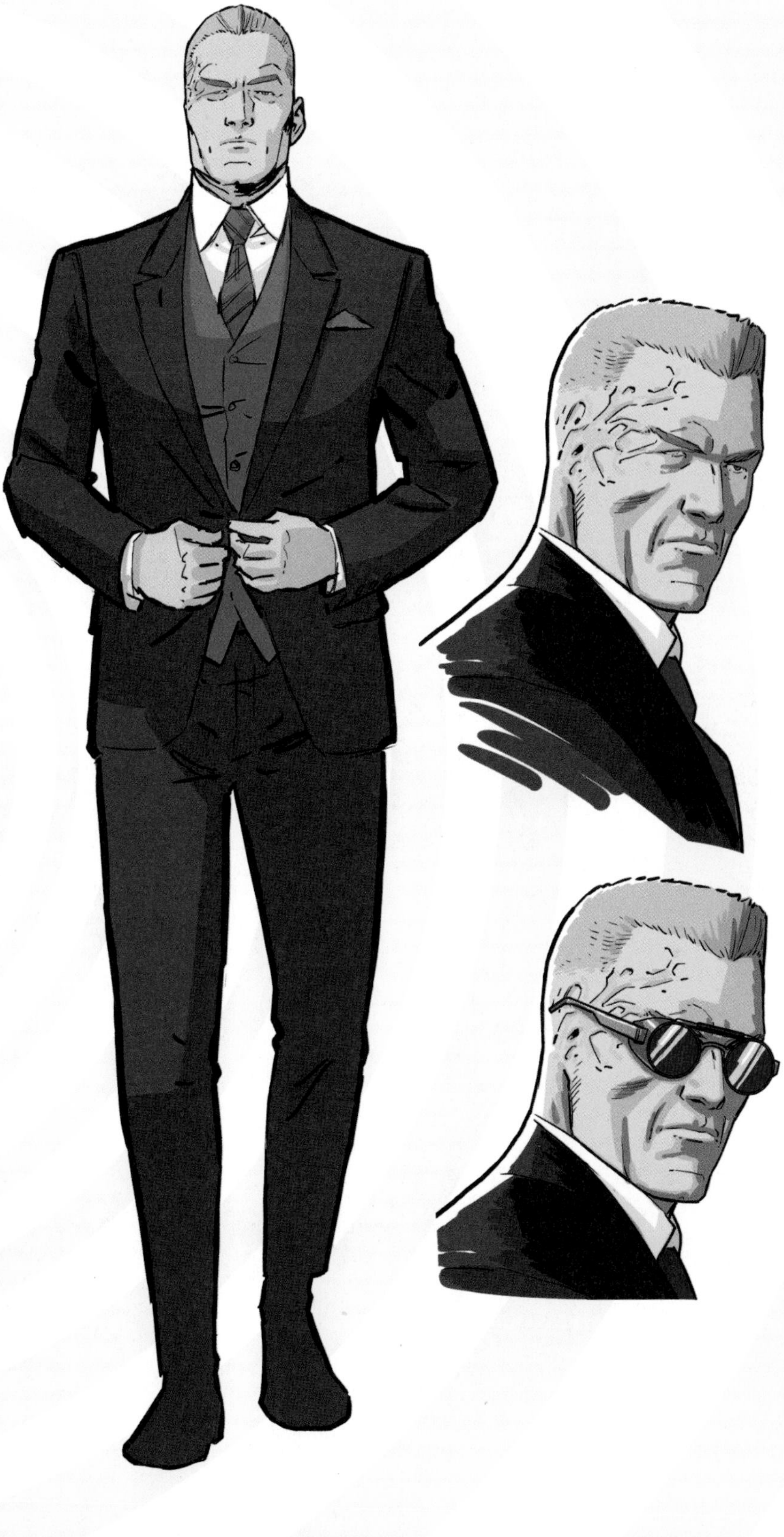

EL RUCIO

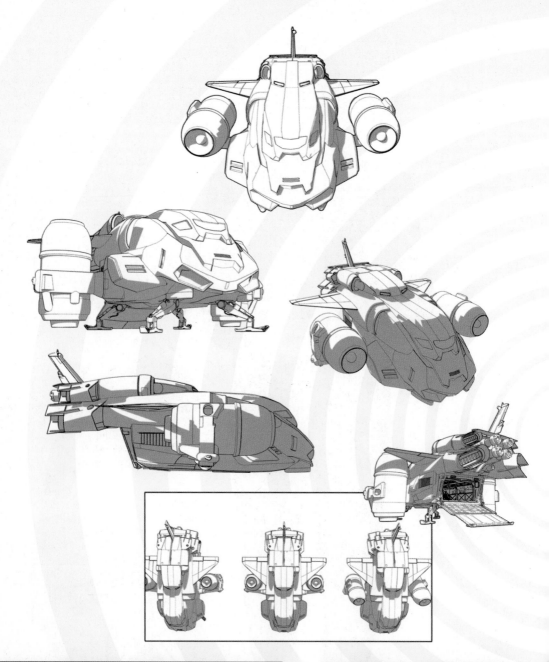

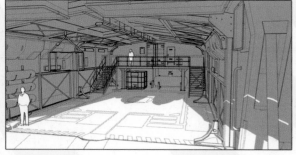

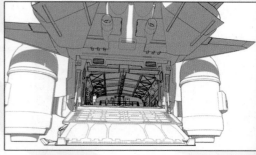